W9-AUX-145

THE WAR OF
1812

Engraving by Alonzo Chappel depicting the battle between the *Constitution* and the *Guerrière*. Courtesy of the Library of Congress

THE WAR OF
1812

A FORGOTTEN CONFLICT

Donald R. Hickey

UNIVERSITY OF ILLINOIS PRESS
Urbana and Chicago

Publication of this work has been supported by a grant from the Oliver M. Dickerson Fund. The Fund was established by Mr. Dickerson (Ph.D., Illinois, 1906) to enable the University of Illinois Press to publish selected works in American history, designated by the executive committee of the Department of History.

First paperback edition, 1995
© 1989 by the Board of Trustees of the University of Illinois
Manufactured in the United States of America
P 13 12 11 10

Library of Congress Cataloging-in-Publication Data
Hickey, Donald R., 1944–
The War in 1812 : a forgotten conflict / Donald R. Hickey.
p. cm.
Bibliography: p.
Includes index.
ISBN 0-252-06059-8 (alk. paper)
1. United States—History—War of 1812. I. Title.
E354.H53   1989
973.5'2—dc19   88-38928
                        CIP
ISBN 978-0-252-06059-5

For my mother and father,
who have always encouraged the pursuit
of knowledge

Contents

Illustrations

Maps

The Voice of America

Hark! the peal for war is rung;
Hark! the song for battle's sung;
Firm be ev'ry bosom strung,
    And ev'ry soldier ready.

On to Quebec's embattled halls!
Who will pause, when glory calls?
Charge, soldiers, charge, its lofty walls.
    And storm its strong artillery.

Firm as our native hills, we'll stand,
And should the lords of Europe land,
We'll meet them on the farthest strand,
    We'll conquer or we'll die!

—A Citizen of Monmouth, NJ
(June, 1812)

On the Conflagrations at Washington

A veteran host, by veterans led,
With Ross and Cockburn at their head—
They came—they saw—they burnt—and fled.

They left our congress naked walls—
Farewell to towers and capitols!
To lofty roofs and splendid halls!

To courtly domes and glittering things,
To folly, that too near us clings,
To courtiers who—tis well—had wings.

Farewell to all but glorious war,
Which yet shall guard Potomac's shore,
And honor lost, and fame restore.

—Philip Freneau
(August, 1814)

Preface

I FIRST BECAME INTERESTED in the War of 1812 in the late 1960s as a graduate student at the University of Illinois. Although the literature on the war was extensive, most studies focused on the military and naval history. The only works that explored domestic developments in any detail were those produced by the great nineteenth-century masters: Richard Hildreth, John Bach McMaster, and especially Henry Adams. I was particularly interested in Federalist opposition to the war, a subject that had never been treated in any systematic way. I explored this topic in my dissertation, "The Federalists and the War of 1812," which was completed in 1972. In the course of my research, I found that I had to study the Republicans and their policies in order to understand what the Federalists were reacting to. As a result, by the time I finished my dissertation, I had learned almost as much about the Republicans as the Federalists.

In the years that followed, I continued to study the war, and I published some of my findings in articles. Other scholars were working on the war, too, but most continued to focus on a narrow range of topics, particularly the military and naval engagements. What we needed, it seemed to me, was a broader treatment of the war—one that dealt with politics, diplomacy, economics, and finance as well as battles and campaigns. We needed a study, in other words, that more fully explored Republican policies and their impact on the nation. Such was the genesis of this book.

It is my hope that this book will serve two ends. As a short, comprehensive study, I hope it will be suitable for students and others interested in a general overview of the war. And as a study that reexamines the sources and contains new material, I hope it will appeal to specialists as well. In short, this work is designed to be both a textbook and a monograph and to appeal to generalists and specialists alike.

In the course of writing this book, I have incurred numerous obligations. Robert McColley (my mentor at the University of Illinois) and Morton Borden (my inspiration at the University of California at Santa Barbara) both urged me to undertake this project and made helpful suggestions along the way. Others who read the manuscript and gave me the benefit of their expertise were Clifford Egan, Edward Skeen, James Broussard, J. C. A. Stagg, and Lowell Blaisdell. I am also indebted to Vance Burke, who shared materials from his extensive personal library, and to the History Department at the University of Connecticut at Storrs, which invited me to take part in a remarkably stimulating seminar in the summer of 1987. I profited greatly from the Classic Texts Seminar, and while living in Storrs I was able to do considerable work on this project.

Wayne State College facilitated my research with three hours of release time from my teaching chores in the spring of 1986 and again in the spring of 1988. The college gave me annual grants to defray some of my research costs, and the Social Science Division provided travel money on two occasions. I am also indebted to the Wayne State Foundation for a Faculty Renewal Grant that facilitated my research in the summer of 1987.

I want to thank the library staff at Wayne State College, particularly Gail Egbers, Jan Brumm, and two generations of interlibrary loan librarians—Mary Jo Gross and Peggy Brown—who proved remarkably adept at locating and borrowing materials for me. For the extensive assistance they afforded me, I owe a special debt to the library staffs at the University of Illinois at Urbana, the University of Colorado at Boulder, the University of California at Santa Barbara, and the University of Nebraska at Lincoln. For supplying me with materials, I am also indebted to the Kansas City Branch of the National Archives, the University of South Carolina Library, the William L. Clements Library at the University of Michigan, the Milton S. Eisenhower Library at Johns Hopkins University, the New York Public Library, the Museum of the City of New York, and the New Hampshire Historical Society.

In my travels around the country, I used resources at a number of other libraries and manuscript depositories. I'd like to thank the staffs at the University of Nebraska at Omaha, Texas Tech University, the University of California at San Diego, the University of California at Berkeley, California State University at Fullerton, the University of

Arizona, Arizona State University, Harvard University, Yale University, Brown University, the University of Connecticut at Storrs, the University of Virginia, the University of North Carolina, Duke University, the Library of Congress, the Massachusetts Historical Society, the American Antiquarian Society, the Essex Institute, the Connecticut Historical Society, the Maine Historical Society, the Historical Society of Pennsylvania, the Maryland Historical Society, the Chicago Historical Society, and the Henry E. Huntington Library and Art Gallery.

For permission to quote from articles I've published, I am indebted to the editors of the *Journal of American History, William and Mary Quarterly, Journal of American Studies, New England Quarterly, Military Affairs, Indiana Magazine of History,* and *Maryland Historian.*

Finally, I want to thank my wife, Connie Clark, for urging me to write this book and for giving me the freedom to do it.

Donald R. Hickey

THE WAR OF
1812

Introduction

THE WAR OF 1812 is probably our most obscure war. Although a great deal has been written about the conflict, the average American is only vaguely aware of why we fought or who the enemy was.[1] Even those who know something about the contest are likely to remember only a few dramatic moments, such as the Battle of New Orleans, the burning of the nation's capital, or the writing of "The Star-Spangled Banner."

Why is this war so obscure? One reason is that no great president is associated with the conflict. Although his enemies called it "Mr. Madison's War," James Madison hardly measures up to such war leaders as Abraham Lincoln, Woodrow Wilson, or Franklin Roosevelt. Moreover, the great generals in this war—Andrew Jackson and Winfield Scott—were unable to turn the tide because each was confined to a secondary theater of operations. No one like George Washington, Ulysses Grant, or Dwight Eisenhower emerged to put his stamp on the war and to carry the nation to victory.

Another reason for the obscurity of this war is that its causes are shrouded in mystery. Some scholars have argued for the primacy of maritime causes, claiming that the United States went to war to force the British to give up the Orders in Council and impressment. In contemporary parlance, the war was fought for "free trade and sailors' rights." Other writers have emphasized western aims—the desire to conquer Canada in order to secure additional farm land or to put an end to British influence over American Indians. Still others have focused on political causes, asserting that the Republicans embraced war as a means of forging party unity, maintaining power, and silencing the Federalists. Yet another group has stressed ideological fac-

1

tors—the desire to uphold the prestige of the republic, preserve national honor, and ensure the continued vitality of republican institutions. The decision for war, in other words, has been attributed to a wide variety of motives.[2]

If the causes of the war are unclear, so too are the consequences. The United States has won most of its wars, often emerging with significant concessions from the enemy. But the War of 1812 was different. Far from bringing the enemy to terms, the nation was lucky to escape without making extensive concessions itself. The Treaty of Ghent (which ended the conflict) said nothing about the issues that had caused the war and contained nothing to suggest that America had achieved her aims. Instead, it merely provided for returning to the *status quo ante bellum*—the state that was before the war.

The prosecution of the war was marred by considerable bungling and mismanagement. This was partly due to the nature of the republic. The nation was too young and immature—and its government too feeble and inexperienced—to prosecute a major war efficiently. Politics also played a part. Federalists vigorously opposed the conflict, and so too did some Republicans. Even those who supported the war feuded among themselves and never displayed the sort of patriotic enthusiasm that has been so evident in other American wars. The advocates of war appeared to support the conflict more with their heads than their hearts, and more with their hearts than their purses. As a result, efforts to raise men and money lagged far behind need.

Despite the bungling and half-hearted support that characterized this conflict, the War of 1812 was not without its stirring moments and splendid victories. The crushing defeat of the British at New Orleans, the rousing victories at Chippewa and Fort Erie, and the naval triumphs on the northern lakes and the high seas—all these showed that with proper leadership and training American fighting men could hold their own against the well-drilled and battle-hardened regulars of Great Britain.

The war also produced its share of heroes—people whose reputations were enhanced by military or government service. The war helped catapult four men into the presidency—James Monroe, John Quincy Adams, Andrew Jackson, and William Henry Harrison—and three men into the vice-presidency—Daniel D. Tompkins, John C. Calhoun, and Richard M. Johnson. The war also gave a significant boost to the political or military careers of other men, most notably Henry Clay, Jacob Brown, and Winfield Scott. Indeed, for many young men on the make, the war offered an excellent launching pad for a career.

Introduction

In some ways, the War of 1812 looked more to the past than to the future. As America's second and last war against Great Britain, it echoed the ideology and issues of the American Revolution. It was the second and last time that America was the underdog in a war and the second and last time that the nation tried to conquer Canada. The war was unique in generating such vehement political opposition and nearly unique in ending in a draw. Although most Americans pretended they had won the war—even calling it a "second war of independence"—they could point to few concrete gains to sustain this claim.

This lack of success may best explain why the war is so little remembered. Americans have characteristically judged their wars on the basis of their success. The best-known wars—the Revolution, the Civil War, and World War II—were all great successes. Although many people remembered the War of 1812 as a success, it was actually a failure, and perhaps this is why it attracts so little attention today.

The obscurity of this war, however, should not blind us to its significance: it was an important turning point, a great watershed, in the history of the young republic. It concluded almost a quarter of a century of troubled diplomacy and partisan politics and ushered in the Era of Good Feelings. It marked the end of the Federalist party but also vindicated Federalist policies, many of which were adopted by Republicans during or after the war. The war also broke the power of American Indians and reinforced the powerful undercurrent of anglophobia that had been present in American culture since the Revolution. Above all, it promoted national self-confidence and encouraged the heady expansionism that lay at the heart of American foreign policy for the rest of the century. Although looking to the past, the war was fraught with consequences for the future, and for this reason it is worth studying today.

Special Notes

Troop figures. All troop figures in this study have been rounded. The precise figures given in contemporary documents are often unreliable because administrative talents were rare and field commanders had an interest in magnifying their victories and minimizing their defeats.

Rate of exchange. Throughout the Age of Jefferson, the rate of exchange between the United States and Great Britain held steady at £1 = $4.44.[3]

Maps. The four maps, which are grouped together at the end of

3

the text, show where the major land and water battles took place as well as the location of most other places mentioned in the text.

Quoted material. All material quoted in the text has been transcribed literally from the sources, including misspelled words, misplaced capital letters, and stray punctuation marks. Any exceptions are noted in square brackets.

Terminology. For the sake of convenience, *Canada* in this study refers to Great Britain's North American provinces even though they were not formally joined in a confederation until 1867. Likewise, the terms *United States* and *America* have been used interchangeably.

CHAPTER 1

The Road to War, 1801–1812

ON MARCH 4, 1801, Thomas Jefferson walked from his boarding house in Washington City, as the nation's capital was then called, to the capitol building, where he was inaugurated as third president of the United States. The walk was short but symbolic. Jefferson pointedly refused to take a carriage, a vehicle he considered a badge of aristocracy.[1] The nation's new leaders favored a more democratic style than their Federalist predecessors. They also planned to adopt a new set of policies. These policies—initiated by Jefferson and carried on by his friend and successor, James Madison—put the United States on a collision course with Great Britain and ultimately led to the War of 1812.

Republicans did not differ with Federalists over the broad objectives of American policy in this era. During the long series of Anglo-French wars that lasted from 1793 to 1815, all Americans agreed that the nation should work to promote prosperity at home while protecting its rights and preserving its neutrality abroad. But what was the best way to achieve these ends? It was this question, more than any other, that divided Americans into two political camps.[2]

Federalists subscribed to the Roman doctrine, proclaimed and popularized by George Washington, that the best way to preserve peace was to be prepared for war.[3] "War is a great calamity," said Federalist Congressman Benjamin Tallmadge, "and the surest way to avoid it, is to be prepared for it." "Even in time of profound peace," echoed the Boston *Weekly Messenger*, "it has been considered a maxim of wisdom to be prepared for war."[4] Toward this end, Federalists implemented a broad program of financial and military preparedness in the 1790s.

5

Their aim was not only to deter war but to put the nation in the best possible position to defend itself in case hostilities erupted.

The Federalists' policy of financial preparedness was based on Alexander Hamilton's program, which was adopted in the early 1790s. This program provided for the federal government to assume responsibility for more than $75,000,000 of indebtedness incurred by the state and Continental governments during the Revolutionary War. It also provided for the imposition of internal and external taxes and the creation of a national bank. Together these measures initiated a financial revolution that restored public credit, created millions of dollars of investment capital, and established a stable and uniform national currency.[5]

To complement their financial policies, the Federalists also expanded the defense establishment.[6] The peacetime army was gradually increased from 840 men in 1789 to 5,400 in 1801. The navy, which had been scrapped after the Revolution, was rebuilt so that by 1801 there were thirteen frigates in service and six ships-of-the-line under construction. The Federalists also began a modest system of coastal fortifications, devoting $1,000,000 to the construction and repair of forts to protect American cities from assault via the sea.[7]

While promoting preparedness at home, the Federalists pursued a pro-British foreign policy abroad. The cornerstone of this policy was the Jay Treaty of 1794, an Anglo-American agreement that regulated commerce and defined neutral rights in time of war.[8] Although the Republicans were always critical of this treaty—one paper called it the "death-warrant to our neutral rights"—there is no denying that it achieved two important ends.[9] It ensured peace with the one nation whose naval power could menace the United States, and it ushered in an era of Anglo-American accord that allowed American commerce— and hence the American economy—to flourish. American exports, which stood at $33,000,000 in 1794, soared to 94,000,000 in 1801, and the entire nation basked in the resulting prosperity.[10]

The only liability of the Jay Treaty was that it was deeply resented by the French, who regarded it as a betrayal of the alliance that had bound them to the United States since the Revolution. France responded to the treaty by unleashing her warships and privateers on American commerce. This led to the Quasi-War, an undeclared naval war that lasted from 1798 to 1801.[11] Although the French seized an estimated $20,000,000 in American mercantile property between 1795 and 1799, the nation's growing trade was so lucrative that these losses caused barely a ripple in the rising prosperity.[12]

The Quasi-War provided the first real test for the Federalist navy— a test that it passed with flying colors. Cruising mainly in the Caribbean (where most of the American shipping losses had occurred), the navy defeated two French frigates, captured over a hundred privateers, and recovered more than seventy American merchant vessels. As a result, rates for shipping insurance dropped sharply all along the Atlantic coast.[13] In the Convention of 1800, which brought this war to a close, the United States waived any claim for compensation for the maritime depredations that had occurred. In return, France agreed to suspend the treaties that had bound the nations together since the Revolution.[14]

By the end of the Quasi-War, the Federalists had been in power for more than a decade, and their policies had served the nation well. Their program of preparedness was in place, and the nation was at peace with France and on especially cordial terms with England. Best of all, because of the mounting profits from neutral trade, Americans were enjoying an unprecedented level of prosperity.

In spite of the success of their policies, the Federalists suffered from several liabilities that doomed them at the polls. The additional taxes necessitated by the Quasi-War and the attempt to suppress opposition with a sedition law alienated many voters. In addition, the Federalists' approach to politics was too elitist for this era of rising democracy, and their foreign policy too pro-British for a people whose revolutionary experience had left them steeped in anglophobia. As a result, the Federalists were defeated in the election of 1800.

When the Republicans took office in 1801, they began to reverse the policies they had inherited. They had no love for the Jay Treaty and no desire to maintain such a close relationship with England—at least not on the terms laid down in this treaty. Moreover, they were committed by their ideology as well as by their campaign promises to reforming public finance and reducing government expenditures. "We shall push you to the uttermost in economising," Jefferson told a Congressional leader in 1801.[15]

Determined to overhaul the nation's finances, the Republicans took direct aim at Hamilton's program. They regarded the national debt as a curse—a source of unearned profit for the rich and a heavy burden on current and future taxpayers. Hence they devoted a large share of the government's annual income to paying off the debt. They were equally hostile to the internal taxes, which they considered an excessive burden on their constituents, particularly in the West. Hence these duties were repealed in 1802. The Republicans had no love for the national bank either. Most considered it an engine of aristocracy of doubtful legality, vulnerable (through stock purchases) to foreign control. The bank was protected by a twenty-year charter, but this charter was not renewed when it expired in 1811.[16]

The Republicans were also determined to cut defense spending. As a matter of principle, they were opposed to a large defense establishment, believing that it fostered special interest groups that posed a danger to republican government. A cut in spending was essential anyway because the internal taxes had been repealed at a time when large sums were being devoted to debt retirement.[17]

Accordingly, the peacetime army was trimmed from 5,400 to 3,300 men in 1802.[18] Many good officers were lost in the process.[19] Although the authorized level of the army was increased to almost 10,000 men during a war scare in 1808, Republican leaders used the expanded officer corps to reward the party faithful.[20] Winfield Scott, who served with these officers in the War of 1812, claimed that most were "imbeciles and ignoramuses." Those from Federalist states, he said, were mainly "coarse and ignorant men," while those from Republican states were "swaggerers, dependants, decayed gentlemen, and others—'fit for nothing else.' "[21] By 1810 incompetence in the officer corps had so demoralized the army that Republican Nathaniel Macon suggested that it might as well be disbanded. The men hated their officers so much that they could not be counted on to obey them in time of war. "The state of that Army," Macon concluded, "is enough to make any man who has the smallest love of country wish to get rid of it."[22]

The Republicans were even more hostile to the navy. "[E]very nation," said one Republican, "which has embarked to any extent, in Naval Establishments, has been eventually crushed by them." "Show me a nation possessed of a large navy," said another, "and I will show you a nation always at war."[23] The Republicans halted construction on the ships-of-the-line and decommissioned most of the frigates. Six of the frigates were subsequently lost to rot or other causes so that by 1812 only seven survived. The only concession that Republicans made to naval defense was the construction of four sloops needed for inshore service in the Tripolitan War (1801–1805).[24]

The Republicans did spend money on coastal fortifications—about $2,800,000 between 1801 and 1812.[25] This was almost three times what the Federalists had spent in the previous decade, but without a fleet to serve as the nation's first line of defense, this sum was wholly inadequate. Most of the nation's great cities remained exposed to attack from the sea.

The Republicans were willing to cut the nation's regular forces because they planned to rely on militia and privateers ("the militia of the sea"). These forces were attractive because they were democratic in character and posed no threat to republican institutions. They were also cheap. Militia did not have to be paid until they were called into service, and privateers actually brought in revenue because their prizes were taxed. But except in New England and the West, the militia were so poorly trained and so badly equipped that they could not be relied on in the heat of battle. There were drawbacks to privateers, too. Although capable of wreaking havoc on an enemy's commerce, they were hardly a match for enemy warships and could offer little protection to the nation's coast or commerce.[26]

The Republicans favored another instrument of war that was also of doubtful value: the gunboats that made up Jefferson's "mosquito fleet." Gunboats were small and inexpensive vessels—"*oyster* boats," one critic called them—that had proved effective in several wars in the Mediterranean, where they could maneuver in waters too shallow for heavier ships.[27] Though perfectly serviceable in calm seas, they were too light to be effective in rough waters. Moreover, time would prove that gun for gun they were more expensive to build and operate than frigates, and they rotted in a year if left unrepaired. Although $1,500,000 was spent on these boats, by 1809 the administration recognized the bankruptcy of the program, and most of the vessels were decommissioned.[28]

❖ ❖ ❖ ❖ ❖ ❖

The Republican policy of retrenchment was popular with most voters, and initially at least it did little harm. England and France concluded the Peace of Amiens in late 1801 and remained at peace until 1803. Although most observers recognized that this was little more than a truce, it nonetheless reduced friction between the United States and the Great Powers and thus gave further impetus to the drive to pare defense expenditures.

The Peace of Amiens also eliminated neutral commercial opportunities. American exports plummeted from $94,000,000 in 1801 to $54,000,000 in 1803. When the Anglo-French war resumed, however, exports began to climb again, peaking at $108,000,000 in 1807.[29] Such was England's restraint in the face of this growing trade that in 1804 James Monroe, the American minister in London, could report: "The truth is that our commerce never enjoyed in any war, as much freedom, and indeed favor from this govt. as it now does."[30]

Little more than a year after delivering this judgment, Monroe accused the British of adopting a plan "to subject our commerce at present and hereafter to every restraint in their power."[31] What had happened in the interval? British officials, jealous of American commercial success and suspecting frauds in the neutral trade, had stepped

9

up enforcement of a British maritime doctrine known as the Rule of 1756.

The Rule of 1756 held that trade closed to a neutral in time of peace could not be opened in time of war. The rule was supposed to prevent American merchants from freighting goods between France and her West Indian colonies when French ships could not get to sea. But American ships circumvented the rule by making a stopover in the United States, thus transforming a direct trade between France and her colonies into a triangular trade. At first tacitly, and then officially in the *Polly* decision (1800), the British held that this re-export trade did not violate their doctrine. As a result, the United States captured most of the trade between Europe and the Caribbean, and re-exports (which constituted about half of America's export trade) soared from $2,000,000 in 1792 to $53,000,000 in 1805.[32]

There was a good deal of grumbling in England over this mushrooming trade. Having driven France's merchant fleet from the high seas, the British were not anxious to see the United States reap the gains. At the very least, they wanted a share of the profits. "[T]he point at issue with the United States on this subject," British officials privately conceded, "is not a question of great importance, but a mere consideration of how the profit taken from the Enemy is to be divided."[33] To insure a share of the trade, the British modified their policy. In the *Essex* decision (1805), the High Court of Admiralty ruled that landing goods and paying duties in the United States was no longer proof of bona fide importation. Thenceforth, American merchants would have to provide additional, though unspecified, proof that ships stopping over in the United States actually broke their voyages.[34]

Given the *Essex* decision, the Royal Navy began seizing American ships engaged in the re-export trade, with paralyzing effect. Insurance rates soared, and American merchants faced staggering losses.[35] The total number of vessels seized was probably three or four hundred; however, most were later released by the British courts. As Monroe put it, England "seeks to tranquilize us by dismissing our vessels in every case that She possibly can."[36] Moreover, the new Whig ministry that assumed office under Lord Grenville and Charles James Fox in 1806 found the *Essex* decision an embarrassment and moved to set it aside. A government decree, issued in May of 1806 proclaiming a blockade of northern Europe (the "Fox Blockade"), implicitly restored the re-export trade to its old status.[37]

In 1805, however, American merchants could not know that the British lion's growl would prove worse than his bite. They only knew that they faced heavy losses if their ships were in fact condemned.

Hence in every major seaport they banded together to petition the government for relief.[38] Federal officials were sympathetic to their appeals, and there was considerable support for sending a special mission to England to resolve the problem.

Other Anglo-American problems also demanded attention. Of these the most important was impressment—the British practice of taking seamen from American ships on the high seas.[39] The rapid growth of American trade in the early national period led to a shortage of able-bodied seamen. To overcome this shortage, British tars were recruited into American service. There was no shortage of volunteers because the pay and working conditions on American ships were so much better than on British warships or even British merchant vessels. As a result, probably a quarter of the 50,000 to 100,000 seamen employed on American ships in this era were British.[40]

The problem with this labor system was that the Royal Navy, on a war footing, needed all the seamen it could get. Hence press gangs from British warships periodically boarded American merchant vessels to reclaim British subjects. This objectionable practice sometimes left American ships dangerously short-handed. Even worse, through accident or design American citizens were sometimes pressed into British service. Between 1803 and 1812 it is estimated that about 6,000 suffered this fate.[41] Although the British government was usually willing to release those Americans whose citizenship could be established, the appeals—which were conducted through diplomatic channels—often took years. In the meantime, American citizens languished in British ships, exposed to the rigors of a harsh discipline and to all the dangers of a war that was not their own.

In the hope of protecting Americans from British press gangs, the United States began issuing certificates of citizenship in 1796. These "protections" (as they were called) were like modern passports, but instead of a photograph they contained a description of the individual to whom they were issued. Age, height, hair and eye colors, and any other distinguishing features were typically included, but often the description was vague. Some British seamen acquired certificates by lying about their place of birth, while others simply bought them from obliging Americans. For a dollar, it was said, a British subject could become an American citizen.[42] Under these circumstances, it is hardly surprising that British officials gave little credence to the documents. "[T]he flagrant and undeniable abuses of the official documents of American Citizenship," said the Admiralty, "have obliged their Lordships to look at all such documents with the utmost distrust."[43]

Although the re-export trade and impressment were the most serious problems that troubled Anglo-American relations in 1805, there were other sources of friction as well.[44] One was the British practice—all too common—of violating American territorial waters. Under international law a nation's waters extended three miles out to sea—the maximum range of shore batteries. Whether through neglect or design, British warships often operated within American waters. The seizure of ships and the impressment of seamen within the three-mile limit was a clear violation of international law that Americans found particularly objectionable.

Another source of friction concerned the British use of blockades. It was the accepted right of a nation at war to blockade an enemy's ports in order to interrupt his trade. Neutral powers had to be given sufficient notice of a blockade, there had to be a continued naval presence before a blockaded port, and the naval force had to be large enough to threaten any vessel seeking to enter or leave the affected port. These were principles that the British recognized in theory but did not always follow in practice.

Still another source of trouble centered on the definition of contraband. It was the accepted right of a nation at war to search neutral merchant vessels on the high seas and to seize any contraband headed for the enemy. But there was no commonly accepted definition of contraband. The United States favored a narrow definition—restricted to war materiel—in order to enhance its commercial opportunities. The British, on the other hand, favored a broad definition—which might include food, naval stores, and even money—in order to deprive their enemy of as many vital supplies as possible. The British were usually willing to pay for dubious items seized—in effect preempting instead of confiscating the articles in question—but this did not mollify American merchants, who were after bigger profits on the continent.

The United States and England also differed over the status of enemy (French) property on neutral vessels. Upholding the *Consolato del Mare*, a fourteenth-century maritime code, the British argued that such property was subject to seizure. The United States favored the newer doctrine of free ships—free goods, which held that any property on a neutral vessel (contraband excepted) was immune to seizure. To the British the key was who owned the property; to Americans it was who owned the ship.

The doctrine of free ships—free goods is sometimes treated as one of the pivotal diplomatic issues of this period, but by 1800 it was of little practical importance. Although Americans had freighted property for France and other European belligerents in the 1790s, by 1800 they had sufficient capital to purchase any merchandise they wished to transport. "We are no longer mere freighters for foreigners," said Republican Barnabas Bidwell in 1806, "but have become the carriers of foreign as well as native produce, on our own capital, and for our own account."[45]

Purchase of foreign property Americanized it and thus protected it from seizure even under the *Consolato del Mare*. Hence in practice Americans had few objections to the enforcement of this doctrine. "If any of our ships are found carrying the property of the enemies of Great Britain," said Republican merchant Samuel Smith in 1806, "let them be punished, we mean not to defend them."[46] Federalists even argued that the United States profited from the *Consolato del Mare*. "The boasted principle of free ships, free goods," Fisher Ames claimed, "would deprive the United States of a great part of the fair profits of their neutrality. Belligerent nations could in that case transact their own affairs, and neutrals would have no gains but freight."[47]

These, then, were the issues that troubled Anglo-American relations in 1805: the re-export trade and impressment most of all, but also contraband, blockades, and violations of American waters. In private talks with the president and in strongly worded public resolutions, members of Congress urged the administration to send a special mission to England to resolve these differences.[48]

Jefferson, however, had long since soured on treaties— particularly commercial agreements—believing that mutual interest was the only reliable guarantee for trade. The day was not distant, he said in 1801, when the United States could dictate international law on the high seas. "[I]n the meantime we wish to let every treaty we have drop off without renewal."[49] Jefferson had little love for the Jay Treaty—"a millstone round our necks," he once called it—and he refused British overtures to renew its commercial clauses when they expired in 1803.[50] He was willing to sanction a limited treaty covering neutral rights— the re-export trade, impressment, blockades, and the like—but he wanted to leave the negotiations to Monroe and to exclude commercial issues altogether. But such was the pressure from Congress that he felt obliged to appoint a special mission to work out the whole range of differences between the two nations. "I found it necessary," he later said, "to yield my own opinion to the general sense of the national council."[51]

To join Monroe in the negotiations, Jefferson chose William Pinkney, a Baltimore lawyer who had penned a particularly able memorial against the Rule of 1756 after the *Essex* seizures. The instructions the secretary of state drew up to guide the American envoys were largely an exercise in wishful thinking because they called for such a broad range of British concessions. But the administration considered only two items essential to a settlement: an end to impressment and the restoration of the re-export trade.[52]

The British refused to give up impressment, which they saw as the only way to prevent wholesale desertions from the Royal Navy. But they did offer to observe "the greatest caution" in impressing British seamen and to afford "immediate and prompt redress" to any Americans mistakenly forced into service.[53] Monroe and Pinkney realized that this fell far short of their instructions, but Britain showed such a conciliatory spirit on the other issues that they decided to conclude an agreement anyway. The result was the Monroe-Pinkney Treaty of 1806, which was in many ways more favorable to the United States than the Jay Treaty had been.[54]

By the terms of the new treaty, the British agreed not to interfere with the re-export trade as long as American ships paid a small transit duty on their stopover in the United States—a duty that was actually smaller than they were accustomed to paying.[55] The British also conceded a narrow definition of contraband, promised to give proper notice of blockades, and agreed to refrain from interfering with American trade within five miles of the American coast. In addition, they promised to reduce the duties paid by American ships in British ports and to allow American merchants continued access to the British East Indies, though on a more restricted basis than provided for in the Jay Treaty. Best of all, the treaty contained a kind of insurance clause that bound the British to indemnify any merchant whose vessel was detained in violation of the treaty.

To American merchants seeking to make a profit in a war-torn world, the Monroe-Pinkney Treaty offered considerable security— against interference with the East or West Indian trade, against hazy definitions of contraband or unannounced blockades, and against impressment or seizure within five miles of the American coast. The treaty also presaged a favorable revision of duties in British ports and assured compensation in the event of violations. Given the state of war in Europe and the relative strength of England and the United States, the British concessions were significant.

What did the United States have to give up in order to win these concessions? Little more than a promise of benevolent neutrality. The nation agreed to employ no commercial sanctions against England that did not apply to other nations, to give up the doctrine of free ships—free goods, to deny the use of American ports to privateers belonging to Britain's enemies, and to prohibit Americans from serv-

James Monroe, by John Vanderlyn. Courtesy of the National Portrait Gallery, Smithsonian Institution

ing in the armed forces of Britain's enemies. Except for the ban on commercial sanctions, these points were of little consequence. Indeed, most were already embodied in American law or were accepted practice under international law. Thus, in this treaty the United States conceded very little that constituted a new obligation.

As favorable as the Monroe-Pinkney Treaty was, it did contain a kicker. Before signing the agreement, the British insisted on appending a note that dealt with France's recently issued Berlin Decree, which proclaimed a blockade of the British Isles. This was a "paper" blockade—illegal because France did not have the naval power to enforce it. In their note the British reserved the right to retaliate against France—any provision in the treaty notwithstanding—if the United States acquiesced in the French decree.[56] The British reservation was extraordinary and put a cloud over the whole treaty, but it did not substantially alter America's diplomatic position. By ratifying the treaty and making some gesture against the Berlin Decree, the United States could still demand that the entire agreement be implemented.

President Jefferson, however, chose not to submit the treaty to the Senate. "To tell you the truth," he reportedly told a friend, "I do not wish any treaty with Great Britain."[57] Jefferson considered the British concessions trifling and was unwilling to give up the weapon of commercial sanctions without a British promise to end impressment. In addition, he was convinced that France and Russia would ultimately prevail in the European war and would force the British to accept a much broader definition of neutral rights. The points contended for by the United States, he insisted, were matters of right. "They are points which Bonaparte & [Czar] Alexander will concur in settling at the Treaty of peace, & probably in more latitude than Gr. Br. would now yield."[58] Even if Britain's enemies failed to win a broad definition of neutral rights, Jefferson was confident that he could achieve his aims by employing economic sanctions.

The rejection of the Monroe-Pinkney Treaty was a great turning point in the Age of Jefferson. Republicans would later claim that the only options the United States had in this era were submission, commercial sanctions, or war. But the Monroe-Pinkney Treaty offered another alternative, that of accommodation. By rejecting this treaty, the United States missed an opportunity to reforge the Anglo-American accord of the 1790s and to substitute peace and prosperity for commercial restrictions and war.

❖ ❖ ❖ ❖ ❖ ❖

After the loss of the Monroe-Pinkney Treaty, Anglo-American relations steadily deteriorated. In the summer of 1807 the *Chesapeake* affair created a full-blown war scare.[59] The U.S.S. *Chesapeake* was an American frigate with a large number of British subjects among its crew. British officials knew that four deserters from the Royal Navy were serving on the vessel but were unable to secure their return through diplomatic channels. Accordingly, Sir George Berkeley, the commander-in-chief of the British squadron at Halifax, decided to take matters into his own hands by ordering naval commanders assigned to his station to recover the deserters, employing force if necessary.

On June 22, 1807, H.M.S. *Leopard* approached the *Chesapeake* and demanded that a boarding party be allowed to search for the deserters. When the American commander demurred, the British vessel fired three broadsides into the ship, killing three men and wounding eighteen others. Unable to defend itself, the *Chesapeake* struck its colors. The British removed the four deserters, and the American ship limped back into port.

The *Chesapeake* affair stirred public outrage throughout the United States. "But one feeling pervades the Nation," Republican Joseph Nicholson said; "all distinctions of Federalism and Democracy are banished."[60] Jefferson ordered all British warships out of American waters, but instead of fanning the flames, he waited for Britain's official response.

The British did not claim the right to search or impress from neutral warships, which were considered an extension of a nation's territory. Hence they disavowed the attack and ordered Berkeley's recall (though he was later given another command). The British also offered to pay reparations and to return three of the deserters, who were apparently American citizens. (The fourth was a British subject and was summarily hanged.) The issue, however, became entangled with others, and a settlement was delayed until 1811. In the meantime, the *Chesapeake* affair continued to fester, contributing to the rising tide of anti-British feeling in America.

❖ ❖ ❖ ❖ ❖ ❖

Shortly after the *Chesapeake* outrage, another problem surfaced that was to bedevil Anglo-American relations even more—the Orders in Council, a series of executive decrees issued by the British government to regulate neutral trade with the Continent.[61] No strangers to commercial warfare, the British had often used their naval power to destroy an enemy's shipping or trade, and sometimes their practices went beyond international law. The Fox Blockade, for example, was too sweeping to be strictly legal.

It was the French, however, who initiated the great commercial war of the Napoleonic era. Although Napoleon's brilliant military triumph at Austerlitz in late 1805 had made him master of the Continent, he could not invade England because her great naval victory at Trafalgar six weeks earlier had made her undisputed mistress of the seas. Hence Napoleon resorted to commercial warfare, claiming that this was "the only way to strike a blow at England and force her to peace."[62] His plan—known as the Continental System—was to destroy British prosperity by cutting off her trade with Europe.

The first Continental decree—the Berlin Decree, issued in 1806— proclaimed a blockade of the British Isles, excluded from French-occupied harbors all neutral vessels that had touched at a British port, and declared all British-made goods lawful prize even when owned by neutrals. The British responded in 1807 with several Orders in Council, the most important of which proclaimed a blockade of all ports from which British goods were excluded and required neutrals who wished to trade with those ports to stop in England and pay transit duties first. Napoleon replied with the Milan Decree, which proclaimed that any neutral vessel submitting to the British trade regulations or even permitting a British search party to board was subject to seizure.

England and France both conceded that their commercial decrees violated international law, but each claimed that it was only retaliating for the illegal acts of the other. The French insisted that the Fox Blockade was the opening round in the commercial war, while the British pointed to the Berlin Decree. Both sides also used the trade war as a pretext for looting neutral commerce. The British seized neutral ships on the high seas, while the French confiscated neutral property in continental ports. For both belligerents, greed and mercantilism played as great a role in the commercial war as higher reasons of state.

The British and French decrees appeared to render trade with the Continent virtually impossible. If American ships complied with the French decrees, they were subject to seizure by the British; and if they submitted to the British decrees, they could be seized by the French. Appearances were deceptive, however, for enterprising merchants could still make a profit in spite of the belligerent restrictions.

The British repeatedly said that they had no intention of ending all trade with Europe. As Spencer Perceval, the British prime minister, put it: "The object of the Orders in Council was not to destroy the trade of the Continent, but to force the Continent to trade with us."[63]

To facilitate this trade, the British in 1809 reduced the scope of their blockade and lowered their transit duties. They also issued thousands of special licenses, mainly to British subjects and European neutrals, that expressly authorized trade with Europe. France herself winked at the license trade and granted exemptions from the Continental System when it suited her interest.[64]

The British permitted Americans to ship goods produced in the United States directly to the Continent, and some merchants managed to cover trade in non-American goods by securing one of the coveted British licenses. In addition, there were a number of holes in the Continental System. At one time or another, Spain, Sweden, Russia, and Denmark welcomed American ships from the British Isles. Indeed, the trade at Europe's periphery was so extensive that John Quincy Adams compared the Continental System to "an attempt to exclude the air from a bottle, by sealing up hermetically the mouth, while there was a great hole in the side."[65] In addition, American merchants sometimes circumvented the system by carrying dual papers or by bribing customs officials in French-occupied ports.

In spite of these opportunities, the losses under the British and French regulations were heavy. Between 1807 and 1812 the two belligerents and their allies seized about 900 American ships.[66] Given these losses, it is little wonder that the repeal of the belligerent decrees became the paramount objective of American foreign policy in the years before the War of 1812.

❖ ❖ ❖ ❖ ❖ ❖

By late 1807 Americans were under heavy pressure from both belligerents. France had begun to enforce the Berlin Decree, and England had reaffirmed the right of impressment and announced her intention of issuing the Orders in Council. Under these circumstances, Republican leaders decided to retaliate by imposing economic sanctions. The restrictive system, as these measures were called, was a series of trade restrictions adopted between 1806 and 1812 to force the belligerents to show greater respect for American rights.[67]

The restrictive system had its origins in the era of the American Revolution. In the 1760s and 1770s the American colonies had employed non-importation and non-exportation against the mother country in the hope of forcing her to change her tax and trade policies. Although these measures had had little impact on British colonial policy, men like Jefferson and Madison interpreted history otherwise. Convinced that America's greatest weapon was her economic power, Republican leaders believed that the United States held the key to the prosperity of Great Britain and, to a lesser extent, of France as well. "Our trade," said the Boston *Chronicle* in 1805, "is the most powerful weapon we can use in our defence."[68] All the United States had to do, the Republicans believed, was to turn the economic screws and the European belligerents would be brought to terms, if not to their knees.

The first restriction adopted was the partial non-importation act of 1806.[69] This law prohibited the importation of a select list of British manufactured goods, but because it excluded few textile or metal products, it did not strike at the heart of Britain's export trade. It was more of a threat than anything else, designed to warn the British of what to expect if they did not show greater respect for American rights. To give the British time to make concessions during the Monroe-Pinkney negotiations, the law was repeatedly suspended and did not go into operation until December of 1807.

Shortly after this law went into effect, the Republicans adopted the embargo, the most comprehensive and controversial of all the trade restrictions.[70] Essentially a non-exportation law, the embargo prohibited American ships and goods from leaving port. In principle the measure was extraordinarily sweeping, and many regarded the cure as worse than the disease. Republican critic John Randolph, for example, compared the embargo to an attempt "to cure corns by cutting off the toes."[71]

In practice, however, the law had numerous loopholes, at least at first. Many ships were able to slip out of port before official news of the embargo arrived and once at sea made no effort to return. Merchants could legally dispatch ships to pick up American property abroad, and some 600 vessels sailed on this pretext. Some ships left port illegally, while others—nominally plying the coasting trade—were "blown" off course to a port in the West Indies or Canada. Foreign ships could still bring cargoes to the United States as long as they left in ballast—a rule they sometimes evaded. There was also a good deal of overland trade, especially along the Canadian frontier.[72]

To enforce the embargo, Secretary of the Treasury Albert Gallatin told Jefferson that government officials would need "arbitrary powers" that were "equally dangerous & odious." The president was undeterred. "Congress," he replied, "must legalise all *means* which may be necessary to obtain it's *end*."[73] Accordingly, the administration asked for and received increasingly broad powers. The climax was the enforcement act of 1809, which gave customs officials sweeping powers and authorized the use of the army and navy to suppress smuggling.[74]

The enforcement campaign was largely successful, but Republicans and Federalists alike became increasingly disillusioned with the whole policy. Likening the embargo to a turtle because the nation was drawing into itself, Federalists spelled the word backwards to illustrate its effects. "O-grab-me," they said, and at one time or another the turtlelike embargo snapped at almost everyone's livelihood.

Economically, the embargo drove the nation into a deep depression, perhaps the worst experienced since the beginning of colonial times. Exports, which had peaked at $108,000,000 in 1807, plummeted (officially at least) to $22,000,000 in 1808.[75] Farmers could not ship their produce to foreign markets, and merchants could not send their ships to sea. For many people, the result was loss and suffering, if not outright disaster.[76]

Politically, the embargo rejuvenated the Federalist party, which only a year or two before had seemed headed for extinction. The howls of protest from commercial New England steadily mounted, and there was even talk of nullification and secession. Although the embargo was conceived of as a substitute for foreign war—as a peaceful means of upholding American rights—it very nearly precipitated civil war.

Yet for all this the embargo elicited hardly a peep from England or France. According to the American minister in Paris, the coercive effects of the measure were overrated. "Here it is not felt, and in England . . . it is forgotten."[77] Napoleon used the embargo as a pretext for seizing American vessels, claiming that they must be British ships in disguise.[78] England was deprived of some of her customary imports, but she found new markets for her exports in South America and welcomed the withdrawal of a commercial rival. A British subject later made fun of the measure: "The late Jeffersonian Embargo was a Rod which produced no other sensation on the rough hide of John Bull, than the pleasurable one which arises from titilation. The poor Animal was delighted, and not suspecting that this philosophical experiment on his Hide was intended to produce pain, he regretted that weariness had ultimately compelled Mr. Jefferson to cease scratching."[79]

In March of 1809—after fifteen months of national suffering—Congress repealed the embargo and non-importation laws and substituted a non-intercourse act.[80] This measure prohibited trade with England and France and their colonies but permitted it with the rest of the world. It imposed both non-importation and non-exportation on the belligerents, but only part of the law could be enforced. Ships and goods from Britain and France could be kept from American ports, but American vessels could not be prevented from going where they pleased once they departed from the United States. American merchants often traded with the British in neutral ports or sailed directly to England, where they were welcomed despite faulty papers.

Given the failure of the embargo, which was far more sweeping, few people expected non-intercourse to work. It was designed primarily to save face, to keep up the appearance of commercial warfare while giving up the rigors of the embargo.

Ever since the early days of the embargo, the administration had expressed a willingness to give up commercial warfare if either belligerent suspended its restrictions on trade. In April of 1809, the British minister in Washington, David M. Erskine, signed a convention providing for the mutual suspension of the British and American restrictions. But the agreement was repudiated in London because Erskine had exceeded his instructions. Hence, non-intercourse was restored against England.[81]

In May of 1810, Congress repealed the non-intercourse act and substituted Macon's bill #2.[82] This law reopened trade with England and France but promised to reimpose non-importation against either belligerent if the other rescinded its restrictions on neutral trade. Seeing an opportunity to hoodwink the United States, Napoleon ordered his foreign minister, the Duc de Cadore, to promise French cooperation. In the so-called Cadore Letter, sent to the American government in August, 1810, France pledged to suspend the Continental Decrees if the United States "shall cause their rights to be respected by the English," presumably by reimposing non-importation.[83]

Napoleon had no intention of making good on this promise. Although some American vessels were released for appearances, the French continued to prey on American shipping, and a new series of French tariffs and export restrictions rendered American trade with the Continent almost impossible. Moreover, in the Trianon Decree (issued at the same time as the Cadore Letter) the Emperor secretly ordered the condemnation of American ships in French hands that had not even violated his decrees. Clearly, Napoleon's plan was not to make concessions to the United States, but to give the appearance of doing so in the hope of further embroiling the new nation with England.[84]

This plan worked because President Madison chose to accept the Cadore Letter at face value. Not only did he hope that Napoleon would live up to his word, but he thought that he could use the French pledge as a lever to force the British to suspend the Orders in Council. The British, however, refused to budge, claiming that the French repeal was spurious. Hence Madison issued a proclamation reimposing non-importation against England and her colonies as of February,

James Madison, by David Edwin. Courtesy of the National Portrait Gallery, Smithsonian Institution

1811. The following month Congress passed a bill to give this proclamation the full force of law.[85]

The second non-importation act was the last coercive measure adopted by the United States before the War of 1812. With this measure the nation had come the full circuit—from non-importation to non-exportation and back to non-importation—as Republican leaders searched in vain for an instrument that would have a significant impact on the belligerents while doing the least damage to the United States. The second non-importation law was probably the best of these measures, although it turned the normally prosperous Anglo-American trade into a stagnant one-sided exchange and led to the accumulation of American capital in England.

❖ ❖ ❖ ❖ ❖ ❖

After the adoption of the non-importation law, Anglo-American relations continued to deteriorate. The American minister to England returned to the United States in early 1811, leaving only a chargé d'affaires in his place. The following July the newly-appointed British minister, Augustus J. Foster, arrived in Washington with a fresh set of demands. Foster threatened retaliation if non-importation were continued. He also declared that Britain would not lift the Orders in Council until France had suspended her decrees for all neutral nations (and not just the United States) and had dropped her tariff and export restrictions as well. In short, the Orders would continue until British goods were freely admitted to the Continent.[86]

Two other developments contributed to the deterioration of Anglo-American relations in 1811. The first was the *Little Belt* incident, a kind of *Chesapeake* affair in reverse. In the hope of deterring impressments, the Navy Department had ordered the heavy frigate *President* to cruise off the coast. On May 16 the *President* clashed with the much smaller *Little Belt,* killing nine of her crew and wounding twenty-three others. The fight took place at night, and it was never clear who fired first. Most Americans saw the engagement as just retribution for the *Chesapeake* affair and celebrated accordingly. The British, on the other hand, were convinced that the *President* was guilty of unprovoked aggression, and some newspapers demanded retaliation.[87] "The blood of our murdered countrymen must be revenged," declared the London *Courier.* "The conduct of America leaves us no alternative."[88]

The other development that contributed to Anglo-American discord in 1811 was the outbreak of a new Indian war on the western frontier. Ever since Pontiac's Rebellion in 1763, the Northwest Territory had periodically erupted in flames. Since the Indians were tied economically and diplomatically to the British, most Americans blamed the uprisings on England. "We have had but one opinion as the cause of the depredations of the Indians," said *Niles' Register;* "they are instigated and supported by the British in Canada."[89]

The threat of an uprising steadily mounted after 1805, when two Shawnee brothers, Tecumseh and Tenskwatawa (better known as the Prophet), sought to build an Indian confederation based on the rejection of the white man's ways and resistance to further land cessions.[90] The Shawnee leaders established their camp at Prophet's Town (at the confluence of the Tippecanoe and Wabash rivers in present-day Indiana) and from there spread their message throughout the West. Tecumseh was a gifted statesman who modeled himself after Pontiac, while the Prophet enjoyed considerable influence as a spiritual leader. The movement became increasingly militant in tone, and a new round of Indian depredations erupted in 1810.[91]

William Henry Harrison, governor of the Indiana Territory, was an ardent expansionist who was determined to crush the Indian conspiracy. "If some decisive measures are not speedily adopted," he told the secretary of war, "we shall have a general combination of all the tribes against us."[92] The administration was reluctant to provoke an Indian war but finally succumbed to Harrison's pleas for troops. By the fall of 1811 Harrison had assembled an army of 1,000 regulars and militia. His plan was to march to Prophet's Town and demand that the Shawnee leaders give up those responsible for the recent depredations.[93]

By the time Harrison's army reached Prophet's Town in November, Tecumseh was on a recruiting mission in the South. Urged on by the Prophet, 600 or 700 Indians attacked Harrison's camp in the pre-dawn hours of November 7. The Indians badly mauled the Americans, who were caught off guard, silhouetted against their camp fires. But the troops held their positions and, using cartridges loaded with buckshot, eventually turned the tide. Most of the Indians enjoyed good cover, though some appeared in the open because the Prophet had promised them immunity from American bullets. The Indians were finally driven off by a counterattack on their flanks, and Harrison burned Prophet's Town the next day.[94]

In the Battle of Tippecanoe, Harrison's army suffered almost 200 casualties, while Indian losses were probably around 100. Nevertheless, the battle was an American victory. The Prophet's spell was broken, and a good many Indians defected from his cause.[95] The battle, however, did little to deter the Indian depredations on the frontier, and the whole region remained unsafe. "Most of the Citizens in this Country," Harrison reported in 1812, "have abandoned their farms and taken refuge in Such temporary forts as they have been able to construct."[96]

The Indian war also intensified American hatred for Britain. Republican newspapers carried accounts of the battle under such headings as "ANGLO-SAVAGE WAR" or "Anglo-Indian War."[97] "[T]he war on the Wabash is purely BRITISH," said the Lexington *Reporter*. "[T]he SCALPING KNIFE and TOMAHAWK of *British savages, is now, again devastating our frontiers.*"[98]

❖ ❖ ❖ ❖ ❖ ❖

With Anglo-American discord mounting, a growing number of Republicans began to talk of war.[99] It was an important, even a momentous step, and yet what were the alternatives? The restrictive system had failed, and in the eyes of most Republicans, to do nothing at all in the face of British encroachments was unthinkable. For years Republican foreign policy had been predicated on the necessity of upholding American rights, and many now regarded war as the only way of achieving this end. "Negociation & commercial restrictions failed to obtain redress," William Plumer of New Hampshire later said: "submission or war were the only remaining alternatives."[100]

War appealed to Republicans because it offered the prospect of winning diplomatic concessions from the British, of forcing them to give up the Orders in Council and impressment and perhaps modify their other maritime practices as well. War was also seen as a way of resolving the nation's long-standing Indian problem. Though this problem was not as crucial as the maritime issues, it did loom large in the West. "The blood of our fellow-citizens murdered on the Wabash by British intrigue," said the Lexington *Reporter*, "calls aloud for vengeance."[101] By conquering Canada, or at least administering a sound drubbing to the British there, the Republicans hoped to sever British ties with American Indians and thus put an end to the nation's recurring Indian wars. In other words, war offered the prospect of winning American diplomatic aims in the Northwest as well as on the high seas.

Republicans also saw war as a way of vindicating American independence. As heirs of the American Revolution, the Republicans were steeped in anglophobia. Extremely sensitive to British slights—as would befit citizens of a new nation—they saw British encroachments as part of a larger plot to keep the United States in a kind of quasi-colonial subjugation. Britain's aim, said Jonathan Roberts of Pennsylvania, was "to make us subserve her interests as a colonial dependency." "If we submit," declared John C. Calhoun, "the independence of this nation is lost."[102]

War was also seen as a way of shoring up republican institutions. The United States was the only democratic republic in the world, and even though most Americans were confident that they were riding the wave of the future, they were acutely conscious of how fragile republican institutions were. If the administration proved incapable of protecting American rights, the people might turn to some other form of government, and the entire republican experiment might collapse. As the editor of the Washington *National Intelligencer* put it, "Not only the rights of the nation, but the character of the government are involved in the issue." "[T]he time is come," added another Republican, "to humble the overgrown monsters [the British]—and to cause our republic to be respected at home and abroad."[103]

Besides upholding independence and preserving republican institutions, war offered the prospect of significant political dividends. A successful war would redound to the Republicans' advantage, while retreat would have just the opposite effect. "The honor of the Nation and that of the party," said a Philadelphia newspaper editor, "are bound up together and both will be sacrificed if war be not declared." "If War is not resorted to," added a Tennessee congressman, "this nation or rather their representatives will be disgraced." "The War machine [must be] put into active motion," said another Republican; "this deed, & this deed alone can save the character of the Democratic party & of the Nation."[104]

War also offered the best means of unifying the Republican party. For years the administration had been under fire from various factions within the party. There was growing resentment, especially in the North, over the domination of the Virginia dynasty. There was also growing frustration over the British and French depredations and the failure of the restrictive system. Many Republicans were critical of the administration for failing to defend the nation's rights or to prepare the nation for war. With the election of 1812 looming ahead, it was imperative for the administration to silence these dissidents and consolidate its hold on the party. "A change in our foreign relations," said a Virginia Republican, "would enable [Madison] to ride triumphant, put down his opponents in Congress & silence the growlings of those who ought to possess his entire confidence."[105]

Besides unifying the Republican party, war also offered the prospect of silencing the Federalists. No doubt Republicans found the Federalist claim—which was constantly repeated—that the restrictive system was a futile, double-edged sword all the more galling because it was so near the truth.[106] A state of war, most Republicans assumed, would put an end to this criticism, for everyone—including Federalists—

would have to rally to the cause. "A declaration of War," said William Plumer, "must necessarily produce a great change in public opinion & the State of parties—British partisans must then either close their lips in silence or abscond." "By war," Elbridge Gerry of Massachusetts told the president, "we should be purified, as by fire."[107]

Thus by 1812 many Republicans had concluded that there were compelling diplomatic, ideological, and political reasons for going to war against England. If all went well, the Republicans could expect to win concessions from the British, vindicate American independence, preserve republican institutions, maintain power, unify their party, and silence the Federalists. With these prospects before them, many Republicans had come to believe that the rewards of war outweighed its risks.

President Madison was by nature a cautious man, but he shared these views. The nation, he believed, was at a crossroads, with the future of the republic at stake. To submit to British practices, he thought, would be to sacrifice "the neutral guaranty of an Independent flag" and to "recolonize our commerce by subjecting it to a foreign authority."[108] Hence, even though Republican policies had left the nation woefully unprepared to prosecute a major war, the President summoned Congress to an early meeting in November, 1811, to consider this very prospect.

CHAPTER 2

The Declaration of War

THE TWELFTH CONGRESS—known to history as the War Congress—convened on November 4, 1811. Republicans across the country showed a keen interest in its proceedings. "Never did the American Congress assemble under circumstances of greater interest and responsibility," said the Boston *Chronicle*. The deliberations of this body, the Washington *National Intelligencer* predicted, "will, perhaps, do more to stamp the character of genuine republican governments than has been effected in this respect since the creation of the world." "The people, the times and the government," added the Salem *Register*, "all require DECISION."[1]

The Republicans had solid majorities in both houses of the new Congress, controlling 75 percent of the seats in the House and 82 percent in the Senate.[2] Yet for years they had been without competent floor leadership and beset by factionalism. "Factions in our own party," said one Republican, "have hitherto been the bane of the Democratic administration."[3] The regular Republicans, who customarily followed the administration's lead, could usually muster a majority, but sometimes they were outmaneuvered by their enemies. Their most implacable foes were the Federalists. Led by Josiah Quincy and James Lloyd of Massachusetts and James A. Bayard of Delaware, the Federalists numbered only 25 percent of the House and 18 percent of the Senate, but they normally voted as a bloc and usually opposed the administration.

The Federalists were sometimes joined by dissident Republicans, such as the Old Republicans, the Clintonians, or the "Invisibles." The Old Republicans were the conscience of the Republican party. Led by the brilliant but eccentric John Randolph of Roanoke, they were a small group of southern agrarians who favored simple government and believed that the administration had embraced too many Federalist policies.[4] The Clintonians, on the other hand, thought the government ought to adopt more Federalist policies. Led by George and De Witt Clinton of New York, they were northern Republicans—mainly from commercial areas—who opposed economic restrictions and favored greater protection for trade.[5] The "Invisibles" (also known as the Smith faction) were a small band of senators headed by Samuel Smith of Maryland, William Branch Giles of Virginia, and Michael Leib of Pennsylvania. They had a reputation for political opportunism, but what actually united them was a common interest in military preparedness and a common dislike of Albert Gallatin and his parsimonious treasury policies.[6] Most of the dissidents also disliked the president. "There is much animosity towards Madison," said a Pennsylvania congressman, "in the Smiths & Gileses & I might say in the Clintons too."[7]

The War Congress also contained a new faction, one capable of providing the leadership and firmness that hitherto had been lacking. These were the War Hawks, a group of about a dozen ardent patriots too young to remember the horrors of the last British war and thus willing to run the risks of another to vindicate the nation's rights. Most of them came from the South or West. The group included Henry Clay and Richard M. Johnson of Kentucky; Felix Grundy of Tennessee; Langdon Cheves, William Lowndes, John C. Calhoun, and David R. Williams of South Carolina; George M. Troup of Georgia; Peter B. Porter of New York; and John A. Harper of New Hampshire.[8] The War Hawks had the respect not only of other Republicans but of the Federalists, too. "Clay, Cheves, Lowndes, and [C]alhoun," said a Massachusetts Federalist, "are confessedly the best informed & most liberal men of the party."[9]

Clay was the most able and articulate of the War Hawks. Although not yet thirty-five and never before a member of the House, he was elected speaker and lost no time in establishing his authority.[10] When Randolph brought his dog into the House, Clay ordered the animal removed—something no previous speaker had dared or cared to do.[11] "The new Speaker is quite popular," commented a Federalist. "He possesses fine talents and presides with dignity."[12] Molding the speakership into a position of power, Clay "reduc'd the chaos to order."[13] By directing debate and interpreting the rules, by packing key committees and acting forcefully behind the scenes, he insured that the War Hawks dominated the Twelfth Congress.

The president sent his annual address to Congress on November 5.

Henry Clay, by an unknown artist. Courtesy of the National Portrait Gallery, Smithsonian Institution

Although Madison had planned a stronger message, Gallatin—who feared the effects of war—persuaded him to tone down his attack on Britain.[14] The only grievance mentioned in the address was the Orders in Council. Accusing England of making "war on our lawful commerce," the president called for war preparations. In view of Britain's "hostile inflexibility," he said, "Congress will feel the duty of putting the United States into an armor and an attitude demanded by the crisis."[15]

According to the Philadelphia *Aurora*, the president's message was "most happily adapted . . . to redeem the public mind from despondence; and to restore the nation to confidence in itself." "It has awakened and invigorated the almost desponding spirits of the people," added the Worcester *Aegis*.[16] Although the War Hawks had hoped for a more spirited address, they agreed to call it a "war message."[17] The House referred the bulk of the message to its Foreign Relations Committee, which Clay had packed with War Hawks.[18] Unwilling to recommend preparations without a promise from the president to support war, the committee conferred with Secretary of State James Monroe. William Lowndes reported that Monroe gave "the strongest assurances that the president will cooperate zealously with congress in declaring war if our complaints are not redressed by may next."[19]

On November 29, Chairman Peter B. Porter read the Foreign Relations Committee's report. It was a stinging attack on British policies—focusing on the Orders in Council but also mentioning impressment—and a ringing plea for action. In the face of British wrongs "so daring in character, and so disgraceful in their execution," the report called on Congress to summon forth "the patriotism and resources of the country." Toward this end, the committee recommended six resolutions that called for filling the ranks of the existing army, raising additional regulars and short-term volunteers, authorizing the use of militia, fitting out the navy, and permitting merchant vessels to arm for defense.[20] In his supporting speech, Porter said that the report was to be understood as a forerunner to war and that only those who favored war should vote for the resolutions. "Do not let us raise armies," he said, "unless we intend to employ them."[21]

The House approved each resolution by a large margin, the majorities ranging from 75 to 112.[22] The only proposal that generated any opposition, the arming of merchantmen, was attacked as a half-way measure that was premature and also dangerous because it might lead to war with several nations. But even this resolution was approved by a 97-22 margin.[23] "There appears to be a greater degree of unanimity in the national legislature," said one Federalist, "than I have observed on any important question, since the conclusion of the revolutionary war."[24]

Appearances were deceptive, however, for different factions in the House supported the resolutions for different reasons. The War Hawks supported them as a prelude to war; commercial Republicans, because they had long advocated stronger defense measures. Some Republicans—the "scarecrow" party—hoped that the mere threat of war would frighten the British into concessions. According to one critic, they believed "that it [would] not be necessary to employ, or even raise the force contemplated."[25] The Federalists, on the other hand, supported the resolutions to avoid the charge of "British gold" and to uphold their traditional commitment to preparedness. "[W]e hope to avoid being amalgamated with [the] British," said one Federalist. These are "measures of the old federal school," said another.[26]

The adoption of the resolutions indicated that a large majority in the House favored war preparations. Members of the Senate were of a like mind, and between December, 1811, and April, 1812, Congress enacted a war program. The Federalists offered little resistance and even supported some of the bills, but dissidents (particularly in the Senate) stymied the administration on several key proposals.[27] As a result, the war program that emerged was not exactly what the administration had wanted.

Five of the measures were designed to support a land war. The most important provided for completing the existing 10,000-man army (whose ranks were barely half full) by raising the bounty for new recruits from $12 to $31 plus 160 acres of land.[28] The other measures provided for raising 25,000 additional regulars and 50,000 one-year volunteers, authorized the president to call out 100,000 militia for up to six months' service, and appropriated $1,900,000 for the purchase of ordnance.[29]

The administration disliked the additional army bill because it was too ambitious. Convinced that sufficient regulars could not be recruited in time for a spring campaign, Madison and his advisors planned to rely on short-term volunteers and militia.[30] But Senator Giles preferred regulars, and he persuaded Congress to raise the authorized level of the army to 35,000 men.[31] Even worse, Congress voted to give the states (rather than the national government) authority to appoint the volunteer officers. This threatened to decentralize the war effort. It also prompted some congressmen—Federalists and Republicans alike—to insist that the new troops were actually militia who could not legally serve abroad—even in Canada.[32]

The administration also failed to secure the authority it sought to arm and classify the militia. Southerners had long favored legislation of this sort because their militia were so poorly armed and organized. Northerners, on the other hand, were reasonably satisfied with existing arrangements and hence opposed any innovations.[33] The House defeated one bill to arm and classify the militia and tabled another to arm the militia.[34]

The measures designed to support a maritime war also ran into trouble. Armed with facts and figures from the Navy Department, Langdon Cheves introduced a bill from the House Naval Committee that called for building ten new frigates. A long-term construction program, Cheves argued, would be relatively inexpensive and would benefit farmers and merchants alike.[35] Cheves was supported by some Republicans as well as by the Federalists. Josiah Quincy delivered a speech on behalf of naval expansion that former Federalist John Adams called "the most important . . . ever uttered" in the House and that even the anti-navy Philadelphia *Aurora* considered "ingenious."[36] "If you had a field to defend in Georgia," Quincy said, "it would be very strange to put up a fence in Massachusetts. And yet, how does this differ from invading Canada, for the purpose of defending our maritime rights?"[37]

Most Republicans, however, were opposed to naval expansion, believing that a fleet was a costly and dangerous expedient that would be overwhelmed by the British navy. "[W]e cannot contend with Great Britain on the ocean," declared Adam Seybert of Pennsylvania. "[O]ur vessels will only tend to swell the present catalogue of the British navy."[38] Most Republicans agreed with Seybert, and Cheves's frigate proposal was voted down by a three-vote margin. James Lloyd offered a similar proposal in the Senate, but it lost by a six-vote margin.[39] The House also rejected proposals to build ships-of-the-line and a naval repair dock.[40] Instead, Congress passed a bill that provided merely for fitting out the existing frigates, purchasing ship timber, and assigning Jefferson's gunboats to those harbors that were most exposed.[41] A bill to build additional coastal fortifications was approved, too, though only after the Senate had slashed the proposed $1,000,000 appropriation in half.[42]

Even more controversial were the administration's plans to finance the war. Secretary of the Treasury Albert Gallatin hoped to use tax revenue to pay the government's regular expenses and loans to finance its war expenses.[43] The details were presented to Congress in January of 1812. Gallatin had earlier estimated that regular expenses for 1812 would be $9,400,000, which could be met from current revenue and a small surplus in the treasury. To finance war-related expenses, he now recommended a loan of more than $10,000,000. Moreover, because a disruption in trade was expected to reduce government revenue at a time when interest charges on the national debt were climbing, Gallatin recommended raising the customs duties and reviving the old internal taxes that had been repealed in 1802.[44]

Gallatin's report was a great shock to most Republicans, few of whom had given any thought to internal taxes. These taxes had contributed to the defeat of the Federalists in 1800, and many Republicans feared that reviving them would undermine their popularity and put a damper on the war spirit. "I cannot think it will necessary at present to resort to *direct taxes & stamp acts*," said William Plumer. "This was the very course that proved fatal to John Adams' administration."[45]

Fearful of the consequences, House Republicans would not even print the report, and Gallatin was subjected to relentless criticism.[46] One congressman accused him of "treading in the muddy footsteps of his official predecessors" and of trying "to chill the war spirit." "If reports are true," said another, the British minister's carriage "is frequently seen at Gallatin's house at such hours of the night as honest men are asleep."[47] A Clintonian paper suggested that Gallatin's aim was to " 'frighten the war-hawks,' and *blow up the cabinet*," and other papers accused him of treachery or apostacy.[48] Many assured their readers that the war could be won without additional taxes.[49]

As unpalatable as the tax issue was, the War Hawks realized that it could not be sidestepped. Hence, in mid-February Ezekiel Bacon, Chairman of the House Ways and Means Committee, introduced a series of proposals to implement Gallatin's program. A bill to borrow $11,000,000 stirred little debate and easily passed both houses.[50] The tax resolutions, however, provoked vigorous opposition even though they merely took the sense of the House and clearly specified that no new duties would be imposed until after war had been declared. There was considerable support for postponing the subject altogether, which prompted one Federalist to wonder whether "the war [would] float the taxes, or the taxes sink the war."[51] In the end the resolutions were approved, which was a triumph for the administration.[52] Members of the House "have got down the dose of taxes," Madison said. "It is the strongest proof they could give that they do not mean to flinch from the contest to which the mad conduct of G[reat] B[ritain] drives them."[53]

On paper the Republican war program was impressive. True enough, Congress had refused to endorse either naval expansion or immediate taxation and had failed to arm and classify the militia or give the president authority to appoint volunteer officers. Nevertheless, those measures that were adopted were more far-reaching than

Albert Gallatin, by Thomas Worthington Whittredge. Courtesy of the National Portrait Gallery, Smithsonian Institution

any since the Quasi-War. In less than four months, Congress had enacted legislation to fill the ranks of the existing army, raise additional regulars and volunteers, call out the militia, purchase ordnance, fit out the navy, build coastal fortifications, and borrow money. Though not exactly what the administration had wanted, the program was nevertheless a giant step in the direction of war.

❖ ❖ ❖ ❖ ❖ ❖

The War Hawks hoped their legislative program would promote patriotism and prepare the American people psychologically and militarily for war. President Madison hoped for the same result, and he used the powers of his office to stimulate the war spirit further. On March 9, 1812, as the war program was nearing completion, the president informed Congress that a British plot to incite disunion in New England had been uncovered. The central figure in this plot was a handsome, if simple-minded and pretentious, Irishman by the name of John Henry.[54]

Born in 1777, Henry had migrated to the United States in 1798. After spending several years in New England, he had moved to Montreal, apparently to pursue the fur-trading business. In 1808 he took a business trip to New England and sent back reports on the state of affairs to British officials in Canada. The following year Sir James Craig, the governor-general of Canada, commissioned Henry to make another trip to New England. War seemed imminent, and Craig wanted more information, particularly on the prospect of exploiting Federalist opposition.

After returning from his second mission, Henry received £200 (about $900) in compensation. Regarding this sum as wholly inadequate, he spent the next two years in England and Canada seeking additional remuneration. He reportedly asked for £32,000 ($142,000) but would settle for an office yielding £500 ($2200) a year. Disillusioned with his lack of success, he fell in with a French rogue who styled himself Count Edward de Crillon but who was actually an accomplished imposter by the name of Paul Emile Soubiran. Crillon persuaded Henry to try to sell his correspondence to the United States government.

The two adventurers came to America, secured a letter of introduction from Governor Elbridge Gerry of Massachusetts, and then proceeded to Washington.[55] There they persuaded the administration to buy the documents for $50,000—the entire budget of the secret service fund. The bargain was sealed on February 8, 1812, but the documents were kept under wraps for another month to give Henry time to leave the country.

Convinced that Henry's papers constituted "formal proof of the Cooperation between the Eastern Junto & the Br[itish] Cabinet,"[56] Madison sent the documents to Congress. In a covering letter, he claimed that they showed that Britain had dispatched a secret agent to New England to promote disaffection and destroy the Union.[57] This was an exaggeration. Although Henry was authorized to put disaffected Federalists in touch with officials in Canada, his primary mission was simply "to obtain the most accurate information of the true state of affairs in that part of the Union."[58]

The *National Intelligencer* expressed hope that Henry's papers would "become a bond of union against a common foe," but their effect was just the opposite.[59] Initially, Republicans greeted news of the plot with indignation, Federalists with embarrassment and chagrin. According to a Republican observer, when the letters were read in the House, one Federalist "began to kick and *squirm*," a second "looked pale— walked the floor in haste," while "great drops of sweat" ran down the face of a third.[60] But closer examination soon revealed that Henry had implicated no one. He had shown his credentials to no one, and he had put no one in touch with Canadian officials. According to one Republican, the Federalists at first "seemed astonished, but the next day they came to the house quite in a passion." After a night's reflection, they were "as mad as they could be."[61]

When the House sought to question Henry, Monroe revealed that the Irishman had left the country and had been promised immunity from interrogation anyway.[62] When the Senate asked if any Americans were implicated in Henry's plot, Monroe conceded that the administration was "not in possession of any names."[63] Moreover, by tracing the treasury warrants Federalists discovered that the documents had been purchased—rather than freely given, as Henry's covering letter had implied. This only added to the Federalists' outrage and to the embarrassment of Republicans.[64]

Federalists considered the whole affair a tawdry political gimmick. A Massachusetts congressman called the publication of the documents "an electioneering trick, calculated for the meridian of Massachusetts."[65] As if to prove him right, Republican newspapers tried to make political capital out of the affair, and one congressman expressed regret that the documents had not been made public sooner to help Republicans in New Hampshire.[66]

The Henry affair proved to be a tempest in a teapot. The letters were hardly worth $50,000 and scarcely a cause for war. It was common practice in those days for governments to use amateur spies to secure information from potentially hostile nations. Because of Canada's weakness vis-à-vis the United States, British officials had employed secret agents on several occasions, and during the war scare that followed the *Chesapeake* affair in 1807–1808, the United States had returned the favor.[67] The real significance of the Henry affair was not that it demonstrated British perfidy or Federalist disloyalty but that it showed the administration's determination to whip up support for its war policy. "We have made use of Henry's documents," Monroe told the French minister, "as a last means of exciting the nation and Congress."[68]

❖ ❖ ❖ ❖ ❖ ❖

Just as the dust raised by the Henry affair was settling, Congress took another step toward war by enacting a ninety-day embargo. This measure was adopted at the insistence of the War Hawks, who considered it a forerunner to war. In mid-March Clay had urged the administration to recommend a short-term embargo to be followed by war unless the U.S.S. *Hornet,* which was expected from Europe shortly, brought news of British concessions. The administration was unresponsive, but Clay kept up the pressure.[69] Finally, on April 1, the president sent a message to Congress recommending a sixty-day embargo.[70] A bill was rushed through Congress in three days, though the Senate extended the embargo to ninety days.[71] Shortly thereafter, a non-exportation act was adopted as a companion measure.[72] Together these laws prohibited American ships from clearing for foreign ports and barred the export of all goods and specie by land or by sea.

The War Hawks insisted that the embargo was designed to protect American property, that its purpose was to keep ships and cargoes in port pending a declaration of war. "[I]t is to be viewed," said Clay, "as a direct precursor to war."[73] But some Republicans supported the embargo as a coercive instrument—as a continuation of the old restrictive system.[74] In addition, some members of the Senate voted to extend the embargo to ninety days because they saw the measure as a negotiating instrument or wished to put off war as long as possible.[75]

The proceedings on the embargo were conducted in secret, but someone (probably John Randolph) leaked word even before the bill was reported from committee. News of the measure soon spread to merchants in Baltimore—perhaps through the agency of Samuel Smith. Calhoun, who thought no one should enjoy any advantage from privileged information, notified Federalist congressmen of the measure, and they sent expresses to northern cities to alert their constituents. Hence, by the time the embargo actually became law, practically everyone in the country already knew about it.[76]

News of the embargo led to a flurry of activity as merchants in virtually every port rushed to get their ships to sea. Freight rates jumped 20 percent, and many vessels were wholly loaded in two days. In Philadelphia shipowners offered seamen $40 a month and in Baltimore as much as $50—which was twice the usual rate. Close to 140 ships cleared from New York City alone, and Boston, reported one merchant, "is all confusion and bustle—& no attention is paid to its being Sunday."[77] Republicans no less than Federalists took part in the frenzied activity. "In this *hurly burley* to palsy the arm of the government," *Niles' Register* conceded, "justice compels us to say, that all parties united."[78]

❖ ❖ ❖ ❖ ❖ ❖

The rush to get ships to sea made a mockery of the embargo, which was supposed to protect American vessels by keeping them in port. "[T]he great body of the people," said *Niles' Register*, "have acted, as though an adjustment of differences with Great Britain, instead of an appeal to the sword, was at hand."[79] Insurance rates—a good indication of public expectations—remained low in early 1812, even for ships sailing to England.[80] "We hear from all quarters," wrote Lowndes in late March, "that the people do not expect war." "[M]any people, even Republicans," wrote William Plumer in May, "do not yet believe the govt is in reality preparing for *actual war.*"[81]

Federalists were particularly skeptical of the war talk. In a highly publicized statement made three years earlier, Josiah Quincy had claimed that the Republican majority "could not be kicked into" war. "[N]o insult, however gross, offered to us by either France or Great Britain," he said, "could force this majority into the declaration of war."[82] Nothing in the years that followed had altered Quincy's opinion. Even after the War Congress had assembled, Quincy claimed that the talk of war was "ludicrous" and that even "the highest toned of the war party" conceded privately that hostilities were unlikely.[83] Most Federalists shared this view. The Republicans, claimed the Boston *Gazette*, "are playing a hypocritical part." Their object was "to provoke the Federalists to their accustomed opposition" so that they could retreat to the restrictive system with the plea that the "British" faction opposed stronger measures.[84]

The government was partly responsible for this skepticism. Talk of war in the past had never led to hostilities, and the signals emanating from the administration were still mixed. As late as March 31, Monroe, sounding very much like a proponent of the scarecrow strategy, told the House Foreign Relations Committee that the war preparations were designed to *"appeal to the feelings of the foreign Govt."*[85] At the time Monroe was writing a series of editorials for the Washington *National Intelligencer,* but not until April 14 did he call unmistakably for war.[86] Ten days later, Madison told Jefferson that "great differences of opinion" still existed over the timing and the form of hostilities.[87]

Perhaps hoping not to tip its hand, the administration kept the British minister in the dark. When Augustus J. Foster asked if the embargo would be followed by war, Madison demurred, claiming that its purpose was to protect commerce and that "one embargo may be inoculated upon another."[88] This made the embargo seem like a continuation of the restrictive system. As late as May 10, Foster was so confused by the signals he was receiving that he wrote to a British consul: "[S]o absolutely are they here without Chart or Compass that I really am at a loss to give you news."[89]

Republicans in Congress were also sending mixed signals. "[T]he war fever," reported a House Federalist, "has its hot and cold fits."[90] It was well known that some Republicans had voted for the embargo as a continuation of the restrictive system, which undermined the War Hawks' claim that it was a preliminary to war. Moreover, members of both houses showed signs of weariness from the long session and were anxious to return home. "I am so fatigued with the doings and not doings of Congress," said Nathaniel Macon in March, "that I sincerely wish myself at home and free from all public engagements."[91]

This sentiment was so prevalent that both houses considered a spring recess even though, as one Republican warned, it would "damp the public Spirit, & paralyze the energies of the nation."[92] The proposed recess was defeated, but many members went home anyway.[93] "The House of Representatives is now thin," reported Macon, "and the members are daily leaving the city." "It is with great difficulty," added Bayard, that "we can get or preserve a quorum in the Senate."[94]

A rumor was also circulated by a Baltimore newspaper that a special diplomatic mission would be sent to England to avert war. The report, which was widely credited and was repeated as far away as London, said that Great Britain had offered to resurrect the Monroe-Pinkney Treaty, with certain modifications favorable to the United States, as a basis for preserving peace. With rumors like this afloat, it is hardly surprising that so many people remained skeptical about the prospects for war.[95]

❖ ❖ ❖ ❖ ❖ ❖

Great Britain, like the United States, was also sending mixed signals, but she was heading in the opposite direction. While the United States was moving toward war, the British were hoping through a series of conciliatory gestures to avert hostilities. The first step in this direction was the settlement of the *Chesapeake* affair in late 1811. After more than four years of sparring, the two powers finally managed to divorce this issue from others and reach a settlement. The British agreed to disavow the attack, pay reparations, and restore the two surviving Americans (the third having died in a Halifax hospital).[96] But this problem had festered so long that its resolution gave little satisfaction to most Americans. Returning the impressed seamen, said the Baltimore *Whig*, was "like restoring a hair after fracturing the skull." It was *"only a sop,"* added the Lexington *Reporter, "to stop the mouth of Congress."*[97]

In the spring of 1812, the British navy began to treat American ships and seamen with new tact. The Admiralty ordered all naval officers to take "especial care" to avoid clashes with the American navy and to exercise "all possible forbearance" toward American citizens.[98] The commanding officers at both Halifax and Bermuda ordered their ships to keep clear of the American coast to avoid incidents.[99] This was particularly significant because the search and seizure of American ships near the coast was so infuriating.

In May of 1812, on the very eve of war, the British offered to give the United States an equal share of the license trade with the continent. Inasmuch as Britain had issued an average of 10,000 licenses a year since 1807, this proposal was significant.[100] In effect, the British were offering to suspend the Orders in Council in practice if American merchants would conduct their trade with Europe under British licenses. But the administration summarily rejected this proposal, believing that accepting it would be tantamount to surrendering American independence.[101]

The British made their greatest concession in June of 1812 just as the United States was declaring war. On June 16—two days before the declaration of war—Lord Castlereagh, the British foreign secretary, announced in Parliament that the Orders in Council would be suspended. A week later the whole system of blockades and licenses was scrapped.[102] Had there been a transatlantic cable, Castlereagh's announcement might have averted war. Madison later indicated that the declaration of war "would have been stayed" if he had known about the repeal of the Orders, and Monroe agreed.[103] But without a cable, it took weeks for the news to reach America, and by then the die was cast.

It was not only slow communication that doomed the British policy of conciliation. At no time did the British announce a new policy toward the United States or even hint that concessions might be made. They themselves were not consciously changing the direction of their policy. They simply offered each concession on an ad hoc basis. As a result, they failed to give adequate publicity to some of their concessions (such as pulling their warships off the coast), and most of the others were made too late to be effective. In short, their policy of conciliation failed because it was not carried out in a timely or intelligent manner.

American officials were also responsible for the failure of conciliation. The American minister in London had returned home in 1811, leaving only a chargé d'affaires in his place.[104] Thus there was no ranking diplomat who might move freely in British circles, no one to perceive that support for the Orders was crumbling. Moreover, Republican leaders were so blinded by their distrust of Great Britain and so burdened by the ideological legacy of the Revolution that they saw significant British concessions as meaningless gestures. The offer to share the license trade, for example, opened the door to a lucrative trade with the Continent, but Republicans saw the proposal as simply a snare designed to recolonize the United States and restore the old navigation system.

❖ ❖ ❖ ❖ ❖ ❖

As much as they distrusted the British, Republican leaders still hoped that the *Hornet* would bring news of concessions. The long-overdue ship finally reached New York on May 19, 1812. Three days later the dispatches it carried were in the hands of officials in Washington.[105] The news, however, was doubly disappointing. Although unofficial reports suggested a softening of British policy, official statements indicated a stubborn adherence to the Orders in Council. The news from France was no better. Reports of continued French depredations had been filtering in for months, and American officials were desperately seeking a definitive statement on the suspension of the Continental Decrees. But no such pronouncement was forthcoming.[106] "The Hornet arrives from france," a Republican senator confided to his diary, "and brings to me satisfactory proof of the perfidy of that Govt."[107] For Americans hoping for concessions from at least one of the belligerents, the *Hornet's* news was disappointing indeed.

The War Hawks had long since agreed that if the *Hornet* did not bring news of British concessions, war would be declared.[108] Although the Constitution entrusted the decision to Congress, the War Hawks

43

wanted the president to take the lead. Madison did not disappoint them. On June 1, less than ten days after the *Hornet's* dispatches had arrived, he sent a secret message to Congress on the subject of Anglo-American relations.[109]

Madison's message was a well-organized indictment of Great Britain for acts hostile to the United States. The British were arraigned for impressing American seamen; violating American waters; establishing illegal blockades, particularly "the sweeping system of blockades, under the name of Orders in Council"; employing a secret agent to subvert the Union; and exerting a malicious influence over the Indians in the Northwest Territory.[110]

The emphasis in the message was on maritime issues. Fully two-thirds of the indictment was devoted to the Orders in Council and other blockades. The issues were not presented in the order of their importance (since the Orders were third), but rather in a rough chronological order that put the most galling grievances first. Hence impressment and the violation of American waters headed the list.

In places Madison's message echoed the Declaration of Independence, a reflection of the Republican view that a second war of independence was necessary to end Britain's quasi-colonial practices of regulating American ships and impressing American seamen. Fearing the charge of executive influence, Madison did not recommend a declaration of war, but the thrust of his message was unmistakable. "We behold . . . on the side of Great Britain," he said, "a state of war against the United States; and on the side of the United States, a state of peace towards Britain."[111]

Madison's message was referred to the House Foreign Relations Committee, which issued its report through Acting Chairman Calhoun on June 3. The report, which was mainly the work of Calhoun, was more spirited in tone than Madison's message, though the content was similar, with the emphasis again on the Orders. "The mad ambition, the lust of power, and commercial avarice of Great Britain," said the report, "have left to neutral nations an alternative only between the base surrender of their rights, and a manly vindication of them." The report closed with a plea for "an immediate appeal to arms."[112]

Shortly after reading this report, Calhoun introduced a war bill that had been drafted by Attorney General William Pinkney.[113] Federalists sought to lift the veil of secrecy so that they could debate the merits of the bill publicly. Although everyone knew that Congress was considering a declaration of war, the Republicans were fearful of debating such an explosive issue openly. Unable to prevail, the Federalists decided to remain silent and to express their views only with their votes.

As a result, the Republicans were able to push the bill through the House in only two days—a remarkably short time for so crucial a measure.[114]

In the Senate the bill ran into more trouble.[115] There was considerable support here for limiting the war to the high seas, a sentiment shared by at least some members of the cabinet. On the very day that Madison sent his war message to Congress (a message that in no way precluded limited war), Monroe penned a note to Gallatin indicating his own views. "I am convinced," he wrote, "that it is very important to attempt, at present, the maritime war only."[116] Gallatin, who feared the effects of war on the nation's finances, agreed, and William Lowndes later claimed that other members of the cabinet shared this view, too.[117]

A limited maritime war in the tradition of '98 appealed to many people because it offered a cheap and direct means of vindicating American rights. The nation would avoid the costs of an extended land war, and the president could end the conflict by executive action without resorting to the sort of time-consuming negotiations that drew out so many wars. The only problem with this strategy was that the British were far more vulnerable in sparsely populated Canada than on the high seas. A maritime war might win some concessions, but it could hardly end in decisive victory.[118]

Although some Republicans favored maritime war, the Federalists were the most vocal proponents of this strategy. Doubtless recalling the successes of the Quasi-War, the Federalists over the years had repeatedly called for arming American merchantmen.[119] Their aim was not to resist British cruisers (which would have been impractical for lightly armed merchantmen) but to oppose the privateers sent out by France and her allies. Between 1806 and 1810, the leading proponent of this strategy, Samuel W. Dana of Connecticut, introduced four resolutions in Congress to authorize merchantmen to arm for defense. Dana was also the driving force behind a pair of Senate bills (introduced in the spring of 1812) that would accomplish the same end.[120] Most Federalists supported these bills (which passed the Senate but were buried in a House committee) as well as every proposal to expand the navy and to build coastal fortifications. Most agreed with Quincy that the nation had a duty to provide "systematic protection of our maritime rights, by maritime means."[121]

No doubt some Federalists supported maritime war simply as the lesser of two evils—not desirable in itself but preferable to full-scale war. Yet for most a war restricted to the high seas offered the best means of upholding the nation's rights, especially if (as was widely assumed) France were included in the reprisals. This would enable Federalist merchants to choose their enemy. Unleashing armed merchantmen against both belligerents, said the Baltimore *Federal Republican* in a widely reprinted editorial, "meets our peculiar approbation."[122]

The Senate referred the war bill to a select committee, which reported it with little change on June 8. The following day, however, Republican Andrew Gregg of Pennsylvania moved to send the bill back to committee with instructions to amend it so that it merely authorized warships and privateers to make reprisals against Britain. This motion carried by a 17–13 vote. Three days later, however, when the modified bill was reported from committee, the Senate reversed itself. A motion to accept the committee's changes failed by a tie vote, 16-16, when the president pro tem, John Gaillard of South Carolina, cast his vote against it. The opponents of maritime war prevailed because one Republican (William Branch Giles) changed his vote, while two others who had not voted on Gregg's motion (Richard Brent of Virginia and Jonathan Robinson of Vermont) now voted to reject the committee's changes. The tie vote meant that the original bill was restored.[123]

Several additional attempts were made to limit the war to the high seas, but these failed. Amendments to include France in a limited maritime war—a "triangular war"—failed, too.[124] Aside from the drawbacks of fighting two powerful foes at once, such a war would deny American warships and privateers the use of French ports.[125] Although proponents of full-scale war prevailed in the Senate, the outcome was long in doubt. It took the Senate two weeks to complete its deliberations, which prompted one member of the House to exclaim: "the suspense we are in is worse than hell—!!!"[126] Finally, on June 17, the Senate approved the original bill by a 19–13 vote.[127] The following day Madison signed the measure into law. Thus on June 18, 1812, the War of 1812 began.[128]

The vote on the war bill—79–49 in the House and 19–13 in the Senate—was the closest vote on any declaration of war in American history. Only 61 percent of the voting members supported the bill. Most representatives and senators from Pennsylvania and the South and West voted for war, while most from the North and East voted against it. But the sectional breakdown was really a reflection of party strength, for the vote on the war bill was essentially a party vote. About 81 percent of the Republicans in both houses of Congress voted for the measure (98–23), while all the Federalists voted against it (39–0).

What did the Republicans hope to accomplish with war? Their chief aim was to win concessions from the British on the maritime issues, particularly the Orders in Council and impressment. Throughout the winter and spring of 1812, these issues had dominated almost every discussion of American grievances, both in and out of Congress. In other words, war was undertaken primarily to secure "free trade and sailors' rights." The advocates of war also hoped to put an end to British influence over American Indians by conquering Canada or at least breaking the power of the British there. But this objective was paramount only in the West.

Republicans also saw the struggle as a second war of independence— a contest that would vindicate American sovereignty and preserve republican institutions by demonstrating to people both at home and abroad that the United States could uphold its rights. In addition, the Republicans saw war as a means of preserving power, unifying their party, and silencing their critics. Political considerations loomed large because (like the Federalists in 1798) the Republicans in 1812 identified the interests of their party with those of the country.

In sum, the Republicans went to war in 1812 to achieve a variety of closely related diplomatic, ideological, and political objectives.[129] The need to take some action was so urgent that Republicans did not wait for their war preparations to mature. This appalled some members of the party, including War Hawk Peter B. Porter, who told the secretary of war in April that it would "be an act of *Madness* fatal to the administration, to declare war at this time."[130] Most Republicans, however, were willing to take the risk. In the words of Congressman Robert Wright, they were willing "to get married, & buy the furniture afterwards."[131]

For some Republicans—members of the "scarecrow" faction—the risks posed by war did not seem great because they expected the British to cave in to American demands. Monroe expressed a common view when he complained that the British had not taken the American threat seriously. "[W]e have been so long dealing in the small way, of embargoes, non-intercourse and non-importation, with menaces of War &c that the British Government has not believed us. Thus the argument of War, with its consequences, has not had its due weight with that Government." A New Hampshire senator made the same point more emphatically. "I have long since adopted the opinion," Charles Cutts wrote, "that if Great Britain would be once convinced that war with this country would be inevitable unless she receded from her unjust pretensions all causes of irritation would be be [*sic*] speedily removed."[132] Given the speed with which Madison later sent out peace feelers, he too may have expected a bloodless victory.[133] In this respect, the declaration of war was a bluff, designed to shock the British into concessions.

❖ ❖ ❖ ❖ ❖ ❖

After the decision for war was made, Congress remained in session to deal with related matters. The most pressing problem was the future of the restrictive system. Although economic coercion had always been defended as an alternative to war—as a peaceful means of upholding the nation's rights—most Republicans were reluctant to give up the system even after war had been declared. The president himself was the chief architect of the restrictive system, and the war in no way dampened his ardor for these measures.[134] Even some of the War Hawks shared his views. Six months into the war, Henry Clay conceded that the nation might be defeated in battle. "But if you cling to the restrictive system," he said, "it is incessantly working in your favor," and "if persisted in, the restrictive system, aiding the war, would break down the present [British] Ministry, and lead to a consequent honorable peace."[135]

Although the ninety-day embargo and non-exportation act were due to expire in July, the non-importation law of 1811 would remain in force unless Congress acted. Ever since the embargo had gone into effect, the treasury department had been flooded with requests from merchants seeking permission to send ships abroad to bring their property home. Gallatin asked local customs officials to investigate the legitimacy of these requests, and, if they were valid, he granted the necessary permits.[136] But because of a specie shortage in England, property could be repatriated from that country only in the form of British-made goods, which would violate the non-importation law. Many people, however, expected Congress to suspend the law, both to enhance the nation's stock of goods and to secure additional revenue to pay for the war.[137]

The drive to modify the non-importation law had the support of the Federalists and commercial Republicans, but it was the South Carolina War Hawks who spearheaded the movement. Calhoun claimed that the non-importation law would "debilitate the springs of war," and Cheves insisted that its suspension would be "a war measure in the strongest sense of the word."[138] Both to reconcile merchants to the war and to enhance the nation's war-making capacity, the South Carolina War Hawks sought the repeal of the non-importation law in early 1812. Their proposal was defeated, at least partly because some Republicans considered it premature.[139]

The day after the declaration of war, Cheves renewed the struggle, introducing a bill to permit the importation of most British goods.[140] Cheves sought to put his bill in the best possible light by portraying it as an anti-tax measure, and he produced a letter from Gallatin showing that several classes of the proposed war taxes—including the hated internal duties—could be dispensed with if non-importation were lifted.[141] The House, however, postponed this measure by a five-vote margin.[142] The following day Republican William M. Richardson of Massachusetts offered a resolution to permit all British imports, but this proposal went down to defeat when Speaker Clay, announcing his "decided opposition to the measure," refused to break a tie vote.[143] The defeat of these measures showed that the Republican majority was determined to use commercial restrictions as well as armed force to bring the British to terms.

Having resolved this question, Congress turned to a closely related one: the complex and murky issue of trading with the enemy. There were many Americans, merchants and farmers alike, who opposed any legislation that would limit their wartime economic opportunities. Jefferson, for one, thought that the preservation of agricultural prosperity was vital to the success of the war policy. "To keep open sufficient markets," he told Madison, "is the very first object towards maintaining the popularity of the war."[144] Toward this end, Jefferson was willing to sanction a broad range of trade with the enemy under special licenses. Madison, however, took a different view. There was an enormous demand for American grain in Spain because of the presence of British troops there, and Madison had no objection to feeding these soldiers. But he preferred to rely on neutral ships to carry the grain, believing that the use of licenses was "pregnant with abuses of the worst sort."[145] Madison's solution would please American farmers but not those merchants who were engaged in the export trade.

Shortly after the declaration of war, Calhoun, who favored minimal restrictions, introduced a narrow enemy trade bill that merely prohibited the export of war materiel and provisions to Canada—the only place where British and American armies were likely to meet. As it made its way through Congress, however, the bill was broadened considerably. The final version prohibited not only exports to Canada but also any seaborne trade with the British Empire. Only one concession was made to the anti-restrictionists: the bill did not prohibit the use of British licenses to trade in non-British ports. This assured that the shipment of provisions to the peninsula in American bottoms would continue.[146]

Another issue that Congress had to deal with before adjourning was that of finance. The $11,000,000 loan authorized in March had brought in only $6,500,000.[147] Hence the administration faced a revenue shortfall. To remedy this, Congress authorized the issue of $5,000,000 in treasury notes. These were short-term notes bearing 5.4 percent interest and redeemable in a year. Although not legal tender, the notes (like those of the old national bank) could be used to pay taxes or to buy public lands. They were expected to serve as a kind of paper money that government creditors would accept in lieu of other forms of payment.[148]

Congress also passed a bill raising the customs duties. The taxes on imported goods (which hitherto had averaged about 17 percent) were doubled, a surcharge of 10 percent was imposed on goods imported in foreign bottoms, and the duties on foreign ships (heretofore 50 cents a ton) were quadrupled.[149] The Republicans, however, postponed any action on the internal taxes.[150] "[I]t was admitted by the ruling party, in debate," said a Virginia Federalist, "that to impose them now, would endanger their success at the next election."[151]

Federalists raised a howl of protest, claiming that Republican tax policy discriminated against the North, where most of the nation's imports were consumed. "[I]s it just and fair," asked Congressman Harmanus Bleecker of New York, "to abandon the internal taxes and impose so much of the burden of the war upon the people of the Northern and Eastern States, the majority of whom are known to be opposed to it?"[152] In effect, the region that opposed the war was being saddled with taxes to pay for it.

Federalists also argued that Republican financial policies were irresponsible. Raising the specter of runaway inflation, Abijah Bigelow of Massachusetts said: "The public credit must be supported, or you put at hazard the best interests of the country—you hazard, indeed, the very existence of the Government."[153] Certainly the refusal to adopt a broadly based tax program coupled with the failure of the loan and the issue of treasury notes augured ill for Gallatin's whole plan of war finance. Indeed, within two years public credit would collapse, and the result would be financial chaos.

Congress closed out the session by establishing regulations to govern privateers, appropriating an additional $500,000 for coastal fortifications, and giving the president the authority he had earlier sought to appoint the officers of the volunteer corps.[154] Congress finally adjourned on July 6, 1812. "The two Houses," said the Boston *Yankee*, "ended their fatiguing and tedious Session of eight months continuance, on Monday Evening."[155] No doubt most Congressmen were thoroughly exhausted, having adopted 143 laws in a session that was longer than any since the Quasi-War.[156]

The *National Intelligencer* predicted that historians would rank the Twelfth Congress next to "the immortal Congress" of 1776. "Under the auspices of the one this nation sprung into existence; under those of the other it will have been preserved from disgraceful recolonization."[157] Though the comparison with '76 was exaggerated, it illustrated the ideological legacy of the Revolution, a legacy that few Republicans were able to shed. For most Republicans, the War of 1812 was very much a second war of independence.[158] But whether the United States could actually vindicate its independence against a foe as powerful as England remained to be seen.

CHAPTER 3

The Baltimore Riots

ACCORDING TO SAMUEL G. GOODRICH, a Connecticut Federalist who later gained fame writing children's books, news of the declaration of war hit "like a thunderbolt."[1] Everywhere people were taken by surprise. Ever since 1805 the nation's leaders had talked of war, and yet always the result was more commercial restrictions. Many people—Republicans and Federalists alike—assumed that war would again be averted, that some excuse would be found to continue diplomatic negotiations.

Most Republicans found the news exhilarating. In Washington, an observer reported "felicitations, shaking of hands, and rejoicings as were never exhibited here before."[2] In Kentucky, there was much cheering, muskets and cannons were fired, and houses were illuminated.[3] In Pennsylvania, "pleasure beam[ed] in the eye of every friend to the government," and in Baltimore people "heartily greeted" a public reading of the president's war message.[4] Not all Republicans shared this enthusiasm, but even the pessimists were relieved that at long last a decisive step had been taken. "War is declared," said Elbridge Gerry of Massachusetts; "God be praised, Our country is safe."[5]

Federalists, by contrast, greeted the news with alarm and foreboding. In New England, bells were rung, shops closed, and flags hung at half-mast.[6] In the middle and southern states, Federalists seemed confused and unsure of what to do. In New York they talked of pursuing a policy of benevolent neutrality, of not obstructing war measures, and in Pennsylvania they considered supporting the war.[7] Many agreed with Felix H. Gilbert of Maryland that even though the declaration of war was an "astounding act of Madness" everyone ought to "rally round the Standard" and contribute to the nation's success.[8] "[H]onor, and patriotism, and love of country," said the Philadelphia *Freeman's Journal,* "will now steel every honest heart and nerve every arm, to support our country through her present difficulties."[9]

Federalists in Congress also talked of supporting the war. On the eve of the final vote, Senator James Lloyd of Massachusetts told Republicans that "whatever may be the issue of your vote, I, for one, will be found in the ranks of my country."[10] After the decision was made, Lloyd and other Federalists reportedly declared "that as the die is now cast, we must all hands play for our country."[11] For a brief moment it looked like the opposition would simply melt away. "The opposition to Government," exulted a Republican paper, "is crumbling to pieces like a 'rope of sand.' "[12]

Republican celebrations, however, were premature. In New England Federalists were never reconciled to the war policy, and in their speeches, sermons, and newspapers, their criticism was unrestrained. The Massachusetts House called the decision for war an act "of inconceivable folly and desperation" that was "hostile to your interests, menacing to your liberties, and revolting to your feelings." The Connecticut House said a nation that declared war "without fleets, without armies, with an impoverished treasury, with a frontier by sea and land extending many hundreds of miles, feebly defended . . . hath not *'first counted the cost.'* "[13]

The best way to bring the war to an end, New England Federalists believed, was to oppose it, using every legal means available. The doctrine of non-opposition was considered "heresy" in New England, Harrison Gray Otis of Massachusetts told a friend in South Carolina. The declaration of war was like any other bad law. "It must be obey[e]d but its mischief may be and ought to be freely discuss[e]d and all due means taken to procure its repeal."[14] New England Federalists attacked not only the war but also those responsible for it. "[A] president who has made this war, is not qualified to make peace," said the Massachusetts House. "Organize a *peace party* throughout your country, and let all party distinctions vanish."[15]

These words were taken to heart by Federalists elsewhere. Several of the leading newspapers in the middle and southern states—the Baltimore *Federal Republican,* the Alexandria *Gazette,* the Philadelphia *United States' Gazette,* and the New York *Evening Post*—already had come out against the war, and they were soon joined by the Charleston *Courier.*[16] Instead of crumbling, opposition to the war got stronger as the summer progressed. Although there were some exceptions, by the fall of 1812 Federalists in the middle and southern states had joined their friends in New England to present a united front against the war.

❖ ❖ ❖ ❖ ❖ ❖

Federalists in Congress also closed ranks. Talk of supporting the war evaporated when Federalists in Washington saw what kind of war it was to be. Attempts to limit the war to the high seas and to include France in the hostilities had been defeated; the restrictive system had been retained and even expanded; and a tax program had been adopted that discriminated against the North. Under these circumstances Federalists in Congress lost all heart for supporting the war. Instead, they united against it.

House Federalists aired their views in a widely circulated address published shortly after the declaration of war. "An Address of Members of the House of Representatives . . . on the Subject of War with Great Britain" appeared in pamphlet form in more than twenty editions and was reprinted in virtually every Federalist newspaper. This document became a rallying point for Federalists across the nation. Written by Josiah Quincy, it was signed by all but two of the thirty-six House Federalists. The only exceptions were Robert Le Roy Livingston, who had left Congress before the declaration of war to take a commission in the army, and Daniel Sheffey, a former Republican who still occasionally expressed independent views.[17]

The address opened with an attack on Republican parliamentary tactics: the use of the previous question to cut off debate, the employment of secret sessions to conceal proceedings, and the arbitrary treatment of motions offered by the minority. House Federalists claimed that these practices posed a threat to republican government. "Principles more hostile . . . to . . . Representative liberty," they said, "cannot easily be conceived."[18]

Next the address explored the "momentous question of war with Great Britain." Although conceding that the Orders in Council and impressment were legitimate grievances, the Federalists argued that these issues would neither justify nor be remedied by a Canadian war. Echoing a familiar refrain, they asked: "how will war upon the land protect commerce upon the ocean?" A far better course, they said, would be to lift the restrictions on trade and to unleash American merchantmen. "It is well known that from the gallantry of our seamen, if merchant vessels were allowed to arm and associate for self defence, they would be able to repel many unlawful aggressions."[19]

Instead, the nation was "rushing into difficulties, with little calculation about the means, and little concern about the consequences." To declare war against such a powerful foe with the people divided and the nation unprepared was to invite disaster. "Let us not be deceived," the address warned. "A war of invasion may invite a retort of invasion." Moreover, war against England might throw the nation into the arms of France. "It cannot be concealed, that to engage in the present war against England is to place ourselves on the side of France, and expose us to the vassalage of States serving under the banners of the French Emperor." War with England, the address concluded, was unnecessary and unwise. It was required by neither "any moral duty" nor "any political expediency."[20]

The Washington *National Intelligencer* published a reply to the address, but it was so labored and tedious that the editor almost apologized for wasting the space.[21] As far as most Republicans were concerned, the time for debate was over. Republicans had always assumed that war would silence their critics, and ever since the previous winter they had ominously hinted at what Federalists might expect if they refused to cooperate. Once war is declared, said Felix Grundy in the halls of Congress, the only question would be "are you for your country or against it." Whenever that decision is made, echoed the Washington *National Intelligencer,* "he that is not for us must be considered as against us and treated accordingly."[22] One of the blessings of war, *Niles' Register* said, is that it would unify the nation and "*weed our country of traitors.*" "A war will prevent all clamors except from *tories,*" added a Philadelphia Republican, "and we shall know how to dispose of them."[23]

After the decision for war was made, Republicans renewed their pleas for unity. "[T]his is no time for debating the propriety of a war," said the *National Intelligencer;* "WAR IS DECLARED, and every patriot heart must unite in its support." "The rightful authority has decreed," said the Republican-dominated Massachusetts Senate. "Opposition must cease." The Rubicon has been passed, added the Augusta *Chronicle;* "he who is not for us is against us."[24]

Many of these pleas carried an open or implicit threat of violence. "When war is declared," said the Baltimore *American,* "there are but two parties, *Citizen Soldiers* and *Enemies—Americans* and *Tories.*" The Wilmington *American Watchman* warned "tories" to watch their step lest they "light a funeral pile on which they themselves will be consumed." And John G. Jackson, a former Virginia congressman who was the president's son-in-law, said: "The war will separate the partisans of England from the honest federalists & *Tar & Feathers* will cure their penchant for our enemy."[25]

Shortly before the declaration of war, Robert Wright, a former governor of Maryland and member of the War Congress, had warned that if "the signs of treason and civil war discover themselves in any quarter of the American Empire . . . the evil would soon be radically cured, by hemp [for hanging] and confiscation [of property]."[26] Thomas Jefferson echoed these views. In a letter written to Madison shortly after the declaration of war, he said: "The Federalists . . . are poor devils here, not worthy of notice. [A] barrel of tar to each state South of the Patomac will keep all in order, & that will be freely contributed without troubling government. To the North they will give you more trouble. [Y]ou may there have to apply the rougher drastics of Govr. Wright, hemp and confiscation."[27] Doubtless Jefferson was speaking half in jest, but other Republicans took the matter more seriously. Most saw war in the same light as the Boston *Yankee*— as a way to "insure peace at home, if not with the world."[28]

❖ ❖ ❖ ❖ ❖ ❖ ❖

Feeling against those who dared to oppose the war ran especially high in Baltimore. A rough and rowdy boomtown founded in 1729, Baltimore was the youngest of the big cities on the eastern seaboard and the only one that was firmly in the Republican camp. By the end of the eighteenth century, the city had become the entrepôt for the export of wheat and flour produced in the backcountry and also had developed close ties with France. A large number of French refugees— mainly from Nova Scotia and Santo Domingo—lived in Baltimore, and the city traded extensively with both France and her West Indian colonies.[29]

By 1812 Baltimore had some 41,000 people—making it the third largest city in the nation—but it was still growing at an explosive pace.[30] A typical boomtown, the city suffered from a shortage of females— only 89 for every 100 males.[31] Although French refugees gave the city a veneer of civilization with their balls, dance halls, and finishing schools, underneath the city was turbulent. The many French, Irish, and Germans in the population hated Great Britain, and so too did most of the native-born Americans. These groups periodically rioted against Federalists or others thought to favor the British cause. Prominent Republicans condoned this violence and sometimes even took part. Samuel Smith, the city's leading Republican, was implicated in more than one political brawl, and Governor Wright once pardoned several people convicted of tarring and feathering a British shoemaker.[32] Federalists considered Baltimore a dangerous example of democracy—the "head-quarters of mobocracy"—a reputation that persisted well into the nineteenth century.[33]

The principal target of Republican fury in 1812 was the *Federal*

Republican, a spirited Federalist newspaper published by Alexander Contee Hanson and Jacob Wagner. Heir to a distinguished colonial name, Hanson had founded the *Federal Republican* in 1808 (when he was only twenty-two) and had consolidated it with Wagner's *North American* the following year.[34] Together these men built their paper into one of the leading prints in the South. "[T]he Federal party," said a contemporary, "has long regarded it as a Telegraph to announce the movements of the Cabinet, and as an Oracle to pronounce the Sentiments of the wisest statesmen of the party."[35] So intense was the paper's Federalism and so vitriolic its style that local Republicans referred to it as "His majesty's paper."[36] "[I]t is the most audacious, shameless, *'lying Chronicle'* in the U. States," said the Richmond *Enquirer.* The "seditious and anti-American" materials that it published, added the Baltimore *Whig,* "put decency to the blush and civic duty to defiance."[37]

As early as 1808 Hanson had incurred the wrath of Baltimore Republicans with a trenchant editorial against the embargo. A lieutenant in the militia, he was court-martialed by his Republican superiors, who claimed that the editorial was "mutinous and highly reproachful to the President."[38] Although Hanson escaped conviction, it was thereafter rumored that a $200 bounty had been offered to anyone who would tar and feather him.[39] Undeterred by such threats, Hanson continued to use his paper to expose Republican folly wherever he found it.

As the nation moved closer to war in the spring of 1812, rumors began to circulate that the *Federal Republican* would suffer violence.[40] While rival papers like the *Whig* (which was controlled by Samuel Smith) and the *Sun* published inflammatory articles, the talk in the coffee houses was "that if war was declared, the paper was so obnoxious that the editors must either alter its tone, or it must be stopped."[41] Taking note of these threats, the *Federal Republican* said that Federalists would not be cowed into silence nor frightened into supporting a war they considered unjust and unwise. Otherwise, "a war would put the constitution and all civil rights to sleep. Those who commenced it, would become dictators and despots, and the people their slaves."[42]

On June 20, two days after the declaration of war, the *Federal Republican* came out squarely against it. Calling the war "unnecessary," "inexpedient," and bearing "marks of undisguised foreign influence," the editors asserted that they would use "every constitutional argument and every legal means" to oppose it. Alluding to the possibility of mob violence, they said they would "hazard every thing most dear" to prevent any attempt to establish "a system of terror and proscription."

Alexander Hanson, by David Edwin. Courtesy of the Library of Congress

If the regular authorities would not protect freedom of the press, the paper concluded, then Federalists would look to themselves.[43]

The paper's defiant stand did not go unnoticed. Almost as soon as this issue hit the streets, rumors began to circulate that there would be violence. The following day, plans were laid at several beer gardens on Fell's Point (the rougher section of town) to destroy the newspaper's office on Gay Street.[44] The next evening, a crowd of several hundred men—mostly Irish, German, and native-born laborers from the Point—gathered at the office. Spurred on by a French apothecary named Philip Lewis, the crowd pulled down the frame building and destroyed the contents inside.[45]

City officials were apprised of the violence but were reluctant to intervene. Federalists asked one constable for help, but he replied that Wagner was "a rascal," and that the mob "ought to put a rope round his neck, and draw him out of town, then hang him on the first tree they came to." [46] Other officials, dragged to the scene by angry Federalists, were frightened by the mob. Although appalled by the violence, Mayor Edward Johnson was reluctant to call out the militia. Instead, he wandered through the crowd, timidly addressing one man after another with expressions like: "my dear fellow, you ought not to do so," or "my dear fellow, you do not know the consequences of what you are doing."[47]

When the mayor approached Lewis, the apothecary said: "Mr. Johnson, I know you very well, no body wants to hurt you; but the laws of the land must sleep, and the laws of nature and reason must prevail; that house is the Temple of Infamy, it is supported with English gold, and it must and shall come down to the ground!"[48] Having said this, Lewis returned to the business at hand, while the mayor and other officials retired from the scene.[49]

In the weeks that followed, mob violence continued to plague the city. One man was forced to flee town because he had reportedly said: "Damnation to the memory of Washington, and all who espouse his cause"; another, because he had said (whether as wish or prediction is unclear) that "the streets of Quebec would be paved with the bones of those troops who should march from the United States to attack Canada."[50] An Irishman also had to flee because he had reportedly ridden express for the *Federal Republican*.[51] Mobs dismantled several ships in the harbor, convinced that they were loaded with provisions for Britain or her allies.[52] The city's black people came in for a share of the abuse as well. Two houses in the black section of town were pulled down because their owners were thought to be sympathetic to

England. A black church was also threatened but was saved when a detachment of militia was called out.[53]

Public officials were often present at these scenes but usually showed more interest in appeasing the mob than in dispersing it. On one occasion Mayor Johnson served on a search committee, hoping to save a house from destruction.[54] On another, customs collector James W. McCulloch refused to let a ship clear for Lisbon, declaring that "he would consider himself as accessory to treason" if he let her sail.[55] Except when the church was threatened, city officials refused to call out the militia. They were unwilling to risk their popularity, and they considered the militia unreliable anyway.

❖ ❖ ❖ ❖ ❖ ❖

Federalists everywhere were appalled by the violence, fearing that it would spread and deter opposition elsewhere. As "Light-Horse" Harry Lee put it: "Mobs [were] justly styled 'sores' political by acrimonious Tom [Jefferson], when his pen was directed by truth, and not by ambition. They must not be allowed to take root in our land, or soon will our tall trees be abrupted from their foundation."[56] "Unless the people are immediately roused," warned another Federalist, "all opposition to the ruling policy will be unnerved, and the influence of these satanic outrages in Baltimore, will spread throughout the state." If the press can be thus silenced, he added, "we are further gone in the road to perdition than I thought possible."[57]

Hanson fully agreed with these sentiments. "In the course of human events," he told a friend, "I shall be in Baltimore to assert my rights with effect."[58] Determined to resurrect his paper, he made arrangements to have it printed in Georgetown and shipped to Baltimore for distribution. Wagner, who had moved to Georgetown to get out of harm's way, subleased a three-story brick building in Charles Street to Hanson for use as an office. Seeking pledges of support, Hanson toured the Maryland countryside in the company of John Howard Payne, a young actor who later gained fame for composing "Home, Sweet Home."[59]

On July 25 Hanson and Payne entered Baltimore to take possession of the Charles Street house. In the days that followed scores of Federalists visited Hanson to welcome him back to the city and to encourage him in his campaign against the war. A number of the visitors—mainly young men from the country, scions of Maryland's finer Federalist families—agreed to stay in order to defend the building from possible attack. General Lee, who was in the city to discuss the publication of his memoirs, also offered to help. Because of his Revolutionary War experience, he was put in charge of the defensive preparations.[60]

Around 9:00 in the morning on July 27, the *Federal Republican* reappeared in the streets of Baltimore. Under a masthead that boldly proclaimed "Baltimore, July 27, 1812—Published at No. 45 So. Charles-Street," the paper carried a caustic and searching editorial on the violence that afflicted the city. The attack on the paper, the editorial said, had been planned for months. Republican papers in the city had repeatedly warned that when war was declared "the office would be demolished, and the proprietors thrown into the fangs of a remorseless rabble." Those who took part in the rioting were merely the "misguided instruments" of more powerful men in Washington: Republican congressmen who denounced opposition to the war and the editors of the Washington *National Intelligencer*, who sought to turn a foreign war into a civil contest.

Who gave "the *specific intimation*" for the attack, the paper said, was unknown, but the evidence pointed to "the monster in Baltimore [Samuel Smith], whose corruption, profligacy and jacobinical heart, were well-suited to place such orders from his superiors in a train of execution." City and state officials were culpable, too, because they had taken no firm action to suppress the lawlessness. The assault on the *Federal Republican* was "a daring and desperate attempt to intimidate and overawe the minority" and "to destroy the freedom of speech and of press." Denouncing the despotism of the mob, the editorial concluded with a defiant announcement that the paper would continue to be published at Baltimore as well as Georgetown.[61]

Incensed by the newspaper's reappearance in their city, Republicans resolved to silence it permanently. Early in the evening of July 27, a group of boys gathered at "Fort Hanson" (as the Charles Street house was called) and began stoning the building and taunting the Federalists inside. The boys were soon joined by adults, mainly Irish, German, and native laborers. The mob was enraged by the appearance of a carriage of arms for the defenders, and the assault continued until most of the windows, shutters, and sashes were broken.[62] The occupants warned the mob to disperse, but the reply from the street was: "Fire, fire, you damned tories! Fire! we are not afraid of you."[63] About 10:00 P.M. the Federalists fired a warning burst into the air. This scattered the mob, but only temporarily, for most of the people returned armed with weapons of their own.[64]

A half block north of the house, a doctor named Thadeus Gale rallied the mob for a fresh assault on the house. "That ball," he said of the warning burst, "was aimed at me—the Tories ought to be hang'd upon this tree." Crying "Follow me," he led the mob back to the house and forced open the front door.[65] As the mob pushed through the

Samuel Smith, by Gilbert Stuart. Courtesy of the National Portrait Gallery

doorway, the Federalists inside opened fire, killing Gale and wounding several others. Once again the mob dispersed, but once again it returned, and for the rest of the night it kept the building under siege.[66]

Hoping to save the house from destruction, the son of the widow who owned it went to Brigadier General John Stricker's home, which was located nearby. When asked for help, the brigadier replied contemptuously: "I am no disperser of mobs."[67] Later, other Federalists urged Stricker to call out the militia, but he refused to do so without an order signed by city officials.[68] Not until 11:00 P.M., when the mob extended all the way to his house and shots could be heard, did Stricker order Major William Barney to summon his troop of cavalry. Barney managed to round up about thirty men but refused to march to the scene of trouble until 3:00 A.M., when two magistrates who would sign the order were at last found.[69]

At the appearance of Barney's force, cries rang out "the troop is coming, the troop is coming," and the mob scattered.[70] But when Barney (who was running for a seat in the House of Delegates) showed more interest in talking than fighting, the people returned. "I come here to keep the peace, and I will keep it," Barney told them. "I am sent here by superior orders, or I would not be here. You all know, that I am of the same political sentiments with yourselves. I pledge you my word and honor, that I will take every man in that house into custody."[71] The mob gave Barney three cheers, after which he entered the house to parley with the Federalists. He apologized for speaking harshly of them and promised to do his best to protect them. But to their demands that he disperse the mob he lamely pleaded lack of authority.[72]

About 4:00 A.M., as Barney was mediating between the two groups, a field piece was pulled down a nearby alley and brought to bear on the house. Hovering about the cannon was Thomas Wilson, the editor of the Baltimore *Sun,* whom one witness said "appeared almost deranged."[73] Declaring that he would not give up the attack on the Federalists "until he had off all their damn'd heads," Wilson encouraged his compatriots to fire the cannon. "We must have blood for blood," he cried. "The civil authority shall not protect these tory murderers: We will not be satisfied till we put them to death."[74] Barney's resolute intervention, however, prevented the cannon from being fired.

About 6:00 A.M. the crowd swelled to 1,500 or 2,000 as waking people from other parts of the city heard of the disturbance and raced to the scene. Mayor Johnson, General Stricker, and other officials also arrived on the scene. When one of the Federalist defenders asked

Stricker where his troops were, the brigadier replied that they were in the street. City officials tried to persuade the Federalists (who numbered about two dozen) to surrender into protective custody, promising to protect their persons and property if they did. Hanson denounced this suggestion, claiming that city officials were duty-bound to disperse the mob and questioning whether they could protect the Federalists anyway.[75] "We should take care what we are about," he said; "we are negotiating with our enemies, or at all events not with our friends."[76]

General Lee was inclined to accept the official promises at face value, and most of the other defenders, weary from the long night of fighting and dreading worse if they hesitated, favored capitulation, too. Although Hanson remained skeptical, he had little choice but to go along with the majority. Stricker assembled a hollow square of militia to guard the officials and Federalists as they marched to the county jail a mile away. The mob hurled cobblestones at the formation, hitting one Federalist in the face and almost knocking down another one, but eventually all the defenders were lodged in the jail.[77]

❖ ❖ ❖ ❖ ❖ ❖

Part of the mob lingered in Charles Street and, quickly betraying official promises, sacked or destroyed almost everything in the house. Other people prowled through the jail yard and talked of revenge. Fearing that the jail might be forced, several Federalists tried to make bail for the defendants, but city officials thought they would be safer in custody. The inmates sought permission to arm, but this request was denied. A large body of militia was called out, but only forty or fifty, mostly Federalists, showed up. Some stayed away because Stricker had ordered the use of blank cartridges, but most simply would not turn out to protect "tories."[78]

In the early afternoon the *Whig* appeared with an inflammatory editorial. Calling the Federalists "murderous traitors," the paper said that the Charles Street garrison should have been leveled and those inside put to death.[79] Mayor Johnson read this "with great anguish and disapprobation" and tried to insure calm by promising that the Federalists would not be allowed to escape or go free on bail.[80] Many people appeared satisfied with this pledge and headed for home. As the ranks of the crowd thinned, city officials dismissed the militia in the hope of convincing people that the trouble was over.[81]

After dinner, however, the crowd at the jail grew in size and unruliness. As darkness closed in, a laborer named George Wooleslager arrived with thirty or forty toughs from Fell's Point. Addressing his comrades, Wooleslager exclaimed: "where are those murdering scoundrels who have come . . . and slaughtered our citizens in cold blood! in that gaol my boys; we must have them out; blood cries for blood!" When the mayor tried to calm them, one of the rioters retorted: "you damn'd scoundrel don't we feed you, and is it not your duty to head and lead us on to take vengeance for the murders committed."[82]

Pushing Johnson and other officials aside, Wooleslager led the mob in a bid to batter down the jail door, when it was opened from within, apparently by the turnkey. The mob rushed in, dismantled the inner doors, and gained access to the cell housing the Federalists. As the mob poured in, the Federalists doused the lights, hoping to escape in the confusion. About half managed to lose themselves in the crowd, but the rest were captured as they were pointed out by a butcher named John Mumma, who could identify them because he had visited the jail earlier in the day.[83]

According to a report later issued by the Maryland House of Delegates, "a scene of horror and murder ensued, which for its barbarity has no parallel in the history of the American people, and no equal but in the massacres of Paris."[84] Nine of the Federalists—including Hanson and Lee—were severely beaten and deposited in a heap in front of the jail. Over the next three hours, they were repeatedly beaten. When they showed no signs of life, they were stabbed with penknives and hot candle wax was dropped into their eyes to determine if they were alive.[85] Women who were present reportedly cried out, "Kill the tories," while children exulted "at the awful scene, clapping their hands and *skipping* for joy."[86] One of the victims, General James M. Lingan, pleaded for mercy, citing his Revolutionary War record, his advanced age, and the needs of his large family, but his pleas were ignored. Amid cries of "Tory," he was stabbed in the chest and died several hours later.[87]

When the mob grew weary of torturing the Federalists, one of the rioters proposed a Revolutionary War song, the chorus of which ran:

> We'll feather and tar ev'ry d—d British tory,
> And that is the way for American glory.[88]

The rioters next considered what to do with their victims, most of whom no longer showed any signs of life. Some wanted to pitch them into the jail sewer or nearby Jones Falls; others thought they should be tarred and feathered or castrated; still others suggested that their bodies be donated to science. At this point, several Republican doctors intervened and, pleading the needs of science, secured custody over the bodies. The victims were carried back into the jail, where their wounds were dressed.[89] The doctors were assisted by the butcher Mumma, who remarked that the victims "had been beat enough to satisfy the devil."[90]

Meanwhile, three other Federalists taken from the jail were also beaten. Hanson's brother-in-law, Daniel Murray, played dead, but a stick was run down his throat to revive him. He later escaped with the help of a rioter who thought "there should be fair play."[91] Another victim, John Thomson, was a big man whose size invited no such mercy. After being beaten into submission in front of the jail, he was stripped, tarred and feathered, and dumped into a cart. As the cart was pulled through town, he was beaten with clubs and stabbed with old rusty swords. One assailant tried to gouge his eyes, another to break his legs with an iron bar. When Thomson feigned unconsciousness, his coat of feathers was set on fire. There was talk of hanging him, but he was spared when he agreed to give the names of his comrades.[92]

Throughout the night liquor flowed freely, and the mood of the mob was ferocious. One eyewitness said: "All I have ever read of the French [Revolution] does not equal what I saw and heard last night. Such expressions as these were current—'We'll root out the damn'd tories.' 'We'll drink their blood.' 'We'll eat their hearts.' "[93] A number of Republican officials, including the mayor and sheriff, tried to stay the fury of the mob, but others refused to help. Congressman Alexander McKim was asked to use his influence, but he declined.[94] Tobias E. Stansbury, a brigadier in the militia and a former speaker of the Maryland House of Delegates, also refused to help, asserting that "he would not protect *tories*, and that he regretted that the house in Charles-street was not battered to the ground, and the persons in there buried in the ruins."[95] Stricker shirked his duty, too. At home when he heard the jail had been forced, he retired to his parlor, leaving orders that he was not to be disturbed. When roused from his bed by an angry Federalist, he said that that he was tired, that his family needed his protection, and that it was "*improbable . . . that any of the prisoners were alive.*"[96]

After the violence had subsided, friends and officials helped the victims slip out of town.[97] The toll was heavy: Lingan lay dead and eleven others were injured. Hanson had suffered internal injuries, a broken nose and finger, wounds to his head and hands, and damage to his spinal cord and collarbones. Although he remained politically active, he never recovered from his injuries, and he died in 1819 at the age of thirty-three.[98] Lee never recovered either. He too had suffered extensive internal injuries as well as head and face wounds.

Shortly after the riots, a friend described him "as black as a negro, his Head cut to pieces."[99] Lee's face remained swollen for months after the riots, and it was said that he was barely recognizable and that even his speech was affected. He later sailed to the West Indies, hoping to recover his health, but remained an invalid until his death in 1818.[100]

❖ ❖ ❖ ❖ ❖ ❖ ❖

Even with his injuries, Hanson managed to publish his newspaper again in early August, and for a third time it caused rioting in Baltimore. The first issue, with its columns draped appropriately in black, was printed in Georgetown on August 3 and shipped to its Baltimore subscribers by mail. When the papers arrived at the post office, a mob gathered and threatened to pull the building down to get at them. The postmaster, Charles Burrall—a Federalist of the old school who wore his hair in a powdered queue—sent an express to Washington asking for federal protection, but his request was denied. Although President Madison conceded that the post office was "under the sanction of the U.S.," he doubted that "any defensive measures, were within the Executive sphere."[101] Mayor Johnson tried to persuade Burrall to send the newspapers back to Georgetown, but the postmaster insisted that all subscribers were legally entitled to the newspaper and that the post office must be defended.[102]

The militia were called out, but there was considerable opposition in the ranks to protecting the paper. Johnson tried to convince the troops that they had been summoned to protect the post office rather than the newspaper. When one of the soldiers protested that "our country is at war, and we will shed our blood to put down all opposition to it," the mayor replied that the *Federal Republican* should never again be published in Baltimore and that he himself "would draw his sword against its re-establishment."[103] At this point, some of the troops charged the mob and easily dispersed it. For almost a week thereafter, however, the city was said to be "much disturbed," and local officials had to place a guard at the post office and proclaim a curfew.[104]

❖ ❖ ❖ ❖ ❖ ❖ ❖

Although the Baltimore riots were as savage as any that had yet occurred in American history, no one was punished for taking part. A grand jury indicted Lewis, Wilson, Wooleslager, Mumma, and others on various charges, but the state attorney general repeatedly declared that they would never be convicted. In fact, only one man was found guilty, and he escaped with a small fine.[105] A member of the jury later declared "that the affray originated with them tories, and that they all ought to have been killed, and that he would rather starve than find a verdict of guilty against any of the rioters."[106] Hanson and his associates were also brought to trial, charged with manslaughter in the death of Gale. They retained the state's top Federalist lawyers— Luther Martin, Robert Goodloe Harper, and Philip Barton Key—and secured a change of venue to Annapolis, a Federalist city. There the jury acquitted them without leaving its box.[107]

The Baltimore riots left a legacy of fear among Federalists in the city—a fear that was fed by continued intolerance. Apparently unrepentant, many Republicans justified the violence or blamed it on the victims. With such a spirit afoot, some Federalists found it prudent to leave town. Those who remained no longer spoke out on the issues.[108] "We were fearful of muttering our sentiments," said one, "lest we in turn might be attacked."[109] Most no longer read the *Federal Republican* because they were afraid to pick it up at the post office, and postmen would not deliver it.[110] Republican terrorism had effectively silenced Federalism in the city, winning a victory on behalf of national unity for the war effort.

The riots left a bitter legacy in Maryland politics. All across the state the violence was condemned, and a voter backlash gave the Federalists control of the House of Delegates.[111] A House committee investigated the riots and issued a report highly critical of city officials.[112] In a separate report, the committee criticized Tobias Stansbury, who was a member of the House, for using "violent and inflammatory expressions, intended and calculated to excite the Mob to break the gaol, and to murder Mr. Hanson and his friends." Stansbury vehemently denied these charges, claiming that "that puppy Alexander Hanson was at the bottom of the whole proceeding."[113] One of the victims of the riots moved that Stansbury be committed to jail by warrant of the speaker to be tried as an accessory to murder. Calmer heads prevailed, however, and the House defeated the motion.[114]

The effects of the riots were felt far beyond Maryland. In their town and county meetings and in their newspapers as well, Federalists everywhere denounced the violence, comparing it to the worst excesses of the French Revolution. The Newport *Mercury* called Baltimore the "Paris of America," and the Pittsburgh *Gazette* said that "the cruelty and barbarity" displayed by the mob was "unexampled in the annals of any civilized country, France excepted."[115] A Boston town meeting expressed fear that the rioting was "a prelude to the dissolution of all free government, and the establishment of a reign of terror."[116] The Hartford *Courant* claimed that the violence revealed the true purpose of the war. "We now see, written in bloody characters, by what means *disaffection must cease.* The war, pretendedly for the freedom of the seas, is valiantly waged against the freedom of the press."[117]

The *Courant* exaggerated, but not by much. Republican mobs drove the Savannah *American Patriot* and the Norristown (Pennsylvania) *Herald* out of business in 1812, and Federalist editors in other towns in the middle and southern states complained that they were warned to change their tune or risk a similar fate.[118] In a number of states, Republican postmasters held up Federalist newspapers, and in New Jersey, there was violence against Federalists at the polls.[119] In Buffalo, a Federalist hotel was demolished, and in Savannah a ship that had traded with Spanish Florida was burned.[120] An opponent of the war was dragged from his house and beaten in New Hampshire, and in Virginia one Federalist was tarred and feathered because he "had offended the militia," and another was threatened with the same fate because he "had exerted himself to suppress the mob."[121]

Republican leaders found this violence embarrassing and accused Federalists of misrepresenting the facts, particularly in connection with the Baltimore riots. *Niles' Register* claimed that Federalists had hired people to travel through Maryland to spread "horrible falsehoods," and Joseph Story insisted that Federalists in New England were circulating "false and exaggerated rumors" to inflame sectional animosity and pave the way for secession.[122] A Republican meeting in Maryland accused Federalists of seeking "to convert the Baltimore atrocities into an electioneering engine," and a Pennsylvania Republican reported that "[t]en thousand copies of a narrative of the late disturbances in Baltimore . . . will be distributed thro this State & Jersey."[123] To counter Federalist propaganda, the Baltimore City Council issued a report on the riots that discreetly avoided using the word *mob* and exonerated city officials. President Madison welcomed this report, calling it "a seasonable antidote to the misrepresentations" of those who blamed the violence "on the friends of true liberty."[124]

Republicans also tried to counter the bad publicity by blaming the violence on the Federalists. Those who expressed opinions obnoxious to the people, said the *Maryland Republican*, "must abide by the consequences." By arming themselves instead of seeking civil protection, said the New York *Columbian*, the Federalists in Baltimore were "guilty of a murderous intent, and [of] wilfully exciting the popular vengeance." "[T]he truth is," added another Republican, "there would have been no disturbance if those men had not armed themselves, without the least cause."[125]

Republican newspapers also tried to show that Federalists in New England were equally guilty of violence. Various illustrations were presented—the roughing up of a Republican congressman in Massachusetts, the destruction of privateers in New Haven and Providence, the closing down of a Massachusetts court, and the mobbing of an army recruiting party in Connecticut.[126] One Republican paper claimed that "more than two thirds of the mobs and riots that have taken place in our country, since the Constitution has been adopted, have proceeded from the federal or tory party," and another insisted that "in principle" Federalist violence was no different from the Baltimore riots.[127] Though there was some merit in these claims, the Baltimore violence was so vicious and brutal and had such a deadly effect on freedom of speech that it was in a class by itself.

The violence in 1812 showed that, like the Federalists in 1798, the Republicans were reluctant to tolerate opposition to their war policy. In 1798 the Federalists had resorted to a sedition law to silence their foes, and some Republicans in 1812 wanted to revive this policy. Judge Story and Attorney General Pinkney both urged the adoption of a sedition law, and other Republicans joined in the cry.[128] "[O]ffenders, conspirators, and traitors are enabled to carry on their purposes almost without check," complained Story. Congress must "give the Judicial Courts of the United States power to punish all crimes and offences against the Government, as at common law."[129] Madison, however, demurred. Unlike most wartime presidents, he had a healthy respect for the civil rights of his domestic foes. Republican mobs, on the other hand, had their own way of suppressing dissent, and the result was a chilling message for all who opposed the war.[130]

Like the sedition act in 1798, the violence in 1812 boomeranged on the war party. The Washington Benevolent Society of Maryland launched a campaign to drum up subscriptions for the *Federal Republican,* and Federalists across the country responded. More than two hundred subscribers were signed up in Boston, another seventy in Providence, and an additional forty-two in Franklin County, Pennsylvania.[131] By December of 1812 $2,000 had poured in.[132] Although this did not cover the paper's losses, which were estimated at $3,000 to $5,000 in the June riot alone, the *Federal Republican* nonetheless flourished.[133] Thus, rather than silencing the paper, the Baltimore mob made the *Federal Republican* one of the most widely read newspapers in the country.

Revulsion against the violence also contributed to Federalist election victories in Maryland, New York, and New England.[134] In addition, the violence politicized the war by showing that, for some Republicans at least, the conflict was merely a pretext for suppressing dissent. The effect was to accelerate the movement of Federalists in the middle and southern states back into opposition. By the fall of 1812, Federalists everywhere opposed the war, not simply because they considered it unjust and unwise but because they saw it as a threat to their basic liberties as well. In short, instead of stifling dissent, Republican violence only added fuel to the growing anti-war fire.

CHAPTER 4

The Campaign of 1812

ON DECEMBER 16, 1811, after the debate on the war preparations had been under way for more than two weeks, John Randolph raised a specter that was to haunt contemporaries and historians alike. "Agrarian cupidity," he said, "not maritime right, urges the war. Ever since the report of the Committee on Foreign Relations came into the House, we have heard but one word—like the whip-poor-will, but one eternal monotonous tone—Canada! Canada! Canada!"[1] Randolph exaggerated, since at no time during the debates did territorial expansion overshadow the maritime issues. Nevertheless, some historians later seized upon his words to prove that this war was undertaken to acquire territory, that the maritime issues were merely a pretext for seizing Canada.[2]

There is no denying that territorial expansionism was a potent force in this era. Republican leaders worked assiduously to pry Louisiana and the Floridas loose from their European overlords, and government and frontiersmen alike pushed Indians off their lands with callous disregard for their rights.[3] Many Americans also coveted Canada, if only to put an end to British influence over American Indians. But the desire to annex Canada did not bring on the war. Rather it was maritime issues—particularly the Orders in Council and impressment. "Canada was not the end but the means," said Henry Clay, "the object of the War being the redress of injuries, and Canada being the instrument by which that redress was to be obtained."[4]

Most Republicans considered Canada a logical target because of its weakness vis-à-vis the United States. Not counting Indians, about 7,500,000 people lived in the United States in 1812, compared to only

500,000 in Canada.[5] The United States also had almost 12,000 regulars in uniform, while Canada could muster only 7,000.[6] Additional enlistments, volunteers, and militia drafts were expected to tip the balance still further in America's favor, especially since Great Britain could ill afford to divert resources from the war in Europe.

Republicans counted on another advantage, too. In Lower Canada, north of the St. Lawrence River, two-thirds of the inhabitants were of French origin and thus of uncertain loyalty. The loyalty of Upper Canada, north of the Great Lakes, was even more problematical because at least a third of the people there were American by birth or descent.[7] Loyal Canadians in this province had remonstrated in 1811 against "the sudden and indiscriminate influx of foreigners, sometimes openly, and at other times secretly hostile to the British Government," but nothing had come of their protest.[8] Despite a request from the administration, the legislature of Upper Canada refused to require men serving in the militia to renounce foreign allegiance.[9] By the time the war began, General Isaac Brock, commander of the British forces in Upper Canada, claimed that most of the people in his province were "essentially bad." They were "either indifferent to what is passing, or so completely American as to rejoice in the prospects of a change of Governments."[10]

Republicans counted on this disaffection to facilitate the conquest of Canada. One reason they had gone to war without adequate preparation was that they expected American troops to be welcomed in Canada. Governor Daniel D. Tompkins of New York predicted that "one-half of the Militia of [Canada] would join our standard," and most other Republicans shared this view.[11] Jefferson claimed that the conquest of most of Canada would be "a mere matter of marching," and Clay boasted that "the militia of Kentucky are alone competent to place Montreal and Upper Canada at our feet."[12] Most Republicans, in other words, expected what John Randolph called "a holiday campaign." With "no expense of blood, or treasure, on our part—Canada is to conquer herself—she is to be subdued by the principles of fraternity."[13]

Federalists did not dispute that Canada might be conquered, but they vigorously denied that it was a legitimate target. They preferred to settle American differences with England on the high seas, believing that a war against Canada was unjust. "Canada has issued no Orders in Council," said Congressman Samuel Taggart of Massachusetts. "She has not impressed our seamen, taken our ships, confiscated our property, nor in any other respect treated us ill. All the crime alleged against Canada or the Canadians, is that, without any act of their own, they are connected with, and under the protection of a nation which has injured us on the ocean."[14]

Federalists regarded the invasion of Canada as not only unjust but also unwise. Ever since the Louisiana Purchase they had openly opposed expansion, believing that any new territory would only enhance Republican strength and undermine national stability. The acquisition of Canada, declared the Maryland House of Delegates, would be "worse than a doubtful boon." It would "enfeeble" the United States, said a Massachusetts Federalist, by increasing those "jarring materials" which made up the country. "The strength of the nation," added a Delaware congressman, is "already too much scattered."[15]

Federalists assumed that Canada would be annexed because Republicans never made clear what they planned to do with the territory once it was conquered. Since Canada was not an end in itself, presumably it would be held for ransom on the maritime issues, but what if the British balked at concessions? As late as 1814 Federalist Joseph Pearson of North Carolina insisted that Republicans had never clarified their position. "Do they mean to plant their standard on the walls of Quebec, apportion out the lands to the conquerors, and sing a requiem to 'free trade and sailors' rights'? These questions never have been satisfactorily answered."[16]

Some Republicans made no secret of their desire to keep Canada, and this sentiment grew as the war progressed. "It appears to be the universal opinion of the Republicans," said the Boston *Chronicle* in 1813, "that the *Canadas* ought in no event to be surrendered. . . . Too much valuable blood has already been shed, and too much treasure expended, to permit us to indulge for a moment the idea of resigning this country." Any treaty that does not secure Canada, a Georgia senator told the president, "will be very ungraciously received."[17] Annexationist fever was particularly strong in the West, where toasts were drunk to the acquisition of Canada, and a resolution on the subject was offered in the Kentucky legislature.[18] According to one critic, by 1814 the message from the West "was unequivocal—Canada must not, shall not be given up."[19]

Long before this, Monroe had conceded that public opinion might make it "difficult to relinquish Territory which had been conquered."[20] In the meantime, the administration had to decide how to govern occupied territory. At the beginning of the war, Congress considered proposals to establish temporary government in Canada and to guarantee the rights of Canadians, but these measures were killed in the Senate.[21] Hence the administration was left to its own devices.

The War Department instructed its commanders in the field to promise Canadians nothing more than protection for their persons, property, and rights.[22] But some officers went further. General William Hull issued a proclamation to Canadians that said: "You will be emancipated from tyranny and oppression, and restored to the dignified station of freemen."[23] Likewise, General Alexander Smyth announced to his men that "[t]he time is at hand when you will cross the streams of Niagara to conquer . . . a country that is to be one of the United States."[24] The War Department approved of Hull's proclamation, and though it reprimanded Smyth, it did so privately.[25] The administration's failure to repudiate either proclamation made it all the more difficult to reconcile domestic opponents to the war.

❖ ❖ ❖ ❖ ❖ ❖

The decision for war was a momentous one, and the president was fully aware of this. When the British minister visited Madison the day after the declaration of war, he found other Republicans shaking hands, "but the President was white as a sheet and very naturally felt all the responsibility he would incur."[26] Nevertheless, Madison did his best to encourage his department heads. According to one observer, "He visited in person, a thing never known before, all the offices of the departments of war and the navy, stimulating every thing in a manner worthy of a little commander in chief, with his little round hat and huge cockade!"[27] This may have given heart to Madison's subordinates, but what the nation really needed was more energy and efficiency, both of which were sorely lacking.

Conditions were particularly bad in the War Department, which was poorly organized and understaffed. According to War Hawk George M. Troup, "In the wretched, deplorably wretched condition of the War Department, it was impossible either to begin the war or to conduct it." The work load of the department, heavy in time of peace, was staggering in time of war. "No man in the country," claimed Troup, "is equal to one-half the duties which devolve on the present Secretary."[28] Although the department had eleven clerks, none had more than a year's experience.[29] Moreover, when the president asked Congress to authorize two assistant secretaries of war, the Senate balked, apparently because the creation of new supply departments was expected to lighten the work load.[30]

The secretary of war, William Eustis, was a good politician, but he lacked administrative skills and never mastered his duties. Overwhelmed by the task before him, he devoted himself to details and failed to give proper direction to the commanders in the field. He sometimes bypassed the chain of command, corresponding directly with junior officers, and, according to one senator, he spent much of his time "reading advertisements of Petty retailing merchants, to find where he may Purchase 100 shoes, or 200 hats." "Our Secretary at War," concluded a Pennsylvania congressman, "is a dead weight in our hands. . . . His unfitness is apparrent to every body but himself."[31]

Conditions in the army were not much better. The senior officers were superannuated and incompetent, most owing their appointments to politics. According to Winfield Scott, "the old officers had, very generally, sunk into either sloth, ignorance, or habits of intemperate drinking."[32] Though there were some promising junior officers, it took time for them to rise to positions of significant authority. The administration had an opportunity to appoint additional officers on the eve of the war, but it was slow to act. "The army appointments," said one Republican, "cannot be made until names from all the states come in, and there is *great tardiness*."[33] According to Scott, the government relied heavily on the recommendations of Republican congressmen, "who unfortunately pressed upon the Executive their own particular friends & dependents, &, in some cases—menials."[34] As a result, few of the new officers had any experience or knew much about the art of war. "Our Army," complained Peter B. Porter in 1813, "is full of men, fresh from Lawyer shops & counting rooms, who know little of the physical force of man—of the proper means of sustaining & improving it—or even the mode of its application."[35]

Most of the enlisted men were inexperienced, and morale in the ranks was low. Infractions of discipline were common, and these multiplied as the army grew. Desertion was common—so common, in fact, that less than four months into the war President Madison felt obliged to issue a proclamation pardoning all deserters who returned to duty within four months.[36] Although Congress outlawed whipping in 1812, army officers had other means of maintaining discipline. Deprivation of pay or spirits, public penance, and paddling were common. In more serious cases, the offender might be branded on the face, his ears might be cropped, or he might be executed.[37]

Those who enlisted in the army at the beginning of the war had a five-year commitment, though later recruits were given the option of enlisting for the duration of the war.[38] At first the bounty was $31 and 160 acres of land, but because enlistments lagged, Congress gradually increased the incentives to $124 and 320 acres of land.[39] This was a princely sum—probably the highest bounty ever paid by any army in the world. The cash bounty alone was as much as many unskilled laborers earned in a year, and even if the land sold for only 50 cents an acre (which is a low estimate), the total bounty was more than most people made in two years. This enormous bounty did much to spur enlistments, though the army did not become an effective fighting force until the last year of the war.

Initially the administration planned to rely on short-term volunteers, but Congress gave the president authority to appoint the volunteer officers only after war had been declared.[40] According to one Republican, the law remained "*a dead letter*" in Pennsylvania because volunteers continued to offer their services to the state instead of the national government.[41] The incentives offered to volunteers were in any case too paltry to be effective. The government paid no bounty but simply allowed volunteers who served at least a month to keep their weapons. Only six regiments were raised during the war, and one army officer claimed that those he inspected were little better than organized bandits who wasted public property, insulted private citizens, and freely engaged in "desertion[,] robbery, [and] disorderly & Mutinous Conduct."[42]

Nor could the militia, who were in disarray everywhere except in New England and the West, play the active role that Republican leaders envisioned for them. They were inefficient and unreliable and costly as well. "The expences of the Militia are enormous," said a Republican general, "& they are of little comparative use, except at the commencement of war, & for special emergencies.—The sooner we can dispense with their services, the better."[43] In short, after a decade of neglect, the nation's land forces were not up to the task at hand.

The system for paying the troops broke down from the beginning. At the start of the war privates were paid $5 a month, non-commissioned officers $7 to $9, and officers $20 to $200.[44] To stimulate enlistments, Congress in late 1812 raised the pay of privates and non-commissioned officers by $3.[45] At $8 a month, privates still earned less than the $10 to $12 that unskilled laborers normally made, but as the bounty increased, army wages soared well above the civilian average.[46]

By law army pay could not be more than two months in arrears "unless the circumstances of the case should render it unavoidable."[47] But even in the first year of the war, when the government had ample resources, administrative inefficiency and slow communication kept many troops from receiving their pay on time. In October, 1812, men who had enlisted five months earlier "absolutely refused to march untill they had recd. their pay," and other troops also mutinied for want of pay.[48] As the war progressed, the problem of paying the troops became almost unmanageable. By the fall of 1814 army pay was frequently six to twelve months in arrears, and in some cases even more.[49]

The system of supply was also grossly inefficient.[50] To cut expenses, Congress had abolished the quartermaster and commissary departments in 1802.[51] Thereafter the army was supplied by civilian agents who were primarily interested in balancing their books. According to one officer, many of the agents were "perfectly ignorant of military affairs."[52] In March of 1812, Congress reestablished the quartermaster and commissary departments, but it was months before either department was staffed and operational, and the authority granted to each was vague and overlapping.[53] The legislation creating these departments, Madison complained, "was so inadequate, that the War office, otherwise overcharged, was obliged for some time to perform the functions of both."[54] Even when operational the supply departments were woefully inefficient, and troops in the field frequently had to go for months at a time without shoes, clothing, blankets, or other vital supplies.[55]

The system for feeding the troops—based on private contract—was even worse. Although most government officials recognized that (in the words of John Armstrong) "all military operations . . . must begin with the belly," this vital service was left in civilian hands in order to save money.[56] It was "madness in the extreme," said one officer, to rely on such a system in time of war.[57] The daily ration was supposed to consist of 20 ounces of beef or 12 ounces of pork; 18 ounces of bread or flour; 4 ounces of rum, brandy, or whiskey; and small quantities of salt, vinegar, soap, and candles.[58] Contractors and subcontractors, however, were so intent on making a profit that they often delivered bad provisions or chiseled on the quantity. "It would be endless to trace the petty villa[i]nies which contractors are daily tempted to commit," said one officer.[59] Although contractors had to sign a binding agreement and post a bond, they were not subject to military law, and it was almost impossible to bring them to heel. "[I]f a contractor fails to make issues," said an officer, "he can only be punished by civil actions."[60] In an emergency, commanding officers could buy provisions, but the cost was likely to be prohibitive, especially in remote areas on the frontier.

Complaints over supply multiplied as the war progressed, and many illnesses and deaths were blamed on the system. One officer complained that the want of food and other supplies had "produced dysenteries and other diseases" that filled his hospital. Another said: "We are literally starving on this end of the line for bread."[61] A doctor at one camp found excrement in the bread, and a food inspector claimed that the flour was so bad that "it would *kill the best horse at*

Sackett's Harbour."[62] Doubtless many agreed with General Edmund P. Gaines that "the irregularity in the Supply and badness of the rations" had done more to retard American operations than anything else.[63] In fact, one general claimed that contractors knocked more men out of combat than the enemy, and another insisted that the men were so badly provided for that the number killed in battle was "trifling" compared to losses from other causes.[64]

Medical science was so primitive that army doctors were almost powerless to combat disease. Though some doctors understood the importance of cleanliness, imposing their views on a camp of careless young soldiers was no easy task.[65] Epidemic diseases such as dysentery, typhoid fever, pneumonia, malaria, measles, typhus, and even small-pox were common and often fatal.[66] Fevers were particularly danger-ous because before the development of aconite (which is derived from the monkshood plant) there was no way to control them.

Most doctors were still committed to the "heroic" practice of medi-cine—which meant they bled and blistered their patients and subjected them to assorted emetics, cathartics, and diuretics designed to purge the body of disease.[67] Doctors also dispensed a large number of drugs, few of which worked. Although opium helped ease pain and intestinal distress, and cinchona (Jesuits' bark) was effective against malaria, most of the drugs were worthless or even poisonous. The most com-mon was mercury—the "Samson of the Materia Medica"—which was usually dispensed in the form of calomel (mercurous chloride). It had no therapeutic value, and it was frequently injurious and occasionally fatal. Those who survived disease usually did so in spite of their treatment rather than because of it.[68]

The nation had better luck with its ordnance. Congress created a department to supervise this branch of the service on the eve of war, and it seemed to function smoothly.[69] The nation already had well-established armories at Springfield, Massachusetts, and Harpers Ferry, Virginia, and additional facilities were built during the war. Hence the government was able to manufacture and repair small arms, produce ammunition, and test ordnance.[70] The army also purchased cannons and small arms from private firms, such as the one in Connecticut owned by Eli Whitney, who developed the concept of interchangeable parts.[71]

The standard weapon of issue during the war was the .70-caliber smooth-bore musket—a muzzle-loaded flintlock that fired a soft lead ball weighing about an ounce. Its effective range was only 100 yards, and it misfired about 15 percent of the time. Fortunately for the

United States, many Americans, particularly in the West, owned rifles. These weapons had grooved barrels, usually with a .40 caliber bore, and an effective range of 300 yards.[72] Powder, in short supply in the Revolutionary War, was amply stocked. More than two hundred powder mills were scattered around the country, though the government purchased most of its powder from several large firms, such as Dupont & Company in Delaware.[73]

❖ ❖ ❖ ❖ ❖ ❖

Given the state of the War Department and the army, the conquest of Canada was likely to be more difficult than Republicans imagined. Canada in this era was often compared to a tree. The taproots were the sea lanes that stretched across the Atlantic to England; the trunk was the St. Lawrence, dominated by Quebec and Montreal; and the outlying communities along the Great Lakes formed the branches. Because the surrounding wilderness was so dense, the western settlements could be supplied only by the water route that followed the river and the lakes. Thus the key to controlling Canada was the St. Lawrence. "It has always been my opinion," said Commodore Isaac Chauncey, "that among the best means to conquer the Canada's was . . . by taking and maintaining a Position on the St. Lawrence—this would be killing the tree by 'girdling'—the branches deprived of their ordinary Supplies from the root, die of necessity."[74]

There was little enthusiasm for an immediate attack on Quebec because it was heavily fortified and lay north of Federalist New England, which was unlikely to provide the necessary men and supplies to make the campaign a success. This left Montreal. Madison conceded the importance of this city, but concentrating on such a target would not allow the administration to take advantage of the war enthusiasm in the West or to protect that region from Indian depredations. Hence the president adopted a plan developed by General Henry Dearborn that called for a three-pronged attack against Montreal, the Niagara frontier, and the Detroit frontier. The attack on Montreal was still supposed to be the main operation, but because of mismanagement at every level, the other operations assumed greater importance.[75]

To manage its operation in the West, the administration chose William Hull, the fifty-nine-year-old governor of Michigan Territory who had a record of distinguished service during the Revolutionary War. Hull eagerly sought a military appointment, though later he claimed that he accepted command of the western army "with great reluctance."[76] Age had taken a heavy toll on him, and a stroke and other personal tragedies had further eroded his strength. The administration was aware of Hull's liabilities, but the only other suitable candidate, Colonel Jacob Kingsbury, was too ill for the job.[77]

In the early summer of 1812, Hull assembled in Ohio an army of 2,000 regulars and militia, some of whom wore signs on their caps that read "CONQUER OR DIE."[78] Hull's marching orders, issued before the declaration of war, called for him to proceed to Fort Detroit, located on the river that linked Lake Erie to Lake Huron. Although Hull had earlier insisted that naval control of Lake Erie was vital to the success of any military operation, he now believed that the presence of a large American army at Detroit might force the British to evacuate the entire region.[79]

To facilitate communication, Hull began the laborious task of carving out of the wilderness a road that would link Urbana, Ohio, to Detroit. Arriving at the Maumee (Miami) River at the end of June, he hired the schooner *Cuyahoga* to take his baggage, papers, and supplies to Detroit. Although Hull did not yet know of the declaration of war, the British learned of it in time to seize the ship as it passed by Fort Malden. This enabled them to learn about Hull's plans as well as the size and condition of his army. "Till I received these letters," said General Brock, "I had no idea General Hull was advancing with so large a force."[80]

Hull reached Detroit on July 5 without further incident. A week later he crossed the Detroit River into British territory with the intention of attacking Fort Malden to the south. Some 200 Ohio militia refused to accompany him, claiming that they could not serve beyond American territory. Hull also had to stop to build carriages for his cannons. But otherwise his prospects looked bright. His army was at least twice as large as the British force defending Fort Malden, and a proclamation he issued to the inhabitants induced many Canadian militia to go home or to defect to the United States. According to Brock, Hull's invasion "was productive of very unfavorable sensations among a large portion of the population."[81]

Hull's prospects, however, soon dimmed. The American commander became increasingly worried about his supply lines to Ohio, which were threatened from Lake Erie by the British and from the West by hostile Indians. Although a detachment of 200 militia had left Ohio loaded with supplies for Hull, the men stopped at the Raisin River, some 35 miles south of Detroit, to await reinforcements from Hull's camp. Hull dispatched 150 men under Major Thomas Van Horne to meet these troops, but the detachment was attacked by a band of Indians led by Tecumseh and forced to return to Detroit. Hull next sent a force of 600 men under the command of Lieutenant

Colonel James Miller to break through to Ohio. After being briefly pinned down by a small group of British and Indians, this force also retreated to Detroit.[82]

Hull received further bad news at the end of July. The tiny American outpost on the island of Mackinac (pronounced Mac-i-naw) between Lake Huron and Lake Michigan had surrendered to a large enemy force.[83] Hull was convinced that this "opened the Northern hive of Indians, and they were swarming down in every direction."[84] Accordingly, he decided to withdraw across the river to Detroit, giving up his plan to attack Fort Malden. "This fatal and unaccountable step," said one of his officers, "dispirited the troops" and "left to the tender mercy of the enemy the miserable Canadians, who had joined us."[85] Hull suggested that it might be prudent to retreat all the way to Ohio, but his militia officers told him the entire army would melt away if he did.[86]

By this time Hull's men were openly questioning his leadership. "He *is* a coward," said one, "and will not risque his person."[87] The militia officers were so alarmed that they considered removing Hull from command, but they gave up the plan when Colonel Miller, the ranking regular army officer, refused to cooperate.[88] Hull made one last effort to break through to Ohio by dispatching 400 picked men under the command of Lewis Cass and Duncan McArthur. This force advanced further than the others but was unable to find the Ohio encampment. By this time Hull's position had become so desperate that he sent an urgent message recalling the troops. But the men had lost all confidence in their general and elected to remain in the wilderness.[89]

Meanwhile, the British had made good use of the reprieve Hull had given them. General Brock had recently arrived with reinforcements, bringing British strength (counting regulars, militia, and Indians) to about 1,600. The contents of a mail bag captured from Van Horne's force informed Brock of the condition of the American army. "I got possession of the letters my antagonist addressed to the secretary of war," said Brock, "and also of the sentiments which hundreds of his army uttered to their friends. Confidence in the general was gone, and evident despondency prevailed throughout."[90]

Crossing the river, Brock brought his cannons to bear on Fort Detroit and mounted a siege. Playing on Hull's fear of the Indians, he arranged to have fall into American hands a bogus document that mentioned a large body of Indians posed to descend on Detroit.[91] Moreover, in demanding the surrender of the American fort, Brock said: "It is far from my inclination to join in a war of extermination, but you must be aware, that the numerous body of Indians who have

Isaac Brock, by an unknown artist. Courtesy of the National Archives of Canada

attached themselves to my troops, will be beyond controul the moment the contest commences."[92] With many civilians in the fort (including members of his own family), Hull was horrified at the prospect of an Indian massacre. "My God!" he exclaimed to a subordinate. "[W]hat shall I do with these women and children."[93]

Facing a siege and the possibility of a massacre, Hull became increasingly despondent. He started keeping to himself, and when he did speak to others his voice often trembled. He took to stuffing huge quids of chewing tobacco into his mouth, apparently oblivious of the spittle that was running down his face and soiling his beard and clothes. He also began crouching in the fort, evidently hoping to dodge incoming artillery shells.[94] Finally, on August 16, 1812, he waved a white flag, surrendering the fort as well as his entire army, including the detachment in the wilderness. "Not an officer was consulted," Lewis Cass said. "Even the women were indignant at so shameful a degradation of the American character."[95]

When Hull later returned to the United States on parole, he was court-martialed. Initially he told the British that lack of powder had forced him to surrender, but Brock's men found huge quantities of munitions in the fort, including more than 5,000 pounds of powder.[96] Later—and with more justice—Hull accused Dearborn of failing to make an adequate demonstration further East, which allowed the British to concentrate their forces in the West.[97] Unimpressed by this logic, the court—which was headed by Dearborn—convicted Hull of cowardice and neglect of duty. The court sentenced Hull to death but recommended mercy because of his "revolutionary services, and his advanced age." The president approved this verdict and remitted the punishment.[98] Hull and his heirs spent the next thirty-five years trying to vindicate his actions.[99]

Several days before surrendering, Hull had ordered the evacuation of Fort Dearborn in Chicago on the grounds that the fall of Mackinac had rendered its defense untenable. The fort was held by about sixty-five regulars and militia under the command of Captain Nathan Heald. Some two dozen civilians were also present. The fort was well stocked, the Indians were known to be unfriendly, and almost everyone was opposed to evacuation. Nevertheless, Heald was determined to obey his orders. On August 15, the evacuation was carried out, ostensibly under the protection of 500 Potawatomi Indians. Not far from the fort, the Indians fell on the whites, killing most of them after surrender terms had been arranged. According to one witness, the Indians beheaded one officer, carved out his heart, and ate it raw.[100]

The loss of Mackinac, Detroit, and Dearborn exposed the entire

Northwest to enemy attack. The effect of these losses, said the Pittsburgh *Mercury*, was to lay open "to the ravages of the merciless foe the whole extent of our western frontier."[101] The only bright spot in the campaign was Captain Zachary Taylor's inspired defense of Fort Harrison in Indiana Territory from a determined Indian assault on the night of September 4–5, the first American victory on land.[102] Otherwise, people in the West had little to cheer about. Thrown into a panic by the prospect of enemy depredations, westerners bombarded the federal government with demands for protection.[103]

Government officials were anxious to meet these demands and to reestablish American control over the Northwest. According to Eustis, the president was determined "to regain the ground that has been lost by the Surrender of Detroit & the army under General Hull, and to prosecute with increased Vigor the important objects of the Campaign."[104] The administration wanted to assign the western command to General James Winchester, a regular army officer, rather than to the local favorite, William Henry Harrison—the hero of Tippecanoe. But Kentucky leaders took matters into their own hands by making Harrison a major general in the militia (even though he was not a citizen of the state) and giving him command of the local troops. Richard M. Johnson and other westerners continued to pressure the administration until Harrison was put in charge of the whole theater of operations.[105]

Harrison spent the fall of 1812 building a huge army that soaked up federal money and supplies at an alarming rate. The War Department ordered one contractor to supply 1,000,000 additional rations to the army, and the price of provisions throughout the West soared.[106] Rumor had it that Harrison's agents paid $50 to $60 a barrel for flour—a charge vigorously denied by the administration paper in Washington.[107] Nevertheless, Harrison conceded that "the Expenses of this Army will greatly exceed the calculations of the Government."[108] Although the administration was alarmed by the mounting costs, the spending worked like a tonic on the western economy and helped keep the war popular despite the military setbacks.

Harrison's intention was to sweep hostile Indians from the region and then retake Detroit, but the onset of winter forced him to give up this plan.[109] Before ordering his troops into winter quarters, however, he dispatched a force under Winchester to the rapids of the Maumee River. Following his own councils, Winchester decided to march from the rapids to the Raisin River in order to protect settlers at Frenchtown (now Monroe, Michigan). Attacked by a force of 1,100 British and Indians, the Americans, who numbered about 850, surrendered on

January 21, 1813. Some 300 Americans were killed, including 30 who were massacred by drunken Indians after the surrender had taken place.[110] "[T]he savages *were suffered to commit every depredation upon our wounded,*" reported a group of American officers; "*many were tomahawked, and many were burned alive in the houses.*"[111] Thereafter, "Remember the Raisin" became a rallying cry throughout the Northwest.

Harrison also sent out raiding parties to destroy Indian villages and provisions. These expeditions were largely successful, thus making the whole region more secure.[112] Nevertheless, after a season of campaigning in the West, the nation had little to show for the blood and treasure it had expended. Sizeable armies had been lost at Detroit and Frenchtown; and Mackinac, Detroit, and Fort Dearborn were in enemy hands.

❖ ❖ ❖ ❖ ❖ ❖

The campaign in the East did not go much better. The War Department let Governor Daniel D. Tompkins of New York select a local man to direct operations on the Niagara front. Tompkins chose Major General Stephen Van Rensselaer, a forty-eight-year-old militia officer with no previous military experience. Known as "the last of the patroons," Van Rensselaer was a rich and powerful Federalist, and Tompkins hoped that his appointment would win other Federalists to the cause. For expert advice, Van Rensselaer was expected to rely on his kinsman and aide, Colonel Solomon Van Rensselaer, who had taken part in the Indian wars of the 1790s and had served for many years as adjutant general of New York. The elder Van Rensselaer shared his command in western New York with a regular army officer, General Alexander Smyth. A political appointee who had received his commission when the army was expanded in 1808, Smyth had published a pamphlet on field maneuvers but was without practical experience. Vain and pompous, he refused to place himself under Van Rensselaer's command despite explicit orders from the War Department to do so.[113]

By October of 1812, more than 6,000 American troops faced a force of perhaps 2,000 British and Indians across the Niagara River. General Van Rensselaer's plan was to seize Queenston Heights on the British side, while Smyth attacked Fort George six miles to the north. But Smyth, unwilling to take orders from a militia officer, refused to cooperate. Even without Smyth's troops, Van Rensselaer still had a decided advantage over the British, and such was his fear of public criticism if he remained inactive that he decided to attack Queenston anyway.[114]

Van Rensselaer planned to send troops across the river on October 11, but this scheme had to be abandoned because, either from treachery or ignorance, an army officer disappeared down the river in a boat loaded with all the oars. Two days later, another attempt was made. Despite a strong current, an advance guard of some 200 men managed to get across the river. The commanding officer, Solomon Van Rensselaer, was wounded six times in the assault, and his men found themselves pinned down by the river by British troops occupying the heights nearby. Captain John E. Wool took charge of the American force and, discovering an unguarded fisherman's path that led to the heights, marched his men to the top. There the Americans drove off a British force commanded by Brock, who had returned from the West to take charge of the British defenses. Brock was killed in a futile bid to retake the heights, and soon there were about 600 Americans in place, now under the command of Lieutenant Colonel Winfield Scott.[115]

At this point Stephen Van Rensselaer ordered the militia on the American side to cross over to reinforce Scott. But the militia, most of whom were "violent democrats" from New York, were disheartened by the sight of the dead and wounded who were ferried back to the United States.[116] Following the example of their Ohio counterparts in the West, they refused to leave American territory. "[T]o my utter astonishment," Van Rensselaer reported, "I found that at the very moment when complete victory was in our hands, the Ardor of the unengaged Troops had entirely subsided. . . . I rode in all directions.—urged men by every Consideration to pass over, but in vain."[117] Without reinforcements, Scott's troops could not resist a fresh assault from the enemy. Driven from the heights, most of the troops—Scott included—surrendered. In all, around 950 Americans were captured on the Canadian side of the river.[118] Local Republicans—never reconciled to General Van Rensselaer's command—blamed him for the defeat, claiming that he had secretly given the British advance warning of the attack.[119]

After this disaster, Van Rensselaer asked to be relieved of his duties, and the War Department, unaware of Smyth's shortcomings, gave him the command. Smyth planned to attack Fort Erie at the south end of the Niagara River, but "Van Bladder" (as his men called him) wasted his time composing bombastic proclamations that even the British found laughable.[120] Sounding more like a postman than a soldier, he told his troops: "Neither rain, snow or frost will prevent the embarkation."[121] Although a preliminary assault in late November destroyed the enemy's outlying positions at Fort Erie, the primary attack was given up when Smyth's officers voted it down, partly because most of the Pennsylvania militia refused to cross the border.[122]

The abandonment of the attack on Fort Erie brought the fighting on the Niagara front to an end. The only thing gained was the death of Brock, a military genius whose loss the Quebec *Gazette* called "a public calamity."[123] As for Smyth, he was bitterly assailed by the New York militia, some of whom even took potshots at him. One soldier called him "a *traitor*, a *tory* and a d—d *coward*," and Peter B. Porter used similar language, which led to a bloodless duel.[124] Shortly thereafter Smyth stole back to Virginia using back roads. Without even the courtesy of an investigation, he was dropped from the rolls of the army in a reorganization mandated by Congress.[125]

❖ ❖ ❖ ❖ ❖ ❖

The third and most important thrust in the campaign was supposed to be against Montreal. To head this operation, the administration selected sixty-one-year-old Henry Dearborn, a Revolutionary War veteran who had been Jefferson's secretary of war. Dearborn—known to his troops as *"Granny"*—had grown fat with prosperity and was no better suited for his command than Hull, Van Rensselaer, or Smyth.[126] He was supposed to coordinate his attack with one on the Niagara front in order to take the pressure off Hull in the West. But enlistments were slow, and most of the available troops had been sent to other fronts. Hence, he remained in New England to recruit men and prepare coastal defenses, which enabled Brock to concentrate his forces in the West and thus bring about Hull's defeat.[127] Such was Dearborn's dilatoriness, and such was the administration's need for a victory, that the War Department finally ordered him to New York to prepare for the attack on Montreal. "Go to Albany or the Lake [Champlain]!" Eustis told him. "The troops shall come to you as fast as the season will admit, and the blow must be struck. Congress must not meet without a victory to announce to them."[128]

It was not until November that Dearborn's army, 6,000 to 8,000 strong, marched from Albany to Plattsburgh on Lake Champlain. A detachment of his troops crossed into Canada and skirmished with the British, but the fighting was inconclusive, and in the darkness the Americans fired on each other. Once again the militia refused to cross the border, standing on their supposed right to serve only in American territory. The whole army soon retreated, and Dearborn gave up this half-hearted attempt on Montreal.[129] A contemporary described his failure as a "miscarriage, without even [the] heroism of disaster."[130]

Henry Dearborn, by an unknown artist. Courtesy of the Eastern
National Park and Monument Association

Thus, America's invasion of Canada in 1812 failed on all three fronts. The "blustering, bullying, mountain laboring campaign," said a Federalist paper in Vermont, had produced nothing but "an unbroken series of disaster, defeat, disgrace, and ruin and death."[131] Armies had surrendered at Detroit, Frenchtown, and Queenston; much of the Northwest had fallen into enemy hands; and no headway had been made against British positions on the St. Lawrence. "The series of misfortunes," said Albert Gallatin, "exceeds all anticipations made even by those who had least confidence in our inexperienced officers and undisciplined men."[132]

The principal reason for America's failure was poor leadership. The administration's strategy was ill-advised, the War Department failed to give proper direction to commanders in the field, and most of the army's senior officers were incompetent. Some of the junior officers, like Winfield Scott, Zachary Taylor, and John Wool, had distinguished themselves; and the rank and file had proven adequate, although most were still raw recruits without battlefield experience. As for the militia, they were a major disappointment. When forced to take the offensive, more often than not they had proven undisciplined, unreliable, and unwilling to leave the country. "[V]olunteer militia," the Washington *National Intelligencer* conceded, "are not precisely the species of force on which to rely for carrying on war, however competent they may be to repel invasion."[133] The entire campaign showed how difficult it was to build an army overnight. "The degraded state in which the military institutions have been retained," concluded the Philadelphia *Aurora*, "comes now upon us with a dismal sentence of retribution."[134]

❖ ❖ ❖ ❖ ❖ ❖

The war at sea went much better for the United States in 1812, though not because of superior leadership in the cabinet. The secretary of the navy was Paul Hamilton, a South Carolina rice planter with little knowledge of naval affairs. Hamilton, an alcoholic, was usually drunk by noon, and Nathaniel Macon said that he was "about as fit for his place, as the Indian prophet would be for Emperor of Europe."[135] Hamilton's one claim to his office was that he was an advocate of preparedness, though parsimonious treasury policies and congressional opposition doomed his schemes to expand the navy.[136]

A decade of Republican hostility had taken a heavy toll on the navy, but seventeen ships still survived in 1812. Seven were frigates. The *Constitution, President,* and *United States* were rated at 44 guns; the *Constellation, Chesapeake,* and *Congress* at 36 guns; and the *Essex* at 32 guns. Another frigate, the *Adams,* was being cut down to a 28-gun corvette. There were also nine smaller vessels rated at 10 to 20 guns. Most of the ships carried more guns than they were rated for, and most also carried extra crewmen.[137]

The frigates were the heart of the navy. Inspired by Philadelphia shipwright Joshua Humphreys, the three heavy frigates—or "44s," as they were called—were longer and sturdier than other frigates. They were capable of carrying heavier guns and were better able to withstand enemy broadsides. In fact, they were "superfrigates," capable of outfighting and outsailing other ships in their class and of outrunning anything larger.[138]

The nation also had the advantage of a rich maritime tradition. Officers and men alike were excellent seamen and skilled marksmen with cannon and small arms. Most of the officers had seen action in the Quasi-War (1798–1801) or in the War with Tripoli (1801–1805). Many of the men had fought in those wars, too, or had served on British warships. The morale of the service was high, and the men were trained incessantly to perfect their skills. In addition, the navy did not face the same logistical problems as the army. The fleet was small, and once supplied a ship could remain at sea for months.[139]

In spite of its high morale, the navy had trouble keeping its ships fully manned. The army siphoned off potential recruits (even some with extensive naval experience) because of the large bounties it offered. The competition from privateers was even greater. Privateering was an attractive alternative to naval service: the tour of duty was shorter (usually a two- or three-month cruise instead of a year's service), the prospect of an armed engagement was less, and the chances of large profits greater.[140]

It was particularly difficult for the navy to find men to serve in the gunboat flotillas attached to the major ports or in the squadrons on the northern lakes. Flotilla duty was dull and lake service rigorous, and neither offered much prospect of prize money. Although men could be transferred from the navy's oceangoing vessels to the lakes or flotillas, this encouraged desertion and discouraged reenlistments.[141]

The usual term of service for navy personnel was a year, and normally there was no bounty.[142] The pay ranged from $6 a month for boys and landsmen to $20 for sailmakers. Ordinary seamen earned $10, able-bodied seamen $12, and gunners $18.[143] Most could earn more on a merchantman and a lot more on a lucky privateer. To compete, the navy began offering incentives on some stations as early as 1812, a practice that became almost universal by the end of the war. By then new recruits could expect to receive a bounty (ranging from $10 to $30), three months' advance pay, and a 25 percent boost in pay.

The navy demanded a two-year commitment in exchange for these incentives but sometimes had to settle for a year or even six months. Even so, the incentives went a long way toward securing the men that were needed.[144]

Even with a full complement of men, the tiny American fleet hardly seemed a match for the Mistress of the Seas. For more than a century Great Britain had ruled the waves, and on paper her naval superiority was overwhelming. She had over a thousand ships on the rolls, half of which were at sea at any given time. Yet her fleet was scattered all over the world in 1812, engaged in patrol, convoy, and blockade duty. Indeed, at the beginning of the war she had only one ship-of-the-line, nine frigates, and twenty-seven smaller vessels at her Halifax and Newfoundland stations. There were additional ships attached to her West Indian stations, but most of these were either unseaworthy or were needed to guard against privateers that threatened Britain's Caribbean trade.[145]

The British were reluctant to divert any warships from the European theater because Napoleon was rebuilding his fleet in the Mediterranean. In addition, they hoped that the repeal of the Orders in Council would put an end to the American war. Even when it became evident that this war was likely to continue, they feared that closing the sea lanes would deprive their troops in Spain and their colonists in the West Indies and Canada of much-needed provisions. Consequently, they retained only a modest naval presence in American waters until 1813.[146]

American officials recognized the nation's fleet might be useful but could not agree on how to deploy it. Monroe wanted to keep the ships in port, while Gallatin thought they should cruise in American waters to protect returning merchantmen, whose value he estimated would be $4,000,000 to $6,000,000 in the first month of the war. Two captains in the service, Stephen Decatur and William Bainbridge, wanted to send the ships abroad to cruise separately, while a third, John Rodgers, thought they should operate in squadrons.[147]

The administration adopted a plan based on Gallatin's and Rodgers's recommendations. The ships were divided into two squadrons (later increased to three) and ordered "to afford to our returning commerce, all possible protection."[148] But this order arrived after Rodgers, who was in charge of one of the squadrons, had already set sail in search of a rich British convoy en route from Jamaica to England.[149] Although he never caught up with the convoy, his cruise nonetheless had a dramatic effect on British naval strategy. Vice Admiral Herbert Sawyer, commander of the Halifax station, had planned to post a British cruiser in front of each American port to intercept returning merchantmen. But when he learned that Rodgers was at sea with a large squadron, he gave up this plan, fearing that his vessels might be picked off one at a time. Instead, he kept his fleet concentrated and spent most of his time searching for Rodgers's squadron. As a result, he was able to make only one sweep through American waters, and his catch was poor. "We have been so completely occupied looking for Commodore Rodgers's squadron," a British officer complained, "that we have taken very few prizes."[150]

Because the British did not patrol American waters, most American merchant vessels were able to reach home safely. "Nearly as great a proportion of homeward bound merchantmen have escaped capture," Governor Tompkins reported, "as has been customary during the last three or four years of peace."[151] The windfall for the United States was considerable. The flood of goods replenished the nation's stockpiles and buoyed the customs revenue. In addition, returning seaman helped fill out the crews of American warships and privateers that were fitting out for sea.[152]

❖ ❖ ❖ ❖ ❖ ❖

Some American warships cruised separately in 1812, and their record of accomplishments was impressive. Captain Isaac Hull, the nephew of the disgraced army general, commanded the U.S.S. *Constitution*, the nation's best frigate. After putting to sea, Hull ran into the Halifax squadron—consisting of a ship-of-the-line and four frigates—which gave chase. Normally, Hull could have outdistanced his pursuers, but he lost his wind. To keep the British at bay, he mounted guns on his stern and undertook several laborious maneuvers to propel his ship. First he used his small boats to tow the ship; then (after discovering that he was in shallow water) he used his boats to drop anchor ahead, his men then pulling the *Constitution* forward (a maneuver known as "kedging"). Later, when a slight breeze picked up, Hull ordered his men to water down the sails to better hold the wind. The chase continued for two days, the British keeping pace by matching Hull's maneuvers. The *Constitution* finally slipped away, eventually putting in at Boston.[153] The escape was the talk of the nation, and even the British conceded that it was "elegant."[154]

Without waiting for new orders, Hull took on supplies and set sail again.[155] On August 19, about 750 miles east of Boston, the *Constitution* (which carried 54 guns) encountered H.M.S. *Guerrière* (49 guns), a ship commanded by Captain James R. Dacres and described by the British *Naval Chronicle* as "one of our stoutest frigates."[156] After outmaneuvering the enemy, Hull's ship delivered a powerful and destructive raking fire. An American on board the British ship said the *Constitution's* double-shotted first fire (700 pounds of metal delivered at close range) sounded like "a tremendous explosion" and forced the *Guerrière* to "reel, and tremble as though she had received the shock of an earthquake."[157]

Although the *Guerrière* returned the fire, her masts were soon destroyed, her hull damaged, and most of her crew knocked out of action. This left Dacres with no choice but to surrender. "[I]n less than thirty minutes, from the time we got alongside of the Enemy," Hull reported, "She was left without a Spar Standing, and the Hull cut to pieces, in such a manner as to make it difficult to keep her above water." Unable to salvage the British ship, Hull removed her crew and ordered her set on fire and sent to the bottom.[158]

During the battle, a seaman on the *Constitution* saw a shot bounce off the ship and exclaimed: "Huzza, her sides are made of iron." Thereafter, the *Constitution* was affectionately known as "Old Ironsides."[159] The American victory was particularly gratifying because the British ship (which had *"Guerrière"* painted on her mainsail and *"Not the Little Belt!"* on her foresail) had been one of the most obnoxious British vessels operating along the coast before the war.[160] The American victory scotched any further talk of keeping the fleet in port, and other naval victories soon followed.

On October 15, the U.S.S. *United States*, a 56-gun frigate commanded by Decatur, was cruising 600 miles west of the Canaries when it encountered a British frigate, H.M.S. *Macedonian* (49 guns), Captain John S. Carden commanding. Although the *United States* was known as "the Wagon" because it was such a poor sailer, Decatur nonetheless outmaneuvered his foe, keeping his distance to take advantage of his powerful long-range guns and his crew's marksmanship. In the ensuing battle, the *United States* got off seventy broadsides, the *Macedonian* only thirty. A sailor on the British ship described the damage done by the American guns: "Grapeshot and canister were pouring through our portholes like leaden hail; the large shot came against the ship's side, shaking her to the very keel, and passing through her timbers and scattering terrific splinters, which did more appalling work than the shot itself."[161]

By the time the *Macedonian* was able to close, she had lost most of her spars and rigging and a third of her crew, forcing Carden to strike his colors. When Decatur boarded the vessel, he found "fragments of the dead scattered in every direction, the decks slippery with blood, [and] one continuous agonizing yell of the unhappy wounded."[162] A

Isaac Hull, by William Strickland. Courtesy of the National Portrait Gallery, Smithsonian Institution

prize crew sailed the *Macedonian* into Newport Harbor, the only time a British frigate has ever been brought into an American port as a prize of war. The government gave the officers and crew of the *United States* $200,000 in prize money, the largest award made for the capture of a single ship during the war. The *Macedonian* remained on the rolls of the American navy for more than twenty years.[163]

Another American victory followed off the coast of Brazil on December 29, 1812, when the *Constitution*, now commanded by Bainbridge, met H.M.S. *Java* (49 guns), a frigate under the command of Captain Henry Lambert. Both captains demonstrated excellent seamanship, but once again superior American firepower and marksmanship carried the day. American gunners destroyed most of the rigging of the *Java* and killed or wounded a large portion of the British crew. "[T]he Enemy was completely dismasted," Bainbridge reported, "not having a Spar of any kind standing."[164] Unable to move, the *Java* surrendered. After removing the crew and passengers (which included Lieutenant General Thomas Hislop, the governor of India), Bainbridge sent the British ship to the bottom.[165]

Several smaller American ships also distinguished themselves. On October 18, 1812, 500 miles off the Virginia coast, the American sloop *Wasp* (18 guns) defeated H.M.S. *Frolic* (16 guns) by firing into the hull of the British ship and killing or wounding almost 80 percent of her crew. Another sloop, the U.S.S. *Hornet* (18 guns), defeated the British sloop *Peacock* (18 guns) in February of 1813 off the coast of British Guiana. The small American frigate *Essex* (which was overloaded with 46 guns) defeated the British brig *Alert* (20 guns) and also captured a troop transport carrying 160 soldiers from Barbadoes to Canada. Although the British captured three American warships—the *Wasp*, *Nautilus* (14 guns), and *Vixen* (14 guns)—the balance was clearly in America's favor.[166] In all, the United States had defeated or captured three British frigates, two sloops, a brig, and a transport, while losing only three vessels of its own. American success was due not only to the superior firepower of the heavy frigates but also to the skillful seamanship and gunnery displayed on all the ships.

The American navy also captured fifty merchantmen, but the real damage to British commerce in 1812 was done by what one Republican called "our cheapest & best Navy"—American privateers.[167] Cruising mainly off the coast of Canada and in the West Indies, these vessels made 450 prizes in the first six months of the war.[168] "Our Privateers," said a Richmond merchant, "bring in Prizes to almost every Port & many of these, of great value."[169] The most successful cruises were made by the *Yankee*, sailing out of Bristol, Rhode Island, which took eight British vessels valued at $300,000, and the *Rossie,* commanded by Joshua Barney of Baltimore, which captured eighteen vessels worth close to $1,500,000.[170]

A Halifax paper reported in July of 1812 that American privateers were "swarming round our coast and in the Bay of Fundy" and that it was "very imprudent for any vessel to sail from this port unless under convoy." Several months later another report from Halifax claimed that "American privateers annoy this place to a degree astonishingly injurious; scarcely a day passes but crews' are coming in that have had their vessels taken and sunk."[171] Similar reports came from the West Indies. A letter from Martinique said that American privateers "have destroyed a great number of our coasting vessels"; another from Guadaloupe claimed that "American privateers are swarming" and that "[t]he navy force upon the station is not sufficient for the protection of the islands." According to a third report, the British naval commander in the Leeward Islands was "mortified at the depredations of the American privateers, it not being in his power to prevent them."[172] "[B]y every account received from the West Indies," the *Times* concluded, "the American privateers are still enabled to range unmolested."[173]

Although British warships in the New World captured more than 150 privateers in the first eight months of the war, the western Atlantic had nonetheless become dangerous for any British merchantman sailing without an escort.[174] Sir John Borlase Warren, who assumed command of the Halifax station in the summer of 1812, conceded "the impossibility of our trade navigating these seas unless a very extensive squadron is employed to scour the vicinity."[175] Armed American vessels threatened British commerce in other seas, too. "*Jonathan's* privateers," complained a correspondent to the *Naval Chronicle,* "have roved with impunity and success to all corners of the earth."[176]

The war at sea gave a tremendous boost to American morale, a boost that was sorely needed because the nation was reeling from the disasters on the Canadian frontier. "Our brilliant naval victories," said an army officer, "serve, in some measure, to wipe out the disgrace brought upon the Nation by the conduct of our generals." "But for the gallantry of our noble Tar's," said another American, "we should be covered with shame and disgrace."[177] There was also considerable pride in humbling the Mistress of the Seas on her own element. "British arms cannot withstand American upon the sea," exulted a Republican congressman. "The bully has been disgraced by an infant."[178]

The British, on the other hand, were stunned by their losses. In more than 200 naval engagements with France and her allies over a twenty-year period they had lost only five battles.[179] Some British subjects, like the editor of the *Times,* acknowledged the merits of American ships and sailors, but most shared the view of the London *Evening Star,* which described the American navy as "a few fir-built frigates, manned by a handful of bastards and outlaws."[180] Given this contempt, the American victories went down hard. "It is a cruel mortification," said a cabinet official, "to be beat by these second-hand Englishmen upon our own element."[181]

Learned essays appeared in the *Naval Chronicle* analyzing the reasons for American success, and the *Times* wondered "[w]hether the Americans are possessed of any secret in the management of their guns, in the fabrication of their powder, or in the size and construction of their shot."[182] Most British subjects concluded that the Royal Navy had been victimized by Yankee trickery—that the "superfrigates" were really ships-of-the-line in disguise.[183] But this implied that British naval personnel were easily duped and could not tell the difference between a battleship and a cruiser.

The naval defeats exposed the British government to growing criticism. Though normally a supporter of the government, the *Times* attacked the ministry's passive war policy. In October of 1812 the paper accused the government of adopting "so drivelling a line of conduct, as to think of waging a war of conciliation and forbearance." "The paramount duty . . . of British Ministers," the paper declared, "is to render the English arms as formidable in the new world as they have become in the old." Two months later the *Times* renewed the attack. "Political cowardice alone," the paper claimed, "prevented Ministers . . . from having a plan matured and ready, for falling upon the sea-coasts of America, blocking up her ports, hindering her privateers from sailing, and capturing or destroying every frigate she might dare to send to sea." The British government, the *Times* concluded, had brought out "the impatient 'dogs of war' muzzled and clogged."[184]

This kind of criticism mounted with each defeat. "[W]e have suffered ourselves to be beaten in detail," said the *Times,* "by a Power that we should not have allowed to send a vessel to sea."[185] "We are satisfied," added the London *Chronicle,* "that every individual in the country must feel humiliated at this succession of disasters, which thus mock and render nugatory our boasted naval superiority."[186] A writer in the *Naval Chronicle* suggested that the best way to retrieve the situation was to maintain a large enough force in American waters to show "that the frontier of England is the high-water mark on every shore: that the British seas are wherever a 32-pounder can be floated."[187]

British officials took this criticism to heart. Besides dispatching additional ships to the New World, they launched a crash program to build heavy frigates.[188] A dozen were constructed during the war, but most were so badly designed and built of such poor materials that they were no match for the American 44s.[189] In addition, the Admiralty secretly ordered British frigates not to cruise alone or "to engage, single handed, the larger class of American ships, which, though they may be called frigates . . . [resemble] line-of-battle ships."[190] The government also ordered all merchantmen in the Atlantic to sail in convoy.[191]

The outcome of the campaign of 1812 was a surprise to people in both countries. The conquest of Canada, which was supposed to be a "mere matter of marching," had eluded the United States, while the war at sea, in which the British were supposed to have a decisive advantage, had gone surprisingly well for America. The campaign, the *Naval Chronicle* concluded, "has been marked by events on land and at sea . . . diametrically opposite to the public expectation."[192] Both sides had been unprepared for the war, which had worked to Britain's advantage in Canada but to America's on the high seas.

Time, however, was on Great Britain's side. In June of 1812 Napoleon had taken the largest army ever assembled, some 600,000 men, into Russia. By the fall of 1812 stout resistance and a lack of supplies had forced him to retreat. The retreat soon turned into a rout, and by the end of the year the Grand Army had melted away. In December *Niles' Register* claimed that "[a]ll Europe, the British islands excepted, . . . now are, or soon will be, at the feet of *Bonaparte*," but the news pouring in from the Continent suggested just the opposite.[193] If Napoleon were in fact defeated, England would be able to concentrate all of her military and naval might against the United States, and there would be little chance for the young republic to take Canada or to win any maritime concessions.

CHAPTER 5

Raising Men and Money

THE CAMPAIGN OF 1812 was both disappointing and embarrassing to Republicans. The string of defeats on the Canadian frontier had dashed all hopes for a quick and an easy victory and had exposed the administration to criticism. The war had never lost its political character, and Republican leaders had hoped that triumphs on the battlefield would disarm their critics and enhance their chances at the polls. "[A] little success," said one Republican, "would silence many who are clamerous." "[I]f our government does not look sharp," said another, "the Federalists will come in again."[1] But except for the naval victories, there was little to cheer about, and the result was growing disillusionment with the management of the war. "Our affirs," Senator Thomas Worthington of Ohio scrawled in his diary on December 1, "is [in] a misreable way[,] defeated and disgraced[,] the revenue extravagantly expended[,] the war not man[a]ged at all."[2]

Although voters usually rally around a wartime president, Madison fared worse in 1812 than he had in 1808.[3] A split in the Republican party and charges of mismanagement very nearly cost him his office. In addition, the Federalists made significant gains in the congressional and state elections. Although the Republicans retained control over the national government and a majority of the state governments, the election results showed that many questioned not only the administration's handling of the war but the wisdom of the war itself.

The presidential campaign opened in February of 1812 when Republicans in the Virginia legislature nominated electors committed to Madison.[4] In the ensuing months Republican caucuses in seven other states followed suit.[5] The regular Republicans in Congress added their endorsement in May of 1812. At a widely publicized meeting (which most people considered the official Republican caucus), eighty-three members of Congress promised to support Madison for the presidency and seventy-one-year-old John Langdon of New Hampshire for the vice presidency. (Langdon declined because of age, which necessitated substituting Elbridge Gerry of Massachusetts.) Nine other members of Congress later added their endorsements, so Madison ended up with the avowed support of about two-thirds of the Republican membership. Most Republican congressmen from New York and other northern states, however, withheld their support because they preferred a northern candidate.[6]

Shortly after the Washington caucus, Republicans in the New York state legislature met to nominate their own candidate. The favorite was De Witt Clinton, the mayor of New York City. Known as the "Magnus Apollo," Clinton was a handsome, popular, and talented statesman from a family long active in politics. Although some New Yorkers were fearful of splitting the party, Clinton won the legislature's endorsement when congressmen returning from Washington brought stories of growing disillusionment with Madison and letters from Postmaster General Gideon Granger urging support for a northern candidate.[7]

Clinton's friends put his case before the people in an address published in the summer of 1812. The address attacked the congressional nominating system and the Virginia Dynasty and charged the administration with mismanaging the war. Virginia's domination of the presidency, the address said, had given rise to charges of "*Virginia influence,*" pitting the agricultural states against the commercial ones. To put an end to this divisiveness, the address recommended Clinton as a man who would provide "vigor in war, and a determined character in the relations of peace."[8]

Clinton's nomination posed a dilemma for Federalists. Should they maintain their purity by supporting a Federal candidate—a course sure to lead to defeat—or should they vote for Clinton, a man long associated with the Republican party but considered friendly to commerce and anxious for peace? In New York and Virginia, the prevailing sentiment was for a Federal candidate, the favorites being Rufus King, John Marshall, and Charles Cotesworth Pinckney.[9] Elsewhere there was considerable support for Clinton because, as one Federalist put it, he "wd. engage, if chosen President, to make immediate Peace with England."[10] The sentiment for Clinton was particularly strong among Federalists in Pennsylvania and Massachusetts. In mid-summer a Philadelphia committee of correspondence sent out a circular recommending Clinton because of "his residence and attachments, his asserted freedom from foreign influence, his avowed hostility to the anti-commercial system, . . . combined with the positive declarations which have been made that he is desirous of the restoration of peace."[11]

To fix their election strategy, Federalists held a convention in New York City in September of 1812. Seventy delegates from eleven states attended, though most were from New York, Pennsylvania, and New Jersey.[12] Rufus King spearheaded the opposition to Clinton, believing that he was nothing more than the "Leader of a Faction." King thought "it was of less importance that the Federalists should acquire a temporary ascendency by the aid of a portion of the Repubs. than that their reputation and integrity shd. be preserved unblemished."[13] Many of the delegates disagreed, not because they had any great confidence in Clinton but because they saw him as the lesser of two evils. As Timothy Pickering of Massachusetts put it, "I am far enough from desiring Clinton for President . . . but I would vote for any man in preference to Madison."[14]

Harrison Gray Otis delivered an impassioned appeal on behalf of Clinton. According to one observer, "Mr. Otis arose, apparently much embarrassed, holding his hat in his hand, and seeming as if he were almost sorry he had arisen. Soon he warmed with his subject, his hat fell from his hand, and he poured forth a strain of eloquence that chained all present to their seats."[15] Otis's appeal carried the day, but the convention stopped short of formally endorsing Clinton, fearing that this would undermine his Republican support. Instead, the delegates simply urged Federalists to support presidential electors "most likely by their votes to effect a change in the present course of measures."[16] The convention made no provision for the vice presidency, but Jared Ingersoll became the accepted candidate when he was nominated by Federalists in Lancaster County, Pennsylvania.[17]

None of the candidates openly campaigned for office, but the followers of each were busy, particularly in the middle states. "Never did I witness a more spirited preparation for an election," said a New Yorker.[18] The war was the principal issue in the campaign. Madison's supporters insisted that the contest was necessary to vindicate the nation's rights and to uphold its independence. "It is a war of right against lawless aggression," said a South Carolina campaign document, "of Justice against perfidy and violence."[19] Republicans also argued that the president could not be blamed for setbacks in the field, that it was unfair "to impute to Mr. Madison the failure of every military expedition, or the defection of every military chief."[20] In response to this, the Clintonians accused Madison's followers of embracing "the

De Witt Clinton, by John Wesley Jarvis. Courtesy of the National Portrait Gallery, Smithsonian Institution

British maxim—*the king can do no wrong,*" and of applying it "to the President in its full force."[21]

The Clintonians sought to win northern support by portraying their candidate as a bold and energetic leader who was friendly to commerce and the navy and in no way tied to France. In pro-war states, Clinton's followers emphasized that he would shorten the war by prosecuting it more vigorously, while in anti-war states he was portrayed as a man who would achieve this end by negotiating with the British. Friends of the administration were quick to exploit this inconsistency. "In the west," said one critic, "Mr. Clinton is recommended as a friend of war . . . in the East he is presented as a friend of peace."[22] A character in a contemporary play echoed this sentiment: "He cannot have *war* and *peace at the same time.*"[23]

The Clintonians claimed that there had been a breakdown in presidential leadership, a charge that some of Madison's followers privately conceded. According to a New Hampshire War Hawk, "many of the friends of the Administration believe, that the Executive are not disposed to prosecute the war with vigor, provided they can find any *hole* through which they can creep out, and avoid the contest."[24] Even in Madison's home state a "horrible spirit of disaffection or distrust" was said to be afoot. "[A]ll the misfortunes of our arms," reported a Virginia Republican, "are here Publicly ascribed to the mismanagement of the Genl Government."[25] Many people wondered whether "Little Jemmy" (who was only five feet four inches tall) was big enough for the job. "Mr. Madison is wholly unfit for the storms of War," Henry Clay confided to a friend. "Nature has cast him in too benevolent a mould."[26]

The Republicans sought to counter charges of Madison's weakness by attacking Clinton's character. One called him "the modern *Cromwell,*" a second described him as a "sprig of upstart nobility," while a third compared him to *"Judas Iscariot."*[27] The Republicans also tried to discredit Clinton by focusing on his alliance with the Federalists. According to a Philadelphia campaign document, this alliance was "unanswerable evidence, that Mr. Clinton has sacrificed his democratic principles on the altar of his ambition." "[C]ourting the interest and votes of the *Essex Junto,*" said another Republican, "ought forever [to] damn him with Democrats."[28]

The means of selecting presidential electors varied from state to state. Half of the states chose their electors by popular vote, while the rest left the decision to the legislature. Each state followed its own timetable, and the results drifted in over a two-month period in the fall of 1812. The outcome was by no means certain. According to congressman Samuel Latham Mitchill, November was "a dark and dismal month" in the White House because news of election defeats coupled with military reverses rolled in "[day] after day, like the tidings of Job's disasters."[29]

The voting followed the same sectional pattern as the vote on the declaration of war. Clinton fared best in the North, Madison in the South and West. The outcome hinged on the results in New York and Pennsylvania, the two populous middle Atlantic states. Clinton needed both to win. He had no trouble in New York, winning all of that state's twenty-nine electoral votes. This result was due mainly to shrewd maneuvering in the legislature by twenty-nine-year-old Martin Van Buren, who henceforth would be known as the "Little Magician."[30] Madison, however, prevailed in Pennsylvania, winning all twenty-five electoral votes and proving again that this state was the "Keystone in the Democratic Arch."[31] The election was "pretty close work," concluded Richard Rush, "and Pennsylvania, as usual, carries the union on her back."[32] Madison was aided in no small degree by Pennsylvania's booming prosperity, which was based on military spending and an extensive overseas trade. "Never did the abundant harvests of Pennsylvania find a quicker or a better market," crowed a Republican campaign document.[33] In all, Madison won 128 electoral votes to Clinton's 89. (By contrast, Madison had defeated Charles Cotesworth Pinckney in 1808 by a margin of 122 to 47.)[34]

The Republicans also lost ground in the congressional elections. The proportion of seats they held fell from 75 to 63 percent in the House and from 82 to 78 percent in the Senate. Their losses were particularly heavy in New York, Massachusetts, and New Hampshire.[35] The Republicans lost control of several states, too. In 1811 they had won every state except Connecticut, Rhode Island, and Delaware. In 1812 they lost these states as well as Massachusetts, New Jersey, and Maryland. They also lost their majority in the New York assembly and suffered small or moderate losses in almost every other state east of the Appalachian Mountains.[36] Although the Republicans remained in charge of the nation's destinies, their popularity appeared to be waning. The Federalists, on the other hand, had every reason to be pleased. By capitalizing on the mismanagement and unpopularity of the war and by exploiting the gruesome violence at Baltimore, they had achieved their most impressive electoral gains since the 1790s.

❖ ❖ ❖ ❖ ❖ ❖

With the elections safely behind them, Republican leaders urged President Madison to strengthen his cabinet. Ever since the previous spring,

Secretary of War William Eustis and Secretary of the Navy Paul Hamilton had been under heavy fire. By the end of the year this criticism had reached such a torrent that it threatened to engulf the president himself. "Our executive officers are most incompetent men," said John C. Calhoun. "We are literally boren down under the effects of errors and mismanagement." "The clamor against the gentlemen who are at the head of the War and Navy Departments," said another congressman, "is loud & very general." If these men are not removed, added a Georgia senator, the president "must be content, with defeat, and disgrace in all his efforts, during the war."[37] Although Madison was reluctant to act, he finally accepted the resignations of both men in December.[38]

To replace Hamilton, Madison chose William Jones, a Philadelphia merchant and former congressman who had fought at Trenton and Princeton and served on a privateer during the Revolution.[39] Though later discredited for mismanaging the national bank, Jones had considerable ability. With some justice, Madison later claimed that he was "the fittest minister who had ever been charged with the Navy Department."[40] Far more knowledgeable about naval affairs than his predecessor, he was a good administrator who brought energy and efficiency to the department and won the admiration of his contemporaries. "I know of Some," said Nathaniel Macon in 1814, "who once thought little of his talents, [but] now consider him, the most useful member of the administration."[41]

It was much harder to find a new secretary of war because this office was such an administrative nightmare. "[W]ith all its horrors & perils," said Gallatin, the office "frightens those who know best its difficulties." Finding a candidate who is "qualified, popular, and willing to accept is extremely difficult."[42] Secretary of State James Monroe agreed to serve temporarily but refused to take the office permanently because he was hoping for a command in the field. Senator William H. Crawford and General Henry Dearborn also declined.[43]

The president finally settled on John Armstrong of New York.[44] Although knowledgeable about military affairs, Armstrong was abrasive and indolent and a known enemy of the Virginia Dynasty. In 1783 he had written the Newburgh Letters inciting the Continental Army to mutiny, and many people considered this "an indelible stain" upon his character.[45] He also had a reputation for intrigue, a reputation that was largely justified.[46] Given his liabilities, his confirmation in the Senate was doubtful. "Armstrong will rub hard, if he gets through at all," said one Republican.[47] Though the Senate finally approved him, the vote was 18–15, with both Virginia senators abstaining.[48]

The new appointments improved the efficiency of the administration but not without a price. Armstrong lived up to his reputation for intrigue and alienated his colleagues. Monroe saw him as a rival for the presidential succession and was constantly at odds with him. Monroe finally told Madison that if Armstrong were not removed he would "ruin not you and the admn. only, but the whole republican party and cause."[49] Gallatin also despised him. Armstrong sided with Gallatin's enemies (particularly in Pennsylvania) and distributed his patronage accordingly. The crowning insult came when he awarded an army staff position to William Duane, the editor of the virulently anti-Gallatin Philadelphia *Aurora*. "The appointment of Duane," lamented Gallatin, "has appeared to me so gross an outrage on decency and self respect . . . that I felt no wish to remain associated with an administration which would employ such a miscreant."[50] By the summer of 1813, William Jones had lost confidence in Armstrong, too. "[M]any begin to believe," he said, "that the 'Old Soldier' [Armstrong's nom de plume] is not a legitimate son of Mars."[51]

❖ ❖ ❖ ❖ ❖ ❖

On November 2, 1812, about a month before the election results were in and the cabinet shuffling had begun, the Twelfth Congress met for its second and last session. This was the same Congress that had declared war four and a half months earlier. Since House officers are chosen for the life of a Congress, Henry Clay resumed his place as speaker. Once again he filled the key committees with supporters of the war.[52] Although a Federalist congressman thought that the advocates of war had "greatly cooled in their zeal," this was not evident in the proceedings.[53]

On November 4 President Madison sent his annual message to Congress.[54] He opened on a positive note, reminding Americans of their health and prosperity. "[I]t is my first duty," he said, "to invite your attention to the providential favors which our country has experienced." Madison was not exaggerating, for the nation was in the flood tide of a wartime boom fueled by huge government expenditures and a mushrooming trade that included large exports of grain to the Spanish peninsula and large imports of manufactured goods from the British Empire.[55]

The president mentioned the defeats on the northern frontier and the victories at sea. He also contrasted British and American Indian policies. "Whilst the benevolent policy of the United States invariably recommended peace and promoted civilization among that wretched portion of the human race . . . the enemy has not scrupled to call to

John Armstrong, by John Wesley Jarvis. Courtesy of the National Portrait Gallery, Smithsonian Institution

his aid their ruthless ferocity." In order to prosecute the war more efficiently, Madison recommended measures to improve the army, upgrade the militia, expand the navy, and restrict trade with the enemy. "The situation of our country," he concluded, "is not without its difficulties.... The spirit and strength of the nation are nevertheless equal to the support of all its rights, and to carry it through all its trials."[56]

Republicans in Congress were receptive to the president's recommendations, but before they could act, a full-scale debate erupted on the merits of the war. House Federalists had remained silent during the proceedings on the war bill the previous June, refusing to debate the issue in secret session. Now, as one Republican put it, they "embraced [the] opportunity to *deliver* themselves of their war speeches with which they were pregnant last session."[57] The Republicans responded with lengthy speeches of their own, and for two weeks the debate raged, pushing other business aside. The exchanges focused on the wisdom of the war and the justice of invading Canada and were so long-winded and repetitious that even John Randolph, who was no fan of brevity, conceded that the debate had become "unnecessarily protracted."[58]

The most provocative speech was delivered by Josiah Quincy of Massachusetts. Taking a swipe at Jefferson, Madison, and Swiss-born Albert Gallatin, Quincy said that for twelve years the nation's affairs had been mismanaged by "two Virginians and a foreigner." The war policy, he claimed, was designed to further the Virginia Dynasty by insuring that James II (Monroe) succeeded James I (Madison). Those New England Republicans who aided the administration were characterized as "toads, or reptiles, which *spread their slime in the drawing room*"—language so coarse that Quincy deleted this passage before publishing his speech.[59]

Republicans hotly denied Quincy's accusations and, according to one War Hawk, "paid him in his own coin, and *with use.*"[60] Not all the speeches were recorded because most were extemporaneous, and a stenographer was not always present to take them down. Stevenson Archer's speech, which was recorded, was probably typical. The Maryland Republican accused Quincy of "secretly advocating, and insidiously endeavoring to effect, a disunion of the States." Archer also articulated a view that most Republicans shared, namely, that Federalists could best work for peace by supporting the war. It is the duty of every good citizen, he said, "to aid in the prosecution of the present war, in order that a speedy and honorable peace might be be [*sic*] obtained."[61]

Both sides talked at length about impressment because, with the Orders in Council repealed, this was the only major issue that separated the two nations. "There is but one point of difference," said a Connecticut Federalist. "But that is a point which we well know, or ought to know, that [England] will not yield until reduced to the last extremity."[62] Republican leaders recognized the importance of impressment, and the administration had already offered to bar all British tars from American ships if Great Britain would give up the practice.[63] Although Britain had rejected this proposal, the administration was anxious to publicize it in order to shore up its position at home and abroad. As one Republican put it, we must "define the grounds of contest . . . that we may stand justified in our own eyes, and in the eyes of the world."[64]

Accordingly, Gallatin drew up a bill that embodied the administration's views. As finally enacted into law, the foreign seaman bill barred from American ships the seamen of any nation that excluded American tars from its ships. The bill also required foreigners seeking American citizenship to reside continuously in the United States for five years. This provision was designed to force those interested in citizenship to give up seafaring because the British claimed the right to impress anyone born in the British Isles, even those who had become naturalized foreign citizens.[65]

The "Impressment Bill" (as contemporaries called it) was attacked by both sides in Congress.[66] Some Republicans thought it was humiliating to give legislative sanction to an offer already rejected by the British. John Clopton of Virginia argued that the bill would "greatly lower the dignity of this nation" and would probably be treated by the British with "scorn and contumely." Joseph Desha thought the measure was tantamount to "begging for peace" and that Americans would be humbling themselves "at the footstool of British corruption."[67] Federalists also distrusted the bill, believing that its main purpose was to undermine opposition to the war. According to Charles Goldsborough of Maryland, the proposal was "a sort of political adventurer, sent out to catch what it may; peace, if it may so happen; if not, what is perhaps more desired—popularity to the war and its authors."[68] Despite these misgivings, a bi-partisan coalition pushed the bill through Congress, and Madison signed it into law.[69]

❖ ❖ ❖ ❖ ❖ ❖

Congress devoted much of its time in this session to debating the larger issues of the war. As valuable as this was for bringing the issues into focus, it did little to strengthen American arms in the field, and this, most Republicans agreed, was essential. "We ought not to calculate on peace," said David R. Williams; "it has become more than ever necessary to prove that we will not only declare war, but can prosecute it with energy and courageous enterprise." "The next campaign," echoed George M. Troup, "must be opened with vigor, and prosecuted to success."[70]

The main problem the nation faced was raising troops. Recruitment lagged behind need for a variety of reasons. Army pay was low and army life hard, and Republicans no less than Federalists were reluctant to enlist. "Money usually can command men," said one Federalist, "but it will take millions to make soldiers of the happy people of this country—nothing short of a little fortune will induce our Farmers or their sons to enter on a life which they cordially despise: that of a common soldier."[71]

The administration made a number of proposals for upgrading the army, and most of these were enacted into law.[72] The most important provided for raising an additional 22,000 regulars for one year of service, thus increasing the authorized level of the army to 57,000 men. This bill offered short-term recruits a bounty of $16 and was designed to replace the volunteer act of 1812, which had failed because it offered no bounty at all. Proponents of the new bill argued that the short enlistment period would attract recruits, while opponents claimed that the term was too short to allow for sufficient training. The bill probably would have been defeated had not Federalists chosen this occasion to deliver most of their speeches against the war.[73] This transformed the vote on the troop bill into a vote of confidence on the war. According to William Lowndes, "there were not half a dozen men who approved [the bill]. . . . The vote was by many considered a vote of approbation to the war."[74]

Congress also tried to spur enlistments by raising army pay. Privates earned only $5 a month, which was less than half what most unskilled laborers made.[75] To lessen the gap, Congress boosted army pay to $8. This also had the effect of increasing the bounty for long-term recruits, which was set at $16 plus three months' pay and 160 acres of land. Under the revised pay schedule, new recruits would receive a cash bounty of $40 instead of $31. On top of this, Congress ordered the army to give all long-term recruits three months' advance pay, which would put an additional $24 into their pockets. Congress also increased the number of officers in each regiment (so that more could concentrate on recruiting) and authorized long-term recruits to sign up for the duration of the war instead of the usual five years.[76]

Congress also prohibited the arrest of any soldier for debt.[77] Although Federalists claimed that this measure was unconstitutional, Ezekiel Bacon of Massachusetts argued that it was necessary to prevent fraud. Some soldiers, he said, created fictitious debts, were arrested, and then released when a friend or relative promised to serve as their bail. These soldiers could not be reclaimed by the army because the courts considered a man the property of his bail until the suit was settled—which could take years.[78]

The practice that Bacon complained of continued even after Congress had legislated against it. In Massachusetts, Judge Joseph Story complained that "the service has suffered exceedingly from *fraudulent arrests*," and there was nothing he could do about it. "[T]he Courts of the United States are expressly prohibited from issuing a writ of *habeas corpus*, except in certain specified cases, and this is not within the exception."[79] An army officer complained that soldiers continued to be arrested for debt in Connecticut, too. "No regard is paid, here," he said, "to the laws or authority of the United States."[80]

Congress also adopted measures to improve the efficiency of the army. The number of staff officers was increased, and some of these were assigned to armies in the field. In addition, to keep better track of supplies, Congress created a superintendent general of military stores and ordered all supply officers to make quarterly reports.[81] Finally, the secretary of war was ordered to draw up a new code of regulations defining the respective duties of the different departments in the army. Armstrong responded to this charge with unaccustomed alacrity. The result was "Rules and Regulations of the Army of the United States," published on May 1, 1813. This manual was so well conceived and so clearly drawn that it became the bible for army operations for years to come.[82]

Although the administration got most of the army legislation it wanted, Congress denied two requests. The War Department sought authority to enlist minors eighteen years or older without the consent of parent, master, or guardian, but Federalists denounced the proposal, claiming that it would violate parental right and contract law and undermine the apprentice system.[83] If the war were as popular as Republicans claimed, said Laban Wheaton of Massachusetts, it would not be necessary "to call to their aid . . . boys without discretion."[84] The Senate was sympathetic to these arguments and killed the proposal.[85] The administration also lobbied for a bill to arm and classify the militia—a measure long advocated by southerners. In the past, schemes of this sort had been defeated by a bi-partisan coalition of northerners in the House. This time the House approved the plan, but it died in the Senate.[86]

Congress also endorsed naval expansion. "Our brilliant naval victories," said an army officer, "have contributed to place that description
of force in a proper point of View."[87] In the flush of excitement
generated by the American triumphs, even President Madison had
come out for naval expansion.[88] The remaining opposition in Congress
was deflated by two grand naval balls, one of which was held on board
the U.S.S. *Constellation* and attended by the president and his cabinet.[89]
Congress subsequently authorized the construction of four ships-of-
the-line (rated at 74 guns), six heavy frigates (rated at 44 guns), six
sloops, and an unspecified number of vessels for service on the northern lakes.[90] This legislation—a fundamental reversal in Republican
policy—committed the nation to a large-scale, long-term construction
program.

As usual, Federalists were virtually unanimous in support of naval
expansion. In fact, so enthusiastic were they that James Milnor of
Pennsylvania suggested that Congress authorize a special naval loan
so that opponents of the war could contribute to maritime defense.
Republicans, however, voted down this proposal, claiming that the
war must be prosecuted as a whole.[91] The various interests in the
country, said Langdon Cheves, "should be all freighted in the same
bark . . . and they should all float or go down together."[92]

Besides endorsing naval expansion, Congress also sought to foster
privateering. Merchants from New York and Baltimore had appealed
to the government to reduce the duties on prize goods, which (counting all the fees) usually amounted to 30 or 40 percent of their value.[93]
Gallatin was opposed to any reduction, claiming that it would cost
the government money without stimulating privateering.[94] Congress
accepted Gallatin's logic and sought instead to promote privateering
by expediting the sale of prize goods and limiting some of the fees. A
pension fund was also established for privateersmen wounded in action. Moreover, to promote the destruction of armed enemy ships
by any means—privateers, submarines, mines, or the like—Congress
authorized the payment of a bounty equal to half the value of each
vessel destroyed.[95]

❖ ❖ ❖ ❖ ❖ ❖

Republicans were able to forge a consensus on army and navy legislation, but tax and trade issues continued to divide them. The most
pressing trade problem concerned the flood of imports that had arrived illegally from the British Empire after the declaration of war.
This problem grew out of the repeal of the Orders in Council in
June of 1812. To American merchants in England, the British action

William Jones, by Gilbert Stuart. Courtesy of the Naval Historical Center, United States Department of the Navy

appeared to pave the way for the restoration of normal trade relations because the administration had earlier promised to lift non-importation if the Orders were rescinded. Seeking guidance, a group of merchants had approached Jonathan Russell, the American chargé d'affaires in London. Russell, who was himself a merchant, "thought it his duty to countenance the idea that shipments made after the revocation of the orders, would be admitted into the United States."[96]

Accordingly, those merchants who already held British-made goods began to ship them to America, while those who held other forms of capital began to convert their funds into goods. When news of the declaration of war reached England at the end of July, the merchants again asked for Russell's advice, and again he advised them to send their property home.[97] The British government, hoping the repeal of the Orders would put an end to the war, allowed these shipments under special license.[98] American merchants in Britain's colonies responded to the news of war by shipping their property home, too.[99]

All of these shipments were made in violation of the non-importation law and thus every ship and cargo was subject to seizure. As word of the shipments spread, merchants in some American ports began to fit out privateers in the hope of reaping an easy harvest.[100] The government, however, ordered American warships and privateers not to interfere with the shipments.[101] Instead, the merchandise was seized by customs officials when it arrived in port. By the end of the year, the government had impounded merchandise whose prime value was $18,000,000 but whose actual value in the American market was close to $30,000,000.[102]

The administration sought to keep the goods under government seal, but federal judges working closely with sympathetic customs officials in Baltimore, New York, and New England released some of the merchandise on bond. Gallatin was dismayed by this but decided that (in fairness to merchants elsewhere) the rest of the goods should be released as well. As a result, the government was left holding $18,000,000 in penal bonds.[103]

Normally, the administration might have prosecuted for the full value of the bonds, but under the circumstances the merchants seemed entitled to more sympathetic treatment. After considering various alternatives, the administration decided to cancel half the value of the bonds and to prosecute for the balance. The secretary of the treasury had authority to pursue this course under a 1797 law, but because of the scope of the problem, the administration decided to seek congressional approval first.[104]

The merchants, however, launched a massive campaign to persuade Congress to cancel the penalties altogether. Claiming that their profits had been modest—only 5 or 10 percent above normal—the merchants argued that they could not afford to pay even half the value of the bonds.[105] Many congressmen, Federalists and Republicans alike, were sympathetic to their pleas. There was considerable sentiment among commercial Republicans for appeasing the merchants in the hope of winning their support for the war. As William M. Richardson of Massachusetts put it: "The merchants are a powerful class of the community, and ought at this crisis to be conciliated."[106] There was also much resistance to bilking the merchants to finance the war. Privately, William Branch Giles called Gallatin's plan a "miserable impracticable attempt to plunder merchants," and Langdon Cheves said that he "would rather see the objects of the war fail . . . than see the long arm of the Treasury indirectly thrust into the pocket of the citizen through the medium of a penal law."[107]

Most Republicans, however, were skeptical of the merchants' claims. Rumors circulated of enormous profits, and some people thought the merchants could afford to pay the bonds and still make a profit. "In many cases," Jonathan Roberts of Pennsylvania claimed, "the profits were immense, three hundred per cent advance, from the hungry demand of an exhausted Market."[108] To most Republicans, the merchants' bonds offered an irresistible alternative to internal taxes. Richard M. Johnson best summarized this view: "I am unwilling to fix upon [the American people] internal taxation until it become[s] indispensable, nor to permit [the merchants] to monopolize advantages without an equivalent."[109] After much soul-searching, Congress finally sided with the merchants, though the decision in the House was close. The result was the passage of a trio of bills that remitted all fines and forfeitures on the goods in question.[110]

The defeat of Gallatin's plan for dealing with the illegal imports deprived the government of $9,000,000 in revenue and brought the whole non-importation system into question. There were some Republicans—including Gallatin himself—who wanted to modify the system in order to raise revenue. Accordingly, Cheves reintroduced his bill from the last session to permit the importation of most British goods. To make the bill more palatable to restrictionists, Cheves included provisions that prohibited judges from releasing impounded goods on bond and provided for closer inspection of ships importing certain products traditionally purchased from Britain's colonies.[111]

Cheves pleaded for the passage of this bill, claiming that the disadvantages of non-importation far outweighed the advantages. "It puts out one eye of your enemy," he said, "but it puts out both your own. It exhausts the purse, it exhausts the spirit, and paralyzes the sword of the nation."[112] Most Republicans, however, were as yet unwilling to give up on economic coercion. Many agreed with a memorial from Baltimore that non-importation was "amongst the most effectual means, which can be used to procure for our Country the blessings of a speedy and honorable peace."[113] Although Federalists did not accept this logic, they too opposed Cheves's bill because they saw it merely as a device "to put further off the dooms-day of direct taxation."[114] Federalists joined with Republican restrictionists to strike out the main clause in the bill. Although the House passed the remnant, it died in the Senate. Thus, the non-importation system remained intact.[115]

Republicans were divided over controlling not only imports but also exports. The enemy trade act adopted shortly after the declaration of war should have prevented most trade with the British, but American citizens continued to supply British subjects in Canada and the West Indies, British fleets in American waters, and British armies in the Spanish peninsula. Most of this trade was conducted under British licenses, some 500 of which were issued by British military and civilian authorities in the first two and a half months of the war. Known as "Sidmouths" or "Prince Regents" (after the authority that issued them), these licenses were usually valid for three to six months. They were extremely valuable, not only for protecting the overseas trade but also as a cover for the coasting trade. The licenses were frequently counterfeited and were openly hawked in American cities, sometimes commanding as much as $5,000.[116]

The British government was particularly anxious to facilitate trade to the peninsula because British armies there were dependent on American provisions. The export of American flour to this region had mushroomed from 105,000 barrels in 1809 to 939,000 barrels in 1812.[117] Since this trade was vital to American agriculture, the government was careful not to obstruct it. The enemy trade act did not prohibit the use of British licenses to trade with non-British ports, and the attorney general's office and the Treasury Department both ruled that American trade with British-occupied Spain and Portugal did not violate the law.[118]

President Madison was never very fond of the license trade, but he tolerated it until early 1813, when he learned of a British order directing officials in the West Indies to favor New England with the licenses.[119] Incensed by this policy, Madison sent a special message to Congress accusing the British of adopting "a system equally distinguished by the deformity of its features, and the depravity of its

117

character." The British policy, the president said, was an "insulting attempt on the virtue, the honor, the patriotism, and the fidelity of our brethren of the Eastern States." To spare New England from temptation, Madison asked Congress to outlaw the use of all foreign licenses. He also asked for a ban on all exports in foreign bottoms because he was convinced that most neutral vessels were British ships in disguise.[120]

Both presidential recommendations ran into stiff opposition in the Senate. A bill to prohibit the use of foreign licenses passed the House but was postponed indefinitely by the Senate.[121] The opposition to non-exportation was even greater. Cheves called non-exportation "a system of self-torture" that would throw the nation "upon the rack of excruciating torment."[122] The House had already rejected two proposals to restrict exports when the president made his recommendation.[123] Though a bill was duly introduced to restrict the export of provisions in foreign bottoms, the prohibition was to remain in effect for only four months. Federalists succeeded in making the bill less palatable—and also more fair—by broadening the prohibition to include all exports. The House passed the bill in this form, but the Senate killed it just as it had killed the ban on foreign licenses.[124]

Congress thwarted the administration not only on trade measures but on tax policy as well. Even though the $11,000,000 loan of 1812 had never been filled, Gallatin was able to balance his books at the end of the year by borrowing short-term money and taking advantage of the $5,000,000 tax windfall generated by the British imports.[125] Balancing the budget in 1813, however, was likely to be more difficult. In January Gallatin estimated that expenses for the coming year would be $36,000,000 but that revenue would be only $17,000,000. This would necessitate raising $19,000,000 with loans and treasury notes, a sum that Gallatin considered prohibitive.[126] "I think a loan to that amount to be altogether unattainable," he told the president.[127] Hence the imposition of new taxes was more essential than ever.

Republicans had no objection to authorizing a $16,000,000 loan and a $5,000,000 issue of treasury notes, but they were still reluctant to move on the tax issue.[128] A proposal to triple the foreign tonnage duties—from $2 to $6 a ton—failed because it was attached to the bill suspending non-importation.[129] The House refused even to consider internal taxes until mid-February, three and a half months into the session. By then most Republicans professed to believe that it was too late to take any action and that the tax windfall from the British imports rendered immediate action unnecessary anyway.[130] Even a proposal to hold a special session in May to deal with the tax issue was initially defeated and was salvaged only by intense lobbying outside of Congress.[131] Thus when the Twelfth Congress adjourned on March 3, 1813, the imposition of internal taxes still lay in the future. The failure to provide "a system of finance . . . adapted to a state of war," admonished a Republican paper, was "wholly inexcusable."[132]

Several days after the adjournment of Congress, the Russian minister in Washington transmitted a formal proposal from his government to mediate an end to the war.[133] The president accepted this proposal, which necessitated another cabinet change because Gallatin, who had grown weary of Armstrong's intrigues and the burdens of the Treasury Department, asked to be appointed to the peace commission. Madison complied with Gallatin's wishes, but rather than permanently lose such a valued member of his official family, he retained Gallatin as nominal head of the Treasury Department, assigning his duties temporarily to Secretary of the Navy William Jones. This arrangement caused the president considerable embarrassment in the Senate, and Gallatin never in fact rejoined the cabinet.[134]

❖ ❖ ❖ ❖ ❖ ❖

The Thirteenth Congress met for its special session on May 24, 1813. Most congressmen were unaccustomed to Washington's hot and sticky summers, and there were some complaints. In June Federalist John Lovett of New York claimed that it was "hotter, in this house, than purgatory." The following month, after meeting in open session for five hours, Lovett reported that "the doors were closed and we were boiled and roasted three hours longer; almost to suffocation."[135] Lovett also complained that it was difficult to sleep because of "the yells and popping [shooting] of our undisciplined Patrols."[136] Doubtless these distractions contributed to the unruliness of the session.

Henry Clay was again elected speaker, and again he packed the key committees with strong war men.[137] But the Republican party was in a weaker position than it had been in the last Congress. As a result of the elections of 1812, the Federalists had increased their strength in both houses. "[W]e have . . . a majority of decided friends of the Administration," said one Republican, "but the opposition have gained considerably in talents."[138] With the Republican majority reduced, this Congress threatened to be more factious than the Twelfth Congress had been.

Nor was the president able to provide effective leadership. At the beginning of the session, a Republican reported that Madison was in "good health & spirits & temper."[139] Yet three weeks later the president was struck down by a "bilious fever"—an intestinal ailment, perhaps

119

dysentery—which kept him bedridden for five weeks and carried him to the very doors of death.[140] "[H]is complaint," said a Republican congressman, "justly excites apprehensions as to the issue."[141] With the president ill and the cabinet divided, it was difficult for the administration to give direction to Congress. "The influence of the president is much less than I supposed," conceded a first-term Federalist senator. "There seems to be little plan or concert in the management of public affairs." "Party sperit," added John C. Calhoun, "is more violent than I ever knew."[142]

President Madison sent his opening address to Congress on May 25. He expressed hope for the Russian mediation proposal, mentioned military and naval developments, and again blasted the British for employing Indian auxiliaries. He also urged Congress to put the nation on a sound financial footing. "This can be best done," he said, "by a well digested system of internal revenue."[143]

Before Congress could tackle the tax issue, it became embroiled with the president over two of his diplomatic appointments. Shortly after the session began, Madison nominated Jonathan Russell, former chargé d'affaires in Paris and London, to serve as United States minister to Sweden. Some senators suspected Russell of mismanaging his earlier diplomatic assignments, and many questioned whether a full-fledged minister was needed in Sweden. When the president refused to confer with a Senate committee to discuss the matter, the Senate rejected the appointment by a vote of 22–14.[144] Russell's rejection, said a Federalist, "is considered here, as being the most important point which has been carried against the administration for ten years."[145]

Shortly thereafter, the president received another jolt when he asked the Senate to confirm John Quincy Adams, James A. Bayard, and Albert Gallatin for the Russian peace commission. Many senators resented the president's precipitous decision to dispatch the envoys to Russia without waiting for Senate confirmation. Many also doubted whether the secretary of the navy could handle his own duties as well as those of the Treasury Department.[146] Although Adams and Bayard were confirmed by large majorities, there was considerable opposition to Gallatin.[147]

Resentment against Gallatin had been mounting ever since he had urged internal taxation on the eve of war, and many Republicans now believed that "The Rat—in the Treasury" (as the Philadelphia *Aurora* called him) was deserting the ship of state at a critical time.[148] "It is freely imputed to him," said a Republican senator, "that he fled to avoid the Odium of the System of taxation . . . which he himself asserted necessary."[149] Gallatin's enemies hoped to take advantage of this resentment to force him from the cabinet. "The scuffle," said one observer, "is to get Gallatin out of the treasury."[150]

The Senate adopted a resolution declaring that the powers of the secretary of the treasury and those of a diplomatic envoy "are so incompatible, that they ought not to be . . . united, in the same person."[151] When the president refused to budge, the Senate rejected Gallatin's appointment by a vote of 18 to 17.[152] Gallatin had been a presidential confidant and cabinet minister for more than twelve years, and according to one Federalist, his defeat (coming on the heels of Russell's defeat) was "the rudest shock the president has ever experienced. It was wholly unexpected."[153]

It was not only the Senate that feuded with the president. There was trouble in the House, too. On June 10, Daniel Webster, a first-term Federalist congressman who was at the beginning of a long and distinguished career, introduced a series of resolutions to secure information on the repeal of the Continental Decrees.[154] At issue was the authenticity of the St. Cloud Decree, a mysterious French document dated April 28, 1811, that purportedly repealed the Continental Decrees. The document was not made public until 1812, and everyone knew that it had been backdated by French officials to make it look like the Continental Decrees had been repealed the year before. Federalists were particularly incensed by France's deception, believing that this kind of trickery had led to the War of 1812. "I declare confidently and boldly," said congressman Harmanus Bleecker, "*that Napoleon has inveigled us into the war. . . .* But for his arts, intrigues, and duplicity, the United States would not now [be] at war with Great Britain."[155] Webster's resolutions were designed to force the administration to acknowledge French perfidy and to bring into question the repeal of the French decrees and by implication the war itself.

The resolutions posed a dilemma for Republicans. Adopting them would force the administration to address an issue that it preferred to ignore, while rejecting them might raise charges of a cover-up. Felix Grundy tried to turn the debate against the Federalists by characterizing their opposition to the war as "moral" treason.[156] Although Federalists hotly denied this charge, it dogged them for the rest of the war.[157] Ultimately all the resolutions were approved by large majorities.[158] This forced the administration to admit that it knew nothing of the St. Cloud Decree until it was made public in 1812. Monroe tried to put the best face on matters by delivering a long report justifying the war, but the damage had been done.[159]

❖ ❖ ❖ ❖ ❖ ❖

The House and Senate debates over policies and appointments pushed financial matters into the background, but only temporarily. In early March the government had been so destitute of funds that Gallatin told the president: "We have hardly money enough to last till the end of the month."[160] Shortly thereafter, the $16,000,000 loan had been opened for subscriptions. Initially there was little response, but the Russian mediation proposal raised hopes for peace and the entire loan was subsequently filled. Three wealthy merchants—David Parish, Stephen Girard, and John Jacob Astor—took two-thirds of the sum offered, though the treasury had to accept a 12 percent discount, which meant that it received only $88 in cash for every $100 in bonds.[161]

The discount on the loan emphasized the need for more tax money, but Congress still seemed reluctant to act. Although most Republicans conceded the need for additional revenue, no one in Congress wanted to take the lead. "The authors of the war," said a Virginia Federalist, "approach the subject with *fear & trembling.*" "Even the most supple courtiers and minions of power," declared another observer, "fear the loss of their Seats."[162] All were anxious to spare their constituents from as much of the burden as possible, and this threatened the entire program. As John W. Eppes of Virginia put it, "every one is for taxing every body, except himself and his Constituents."[163] Federalists were particularly skeptical of Republican resolve. The internal taxes had been repeatedly postponed, and most Federalists expected them to be put off again.[164]

Much to the surprise of their enemies, the Republicans closed ranks and enacted virtually the entire tax program. The new duties were designed to yield $5,500,000.[165] They included a direct tax on land, a duty on imported salt, and excise taxes on stills, retailers, auction sales, sugar, carriages, and bank notes and other negotiable paper. All the taxes were to go into effect on the last day of 1813 or the first day of 1814, which showed that Republicans were still determined to put off "the dooms-day" of internal taxation as long as possible. The direct tax was levied for a year only, but the other duties were to remain in effect until a year after the end of the war.[166]

The most important of the new levies was the direct tax, designed to yield $3,000,000. Federalists had imposed a $2,000,000 direct tax in 1798 during the Quasi-War, but the method of assessment was so complicated and collection was so difficult that as late as 1812 close to $100,000 was still uncollected, mainly in the South.[167] Republicans hoped to avoid this problem by giving discounts of 10 or 15 percent to any state willing to pay its quota directly into the federal treasury.[168] Seven states took advantage of this provision, but the rest declined because they would have to raise their own taxes.[169] Federalist states had an additional reason for refusing to assume the direct tax. According to the Rhode Island Assembly, paying the tax "would release the General Government from the odium of collecting a tax which their own mad policy has brought upon the country."[170]

Congressional action on tax legislation came none too soon, for the administration came back to Congress in mid-July with a request to borrow an additional $7,500,000. According to the acting secretary of the treasury, Jones, this money was needed to cover an unanticipated deficit and to defray costs in early 1814 before a loan for that year could be filled.[171] Congress passed the necessary legislation, and the loan was filled at a discount of 11.75 percent, which was slightly less than the discount on the previous loan.[172] No doubt this was a reflection of the continued optimism generated by the Russian peace initiative as well as the progress Congress had made on tax legislation.

❖ ❖ ❖ ❖ ❖ ❖

Even though the administration finally got the tax program it wanted, it still had trouble with Congress over trade restrictions. The only restriction adopted in this session was a ban on the use of British licenses. Although the previous Congress had balked at such a ban, the courts had come to the administration's aid. At the end of 1812 the U.S.S. *Chesapeake* had seized the *Julia,* an American ship trading with Lisbon under a British license, and the courts had upheld the seizure. Basing his decision on the common law, Judge Joseph Story ruled that using a British license to supply British armies (even through a neutral port) constituted illegal intercourse with the enemy.[173] Congress sustained this decision in the summer of 1813 by adopting legislation that outlawed the use of all enemy licenses. Thenceforth, American ships carrying British licenses would be treated like enemy vessels.[174]

The administration was pleased with the court decision and the license law, but these measures did not halt the flow of provisions to British men-of-war in American waters. Coasting vessels continued to ply this trade, and so too did neutral vessels, many of which were actually British ships in disguise. Madison was incensed by this trade. He also resented a British decision to blockade the middle and southern states while leaving New England's ports open. Determined to put an end to the flow of goods to the enemy and to the "insidious discrimination between different ports of the United States," the president sent a confidential message to Congress on July 20 recommending an embargo on all exports.[175] The president's proposal was treated roughly in both houses of Congress. The House referred the message to its foreign relations committee, which recommended against an embargo. The House overrode this recommendation and passed the necessary legislation, but it was defeated in the Senate.[176] Madison was dismayed by the Senate's action, claiming that an embargo would have "driven the enemy out of Canada, expelled him from our waters, and forced him to retire from Spain and Portugal."[177] Nor was the president pleased when the House rejected proposals to expand the scope of the enemy trade act and prohibit the export of provisions and naval stores in foreign bottoms.[178] Neither house, it seemed, was enthusiastic about restricting trade with the enemy.

Blocked in Congress, the administration fell back on its executive powers. On July 29, the day after the embargo was defeated, the secretary of the navy issued a general order to all naval commanders, directing them to seize any vessel, whatever its flag, that was headed toward enemy ships in American waters or enemy stations in American territory. A week later, the War Department issued a similar directive to the nation's army officers.[179]

Before adjourning, Congress sought to give another boost to privateering. In a letter to a House committee, William Jones took issue with Gallatin's argument (voiced during the previous session) against reducing the duties on prize goods. Jones claimed that excessive duties had sharply curtailed privateering and that the revenue from prize goods was now "very inconsiderable."[180] Jones recommended a reduction in the duties, and Congress responded by approving a 33 percent decrease.[181] The purpose of this measure, said Federalist John Lovett, was "*to bore a hole through the Non importation Law, large enough to throw a little money . . . in the hands of the Admin.*"[182] Congress also sought to encourage privateers to hold on to their prisoners of war (instead of releasing them at sea or in a neutral port) by offering a bounty of $25 for each prisoner brought to the United States. The balance of prisoners held by the two warring nations was running against the United States, and the government was anxious to redress the balance.[183]

Congress adjourned on August 2, 1813, thus bringing to a close a difficult nine months for the president. At the beginning of this period, Madison was nearly defeated in a close election, and at the end he suffered through a lengthy illness that almost took his life. In between, he had to contend with a recalcitrant Congress that blocked two of his appointments, questioned his position on the repeal of the French decrees, rejected his proposals for trade restrictions, militia reform, and the enlistment of minors, and dangerously delayed the adoption of new taxes.

The Senate was particularly obstreperous. The "Invisibles," led by William Branch Giles, Samuel Smith, and Michael Leib, had frequently sided with the Federalists, not because they opposed the war but because they opposed the administration and its management of the war. I "never saw or heard of so much personal rancor and private intrigue," said Republican Alexander Dallas, who was visiting from Philadelphia. "[T]he malcontent junto, of self-called Republicans, was worse" than the Federalists.[184] Nor were the malcontents amenable to criticism. When the semi-official *National Intelligencer* suggested that opposition to Gallatin's diplomatic appointment was based on jealousy of "his virtues and transcendent talents," dissident senators responded angrily, calling the paper's British-born editor "a d—d little mischief making 'English-man.' "[185]

By the end of the session the Senate had become so unmanageable that the vice president, Elbridge Gerry, refused to follow custom and vacate his seat as presiding officer. This prevented the election of a president pro tem and thus insured that if death took both the ailing Madison and the elderly Gerry (who was sixty-nine), the presidency would pass on to the speaker of the house, Henry Clay, instead of to Giles or to one of the other "malcontents" in the Senate.[186]

Yet Congress did not entirely repudiate presidential leadership or ignore its responsibilities for prosecuting the war. A good deal of much-needed war legislation was adopted in these two sessions. The army was expanded and the general staff and supply system improved. The pay of the troops was increased and so too was the recruitment bounty. In addition, the navy was expanded, privateering encouraged, new loans and taxes authorized, and a ban on the use of British licenses adopted. But time was running out on the United States, and whether this legislation would translate into battlefield victories was by no means certain.

CHAPTER 6

The Campaign of 1813

WHEN THE SPRING THAW opened the campaigning season in 1813, the United States was in a stronger position than it had been in 1812. The addition of John Armstrong and William Jones to the cabinet had improved the leadership in Washington, and there were better commanders in the field, too. Although no competent officers had been found to take charge of the Niagara and St. Lawrence fronts, William Henry Harrison had succeeded William Hull in the Northwest, and Andrew Jackson was emerging as a leader in the Southwest. Moreover, Armstrong had adopted the policy of advancing talented young officers to positions of authority. Thus men like Winfield Scott and Zebulon Pike were able to play a larger role in 1813 than they had in 1812.[1]

The troops in the line were also better. Although enlistments still lagged behind need, the combination of better pay and higher bounties had attracted large numbers to the service. By the spring of 1813, there were about 30,000 men in uniform—more than twice as many as when the war began.[2] Although most of the troops were still inexperienced, the campaign of 1812 had turned some into seasoned veterans. In addition, the staff and supply legislation passed the previous winter, coupled with Armstrong's new code of regulations, promised to make army operations more efficient. To insure tighter control, Armstrong also had divided the nation into nine districts, putting a regular officer in charge of each sector with orders to report directly to the War Department.[3]

In spite of these reforms, the road to victory was beset with obstacles. The campaign of 1812 had demonstrated that conquering Canada was no easy task and that the British would not simply cave in to

American demands. Under these circumstances, the nation had little choice but to prepare for a vigorous campaign in the hope of bringing the British to terms. "I have no belief in an honorable peace," said one Republican, " 'till We give them a drubbing on Land."[4] Speed was important because the tide in Europe was running in Britain's favor. If the United States were to prevail in the New World before Britain was freed from her commitments in the Old, the nation had to act quickly and decisively.

❖ ❖ ❖ ❖ ❖ ❖

American strategy in 1813 once again focused on targets in Upper Canada. Quebec was ignored because it was so heavily fortified, and even Montreal was considered too well defended to be a primary target. Instead, the administration's plan—which was developed by Armstrong—called for attacking Kingston (Britain's principal naval base on Lake Ontario), then York (a secondary naval base), and finally Fort George and Fort Erie (which anchored the enemy's defenses on the Niagara River). Success against these targets was expected to pave the way for operations against other British strongholds and to produce a favorable effect on the spring elections in New York.[5]

The key to the campaign was control of the Great Lakes—particularly Ontario and Erie. Because of the dense wilderness and lack of good roads, the lakes offered the only efficient means of moving men and materiel along the northern frontier. Thus whoever controlled the lakes controlled the whole border region. Command of Lake Ontario was particularly important because it was close to the centers of population in the East and served as a vital link between the St. Lawrence River and British outposts in the West.[6]

At the beginning of the war, the British held undisputed sway over both lakes. On Lake Ontario they had six vessels that mounted 8 to 22 guns, while the United States had only the *Oneida* (19 guns). On Lake Erie, the British had another six ships mounting 2 to 17 guns, while the United States had only the *Adams*, an army vessel of 6 guns that fell into British hands with Hull's surrender.[7] British control of Lake Erie played a central role in Brock's success in 1812. While Hull had to supply and reinforce his troops by using undeveloped and exposed roads, Brock was able to use the lake. This enabled him to capture Detroit while still maintaining effective resistance along the Niagara frontier.

American officials were aware of the importance of controlling the lakes but had hoped that a few well-aimed strokes would destroy British power in Canada and render the whole question academic. It was only after Hull's defeat that the administration resolved to secure command of the lakes. "[W]ithout the ascendency over those waters," Madison said, "we can never have it over the savages, nor be able to secure such posts as Mackinaw." "The success of the ensuing Campaign," added the secretary of the navy, "will depend absolutely upon our superiority on all the Lakes—& every effort, & resource, must be directed to that object."[8]

Accordingly, in September of 1812, the administration ordered Captain Isaac Chauncey, a forty-year-old veteran naval officer, "to assume command of the naval force on lakes Erie and Ontario, and to use every exertion to obtain control of them this fall."[9] The nation already had a naval base at Sackets Harbor, New York, on Lake Ontario, and Chauncey now chose Presque Isle (Erie, Pennsylvania) for his base on Lake Erie. By purchasing merchant vessels and converting them into small warships, and by launching an energetic program to build larger ones, Chauncey hoped to wrest control of the lakes from the British.[10]

British officials fully appreciated the significance of Chauncey's challenge. "The enemy," reported Brock, "is making every exertion to gain a naval Superiority on both Lakes which if they accomplish I do not see how we can retain the Country."[11] The British were determined to match America's building program, but this was no easy task. Unlike the United States, Great Britain had to ship most of her naval equipment across the Atlantic and then over a Canadian water route that was both long and exposed. Moreover, for the first nine months of the war, British forces on the lakes were under the direction of the Provincial Marine, a transport service administered by the army. The men who ran this service were old and ill-equipped for energetic action. Not until March of 1813 was Sir James Yeo, a Royal Navy captain, put in charge. In spite of these liabilities, the British were able to maintain parity on Lake Ontario. On Lake Erie, however, they lacked the manpower and resources to compete effectively. As a result, they lost control of this lake, which changed the whole course of the war in the West.[12]

There was little action on Lake Ontario in the early months of the war, but by the end of 1812 the United States had enough ships to challenge the British for control. Thereafter, the balance of power tipped back and forth between the two nations depending on the progress of their building programs and the deployment of their ships. Both fleet commanders—Chauncey and Yeo—were cautious men. Hence even though they skirmished, neither attempted a decisive blow. The United States suffered the only significant loss on August

8, 1813, when two of its best schooners, the *Hamilton* (9 guns) and the *Scourge* (10 guns), went down in a storm. (These ships have recently been found—perfectly preserved in 300 feet of water.)[13]

Although the two commanders avoided any decisive fleet action, each made a determined bid to destroy the other's naval base. American strategy called for attacking Kingston first, but Dearborn and Chauncey persuaded Armstrong to substitute York (present-day Toronto). A small community of about 600 people, York was the capital of Upper Canada and a secondary base at the western end of Lake Ontario. Dearborn and Chauncey were convinced that the destruction of the British ships at York would give the United States command of Lake Ontario and thus greatly facilitate American operations elsewhere in the region.[14]

In late April, 1813, Chauncey departed from Sackets Harbor with a force of 1,700 troops under the command of General Zebulon Pike, a capable young officer who had already gained fame as an explorer. On April 27 the American force landed west of York, which was defended by 700 British and Indians under the command of General Sir Roger Sheaffe. Supported by Chauncey's fleet (which had to fight gale-force winds), Pike's army attacked the town and overwhelmed its defenders, forcing Sheaffe to retreat to the interior.[15]

The British suffered 150 killed and wounded and 290 captured in the Battle of "Little York." The Americans sustained 320 casualties, most of which were caused by the explosion of the garrison's magazine, which contained several hundred barrels of powder and a large quantity of ammunition. "The explosion was tremendous," said an American who witnessed it. "The column was raked from front to rear."[16] The blast caused so many injuries that army doctors waded "in blood, cutting off arms, legs & trepanning [boring holes in] heads." One of the surgeons claimed that he "cut & slashed for 48 hours, without food or sleep."[17] Among the casualties was General Pike. "A large Stone," said a fellow officer, "Struck him in the forehead and Stamped him for the Grave."[18]

American soldiers, already angry over the explosion, found a scalp hanging in one of the government buildings in York and used this as an excuse to loot the town. They were joined by British subjects who had come in from the countryside. "Every house they found deserted was completely sacked," said a local resident.[19] The Americans carried off enemy provisions and military stores. They also destroyed a printing press (which prevented the provincial government from publishing its laws); took a government mace (which was returned in 1934); and stole books from the subscription library (most of which were returned by Chauncey after the war). The government buildings in York were also put to the torch. The British later used this as a justification for burning Washington.[20] Despite the heavy toll, the capture of York was an important victory. The United States seized one British ship, and the British destroyed another as well as a large quantity of naval stores. This helped the United States maintain parity on Lake Ontario and hampered British operations on Lake Erie. "The ordnance, ammunition and other stores for the service on Lake Erie," said a British official, "were either destroyed or fell into the enemy's hands when York was taken."[21]

York was so indefensible that in July of 1813 Chauncey attacked again. A small detachment of soldiers and sailors landed unopposed on July 31. The Americans again carried off military and naval stores and burned the public buildings. They also destroyed a lumberyard and several boats. In their search for public property, they were assisted by disaffected British subjects. "[T]he Number of Enemies & Spies," complained a local merchant, "are beyond all conception."[22] The Americans also seized British soldiers who were confined in the jail or hospital, carrying off those who were fit and paroling those who were not.[23]

The British returned the favor in May of 1813 by attacking Sackets Harbor. At dawn on May 29 Commodore Yeo's fleet landed 750 troops under the command of Colonel Edward Baynes on the American shore. The American base was defended by 400 regulars and 500 militia under the direction of General Jacob Brown of the New York militia. The Americans made good use of the cover afforded by their defensive works and the surrounding forest. Although the militia soon fled, the regulars held fast, pouring on a steady stream of fire that forced the British to withdraw. "I do not exaggerate," said one British soldier, "when I tell you that shot, both grape and musket, flew like hail."[24] The British suffered 260 killed, wounded, and missing, while American losses were only about 100. Although the British attack was a failure, a large quantity of American supplies was burned when several men told the young American naval officer in charge that defeat was imminent. Brown was furious, calling this "as infamous a transaction as ever occurred among military men."[25]

❖ ❖ ❖ ❖ ❖ ❖

Although no decisive action occurred on Lake Ontario in 1813, the results of the campaign on Lake Erie were quite different. When Chauncey assumed command of the lakes in the fall of 1812, he dispatched Lieutenant Jesse Elliott to Lake Erie to build and buy ships suitable for naval service.[26] As Elliott was fitting out two schooners on the Niagara River near Buffalo, he learned of the arrival of two British ships at Fort Erie to the south. These were the *Detroit* (formerly the American ship *Adams*), mounting 6 guns, and the *Caledonia*, a private armed vessel mounting 2 guns. Elliott decided to try to take the ships by surprise. "[A] strong inducement," he wrote, was "that with these two Vessels added to those which I have purchaced and am fitting out I should be able to meet the remainder of the Brittish force on the upper Lakes."[27]

In the early morning hours of October 9, 1812, Elliott set sail upriver with his two schooners and about 100 men. Taking the British by surprise, the Americans overpowered them and made off with the ships. The *Caledonia* was navigated safely to the American shore, but the *Detroit* was carried off by the river current and ran aground. She was pounded by fire from both shores and finally burned by the Americans.[28] The loss of these vessels and the supplies they carried— the hold of the *Detroit* was loaded with ordnance captured at Detroit— was a serious blow to the British. "This event is particularly unfortunate," said Brock, "and may reduce us to incalculable distress."[29]

By the end of 1812 Chauncey was searching for an experienced officer to assume command of Lake Erie when he learned that Commodore Oliver H. Perry, a twenty-seven-year-old officer who was in charge of a flotilla of gunboats at Newport, was looking for more exciting service. "You are the very person," said Chauncey, "that I want for a particular service, in which you may gain reputation for Yourself and honour for your country."[30] Thenceforth, Chauncey devoted himself exclusively to Lake Ontario, giving Perry a free hand on Lake Erie.[31]

Perry arrived at Presque Isle in the spring of 1813. Although plagued by recurring bouts of "bilious fever"—probably dysentery— he worked at a frantic pace to complete four ships that were under construction there. To these he added five vessels stationed on the Niagara River—the *Caledonia* and four merchantmen purchased by Elliott. Moving these ships upriver against a steady wind was exceedingly difficult and was accomplished only with the assistance of 200 soldiers supplied by General Dearborn and only after the British had evacuated Fort Erie. Getting the ships to Presque Isle posed additional dangers because the British fleet on Lake Erie was cruising nearby. Even after all the ships were at Presque Isle, the larger ones had to be stripped of their guns and lifted by floats over a sand bar to reach deep water. This was accomplished in early August when the British fleet unaccountably withdrew.[32]

Before his fleet could be ready for action, Perry had to find a way to fill out his crews.[33] At one point he became so exasperated with this task that he asked to be transferred, even offering to return to his old station at Newport.[34] Perry blamed his problems on Chauncey, claiming that the senior officer had kept the best sailors for himself and sent only "a Motley set, blacks, Soldiers and boys."[35] General Harrison was more cooperative, furnishing Perry with 100 of his best Kentucky sharpshooters and all the seamen he could find in his army.[36] With this ragtag crew, Perry took command of the *Lawrence* (20 guns) and assigned the *Niagara* (20 guns) to Lieutenant Elliott. The fleet of nine vessels then set sail for Put-in-Bay, located in the Bass Islands at the western end of the lake. This afforded a good vantage point for watching the British fleet, now anchored near Fort Malden.[37]

The commander of the British squadron was Captain Robert H. Barclay, an experienced naval officer who had served with Lord Nelson at Trafalgar and had lost an arm in the service (which prompted Indians to call him "our father with one arm").[38] Barclay's fleet of six ships was inferior to Perry's force, especially at close range. Like Perry, Barclay faced a manpower shortage that could be remedied only by using soldiers. He was also short of naval guns and had to use guns taken from Fort Malden to equip his best ship, the *Detroit* (named after the ship lost the previous year). These guns could be fired only by shooting a pistol over the touch hole.[39]

Barclay also had to contend with a food shortage because British officials at Amherstburg had to feed a large body of Indians, said to number 14,000.[40] "The quantity of Beef, and flour consumed here is tremenduous," Barclay complained; "there are such hordes of Indians with their *Wives,* and *children."* By early September Barclay reported that "so perfectly destitute of Provisions was the Post, that there was not a days flour in Store, and the Crews of the Squadron under my Command were on Half Allowance of many things." Desperately short of supplies and goaded on by the army, Barclay decided "to risk everything" to open his lines of communication.[41] Accordingly, he sallied forth to meet Perry's fleet.

On September 10, 1813, the opposing squadrons came within sight of each other. Perry had carefully prepared for action, spreading sand on his decks to prevent his men from slipping on the water that would be splashed up or the blood that would be spilled. The Americans had the weather gage (the wind at their backs), which Barclay claimed was "a prodigious advantage" because it enabled Perry to choose his distance.[42] The British opened at long range, which was their best strategy, but Perry soon moved in to take full advantage of his fire power. "I made sail," he said, "and directed the other vessels to follow, for the purpose of closing with the enemy."[43] Elliott, however, held the *Niagara* back, preferring for reasons that have never been satisfactorily explained to rely on his long guns. This meant that Perry fought the British ships at close range with only minimal assistance from his second largest ship.

The *Lawrence* repeatedly traded broadsides with the two largest British ships, the *Detroit* (21 guns), which was Barclay's flagship, and the *Queen Charlotte* (18 guns). The fire was so intense that a British marine who had been at Trafalgar claimed that "that was a mere flea-bite in comparison with this."[44] After two hours of fighting, all three ships were seriously damaged. Perry's crew had suffered more than 80 percent casualties, forcing the commodore to call up the wounded from below to aid in the fight. Although his ship had become a floating hulk, Perry refused to surrender. Instead, he hopped into a small boat manned by several sailors and rowed to the *Niagara*, miraculously escaping injury from the rain of fire around him.

Taking command of the *Niagara*, Perry sailed back into the heart of the British fleet, this time exchanging fire with three ships on each side. When the *Detroit* and *Queen Charlotte* became fouled, they were shot to pieces by the *Niagara* and two American schooners. Three hours into the battle, the larger British ships had been destroyed, and the first and second in command on all six British vessels had been killed or wounded. Barclay himself had to be carried below. His good arm was now mangled, and he had sustained a deep thigh wound as well as several lesser wounds. Four of the British ships struck their colors. Two others tried to escape but were run down and forced to surrender, too. When the victors boarded the *Detroit*, they found a pet bear lapping up blood on the decks and two Indians (who were supposed to be musketeers in the tops) hiding in the hold.[45]

Perry's victory on Lake Erie was a tribute to his courage and coolness under fire and to the effective use of his superior resources. On the back of an old letter he wrote a note to Harrison that added even more luster to his name: "We have met the enemy and they are ours: Two Ships, two Brigs[,] one Schooner & one Sloop."[46] Perry's triumph was celebrated all over the nation. "Every demonstration of joy and admiration," reported the secretary of the navy, "was exhibited as far and as fast as the roar of cannon and splendour of illumination could travel."[47] To show its appreciation, Congress voted Perry and his men $260,000 in prize money and three months' pay. (The largest share of prize money—$12,750—actually went to Chauncey, who was nominally in command. Perry got $12,140, Elliott $7,140, and the other

Oliver H. Perry, by George Delleker. Courtesy of the National Portrait Gallery, Smithsonian Institution

officers and men sums ranging from $215 to $2,295.)[48] The British *Naval Chronicle* called Perry's victory "a miscarriage, of minor importance," but British officials knew better.[49] The battle was the most important fought on the Great Lakes during the war. It changed the balance of power in the West and enabled the United States to recover all that it had lost in 1812.

❖ ❖ ❖ ❖ ❖ ❖

By the time Perry's victory had secured Lake Erie, the campaign in the Northwest was already under way. In March of 1813, with the treasury nearly empty, Gallatin had recommended "reducing the Western expenditure to what is necessary for defensive operations, relying exclusively on the possession of the Lakes for any thing of an offensive nature."[50] Armstrong, who was himself an advocate of economy, was happy to comply. He had no confidence in Harrison and preferred to concentrate American resources further east anyway. Hence he restricted Harrison's authority to call out the militia, draw supplies, or engage in offensive operations.[51] Forced on the defensive, Harrison ordered the construction of a new fort on the Maumee Rapids in Ohio. Built under the supervision of Eleazer Wood, one of the first graduates of West Point, Fort Meigs was exceptionally strong. Ringed by picket logs and reinforced by mounds of dirt, it was protected by blockhouses and batteries that commanded all approaches.[52]

Because the British still controlled Lake Erie and had a sizable army in the Northwest, they were able to take the offensive in the spring of 1813. Prodded by Tecumseh and his followers, General Henry Procter assembled an army of 900 regulars and militia and 1,200 Indians to attack Fort Meigs, which was defended by only 550 men under Harrison. Procter hoped to bring the defenders to their knees by using his artillery and mounting a siege. The artillery bombardment began on May 1, but most of the cannon balls fell harmlessly on the dirt mounds. "The Enemy," Procter reported, "had during our Approach so completely entrenched, and covered himself as to render unavailing every Effort of our Artillery."[53]

On May 5 a 1,200-man relief force under the command of General Green Clay arrived from Kentucky. The Kentuckians drove some of the British units from their positions, but in their disorganized pursuit of the enemy, almost half of the Americans were killed, wounded, or captured. Harrison complained that the "excessive ardour" shown by the Kentuckians was "scarcely less fatal than cowardice."[54] Over Tecumseh's protests, the Indians massacred some of the prisoners. The Shawnee chief was appalled at Procter's inability to halt the slaughter. "Begone!" he reportedly exclaimed, "you are unfit to command; go and put on petticoats."[55]

By this time, most of the Indians, perceiving that the siege was a failure, deserted with whatever plunder they could find. At the same time, the Canadian militia informed Procter that they had to return home to plant their crops. Hence on May 9 Procter lifted the siege and marched his troops back to Canada. The United States had suffered 320 killed and wounded and 600 captured. British losses (excluding Indians) were only about 100. Still, the British had been unable to capture the fort, largely because it was so well built.[56]

In late July Procter invaded Ohio again, this time with a force of 5,000 regulars, militia, and Indians. Following a plan developed by Tecumseh, the British hoped to lure the defenders out of Fort Meigs by staging a sham battle nearby. When this plan failed, Procter detached part of his force for an attack on Fort Stephenson on the Sandusky River. This small post was defended by 160 men under twenty-one-year-old Major George Croghan. Convinced that the fort was indefensible, Harrison ordered Croghan to abandon it. But Croghan refused. "We have determined to maintain this place," he wrote Harrison, "and by heavens we can."[57] In the face of such determination, Harrison relented.

Procter attacked Fort Stephenson on August 2 with some 400 troops and a large body of Indians. When the British reached a ditch at the edge of the fort, they were cut down by Kentucky sharpshooters and a concealed cannon. Calling this "the severest Fire I ever saw," Procter gave up the attack and ordered his troops back to Canada. He blamed the defeat on the Indians, who had clamored for action and then disappeared when the fighting began. "A more than adequate Sacrifice having been made to Indian Opinion," he said, "I drew off the brave Assailants."[58]

The attack on Fort Stephenson was the last British offensive in the Northwest, for the following month Perry's victory deprived them of control of Lake Erie. Unable to secure supplies by water, Procter decided to withdraw via the Thames River to the interior. "The Loss of the Fleet is a most calamitous Circumstance," he wrote. "I do not see the least Chance of occupying to advantage my present extensive Position."[59] Tecumseh bitterly opposed the retreat and publicly compared Procter to "a fat animal, that carries its tail upon its back, but when affrighted . . . drops it between his legs and runs off."[60] But the only concession that he could win from the British general was a promise to make a stand somewhere on the Thames.

While Perry repaired his fleet so that it could be used to transport men and supplies, Harrison raised additional troops. Already he had persuaded Governor Isaac Shelby of Kentucky to take the field in person. Known as "*old King's mountain*" because of a battle he had fought in during the Revolutionary War, the sixty-three-year-old Shelby delivered a stirring plea urging Kentuckians to turn out for service. "I will lead you to the field of battle," the governor's widely circulated handbill proclaimed, "and share with you the dangers and honors of the campaign."[61] More than 3,000 Kentuckians—many of whom were "but lads and quite careless"—responded to the call.[62] This raised Harrison's total strength to about 5,500 men. Although a large number of Ohioans responded to a similar call from their governor, these men had to be turned away—much to their chagrin—because of a lack of supplies to sustain them.[63]

Harrison's army rendezvoused at the western end of Lake Erie in late September of 1813. Most of the Kentucky troops had brought their horses, which were left in a large corral constructed for that purpose. Only 1,200 highly trained volunteers under the command of Congressman Richard M. Johnson were permitted to take their mounts into battle. The Americans occupied Detroit and Malden, which the British had abandoned in their flight to the interior. Although 150 Pennsylvania militia refused to cross the border, the Kentucky militia had no such qualms. Thus most of Harrison's army crossed into Canada, and the pursuit of Procter began in earnest.

Harrison did not expect to catch up with the British army, but Procter moved at a leisurely pace and failed to destroy all the bridges behind him. The Americans soon came across baggage and supplies discarded by the British. They also captured, on the Thames, two gunboats carrying Procter's spare ammunition. With the Americans closing in, Procter decided to make a stand near Moraviantown, about 50 miles east of Detroit. Procter's force consisted of over 800 regulars (most of whom had been on short rations for two days) and 500 Indians. The men were arrayed in open order in two thin lines extending from the river to a large swamp.

Harrison approached the enemy on October 5 with 3,000 men, including Johnson's regiment. Finding the British lines thin, Johnson asked for permission to make a frontal assault with his mounted troops. Although a cavalry charge like this was extremely unorthodox, Harrison agreed to the plan. "The American backwoodsmen ride better in the woods than any other people," he said. "I was persuaded too that the enemy would be quite unprepared for the shock and that they could not resist it."[64]

Shouting "Remember the Raisin!"—the rallying cry commemorat-

William Henry Harrison, by Rembrant Peale. Courtesy of the
National Portrait Gallery, Smithsonian Institution

ing the massacre in January, 1813—Johnson's troops galloped toward the enemy. The right wing easily burst through the British line and then dismounted and caught the British in a crossfire, forcing them to surrender. "It is really a novel thing," said an American officer, "that raw militia stuck upon horses, with muskets in their hands instead of sabres, should be able to pierce British lines with such complete effect." The Indians continued their resistance longer, but when word spread that Tecumseh had been killed, most of them fled. Johnson (who suffered several disabling wounds in the engagement) was credited with killing Tecumseh, which helped catapult him into the vice presidency in 1836. The Americans took clothing, hair, and even patches of skin from Tecumseh's body for souvenirs. "I [helped] kill Tecumseh and *[helped] skin him*," a veteran of the campaign recalled a half century later, "and brot Two pieces of his yellow hide home with me to my Mother & Sweet Harts."[65]

The Battle of the Thames was a great victory for the United States. Although the casualties on both sides were light, 600 British soldiers were captured. The Americans also captured a large quantity of war materiel, including a cannon that had been taken at Saratoga in 1777 and then lost by Hull in 1812. Procter had panicked badly during the retreat. Although he tried to blame the disaster on his subordinates (as was his custom), a military court convicted him of misconduct and sentenced him to be reprimanded publicly and suspended from duty for six months. The Prince Regent rescinded the suspension, but the reprimand was read before every regiment in the British army.[66]

Harrison and Perry worked up a plan to retake Mackinac, but bad weather forced them to abandon the scheme.[67] Retaking this outpost was not essential anyway because the Battle of the Thames had undermined British power in the Northwest and shattered Tecumseh's Indian confederacy. Harrison later resigned in disgust over Armstrong's open enmity, claiming that "the most malicious insinuations had been made against me at Washington."[68] Nevertheless, he and Perry had turned the tide in the West and had secured the whole region to the United States. As proof of the new state of affairs, Harrison joined with Lewis Cass on July 22, 1814, in signing a treaty with some of the northwestern tribes that bound them to wage war against Britain.[69]

❖ ❖ ❖ ❖ ❖ ❖

The campaign along the Niagara front also had a promising start, but in the end reverses and mismanagement cost the United States all that it had gained. The principal target of American troops here was Fort George, located on the Canadian side where the Niagara River flows into Lake Ontario. The British fort was garrisoned by 1,100 regulars and militia under the command of General John Vincent. There were an additional 750 British troops stationed at other posts along the Niagara frontier, and several hundred militia from the surrounding area were available for duty as well.[70]

In May of 1813 the United States assembled a force of 4,500 troops across from Fort George. On May 24 American artillery units opened fire on Newark, a small town near Fort George that housed some of the British soldiers. Three days later Chauncey laid down an artillery barrage from the lake to cover a landing of American troops west of the fort. The landing—a joint operation directed by Winfield Scott and Commodore Perry—put American troops in a position to attack the fort from the rear. The British came out to meet the invaders but were outgunned and outnumbered. Forced to give ground, they abandoned the fort and fled south. Scott pursued the British but was ordered to return to Fort George by General Morgan Lewis, who was temporarily in command. The British lost 350 killed, wounded, and captured in the Battle of Fort George, compared to American losses of only 140.[71]

Since the loss of this fort exposed British positions all along the Niagara frontier, Vincent ordered the evacuation of the other British garrisons—Fort Chippewa, Queenston, and Fort Erie—each of which was subsequently occupied by American troops. Although the United States now controlled the entire frontier, the failure to follow up on the initial victory proved costly, for Vincent was able to regroup his forces at Burlington Heights (now Hamilton) at the western end of Lake Ontario. Recognizing his mistake, Lewis ordered two brigades— about 2,600 men—to pursue the British. These troops were under the command of two political generals, William Winder and John Chandler, neither of whom had much military experience. About half of the American troops made camp at Stoney Creek, seven miles from the British camp.[72]

In the predawn hours of June 5 a British force of 700 men under the command of Colonel John Harvey silently approached the American camp. Having learned the countersign from a paroled prisoner, the British captured or bayoneted the American sentries and then launched their attack. The surprise was complete. According to one British soldier, "our men set up a tremendous shout, which continued along the whole line, and was the cause of throwing the enemy into the greatest disorder and confusion imaginable."[73] The Americans were forced to retreat, and in the confusion both Winder and Chandler blundered into British units and were captured. Although the United

States suffered fewer losses—about 150 men compared to 200 for the British—the Americans had left the British in control of the field. The retreat from Stoney Creek, coupled with the appearance of Yeo's fleet, rendered American positions on Canadian soil less secure, and General Dearborn, who was now in command, ordered all the garrisons on the Canadian side of the river evacuated except Fort George.[74]

Hoping to restore American prestige and put an end to the growing number of British depredations, Dearborn ordered Lieutenant Colonel Charles Boerstler to take 500 men to attack a small British outpost about 16 miles from Fort George. A Canadian woman, Laura Secord, became a national hero when she walked 20 miles through unfamiliar territory to warn the British and their Indian allies. On June 24 at Beaver Dams, a party of Indians under a Frenchman, Captain Dominique Ducharme, ambushed Boerstler's force. After the fighting began, British reinforcements under the command of Lieutenant James Fitzgibbon arrived. Although the British and Indians were outnumbered, Fitzgibbon ran a good bluff by exaggerating the size of his force and raising the specter of an Indian massacre. Frightened by this prospect, Boerstler surrendered.[75] When news of this defeat reached Washington, Republican congressmen were so furious that they forced the administration to remove Dearborn from command. "The news of Boe[r]stler's capture threw us into an indignation," said Charles J. Ingersoll. "We have deposed Gen. Dearborn, who is to be removed to Albany, where he may eat sturgeon and recruit."[76]

The British now took the offensive and brought the war home to Americans all along the Niagara frontier. On July 5 a small party of Canadian militia crossed the river, attacked a blockhouse called Fort Schlosser, and made off with the supplies there. A week later another British force burned the military post at Black Rock and carried off additional supplies. These raids were designed to force the American troops to evacuate Fort George or to overextend themselves.[77]

Fort George, which was now under the direction of General George McClure of the New York militia, had become increasingly vulnerable. Most of the regulars had been transferred east, leaving only 250 men to defend the entire frontier. In addition, lack of pay had turned McClure's best militia into "a disaffected and ungovernable multitude," and attempts to recruit additional militia had failed.[78] Everyone knew that the pay was in arrears and that (despite the onset of winter) the only housing available was tents. Few militia were willing to serve in Canada anyway. Hence, on December 10, 1813, McClure decided to abandon Fort George, though before doing so he burned Newark to deny British troops shelter there. The inhabitants were given only twelve hours' notice in zero-degree weather to vacate their homes.[79] "[E]very building in Newark is reduced to ashes," McClure reported; "the Enemy is much exasperated and will make a descent on this frontier if possible."[80]

McClure's prediction proved correct. General Sir Gordon Drummond, who had assumed command of the British forces in this theater of operations, was furious over the callous treatment of Newark's civilians and authorized retaliation. On December 18 a British force of 550 men surprised the American sentries at Fort Niagara (across the river from Fort George), extracted the password, and then secured access to the fort. The American commander was reportedly drunk at his home three miles away, and those in the fort had taken no precautions. "Our men," said General McClure, "were nearly all asleep in their tents, the Enemy rushed in and commenced a most horrid slaughter."[81] The British inflicted eighty casualties (mostly by bayonet) and took 350 prisoners, while suffering fewer than a dozen casualties themselves. The British also acquired a huge quantity of war materiel. According to Governor Daniel Tompkins, "The quantity of cannon, muskets, shot, shells, powder, fixed ammunition, clothing & other supplies in Fort Niagara was immense. The acquisition of them will be of the greatest importance to the British, & an irreparable loss to us."[82] The British retained control of Fort Niagara—an important beachhead on American territory—until the end of the war.

Another British force under General Phineas Riall crossed into American territory on December 18 and destroyed Lewiston as well as two smaller towns nearby.[83] The Indians who accompanied Riall got drunk and left a ghastly scene at Lewiston. According to an American who later visited the town: "The sight we here witnessed was shocking beyond description. Our neighbors were seen lying dead in the fields and roads, some horribly cut and mangled with tomahawks, others eaten by the hogs."[84]

American officials tried to rally the militia to end these depredations but without much success. Most of the men in the region had already stood several drafts and were reluctant to serve again. According to McClure, even those who responded to the call were more interested "in taking care of their families and property by carrying them into the interior, than helping us to fight."[85] Few were willing to serve under McClure anyway. He was blamed for the recent reverses and was so universally detested that he had to withdraw from the front. "The gross insults which I have received from many at Buffalo," he said, "will apologise for my absence."[86]

General Amos Hall, who succeeded McClure in command, was able to raise 2,000 militia to meet a British force of 1,400 regulars and Indians near Black Rock in late December, but the Americans were routed. On December 30 the British put both Black Rock and Buffalo to the torch.[87] Lewis Cass, who saw Buffalo a week later, called it "a scene of distress and destruction such as I have never before witnessed."[88] Thus by the end of the year, the Niagara Valley was in flames, and the American position along the entire front had collapsed. "The whole frontier from Lake Ontario to Lake Erie," lamented Governor Tompkins, "is depopulated & the buildings & improvements, with a few exceptions, destroyed."[89]

❖ ❖ ❖ ❖ ❖ ❖

The Niagara frontier was exposed in the second half of 1813 because most of the regulars stationed there had been shipped east for service on the St. Lawrence front. Although a major offensive in this theater was not part of the administration's original planning, from the beginning Armstrong had waffled on the objectives of the campaign. Even before the campaign had begun, he had suggested other targets to his generals. Although still committed to attacking Kingston, he asked the cabinet in July to approve Montreal as an alternative. Then in October, after the British had reinforced Kingston, he ordered his generals to attack Montreal. By this time, however, it was so late in the season that the chances for success were remote.[90]

It was not only the War Department's indecision that doomed the campaign against Montreal. The United States had suffered a major setback on Lake Champlain as well. This lake, which lies between New York and Vermont, empties into the Richelieu River, which in turn flows into the St. Lawrence River between Montreal and Quebec. Together these waterways form a natural invasion route that could be used to ferry troops and supplies in either direction. Whoever controlled these waters—particularly Lake Champlain—controlled the whole region.

The United States held the balance of power on Lake Champlain until mid-1813, when Lieutenant Thomas Macdonough, who was in charge of the American flotilla, ordered Lieutenant Sidney Smith to patrol the northern reaches of the lake with the the *Eagle* and *Growler,* each of which mounted eleven guns. On June 3 the over-eager Smith sailed into the shallow waters of Isle-aux-Noix, a small fortified British island at the northern end of the lake. When Smith tried to withdraw, he found that his ships could not maneuver because the water was too shallow. The British mounted an artillery attack from the shore, and after a three-and-a-half hour engagement both ships were disabled and forced to surrender.[91] The acquisition of these vessels, which were renamed *Chub* and *Finch*, gave the British naval superiority on Lake Champlain and deprived the United States of an important supply route. "The loss of our command of Lake Champlain at so critical a moment," said Madison, "is deeply to be regretted."[92]

If the lateness of the season and the loss of Lake Champlain undermined the chances for a successful campaign, so too did poor leadership in the field. The man who assumed command in this theater after Dearborn's removal was General James Wilkinson, a longtime Spanish spy with an appetite for booty and intrigue. Winfield Scott (who was once suspended from the army for publicly maligning Wilkinson) considered him an "unprincipled imbecile," and John Randolph claimed that the brigadier was the only man he knew "who was from the bark to the very core a villain."[93]

Wilkinson had long commanded troops in the Southwest, but his despotism in New Orleans during the Burr Conspiracy in 1807 and his known ties to Spanish officials had thoroughly alienated local Republicans. Moreover, he had so mismanaged his command in 1809 that he lost nearly half his army—over 1,000 men—to disease and desertion. By 1813 it was said that Louisiana militia in many parts of the state "*positively refused to serve under General Wilkinson*" and that the state's two senators would go into opposition unless he were removed from command.[94]

To quell this incipient rebellion, the administration ordered Wilkinson to the Canadian frontier. After a leisurely trip north, Wilkinson established himself at Sackets Harbor and assumed command over the whole eastern theater of operations. But General Wade Hampton, who headed a force at Plattsburgh, considered his superior so despicable that he refused to obey him. Armstrong tried to coordinate operations by visiting the field in person, but his efforts were futile.[95]

The plan of operations was vague, but ultimately Montreal was the target. Wilkinson was supposed to lead 7,000 men down the St. Lawrence River and approach from the west, while Hampton was to approach with 4,500 men from the south. The campaign did not get under way until October, and neither commanding officer showed much confidence in the plan. Moreover, when Armstrong left the front in early November, any prospect of cooperation between the two generals vanished.[96]

Hampton remained in upper New York in September and October, waiting for specific orders from the War Department. Finally, he decided to invade Canada by following the Chateaugay River, which empties into the St. Lawrence not far from Montreal. Most of Hampton's militia (about 1,000 men) refused to cross the border, and even his regulars were undependable. "The perfect *rawness* of the troops," he complained, "has been a source of much solicitude to the best informed among us."[97] To repel Hampton's invasion, Lieutenant Colonel Charles de Salaberry organized 1,400 French Canadian militia behind extremely strong defensive works.

The Battle of Chateaugay took place on October 26. Unable to get any of his troops around the Canadian position for an attack from the rear, Hampton ordered a frontal assault. But de Salaberry's troops raised such a din with shouting and bugles that the Americans fell back, convinced that they faced a huge army. "[T]his *ruse de guerre*," said a Canadian, "had the desired effect, for we afterwards learned from the prisoners that they rated our force at five to six thousand."[98] Actual casualties on either side were light, but Hampton gave up on the invasion and returned to the United States.[99] Moreover, when he saw an order signed by Armstrong for the construction of winter quarters, he concluded that the administration had no real interest in pressing the invasion. "This paper sank my hopes," he said, "and raised serious doubts of receiving that efficatious support which had been anticipated."[100]

Wilkinson proved no more eager to carry out his part of the operation. He wanted the administration to order the attack (so that he could avoid blame if it failed), and he suggested that "in case of Misfortune[,] having no retreat, the army must surrender at discretion."[101] Departing from Sackets Harbor in mid-October, he did not begin his descent down the St. Lawrence until November 5. From the beginning, he was hampered by problems: personal illness, bad weather, and harassment from an 800-man force in his rear commanded by Colonel Joseph Morrison. Wilkinson tried to combat his illness by consuming massive quantities of laudanum. He conceded that this gave him "a giddy head," and according to one officer, during the descent down the river "the general became very merry, and sung and repeated stories."[102]

When Wilkinson reached Chrysler's Farm, he determined to crush Morrison's force, but being too unwell to conduct the operation himself, he put General John P. Boyd in charge of 2,000 troops to accomplish the task. Boyd attacked on November 11 but could not dislodge the British regulars from their positions. Despite their inferior numbers, the British drove the Americans from the field with a counterattack. British casualties in the Battle of Chrysler's Farm were about 180, while the Americans lost 340 killed and wounded and 100 captured.[103]

By this time Wilkinson realized that Hampton would not join forces with him. He used this as an excuse for calling off the campaign and going into winter quarters at French Mills just south of the St. Lawrence River. Here his troops suffered from the severe winter weather. "You can almost gather the Atmosphere in by handfulls as you do Water," said one officer. "Several Sentinels, have frozen to death on post and Many are badly frostbitten."[104] The men also suffered from bad provisions and a scarcity of hospital stores and other supplies. "Even the sick had no covering except tents," reported an army doctor. "Under these circumstances sickness and mortality were very great."[105]

Wilkinson roused himself for one more foray into enemy territory in March of 1814. Leading some 4,000 men into Lower Canada, he aimed to menace Montreal and thus force the British to transfer troops from Upper Canada to protect the city.[106] On March 30 he found himself at La Colle Mill, a stone fortification protected by thick walls and garrisoned by 180 men. Wilkinson laboriously brought up three small field pieces to assault the mill, but the cannon shot made little impression. The British were subsequently reinforced and then retired to a blockhouse on the north side of La Colle River. Since the British had several armed vessels on the river, Wilkinson gave up the attack and retreated to the United States. In the Battle of La Colle Mill, the British lost about 60 men, the Americans more than 150. Wilkinson later claimed that his ill-conceived invasion had had a tonic effect on the army. Shortly thereafter, he was removed from command, thus bringing to an end his long and checkered career as an army officer.[107]

✤ ✤ ✤ ✤ ✤ ✤

There was also fighting on the southern frontier in 1813, though here the Creek Indians fought alone, without any assistance from the British. The Creeks occupied most of present-day Alabama and were loosely allied with neighboring tribes in a large confederation. Many half-breeds living with the tribe had adopted the white man's ways, and by contemporary standards the Creeks had a comparatively advanced civilization. Though still primarily hunters, they practiced agriculture, raised livestock, owned slaves, and had an effective form of tribal government.[108]

Niles' Register claimed that the United States had treated the Creeks "with the utmost gentleness and generosity" and that the Indians had "no possible cause of complaint."[109] But the Creeks, like the Indians in the Northwest, had long been nursing grievances against Americans for encroaching upon their lands. Tecumseh had visited the tribe in 1811, hoping to persuade the Creeks to return to their traditional ways and to join his crusade against the white man. "Let the white race perish!" he told the Creeks. "Burn their dwellings—destroy their stock—slay their wives and children, that the very breed may perish."[110] Although the older chiefs withstood Tecumseh's entreaties, a young faction—known as the Red Sticks—was more receptive. The Red Sticks were emboldened by the Anglo-Indian victories in the Northwest and by promises of aid from Spanish officials in Florida.[111]

A small band of Red Sticks traveled to the Northwest to visit Tecumseh in 1812. These Indians took part in the River Raisin massacre at the beginning of 1813 and departed for home filled with hatred for Americans and with visions of rolling back white settlements all along the frontier. When the Indians reached the mouth of the Duck River south of Nashville in Tennessee, they murdered several white people living there. To keep peace with the whites, the old Creek chiefs ordered the guilty Indians hunted down and killed. This precipitated a civil war in the tribe, and most of the old chiefs had to flee to the American Indian agent for protection. With the Red Sticks in the ascendant, Indian raids in the Southwest increased.[112]

In July of 1813, a group of Red Sticks visited Pensacola to trade for European goods and to pick up arms promised by Spanish officials. On July 27, as the Indians were returning with their pack train, they were attacked eighty miles north of Pensacola by 180 Mississippi militia. In the skirmishing that followed—known as the Battle of Burnt Corn—the Americans ended up with most of the supplies, but they were driven from the field, which further emboldened the Indians. This was the opening battle in the Creek War. It transformed what had been a civil war in the Creek confederation into a larger war with the United States.[113]

The Creeks retaliated on August 30 by attacking Fort Mims, a stockade forty miles north of Mobile. The fort was occupied by 300 people, including 120 militia under the command of Major Daniel Beasley, a regular army officer. Beasley took his duties lightly and did not adequately prepare the fort for defense. Ignoring a warning from slaves who had spotted Indians earlier in the day, the Americans were caught by surprise and overwhelmed. The Indian assailants paid dearly, losing at least 100 killed and many more wounded. But they killed close to 250 of the defenders, including many women and children. "[M]y warriors," said William Weatherford, a half-breed chief, "were like famished wolves, and the first taste of blood made their appetites insatiable."[114] The only survivors were a few whites who escaped into the woods and some black slaves who were carried off by the victorious Indians.[115]

Early reports greatly exaggerated the number of people killed at

Fort Mims and "spread consternation through the Territory."[116] "Our settlement is overrun," reported one westerner, "and our country, I fear, is on the eve of being depopulated."[117] The Fort Mims massacre stirred up people in the Southwest, much as the River Raisin massacre had galvanized people in the Northwest. Expeditions against the Indians were mounted from Georgia and the Mississippi Territory. Although these campaigns took a heavy toll on the Indians, the results were inconclusive.[118]

People in Tennessee also responded to the call for action. Although the heart of the Creek country was least accessible from this state, by the fall of 1813 some 2,500 militia had gathered to undertake a punitive expedition. The troops included young Sam Houston and Davy Crockett, who reportedly kept "the camp alive with his quaint conceits and marvelous narratives."[119] Andrew Jackson, a major general in the Tennessee militia, took charge of the troops even though he was still recovering from bullet wounds suffered in a brawl with Jesse and Thomas Hart Benton. A tough Indian fighter who was already known as "Old Hickory," Jackson planned to wipe out the hostile Indians and then seize Spanish Florida. "The blood of our women & children," he told his troops, "shall not call for vengeance in vain."[120]

Marching rapidly south, Jackson built Fort Strother on the Coosa River to serve as a forward base for his operations. On November 3, his most able lieutenant, General John Coffee, attacked an Indian village at Tallushatchee. Using tactics pioneered by Hannibal 2,000 years before, Coffee formed his men into a semicircle around the village, induced the Indians to attack, and then closed the loop. Coffee sustained fewer than 50 casualties in the Battle of Tallushatchee, while the Indians suffered at least 200 killed and 84 women and children captured.[121] "[T]he enemy fought with savage fury," reported Coffee, "and met death with all its horrors, without shrinking or complaining: not one asked to be spared, but fought as long as they could stand or sit."[122]

Several days later Jackson learned that 1,100 hostile Creeks were besieging a town of friendly Indians at Talladega. Jackson marched 2,000 men to the town and on November 9 used the same tactics as Coffee to envelop the hostile Indians. This time, however, the Indians found a weak spot in the American line and managed to break through and effect their escape. The Battle of Talladega was nonetheless an American victory, for the Indians left 300 dead on the field while Jackson's losses were only about 100.[123]

At this point, Jackson had to suspend operations and return to Fort Strother because his provisions were low. Like so many generals in this war, Jackson had to contend with recurring problems with his contractors. "The difficulties and delays of The Campaign," he said, "are to be ascribed, primarily, to The negligence of The Contractors."[124] In addition, many of his troops, whose terms of service had expired, wanted to go home. On several occasions Jackson had to threaten volunteers with militia or militia with volunteers in order to keep his army intact. Twice he leveled his own gun against men threatening to leave. Were this not enough, the governor of Tennessee was beginning to lose heart, and Jackson had to persuade him to continue the campaign. It was only by sheer force of will that the Tennessee general kept his army together and the campaign alive.[125]

Ultimately, Jackson had to permit most of his troops to go home. But by early 1814 reinforcements had arrived, raising his strength to 1,000 men. Resuming the offensive, Jackson marched into the very heart of Creek country, where he fought two engagements: one at Emuckfau on January 22 and the other at Enotachopco Creek two days later. The fighting in both battles was intense, but each time the outcome was inconclusive. Jackson sustained about 100 casualties, while the Indians probably lost twice this number.[126]

After returning again to Fort Strother, Jackson stockpiled supplies and waited for fresh troops. Tales of his campaign stimulated recruiting in Tennessee, and by February of 1814 his army was 4,000 strong. Among the new arrivals were 600 regulars. Jackson hoped that these troops would give "Strength to my arm & quell mutiny," but he continued to have trouble with the militia.[127] When one young soldier, John Woods, refused to obey orders, Jackson ordered him court-martialed. The defendant was convicted and shot—the first execution of a militiaman since the Revolution. "An army cannot exist where order & Subordination are wholly disregarded," Jackson said in defense of his actions.[128] The sanguinary lesson was not lost on his men. According to Jackson's aide, "a strict obedience afterwards characterized the army."[129] In this campaign, as in others, Jackson got the most out of his men because they feared him more than they feared the enemy.

Jackson learned from friendly Indians that about 1,000 hostile Creeks had established themselves on a peninsula called Horseshoe Bend on the Tallapoosa River. The Indians had fortified the land approach and placed their canoes on the river in case they had to flee. Jackson marched to the scene with about 3,000 men and carefully laid plans for an attack. The battle began on March 27, 1814, when friendly Indians swam the river and made off with the Creek canoes. After fruitlessly pounding the enemy breastworks with cannon fire, Jackson launched a frontal assault. At the same time, troops across the river

Andrew Jackson, by Ralph Whiteside Earl. Courtesy of the National Portrait Gallery, Smithsonian Institution used the Creek canoes to attack from the rear. The Battle of Horseshoe Bend was a slaughter: most of the Creeks preferred death to surrender and those who tried to escape were shot down. Even Jackson admitted that the *"carnage* was *dreadfull."*[130] Close to 800 hostile Indians perished, while Jackson's own force sustained only 200 casualties.[131] "The fiends of the Tallapoosa," Jackson said triumphantly, "will no longer murder our Women and Children, or disturb the quiet of our borders."[132]

The half-breed chief William Weatherford later surrendered to Jackson. "My people are no more!!" he reportedly said. "Their bones are bleaching on the plains of Tallushatches, Talladega, and Emuckfau."[133] Weatherford lived out his days as an affluent and respected Alabama planter, but the full-blooded Creeks did not fare so well. "They . . . [have] forfeighted all right to the Territory we have conquered," Jackson wrote.[134] Even though many of the Creeks had sided with the United States, on August 9, 1814, Jackson forced all the tribal leaders to sign the Treaty of Fort Jackson, which stripped the Indians of more than 20,000,000 acres of land—over half of their territory. Such a massive land grab pleased Jackson's western supporters but left most government officials aghast.[135]

Jackson's victories in the Southwest, coupled with those of Perry and Harrison in the Northwest, greatly increased American security on the western frontier. The only problem with these victories was that they had occurred in regions too remote to have a decisive effect on the outcome of the war. On the more important fronts—along the Niagara and St. Lawrence rivers—the United States had made no headway in its efforts to dislodge the British. After two years of campaigning, Canada still remained in British hands, and victory seemed as remote as ever.

❖ ❖ ❖ ❖ ❖ ❖

If the war on land went better for the United States in 1813, the war at sea went worse. This was to be expected because the ocean was Britain's element. The British had been slow to exploit their naval superiority in the first six months of the war, which had led to considerable domestic criticism.[136] In response, the government in early 1813 increased its naval force in American waters to 10 ships-of-the-line, 38 frigates, and 52 smaller vessels.[137]

The government also lectured John Borlase Warren, who was put in charge of British naval forces in the North Atlantic and Caribbean, on what was expected of him in the ensuing campaign. "It is of the highest importance to the *character* and interests of the country," wrote the Admiralty, "that the naval force of the enemy should be quickly and completely disposed of." Warren was "to bring the naval war to a termination, either by the capture of the American national vessels, or by strictly blockading them in their own waters."[138]

Warren had already established a blockade from Charleston, South Carolina, to Spanish Florida in the fall of 1812.[139] With his enlarged fleet, he extended this blockade in early 1813 to the Chesapeake and Delaware bays and then to other ports and harbors in the middle and southern states. Thus by November, 1813, the entire coast south of New England was under blockade. Warren exempted New England from the blockade, both to reward her for opposing the war and to keep up the flow of provisions to Canada and the British West Indies. (By this time, British troops in the Spanish peninsula no longer needed American grain.)[140]

The British blockade had a deadly effect on the United States. Foreign trade dropped sharply and government revenue dried up. "Commerce is becoming very slack," reported a resident of Baltimore in the spring of 1813; "no arrivals from abroad, & nothing going to sea but sharp [fast] vessels."[141] By the end of the year, the sea lanes had become so dangerous that insurance for ocean-going vessels had soared to 50 percent of the ship's value.[142]

With British warships hovering nearby, the coasting trade had become perilous, too, forcing American merchants to resort to overland transportation. But there were few good roads, and even the best broke down under heavy use and the on-going assault of the elements. "The roads [in Virginia] . . . are worse than usual," Nathaniel Macon reported in March of 1813; "it takes 38 hours to travel from Fredericksburg to Alexandria the distance 50 miles." "The road is literally cut hub deep," wrote a New Jersey traveler in May; "wagons innumerable [are] passing and repassing from Trenton to New York with goods."[143]

The lack of good transportation created gluts and shortages throughout the American economy. Sugar which sold for $9 a hundredweight in August of 1813 in New Orleans commanded $21.50 in New York and $26.50 in Baltimore. Rice selling for $3 a hundredweight in Charleston or Savannah brought $9 in New York and $12 in Philadelphia. Flour, which was $4.50 a barrel in Richmond, went for $8.50 in New York and almost $12 in Boston.[144] Such was the demand for flour in New York that a traveler reported seeing 2,000 barrels en route to the city. "Every hut, blacksmith's shop, house, shed and hovel is filled with flour," he said; "10, 20, 60, 100 Barrels in a place, and piled on the sides of the road, and many loads thrown down in the mire."[145]

Because the blockade curtailed imports from abroad, a panic set in at the end of 1813 which drove up prices. "A rage for speculation," reported a Philadelphia merchant, "has seized our traders."[146] Coffee, tea, sugar, salt, cotton, molasses, and spices suddenly doubled, tripled, or even quadrupled in price. The "*mania* for *commercial speculations* and monopolies," said the New York *Columbian*, is "extensive and increasing."[147] One Republican paper called the speculation "criminal," and another urged people to boycott overpriced goods.[148] The press insisted that there were ample stocks of most commodities on hand, but not until early 1814, after the arrival of a truce ship raised hopes of peace, did the bubble burst and prices tumble.[149]

❖ ❖ ❖ ❖ ❖ ❖

The British used their naval power not only to put economic pressure on the United States but also to bring the war home to the American people, especially in the Chesapeake Bay. Warren, who had no stomach for raiding and plundering, assigned the command in these waters to Admiral Sir George Cockburn (pronounced Co-burn). Cockburn was a bold and able officer in the prime of a long and distinguished naval career.[150] Guided through the countryside by runaway slaves, he devoted the spring of 1813 to plundering the Chesapeake. His immediate aim was to destroy American warships, burn government supplies, and ruin the coasting trade. His larger purpose was to show Americans the futility of resisting British power and the perils of making war on the Mistress of the Seas.[151]

In late April Cockburn sailed into the Upper Chesapeake, attacked and burned Frenchtown, Maryland, and destroyed the ships that were docked there. The following month his forces swept aside the local militia and looted and burned three other Maryland towns: Havre de Grace, Georgetown, and Fredericktown. To drive home the purpose of the campaign, a British naval officer told people in Havre de Grace: "you shall now feel the effects of war."[152] Cockburn next marched his men to Principio, where a cannon foundry and sixty-eight cannons were destroyed. For twelve days the British moved freely on American soil without meeting effective resistance.[153] "On my way from Philadelphia to Washington," recalled a Republican congressman, "I found the whole country excited by these depredations. Cockburn's name was on every tongue, with various particulars of his incredibly coarse and blackguard misconduct."[154]

In mid-June Warren returned to the Chesapeake with reinforcements, determined to attack Norfolk, Virginia, a regional commercial center that was harboring the frigate *Constellation*. General Robert B. Taylor, who was in charge of the local defenses, prepared for the attack by assembling 700 militia and fortifying Craney Island, which commanded the approaches to Norfolk. Warren detached 2,500 men to land on the mainland west of the island and 1,500 to approach in barges. But the assault forces ran into so many natural obstacles and such heavy artillery fire that Warren ordered a retreat.[155]

The British next attacked Hampton, Virginia, with a force of 2,000 men. The 450 militia defending the town were brushed aside, and those civilians found in Hampton were subjected to all kinds of abuse.[156] According to Charles Napier, a young British officer who later gained fame in India, "every horror was committed with impunity, rape, murder, pillage: and not a man was punished!"[157] The British blamed the excesses on the Chasseurs Britannique—French prisoners of war who had enlisted in British service to escape confinement. These troops were withdrawn from combat and sent to Halifax, where they continued to terrorize civilians. "The Inhabitants of Halifax are in the greatest alarm about these fellows," said a British official.[158]

The British depredations caused a great deal of bitterness in the Chesapeake. *Niles' Register* called Warren the "spoiler in the Chesapeake" and dubbed his troops "water-*Winnebagoes*"—an allusion to the most militant Indians in the Northwest. Cockburn drew even greater fire. "[T]he wantonness of his barbarities," said *Niles*, "have gibbetted him on infamy."[159] Some Americans, however, benefited from the British presence. When they met with no resistance in an area, the British usually paid for the provisions they needed. Those willing to do business with the invaders—and there were many—profited handsomely. In addition, about 600 runaway slaves who found sanctuary with the British were given a choice of either enlisting in the service or settling in the West Indies.[160] This was a matter of grave concern to southerners. "All accounts agree," a northern congressman reported, "that [the British] are recruiting rapidly from the Plantations; . . . there begins to be loud howling on this subject."[161]

❖ ❖ ❖ ❖ ❖ ❖

There were fewer naval engagements in 1813 than in 1812 because most American warships were bottled up in port. Even those that managed to escape often returned empty-handed because British warships now sailed in squadrons and British merchantmen in convoys.

The Navy Department ordered American warships to cruise separately and to avoid battle except under the most favorable circumstances. Their mission was "to destroy the commerce of the enemy, from the cape of good Hope [off the tip of South Africa], to cape clear [off the Irish coast]."[162] There were only four naval duels in this campaign, and three of these ended in defeat for the United States.

In May of 1813 James Lawrence, who had earlier commanded the U.S.S. *Hornet* in its victory over the *Peacock,* was given command of the *Chesapeake* (50 guns) when the captain assigned to this vessel asked to be relieved because an old war wound had flared up.[163] The *Chesapeake* was fitted out in Boston, but Lawrence had trouble finding experienced seamen for his crew. Many of the ship's veterans refused to reenlist because of a dispute over prize money, forcing Lawrence to accept raw recruits.[164]

Hovering off the coast of Boston were two British frigates, the *Shannon* (52 guns), commanded by Captain Philip Broke, and the *Tenedos* (38 guns). Broke had been cruising in the *Shannon* since 1806, and unlike most British naval commanders, he drilled his crew in gunnery. According to a British officer who was assigned to the American station, "The *Shannon's* men were better trained, and understood gunnery better, than any men I ever saw."[165] As the *Chesapeake* was preparing to sail, Broke sent the *Tenedos* away and dispatched a challenge to Lawrence for a meeting "Ship to Ship, to try the fortunes of our respective Flags."[166] Lawrence sailed before this challenge arrived, but he needed no invitation.

On June 1 the *Chesapeake* emerged from port flying a banner that read "Free Trade and Sailor's Rights." Lawrence made for the *Shannon,* but for reasons that are unclear, he passed up a chance to cut across the British ship's stern and rake her. Instead, the two ships lined up parallel to each other and exchanged broadsides at close range. Superior gunnery carried the day for the *Shannon.* The *Chesapeake* lost control, was subjected to a murderous raking fire, and then boarded. Lawrence was mortally wounded but before dying uttered those words that gave him immortality: "Don't give up the ship." His men, however, suffered heavy casualties and had no choice but to surrender. The British took control of the *Chesapeake* and sailed her into Halifax as a prize of war. The vessel was later taken to England, broken up, and her timbers used in the construction of a flour mill.[167]

The *Shannon's* victory, which was accomplished in only fifteen minutes, provided a great boost to British morale. It was the first defeat of an American frigate in the war and ended a long string of American naval victories. The British people were ecstatic. "Captain Broke and his crew," said the London *Morning Chronicle*, "have vindicated the character of the British Navy."[168] The *Naval Chronicle* called the British triumph "the most brilliant act of heroism ever performed," and the news was greeted in Parliament with the "loudest and most cordial acclamations from every part of the House."[169] Broke was made a baronet, given the key to London, and showered with gifts from an appreciative nation.[170]

Lawrence, on the other hand, was given a hero's funeral in New York City that was reportedly attended by 50,000 people.[171] He was honored in a poem by Philip Freneau and eulogized in newspapers across the nation.[172] "*The brave, the noble Lawrence is no more,*" said the *Maryland Republican*. "He who added the last brilliant trophy to our triumphal diadem [with his victory over the *Peacock*], the bed of glory has received."[173] Lawrence's words—"Don't give up the ship"—became the motto of the young navy and replaced "free trade and sailors' rights" as the rallying cry of the war. Perry paid Lawrence the highest tribute by naming his flagship on Lake Erie after him.

The United States frigate *Essex* (46 guns), Captain David Porter commanding, had better luck though ultimately she too was captured. Porter was never happy with the *Essex*. She was so overloaded with guns and such a bad sailer that he regarded her as "the worst frigate in the service."[174] Nevertheless, he made the most of his cruise in the ship. Rounding the Horn in late 1812, the *Essex* became the first American warship to sail in the Pacific. For over a year Porter cruised in those waters, destroying British whale ships, taking prizes, and living off the enemy. "The valuable whale Fishery there is entirely destroyed," he reported, "and the actual injury we have done [to the British] may be estimated at two and a half millions of dollars."[175]

In late 1813 the British dispatched a squadron of three ships under the command of Captain James Hillyar to track down the *Essex* and destroy her. Two of the British ships, the *Phoebe* (46 guns) and the *Cherub* (26 guns), caught up with the *Essex* in Valparaiso, Chile. Porter could have destroyed the *Phoebe* when she docked next to the *Essex* in port, but preferring to respect Chile's territorial waters, he sought to persuade Hillyar to fight a duel at sea. Even though the crew of the *Essex* goaded the British with insulting songs, Hillyar refused the challenge. Instead, the two British ships cruised beyond the harbor, waiting for an opportunity to act in concert against the American vessel.[176]

On March 28, 1814, Porter made a run for the sea, but a sudden squall destroyed his topmast, forcing him to seek sanctuary in a small bay. Although the *Essex* was in Chilean waters, the *Phoebe* closed to take advantage of the American ship's distress, and the *Cherub* soon followed. After a hard-fought contest, the *Essex* was forced to strike her colors. Porter bitterly assailed the British officers, not only for refusing a duel but also for attacking the *Essex* while she was in a crippled state in neutral waters. He also accused the British of continuing their fire after the *Essex* had struck her colors. The British, however, denied any wrongdoing.[177]

Two smaller American warships also fought duels with the British. On August 14, 1813, the U.S.S. *Argus* (10 guns) was defeated off the coast of Ireland by H.M.S. *Pelican* (11 guns). The crew of the *Argus* was probably suffering from the aftereffects of having captured a prize loaded with wine the night before. The key to the *Argus*'s defeat was its failure to rake the enemy even though in a perfect position to do so. Another American ship, the *Enterprise* (16 guns), fought H.M.S. *Boxer* (14 guns) on September 5, 1813, off the coast of Maine. The two vessels exchanged broadsides for over an hour before the British ship surrendered. Both captains were killed in the engagement.[178]

With most of the American fleet bottled up in port or simply overmatched by the British, privateers had to shoulder a heavier burden, though the pickings were slimmer than they had been in 1812. It was difficult to find prizes on the open seas because most British merchantmen now traveled in convoy. The captain of one privateer reported "vexing the whole Atlantic" without sighting a single enemy vessel.[179] To find prizes, privateers had to cruise in the British West Indies or near the British Isles, for it was only in these waters that merchant ships traveled without an escort.

The most spectacular cruise was made by the *True-Blooded Yankee*, a small vessel fitted out by an American living in Paris. On a thirty-seven-day cruise in waters around the British Isles, this ship took twenty-seven prizes, occupied an Irish island for six days, and burned seven vessels in a Scottish harbor.[180] "She outsailed everything," marveled a British naval officer; "not one of our cruisers could touch her."[181] The *Scourge* and *Rattlesnake* found equally good hunting in the North Sea. Between them they took twenty-three prizes, which were sent into Norwegian ports for condemnation. The *Scourge* made another successful cruise and then took additional prizes on her way home.[182] Other privateers also enjoyed successful cruises in 1813, and this species of warfare continued to bedevil the British, especially in their own waters.

The outcome of the campaign should have occasioned no surprise: the American victories on land and the British victories at sea accorded with the general strengths of the two nations. Although Americans could be justly proud of their triumphs, final victory continued to elude them, and now, more than ever, time was running against them. In October of 1813 Great Britain's allies had defeated Napoleon in the decisive Battle of Leipzig. Coupled with the British triumphs in Spain, this foreshadowed Napoleon's doom. With these victories behind them, the British began diverting men and materiel to the New World, and this changed the whole complexion of the American war. Having failed to conquer Canada in 1812 or 1813, the United States would not get another chance. When the campaign of 1814 opened, the British were on the offensive.

CHAPTER 7

The Last Embargo

By THE TIME the Thirteenth Congress convened for its second session on December 6, 1813, there was a note of apprehension in the air. Despite the victories in the Northwest and Southwest, the news from the other fronts was uniformly bad. Canada was still in British hands, the British fleet had invaded American waters, and the tide of war appeared to be turning against the United States. "[T]he result of the last campaign," lamented a Republican, has "disappointed the expectations of every one." "[I]n spite of some gleams of success," added a Federalist, "[w]e are further off our object than at first."[1]

Fortunately, the president had fully recovered from his summer illness and was again able to assume the mantle of leadership. "The little president is back, and as game as ever," said one of his supporters.[2] In his opening address to Congress, Madison announced that the British had rejected the Russian mediation offer. Putting the best face on events, he enumerated American victories and insisted that "the progress of the campaign has been filled with incidents highly honorable to the American arms." He also pointed out that "the privations and sacrifices" necessitated by the war were offset by "improvements and advantages of which the contest itself is the source." Among these were the development of manufacturing and a permanent increase in the defense establishment. In short, "the war, with its vicissitudes, is illustrating the capacity and the destiny of the United States to be a great, a flourishing, and a powerful nation."[3]

Madison's optimism was strained though not entirely unwarranted, for on December 30 a truce ship arrived with the first good news from England since the repeal of the Orders in Council. Although the

British had rejected the Russian mediation proposal, they offered to open direct negotiations with the United States. The president accepted this offer and nominated John Quincy Adams, James A. Bayard, Henry Clay, and Jonathan Russell to serve on the peace commission. When Madison later learned that Albert Gallatin was still in Europe, his name was added to the list, too.[4]

There was some opposition in Federalist circles to Clay, who was considered too strong a War Hawk, and to Russell, who was variously described as "a bankrupt merchant" and "a time-serving wretch."[5] Nevertheless, it was a strong commission, and the Senate confirmed each nomination by a large majority. Since the negotiations were expected to take place in Sweden, the Senate also approved Russell's nomination as United States minister to that country. This was an important victory for the administration because the Senate had rejected this nomination by a large majority the previous summer.[6]

The appointment of the peace commissioners necessitated other changes in the government. With Clay's departure, the House had to pick a new speaker. Friends of the administration backed Felix Grundy, while opponents supported Langdon Cheves. Both were War Hawks, but Cheves was a known enemy of the restrictive system, and he won, 94–59. The voting was secret, but Cheves apparently garnered the support of the Federalists and dissident Republicans as well as some of the regular Republicans.[7]

Since all now conceded that Gallatin had forfeited his position in the cabinet, members of the Senate urged the president to fill this vacancy, too.[8] Secretary of the Navy William Jones, who was overseeing the Treasury Department, was anxious to be relieved of the extra duties anyway. "I am as perfect a galley slave as ever laboured at the oar," he told a friend; "the duties of both [offices] have become intolerable."[9] Unable to persuade more capable men to take the post, Madison offered it to Senator George W. Campbell of Tennessee.[10] Although Campbell was an able politician, he lacked the necessary skills for so demanding a job. Jonathan Roberts claimed that he "wanted promptness of action, & more knowledge of finance," and William Jones concluded that he was "entirely out of place in the Treasury."[11] The appointment had the added effect of depriving the administration of an important ally in Congress. "He will be much missed in the Senate," said Nathaniel Macon. "I am at a loss to guess, who now will be the defender of the administration in the Senate."[12]

Madison also had to appoint a new attorney general. The attorney general was not a full-time executive officer but simply the government's legal counsel. He was not expected to live in Washington nor

William Pinkney, by Charles B. King. Courtesy of the Maryland Historical Society

to give up his legal practice elsewhere. In early 1813, however, the House passed a bill requiring the attorney general to reside in Washington. Although the bill ultimately died in the Senate, by this time incumbent William Pinkney, who had a lucrative legal practice in Baltimore, had resigned.[13] This was a significant loss to the administration: Pinkney was an accomplished statesman who was considered by many to be "the first Lawyer in the Nation."[14] As his replacement, Madison chose Richard Rush of Philadelphia. Rush was a brilliant young attorney and a rising star in the party, but he lacked Pinkney's stature and experience.[15]

The president also replaced his postmaster general. Although this was not a cabinet-level position, the postmaster general had enormous patronage—over 3,000 postmasterships—and none of his appointments required Senate or even presidential approval. The man who had held this post since 1801 was Gideon Granger, a Connecticut Republican who in recent years had quietly doled out patronage to opponents of the administration. Since postal officials often read the mail that passed through their hands, these appointments caused regular Republicans considerable dismay.[16] Granger also had supported Clinton for the presidency and was considered by many to be an opponent of the war. Indeed, one War Hawk described him as "a violent *peacable* man, and a strong anti-Madisonian."[17]

When the postmastership in Philadelphia fell vacant in early 1814, regular Republicans in the state urged the appointment of Richard Bache.[18] The president himself urged Bache's candidacy, but Granger chose Michael Leib, an anti-administration senator.[19] This elicited a vigorous protest from Pennsylvania. Harrisburg merchants complained that with Leib as postmaster they could not safely transmit money to Philadelphia, and a Republican editor insisted that even the governor was reluctant to use the mails.[20] Madison finally dismissed Granger and appointed Governor Return J. Meigs of Ohio in his stead, though not before Republicans in Congress had initiated a full-scale investigation into postal matters.[21] "The fall of G—r," said a New York senator, "will deprive the faction hostile to the Administration of their most efficient man, who has for seven years past been engaged in thwarting the measures taken by the Government."[22]

❖ ❖ ❖ ❖ ❖ ❖

Madison made few recommendations to Congress in his opening address, preferring to rely on special messages or informal conferences to make his wishes known. Once again, however, congressional action on war legislation was delayed by Federalist opposition. "There is every appearance," said Jonathan Roberts, "that the minority will Contest every inch of ground—I look for one of the most procrastinated & angry debates . . . that has ever occurr[e]d in Congress."[23] Federalists renewed their attack on the Canadian strategy and denounced Republican demands that they support the war without questioning its justice or necessity. "It savors too much of the old tory doctrine of passive obedience and non-resistance," said one Federalist. "It is repugnant to the genius of our free institutions."[24]

House Federalists made two proposals to restrict the war to defensive operations. Daniel Sheffey of Virginia offered an amendment to an army bill that would limit the service of the troops "to the defence of the territories and frontiers of the United States," and William Gaston of North Carolina submitted a resolution proclaiming that, "pending the negotiation with Great Britain, it is inexpedient to prosecute military operations against the Canadas for invasion or conquest."[25] Republicans were exasperated by these proposals. Thomas B. Robertson of Louisiana expressed "astonishment and indignation" at Sheffey's amendment, claiming that he had never heard of "a proposition more fraught with mischief, more parricidal in its nature."[26] House Republicans closed ranks to vote down both proposals by large majorities.[27]

The Republicans tried to counter Federalist arguments by demonstrating that the war was defensive in character. John C. Calhoun argued that "a war is offensive or defensive, not by the mode of carrying it on, which is an immaterial circumstance, but by the motive and cause which led to it."[28] But Federalist Zebulon R. Shipherd of New York replied that if this were true then every war was defensive: "When a nation declares war it always complains that it has been injured; and, if the gentleman is correct, all wars are defensive."[29]

Republicans also tried to blame the war on the Federalists, arguing that opposition to the government had encouraged the British to persist in their policies. "If that American feeling had prevailed everywhere which ought to animate the bosoms of every man," said James Fisk of Vermont, "we should never have had occasion to go to war." Fisk claimed that Federalist opposition was linked to British gold. "[I]f you could open the secret archives of the enemy," he said, "you would find that money has a little influence somewhere."[30] Felix Grundy also joined in the attack, renewing a charge he had made the previous session: "I then said, and I now repeat, that those who systematically oppose the filling of the loans, and the enlistment of soldiers, are, in my opinion, guilty of moral treason."[31]

The debate dragged on for weeks and even spilled over to routine appropriations bills, which was almost unheard of.[32] "[T]his is the [most] talking legislature, that I have Seen," said veteran Congressman Nathaniel Macon. "Both Houses," added the Washington *National Intelligencer*, "are engaged in an unlimited, and, it would almost appear, interminable Debate on the State of the Union."[33] The speeches were so long-winded and repetitive that attendance in the House dropped off sharply. "[W]e have . . . some very moving Speeches," said Macon wryly, "so much so that more than half the chairs are vacant and some times the stenographers are absent."[34] For those who remained the experience was tedious and frustrating. Twice John C. Calhoun almost became involved in duels with Federalists, and in general Republicans were less tolerant of Federalist opposition than they had been in the past.[35]

❖ ❖ ❖ ❖ ❖ ❖ ❖

Raising troops was still a top priority with Republicans. Although the increase in pay and bounty the year before had attracted many new recruits, by the end of 1813 enlistments had slowed considerably. "[I]t Seems to be general opinion," said Macon, "that the recruiting of men by enlistment is every where nearly at an end."[36] Worse still, many of those who had enlisted for five years in 1808–1809 or for a year in 1812–1813 would soon be discharged. If Congress did not act, there was a real danger that the army would simply melt away.

The secretary of war, John Armstrong, who had lingered in New York at the end of the last campaign, aired his views in an anonymous article published in the Albany *Argus*. Convinced that voluntary enlistments would never produce the necessary troops, Armstrong called for drafting 55,000 militia into the regular army. To command these troops, he recommended the appointment of a lieutenant general of "deep and comprehensive views"—no doubt thinking of himself.[37]

Congress had little faith in Armstrong and no interest in his conscription plans.[38] Instead, congressional Republicans sought to bolster enlistments by raising the bounty again. Hitherto new recruits had received $40 in cash, a $24 advance in pay, and 160 acres of land. Thenceforth they would receive $124 in cash and 160 acres in land. To stimulate enlistments still further, Congress offered an $8 premium to anyone who secured a recruit.[39] Federalists protested that amateur recruiting agents would overrun the country, but Robert Wright replied that the government needed some means to offset the "treasonable sentiments" of those who discouraged enlistments. "When every effort was used by the minority to defeat the recruiting service," he said, "there ought to be a counter *projet* on the part of Government."[40]

Congress also authorized the president to reenlist the army's short-term men for longer periods and to raise additional riflemen. This legislation, coupled with a reorganization in the artillery and cavalry corps, raised the authorized level of the army to 62,500.[41] In accordance with a recommendation from the administration, Congress also adopted a law to secure the obedience of recalcitrant militia. The new law gave military courts broad authority to try delinquent militia in absentia and to compel the attendance and testimony of witnesses.[42]

Robert Wright wanted to give military courts authority to try civilian spies as well. He argued that it was impossible to secure a conviction for treason in civilian courts because the constitutional requirements were so strict.[43] Federalist Richard Stockton of New Jersey called Wright's proposal "monstrous," claiming that it would "subvert every principle of civil liberty."[44] Most Republicans evidently agreed. Although Wright's resolution was adopted, no bill on the subject was ever reported.[45]

Congress also passed a pair of laws to bolster American operations at sea. One measure appropriated $500,000 for the construction of a floating battery, which was actually a steam-powered frigate designed by Robert Fulton.[46] Federalists objected to so large an expenditure for an experimental project, but Republicans countered that the expense was justified because of the danger posed by British warships in American waters.[47]

Congress also quadrupled the $25 bounty that was paid for prisoners of war brought in by privateers.[48] Federalists considered the additional premium excessive, but once again Republicans argued that circumstances justified the expense.[49] The British had accumulated 2,000 more prisoners than the United States, and, according to an American official, they had "discontinued the system of *releases on account.*"[50] The object of the bill, said Congressman Alexander McKim, "was to get as many prisoners of war as we could, to balance accounts with the enemy, and enable us to redeem our fellow-citizens from captivity."[51]

❖ ❖ ❖ ❖ ❖ ❖

Congress had to make further provision not only for fighting the war but also for financing it. In January of 1814, before surrendering the Treasury Department to Campbell, William Jones presented his budget for the coming year. He estimated that the government's income would be only $16,000,000 while its expenses would be $45,400,000. This meant that $29,400,000 would have to be raised by loans and treasury notes. Since the cost of servicing the national debt was growing while revenue was declining, the government was actually using money from new loans to pay the interest on old ones. This violated Gallatin's original plan of war finance, and hence Jones recommended a new round of taxes.[52]

Having adopted a comprehensive system of internal duties only a few months earlier, congressional Republicans were in no mood for additional taxes. Instead, they authorized a $25,000,000 loan and the issue of $10,000,000 in treasury notes.[53] Federalists attacked these measures as unsound. Alexander Contee Hanson, who was still suffering from injuries sustained in the Baltimore Riots but was now a member of Congress, called the Republican system of war finance "deceptive and disingenuous." To float new loans to pay the interest on old ones, he said, was "to adopt a most desperate system of fiscal gambling."[54]

Calhoun responded that the government had no choice but to borrow the money it needed. If the money were withheld, he said, "it must communicate a fatal shock to public credit." The result, said the *National Intelligencer*, would be "the bankruptcy of the Treasury; confusion and anarchy at home; and . . . an ignominious submission to whatever terms the arrogance of the enemy might dictate!"[55]

Although irked by Federalist opposition, most Republicans recognized that the government's financial position was precarious. To shore up this position, many Republicans favored a national bank. Pro-bank Republicans had been unable to save the first national bank when its charter had expired in 1811 even though they had the unanimous support of the Federalists.[56] But now, as a measure of war finance, a national bank had considerably greater appeal. In December of 1813 a group of businessmen in New York City urged Congress to establish a bank. "Among the most obvious and important advantages which the Government would acquire," they said, "would be the means of borrowing . . . money for the public service."[57]

The House Ways and Means Committee agreed. On February 19, 1814, John W. Taylor of New York reported a bill from committee for creating a national bank in Washington, D.C. The bank would have no branches and thus would not compete with state banks or control them. The bill set the bank's capital stock at $30,000,000 and required the bank to lend the government $6,000,000 to buy bank stock plus an additional $15,000,000 to finance the war. The whole scheme was little more than an attempt to float paper money in the guise of bank notes. Many Republicans doubted the wisdom of the plan. Some preferred to rely on treasury notes, while others insisted that additional revenue was unnecessary. The proposal was finally killed by a rash of armistice rumors that swept through the country in April.[58]

The fears voiced for the nation's financial health were nonetheless well-founded. Although some Federalists had quietly subscribed to the war loans in 1812 and 1813, most Federalist bankers, who controlled the bulk of the nation's liquid capital, had remained aloof.[59] The British offer to open peace talks, however, had generated considerable optimism in 1814, and some bankers wanted to take part in the new loan, especially since it was likely to be offered on favorable terms.[60]

Federalist bankers from Boston and Philadelphia met in April to work out a common policy. They agreed to subscribe to the loan but only if the administration dropped its demand for an end to impressment. When the administration refused to budge, the bankers withheld their support.[61] Some New England Federalists did not approve of taking part in the loan anyway. "As to *Federalists* who loan their money," said Timothy Pickering, "I know not any punishment they do not deserve."[62]

Although representatives of the government ran newspaper ads in Boston offering to keep the names of subscribers secret, the loan of 1814 failed.[63] When the Treasury put up $10,000,000 in May, it received subscriptions for $9,800,000, but the principal subscriber was Jacob Barker of New York, who took $5,000,000. Federalists scoffed at Barker's ability to raise so much capital, and even Republicans were skeptical.[64] Eventually he defaulted on $1,500,000 of his contract. Since other subscribers defaulted on $400,000, the government realized only $7,900,000 from the loan. Moreover, it had to accept $88 in cash for every $100 in bonds issued and guarantee to increase the discount if future subscribers received a better deal.[65]

Two months later, the administration put up another $6,000,000 of the loan, but subscribers would take only $2,900,000 even at $80 a share, which was a 20 percent discount. The administration had to accept this offer out of sheer necessity, but because of defaults, the total amount realized was only $2,500,000. Moreover, the Treasury had to issue additional bonds to the subscribers of the May loan so that they would receive the same discount. In all, the government issued $4,000,000 in bonds to raise $2,500,000 in cash.[66] All of this suggested that public credit was sinking and that the government teetered on the brink of bankruptcy.

❖ ❖ ❖ ❖ ❖ ❖

With the nation's military prospects dimming and public credit in decline, the administration looked for other ways to put pressure on the enemy. The president had lost none of his faith in commercial sanctions, and this was the only major weapon still left in the nation's arsenal. Madison was also determined to stamp out trade with the enemy, which flourished all along the common border in the north and on the maritime frontier in the east and south. "We have been feeding and supplying the enemy," complained a Republican newspaper, "both on our coast and in Canada, ever since the war began."[67]

Most of this traffic was carried on with Canada. Extensive trade along the Canadian-American border was well established before 1812 despite the non-importation law, and the war did little to halt it.[68] Indeed, one of the reasons the British left New England unblockaded was to facilitate this trade. At the beginning of the war, British officials in Canada explicitly authorized the export of all goods to the United States (war materiel and specie excepted) and ordered British subjects in the maritime provinces not to molest the goods or vessels of American citizens "so long as they shall abstain, on their parts, from any Acts of Hostility."[69] Americans living near the frontier were happy to accept this modus vivendi. Anxious to acquire British textiles, plaster of paris, pottery, salt, and sugar products, they freely offered provisions and naval stores in return.[70]

Much of the trade with Canada was carried on by sea, and as long as it was conducted in neutral vessels, it did not violate American law. Neutral ships ferried particularly large quantities of American food from Massachusetts (which then included Maine) to the maritime provinces. "Since I have been here (about 15 days)," wrote an American from Halifax in late 1812, "upwards of 20,000 barrels of flour have been brought in by vessels under Swedish and Spanish colors—most of the shipments are from Boston."[71]

The bulk of the seaborne trade, however, was conducted in American vessels—a clear violation of the enemy trade act. Coasting vessels, which did not have to enter or clear from a customs house, traded directly with Nova Scotia and New Brunswick or rendezvoused with neutral vessels at sea. Islands were often used as "drops" for the exchange of goods, and collusive captures were common.[72] In one notorious case, the tiny privateer *Washington* "captured" two heavily-laden ships from Halifax worth more than $100,000. Although customs officials seized the prizes, the Supreme Court later restored them to their captors. Justice William Johnson conceded "that the voyage of these vessels was loaded with infamy," but "the evidence is not sufficient to fasten on the captors a participation in the fraud."[73]

American merchants commonly ransomed captured vessels for 5 or 10 percent of their value. "A brisk *business* is now carrying on all along our coast," said the Boston *Centinel* in 1813, "between the British cruisers and our coasting vessels, in ready money."[74] Though this practice was sanctioned by the American government, it was sometimes a cover for illegal trade. Moreover, British merchants who wished to ship their merchandise directly to the United States could usually secure neutral papers from obliging Swedish officials at St. Barthelemy in the Caribbean. Although the United States denounced this practice, the Swedish government was slow to curtail it.[75] In the meantime, some customs officials hired experts to distinguish between British and non-British goods. In practice, however, it was almost impossible to determine the source of any product unless those perpetrating the fraud slipped up. In one case, for example, customs officials in Boston confiscated a $130,000 shipment because thread pulled out of the woolens had left a visible impression of the word *London*.[76]

There was also a great deal of overland trade between Canada and the United States. Merchants in the interior often used inland waterways, such as Lake Ontario and the St. Lawrence River, or Lake Champlain and the Richelieu River. Some merchants outfitted privateers on these waters and made dummy captures of goods purchased by their agents in Montreal. Others informed on themselves (which entitled them to a third of the proceeds) and then used various legal maneuvers to secure additional relief.[77]

Nor was the illicit trade confined to the northern frontier. Amelia Island, a Spanish possession at the mouth of St. Marys River in Florida, was the principal outlet for southern produce and the main source of British goods for people living in the South. Shortly before the war, Gallatin received reports "that British goods to an immense amount have been imported into Amelia Island, with the view of smuggling the same into the United States."[78] There were also reports of illegal slave imports from the Spanish island.[79]

Lake Barataria, with its ready access to the sea, was the funnel through which illegal goods flowed into Louisiana. The Baratarian pirates had established a settlement on Grand Terre Island in Barataria Bay in southern Louisiana. Though technically privateersmen sailing under commissions issued by France and Cartagena (a city state in present-day Colombia), the pirates preyed indiscriminately on commerce in the Gulf of Mexico and smuggled their booty into New Orleans.[80] "Our whole coast Westwardly of the Balize," reported a naval officer in 1812, "is at this moment, infested with *pirates* and *smugglers*."[81]

Most merchants in New Orleans had no qualms about buying smuggled goods because the profits were so high. "Smuggling is carried on to a great degree," reported an observer; "fortunes have been made in a few Months."[82] The smugglers operated openly, and according to one official, they "even dared to rescue property which had been Seized by the Officers of the Customs."[83] In one case, a customs official was killed and two others were wounded in an armed clash with smugglers.[84]

The collector at New Orleans repeatedly asked for military assistance, but General Wilkinson (who probably profited from the trade) was unwilling to cooperate.[85] Nor could the navy help. "[T]he force heretofore under my command," said the ranking officer on the station, "had been rendered by decay, altogether inadequate to the protection of the coast, and the support of the revenue laws, even in a time of peace."[86] The administration promised assistance but insisted that the real problem was local complicity. "I will not dissemble," William Jones told the New Orleans collector in 1813, "that whilst the inhabitants of Louisiana continue to countenance this illegal commerce and the Courts of justice forbear to enforce the laws against the offenders, little or no benefit can be expected to result from the best concerted measures."[87]

The experience of customs agents in New Orleans typified that of most border officials during the war. Even before the war, collectors on the northern frontier had complained of the difficulty of enforcing the non-importation law. "Large combinations," wrote the Sackets Harbor collector in early 1812, "appear to be forming to render the Non-importation law, unpopular and intimidate those who will assist in inforcing the law. The public houses in this quarter are kept by violent partisans in their interest. Every friend to the law is misused at them; by a gang of villains kept for that purpose."[88] The wartime expansion of the restrictive system did not make enforcement any easier. After Vermont repealed a law against trading with Canada, the customs collector there claimed that illegal trade was conducted "in a public and open manner."[89]

Widespread complicity rendered government officials helpless. Before meeting his death in the Battle of York, Zebulon M. Pike sought to prosecute smugglers near Plattsburgh, but no court would take cognizance because even the judges had a hand in the trade.[90] In Eastport, Maine, a volunteer army officer reported that some 200 merchants were engaged in trade with the enemy and that 86 British subjects were present to facilitate the trade. When the officer tried to suppress the traffic, he was threatened with tar and feathers and eventually jailed for fictitious debts.[91] Other army officers later assigned to the station profited from his example by looking the other way. According to an anonymous correspondent of the War Department, they showed a "blind indifference and almost total disregard . . .

to the prosecution of an illicit trade."[92] Government officials were also stymied in Provincetown, Massachusetts, on the tip of Cape Cod. Local merchants, said a customs official, were so deeply involved in illegal trade that "his Inspecters dare not now attempt to search Stores or Houses there, for smuggled Goods, as the mass of the population are interested in their concealment, and so far from giving assistance, threaten such opposition as renders the attempt . . . futile."[93]

Nor were government officials able to keep provisions from British fleets in American waters. "The fact is notorious," declared the Lexington *Reporter*, "that the very squadrons of the enemy now annoying our coast . . . derive their supplies from the very country which is the theatre of their atrocities."[94] Although royal officials sometimes threatened coastal towns with destruction if their needs were not met, the use of force was rarely necessary. Admiralty procurers paid for provisions in cash, and there was no shortage of volunteers to supply their wants. Chesapeake Bay, Long Island Sound, and Vineyard Sound teemed with tiny coasters ferrying supplies to the British fleets stationed there. Some sixty vessels were reportedly engaged in this traffic in Long Island Sound alone.[95] Although most trade with the Royal Navy was clandestine, the harbor at Provincetown, Massachusetts, was openly used by British ships seeking provisions or refuge from winter storms. According to one report, small coasters and fishing vessels regularly carried "Fresh Beef, vegitables, and in fact all Kind of supplies" to these ships.[96]

The trade with the enemy knew no political or social barriers. Although Republicans blamed the traffic on Federalists, members of both parties were involved. Republican John Jacob Astor used various ruses to import furs from Canada, and while cruising in the *Rossie* Joshua Barney caught a ship, owned by Maine Republican William King, that was carrying a fraudulent manifest and British goods.[97] Barney let the ship go, fearing that "such a seizure at this time would be made a handle by the enemies of the administration."[98] Another Republican, Jacob Gibson of Maryland, was described as a "flaming democrat and war-man," but because of his friendship with British navy officials, he was allowed to export produce to the mainland from his island in the Chesapeake.[99] Local Republicans freely admitted that if Gibson had been a Federalist "he would have been tarred and feathered and his house pulled down."[100]

❖ ❖ ❖ ❖ ❖ ❖

Such was the extent of this illegal trade and such was the administration's faith in economic coercion that Madison decided in late 1813 to seek a broad range of new restrictions. The government hoped not only to stamp out trade with the enemy but also to increase the economic pressure on Britain. In a confidential message sent to Congress on December 9, the president said: "To shorten, as much as possible, the duration of the war, it is indispensable that the enemy should feel all the pressure that can be given to it." Toward this end, the president recommended four new restrictions: (1) an embargo prohibiting all American ships and goods from leaving port; (2) a complete ban on the importation of certain commodities customarily produced in the British Empire, such as woolen and cotton goods and rum; (3) a ban against foreign ships trading in American ports unless the master, supercargo, and at least three-quarters of the crew were citizens or subjects of the flag flown by the ship; and (4) a ban on ransoming ships. Together these measures were designed to halt the flow of supplies to British armies in Canada and Europe and British fleets in American waters, tighten the non-importation system, prevent the British from fraudulently using neutral flags, and put an end to the use of ransoming as a cover for illegal trade.[101]

Congress had rejected the president's recommendation for an embargo the previous summer but was more compliant this time. The Senate, which had killed so many other restrictive proposals, was now willing to follow the administration's lead, in part because of the exigencies of war. In addition, public pressure had been exerted on three senators who had opposed the embargo in the previous session. "Messrs Giles, and Stone and Anderson," said the *National Intelligencer,* "have *thought better* of their votes, and will now yield their suffrages in favor of the measure."[102]

Federalists fought a spirited but futile rear guard action against the embargo, offering a host of amendments to ameliorate its impact and outlining its likely effects on commerce, agriculture, and government revenue.[103] Zebulon Shipherd called the measure "an engine of tyranny, an engine of oppression," and the Maryland House of Delegates later compared it to one of the coercive acts adopted by Britain in 1774. "[T]he bitter tribulation of the Boston port bill," said the delegates, "is again to be realized on an infinitely more extended scale."[104]

The Republicans met these attacks with a stony silence. "[T]he duty of the friends to the embargo," said the *National Intelligencer,* "was to act, not to speak."[105] Thus only eight days after submitting his request to Congress, Madison signed the embargo into law.[106] One of the reasons that Congress acted so quickly was that news of the measure had leaked to the press. According to one Federalist, congressional action on the proposal was "the subject of newspaper paragraphs" and was "as well known in the principal cities of the Union as in this Hall."[107] Modeled after the enforcement act of 1809, the embargo of 1813 was more sweeping than any previous restriction. All ships were embargoed in port and the export of all goods and produce prohibited. The coasting trade was outlawed except in bays, rivers, sounds, and lakes, and fishing vessels could venture to sea only after posting heavy bonds. Government officials were given broad powers to enforce the law, and the penalties for violation were heavy.[108]

The embargo proved too sweeping even for its supporters. A week after the measure became law, Treasury Secretary Jones sent a circular to all customs officials interpreting a section of the law that appeared to sanction seizures on the vaguest of suspicions. Jones instructed collectors to impound goods only if circumstances clearly indicated that a violation was intended.[109] Congress also had to pass legislation to ameliorate the harshest effects of the measure. Nantucket, an island thirty miles off the coast of Massachusetts, was given special permission to import food and fuel, and coasting vessels trapped away from home were allowed to return.[110]

The embargo could not halt all trade, but according to the customs collector at Boston, the only loophole was a clause that allowed privateers to sail. After leaving port, these vessels sometimes discharged their crews and sold their provisions abroad.[111] Federalist fishermen in Boston complained that their Republican counterparts in Marblehead were permitted to go to sea while they were not, but in general the measure was fairly enforced.[112] The main problem, as Federalists pointed out, was that it further undermined American prosperity and cut into government revenue. It punished the entire nation, said one Federalist, "because of a few sinners."[113]

❖ ❖ ❖ ❖ ❖ ❖

Even though the president finally got the embargo he wanted, Congress was unresponsive to his request for other restrictions. Most Republicans were reluctant to go as far as the president, even in time of war. Moreover, the same truce ship that brought news of Britain's peace initiative at the end of December also brought reports of Napoleon's defeat at Leipzig. This battle shattered the Continental System and opened all of northern Europe to British trade.[114] As a result, the restrictive system as a coercive instrument lost much of its effectiveness. Although bills were introduced to tighten the non-importation system and outlaw the ransoming of ships, these proposals did not become law.[115]

Besides killing the prospects for additional restrictions, the news from Europe also led to a clamor for the repeal of the embargo and non-importation law. Federalists made several attempts to repeal these laws, and Republicans, looking for ways to generate badly needed revenue, lent a sympathetic ear.[116] Even Robert Wright, a pro-embargo Republican, wondered if it might not be wise to sheathe "the two-edged sword, the embargo . . . during the [peace] negotiation."[117] Madison himself eventually came around to this view, and on March 31, 1814—less than four months after recommending the new restrictions—he asked Congress to repeal both the embargo and non-importation act. Goods that were owned by the enemy, he said, should still be barred from the United States. The export of specie should also be banned to prevent an unfavorable balance of trade from draining the nation's banks.[118]

Madison's change of heart stunned nearly everyone. "The shock produced by this political earthquake," said a Republican newspaper, "is tremendous."[119] The president's about-face was greeted with "utter astonishment" in Washington and caused a particular sensation among the most devoted restrictionists, some of whom were said to be "pretty warm . . . and a little violent."[120] According to one observer, there was "much pouting and no small degree of execration . . . among [the president's] zealous supporters, some of whom, I am told, will oppose the Bill with bitterness in the House, as they certainly do out of it."[121] Most Republicans, however, were willing to follow the president's lead. "[I]n the present state of *Europe*," said *Niles' Register*, "it is pretty generally agreed that the embargo ought to be raised."[122] With victory at hand, longtime opponents of the restrictive system found it difficult to contain their joy. "I have not for a long time seen the feds look in as so good humor," commented Nathaniel Macon; "they have all a smile on their countenance."[123]

A bill repealing the embargo and non-importation law passed both houses by large majorities.[124] In fact, the mood of Congress had swung so much against restrictions that another bill to outlaw the export of specie failed to win a majority in either house.[125] John C. Calhoun doubted whether even "the most strenuous efforts of our custom-house officers" could halt the export of specie, and a Federalist said "you might as rationally . . . prevent the ebb and flow of the tide."[126] With the repeal of the embargo and non-importation act and the defeat of the ban on specie exports, Americans were now barred only from trading directly with the enemy, importing enemy-owned goods, or using enemy licenses.

❖ ❖ ❖ ❖ ❖ ❖

Schemes to raise men and money and restrict trade with the enemy consumed much of the administration's time during the war, but other war-related issues demanded attention, too. Among these was the regulation of enemy aliens.[127] More than 10,000 British subjects lived in the United States during the war, mainly in New York and Pennsylvania.[128] Most were permanent residents who for one reason or another had never taken out citizenship papers. Though few posed any real threat, all were enemy aliens, and the government had to devise regulations to insure that they provided no aid or information to the enemy.

The basic legislation governing American policy was the alien enemies act of 1798, which was still in force in 1812. This law gave the government broad powers over enemy aliens but also decreed that they be accorded a "reasonable time" to depart from the United States with their property.[129] Shortly after the declaration of war, Congress fixed the grace period at six months.[130] At the same time, the State Department ordered all enemy aliens who remained in the country to register with United States marshals.[131]

Initially, government officials treated British subjects with indulgence, stretching the letter of the law to avoid hardship. The State Department freely granted passports for the removal of property long after the grace period had expired, and many aliens—known and trusted in their communities—did not bother to register.[132] Although the government in early 1813 ordered enemy aliens to move to a place (chosen by the local marshal) that was at least forty miles from the tidewater, all except merchants could secure permission from the marshal to remain, and even merchants could seek an exemption from the State Department.[133] Such were the indulgences granted by the government that in May of 1813 Monroe told a British official that enemy aliens enjoyed "almost equal rights with American Citizens."[134]

By this time, however, the administration had already begun to adopt tougher policies. In February of 1813 the government prohibited enemy aliens from traveling without a passport secured from a marshal or customs collector.[135] The following July, in response to British depredations in the Chesapeake, the State Department stopped granting passports for the removal of British property. "[T]he conduct of Great Britain," Monroe said, "has not been such as to authorise a relaxation of the rules."[136] Then in November, John Mason, who had been put in charge of enemy aliens (as well as British prisoners of war) adopted tougher rules to prevent British subjects who had moved to the interior from visiting the enemy. "[T]he lenity shown Enemy Aliens," he complained, "has been frequently abused." To avoid future abuses, Mason ordered all British subjects living beyond the tidewater to sign "a parole of honor" not to travel more than five miles from their assigned place or to correspond with the enemy.[137] This completed the government's code of regulations. Even with the later restrictions, American policy toward enemy aliens remained comparatively lenient.

The administration also had to establish rules to regulate the treatment of prisoners of war, and this proved far more vexing.[138] Although there was no international agreement on the subject, warfare in this era was carefully limited and highly professional, and each nation professed to favor humane treatment. The precedents, however, were vague, and prisoners on both sides complained of crowded, cold, and dirty housing, foul rations, and physical abuse.[139]

Since officers were considered gentlemen, they received special treatment. Most were given the freedom of a town or larger area, and some were sent home on an extended parole with the understanding that they refrain from fighting until officially exchanged. Militia were sometimes sent home, too, because they were considered part-time soldiers. Enlisted men, on the other hand, were usually confined until they were actually exchanged. The United States favored the use of state penitentiaries located near (but not too near) the northern frontier, particularly in Massachusetts and Kentucky. Great Britain, on the other hand, utilized a host of prison ships and jails scattered all over the British Empire, the most notorious of which was Dartmoor, a cold, damp, and bleak prison located on the moors of Devonshire.[140]

In theory men taken at sea were treated like those captured on land, but in practice Britain handled them differently. Some 2,200 Americans who were in the Royal Navy when war broke out refused to fight against their country. They were confined as prisoners of war but were not deemed eligible for release or exchange until their citizenship was proven. Once their citizenship was established, those who had been impressed into British service were released, while those who had volunteered (or had been impressed and then accepted the royal bounty) were exchanged. Because communication was slow and documentation that satisfied the British was hard to find, most of these men languished in prison for the duration of the war.[141] The United States, by contrast, discharged all British seamen who claimed to be deserters from the Royal Navy.[142] Much to the dismay of the Navy

Department, however, Captain David Porter allowed his men to tar and feather a British subject who was discharged from his ship.[143]

In order to discourage privateering, the British refused to parole or exchange anyone from a privateer that mounted fewer than fourteen guns. In addition, royal officials held some mariners trapped in the Britain Isles in 1812 as prisoners of war and sought to make prison life hard on all maritime prisoners in the hope of inducing them to enlist in the Royal Navy. Great Britain also insisted that British prisoners who were put on a neutral vessel at sea or dropped at a neutral port by American privateers were not on parole. These men, the British claimed, had been released outright and were not subject to exchange. The British objective was to force American privateers to keep their prisoners until they returned to the United States, an inconvenience that was likely to interfere with normal cruising.[144]

To regularize the treatment and exchange of prisoners, the two warring nations negotiated a series of conventions. The first was signed in Halifax on November 28, 1812.[145] American officials were unhappy with this agreement, and hence a new one was signed on May 12, 1813. The new convention bound both nations to treat prisoners "with humanity, conformable to the usage and practice of the most civilized nations during war." It prohibited corporal punishment, fixed the daily ration, defined the terms of parole, authorized the use of cartel ships for exchanges, and set the places where exchanged prisoners were to be delivered. The convention also established the rates of exchange. (A rear admiral or major general was worth thirty privates; a petty officer or non-commissioned officer was worth two).[146]

This agreement was never ratified by England. Besides mandating a more varied and generous ration than British officials favored, the convention provided for paroling maritime prisoners at sea. Nevertheless officials of both countries in the New World generally adhered to the terms of the agreement. Only in 1814, after learning that American prisoners in Halifax, Jamaica, and Barbadoes had been put on a smaller ration, did American officials reduce the ration of British prisoners in the United States.[147]

Both sides adopted liberal parole policies in 1812, but this changed when a bitter controversy erupted over the treatment of prisoners of doubtful nationality.[148] In the Battle of Queenston, the British had captured a large number of American soldiers, including twenty-three—mostly Irishmen—who had been born in the British Isles. Although some of these men were naturalized American citizens and others had lived in the United States for many years, royal officials considered them British subjects. The twenty-three were therefore clamped into irons and shipped to England to be tried for treason. The men reportedly offered to atone for their "treason" by taking up arms against the United States, but this did not appease the British government.[149]

Winfield Scott, who was himself captured at Queenston, protested British actions but to no avail. When Scott was later paroled, he went to Washington to inform American officials of the problem.[150] The president secured authority from Congress to retaliate and then ordered twenty-three British soldiers put in close confinement as hostages for the safety of the Americans.[151] Sir George Prevost, governor-general of Canada, responded by confining forty-six American officers and non-commissioned officers and threatened to put two Americans to death for every British soldier executed. Prevost also threatened "to prosecute the war with unmitigated severity" if any of the British prisoners were harmed.[152] American officials responded by confining British officers in American hands, which prompted the British to confine the remaining American officers they held. Thus by early 1814, all the officers held by either side in the New World were in close confinement with the threat of retaliatory execution hanging over their heads.[153]

British officials were livid over the threat of American retaliation, and most English newspapers followed their lead. "If Mr. Madison dare to retaliate by taking away the life of one English prisoner," warned the London *Courier*, "America puts herself out of the protection of the law of nations, and must be treated as an outlaw. An army and navy acting against her will then be absolved from all obligation to respect the usages and laws of war." The confinement of the British officers, added the *Times,* was "a wanton and barbarous act of cruelty." Any violence against them would "justify severe retaliation."[154]

Some Federalists agreed with the British. The Maryland House of Delegates protested against the "system of sanguinary retaliation" which jeopardized American prisoners to protect "British traitors." Gouverneur Morris went further. "[I]f the horrible project of murdering our prisoners because the enemy executes her traitorous subjects in our service be carried into effect," he said, "we shall soon be divested of everything which can check the savage temper of barbarous nations."[155]

In Worcester, Massachusetts, Federalists complained that British officers were confined under intolerable conditions in the local jail. "We have never witnessed a more powerful excitement of the tender sympathies of *the friends of peace,*" commented a Republican paper, "than by the *cruel duress* imposed upon these *'unfortunate captives'!*"[156]

Winfield Scott, by an unknown artist. Courtesy of the National Portrait Gallery, Smithsonian Institution

When the sheriff failed to search visitors to the jail, someone (presumably a Federalist) gave a pistol to the incarcerated officers, and nine of them escaped. Five were recaptured, but the others made their way to Canada. The state of Massachusetts subsequently prohibited the use of its jails for this purpose.[157]

The question of retaliation raised the whole issue of allegiance, much as the subject of impressment did. Langdon Cheves took a broad view of the matter and probably spoke for most Americans. "[T]he right of retaliation," he said, "does not depend on questions of allegiance, naturalization, or expatriation, but on the laws and usages of civilized war." These laws "concede to belligerent sovereigns the right of protecting by retaliation, if necessary, not only their naturalized subjects, but all those who fight under their banners."[158]

Ultimately, good sense prevailed on both sides, and none of the prisoners were harmed. The United States authorized General William Winder, who was captured by the British and later paroled, to negotiate an exchange of all confined prisoners. But Winder, who was sympathetic to the British position, signed an agreement on April 15, 1814, that excluded the original twenty-three sent to England and the first round of hostages held by each side. Although American officials refused to ratify the agreement, the British had already released their hostages.[159] Later, American officials learned that the original twenty-three prisoners were being treated no differently from other American prisoners in England. Hence on July 16, 1814, they signed a new convention that confirmed the terms of the April agreement and provided for the exchange of all remaining hostages. The original twenty-three remained in British hands until after the war, when all but two (who had died of natural causes) were returned to the United States.[160]

There were other incidents like this one. On numerous occasions the British learned that men captured in battle or taken from American warships or privateers had been born in the British Isles. Royal officials often threatened to try such men for treason, but in each case the prospect of American retaliation forced them to relent. Thus no one fighting on America's side during the war was actually prosecuted by the enemy for treason.[161]

❖ ❖ ❖ ❖ ❖ ❖

All in all, the administration had reason to be satisfied with its accomplishments in the winter of 1813–1814. Besides facing down the British on the prisoner-of-war issue, the administration got most of what it wanted from Congress. By the time it adjourned on April 18—almost four and a half months after convening—Congress had increased the recruitment bounty, provided for the extension of short-term enlistments, strengthened martial law, appropriated money for a steam frigate, raised the bounty for prisoners of war, and authorized a new loan and a new issue of treasury notes. Moreover, in sharp contrast to the previous session, the Senate had confirmed all of the president's appointments, and the House had been far less indulgent of Federalist opposition. On several occasions House Republicans had responded to Federalist arguments with silence or had used the previous question to cut off debate.[162] All of this suggested that the Republicans were at last closing ranks.

The administration failed to get its way on only three issues. Most of the president's requests for additional trade restrictions were ignored. So too was his recommendation that French warships and privateers be explicitly authorized to use American ports.[163] The president hoped to insure continued access to French ports for American privateers, but Congressional Republicans (fearing the cry of French influence) buried this proposal in committee.[164] The president also asked Congress to retain the double duties on imports beyond the end of the war in order to protect American manufactures.[165] No action was taken on this proposal because neither Republicans nor Federalists were ready for such overt protectionism. Even Daniel Webster, the great champion of protection in later years, declared that he was in no hurry "to see Sheffields and Birminghams in America."[166]

These setbacks for the administration were minor. Far more ominous were the growing difficulties that the government faced in prosecuting the war. Public credit was declining, trade with the enemy continued, and the tide of the conflict appeared to be turning against the nation. Moreover, developments in Europe had stripped the nation of its last great weapon. Commercial sanctions had been at the heart of Republican foreign policy ever since 1806, but the collapse of French power on the Continent had rendered them useless. When the embargo was repealed, Daniel Webster had expressed hope that "the immense losses and sufferings which the people of the United States have endured, uselessly endured, under the operations of the restrictive system, will insure a long abhorrence of its memory."[167] Webster got his wish. The embargo of 1813 was the nation's last great trade restriction. Never again would the United States cut off all its trade to achieve a foreign policy objective.

CHAPTER 8

The British Counteroffensive

By the time the campaign of 1814 opened, the initiative in the war had shifted to the British. The Battle of Leipzig the previous October had forced Napoleon to retreat to France with the Allies in pursuit. At the same time, a British army under the Duke of Wellington had broken the back of French resistance in Spain and invaded France from the south. On March 31, 1814, the Allies entered Paris—the only time that Russian troops have ever occupied the French capital. Napoleon abdicated on April 11 and shortly thereafter was exiled to the Mediterranean island of Elba. For the first time in more than a decade, Europe was at peace.[1]

Federalists joyfully celebrated the defeat of the Anti-Christ, and some Republicans joined them.[2] "I rejoice with you," Jefferson told a friend, "in the downfall of Bonaparte. This scourge of the world has occasioned the deaths of at least ten millions of human beings."[3] Federalists assumed that Napoleon's defeat would pave the way for peace with England, but Republicans were skeptical.[4] The United States was now alone in the field against England, and most Republicans expected the British to be vindictive. "We should have to fight hereafter," said Joseph Nicholson, "not for 'free Trade and sailors rights,' not for the Conquest of the Canadas, but for our national Existence."[5] As the character of the war changed, so too did the nation's motto. "Don't give up the soil" gradually replaced "Don't give up the ship."[6]

Ever since Leipzig, the British had been cautiously detaching veterans from the peninsular campaign for service in America. After Napoleon's exile, the trickle of troops to the New World turned into a torrent. By September of 1814 some 13,000 veterans had reached Canada, bringing British troop strength there to 30,000. Additional men continued to arrive, so that by the end of the year there were close to 40,000 British troops in the American theater.[7] With the balance of power shifting in their favor, many Englishmen wanted to punish the United States. "I have it much at heart," Cochrane declared, "to give [the Americans] a complete drubbing before peace is made." "Chastise the savages," said the *Times;* "for such they are, in a much truer sense, than the followers of Tecumseh or the Prophet."[8]

Fortunately for the United States, the American army was steadily improving with experience. Two years of campaigning had weeded out many incompetent officers, and Secretary of War John Armstrong, who was a fair judge of talent, continued to push capable young men ahead. "[I]t was under the auspices of his administration," a sympathetic Congressman later said, "that Wilkinson, Hampton, Lewis, and Boyd had to make room for *Brown, Scott, Gaines, Ripley,* and *Macomb.*"[9] Moreover, despite the large number of discharges in the winter of 1813–1814, the enhanced bounty attracted a host of new recruits and induced many veterans to reenlist.[10] As a result, by the spring of 1814, there were about 40,000 men in uniform—a third more than the year before. Enlistments continued to mount in the remaining months of the war, so that by early 1815 the total was close to 45,000.[11]

❖ ❖ ❖ ❖ ❖ ❖

Although military experience and naval power gave Britain a decided edge in the campaign, the United States still held the advantage in the West. America controlled Lake Erie, and its supply lines to the West were shorter and less exposed. Moreover, the Battle of the Thames had destroyed Tecumseh's confederacy, depriving the British of many of their Indian allies. In order to exploit these advantages, American officials decided once again to concentrate on Upper Canada. The plan was to destroy British power on Lake Huron by retaking Mackinac, drive the British from the Niagara frontier, and then seize other British posts on Lake Ontario. If this campaign were successful, then Kingston and Montreal might be attacked.[12]

Command of the Great Lakes continued to play a pivotal role in the campaign. The British had fortified Mackinac, hoping to develop it into a naval base for Lake Huron, though this lake was so far west that neither side could actually claim control. On Lake Erie the United States remained firmly in command, while on Lake Ontario the balance of power continued to shift back and forth. Both commanders on

Lake Ontario—Chauncey and Yeo—remained cautious, unwilling to engage in combat without overwhelming superiority. Instead, each hoped to achieve control by putting ever larger ships into service. At the beginning of the campaign, Yeo launched the *Prince Regent* (58 guns) and the *Princess Charlotte* (42 guns). Chauncey countered with the *Superior* (62) and the *Mohawk* (42). Later in the year, the British launched the *St. Lawrence* (112 guns) and the *Psyche* (55 guns) and began construction on two additional ships-of-the-line. The United States countered by laying down two battleships of its own, the *New Orleans* and *Chippewa*, each of which was capable of mounting over 100 guns. None of the battleships were ready for service before the end of the war, and no naval engagements were fought on Lake Ontario. Instead, on this lake, as on the other Great Lakes, the fleets were used mainly to support land operations.[13]

In accordance with American strategy, the navy prepared to attack Mackinac in the summer of 1814. Captain Arthur Sinclair, who had succeeded Perry on Lake Erie, took several vessels from that fleet and transported 700 men under Major George Croghan to Lake Huron. After destroying an unoccupied British post at St. Joseph and seizing British property at Sault Sainte Marie, the American flotilla rendez-voused at Mackinac in late July.[14] According to Sinclair, the island was "a perfect Gibralter, being high inaccessible Rock on every side except the West."[15] Sinclair was unable to elevate his naval guns enough to hit either of the British forts and could give little support to Croghan's men when they landed in a dense forest on the western side of the island.

Lieutenant Colonel Robert McDouall, who was in charge of the defense of Mackinac, was waiting for the Americans with 200 soldiers and several hundred Indians hidden in the forest. In the ensuing battle, which took place on August 4, the Americans became lost and confused and were driven off with seventy-five casualties and the loss of two schooners.[16] Two other American ships were left behind to blockade Mackinac but were captured by surprise the following month. This ended America's naval presence on Lake Huron, and Mackinac (like Fort Niagara) remained in British hands until the end of the war.[17]

On Lake Erie, Colonel John B. Campbell loaded 700 American troops into several vessels and on May 15 attacked Port Dover. Since this town was supposed to be inhabited by "revolutionary tories and halfpay officers," some of whom had taken part in the burning of Buffalo the previous winter, Campbell ordered it put to the torch.[18] "A scene of destruction and plunder now ensued," reported a Pennsylvania soldier, "which beggars all description. In a short time the houses, mills, and barns were all consumed."[19] Although a court of inquiry reprimanded Campbell, British officials were not appeased. Later in the year they used Campbell's lawlessness as a pretext for plundering the Chesapeake.[20]

On Lake Ontario, the British took the offensive against Fort Oswego, a crudely built garrison that was an important depot in the pipeline supplying Sackets Harbor. In early May Captain Yeo ferried some 750 men under General Gordon Drummond to the American fort, which was defended by 300 men under Lieutenant Colonel George E. Mitchell. In their first attack on May 5, the British were repulsed, but the following day they they drove Mitchell's men off. The British suffered 125 casualties, the Americans about 70. Drummond made no attempt to hold this fort. Instead, he ordered his men to destroy the post and withdraw with whatever munitions they could carry.[21]

Another engagement took place in this region when an American flotilla under Master Commandant Melancthon Woolsey ferried thirty-four large naval guns from Oswego to Sackets Harbor in order to arm the American ships under construction there. With a powerful British fleet nearby, Woolsey began his voyage on the night of May 29, taking refuge the next day in Sandy Creek about sixteen miles from Sackets Harbor. Here he was protected by 150 riflemen and 200 Oneida Indians, who took cover in the surrounding woods. Convinced that the American flotilla was undefended, Captain Stephen Popham, who had sailed up the river with 200 men, ordered an attack. Popham's force was cut to shreds by the American sharpshooters and their Indian allies. More than seventy British soldiers were killed or wounded, and the rest were captured, while the American force sustained only a few casualties. As a result of this victory, Woolsey got most of the naval guns to Sackets Harbor, thus insuring American parity on Lake Ontario.[22]

❖ ❖ ❖ ❖ ❖ ❖

The heaviest fighting on the northern frontier took place along the Niagara River. The United States took the offensive on July 3 when Jacob Brown led 3,500 men across the river into Canada. Brown's best troops were those trained by Winfield Scott, who regularly drilled his men for seven hours a day. These troops dressed in gray jackets and white trousers because cloth for blue uniforms was unavailable. They fought so well in the campaign that their uniforms—"cadet's gray"—became the standard dress for students at West Point.[23]

The American force invested Fort Erie, compelling the small British garrison there to surrender. From here Brown ordered his army to

Jacob Brown, by an unknown artist. Courtesy of the National
Portrait Gallery, Smithsonian Institution

proceed north in search of the main British force. On July 5, as the Americans approached the Chippewa River, they were harassed by Indians in a nearby forest. Former congressman Peter B. Porter took charge of a band of militia and Iroquois (roused by the aging Seneca chief Red Jacket) and drove the hostile Indians off. But when Porter's troops encountered British regulars, they retreated in disorder.[24]

At this point Scott appeared on the scene with a body of regulars that ultimately numbered about 1,500. Soon he was fully engaged with a British force of about equal size under General Phineas Riall. Despite the hail of artillery fire, Scott's well-disciplined troops maintained their formation and advanced toward the enemy. Riall, who thought the gray uniforms signified militia, was stunned by the tight discipline of the American troops. "Those are regulars, by God," he reportedly exclaimed, thus contributing to an American legend.[25] Scott's men mounted a bayonet charge which broke the British right flank and forced Riall to retreat across the river. In the Battle of Chippewa, the British suffered 500 killed, wounded, and missing, while American losses were only 325. The American victory was a direct result of the long hours Scott had spent drilling his troops.[26]

Brown next moved his entire army across the Chippewa River, hoping to link up with Chauncey for a combined assault on British bases.[27] But Chauncey was ill and, as usual, slow to commit his fleet to action. In addition, he resented Brown's intimation that the navy should carry the army's supplies. In a note to Brown, he said: "[T]he Secretary of the Navy has honoured us with a higher destiny—we are intended to seek and to fight the enemys fleet—This is the great purpose of the Government in creating this Fleet and I shall not be diverted in my efforts to effectuate it, by any sinister attempt to render us either subordinate to or an appendage of the army."[28]

Even without naval support, Brown was determined to seek out the enemy. On July 25 the American army clashed with the British at Lundy's Lane several miles north of the Chippewa River not far from Niagara Falls. Scott—always aggressive—attacked a British force 1,600 to 1,800 strong with only 1,000 men. Both sides were reinforced until by dusk the Americans had 2,100 men in the field and the British about 3,000. The confused and bloody battle dragged on well into the night and almost entirely drowned out the roar of Niagara Falls in the background.

Scott's troops pushed back the British left flank and were then reinforced by a detachment under General Eleazar W. Ripley. At the same time, Colonel James Miller's men overran a powerful battery in the center of the British line. British veterans from the Napoleonic

Wars claimed they had never seen such determined charges as the Americans made. "[T]he Americans charged to the very muzzles of our cannon," said one observer, "and actually bayonetted the artillerymen who were at their guns."[29] The British repeatedly counterattacked to regain this battery but were unsuccessful. Brown finally ordered a retreat, which brought the battle to an end.

Colonel Miller described the five-hour Battle of Lundy's Lane as "one of the most desperately fought actions ever experienced in America," which was no exaggeration.[30] The cost to both sides was high. Brown and Scott were wounded, the latter so seriously that he was knocked out of the war. Both of Britain's senior officers, Riall and Gordon Drummond, were also wounded, and Riall was captured when his aides carried him into a detachment of Americans on the British flank. In all, the United States suffered 850 killed, wounded, or missing. Total British losses were about 875. Even though the United States had withdrawn from the field, the losses were about equal, and the battle was a draw.[31]

On August 3 the British dispatched 600 men under the command of Lieutenant Colonel John Tucker across the Niagara River. Their mission was to destroy the supply depots at Buffalo and Black Rock in the hope of forcing the United States to abandon operations on the Canadian side of the river. At Conjocta Creek the British met some 300 American riflemen under the command of Major Lodowick Morgan. Morgan had destroyed the bridge across the river, and the destructive fire from his troops prevented the British from fording. Complaining that his men "displayed an unpardonable degree of unsteadiness," Tucker gave up the attack and returned to Canada.[32] The casualties on both sides in the Battle of Conjocta Creek were light.[33]

The British next turned their attention to Fort Erie. The American army—about 2,100 strong and now under the command of General Edmund P. Gaines—had retired to this fort and greatly strengthened it. On August 13 the British began to pound the fort with artillery fire. Then at 2:00 A.M. on August 15, in a heavy rainstorm, three columns totaling 2,100 men advanced on the fort with fixed bayonets. Most of the British troops had been ordered to remove their flints to insure surprise. When the attack got under way, the main column stalled, but the other two—led by Colonel Hercules Scott and Lieutenant Colonel William Drummond—penetrated one of the fort's bastions and engaged the American defenders in close combat for nearly two hours.[34]

Gaines and other Americans heard the British officers calling out to "give the Damned Yankee rascals no quarter."[35] The British were finally dislodged when a powder magazine blew up. "The Explosion," reported Gaines, "was tremendous—it was decisive."[36] Both commanding British officers were killed. In all, the British suffered 360 killed or wounded and almost 540 captured or missing. "Our loss has been very severe," reported a British officer, "and I am sorry to add that almost all those returned 'missing' may be considered as wounded or killed by the explosion, and left in the hands of the enemy."[37] Total American losses were only about 130. As the lopsided casualty figures suggest, the Battle of Fort Erie was a great victory for the United States.[38]

Having failed to take Fort Erie by storm, the British mounted three heavy batteries about 500 yards north of the post, hoping to bombard it into submission. Brown, who had resumed command even though he was still recovering from wounds sustained at Lundy's Lane, was advised by his subordinates to evacuate the fort, but he preferred to try to knock out the British guns. His plan was "to storm the batteries, destroy the cannon and roughly handle the brigade upon duty, before those in reserve could be brought into action."[39]

Two assault forces were formed. One consisted of 1,200 men, mainly New York militia, under Peter Porter; the other was a brigade of regulars under James Miller. In a driving rainstorm in the middle of the night on September 17, the American troops surprised the British and after severe fighting overran two of their batteries, spiked the guns, and then retired. The engagement was costly to both sides. The British suffered over 600 casualties, the United States a little over 500.[40]

An American officer later described this sortie as "the most Splendid achievement" of the campaign.[41] General Brown was particularly delighted with the courage and discipline shown by the militia, who so often in the past had been a disappointment. "The Militia of New York," he said, "have redeemed their character. They behaved gallantly."[42] The sortie from Fort Erie was the last in this series of bloody but indecisive engagements on the Niagara front. Fort Erie was evacuated and blown up on November 5.[43] The battles of Chippewa and Lundy's Lane and the two engagements at Fort Erie contributed to the nation's military tradition by demonstrating that American troops could hold their own against British regulars in close combat. But Brown's invasion had nonetheless been blunted, and despite the carnage little of strategic importance had been accomplished.

❖ ❖ ❖ ❖ ❖ ❖

Although the heaviest fighting took place on the Niagara front, the British concentrated most of their troops further east. It was here—

in upper New York—that they launched their only major offensive on the northern frontier. After building up their troop strength in this theater, British officials ordered Sir George Prevost, the governor-general of Canada, to take the offensive. "If you shall allow the present campaign to close without having undertaken offensive measures," said one dispatch, "you will very seriously disappoint the expectations of the Prince Regent and the country."[44] In response to this mandate, Prevost devised a plan to march down the western side of Lake Champlain in order to attack Plattsburgh. He had no intention of holding the town but hoped to occupy some territory in order to give his government a bargaining chip in the peace negotiations.[45]

Having amassed an army of more than 10,000 men, Prevost crossed into the United States on August 31, 1814. To minimize opposition, he issued a proclamation promising to treat civilians kindly and urging them to sell supplies to the British army.[46] Secretary of War Armstrong, who did not expect the British to mount a major attack in this region, had ordered 4,000 troops under General George Izard to leave Plattsburgh for Sackets Harbor.[47] This left the burden of defense on General Alexander Macomb, who had only 3,400 troops at his disposal, many of whom were raw recruits. Although some members of his staff urged Macomb to retreat, he refused. "The eyes of America are on us," he said. "Fortune always favors the brave."[48]

Macomb sent skirmishing parties—consisting mainly of militia—to slow the British march, but these troops were brushed aside. "So undaunted . . . was the Enemy," Macomb reported, "that he never deployed in his whole march always pressing on in Column."[49] Prevost halted his men on September 6 on the north side of the Saranac River. Here he waited for support from the British fleet on Lake Champlain. This gave Macomb time to shore up his defenses and to summon additional militia from New York and Vermont.[50]

The British had won control of Lake Champlain the previous summer when they captured the *Eagle* and *Growler,* but both nations had been building ships, and the two fleets were now about evenly matched.[51] The British squadron was commanded by Captain George Downie and consisted of the *Confiance* (37 guns), *Linnet* (16), *Chub* (11), *Finch* (11), and twelve gunboats mounting a total of 17 guns. The *Confiance,* which had a furnace for hot shot, was the largest ship on the lake—far superior to anything the United States had—but she was not quite ready for action. In fact, the last workmen did not leave her until just before she reached Plattsburgh Bay. Downie was opposed by thirty-year-old Lieutenant Thomas Macdonough, whose fleet consisted of the *Saratoga* (26 guns), *Eagle* (20), *Ticonderoga* (17), *Preble* (7), and ten gunboats carrying a total of 16 guns. Although the British had a decided advantage in long guns, the United States had the edge in short guns or carronades.[52]

Macdonough anchored his fleet near Cumberland Head in Platts-burgh Bay to await Downie's attack. The American ships were positioned in such a way that the British could not use their long guns to good effect. Instead, they would have to move in close, where Macdonough's guns were likely to be more effective. Macdonough also put out the anchors of his larger ships so that if necessary he could wind the vessels around and bring fresh batteries to bear on the enemy. This, as it turned out, gave him a decisive advantage in the battle that ensued.

At 8:00 A.M. on September 11, Downie rounded Cumberland Head and made for Macdonough's fleet. The British ships took heavy fire from Macdonough's long guns as they approached, but Downie brought his ships around in good order. Once in position the *Confiance* delivered a withering broadside to the *Saratoga*, killing or wounding forty of her crew. The sailors on the American ship were momentarily stunned and disheartened, but a rooster, whose coop had been smashed, flew into the ship's shrouds and crowed loudly. The Americans took heart from this omen, let out a cheer, and resumed the battle.[53]

Early in the contest each side lost a ship. H.M.S. *Chub* drifted out of control toward the shore, where she surrendered to American troops. The U.S.S. *Preble* was also disabled and drifted out of the battle. Both commanding officers were hit during the battle. Downie was killed instantly when struck by a carriage knocked loose from a cannon. His watch was flattened by the blow, marking the exact time of his death. Macdonough was twice knocked down and dazed, first by the head of a decapitated midshipman and then by flying debris.[54]

The *Saratoga* was twice set on fire by hot shot from the *Confiance*, and eventually her entire battery was silenced by enemy fire. But Macdonough was able to wind his ship around by using the anchors he had set before the battle. This enabled him to bring a fresh battery into the contest. Lieutenant James Robertson, who had taken command of the *Confiance* after Downie's death, tried to bring his ship around by employing the same maneuver, but without advance preparation his lines became fouled. The *Confiance* took such a terrific pounding from Macdonough's fresh battery—105 shot-holes were later counted in her hull—that members of the crew refused to continue the fight. According to Robertson, "the Ship's Company declared

Thomas Macdonough, by Thomas Gimbrede. Courtesy of the
National Portrait Gallery, Smithsonian Institution

they would stand no longer to their Quarters, nor could the Officers with their utmost exertions rally them."[55]

Two and a half hours into the battle, *Confiance* surrendered. The *Linnet* followed suit. The *Finch,* which had lost control and run aground off Crab Island, also surrendered. Only the gunboats, which had withdrawn in the heat of battle, escaped. Echoing Perry after his great victory on Lake Erie, Macdonough sent a message to the secretary of the navy that read: "The Almighty has been pleased to Grant us a Signal Victory on Lake Champlain in the Capture of one Frigate, one Brig and two sloops of war of the enemy."[56]

Meanwhile, Prevost had ordered his men to attack Macomb's position on land. British troops under the command of General Sir Frederick Robinson crossed the Saranac River and routed the militia on the other side. According to Robinson, his men "dashed down a very steep and high bank, and forded the river like so many foxhounds, driving the Doddles in all directions."[57] Robinson's men paused to wait for reinforcements, but just then Prevost learned of Downie's defeat on the lake. Fearing that his supply lines would be menaced by the American fleet and the militia that were pouring into the region, Prevost ordered a retreat. According to Robinson, the British withdrawal was conducted "in the most precipitate and disgraceful manner."[58] The retreat was so unexpected that the British were eight miles away before Macomb realized what had happened. Casualties in the Battle of Plattsburgh were light, each side losing about 100 men. The British lost an additional 300 men to desertion during the withdrawal. They also abandoned huge quantities of war materiel.[59]

The retreat of such a large force after so little fighting created consternation in both Canada and England. Prevost had already alienated many of his veteran officers by insisting on proper dress, and the retreat served only to increase this antagonism.[60] According to one observer, "The recent disgraceful business of Plattsburg has so completely irritated the feelings of the whole army, that it is in a state almost amounting to mutiny." "All ranks of people," added a British newspaper, "were clamorous against Sir George Prevost."[61] Ultimately Prevost was recalled to England to answer for his failure, but he died before he could present his case.

Macdonough, on the other hand, was showered with praise and rewards. He received a gold medal from Congress, 1,000 acres of land in Cayuga County from New York, and 100 acres on Cumberland Head from Vermont. He was also given valuable keepsakes by other cities and states.[62] "In one month," he said, "from a poor lieutenant I became a rich man."[63]

The battles on Lake Champlain and at Plattsburgh closed out the fighting on the northern frontier in 1814. In spite of growing British strength in Canada, the fighting here continued to be indecisive. Neither side could claim any significant conquests, and control of the lakes was divided. Thus, after three years of campaigning, the war on the Canadian-American frontier was still a stalemate.

❖ ❖ ❖ ❖ ❖ ❖

British operations on the Atlantic Coast were more successful than those on the Canadian frontier because here they could use their fleet to support their troops. The British targeted two areas for amphibious operations in this theater: Maine and the Chesapeake Bay. British officials coveted northern Maine because it jutted into Canada, hampering overland transportation between Quebec and Halifax. The Canadian-American boundary was in dispute here, and by occupying part of Maine the British hoped to rectify the border in their favor. Accordingly, in June of 1814 the British government ordered Sir John Sherbrooke, governor of Nova Scotia, to occupy "that part of the District of Maine which at present intercepts the communication between Halifax and Quebec."[64]

On July 11, Captain Thomas Hardy transported 1,000 men under the command of Lieutenant Colonel Andrew Pilkington from Halifax to Eastport, Maine, located on Moose Island. Although occupied by the United States, Moose Island was claimed by both nations. Eastport was protected by Fort Sullivan, whose garrison of eighty-five men surrendered to the overwhelming British force. On September 1 Admiral Edward Griffith ferried 2,500 men under Sherbrooke to Castine in the Penobscot River. The American defenders were again overmatched. Hence they blew up their fort and fled. The British next sailed up the Penobscot, meeting only token resistance along the way. Captain Charles Morris was forced to burn the U.S.S. *Adams*, a 28-gun corvette that had taken refuge at Hampden. The British occupied the river up to Bangor, where they seized or destroyed a number of merchant vessels. Later they occupied the port town of Machias. This gave them effective control over 100 miles of the Maine coast.[65]

The British seized all public property in eastern Maine and some private property as well. The inhabitants were given a choice of taking an oath to keep the peace or of leaving the area. They were also urged to take an oath of allegiance to the British Crown. Those who took this oath were accorded the same commercial privileges as British subjects. Castine became a British port of entry and a resort town for British military officers on leave. Most of the inhabitants welcomed the region's new status because it meant increased trade with New Brunswick and Nova Scotia.[66] "[I]t is scarcely possible to conceive the joy of the inhabitants," said a Massachusetts newspaper. "At the striking of the flag, some huzza'd, and others, men of influence, observed, *'now we shall get rid of the tax gathers,' 'now the damned democrats will get it.'* "[67]

American officials halted all mail service to the occupied territory and hatched a plan for reconquest. The plan called for sending an army of regulars and militia overland to make an assault on Castine from the rear. The War Department asked Governor Caleb Strong of Massachusetts to call up the necessary militia and to provide part of the funding, but since the state's resources were stretched thin, Strong refused to cooperate. In addition, his advisors told him that it would be almost impossible to succeed without "a naval force that shall command the Bay of Penobscot."[68] The administration finally shelved the plan when it was leaked to the press. Hence eastern Maine (like Mackinac and Fort Niagara) remained in British hands until the war was over.[69]

❖ ❖ ❖ ❖ ❖ ❖

Far more demoralizing to Americans than the occupation of Maine was the invasion of the Chesapeake. In the summer of 1814 the British government ordered General Robert Ross "to effect a diversion on the coasts of the United States of America in favor of the army employed in the defence of Upper and Lower Canada."[70] At the same time, Prevost, who was angry over American depredations in Canada, asked Admiral Alexander Cochrane (who had succeeded John Borlase Warren as the naval commander on the Atlantic station) to "assist in inflicting that measure of retaliation which shall deter the enemy from a repetition of similar outrages."[71]

Both Ross and Cochrane regarded the Chesapeake as the best place to achieve their goals. The bay's extensive shoreline was almost entirely exposed, and the region's two most important cities—Washington and Baltimore—offered inviting targets. A successful attack on the nation's capital would be a great blow to American pride, while an assault on Baltimore would garner considerable prize money and put an end to the use of that city as a base for privateering.[72]

The British had plundered the Chesapeake with impunity in 1813. This prompted the United States to put Captain Joshua Barney, a Revolutionary War hero and accomplished privateer captain, in charge of a flotilla of gunboats and barges in the hope of deterring future raids.[73] Barney's flotilla prevented the British from sending out small foraging parties but was no match for the British fleet and became a target of attack itself. At the appearance of a British squadron in the spring of 1814, Barney was forced to take refuge in the Patuxent River.

The British established a base on Tangier Island and then dispatched a naval force under Captain Robert Barrie to destroy Barney's boats. Twice Barrie engaged Barney in a tributary of the Patuxent but was driven off when Decius Wadsworth, the commissary general of ordnance, mounted an artillery attack from the shore. This enabled Barney to get his boats back into the Patuxent's main branch, though they remained bottled up and later had to be destroyed to prevent them from falling into enemy hands.[74]

These operations were conducted perilously close to the nation's capital, but little was done to prepare Washington for defense. "The shameful neglect of the administration to provide an adequate defence for the capital," said a Federalist newspaper, "is a just cause of loud complaint among all parties."[75] Armstrong was convinced that Washington would never be attacked because it had no strategic significance. "Baltimore is the place," he said; "that [city] is of so much more consequence."[76] Nor did Armstrong believe that fortifications were the best means of protecting cities. "[B]ayonets," he claimed, "are known to form the most efficient barriers."[77] With an eye on economy, Armstrong also believed that militia should be called out only after the target of British operations was known.[78]

Other officials in Washington were slow to perceive the danger, too. Not until July 1 did the president authorize the creation of a special military district embracing the nation's capital. Madison put General William Winder in charge of the new district. Although Winder gave the impression of being knowledgeable about military affairs, the only action he had seen was in the Battle of Beaver Dams the previous year, when he had been captured by the enemy. His only real asset was that he was the nephew of the Federalist governor of Maryland, whose cooperation was deemed essential for the proper defense of the region.[79]

Winder had only 500 regulars at his disposal, and the militia called into service were slow to respond. Winder's inexperience told early, and he seemed overwhelmed by the task before him. He spent much of his time traveling through the countryside inspecting the terrain, while the real work of planning strategy and preparing defense works remained undone. In fact, Winder moved around so much that one of Armstrong's directives—which was characteristically sent by regular mail—followed the district commander around for more than three weeks.[80] The British seemed to sense the confusion in all this. "Jonathan is so confounded," said a naval officer, "that he does not know when or where to look for us, and I do believe that he is at this moment so undecided and unprepared that it would require little force to burn Washington."[81]

By mid-August Cochrane and Ross were in the Chesapeake with twenty warships and several transports filled with veterans from the Peninsular War. Also present was Admiral George Cockburn, who knew the area because he had overseen predatory raids the previous year. After sailing up the Patuxent River, the British landed 4,500 men at Benedict, Maryland, on August 19–20. On the twenty-second the troops reached Upper Marlboro, where they were joined by Cockburn.

Ross ordered a halt at Upper Marlboro to consult with his spies. "Having advanced to within sixteen miles of Washington," he said, "and ascertaining the force of the enemy to be such as might authorise an attempt at carrying his capital, I determined to make it."[82] Leaving 500 marines at Upper Marlboro, Ross marched his troops toward Bladensburg, where he could cross the Eastern Branch of the Potomac and approach Washington from the northeast. Cochrane, who remained with the fleet, evidently got cold feet, for on the twenty-fourth he ordered a retreat, but Cockburn persuaded Ross to continue.

By this time American officials realized the capital's peril and began frantically putting the city in a state of defense. Winder recognized the city's vulnerability from the northeast and ordered most of the bridges there destroyed. There was no attempt, however, to harass the enemy or obstruct his approach even though he was marching through a dense forest. Secretary of State James Monroe volunteered to serve as a cavalry scout—surely the only time a member of the cabinet has served in this capacity. The information he picked up was not vital, though several times he found himself perilously near British units.[83]

Additional militia were called out, but there was scarcely enough time to prepare them for battle. Most of the men were short of sleep and hungry. The militia were joined by some regulars and by about 500 sailors and marines under Barney's command. The American force—perhaps 7,000 troops in all—was arrayed in three lines facing the eastern branch of the Potomac River. The third line was too far away to support the first two, and Monroe (who had no authority in the matter) redeployed the troops so that the second line could not support the first. General Tobias Stansbury, the Maryland militia officer in charge of these troops, realized that the new deployment was potentially disastrous, but believing that Monroe's order had Winder's approval, he made no attempt to countermand it. The president and other civilian officials arrived on the scene just before the battle began and were of the verge of crossing the bridge into the approaching British columns when they were warned off by a volunteer scout. No doubt the 100-degree temperature added to everyone's discomfort.[84]

About 1:00 P.M. on August 24, just as the last militia took their places, the British appeared on the opposite side of the river. What they saw did not impress them. Most of the American troops, said one officer, "seemed [like] country people, who would have been much more appropriately employed in attending to their agricultural occupations, than in standing, with their muskets in their hands." One British officer, fooled by their motley appearance, was not even sure they were Americans. "Are these Yankees?" he asked, "or are they our own seamen got somehow ahead of us?"[85]

The defenders had neglected to destroy the bridge (though the water was shallow enough to ford anyway), and first one British brigade and then another got across the river. The British outflanked the first American line, forcing it to fall back. Among those wounded in the initial assault was the former attorney general, William Pinkney. Just as the British were attacking the second line, Winder—who had radiated confusion and defeatism from the outset—ordered it to fall back. The withdrawal turned into a rout—immortalized in wit and poetry as "the Bladensburg races."[86] The British use of small Congreve rockets, which did little actual damage but terrified even hardened veterans, contributed to the panic.

Only Barney's troops, who anchored the third line, held firm, tearing into the advancing British units with grapeshot from their heavy naval guns. The British routed the militia protecting Barney's flank and then stormed his position. By this time Barney had run out of ammunition anyway. Although he was wounded and captured, most of his men got away. By 4:00 in the afternoon, the British controlled the battlefield. "The rapid flight of the enemy," said Ross, "and his knowledge of the country, precluded the possibility of many prisoners being taken."[87] The United States suffered only 70 casualties in the Battle of Bladensburg, while the British sustained 250. The disparity in these figures suggests that with more disciplined troops the United States might have prevailed.[88]

By the time the battle was over, most people—soldiers, officials, and residents alike—had fled from Washington. Dolley Madison oversaw the removal of cabinet records and White House treasures but had to leave her personal property behind.[89] Most of the other government records were saved, though House clerks were thwarted by the lack of transportation. "Everything belonging to the office," they reported, "might have been removed in time, if carriages could have been procured; but it was altogether impossible to procure them, either for hire, or by force."[90]

The secretary of the treasury, George Campbell, had given the president a pair of dueling pistols, but Madison had no occasion to use them. He left them in the White House, from which they were stolen by local predators. By prearrangement, the president and cabinet were supposed to rendezvous in Frederick, Maryland, but Madison departed with Attorney General Richard Rush for Virginia instead. On the way they were joined by Monroe and were reportedly subjected to various insults for mismanaging the war.[91]

The British marched into Washington about 8:00 P.M. Ross looked in vain for someone to parley with in order to establish the terms of surrender. A group of British officers headed by Cockburn entered the White House. "[W]e found a supper all ready," one recalled, "which many of us speedily consumed . . . and drank some very good wine also."[92] Having satisfied their appetites, the British took some souvenirs and then set fire to the building. According to an American who later viewed the ruins, nothing survived but "unroofed, marked walls, cracked, defaced, blackened with the smoke of fire."[93] The British also burned the Capitol building (which included the Library of Congress), the treasury, and the building housing the war and state departments.[94]

Dr. William Thornton, an English-born Federalist who was the superintendent of patents, saved the patent office by convincing the British that it contained private property—"models of the arts . . . useful to all mankind"—and that to burn it "would be as barbarous as formerly to burn the Alexandrian Library, for which the Turks have been ever since condemned by all enlightened nations."[95] Captain Thomas Tingey, acting on standing orders, set fire to the navy yard, which was the best-stocked naval facility in the country. Tingey also burned two fine new ships that were under construction, the heavy frigate *Columbia* and the sloop *Argus*.[96]

Some British officers took special pleasure in the destruction they wrought. "Cockburn was quite a mountebank," reported the *National Intelligencer*, "exhibiting in the s[t]reets a gross levity of manner, displaying sundry articles of trifling value of which he had robbed the president's house." Although most private buildings were spared, Cockburn personally supervised the destruction of the office of the semi-official *National Intelligencer*, amusing spectators "with much of the peculiar slang of the Common Sewer in relation to the editors."

George Cockburn, by W. Greatbatch. Courtesy of the National
Archives of Canada

The paper's owners took this surprisingly well. When the *Intelligencer* resumed publication, it carried an editorial praising the British for their restraint. "Greater respect was certainly paid to private property than has usually been exhibited by the enemy in his marauding parties. No houses were half as much *plundered* by the enemy as by the knavish wretches about the town who profited of the general distress."[97]

The fires set by the British burned all night. "The sky was brilliantly illuminated by the different conflagrations," reported a British officer.[98] A pair of storms followed the next day, one of which was so violent that it blew down several buildings, killing some British soldiers inside.[99] Others perished when a dry well containing powder exploded. "The effect was terrific," said the *National Intelligencer*. "Every one of [the] soldiers near was blown into eternity, many at a greater distance wounded, and the excavation remains an evidence of the great force of this explosion."[100] The British departed from the city on August 25, re-embarking at Benedict on the thirtieth. They left their wounded behind. Barney, who had been treated kindly by the British, promised to look after them.[101]

Meanwhile, a sizable British naval force under Captain James Gordon had sailed up the Potomac River to support Ross's invasion. The ships did not reach Fort Washington—ten miles below the capital—until August 27, two days after Ross had begun his retreat. The commander of the fort, Captain Samuel T. Dyson, was drunk at the time and ordered the fort abandoned. For this he was later cashiered from the service. The abandonment of Fort Washington exposed Alexandria, an affluent Federalist city six miles upriver.[102]

Although the residents of Alexandria formally capitulated and turned over all public stores, Gordon considered their shipping and mercantile wealth fair game. His squadron sailed off with twenty-one prize ships filled with 16,000 barrels of flour, 1,000 hogsheads of tobacco, 150 bales of cotton, and $5,000 worth of sugar, wine, and other commodities. The withdrawal was harrowing. Batteries were established along the river to harass Gordon, and American troops fired down on his decks from the riverbank. Gordon's larger ships ran aground, forcing him to unload and then reload his heavy naval guns. In spite of all this, he reached the Chesapeake Bay with his squadron and booty intact.[103] British naval officials applauded the feat, one calling it "as brilliant an achievement . . . as grace the annals of our naval history."[104]

Meanwhile, Madison and his cabinet had returned to Washington on August 27. Some people blamed the destruction of the capital on the president, and rumors were afloat that his life was in danger.[105]

Graffiti appeared on the walls of the Capitol that read: "George Washington founded this city after a seven years' war with England—James Madison lost it after a two years' war."[106] Most people in the capital, however, blamed Armstrong, a northerner who many thought had intentionally sacrificed the city. "Universal execration follows Armstrong," said one resident. "The Cittizens sware," said another, that if he returns to the city "they will hang him on the Walls of the Capitol."[107] Local militia refused to take further orders from Armstrong, and after meeting with the president, he retired to Baltimore and subsequently submitted his resignation.[108] Blaming his fall on Monroe, Armstrong said: "I was supposed to be in some body's way [for the presidency] and it became a system to load me with all the faults and misfortunes which occurred."[109] As if to prove him right, Madison named Monroe acting secretary of war for the second time during the conflict.

The burning of Washington was denounced on both sides of the Atlantic. The destruction of the capital, said the *Annual Register,* "brought a heavy censure on the British character, not only in America, but on the continent of Europe."[110] Some members of Parliament joined in the criticism, and so too did opposition newspapers. "The Cossacks spared Paris," said the London *Statesman,* "but we spared not the capitol of America."[111] Most Englishmen, however, rejoiced at the obvious embarrassment of their enemy and considered the destruction of Washington just retaliation for American depredations in Canada. The Prince Regent called the Chesapeake campaign "brilliant and successful," and Ross was officially commended.[112] The park and tower guns in London were fired at noon three days in succession to celebrate the victory, and the *Times* and *Courier* were reportedly "nettled that [British] commanders did not date their despatches from the Capitol."[113]

❖ ❖ ❖ ❖ ❖ ❖

In early September the British decided to follow up on their success at Washington by attacking Baltimore. This city was an attractive target, not only because it was a large commercial center and an important base for privateers but also because it was such a hotbed of anglophobia. "I do not like to contemplate scenes of blood and destruction," said a British naval officer; "but my heart is deeply interested in the coercion of these Baltimore heroes, who are perhaps the most inveterate against us of all the Yankees."[114] Ever since early 1813 Samuel Smith, a United States senator and major general in the militia, had been working with other volunteers to prepare the city for defense. By the middle of 1814, Smith had gathered 10,000 to 15,000 troops (mostly militia) and had every available man building earth-works.[115]

Ross landed his army—about 4,500 men—at North Point at 3:00 A.M. on September 12. Five hours later the troops began their march to Baltimore fourteen miles away. About half way to the city they met a force of 3,200 militia under the command of General John Stricker. The British softened the American lines with artillery and then launched a frontal assault that forced the Americans to retreat. The Americans lost 215 men, the British 340.[116] Although the Battle of North Point was a British victory, it was a costly one, for Ross was killed by a sharpshooter. "It is impossible to conceive the effect which this melancholy spectacle produced throughout the army," recalled a British officer.[117] Ross's body was shipped to England in a cask of rum for burial, and thereafter the British gave no quarter to snipers.

Colonel Arthur Brooke assumed command after Ross's death and resumed the march to Baltimore. On September 13 the British came within sight of the city's defenses. Unable to secure any naval support or to lure the Americans out from behind their defensive works, Brooke decided not to attack. The British departed at 3:00 A.M. the next morning.[118] The Americans were delighted to see the British leave and made only a nominal attempt to pursue them. "[W]hen you fight our citizens against British regulars," said Smith, "you are staking dollars against cents."[119]

Meanwhile, Cochrane had brought up his bomb and rocket ships to attack Fort McHenry, which was defended by 1,000 men under the command of Major George Armistead. Cochrane's hope was to silence the guns of the fort so that he could bring his lighter ships into Baltimore Harbor to bombard the American lines. The British fired more than 1,500 rounds at the fort over a twenty-five-hour period on September 13 and 14. About 400 of these rounds found their mark. The Americans could not respond because their guns were not as powerful as the British mortars, which were capable of firing 200-pound shells over 4,000 yards. The damage to the fort, however, was minimal. Only four Americans were killed and twenty-four wounded. The British also failed to silence the guns on nearby Lazaretto Point. Cochrane put 1,200 men in barges to slip down the Patapsco, evidently to attack the city from the southwest, but these troops were driven back by heavy fire from the shore.[120]

Francis Scott Key, a Georgetown Federalist who had come to Balti-more with a volunteer artillery company, had boarded a British ship to secure the release of a prisoner. Although he achieved his mission, the British kept him on board until after the attack on Fort McHenry was over. Key paced the ship all night, witnessing the bombardment. On the morning of the fourteenth, after seeing the fort's huge flag still flying, he was inspired to write "The Star-Spangled Banner," which he put to an eighteenth-century British drinking song, "To Anacreon in Heaven." ("The bombs bursting in air" were the British mortar shells that exploded above the fort; "the rockets' red glare" refers to Congreve rockets.) Key's song became an instant hit, but not until 1931 did Congress make it the national anthem.[121]

The Battle of Baltimore ended the Chesapeake campaign. Local reports indicated that during the campaign British troops had looted private property, destroyed church property, and even opened coffins in their search for booty. "[T]heir conduct," said Congressman Robert Wright, "would have disgraced cannibals."[122] The entire campaign served to enhance the legacy of bitterness left from the previous summer. *Niles' Register* called Cockburn a "*Great Bandit*" and proposed that Ross's death be commemorated with a monument dedicated to "THE LEADER OF A HOST OF BARBARIANS, who destroyed the capitol . . . and devoted . . . Baltimore, to rape, robbery and conflagration."[123]

The British were also accused of fomenting a slave rebellion. Although this was untrue, Cochrane did issue a proclamation that promised all interested Americans a "choice of either entering into His Majesty's Sea or Land Forces, or of being sent as FREE Settlers, to the British Possessions in North America or the West Indies."[124] Some 300 runaway slaves took advantage of this offer and entered British service. According to Cochrane, they showed "extraordinary steadiness and good conduct when in action with the Enemy."[125] When the British departed, they carried off more than 2,000 runaways, most of whom settled in the maritime provinces.[126]

❖ ❖ ❖ ❖ ❖ ❖

Although the British did not realize it at the time, the Chesapeake campaign was the high water mark of their counteroffensive in 1814. Their next campaign—against the Gulf Coast—ended in disaster.[127] This region attracted the British because it was sparsely populated and lightly defended. There were many potential allies here, including Indians, particularly the Seminoles and Creeks, and black people, both slave and free. In addition, there were Spanish and French people living in West Florida and Louisiana who had never become reconciled to American rule. Finally, there were the Baratarian pirates—a lawless band of thieves and smugglers, perhaps 1,000 strong—who lived on Grand Terre Island in southern Louisiana.[128]

New Orleans, located a hundred miles up the Mississippi River, was a particularly tempting target. With a population of almost 25,000, it was the largest city west of the Appalachian Mountains. It was also the principal outlet for western commodities, and millions of dollars in produce was blockaded in the port. Scottish naval officers like Cochrane were known to have a keen eye for booty, and the British brought cargo ships with them to carry off their plunder.[129] Indeed, British prisoners of war and deserters claimed that the watch-word and countersign on the morning of the Battle of New Orleans was "beauty and booty."[130]

Initially British officials saw this campaign as a means of taking pressure off Canada. But by the time the operation got under way, the objective had changed. General Ross—who was supposed to lead the expedition—was instructed "to obtain command of the embouchure [mouth] of the Mississippi, so as to deprive the back settlements of America of their communication with the sea" and "to occupy some important and valuable possession, by the restoration of which the conditions of peace might be improved, or which we might be entitled to exact the cession of, as the price of peace." Ross was to encourage the free inhabitants to revolt but was to make no binding promises about the future. "[Y]ou must give them clearly to understand that Great Britain cannot pledge herself to make the independence of Louisiana, or its restoration to the Spanish Crown, a *sine qua non* of peace with the United States."[131]

As a preliminary to the main expedition, in May of 1814 Cochrane dispatched a shipload of arms to Indians on the Apalachicola River in Spanish Florida. George Woodbine, an Indian trader, was given a brevet commission as captain of the marines and appointed agent to the Indians. He distributed the arms and trained the Indians in the use of the bayonet.[132]

The next step for the British was the occupation of Pensacola, a Spanish port city that had the best harbor on the Gulf Coast and enjoyed excellent access to the interior. With the blessing of Spanish officials, Major Edward Nicolls led 100 British troops into the city on August 14. He subsequently expanded his occupation force by recruiting Indians and (much to the dismay of the Spanish) local slaves.[133] On August 29, Nicolls issued a proclamation calling on the "Natives of Louisiana . . . to assist in liberating from a faithless and imbecile government, your paternal soil."[134]

The following month Nicolls led an expedition to Mobile, a port city in West Florida that the United States had seized from Spain in 1813. This city was protected from seaborne attack by Fort Bowyer, which was located on a peninsula in Mobile Bay and defended by 160 regulars under the command of Major William Lawrence. On September 12 a British force of 225 marines and Indians was put on shore, and three days later a naval squadron under Captain William H. Percy bombarded the fort. The British land force, however, was too small to take the post, and the waters of Mobile Bay were too shallow for the British ships. Hence the attack was abandoned. The British lost their flagship, the *Hermes* (22 guns), which ran aground within range of American guns and had to be destroyed. The British also sustained about seventy casualties compared to only about ten for the United States.[135]

Andrew Jackson, who had assumed command of the Gulf Coast region in May of 1814, was convinced that Pensacola was the key to British operations in the region. "Pensacola," he said, "is more important to the British arms than any other point on our South or Southwest."[136] Officials in Washington, however, feared that any military action against this city might lead to war with Spain. Hence in late October the secretary of war ordered Jackson not to invade Florida. This directive, however, arrived too late to affect Jackson's plans.[137]

On November 7, 1814, Jackson attacked Pensacola with a force of 4,100 regulars, militia, and Indians. The Spanish governor, who had perhaps 500 troops at his disposal, could not decide whether to surrender or defend the city, and Jackson marched in almost unopposed. Disgusted, the British blew up the forts on Pensacola Bay and retired to the Apalachicola River.[138] With its forts destroyed, Pensacola was neutralized, and Jackson abandoned the city and marched to Mobile. Almost belatedly—since he fully expected the British to attack Mobile first—he raced to New Orleans, arriving in the Crescent City on December 1.[139]

Jackson found that little had been done to prepare New Orleans against attack. Before being transferred north in 1813, Wilkinson had squandered the public funds under his control, and people throughout Louisiana radiated disloyalty and defeatism.[140] "The War of the U.S. is very unpopular with us," John Windship, a transplanted New Englander, reported in early 1814. French and Spanish residents, who constituted a large majority of the population, were called up for militia duty in New Orleans but "absolutely refused to be marched" and "declared themselves liege subjects of Spain or France." If the British should attack, Windship concluded, "there is no force competent to repell them."[141] There was also a growing scarcity of cash in New Orleans, and local banks refused to advance the government money. "*[F]ew, very few*," lamented an American army officer, "are disposed to aid the General Government in the present crisis."[142]

Jackson's arrival had a dramatic effect on the people. "General Jackson," wrote one contemporary, "electrified all hearts." "His immediate and incessant attention to the defence of the country," said another, "soon convinced all that he was the man the occasion demanded."[143] After making a detailed study of the area, Jackson ordered all the water approaches from the gulf blocked and batteries established at strategic points. He also established an excellent intelligence system to keep abreast of enemy movements.[144] In addition, he issued a proclamation calling on everyone to assist in the defense of the city. "Those who are not for us," he said, "are against us, and will be dealt with accordingly."[145] Jackson's energetic actions dissipated the defeatism that had prevailed in the city. According to one witness, "The streets resounded with *Yankee Doodle, the Marseilles Hymn, the Chant du dePart,* and other martial airs."[146]

Governor William Claiborne called out all the militia in the area, and troops began to pour in from miles around. John Coffee force-marched 850 Tennessee riflemen from Baton Rouge, covering 135 miles in three days. Jackson already had appealed to free black men to enlist in the regular army, and he now accepted the services of a special corps of black troops, mostly refugees from Santo Domingo, raised by Colonel Jean Baptiste Savary. Speaking on behalf of the white citizens, Governor Claiborne lodged a protest, but Jackson brushed his objections aside.[147]

The Baratarian pirates also offered their services. Even though an American naval force had destroyed their base on Grand Terre Island in September, the Baratarians rejected British overtures to side with them.[148] Instead, they pleaded with American officials to accept their services. According to one observer, "this transition from piracy to Patriotism" was due to the influence of Edward Livingston. The pirates had promised Livingston $20,000 if he could secure their acquittal on charges of violating the trade laws, and he advised them to enlist under the American banner.[149]

Although Jackson had once described the pirates as "hellish Banditti," he could use more men and desperately needed the artillery and ammunition the pirates had.[150] Hence he reluctantly accepted their offer. The Baratarians not only augmented Jackson's force but proved to be excellent artillerymen. Their knowledge of the local terrain was also invaluable. Jean Laffite (or Lafitte), the Baratarian leader, got along so well with Jackson that he became the general's unofficial aide-de-camp. Such was the Baratarians' contribution (and such was their influence in the state) that after the war the Louisiana legislature asked Madison to pardon them, which he did. Although

Laffite later resumed his privateering career and served as a spy for the Spanish, the park commemorating the Battle of New Orleans is now called Jean Lafitte National Historical Park.[151]

Meanwhile, the British had been assembling a large army—about 10,000 strong—in Jamaica for their Gulf Coast campaign.[152] After Ross's death, the command was assigned to General Edward Pakenham, the Duke of Wellington's brother-in-law. Pakenham was an able and experienced officer. According to one subordinate, he was "a hero, a soldier, a man of ability in every sense of the word."[153] At the end of November most of the British troops were put on board transports in a large convoy—commanded by Cochrane—and shipped to the Gulf Coast.[154]

On December 5 the convoy arrived off the coast of Florida. British officials, hoping to use the Indians in a diversion, issued a proclamation promising to help them recover lands "of which the People of Bad Spirit have basely robbed them."[155] The Indians who responded, however, were unimpressive. Hence the British, who hardly needed Indian assistance anyway, decided to proceed without them. Although the British initially had planned an overland campaign against New Orleans from Mobile, they now decided to attack from the sea instead. Accordingly, the convoy weighed anchor and sailed west, reaching Cat Island—about 80 miles from New Orleans—on December 13.[156] From here the British could attack either from the east via Lake Borgne, from the north via Lake Pontchartrain, or from the northeast via the land mass between the lakes, which was known as the Plain of Gentilly.

Because they lacked the necessary small boats to operate further north, the British decided to attack through Lake Borgne.[157] As they moved toward the lake, they found their way blocked by Lieutenant Thomas Ap Catesby Jones, who had five gunboats and 185 men. Jones had been sent to keep an eye out for the British, not to do battle with them. But he lost his wind, and since his boats were not equipped with oars, he had little choice but to prepare for battle. To destroy the American force, the British sent an assault force of forty-five boats and 1,200 men under the command of Captain Nicholas Lockyer. In the engagement that followed on December 14, the British prevailed but suffered about 100 casualties. Jones lost about forty killed and wounded. The rest of his men were captured. Although the United States could ill afford to lose Jones's boats, the battle delayed the British advance to New Orleans, allowing additional time for defensive preparations.[158]

Having disposed of Jones's force, the British established a base on Pea Island. The weather was cold and windy, and although primitive shanties were erected for the officers, everyone suffered. The morning of December 19, said Admiral Edward Codrington, "produced a N.-W. gale, as bitter cold as we could have felt in England; and the nights of the 19th and 20th were so severe as to produce ice an inch thick in [water] tubs." The bad weather continued for another a week. "Neither day nor night," Codrington complained, "can we contrive to make ourselves comfortably warm."[159]

After hiring some Spanish and Portuguese fishermen as guides, the British advanced across Lake Borgne to Bayou Bienvenu and thence to Bayou Mazant. From here they took a canal to Jacques Villeré's plantation, which was located on the Mississippi River eight miles below New Orleans. On December 23 a British advance party of 1,600 men, commanded by Colonel William Thornton, occupied Villeré's house, which served as the British headquarters for the rest of the campaign. Thornton's men captured thirty militia in the process, but Villeré's son escaped to warn Jackson of the British approach.[160]

Jackson was determined to meet the British well beyond New Orleans and to fight them before they were at full strength. Hence as soon as he learned of Thornton's arrival at Villeré's, he rounded up 1,800 men and marched them to within a mile of the British position. Jackson's men were supported by two ships, the *Carolina* (14 guns) and the *Louisiana* (22 guns). At 7:30 at night on December 23, the *Carolina* opened fire on the British camp.[161] The attack caught the invaders by surprise. A British officer described the scene: "flash, flash, flash, came from the river; the roar of cannon followed, and the light of her own broadside displayed to us an enemy's vessel at anchor near the opposite bank, and pouring a perfect shower of grape and round shot, into the camp."[162]

Shortly thereafter Jackson ordered his army to attack. The British troops, who were now under the command of General John Keane, were unaware of Jackson's presence and were again caught by surprise. Much close fighting ensued, resulting in a large number of bayonet wounds. The lines were not clearly drawn, and in the darkness, smoke, and fog there was considerable confusion on both sides. Friendly troops fired on each other or blundered into enemy lines. By the time the battle ended, the British had suffered 275 casualties, the Americans 215.[163]

British reinforcements began to arrive the following day, and the day after that (Christmas Day) Pakenham himself arrived with additional troops, bringing total British strength to more than 4,000 men. Unaware that his army was much larger than Jackson's, Pakenham failed to press his advantage. This enabled Jackson to pull back unmolested and establish a new line behind a canal about two miles from the British. In the days that followed, the Americans constructed earthworks along the edge of the canal between a cypress swamp on the east and the Mississippi River on the west.[164] At the same time, the American ships in the river continued to bombard British positions, while Tennessee and Choctaw sharpshooters harassed British pickets. The British found the sniper fire particularly infuriating. "[T]o us," said an officer, "it appeared an ungenerous return to barbarity."[165]

Pakenham was none too sanguine about his chances of getting to New Orleans but decided to proceed with the campaign. To protect his flank, he had to knock the American ships out of action. Accordingly, he ordered a furnace for hot shot built and then on December 27 launched a massive artillery attack against the vessels. Contrary winds made it difficult for the ships to pull back, and the *Carolina* caught fire and blew up. The *Louisiana* was saved only because her crew ran tow lines to the opposite shore and pulled her out of range.[166]

The next day—December 28—Pakenham ordered his troops to advance in two columns toward the American lines, which were now defended by about 4,000 men. The British suffered such intense fire, not only from the American troops but also from the *Louisiana* (which fired 800 rounds), that Pakenham gave up the attack and ordered a withdrawal. In this engagement, the losses on both sides were light: perhaps thirty-five for the United States and fifty-five for the British.[167]

Jackson again used the respite to good advantage to strengthen his position. He extended his defensive works further into the swamp, so that his line was now a mile long. He also established additional artillery batteries in his line, bringing the total to eight. As a hedge against disaster, he built two additional lines closer to the city in case his men had to fall back. In addition, he ordered the construction of a defensive line on the western side of the river to be anchored by naval guns from the *Louisiana*.[168]

On December 31 Pakenham established four new batteries of heavy guns that had been laboriously brought up from the fleet. The batteries were placed behind casks of sugar, which the British mistakenly believed would offer as much protection as sand. The following day—January 1, 1815—the British began bombarding Jackson's main line. The heavy British artillery was supposed to destroy the American earthworks but most of the rounds overshot their mark. Although caught unprepared, the Americans recovered quickly and responded with cannon fire of their own. Their shot easily penetrated the sugar casks, dismounting the British guns and killing the gunners. "Our fire slackened every moment," said a British officer; "that of the Americans became every moment more terrible, till at length, after not more than two hours and a half of firing, our batteries were all silenced."[169] In this artillery duel, the British suffered about seventy-five casualties, the Americans about thirty-five.[170]

Pakenham now waited for reinforcements that were en route to his camp. Each soldier brought a cannon ball in his knapsack to replenish the supply in the front lines. When a boatload of these troops overturned on Lake Borgne, the extra weight carried many of the soldiers to the bottom.[171] Those troops who made it safely to Pakenham's camp raised his total strength to about 6,000 men. Meanwhile, Cochrane had taken advantage of the lull in the fighting to dam Villeré Canal. He hoped to bring boats through the canal in order to ferry 1,500 troops across the Mississippi River. The number of boats actually brought forward, however, made it possible to move only 600 troops to the opposite shore.[172]

The British battle plan called for Colonel William Thornton to lead the 600 troops across the river and launch a night attack against the American position there, which was defended by about 700 ill-trained Louisiana and Kentucky militia under the command of General David Morgan. Thornton was to seize the American guns and turn them on Jackson's main line across the river. Then at dawn Pakenham's principal force, about 5,300 strong, was to advance in three columns across Chalmette's plantation to Jackson's main line, which was now defended by 4,700 men.[173]

Thornton fell behind schedule and did not launch his attack until nearly daylight on January 8. His troops completely routed the militia and gained possession of the American guns, one of which was a brass howitzer that carried the inscription "taken at the surrender of York town 1781." Thornton's troops, however, had no chance to follow up on this victory. The British attack on the other side of the river had stalled, and Thornton was ordered to withdraw.[174]

The main British force attacked about an hour and a half after Thornton. A fog covered the advance for a time, but it lifted suddenly, leaving the British troops completely exposed to American fire. When the British got within 500 yards, the Americans began firing their cannons. When they were within 300 yards, American riflemen opened up; and when they got within 100 yards, those with muskets opened fire. "The atmosphere," said one American, "was filled with sheets of fire, and volumes of smoke."[175] The effect of this fire— particularly the grape and canister from the American artillery—was utterly devastating. According to a British veteran of the Napoleonic Wars, it was "the most murderous [fire] I ever beheld before or since."[176]

All along the battle line the British were mowed down before they could get near the American earthworks. Only a small column advancing along the river got to the American line, but these troops suffered such a withering fire that they had to fall back. The fire was so intense that many hardened British veterans turned and fled. Others hit the ground and remained there until the battle was over. Pakenham did his best to rally his men, but as he rode across the battlefield he made a conspicuous target. One horse was shot out from under him, and shortly after commandeering another, he was "cut asunder by a cannon ball."[177]

General John Lambert, who took command after Pakenham fell, broke off the engagement. It had lasted only a half hour on the eastern side of the river, and yet the toll was terrific. One eyewitness said the field was a terrible sight to behold, "with dead and wounded laying in heaps"—all dressed in scarlet British uniforms.[178] Those who had thrown themselves to the ground in the heat of battle got up when the fighting ended. A few fled but most surrendered. One officer who was far from American lines reportedly surrendered because "*these d—d Yankee riflemen can pick a squirrel's eye out as far as they can see it.*"[179]

Lambert asked for an armistice to remove the wounded and bury the dead, which Jackson accepted. The British hastily interred their dead in common graves. "[T]he bodies [were] hurled in as fast as we could bring them," recalled an officer.[180] Pakenham's body was shipped to England for burial. "Our lamented General's remains," said a fellow officer, "were put in a cask of spirits and taken home by his Military Secretary." [181] Although Cochrane urged Lambert to renew the attack, the British general refused, convinced that this would only lead to more slaughter. The battle was therefore over.[182]

The battle on January 8, 1815—which was *the* Battle of New Orleans—was the most lopsided engagement of the war. The British lost over 2,000 men (including close to 500 captured). The United States, by contrast, lost only about 70 men, and only 13 on Jackson's side of the river.[183] "[T]he vast disparity of loss," said the *National Intelligencer,* "would stagger credulity itself, were it not confirmed by a whole army of witnesses."[184] During the major engagements in the New Orleans campaign—from December 23 to January 8—the British lost 400 killed, 1,500 wounded, and 550 missing or captured—a total of 2,450 men. The United States, by contrast, suffered only 50 killed, 200 wounded, and 100 missing or captured, for a total loss of 350 men.[185]

The British held their positions for another ten days, and additional skirmishing occasionally took place. Cochrane also brought his fleet into action by sending a squadron of ships up the Mississippi to bombard Fort St. Philip, which was located sixty-five miles downriver from New Orleans. The British reportedly spent seventy tons of shells and 20,000 pounds of powder in the assault but failed to batter the fort into submission.[186] This was the last battle in the series of engagements around New Orleans. When the British withdrew from the area, they carried off some runaway slaves but left behind eighty seriously wounded soldiers and a large quantity of war materiel.[187]

Jackson realized that the British attack was over but was reluctant to loosen his grip on the city.[188] This exasperated local residents. In late December Jackson had heard that the Louisiana legislature was considering capitulation. Although skeptical of the report, he asked Governor Claiborne to investigate and if the report proved true "to blow up the legislature."[189] Claiborne responded by dispatching armed men to close down the legislature. Although the legislators reconvened several days later, they were much perturbed with Jackson. When they later voted their thanks to those who had saved the city, Jackson's name was conspicuously absent from the list.[190]

Jackson had proclaimed martial law in New Orleans on December 16, mainly to prevent spies from moving freely into and out of the city.[191] Although reports of peace arrived as early as February 19, 1815, he refused to lift martial law until official news came on March 13.[192] In the meantime, he continued his dictatorial rule in the city. When a member of the legislature wrote a newspaper article complaining, Jackson had him jailed, and when the federal district court judge, Dominick A. Hall, ordered the victim released, Jackson had the judge jailed. When the war ended, Hall fined Jackson $1,000 for contempt of court.[193] "[T]he only question," said the judge, "was whether the Law should bend to the General or the General to the Law."[194] (In 1844 Congress refunded Jackson's fine with interest—$2,732 in all.)[195]

Jackson also dealt severely with 200 Tennessee militia who had allegedly deserted in September of 1814. Although ordered out for six months' of duty, the men were convinced that they could be required to serve only three months and hence had gone home. Jackson ordered the men seized and tried by military tribunal in Mobile in December of 1814. The court found them guilty. Most were sentenced to forfeit part of their pay and make up lost time and then were drummed out of camp with their heads partly shaved. The six ringleaders—a sergeant and five privates—did not get off so easily. Convicted of desertion and mutiny, they were executed by a firing squad on February 21, 1815. Although the Battle of New Orleans catapulted Jackson into the limelight, his enemies never let the public forget his severe brand of military justice.[196]

The fighting was not quite over on the Gulf Coast, for having failed at New Orleans, the British turned again to Mobile as a consolation prize. In early February, Fort Bowyer was surrounded on three sides by warships, and 5,000 men under General Lambert were put on shore. The British landed cannons, which were placed within 100 yards of the fort. On February 11, after some light skirmishing, Major William Lawrence, who had only 375 men with which to defend the fort, surrendered. This closed out the campaign, since news of peace arrived before the British could take Mobile itself.[197]

The United States made a good showing in the fighting on land in the campaign of 1814. On the northern frontier, American troops had defeated the British at Chippewa, fought them to a draw at Lundy's Lane, and beat them twice at Fort Erie. American forces also had compelled the British to retreat from Plattsburgh—a result of Macdonough's great victory on Lake Champlain. On the Atlantic Coast the British had occupied eastern Maine and burned the nation's capital but had been repulsed at Baltimore. Moreover, they had suffered one of the greatest military disasters in British history when they attacked New Orleans. The American victories were largely a tribute to good leaders—Scott, Brown, Macomb, and Macdonough in the North; Smith at Baltimore; and Jackson at New Orleans. After two years of campaigning, Madison finally had found competent generals to fight his war.

❖ ❖ ❖ ❖ ❖ ❖

The war at sea continued to favor the British in 1814. The most effective use of British sea power was still their blockade. The Royal Navy had blockaded the middle and southern states in 1812–1813, and in April of 1814 the blockade was extended to New England. The British decided to close New England's ports to put an end to neutral trade and to prevent warships there from getting to sea.[198] President Madison responded with a proclamation denouncing the entire blockade as illegal. Even the British, he said, did not have a fleet large enough to enforce a blockade extending all the way from Maine to Georgia. The administration hoped that European neutrals anxious to trade with the United States would oppose the blockade, but after the fall of Napoleon no one cared to challenge the Mistress of the Seas on her own element.[199]

The extension of the British blockade further curtailed American trade and reduced government revenue. American exports, which had reached $61,300,000 in 1811, steadily plunged during the war to a low of $6,900,000 in 1814. There was a similar decline in imports, from $53,400,000 in 1811 to $13,000,000 in 1814. Even though the customs duties had been doubled at the beginning of the war, revenue from this source fell from $13,300,000 in 1811 to $6,000,000 in 1814.[200]

The economic bottlenecks that had appeared in 1813 worsened in 1814 as the gluts and shortages in every market increased. Merchants and fishermen could not send their ships to sea, and farmers could not ship their produce to foreign markets. The shipping industry was particularly hard hit. The tonnage of American ships engaged in foreign trade dropped from 948,000 in 1811 to 60,000 in 1814.[201] Although some of these losses were offset by new economic activities—such as privateering and manufacturing—the overall effect of the war on the American economy was decidedly negative.[202]

Great Britain's naval presence was felt in other ways. The number of predatory raids increased in 1814, particularly along the lengthy and exposed New England coast, which heretofore had been untouched. "The eastern coast of the United States is much vexed by the enemy," reported *Niles' Register* in July.[203] Although the larger cities enjoyed a measure of protection from coastal fortifications, the smaller ones were more vulnerable. The British, said *Niles*, "seem determined to enter the little out ports and villages, and burn every thing that floats."[204] In one such raid, a British squadron sailed up the Connecticut River and destroyed twenty-seven vessels valued at $140,000.[205] Militia were repeatedly called out to guard against raids like this, and life in many cities—large and small alike—was thoroughly disrupted.[206]

The Royal Navy also cut off the nation's coastal islands from the mainland. Although Nantucket was dominated by Republicans, by August of 1814 the threat of starvation was so acute that the island had to declare its neutrality. In exchange for surrendering its public stores, supplying British warships, and discontinuing the payment of federal taxes, Nantucket won the right to import provisions and fuel from the mainland and to fish in nearby waters. As a bonus, Admiral Cochrane worked for the release all Nantucketeers who were being held as prisoners of war, though the conflict ended before he could achieve this end.[207]

Other exposed towns also came to terms with the British. On Cape Cod many paid tribute to avoid bombardment and plundering.[208] On Block Island (which was part of Rhode Island) people were "in the daily habit of carrying intelligence and succour to the enemy's squadron," which prompted American officials to cut off all trade with the island.[209] British officers were shocked by the eagerness with which Americans pursued their own interest at the expense of the nation's. "Self, the great ruling principle," said one, "[is] more powerful with Yankees than any people I ever saw."[210]

❖ ❖ ❖ ❖ ❖ ❖ ❖

Most American warships were bottled up in port in 1814, and the navy actually suffered its greatest losses to British troops operating inland. The occupation of Washington forced the destruction of the *Columbia* (rated at 44 guns) and the *Argus* (rated at 22), and the seizure of eastern Maine led to the burning of the *Adams* (28 guns). Ships in the North had the best chance of getting to sea because westerly winds sometimes blew blockading vessels off their assigned stations. Finding enough experienced seamen for a crew, however, was not always easy because of competition from privateers and the army.[211]

The nation's greatest loss at sea in this campaign was the *President*, a heavy frigate mounting fifty-two guns. This vessel had such a fine reputation that in 1812 Captain William Bainbridge, who commanded the *Constitution*, had offered John Rogers $5,000 to trade ships.[212] Rogers had refused, which enabled Bainbridge to make his reputation in the *Constitution*. By 1815 Captain Stephen Decatur commanded the *President*. Taking advantage of a severe snowstorm, he sailed out of New York harbor. Though considered a good sailer, the ship ran aground on a sand bar and got so twisted around before breaking free that she lost much of her speed.[213]

The *President* was subsequently chased by a squadron of British ships that included three light frigates, the *Endymion* (40), *Pomone* (38), and *Tenedos* (38). In an engagement that took place on January 15, Decatur managed to disable the *Endymion*, but he lost a fifth of his crew and his ship was crippled. Hence he surrendered to the other frigates.[214] The *President* was later condemned by the British and sold at public auction in Bermuda for $65,000.[215]

The *Constitution* (52), on the other hand, continued her run of good luck. Commanded now by Captain Charles Stewart, she slipped out of Boston harbor in December of 1814. On February 20, 1815, 200 miles from Madeira, she met two British ships, the *Cyane* (34), Captain Gordon Falcon, and the *Levant* (20), Captain George Douglass. The British commanders were so confident of their seamanship that instead of fleeing they engaged the *Constitution*. The American ship was superbly handled by Stewart and his men, and their gunnery was equally sharp. The *Constitution* was able to rake both her antagonists without being raked herself, and as a result both British ships were forced to surrender. The *Constitution* had to abandon her prizes when chased by a British squadron, but "Old Ironsides" made it back to port with her reputation much enhanced.[216]

The United States constructed six new sloops during the war. Like the heavy frigates, they were designed to outsail any ship they could not outfight. Although finding guns and crews for these vessels was difficult, three of them—the *Hornet* (20), *Peacock* (22), and *Wasp* (22)—made successful cruises in 1814. These vessels captured a number of British ships, including the *Penguin* (19), *Reindeer* (19), *Avon* (18), and *Epervier* (18), the last of which was carrying $128,000 in specie. The British, in turn, captured the *Frolic* (22), *Syren* (16), and *Rattlesnake* (16). The *Wasp* was lost at sea when she went down with all hands for unknown reasons.[217]

In 1814 the United States launched two ships-of-the-line, the *Independence* in June and the *Washington* in October. Apart from a small battleship given to France during the Revolution, these were the first such vessels constructed in America. Both were poorly designed and neither was ready for sea before the end of the war. Robert Fulton launched the world's first steam frigate, *Fulton the First*, in October of 1814. This vessel was built for the protection of New York harbor, but the war ended before she could be given a fair test. Fulton and others also did pioneering work in the development of submarines and mines (which contemporaries called "torpedoes"). Several attempts were made to use crude submarines to attach mines to blockading British ships but without success.[218]

❖ ❖ ❖ ❖ ❖ ❖

American warships and privateers continued to harass British commerce in the last year of the war. According to the *Naval Chronicle*, "The depredations committed on our commerce by American ships of war, and privateers, has attained an extent beyond all former precedent." "On the ocean, and even on our own coasts," said the *Morning Chronicle*, "we have been insulted with impunity."[219] Although warships usually burned their prizes to prevent them from being retaken, privateers generally put a prize crew on board to try to get the vessel back to port.

The Atlantic swarmed with so many American privateers and British warships in 1814 that some English merchantmen were captured and recaptured several times. Insurance rates for British ships sailing from Liverpool to Halifax jumped to 30 percent, and underwriters publicly complained about their losses.[220] "Each daily book at L[l]oyd's," said one, "presents a *tremendous* list for our contemplation."[221]

The favorite haunt of American privateers in 1814 was the British Isles. British merchantmen trading in these waters were not required to sail in convoy and thus made easy targets for privateers, which "in summer weather and light breezes eluded all attempts of the king's ships to catch them."[222] American privateers were particularly active in the Irish Sea, and insurance rates for ships trading between England and Ireland rose to an unprecedented 13 percent.[223] According to the *Naval Chronicle,* this rate was *"three times higher* than it was when we were at war with all Europe!"[224]

People living in Greenock, an unfortified city on the coast of Scotland, reportedly gave up their trade with the Continent and "live[d] in constant apprehension of a visit from an American national ship or privateer."[225] Merchants in Bristol complained that American depredations had "increased to a most alarming extent," forcing them to suspend much of their trade.[226] In Glasgow, merchants bitterly protested the lack of protection, calling the situation "discreditable to the directors of the naval power of the British nation."[227] There were similar complaints from London and Liverpool.[228] "[I]n the chops of the Channel . . . in our own seas," said a member of Parliament, "the American privateers had come and carried off our vessels."[229]

In the interest of economy, the British government had demobilized part of its fleet after Napoleon's defeat, including some of the smaller vessels that had the best chance of catching privateers.[230] Much to the chagrin of protesting British merchants, the Admiralty still claimed that "there was a force adequate to the purpose of protecting the trade, both in St. George's Channel and the Northern Sea."[231] The Admiralty also criticized British merchants for not sailing in convoy, though, as the *Times* pointed out, even convoys were sometimes unsafe. "The American cruisers," the paper said, "daily venture in among our convoys, seize prizes in sight of those that should afford them protection, and if pursued 'put on their sea-wings' and laugh at the clumsy English pursuers."[232] Such was the public outcry that members of the opposition were able to secure a Parliamentary investigation into the conduct of the war at sea.[233]

A number of privateers recorded spectacular cruises in 1814. The *Prince-de-Neufchatel* captured or destroyed $1,000,000 in British property in a single cruise. The *Governor Tompkins* stripped and burned fourteen prizes in the English Channel, while the *Harpy* returned to the United States after a twenty-day cruise with booty worth more than $400,000.[234] Captain Thomas Boyle, who commanded the *Chas-*

seur—"the pride of Baltimore"—added insult to injury by sailing into a British port and issuing a proclamation that mocked British blockade notices. Boyle announced a blockade of "all the ports, harbours, bays, creeks, rivers, inlets, outlets, islands and sea coast of the united kingdom of G. Britain and Ireland."[235]

Even when privateers were cornered by British warships, they sometimes offered stout resistance. In September of 1814 British boarding parties from nearby royal ships attacked the *General Armstrong* while she lay in a neutral port in the Azores. Ultimately the privateer was abandoned by her crew, but the British had suffered close to 200 casualties compared to only nine for the United States. "The Americans," said an English observer, "fought with great firmness, but more like bloodthirsty savages than anything else."[236] British officials were so embarrassed by their losses in this engagement that they refused to allow any mail on the vessels that carried their wounded back to England.[237]

The following month H.M.S. *Endymion* (40) found herself becalmed off Nantucket in sight of the privateer *Prince-de-Neufchatel* (17). The American ship had just completed a successful cruise and had more than $200,000 in prize goods on board. She had manned so many prizes that her original crew had shrunk from 150 to 40. The captain of the British frigate sent his boats to take the American vessel, but the attack failed. The British lost 100 men, while the Americans lost only 30. The privateer had only 10 healthy seaman at the end of the engagement, but she managed to escape and reached port safely.[238]

Privateers were built for speed rather than fighting, and usually they fled when they saw British warships. There were, however, exceptions. On February 26, 1815, near Havana, Cuba, the *Chasseur* (15), still commanded by Captain Boyle, fell in with H.M.S. *St. Lawrence* (13). Mistaking the British vessel for an armed merchantman, Boyle closed. By the time he discovered his mistake, it was too late to escape. "I should not willingly perhaps, have sought a contest with a king's vessel," he reported, "knowing it was not our object; but my expectations were at first a valuable vessel and a valuable cargo also."[239] After a bloody fifteen-minute engagement, the *St. Lawrence* struck her colors.[240] This, of course, was an exceptional case, for the Royal Navy succeeded in capturing many privateers. But those that remained free thoroughly disrupted British commerce.

All in all, the campaign of 1814 turned out well for the United States. Although thrown on the defensive, the nation was able to defeat British offensives everywhere except in Maine and Washington. In all three campaigns during the war (1812, 1813, and 1814), the defending side had fared better than the attacking side. Perhaps this was because most offensive operations required moving men and materiel long distances over rough and heavily wooded terrain. Thus, after three years' of campaigning, neither the United States nor Great Britain could claim any great advantage in the war, let alone victory. Militarily, the War of 1812 ended in a draw.

CHAPTER 9

The Crisis of 1814

BY THE FALL OF 1814 it was clear to everyone that the United States faced a crisis. The war had changed dramatically since the beginning of the year. Freed from the contest in Europe, Great Britain was able to mount one campaign in the Chesapeake and prepare a second against the Gulf Coast while still maintaining a large army in Canada. "We are contending with an exasperated foe," said a Republican paper, "whose mighty power will soon be levelled at our liberties."[1] Menaced on every front, Americans viewed the war with a growing sense of foreboding. "Our affairs," said the secretary of the navy, William Jones, "are as gloomy as can well be." "These may be truly said to be *the times that try men's souls,*" added the New York *National Advocate.*[2]

The most pressing problem the nation faced was raising troops to wage the next campaign. Although the actual strength of the army was about 40,000, the reporting procedures were so bad that the administration thought there were only about 30,000 men in uniform.[3] Even though the army was larger than supposed, it was still well below the authorized level (62,500) and well below the nation's needs.

Without enough regulars to protect its frontiers, the nation was forced to rely increasingly on militia, but these troops were costly and inefficient. James Monroe estimated that it took three times as many militia to do the work of regulars. Relying on citizen soldiers had other disadvantages. Besides disrupting normal life, frequent calls deprived the regular army of potential recruits because men anxious to avoid militia duty paid large premiums for substitutes.[4] Although most Americans recognized the liabilities of militia, few were optimistic about raising additional regulars by conventional means. "[I]t is nonsense to talk of regulars," said Jefferson. "[W]e might as well rely on calling down an army of angels from heaven."[5]

The administration had trouble not only raising troops but also controlling those already in the service. Dueling became so prevalent among officers in 1814 that the War Department had to threaten to dismiss those who engaged in the practice.[6] More serious was the problem of desertion, which increased dramatically in 1814 because of bounty-jumping. "Desertion prevails to an allarming Extent among the Recruits before they join the Army," complained George Izard in July of 1814.[7] A statistical study has shown that 12.7 percent of American troops deserted during the war, and almost half of these were recruited in 1814.[8] In the last year of the war it was not uncommon for newspapers to run side by side ads that offered bounties for new recruits and rewards for the capture of deserters.[9]

How to deal with deserters posed a dilemma. Executing those who were caught might serve as a deterrent to others, but, as one officer pointed out, this undermined the recruiting service.[10] Moreover, men who deserted when sickness was prevalent, pay in arrears, or rations short seemed entitled to a measure of mercy. Typically what the government did was to sentence first-time deserters to death and then pardon them, while reserving execution for repeat offenders.[11]

As the incidence of desertion increased, however, some people called for tougher measures. "Examples must be made of Deserters," said William Jones, "as the evil is greatly increasing." "We believe nothing would put a stop to this growing evil sooner," added the Lexington *Reporter,* "than the *certainty* of suffering *death* for the *first* offence."[12] The president, however, preferred a more cautious policy. In June of 1814, he issued a proclamation (as he had in 1812) promising to pardon all deserters who surrendered within three months. In addition, the War Department authorized a $50 reward for the capture of deserters.[13] But the problem continued to plague the nation, and the number of executions carried out by the army steadily mounted: from 3 in 1812, to 32 in 1813, to 146 in 1814.[14]

The nation was also plagued by financial problems. Financial conditions had deteriorated badly since the beginning of the year. The $6,000,000 loan offered in July had netted only $2,500,000 at a 20 percent discount.[15] This left the government far short of the funds it needed for 1814, and the prospects for raising money in 1815 were bleaker still. "Something must be done and done speedily," said William Jones, "or we shall have an opportunity of trying the experiment of maintaining an army and navy and carrying on a vigorous war without money."[16]

The service chiefs were already scrambling for funds to meet their most pressing obligations. Secretary Jones reported that the Navy Department was "destitute of money in all quarters" and that he had no funds for even "the most urgent contingent purposes."[17] Stephen Decatur was unable to meet the operational expenses of his ship, and Isaac Chauncey complained that his men were "very clamorous for their pay."[18] In some port cities the lack of funds brought recruiting to a standstill. "Not a man can be procured here," said one officer. "[M]en will not ship without cash," declared another. "With treasury notes," added a third, "it will be impossible to enter men for the service in this part of our country."[19]

The War Department faced similar problems. Lack of funds idled the Springfield armory, and according to General Thomas Pinckney, recruiting was "completely at a stand for want of the necessary means to carry it on."[20] In Virginia, militia from "the most democratic part" of the state mutinied for want of pay, and in New Hampshire paying off discharged militia with treasury notes "disaffected many of them against the cause of their country."[21] Elsewhere discharged militia remained in camp for want of funds or sold their government claims at a sizable discount.[22] The pay of many regulars was six to twelve months in arrears and in some cases even more.[23] According to one Federalist, it was notorious that the army paymaster "was unable to meet demands for paltry amounts—not even for $30."[24]

The lack of funds was felt in other ways. An army officer reported that recruits who received no bounty considered themselves in the service only as long as they were actively campaigning and that his authority over them was "slender, Limited and uncertain."[25] In one district lack of funds prevented army officials from pursuing deserters or paying the reward advertised for their return.[26] In New England government officials could not afford to care for prisoners of war, and in New York the apothecary general was completely destitute of supplies.[27] "The Supply of Hospital stores . . . for the use of Our Armies on the Northern & western Frontier," he said, "has been for some time exhausted."[28] Having stretched public credit to the limit, many government officials and contractors had to borrow money on their own signatures to get badly needed supplies.[29]

The government also had trouble meeting its obligations abroad. Funds were needed to support the diplomatic corps, pay the interest on that portion of the national debt held overseas, and provide for the care of American prisoners of war in England. Unable to raise the money it needed, the government fell $128,000 in debt to its Dutch bankers and had to rely on advances from the House of

Baring in England. By the end of 1814, these advances totaled almost $200,000.[30]

Public credit, already slipping badly, received another blow in November when the government defaulted on the national debt. Unable to pay the interest in specie (as required by law), the Treasury Department offered bondholders in Boston treasury notes, depreciated bank paper, or government bonds.[31] War bonds fell to 75 percent of their nominal value in most cities and were quoted as low as 60 percent in Boston. Treasury notes also declined in value, often circulating at a 15- to 25-percent discount.[32] To make matters worse, the government defaulted on the notes that fell due in late 1814.[33] By this time, most banks were unwilling to accept treasury notes as security for government loans, and only the neediest of government contractors would take them in the course of business.[34] "I[t] is impossible to procure wood, labour, or forage, without Cash," reported a deputy commissary in New Hampshire.[35] Even in the specie-rich West, banks refused to lend money because of "the great amt. of Bills drawn on the Govt. returning under Protest—or unpaid."[36]

The government's financial woes were further compounded by the suspension of specie payments in the summer of 1814. After the dissolution of the national bank in 1811, the number of state banks had risen dramatically, from 117 in 1811 to 212 in 1815.[37] According to the Washington *National Intelligencer,* new banks had sprung up "like a crop of mushrooms in a night," and many were "unincorporated and irresponsible."[38] Without a national bank to restrain them, the banks greatly increased their note issue, both to accommodate needy customers and to invest in war bonds. From 1811 to 1815 the face value of bank notes in circulation rose from $66,000,000 to $115,000,000.[39]

During the same period the amount of specie in the country actually declined. The dissolution of the national bank drained $7,000,000 to pay off European stockholders, and during the war specie flowed from the middle and southern states to New England and from there into Canada to finance illegal imports and the purchase of British government notes and British bills of exchange. According to contemporary reports, $2,000,000 in gold was shipped from the United States to Canada in early 1814 and another $1,800,000 the following summer.[40] "The Specie is constantly going in Cart Loads to Canada," said a Massachusetts Federalist. Between New England and Canada, "there is an uninterrupted trade in Bills of the British Gov't."[41] The result was an acute shortage of hard money. "[T]he scarcity of money throughout the UStates," claimed a Virginia firm, "has never been equalled."[42]

With their specie reserves shrinking and their note issue expanding, many banks found themselves in a precarious position. In August of 1814 the British invasion of the Chesapeake started a run on the banks in Washington and Baltimore, forcing them to suspend specie payments. Other banks in the middle and southern states quickly followed suit, and eventually those in the West did, too. Only the New England banks, which had large specie reserves and were closely regulated by state law, held out. But even they had to retrench in order to remain solvent.[43]

Once the banks went off a specie-paying basis, they stopped honoring each other's notes. As a result, the administration could no longer transfer funds from one part of the country to another. Although government surpluses accumulated in some banks in the middle and southern states, federal funds were quickly exhausted in Boston, New York, and Philadelphia, where most of the interest on the national debt was due. The suspension of specie payments hurt the government in another way. Bank paper circulated at a 15- to 30-percent discount, and yet the Treasury accepted it at par for taxes and loans. With only depreciated bank notes and treasury notes coming into the Treasury, the government had no currency that could readily be used to meet its obligations.[44] For all practical purposes, public credit was extinct and the government was bankrupt. "[P]ublic as well as private, credits," said a government contractor, "are lower than I have ever known either before."[45]

❖ ❖ ❖ ❖ ❖ ❖

Were these problems not vexing enough, the adminstration also had to contend with trade with the enemy. Although the embargo and non-importation acts had been repealed the previous spring, Americans were still barred from trading with the British or importing British-owned goods. Nevertheless, the influx of British troops into the New World created such a demand for provisions that trade with the enemy rose dramatically in 1814. Smugglers and government officials waged a running battle, and the smugglers were winning.

The mushrooming trade with Canada was particularly alarming. This trade brought British goods into the United States, drained specie from American banks, and put food in the mouths of British soldiers. Much of the trade was carried on by sea, and not all of it violated American law. When the British seized eastern Maine in September of 1814, they made Castine a port of entry. Swedish vessels ran immense quantities of British-made goods from Castine up the Penobscot River to Hampden, and from there the merchandise was distributed to other parts of New England. Neutral ships flying Swedish and Spanish colors also operated on Lake Champlain.[46] The trade with Canada ran heavily against the United States, draining specie from the nation's banks. Nevertheless, the government condoned it as long as it was conducted in neutral ships. "A neutral vessel and Cargo coming from any part of the British dominions," said a Treasury official, "may be admitted to an entry in any part of the United States."[47]

The overland trade—both with British-occupied Maine and with Canada—was even greater. Cattle, grain, and other provisions flowed into Castine and other parts of occupied Maine in enormous quantities. "The trade appears as free & open as in time of peace," said William Eustis; "20, 30, & 50 waggon loads are passing almost daily."[48] Livestock and provisions also poured across the border into Canada. "From the St. Lawrence to the Ocean," reported George Izard in the summer of 1814, "an open Disregard prevails for the Laws prohibiting Intercourse with the Enemy. The Road to St. Regis is covered with Droves of Cattle, and the River with Rafts destined for the Enemy."[49] As a result of this trade, British troops feasted on American provisions. "[T]wo thirds of the army in Canada," Governor George Prevost boasted in August of 1814, "are at this moment eating beef provided by American contractors, drawn principally from the States of Vermont and New York."[50]

Americans also shipped naval stores to Canada. On several occasions Lieutenant Thomas Macdonough seized ship timber and other materials destined for British warships on Lake Champlain.[51] Military intelligence flowed across the border as well. "The turpitude of many of our citizens in this part of the country," Macdonough complained, "furnishes the Enemy with every information he wants."[52]

American officials found it difficult to halt this growing trade. Customs officials could not legally search every type of vehicle or make preventive seizures, and the enemy trade act of 1812 was so loosely drawn that some exports to Canada were actually legal. Revenue officials in Vermont were further hampered by a series of unfavorable judicial decisions. The state courts had ruled that the inspectors employed by customs officials had no authority to make seizures and were liable to damages even if the merchandise they seized was condemned.[53]

Federal attorneys could offer little help because it was difficult to indict and almost impossible to convict smugglers. Moreover, the attorney general had ruled that visiting the enemy was not illegal. The prosecution had to prove that the accused furnished "improper information" or "supplies."[54] Canny New England farmers circumvented the law by marching their livestock to the border, where a Canadian cohort would entice the animals across with a basket of corn.[55] According to the Salem *Gazette,* smuggling had become "the most lucrative business which is now carried on." The profits were so great that smugglers could "afford to lose one half by custom house spies, and yet make money faster than those who follow the 'dull pursuits' of regular business."[56] Moreover, anyone who interfered with the trade risked a damage suit or worse. A Vermont militia officer who sought to prevent livestock from reaching Canada was thrown into jail, and a mob assaulted a Boston customs official who had seized a wagonload of suspected British goods. In the interior, the possibility of violence was greater. Two revenue officers were killed and two others wounded in a clash with smugglers near Belfast, Maine.[57] According to General Izard, "Nothing but a Cordon of Troops, from the French Mills [in northern New York] to Lake Memphramagog [in northern Vermont] could effectually check the Evil."[58]

❖ ❖ ❖ ❖ ❖ ❖

Lack of men and money and mounting trade with the enemy all contributed to the crisis of 1814. So too did deteriorating economic conditions, which eroded the nation's tax base and generated political discontent, especially in New England. In spite of their many differences, the South and New England shared a common fate in this war. In different ways both were tied to the sea and both experienced economic hardship. The middle and western states, by contrast, fared much better. In these states money could still be made, especially from government contracts and manufacturing, and the result was considerable prosperity.

Pennsylvania fared particularly well. Most of the army's principal supply officers used Philadelphia as a base of operations, and one of the army's two major supply routes ran from Philadelphia to Pittsburgh and thence further west. Large quantities of army supplies were purchased in the state, and a great deal of money passed through Pennsylvania's banks. In the last quarter of 1812 alone, the Treasury Department deposited more than $1,000,000 in two Philadelphia banks.[59] "The pressure of the war," said a Philadelphia merchant in 1813, "has been as yet but little felt." "The war-hawks," added a Federalist newspaper, "are thriving and fattening upon the hard earnings of the industrious and peaceable part of the community."[60]

According to one report, more buildings were constructed in Philadelphia in the summer of 1814 than at any time in memory. "Real

Estate in Town & Country has in general considerably advanced since the war." said a merchant. "Lands are at least 1/3 higher & many plantations have sold for double what they would have brought three years ago." Not until the fall of 1814, when several business failures in New York sent shock waves through Philadelphia, did business finally slow down.[61]

New York prospered even more. People in the Empire State were deeply involved in the trade with the enemy, but the real source of their prosperity was the largess of the federal government. The second of the army's two major supply routes originated in New York City and ran through Albany to the northern frontier.[62] To support American troops in the state, the federal government spent enormous sums of money. Though the price of rations varied, it usually cost about $500,000 to feed 10,000 troops for a year, and more than $1,000,000 to pay their wages.[63]

One army contractor in New York sold $500,000 in rations in 1812, $250,000 over three months in 1813, and $850,000 over a seven-month period in 1814. Another received $270,000 from the government over a three-month period in 1814, and this covered less than half of his expenses.[64] The army paymaster also disbursed large sums in the state—$400,000 to pay soldiers in the last three months of 1813 alone.[65] Government expenditures had a particularly buoyant effect on New York agriculture. "The market for the produce of the farmer," said Governor Daniel Tompkins in late 1812, "has experienced an unexpected and unusual rise."[66]

The middle states benefited not only from war contracts but also from manufacturing. Many small industrial plants established during the early years of the restrictive system flourished during the war.[67] In Pennsylvania, Republican leaders saw manufacturing as the nation's salvation because, unlike commerce, it did not lead to foreign entanglements. "Years of experience," said Governor Simon Snyder in late 1811, "must convince us that foreign commerce is a good but of a secondary nature, and that happiness and prosperity must be sought for within the limits of our country and not in foreign connections."[68]

Like the middle states, the West also prospered during the war. Military operations in this region brought in large sums of federal money, particularly to Kentucky and Ohio. More than $400,000 was sent to these two states in late 1812, and a contractor there said this was "but a drop in the Bucket." An additional $1,000,000 would be needed for the first three months of 1813.[69] The Miami Exporting Company of Cincinnati—which was actually a bank—took in over $1,000,000 in government drafts in a seven-month period in 1812–

1813.[70] In fact, the government spent so much on its western operations in the first year of the war that John Armstrong accused westerners of gouging—of selling produce at three times the peace price and of putting everyone on the payroll. "The war is [considered] a good thing," he grumbled, "and is to be nursed."[71]

According to Henry Clay, so much specie flowed into the West during the war that eastern bills of exchange (which normally sold at a premium) began passing at a discount. In effect, the West's traditional debtor relationship with the East was temporarily reversed. Clay attributed this state of affairs to "the effects of the War, and the military operations in that quarter."[72] Western banks were able to build up large specie reserves and only reluctantly suspended payment when the banking collapse came in 1814. According to Congressman Joseph Hawkins, "the banks of Kentucky and Ohio (where specie abounded) had at length been compelled in self-defence to stop payment."[73]

Western cities—Pittsburgh, Cincinnati, Lexington, Louisville, and St. Louis—all enjoyed a booming prosperity during the war.[74] A Boston merchant visiting Lexington in 1813 was surprised at the prosperity he saw. "I find in this country an entire reverse of New-England in regard to business. Here there is no competition, and every thing [is] brisk and profitable. The war, so far from depressing the people of the Western States, is making the greater proportion of them rich."[75] Rural areas also benefited because of the army's huge appetite for provisions. Commodity prices rose, and western farmers had a ready market for their produce.[76] Even after military expenditures fell off in 1814, the western economy continued to flourish. "Blessed with bountiful crops," said Governor Isaac Shelby in late 1814, "we have great reason . . . to congratulate each other on the plentiful appearance which our country exhibits."[77]

In sharp contrast to the middle and western states, the South suffered during the war. People living in the Chesapeake region made their share of money from privateering, manufacturing, and government contracts, and when the militia were called out in 1813 and 1814 federal money flowed into the region. But the South was heavily dependent on the export of agricultural produce, and this trade practically ceased in 1813 when the British stopped issuing licenses and established their blockade.

Commodity prices began to sag at the end of 1812 and then dropped precipitously in 1813. In response Georgia, Maryland, and North Carolina enacted stay laws to protect debtors.[78] Conditions got worse in 1814, when Virginia wheat fell below 50 cents a bushel, and farmers began feeding it to their livestock.[79] Tobacco farmers fared no better.

A Virginia congressman complained in 1812 that he had "not Sold a Single pound of my Small crops of tobacco for the three Last years," and by 1814 Jefferson reported that tobacco was "not worth the pipe it is smoked in."[80] "The whole country watered by the rivers which fall into the Chesapeake," concluded John Randolph, "is in a state of *paralysis.*"[81] People living in the lower South were also dependent on the export of produce, and they too suffered from the war. "I believe that if the war should last three years longer," William Lowndes said in 1814, "I shall not be worth more than 50 negroes after paying my debts."[82]

New England also suffered during the war, although some critics have suggested otherwise. In late 1814, *Niles' Register,* a Republican magazine published by Hezekiah Niles in Baltimore, cited statistics showing that between 1810 and 1814 specie deposits in Massachusetts banks had risen from $1,600,000 to $6,400,000. This increase was the result of a favorable balance of trade with the rest of the Union, and Niles claimed that it was proof of Massachusetts' prosperity.[83]

In normal times Niles might have been right, but the times were anything but normal. In fact, the banks in Massachusetts pursued a conservative fiscal policy throughout this period, increasing their loans by only 33 percent and their note issue by only 25 percent.[84] Moreover, once the banks in the South and West suspended specie payments, those in New England had to retrench, calling in existing loans and refusing to make new ones. "The solid banks," said John Quincy Adams, "were enabled to maintain their integrity, only by contracting their operations to an extent ruinous to their debtors, and themselves."[85] As a consequence, money became so tight that even the state governments could not borrow the funds they needed.[86]

Many New Englanders, to be sure, prospered during the war. Most farmers fared well, and some money could be made from privateering, manufacturing, and trade with the enemy. Those with government contracts also prospered. Paul Revere and Eli Whitney, for example, both supplied munitions to the army.[87] But New England was too far east to profit from the big army contracts, and few regulars were stationed in the region. New England also called out fewer militia than any other region, and the state governments had to bear a larger share of the cost because of a shortage of government funds and a dispute over the command of the troops.[88] Indeed, of the $12,600,000 expended by the federal government simply to pay the wages of militia during the war, only 3.5 percent went to New England.[89]

With extensive commercial and fishing operations, New England was too dependent on the sea to prosper in any war with a great naval power. Massachusetts alone owned more than a third of the nation's shipping tonnage.[90] By the fall of 1813 there were 250 idle ships in Boston harbor, and people were moving out of the city to look for work elsewhere.[91] Many of the ships rotted from inactivity—a significant capital loss. Conditions worsened in 1814. By the end of the year, it cost as much as 75 percent of a ship's value to insure it for a voyage, and a Boston firm reported that it was "extremely difficult" to sell anything except for immediate consumption and impossible to buy anything except for cash.[92]

Other seaports in New England experienced a similar fate. Property values in Newburyport plummeted 37 percent during the war, and the number of people on public relief rose from 20 to 244.[93] "In Newburyport," said a contemporary, "the Rich have become poor, & those, who were in comfortable Circumstances, are Mendicants."[94] Summing up, a Massachusetts Federalist said: "We are in a deplorable situation, our commerce dead; our revenue gone; our ships rotting at the wharves. . . . Our treasury drained—we are bankrupts."[95]

❖ ❖ ❖ ❖ ❖ ❖

Prosperity in the middle and western states no doubt contributed to the popularity of the war, but deteriorating economic conditions had the opposite effect in New England. By the fall of 1814, all eyes were on what a New Jersey Federalist called "the cloud arising in the East," a cloud that was "black, alarming, portentous."[96] Growing sectionalism in New England was a source of grave concern to Republicans. "[I]t is too plain," Williame Duane told Jefferson, "that we are not all *republicans nor all federalists*—and the spirit of faction in the East . . . has been too much encouraged."[97] A Philadelphia Republican expressed fear that the moderates in New England "would be driven of[f] the stage by Marats Robenspears Bounapartes etc.," and the Russian minister claimed that "[t]here is not a state in Europe which, in similar circumstances, would not have been considered on the eve of revolution."[98]

President Madison was particularly worried about New England disaffection. William Wirt described him in October of 1814 as "miserably shattered and woe-begone." "His mind seems full of the New England revolt," said Wirt; "he introduced the subject & continued to press it, painful as it obviously was to him."[99] The following month the subject still weighed heavily on the president's mind. "You are not mistaken," he wrote a friend, "in viewing the conduct of the Eastern states as the source of our greatest difficulties in carrying on the war; as it certainly is the greatest if not the sole inducement with the enemy to persevere in it."[100]

Throughout the war the Republicans had hoped that favorable election results would shore up their majorities and silence the opposition, but their hopes were never fulfilled. In the elections of 1812, the Federalists had gained control of six of the eighteen states (Massachusetts, Connecticut, Rhode Island, New Jersey, Delaware, and Maryland).[101] The following year they lost New Jersey but won Vermont and New Hampshire, which gave them control over all of New England. In 1814 they retained control of these same seven states.[102]

The Republicans fared no better in congressional elections. Most states held their elections for the Fourteenth Congress in 1814 even though this Congress did not convene until the end of 1815. In the House, Republican strength, which had declined from 75 percent in the Twelfth Congress to 63 percent in the Thirteenth, rose slightly to 65 percent in the Fourteenth Congress. In the Senate, however, Republican strength continued to slide: from 82 percent in the Twelfth Congress to 78 percent in the Thirteenth, to 67 percent in the Fourteenth. Although the leading Senate "Invisibles"—Samuel Smith, William Branch Giles, and Michael Leib—were not returned to the Fourteenth Congress, the regular Republicans were little better off than they had been in the Thirteenth Congress.[103]

Thus in neither Congress nor the country were the Republicans able to win the decisive majorities they sought. Although they counted on the war to enhance their popularity and silence the Federalists, the effect of the conflict was just the opposite. In New England especially, the war served as a catalyst for a Federalist revival. As a result, Federalists achieved a more commanding position in this region than at any time since the 1790s.

It was not only the Federalists who opposed the administration. Many Republicans did, too. The Clintonians and "Invisibles" disliked the administration's management of the war, and the Old Republicans objected to the war itself. The election of 1812 had revealed deep-seated hostility to the Virginia Dynasty, and by 1814 even regular Republicans had become disillusioned with the party's leadership. "If we have another disastrous campaign in Canada," said George Hay of Virginia, "the republican cause is ruined, and Mr. M[adison] will go out covered with the Scorn of one party, and the reproaches of the other." "Without a change in the management of the war on the Canadian frontier," added Nathaniel Macon, "the republican party must go down[.] The people of every part of the Nation, will be disgusted with an administration, who have declared war, without ability to conduct it, to a favorable issue."[104]

With the disasters of 1814—particularly the burning of Washington—the president and his advisors suffered a further loss in public esteem. "The President is much railed at by many of the Democrats," said a Philadelphia merchant. "The whole administration is blamed for the late disastrous occurrences at Washington," declared a Virginia Republican. "Without money, without soldiers & without courage," said Rufus King, "the President and his Cabinet are the objects of very general execration."[105]

❖ ❖ ❖ ❖ ❖ ❖

The shortage of men and money, expanding trade with the enemy, deteriorating economic conditions, growing disaffection in New England, and discontent within the Republican party—all of these contributed to the crisis of 1814. To compound the nation's problems, a new round of cabinet changes made it difficult for the administration to respond to the crisis quickly. John Armstrong had resigned from the War Department in August of 1814 after being blamed for the burning of Washington.[106] In September Secretary of the Treasury George W. Campbell, who suffered from poor health and was overwhelmed by the nation's complex financial problems, followed suit.[107] That same month William Jones, who had fallen deeply into debt, announced that he would resign from the Navy Department no later than December 1.[108] These resignations forced the president to scramble for replacements.

Monroe, who had taken over as acting secretary of war after Armstrong's departure, accepted the position on a permanent basis.[109] Madison offered Monroe's old State Department post to Daniel D. Tompkins, governor of New York, but he declined, fearing that his enemies would ruin him if he left the state before justifying some unauthorized defense expenditures.[110] Madison therefore left Monroe in charge as acting secretary of state. The Navy Department, always a difficult post for Republicans to fill, was offered to Captain John Rodgers, but he declined after learning that he would have to give up his naval commission. The president's next choice was Benjamin W. Crowninshield, a Massachusetts merchant who accepted the post only reluctantly. Although able enough, Crowninshield was without political clout and did not assume office until the war was nearly over.[111]

Alexander J. Dallas of Pennsylvania took over as head of the Treasury Department. Although he had refused to join the cabinet earlier in the year, with Armstrong now gone Dallas agreed to serve, even though he regarded the Treasury Department as "the forlorn hope of executive enterprize."[112] A Jamaica-born lawyer educated in Great Britain, Dallas sported aristocratic clothing, had a bearing of social

Alexander J. Dallas, by Gilbert Stuart. Courtesy of the Pennsylvania Academy of Fine Arts

and intellectual superiority, and was known to be conservative on many issues.[113] A Virginia Republican described him as "a man of great labor and some talents" but without "that weight of character, which the times require."[114] Many Pennsylvania Republicans disliked Dallas, but such were his known talents and such was the deplorable condition of the Treasury that even his enemies agreed to accept his appointment. "Tell *Doctor* Madison," Senator Abner Lacock reportedly said, "that we are now willing to submit to his Philadelphia lawyer for head of the treasury. The public patient is so very sick that we must swallow anything the doctor prescribes, however nauseous."[115]

❖ ❖ ❖ ❖ ❖ ❖

Thus, amidst a deepening national crisis and with his cabinet in a state of flux, President Madison summoned the Thirteenth Congress for its third and last session. Normally Congress met in November or December, but the previous spring congressional Republicans had called for an October meeting.[116] By August, however, the nation's military and financial situation had deteriorated so badly that Madison pushed the date up to September 19. An early meeting was essential, he said, to deal with "great and weighty matters."[117]

Many congressmen were surprised at the extent of damage they found in Washington. "The ruins of the public edifices," said Jonathan Roberts, "is more complete than I had anticipated."[118] With government buildings destroyed, everyone had to find new quarters. Madison stayed for a month with his brother-in-law, Richard Cutts, and then moved into the Octagon House, the former residence of the French minister. Cabinet officials rented private buildings to house their departments.[119] With the exception of the French mission, the diplomatic corps fled to Philadelphia, the Russian minister complaining that Washington had "become still more uncomfortable and more expensive than before."[120] Crawford's Hotel, a popular Georgetown haunt for congressmen and capital visitors, was more crowded than usual. "I am surrounded," said William Wirt, "by a vast crowd & bustle of legislators and gentlemen of the turf assembled for the races which commence here tomorrow."[121]

Congress commandeered the patent office—the only undamaged government building. According to William Jones, members of Congress were "in bad temper, grumbling at everything."[122] No doubt the cramped quarters contributed to this mood. Federalist Daniel Webster called the new chambers "confined, inconvenient, and unwholesome," and Republican Jesse Bledsoe said that the representatives' room was "too small" and that "Every Kind of privation is enormous."[123]

President Madison dispatched his opening address to Congress on September 20. Hoping to put the best face on events, he brushed aside British victories in order to focus on American triumphs. But he could not deny that a crisis was at hand. "It is not to be disguised," he said, "that the situation of our country calls for its greatest efforts." Appealing to the spirit of Seventy-Six, Madison expressed confidence that the American people would "cheerfully and proudly bear every burden of every kind which the safety and honor of the nation demand."[124]

Madison was not optimistic about the prospects for peace, and he gave force to this point in mid-October by sending a bundle of diplomatic documents to Congress. These documents, just received from the nation's peace envoys in Europe, showed that, while the United States had dropped its own demands, Britain would not restore peace without certain concessions. The British demanded the creation of an Indian reservation in the Old Northwest, territorial concessions in northern Maine and Minnesota, American demilitarization of the Great Lakes, and an end to American fishing privileges in Canadian waters. These terms demonstrated that the two nations were still far apart and that an early end to the war was unlikely.[125]

❖ ❖ ❖ ❖ ❖ ❖

Given the deepening crisis, all Republicans agreed on the need for forceful measures. "I am deeply impressed with the importance of the present crisis," said Joseph Varnum of Massachusetts, "and the importance of the adoption of strong and energetic measures." "If ever a body of men held the destinies of a country in their hands," John C. Calhoun told the House, "it [is] that which [I am] now addressing."[126] The only problem was that Republicans could not agree on the best way to meet the crisis. The administration favored extreme measures—raising an army by conscription and creating a national bank—but these proposals stirred so much controversy that neither became law. Although congressional Republicans had shown signs of closing ranks in the previous session, at the height of the war crisis they remained divided.

Federalists also conceded that a crisis was at hand. "I admit the distress of the nation exists to the full extent stated," said Senator Jeremiah Mason of New Hampshire. "We see and feel it, and have too much reason to believe it will soon become universal. The crisis demands all the wisdom and virtue of the country."[127] But like the Republicans, the Federalists were also divided. In the hope of working out a common policy, congressional Federalists held a grand strategy meeting at Crawford's Hotel. The meeting revealed much difference of opinion over whether to support the war. A committee was appointed to study the matter, and it issued a report just after the British peace terms were made public. The report declared that the character of the war had changed and urged Federalists to support bills to raise men and money.[128]

Federalists from the middle and southern states responded favorably to the report. Appalled by the British terms, most now agreed that it was their duty to support the war. Alexander Hanson, the hero of the Baltimore riots, rose in the House to denounce the British terms and to pledge his support for "the most vigorous system of honorable war, with the hope of bringing the enemy to a sense of justice."[129] Other Federalists from the middle and southern states joined in the cry, calling the British terms "arrogant," "inadmissible," "humilating," and "disgraceful." Most agreed with the Alexandria *Gazette* that whatever the war's origins it had "from the arrogance of the enemy, become a war of necessity."[130]

Federalists in New England, however, took a different view. They were more appalled by the views of their friends to the south and west than by the terms themselves. Most agreed with the Boston *Gazette* that, having declared war and failed, the United States must now pay the price.[131] "I have uniformly thought that G. Britain might justly demand Some *indemnity*," declared Timothy Pickering.[132] "We shall have no objection here to better terms," added Harrison Gray Otis of Massachusetts. "But I religiously believe, that 90 out of every 100 men in this State would if left to themselves prefer *treating* on the proposed basis *at least*, to the continuance of the war one day."[133]

Although Federalists seemed to be deeply divided by the crisis, the breach in their ranks was more apparant than real. No sooner had Federalists from the middle and southern states proclaimed their support for the war then they began to drift back into New England's camp. "[T]he opposition," said one Republican, "continues as malignant and unreasonable as ever, with a few honourable exceptions only."[134] This was partly the result of New England's influence, which was always a potent force in party councils, but other factors played a role, too.

In October Monroe publicly called for pushing the war into Canada again, telling Congress that this was the best way to secure the friendship of the Indians, protect the coast, and win peace.[135] "The great object to be attained," Monroe told General Jacob Brown, "is to carry the war into Canada, and to break the British power there, to the utmost practicable extent."[136] Monroe's plans convinced many Federalists that (as one New Englander put it), the "character of the war [had] not changed" and the administration was still "eager for conquest and aggrandizement." "The Notion of some Federalists," concluded Gouverneur Morris, "that this War had become defensive . . . must vanish with Mr Munroe's late Declaration that their Object is to conquer Canada."[137]

Federalists were alienated not only by the administration's military strategy but also its political exclusiveness. There was a good deal of speculation, even among New Englanders, about the possibility of Federalists joining the cabinet. The Federalist caucus that recommended supporting the war had called for "an entire change of the Heads of Departments," and establishing a bi-partisan cabinet was a common theme in Federalist speeches and editorials.[138] Some Republicans responded favorably to these overtures. George Hay told Monroe that the president "ought to accede to the proposal of the federalists in relation to the cabinet," and many other Republicans—including some in Congress—agreed.[139] But the president demurred. According to Hanson, Madison thought it would be "a passport to the Presidency" if he acknowledged the talents of a Federalist by appointing him to the cabinet.[140]

In late November, after Vice President Elbridge Gerry died, Federalists tried to install Rufus King as president pro tem of the Senate. Often mentioned as a potential cabinet member, King was well regarded by both parties. Even Republicans, said a Federalist, considered him "the very *Oracle.*"[141] Senate Republicans, however, refused to elevate him to so high a post. With the vice presidency vacant and Madison once again ailing, Republicans were unwilling to put a Federalist next in the line of succession.[142] According to a letter from Washington published in a Federalist paper, "Mr. Madison had declared, that the democratic *party* would be put down, if Mr. King was chosen," and "Mr. Eppes had declared . . . that '*he would assist to* TAR AND FEATHER *the democratic Senator who dared vote for Mr. King.*' "[143] Annoyed by these rebuffs, Federalists murmured that the administration was not interested in conciliation and that the war was still a party war. "The delusion has vanished," said a Federalist paper. "The call to union means nothing."[144]

Exasperated by the administration's war strategy and politics, Federalists from the middle and southern states were already deserting the war movement when a new set of British terms was submitted to Congress on December 1. These showed that Great Britain was willing to restore peace on the basis of *uti possidetis,* which meant that each

Rufus King, by Gilbert Stuart. Courtesy of the Frick Art Reference
Library

side would retain whatever territory it held.[145] If these terms were acceded to, the United States would lose eastern Maine but little else. This was a settlement that Federalists everywhere could live with, and doubtless many Republicans could, too.

Fearing the impact these dispatches might have on the war spirit, Republican congressmen at first tried to suppress them, and when they were published, the *National Intelligencer* professed to believe that the prospects for peace were still "very faint."[146] No one was fooled, least of all the Federalists, most of whom thought peace was near. According to a New Hampshire Republican, "informed men of both parties in this part of the country" expected peace within a few months.[147] The result was a flood of peace rumors that continued until the war was over.[148]

Heartened by the news and unwilling to encourage the administration to hold out for better terms, Federalists from the middle and southern states closed ranks behind their friends from New England. "The war-pitch," recalled a Republican congressman, "fell as much at Washington as it did in London. The salutary apprehension of October turned to hopeful confidence in December. The nerve of opposition was strung afresh."[149]

❖ ❖ ❖ ❖ ❖ ❖

Although partisanship played an important role in this session (as it did throughout the war), the first issue that Congress faced was not a party issue at all, but a sectional one—the question of relocating the nation's capital. Many northerners saw the destruction of Washington as an opportunity to move the capital from the swampy wilderness on the Potomac to a more urban and cosmopolitan setting in the North. "The removal of the seat of government," said John Quincy Adams, "may prove a great benefit."[150] City officials in Philadelphia, anxious to regain the capital they had lost in 1800, promised suitable accommodations, and most congressmen appeared to be favorably disposed.[151] "The Majority Seem determined to go," said Nathaniel Macon, "& Philadelphia Seems to be the place."[152]

On September 26, Jonathan Fisk of New York introduced a resolution calling for the appointment of a committee to study the expediency of temporarily moving the capital. Fisk, doubtless thinking of New York or Philadelphia, favored "a place of greater security and less inconvenience" and "a place more connected with the moneyed interest of the nation."[153] But southerners, fearing that any move might become permanent, claimed that abandoning Washington would set a bad precedent and would be unfair to those who had invested in the city. "[I]f the Seat of Government was once set on wheels," Macon warned, "there was no saying where it would stop."[154]

Fisk's resolution was approved, and a committee was appointed to study the matter. Although the committee recommended against removal, the House rejected this recommendation on a close vote when Speaker Langdon Cheves of South Carolina stunned nearly everyone by voting for removal.[155] "The reason for this vote," he said, "was, that this District could not be defended except at an immense expense."[156] A bill was accordingly prepared that provided for moving the seat of government to Philadelphia for the duration of the war. Only two concessions were made to the opponents of removal: money was appropriated to rebuild Washington and a pledge was made to return to the city after the war.[157]

When the bill was put to a vote in the House, it was defeated by a nine-vote margin, largely because several Republicans (including three from Pennsylvania) succumbed to executive influence.[158] After defeating this bill, Congress approved another that merely provided for rebuilding Washington.[159] A companion measure authorized the purchase of Thomas Jefferson's 10,000-volume library. The British had burned the original Library of Congress, and Jefferson's collection (which was appraised at $23,950) became the basis for a new library.[160]

❖ ❖ ❖ ❖ ❖ ❖

With the location of the capital resolved, Congress turned to other matters more directly related to prosecuting the war. On October 17 Monroe submitted a report to Congress outlining his recommendations for raising troops.[161] He estimated that 100,000 men would be needed to prosecute the war successfully in 1815. Since the regular army was believed to contain only about 30,000 men, it would be necessary to raise 70,000 more. Monroe rejected militia as too costly and inefficient. Instead, he called for raising 40,000 volunteers for local defense and 30,000 regulars for use against Canada.

Monroe saw no difficulty in raising the volunteers since their duties would be confined to the locality in which they were raised. Recruiting additional regulars, however, would not be easy. Monroe presented several options but made it clear that he favored the most extreme, a conscription plan that called for dividing all eligible males into classes of 100 men each and requiring each class to furnish four recruits, with replacements in case of casualties. Each recruit would receive the standard land bounty from the government, but any cash bounty would have to come from other members of his class.

Anticipating criticism, Monroe argued that "the conservation of the

State is a duty paramount to all others" and that the militia provided a precedent for compulsory service.[162] Monroe pointed out that several states had employed draft schemes during the Revolution and that New York had adopted a similar system in 1814.[163] He also said that his proposal was modeled after a plan drawn up by Secretary of War Henry Knox in 1790. Although this plan never became law, it had the blessing of President Washington.[164]

There was little enthusiasm for Monroe's plan and little likelihood that it would become law. Hoping to forge a consensus behind a compromise proposal, Senator William Bibb of Georgia drew up a bill that provided for using Monroe's system of classification and draft to raise 80,000 militia for two years' service. The men would serve under officers appointed by the state, and their service would be restricted to their own or an adjoining state. Bibb's bill offered military exemptions to those men who provided recruits for the army, but otherwise it did not raise regulars. Instead, it raised militia for long-term local service.[165] The bill pleased neither those Republicans who wanted to carry the war into Canada nor the Federalists, who were horrified at any scheme that savored of a French-style conscription.

The bill was reported from committee by Senator William Branch Giles on November 5.[166] Republican Joseph Varnum, who told a friend that "no Man can entertain a more despi[c]able Idea of Mr. Giles' Militia Bill than I do," delivered a long speech against the measure, detailing its technical flaws.[167] Varnum called the proposal "extremely impolitic" and claimed that it was based on "unusual and arbitrary principles" and that it was "totally incompetent to effect the object" for which it was designed.[168] Federalists joined in the attack, challenging the bill's constitutionality. Robert H. Goldsborough of Maryland said that raising troops in this manner was "a palpable and flagrant violation of the constitution," and David Daggett of Connecticut claimed that the measure was "not only unconstitutional" but "unequal, unjust, and oppressive."[169] In spite of these objections, the Senate passed the bill by a comfortable margin.[170]

The debate then shifted to the House, where young Charles J. Ingersoll, a Pennsylvania Republican, praised the bill: "You may call it by what odious ugly name you will—conscription or what not—but it is the only sufficient, the only republican, the only fair, the only equal plan for applying the physical means to the end of common military defence and protection." Ingersoll asserted that "vast improvements have taken place in the military art" in the past twenty years. All of Europe had adopted these improvements, "and this country will be left lamentably behind in the march of mankind, unless, like the rest, it adopts them too."[171]

Ingersoll's appeal to European precedents was unlikely to convert any Federalists, though proponents of the bill did offer them a sop by lowering the term of service to a year. The limitation on local service was also dropped in the hope of winning the support of the Canadian enthusiasts. In addition, in case any state failed to comply with the law, the president was authorized to call directly on militia officers. In this form the bill passed the House and was returned to the Senate.[172] The two houses, however, were unable to resolve their differences, and on December 28 Rufus King took advantage of light attendance in the Senate to propose indefinite postponement. His motion carried by a one-vote margin.[173] According to one Republican, "Prospects of peace, contrivances of party, and differences of opinion in the dominant party" all conspired to kill the measure.[174]

One of the reasons that Republicans did not insist on conscription was that Federalists in New England were talking openly of resistance. "Our Citizens," said a Connecticut Federalist, "are not yet prepared to submit to a *conscription Law,* or to advance all their resources to support a war of Conquest."[175] In Massachusetts, people at a large public meeting adopted a resolution pledging to bid defiance to the law: "WE DARE NOT SUBMIT, AND WILL NEVER YIELD OBEDIENCE."[176] Daniel Webster called on the New England states to nullify the measure—"to interpose between their citizens & arbitrary power"—and Republicans in the Connecticut legislature joined with Federalists in denouncing the bill and in urging the governor to call a special session if it became law.[177] Since the bill died in the Senate, New England's defiance was never put to a test.

Another measure that generated opposition in New England was a new enlistment law. Like the conscription bill, this measure was drawn up by William Bibb and introduced in the Senate by William Branch Giles on November 5.[178] It provided for doubling the land bounty, so that new recruits would receive 320 acres of land as well as $124 in cash. It also authorized the enlistment of minors eighteen or older without the consent of parent, guardian, or master, and it exempted from militia duty anyone who provided a recruit for the regular army at his own expense—presumably by paying a large cash bounty. (The government would still pay the land bounty.)

Federalists in both houses denounced the provision for minor enlistments. Cyrus King of Massachusetts said the proposal struck at "the best feelings of the heart" and was "inhuman, immoral, and oppres-

243

sive." According to Thomas P. Grosvenor of New York, the bill would have the effect of "jeopardizing the good order of the community, violating contracts, disturbing the sacred rights of natural affection, and all the felicities of domestic life."[179] In an obvious attempt to frighten southerners, Daniel Webster declared that the bill could serve as a precedent for taking slaves from their masters.[180] Republicans made little attempt to reply to these arguments. The only concession they made was to give minors a four-day grace period in which to cancel their enlistments. Thus amended, the bill passed both houses and was signed into law on December 10.[181]

Like the conscription bill, the enlistment law unleashed a storm of opposition in New England. Theodore Dwight, a Federalist editor and pamphleteer, told a Connecticut congressman: "We do not believe your right to annul the laws of the States [governing minors], & do not intend you shall do it in Connecticut."[182] There was talk in Connecticut of prosecuting army officers who enlisted minors, and state judges routinely discharged minors from the service.[183] In Massachusetts a state judge discharged a minor because his consent papers had been signed by only one parent. According to an army officer, this threatened the legality of all minors enlisted in Massachusetts—about 2,500 soldiers.[184] Both Massachusetts and Connecticut passed laws prohibiting the enlistment of minors without consent, though the Bay State judiciously waited until after the war was over and recruiting had been suspended. The Connecticut assembly also strengthened its *habeas corpus* laws to facilitate the release of minors who were recruited into the service.[185]

A third army bill taken up by Congress met with little opposition and in fact had the full support of Federalists. This legislation was framed initially to raise the 40,000 volunteers for local defense that Monroe had called for, but after the defeat of conscription it was modified so that it also raised troops for use on the northern frontier. In its final form, the bill authorized recruiting 40,000 volunteers— which Monroe planned to use in Canada—and accepting up to 40,000 state troops into federal service for local defense.[186]

This bill represented a significant departure from existing policy: hitherto the administration had opposed state armies, fearing that they would siphon off potential recruits from the regular army. Many states, however, preferred state troops over militia because they were more professional and less disruptive. Virginia had authorized a state army in early 1813, mainly out of fear of a slave revolt. This army was disbanded several months later at the request of the national government, but only after the administration promised to keep a body of regulars at Norfolk and pay the expenses of some militia called out without federal authority.[187]

The New England states could not be placated so easily. Connecticut authorized a state army in 1812, and Massachusetts and Rhode Island followed suit in 1814. At first the administration was reluctant to sanction the use of these troops, but by the summer of 1814 British raids along the coast had become so common that the War Department relented. The administration agreed to accept Rhode Island's troops into federal service in lieu of militia, and other states, at least seven of whom had authorized armies, clamored for the same treatment. The new law put Congress's stamp of approval on the practice.[188]

❖ ❖ ❖ ❖ ❖ ❖

Congress also dealt with naval affairs in this session, even though most of the nation's ships were bottled up in port. On November 15, shortly before leaving office, Secretary of the Navy William Jones delivered a report to Congress making several recommendations for overhauling the service. To facilitate naval administration, he called for the creation of a board of commissioners that would be responsible for overseeing the construction of warships, the procurement of naval stores, and the deployment of the fleet. There was little objection to this proposal.[189] Now that the nation was committed to a long-term construction program, a more efficient means of administering the service was needed. Hence Congress passed the necessary legislation with little debate.[190]

Jones also recommended establishing a school to train officers for the navy. This was the first of many times that Congress considered the matter, but not until 1845 was the Naval Academy at Annapolis established. Jones's final recommendation called for a system of compulsory service to insure an adequate supply of seamen for the navy. The fleet, Jones said, was desperately short of men, and conscription was justified because most seamen escaped militia duty. But this proposal smacked too much of the British practice of impressment to receive any serious consideration.[191]

Congress also passed another naval expansion bill. With most of the nation's larger warships blockaded in port, smaller vessels had come to play a greater role in the war. American privateers had been particularly effective against British commerce. "The effects of their enterprises against the commerce of the enemy," said a Virginia congressman, "had been great and important." A fleet of "small, swift-sailing vessels . . . would, in all probability, conduce to put a speedy end to the war, by the impression it would make on the enemy's commerce."[192] In accordance with this thinking, Congress authorized the purchase or construction of twenty schooners carrying eight to sixteen guns.[193] The conflict ended, however, before any of these vessels could be put to sea.

❖ ❖ ❖ ❖ ❖ ❖ ❖

The financial problems the nation faced were every bit as pressing as its military problems, and this issue also created divisions in the Republican party. Before leaving office in late September, George Campbell delivered his last financial report to Congress. Conceding that Gallatin's plan of war finance had broken down, Campbell said that it was no longer possible to finance the war with borrowed money. "The experience of the present year," he said, "furnishes ground to doubt whether this be practicable." Estimating a revenue shortfall of $11,700,000 for the balance of 1814 and heavy expenses for 1815, Campbell recommended that Congress impose new taxes and raise the interest rate on treasury notes.[194]

While Congress waited for Campbell's successor to make more detailed recommendations, the Virginia paper money advocates seized the initiative. Thomas Jefferson, who had never been fond of bank paper, wrote to friends to urge the expediency of paper money both to finance the war and to serve as a circulating medium. "Congress may now borrow, of the public and without interest," he told a friend, "all the money they may want to the amount of a competent circulation, by merely issuing their own promissory notes." "[O]ur experience," he told Madison, "has proved [paper money] may be run up to 2. or 300 M[illion] without more than doubling . . . prices."[195] Monroe shared Jefferson's views, and so too did a number of congressmen, including Nathaniel Macon, who was fond of saying that "*paper money never was beat.*"[196] Madison, however, was cool to the idea.

On October 10 John W. Eppes, another advocate of paper money,[197] introduced a compromise proposal from the House Ways and Means Committee. It called for new taxes and a new issue of interest-bearing treasury notes "in sums sufficiently small for the ordinary purposes of society." Unlike the treasury notes already in circulation, the new notes would not be redeemable in specie, though they could be exchanged for bonds or used to pay taxes or buy public lands. Since they were designed to serve as a national currency, they were essentially a form of paper money.[198]

While Congress was mulling over Eppes's proposal, Dallas submitted his first report on public finance. Although Madison had urged him to be conciliatory to Congress, the Philadelphia financier refused to pull his punches.[199] He painted an even bleaker picture of public finance than Campbell had, estimating a revenue shortfall for the year of $12,300,000. Dallas asked for authority to borrow money and to issue additional treasury notes, but he rejected Eppes's scheme for relying on treasury notes as a circulating medium because of their high interest rate and their exposure "to every breath of popular prejudice or alarm." Instead, Dallas argued that the best way to put the nation on a sound financial footing was with new taxes and a national bank.[200]

Later in the session Dallas sent two additional reports to Congress. The first, dated December 2, outlined the Treasury's problems in paying the national debt.[201] The second, submitted on January 17, contained Dallas's estimates for 1815. Disbursements for the year were expected to top $56,000,000 (including $15,500,000 merely to service the debt), while income—even with new taxes—would be a paltry $15,100,000. This meant that the government would have to raise $40,900,000 through loans and treasury notes.[202]

According to George Ticknor, who was in the gallery when Eppes read this report to the House, Republicans were dumbfounded by Dallas's figures. "You can imagine nothing like the dismay with which [Dallas's report] has filled the Democratic party," he said. "All his former communications were but emollients and palliations, compared with this final disclosure of the bankruptcy of the nation." After reading the report, Eppes "threw it upon the table with expressive violence" and, turning to Federalist William Gaston, half in jest said: "Well, sir, will your party take the Government if we will give it up to them?" "No, sir," replied Gaston, "not unless you will give it to *us* as we gave it to *you*."[203]

❖ ❖ ❖ ❖ ❖ ❖

Congress's first order of business was to give Dallas the authority he needed to raise money to cover expenses for 1814. There was little opposition to authorizing an additional $10,500,000 in treasury notes.[204] Dallas also wanted to borrow $3,000,000 to replace an equivalent sum of government bonds that had been shipped to Europe for sale there.[205] Federalists tried to limit the interest on the new loan to 8 percent and to pledge specific taxes for the loan's redemption (which was the practice in England), but their amendments were defeated and the bill passed essentially unchanged.[206]

The administration was able to borrow only a fraction of the $3,000,000 authorized by Congress. Three New York banks agreed to accept $600,000 in bonds in exchange for short-term money. The banks paid $80 for each $100 in bonds, and since they paid in depreciated bank notes, the government actually got the equivalent of only $65—which worked out to $390,000 specie value. The subscribers to the earlier loans in 1814 now clamored for additional bonds to make up the 15 percent difference, but the Treasury refused to bow to their demands until Congress finally mandated payment in 1855.[207]

Raising the $40,900,000 that Dallas had said would be necessary for 1815 seemed impossible. Dallas had recommended that the government issue $15,000,000 in treasury notes and try to borrow $25,000,000.[208] But the chances of borrowing this sum were so remote that Congress decided to reverse his figures. The war ended before the necessary legislation was passed, but ultimately Congress authorized $25,000,000 in treasury notes and a loan of $18,500,000.[209]

Besides authorizing additional loans and treasury notes, Congress also imposed new taxes. As unpalatable as this was, everyone recognized that as long as the war continued there was no other way to restore public credit. Accordingly, members of the Ways and Means Committee met and, with "the British list of taxes before them," drew up bills for a host of new internal duties.[210]

Seven of the bills became law.[211] The most important imposed a direct tax of $6,000,000. This was twice the direct tax levied in 1814, and it was to be collected annually instead of just once. Any state could secure a 10- or 15-percent discount by paying the tax directly into the Treasury, but in contrast to 1814, when seven states had taken advantage of this provision, only four did in 1815.[212] Congress also imposed a tax of 20 cents on each gallon of spirits distilled in the United States. This duty, which was above and beyond the tax imposed on stills in 1813, was greater than the tax that had precipitated the Whiskey Rebellion in 1794.[213]

Southern and western Republicans protested that both the direct tax and the "whiskey" tax bore too heavily on their constituents. "[I]f any thing could revolt our citizens against the war," Jefferson declared, "it would be the extravagance with which they are about to be taxed. . . . The taxes proposed cannot be paid."[214] Most northerners, however, considered the taxes fair, and Federalists took special delight in forcing those responsible for the war to pay for it. "You must 'pay for the whistle which you have purchased,'" said Grosvenor.[215]

The other revenue bills were less controversial. Taxes were imposed on various goods manufactured in the United States, including iron products, candles, hats, umbrellas, paper, saddles, boots, beer, tobacco, leather, jewelry, and gold, silver, and plated ware. Gold and silver watches were also taxed as was household furniture valued at more than $200. In addition, the existing duties on auctions sales, retailers, and postage were increased by 50 to 100 percent, and the duty on carriages by a lesser amount.

All the taxes were to remain in effect until public credit was restored. The total amount that accrued from all the internal taxes—including those adopted in 1813—was $13,700,000 in 1815.[216] Although the Republicans were slow to impose internal taxes during the war, the system finally adopted was the most sweeping enacted before the Civil War—far more sweeping than anything envisioned by the Federalists in the 1790s.

❖ ❖ ❖ ❖ ❖ ❖

Even more controversial than the tax bills was Dallas's plan for a national bank. Historically, Republicans had opposed a bank, but as the nation's financial situation deteriorated, congressional support for a bank mounted. Proponents saw a number of advantages to a bank: as a source for a national currency and government loans, as a means of transferring funds across the country, and as a vehicle for establishing a more orderly system of public and private finance. But even the bank's proponents could not agree on the details, and there was opposition to the project in both parties. Some Republicans still regarded a national bank as a dangerous and unconstitutional expedient that would open the door to commercial tyranny, and many Federalists feared that it would be "a mere machine for manufacturing paper money."[217]

In his first report to Congress on October 17, Dallas outlined his own plan for a bank. Much to the dismay of some Republicans, the bank he recommended was an enlarged version of the first national bank—devised by Alexander Hamilton in 1791—though it was to have much closer ties to the government. Like the first bank, Dallas's bank would have a twenty-year charter and maintain its central office in Philadelphia (still the nation's financial capital), with branch offices in other cities. The bank's capital stock was set at $50,000,000, five times the capital of the first national bank. Of this, $30,000,000 would be offered to the public. Subscribers would have to put up at least one-fifth of the purchase price in specie and the balance in war bonds or treasury notes. The government would take the remaining $20,000,000 in stock in exchange for war bonds. The bank would be governed by fifteen directors, five of whom (including the presiding officer) would be chosen by the administration. The bank's notes could be used to settle all obligations with the federal government, and the bank would be required to lend the government up to $30,000,000 at 6 percent interest.[218]

Speaker Cheves had taken care at the beginning of the session to pack the House Ways and Means Committee with pro-bank men, though the chair was still held by the hostile Eppes.[219] On November 7, Jonathan Fisk introduced a bill from committee that provided for incorporating a bank along the lines sketched out by Dallas.[220] Although Dallas had not mentioned the possibility of suspending specie payments, Fisk's bill expressly authorized the president to take this action. Federalists were appalled by the entire proposal, fearing that the government would exert too much control over the bank and that the institution would flood the country with bank notes. According to William Gaston, the bank's specie would be so limited that any sizable loan to the government would necessitate an immediate suspension of specie payments.[221]

Many Republicans—including John C. Calhoun—agreed with the Federalists. Calhoun forced a series of amendments that fundamentally changed the bank's character by making it more autonomous. The government's right to purchase bank stock and to select bank directors was eliminated; so too was the forced loan to the government, the Treasury's mandatory acceptance of the bank's notes, and the authority to suspend specie payments. The bank was also scaled down to $30,000,000, and the stock could be purchased only with specie or with treasury notes hereafter issued.[222] Nothing was left of Dallas's proposal, said a Republican, "except the name—every feature and every important principle is changed."[223]

Dallas vigorously protested that in this form the bank would benefit neither the government nor the country. If the administration issued the large number of treasury notes needed to float the bank, he warned, it would "have an injurious effect upon the credit of the Government; and, also, upon the prospects of a loan for 1815."[224] These arguments carried some weight in the House. There was also a backlash among regular Republicans against "Calhoun & [the] other giddy young men" who had spearheaded the drive to change the original bill.[225] As a result, Calhoun's bill was voted down by a large majority.[226]

The Senate, which had been waiting for the House to act, now took the initiative. On December 2 Rufus King reported a bill from committee that incorporated a bank along the lines favored by Dallas. The bill passed the Senate by a three-vote margin but was narrowly defeated in the House when Speaker Cheves voted against it.[227] Calling the proposed bank "a dangerous, unexampled," and even "a desperate resort," Cheves claimed that it would never achieve the ends for which it was created.[228]

The House subsequently reconsidered this vote and then sent the bill back to committee. Federalists Richard Stockton and Thomas Oakley pledged to vote for a modified bank bill and expressed confidence that "they would be joined by a majority of their political friends."[229] The committee produced a bill that once again provided for a small, autonomous bank—one that was free from government control, did not have to loan the government money, and could not suspend specie payments. In addition, it did not have to commence operations until 1816. In this form, the bill won the support of both parties and was approved by large majorities in both houses.[230] Not everyone was happy with the bill, but most preferred this bank to Dallas's version or to no bank at all. As Daniel Webster put it: "We were obliged to make a bank or let Dallas's plan go."[231]

The bill was sent to the president on January 23, 1815. Dallas, who considered Congress so unmanageable that he was already contemplating resigning, was incensed. "I asked for bread," he said, "and [Congress] gave me a stone. I asked for a Bank to serve the Government during the war; and they have given me a commercial Bank, to go into operation after the war."[232] Taking Dallas's views to heart, Madison vetoed the bill. The proposed bank, he said, would not "answer the purposes of reviving the public credit, of providing a national medium of circulation, and of aiding the Treasury."[233]

Rebuffed by the administration, congressional Republicans met in caucus and decided to resurrect the original bill—the one favored by Dallas.[234] Accordingly, on February 6 James Barbour reintroduced this bill in the Senate. Republicans refused to send the bill to committee, claiming that the matter already had been discussed enough and that everyone understood the issues. After beating back a series of amendments, Republicans pushed the bill through the Senate by a two-vote margin. The House also refused to commit or amend the bill, but before a vote on the measure could be taken, news of peace arrived. This gave the bill's enemies an opening. The bill was first tabled and then postponed indefinitely by a one-vote margin. This killed the project for the session.[235]

❖ ❖ ❖ ❖ ❖ ❖

Another issue that Congress had to grapple with in this session was trade with the enemy. On September 22, Republican James Fisk of Vermont, whose own state was as guilty as any, offered a resolution to strengthen the enemy trade act of 1812.[236] The House approved the resolution, but for the next two months Congress devoted its attention to other matters, waiting for the administration to take the lead on the trade issue. Finally, on November 19, Dallas sent a report to the House outlining the government's enforcement problems and recommending legal remedies.[237]

Armed with Dallas's report, the House Ways and Means Committee drew up a new enemy trade bill, which Eppes introduced in early December.[238] This bill gave government officials more extensive powers than any previous trade restriction, including the enforcement act of 1809 and the embargo of 1813. According to the *Federal Republican,* "The Bill contains novel, extraordinary, and dangerous provisions, at war with the principles of our free constitution and the established rights of the citizen. It creates a swarm of irresponsible petty tyrants, spies and informers who are clothed with powers exceeding those, of the highest officers of the government."[239]

The bill authorized customs officials to search without warrant any land or water craft or any person suspected of trading with the enemy and to seize any goods suspected of being illegally imported or of being on their way to the enemy. With a warrant, customs officials could also search any building suspected of containing goods which were likely to be shipped to the enemy or which might have been imported from enemy territory. Inspectors were classified as customs officials, and all such officials were empowered to raise posses and were rendered virtually immune to damage suits. The penalties established in 1812 for trading with the enemy were increased, and no one was permitted to visit the enemy without a presidential or gubernatorial passport.[240]

Federalists offered a host of amendments to the bill, and when these failed, they tried to prevent a quorum by absenting themselves from the House.[241] But Republicans mustered enough votes to push the bill through both houses, and the president signed the measure into law on February 4, 1815.[242] The new law never received a fair test, however, because it expired two weeks later with the restoration of peace. The law was extreme, but whether it would have worked may be doubted. The enforcement machinery of the customs department remained primitive, and people living on the frontier showed a remarkable determination to keep profitable avenues of trade open. In the contest between the government and smugglers, most of the advantages still lay with the latter.

❖ ❖ ❖ ❖ ❖ ❖

By the time Congress adjourned on March 3, 1815, the crisis the nation faced had passed, but only because peace had been restored. During the long session, legislation had been adopted to raise the land bounty, permit the recruitment of minors, establish a volunteer corps, accept state troops into federal service, create a board of naval commissioners, build commerce raiders, curtail trade with the enemy, issue treasury notes, and authorize additional loans and taxes.

Under normal circumstances, this might have been an impressive record of legislation, but given the crisis many people expected more. The administration had asked Congress for energetic and controversial measures, but these measures had divided Republicans and united Federalists. As a result, neither of the administration's two key proposals—conscription or the national bank—had become law. "The efficient and manly measures proposed by the executive," complained a Pennsylvania Republican, "were all either totally rejected, or frittered down into insignificance."[243]

It was not simply that Congress failed to adopt key administration proposals. It was slow to take any action at all. Even though Congress had convened on September 19, no war legislation of any consequence was adopted until December, and the pace of action remained slow throughout the session. Most Republicans attributed the delays to the *"inertia"* of Congress, the "perverseness" of independents like Calhoun and Cheves, or the "turpitude of federalism."[244] "Our misfortune," said Joseph Varnum, "is that we have a number of young Politicians who, although ardent & honest, Suffer themselves to be misled by the pla[u]sible Arguments of the Opposition."[245]

The failure of Congress to take energetic action led to growing criticism in the press. The Worcester *National Aegis* accused Congress of "wasting two or three months in useless debate," and the Boston *Yankee* echoed this charge.[246] The New York *National Advocate* suggested that congressmen were "forgetful, or, at least, unmindful of the spirit that prevails among the people," and the Philadelphia *Aurora* said that if the British had bribed Congress "that body could not more effectually have served their employer than has been done by procrastination and idle debate."[247]

No doubt the record of Congress would have been more impressive if Republicans had been able to close ranks or win over the Federalists. But such was not to be. In spite of the crisis, Republicans remained divided, and in spite of their pledges of support, Federalists found few measures they could actually vote for. "Instead of uniting with the majority to defend the country," said a Republican newspaper, "they [were], if possible, more infuriate in their opposition than ever."[248]

The specter of New England disaffection also weighed heavily on Congress. Two months into the session, Republican Charles J. Ingersoll openly discussed the objectives of a meeting in Hartford sponsored by New England Federalists. "Since we assembled," he said, "a most alarming temper has appeared . . . among some of the Eastern States; and it is said to be intended, by the agitation of the Hartford Convention, to proceed deliberately to the disintegration of New England from the Union."[249] Although Ingersoll discounted the possibility of secession, many other Republicans did not. Throughout this session, Republican leaders had to contend with not only a foreign war but also the possibility of domestic war. "A lowering sky begins to shroud the political horizon," said the Hartford *American Mercury*, "and clouds black with uncommon vengeance over-hang us, and portend a dreadful storm."[250]

CHAPTER 10

The Hartford Convention

THE WAR OF 1812 was America's most unpopular foreign war. It generated more intense opposition than any other war in the nation's history, including the war in Vietnam. Although most scholars have focused on New England's opposition, Federalists in the middle and southern states opposed the conflict, too. Except for two brief periods—one in the summer of 1812 and the other in the fall of 1814—the party presented a united front against the war.

In Congress Federalists voted as a bloc on almost all war legislation. They unanimously opposed the declaration of war in June of 1812, and thereafter they voted against almost every proposal to raise men or money, to foster privateering, or to restrict trade with the enemy. The only war measures they supported were those they considered defensive—mainly bills to increase the navy or to build coastal fortifications. "The Federal party," said the Salem *Gazette* in 1814, "have steadily at all times . . . maintained that in time of Peace, as well as in War, the nation ought to be protected and defended by a Navy and by Fortifications."[1]

The House took 305 roll-call votes on war-related measures between June 1, 1812 (when Madison sent his war message to Congress), and February 13, 1815 (when news of the peace treaty reached Washington). Federalists achieved an index of relative cohesion of 94.4 percent on these measures: on the average war measure almost 95 percent of House Federalists voted together. The Senate took 227 roll-call votes on war-related measures, and here Federalists achieved a cohesion of 92.5 percent. Since a cohesion of 70 percent is considered a sign of party solidarity, the record of the Federalists is extraordinary—surely the most remarkable record of bloc voting in any war in the nation's history.[2]

Why did Federalists oppose the war? For one thing, they saw it as a party war designed to further the interests of Republicans and to silence the opposition—a view that was reinforced by the Baltimore riots in 1812 and the refusal of the administration to take Federalists into the cabinet in 1814. "I regard the war, as a war of party, & not of the Country," said Rufus King in 1812. "[T]he people are no more obliged . . . to approve and applaud the measure," added the Philadelphia *United States' Gazette*, "than . . . any other party project."[3]

Federalists also feared that the war would throw the nation into the arms of Napoleon, who was variously described as "the great destroyer," the "monster of human depravity," and "the arch-Fiend who has long been the curse & Scourge of the European World."[4] The initial protests against the war, particularly in New England, often expressed greater fear of a French alliance than of the war itself. "The horrors of war, compared with it, are mere amusement," said Timothy Dwight. "The touch of *France* is pollution. Her embrace is death." French dominion, added William Ellery Channing, threatened not just the wealth, but *"the minds, the character, the morals, the religion* of our nation."[5]

Even after the danger of a French alliance had receded, Federalists continued to oppose the war because they considered it an "offensive" war aimed at Canada. Although willing to support a war to protect American commerce or to defend the nation's frontiers, they refused to sanction the conquest of Canada. "Let it not be said," Congressman Morris Miller of New York told the Republicans in 1813, "that we refuse you the means of defence. For that we always have been—we still are ready to open the treasure of the nation. We will give you millions for defence; but not a cent for the conquest of Canada—not the ninety-ninth part of a cent for the extermination of its inhabitants."[6]

Even if the invasion of Canada succeeded, Federalists were convinced that the war would do more harm than good. "Whether we consider our agriculture, our commerce, our monied systems, or our internal safety," declared the Alexandria *Gazette*, "nothing but disaster can result from it."[7] Nor did Federalists expect the nation to win any concessions from the enemy, certainly not on an issue as vital as impressment. "No war of any duration," said James A. Bayard, "will ever extort this concession."[8]

In sum, Federalists saw the war as a costly, futile, and partisan venture that was likely to produce little good and much evil. The best way to bring the conflict to an end, most Federalists agreed, was to oppose it. Hence they wrote, spoke, and preached against the war; they discouraged enlistments in the army and subscriptions to the war loans; and they vigorously condemned all who supported the war and worked for their defeat at the polls.[9]

❖ ❖ ❖ ❖ ❖ ❖

Even though Federalists everywhere opposed the war, those in New England went the farthest. Because they were the dominant party, Federalists here did not have to worry about persecution or violence from an outraged majority. Moreover, they shared an abhorrence of the war—frequently grounded on religious principles—that was unmatched elsewhere (except perhaps in Maryland, where the Baltimore riots had radicalized the party). "[E]ach man who volunteers his services in such a cause," said a Massachusetts preacher, "or loans his money for its support, or by his conversation, his writings, or any other mode of influence, encourages its prosecution . . . loads his conscience with the blackest crimes."[10]

Federalists in New England were also able to use the machinery of state and local government to obstruct the war effort. In Hartford, Federalists sought to end loud demonstrations by army recruiters by adopting a pair of city ordinances that restricted public music and parades.[11] In New Bedford, Federalists denounced privateering and voted to quarantine all arriving privateers for forty days—ostensibly on medical grounds.[12] And in Boston, the Massachusetts legislature threatened to sequester federal tax money if militia arms due to the state under an 1808 law were not delivered.[13]

New England Federalists made their opposition felt in other ways. In Massachusetts, after a Republican paper denounced Federalists for applauding naval victories in a war they opposed, Josiah Quincy sponsored a resolution in the state senate declaring that "in a war like the present . . . it is not becoming a moral and religious people to express any approbation of military or naval exploits, which are not immediately connected with the defence of our sea coast and soil."[14] The senate adopted this resolution, and it remained on the books until 1824, when Republicans finally succeeded in expunging it from the record.[15]

In Connecticut, Federalists were accused of aiding the enemy in the "blue light" affair. In late 1813 a squadron of ships under Stephen Decatur tried to slip out of New London harbor at night but was driven back by the British fleet. Decatur later complained that someone had signaled the British by flashing blue lights.[16] Whether the signals were

Josiah Quincy, by Gilbert Stuart. Courtesy of the Museum of Fine Arts, Boston

given by a British spy or an American citizen is unknown, but Republicans were quick to fix the blame on Federalists. It was "the blackest treason," declared *Niles' Register*.[17] Connecticut Federalists demanded a congressional investigation to clear the air, but there was no way of ascertaining the truth.[18] By then "blue light Federalist" had already entered the political lexicon. According to one Federalist, the phrase had become an "ornament or embellishment to a speech, such as Old tory, British gold, Henryism, &c."[19]

❖ ❖ ❖ ❖ ❖ ❖

The most persistent source of conflict between New England and the federal government was over the control and deployment of the militia. This was no small matter because the militia played such a vital role in the nation's defense. The militia problem, in turn, raised the larger issue of who was responsible for New England's defense. Was it the federal government or was it the states? Federalists never found a satisfactory answer to this question, and the result was the Hartford Convention, a regional conference convened to air New England's grievances.[20]

The New England militia were among the best in the nation. They were well-armed and well-trained and had repeatedly distinguished themselves during the Revolution. The troops were organized in accordance with the uniform militia act of 1792, which meant that each company had sixty-four privates plus officers and musicians. Five companies made up a battalion, ten constituted a regiment, forty a brigade, and eighty a division. In actual practice there were variations to this pattern, but in New England, more so than elsewhere, the militia measured up to federal specifications.[21]

The first clash over the militia took place in the summer of 1812. On June 22, four days after the declaration of war, Brigadier General Henry Dearborn, the army's ranking officer in New England, ordered out forty-one companies of militia in Massachusetts, five companies in Connecticut, and four in Rhode Island. The War Department was sending the regulars in New England to the northern frontier and wanted the militia to garrison the empty forts that would be left behind. But to facilitate deployment and control, Dearborn asked for *detached* companies without a full complement of officers. This assured that the regular officer in charge of each post would retain control and would not be outranked by a militia officer.[22]

All three governors—Caleb Strong of Massachusetts, Roger Griswold of Connecticut, and William Jones of Rhode Island (no relation to the secretary of the navy of the same name)—refused to meet the requisition. Acting with the full support of their councils (and in the case of Massachusetts, with the approval of the state supreme court as well), the governors grounded their refusal on the Constitution. Strong and Griswold argued that, internal disorders aside, the militia could not be called out unless the country were invaded or were in imminent danger of invasion, and that no such contingency existed.

Moreover, since the states were constitutionally charged with appointing the militia officers, the Connecticut council and the Massachusetts court held that their troops could not serve under regulars. Rhode Island, on the other hand, did not raise this objection, doubtless because Dearborn's order called for a suitably high-ranking state officer to accompany the troops. Governor Jones merely said that the militia would be called out when, in his opinion, the Constitution required it.[23]

The three governors refused to comply with Dearborn's request both to protest the war and to insure that they retained control over their militia. Convinced that the assault on Canada was unjust and unwise, they were unwilling to subject their militia to the rigors of garrison duty in support of the venture. Moreover, rumors were rife that if the militia were federalized, they would be marched to Canada.[24] Already citizen soldiers from New York, Pennsylvania, and the western states were being called up for service on the northern frontier, and New Englanders feared that their militia would meet the same fate.[25] In order to dissociate themselves from an unjust war and to retain control over their only means of defense, New England officials refused to comply with Dearborn's request.

President Madison condemned this decision, claiming that it was based on "a novel and unfortunate exposition" of the Constitution and that it challenged the very basis of the Union. If the United States could not call up militia in time of war, he said, "they are not one nation for the purpose most of all requiring it."[26] Joseph Story claimed that every judge on the Supreme Court agreed with the administration's position, and Eustis and Dearborn argued that the president could bypass the governors and call the militia directly into service.[27] But Madison—ever cautious—refused to press the matter. Although privately he expressed hope that the militia would turn out voluntarily, none did.[28]

❖ ❖ ❖ ❖ ❖ ❖

Even though New England leaders were uncooperative in 1812, they had no objection to calling out their militia when the enemy actually threatened. In different ways, too, each state tried to resolve the command problem. Connecticut was the least flexible. Her officials were unwilling to place the militia under United States officers under any circumstances. To assure control, they simply assigned a high-ranking state officer to any troops called into service. Massachusetts and Rhode Island were more cooperative and tried to compromise whenever possible. But in the end their compromises broke down, and they found themselves in much the same position as Connecticut.

Connecticut officials called out their first militia in June of 1813 to protect Decatur's squadron of ships in New London harbor. Governor John Cotton Smith (who had succeeded Griswold) said that he was "heartily disposed" to assist Decatur, and militia and state troops remained on duty in the city for about five months.[29] Although the number of troops in service fluctuated, it was usually about twenty companies, many of which were understrength. Normally these troops would have rated no more than a brigadier general, but the army's representative in the city, Brigadier General Henry Burbeck, would outrank any militia officer of the same grade. Hence state officials assigned the command to Major General William Williams. Burbeck was a Federalist and acceded to this arrangement. Although under a state officer, the troops were considered in federal service and were supplied and paid by the federal government.[30]

This arrangement worked smoothly enough in 1813, but the following year it broke down. In early 1814 Burbeck began to quarrel with state officials, perhaps because he resented his anomalous position. In addition, he came under growing fire from political enemies in New England. A Boston Republican told Monroe that Burbeck had repeatedly said "that the war is unjust, unnecessary & impolitic, & that the administration have not talents to carry it on." Similarly, friends of the government in New London told the president that Burbeck "has not the confidence of any of the Republicans, and they think him not deserving the confidence of the Administration."[31] In response to these complaints, the War Department transferred Burbeck out of the district in May of 1814.[32]

After Burbeck's departure, the regular command in New London devolved temporarily on Colonel Jacob Kingsbury. State officials described Kingsbury as "a *Connecticut Man* in every respect" and a "*discreet* and excellent officer"—meaning that he was a good Federalist.[33] Neither his rank nor his politics disposed Kingsbury to challenge the state. Instead he accepted the existing command arrangement and expressed hope that Connecticut would "avoid as far as possible, the burdens of this war."[34]

Kingsbury was the army's ranking officer in New London until July of 1814, when the new district commander, Brigadier General Thomas H. Cushing, arrived on the scene. Fresh from Massachusetts, where a compromise had enabled him to command the militia, Cushing would settle for nothing less in Connecticut. Able and charming, he soon won the hearts of the people in the city and the respect of many officers in the militia. Unlike Burbeck, however, he insisted on commanding any troops called into service.[35]

Shortly after Cushing's arrival, a British fleet appeared off the coast. State officials responded by calling out a brigade of militia. These troops and their replacements remained on duty for about three months. During the first month they were under the direction of two militia brigadiers, first Jirah Isham and then Levi Lusk, both of whom considered themselves under Cushing's command. This arrangement evidently met with the approval of the militia as well as the people of New London.[36] "Brigr Gen Cushing is the Gentleman and the Soldier," said Isham. "His vigilance, his attention to our Troops, his attachment to this State, his opposition to any surrender of our State rights . . . all conspire to forbid his being superseded in the command here."[37] State officials, however, were determined to put their own man in charge. Hence Governor Smith ordered Major General Augustine Taylor to take command.[38]

Taylor arrived in New London in September. Acting on orders from the governor, Lusk put his brigade under Taylor's command.[39] Cushing was furious. Summoning Lusk to an interview, he warned the state officer that if he disobeyed orders he would "be considered as engaged in a mutiny, & be treated accordingly" and that if he withdrew his troops "it would be considered as desertion and treated accordingly."[40] When these warnings failed, Cushing threatened to use force and even paraded his regulars in front of Taylor's headquarters. Unwilling to be intimidated, Taylor called out the militia for inspection. Badly outnumbered and facing the prospect of a hopeless and bloody confrontation, Cushing retired from the field.[41] But claiming that the militia had been withdrawn from national service, he ordered federal agents to stop supplying and paying them.[42] This meant that for the last five months of the war, from September, 1814, to February, 1815, the state had to assume responsibility for any militia called into service.

Officials in Massachusetts were more flexible, largely because of the influence of Governor Strong. Unlike the governor of Connecticut, who insistently focused on the command issue, Strong was more interested in securing proper deployment of the troops. When he refused to meet the War Department's initial request in 1812, he left the command issue to his supreme court while addressing himself to the absence of any immediate threat and to defects in Dearborn's plan of deployment. Shortly thereafter, he demonstrated that effective use of the militia was his chief concern by dispatching three companies for service under a regular army officer on the Maine frontier. These troops remained on duty for three months in 1812, commanded by a regular officer and supplied by the federal government.[43]

There were few calls on the Massachusetts militia in 1812 or 1813, but the following year was different. In the spring of 1814, the British blockaded the Massachusetts coast and began raiding and ransoming exposed towns. Royal officials took special interest in those ports that harbored American warships. At first, state officials eagerly cooperated with Commodore William Bainbridge to protect his squadron in Boston harbor. Small detachments of militia were called out for service at Marblehead and Charlestown, and an additional 3,000 troops were held in readiness. Later, however, state officials complained that the ships at Charlestown were a liability and urged Bainbridge to move them to an unprotected part of the harbor to spare Boston from bombardment. Bainbridge indignantly rejected this proposal.[44] He also let it be known that if Boston surrendered to the British without offering resistance (as Alexandria, Virginia, had done), "*he should certainly Fire upon the Town.*"[45]

Massachusetts officials also had trouble with the army. In the spring of 1814 the state struck a bargain with District Commander Thomas Cushing to coordinate efforts to defend Boston. Governor Strong agreed to permit Cushing to command any militia called out to garrison the forts in the harbor or to protect other vital points near Boston. In return, Cushing promised to interpose no regular officer between himself and the militia, agreeing in effect to keep the militia and regular units under his command entirely separate. This arrangement seemed to satisfy everyone, but before it could be put to the test of a full-scale alarm, Cushing was transferred to Connecticut.[46]

Cushing was succeeded by Dearborn, who assumed command in June of 1814. Dearborn continued Cushing's command arrangement but evidently thought it applied only to Boston. Hence in July, when he called out 1,300 militia because of "the threats and daily depredations of the Enimy," he put a regular officer in charge of each of the posts to which the troops were assigned.[47] Moreover, in accordance with the new code of army regulations drawn up by John Armstrong in 1813, Dearborn organized the troops into companies of 100 men each. In thus dismantling the state's existing organization (which was based on sixty-four-man companies), Dearborn deprived some officers

of their command, forced some men to serve under unfamiliar officers, and subjected all to a new system of drill and tactics. For men
who regarded their militia duties with a deep sense of pride and
tradition, this was a serious affront.[48]

Dearborn's actions led to a host of complaints from displaced officers
and disaffected men alike. Such were the objections that when Dearborn asked for an additional 5,000 men in September, Governor
Strong complied but insisted on placing the troops under state officers.[49] Strong took this step reluctantly (because the state would have
to supply and pay the troops), and he continued to cooperate with
federal officials whenever possible. He allowed those units already in
federal service to finish their tours, and he supplied 300 troops for
service under a United States officer in Portsmouth. Moreover, in an
effort to continue the arrangement for the defense of Boston, he
assigned 1,400 men to serve in the harbor ports under Dearborn's
son, Henry A. S. Dearborn. Although the younger Dearborn was a
brigadier in the militia, he was allowed to take his orders from his
father.[50]

Governor Strong also sought to cooperate with federal officials in
the defense of Maine, which was too remote to be properly supervised
from Boston. Shortly after the breakdown of the command agreement
in Massachusetts, Strong dispatched his aide-de-camp, Lieutenant Colonel William H. Sumner, to stave off trouble in Maine. Sumner's
principal task was to organize the defense of Portland, whose open
harbor and exposed shipping invited attack.[51] Portland had been
burned by the British in 1775, and the townspeople feared that "the
destressing scenes" of the Revolution would be repeated again.[52]

With the governor's aide serving as mediator, a plan for defending
the city was drawn up by the Portland Committee of Public Safety,
Brigadier General John Chandler of the United States Army, and
Major General Alford Richardson of the state militia. The plan called
for maintaining 1,900 militia in service, some commanded by state
officers and others by regulars.[53] This arrangement met with "the
greatest satisfaction" of all concerned, and state officials complimented
Sumner on leaving Portland "in so tranquil a state."[54]

This tranquillity, however, did not last, for state officials had reck-
oned with neither the plans of the War Department nor the wishes of
the Republican militia of Maine. On September 20, the day after
the troops were called into service, orders arrived from Washington
transferring Chandler to Portsmouth and assigning the command in
Portland to Lieutenant Colonel Horatio Stark. Although Stark was
conciliatory enough, his rank seriously compromised the command

agreement. The militia, in any case, had already begun to voice objections against serving under regular officers.[55]

Part of the problem was in Richardson's division. Some of the men deserted and had to be brought back by force, and some of the officers protested against serving under regulars.[56] The militia from Oxford County were even more troublesome. Although this county was the most Republican in the state, its militia showed little interest in making sacrifices for the war.[57] According to Sumner, they were "undisciplined, badly armed, miserably provided, and worse commanded." Such was the "spirit of disaffection" among these troops that Sumner could see no way of implementing the command agreement except by using force, which meant using militia against militia.[58] Since a British attack on Portland seemed imminent, Sumner decided instead to put all the troops under Richardson's command. This quieted the men in Richardson's own division, though the Oxford militia remained obstreperous for the duration of the campaign, often refusing to perform routine duties or to take orders from anyone.[59]

Officials in Boston were distressed by the breakdown of the Portland agreement, but believing that Sumner had done all he could, they supported his resolution of the problem.[60] But this meant that in Maine, as well as in Massachusetts proper, most of the militia were serving under state officers. Hence, Massachusetts, like Connecticut, had to assume financial responsibility for militia called into service in the last five months of the war.

Officials in Rhode Island also tried to cooperate with the army, but they too met with disappointment. Although Rhode Island was spared from British raids in the first two years of the war, by the summer of 1814 her citizens were apprehensive. American officials had long recognized that the state offered an attractive target for enemy operations because of its accessibility by water in all seasons, its spacious and weatherproof harbor, and its ample stock of provisions.[61] The British had occupied Newport during the Revolution, and the inhabitants feared that they would "experience the horrors of War and Conquest" again.[62]

In the hope of forestalling an attack, Governor Jones called out four companies of militia in the summer of 1814. These troops were placed in federal service, partly in the hope of getting federal money and partly out of respect for the regular officer in charge of the city's garrison. But federal agents in Rhode Island were so destitute of funds that the state had to pick up the bill for these as well as five additional companies called out to protect Connecticut.[63] "From the present State of the Treasury," Monroe told Governor Jones, "much dependence must be placed on the local authorities and the banks of your State."[64] Thus Rhode Island, like her two sister states, found herself burdened with her defense costs in the last months of the war.

❖ ❖ ❖ ❖ ❖ ❖

Trouble over the militia was not restricted to the staunchly Federalist states in southern New England. There were also difficulties in New Hampshire. This state had a Republican governor in the first year of the war, and he readily complied with requests for troops and agreed to place them under regular army officers.[65] By 1814, however, Federalists had won control of the state and they were less cooperative. In the spring of that year, Governor John Taylor Gilman reported that such was the fear of an enemy attack on Portsmouth (where the ship-of-the-line *Washington* was under construction) that people there were "moving their Shipping up the River and Valuable Effects out of Town."[66] To protect the city, Gilman called out seven companies of militia, but he refused to place the troops under regular officers. Federal agents responded by withholding supplies, and Gilman, acting on the advice of the state legislature, sent the men home.[67] Later that summer, however, when the British again threatened Portsmouth, Gilman called out 1,500 men, and this time he let them serve under regular officers.[68]

There was also trouble in Vermont. In September of 1813 Republican Governor Jonas Galusha ordered a brigade of militia to New York to assist General Wade Hampton in his ill-fated foray into Canada. The following month, after an inconclusive election, the Vermont legislature chose Federalist Martin Chittenden as governor. Chittenden waited until Hampton's campaign was over and then issued a proclamation ordering the militia home. The troops, he said, were needed for local defense and could not serve under regular officers anyway.[69]

Chittenden dispatched Brigadier General Jacob Davis to New York to execute the order. When Davis arrived in Plattsburgh, he was arrested for sedition, and a group of Republican officers sent Chittenden an open letter refusing to obey his order.[70] Denouncing the governor's proclamation as "a gross insult," the officers said: "An invitation or order to desert the standard of our country will never be obeyed by us."[71] Although the officers insisted that the proclamation had been circulated among the troops without effect, many soldiers had already returned home. The campaign was over, and the remaining men were soon discharged anyway.[72]

The matter, however, did not end here. A Republican paper called

Chittenden's recall order "the most scandalous & unwarrantable stain on the political history of America" and suggested that the governor be tried for treason.[73] Several weeks later Solomon Sharp of Kentucky introduced a series of resolutions in Congress calling for Chittenden's prosecution. The governor's proclamation, said Sharp, "was in direct violation of the statute, which makes it penal to entice the soldiers in the service of the United States to desert."[74]

Although Congress took no action on Sharp's proposal, Harrison Gray Otis introduced a resolution in the Massachusetts legislature promising to support the people of Vermont in "their constitutional rights whenever the same shall be in danger of infringement from any quarter."[75] This resolution was tabled, though it elicited sharp reproofs from both New Jersey and Pennsylvania. We view "with contempt and abhorrence," said the New Jersey legislature, "the ravings of an infuriated faction, either as issuing from a legislative body, a maniac governor, or discontented or ambitious demagogues."[76]

There was further trouble in 1814. In April General James Wilkinson asked Chittenden to call up troops to protect American positions on the eastern side of Lake Champlain. Chittenden responded by ordering 1,000 men to Vergennes and 500 to Burlington.[77] But these troops—like their compatriots in Massachusetts—deeply resented being reorganized into 100-man companies. In Vergennes, the officers—Federalists and Republicans alike—were slow to muster their men and were reportedly "very lavish with their furloughs." According to an observer, the officers were only interested in their pay and popularity and the men were "undisciplined & insubordinate."[78] The situation was no better at Burlington. Here the men were so incensed by the reorganization scheme that they refused to be mustered. Instead, they simply "discharged themselves."[79]

Later in the year, when the British threatened Plattsburgh, Chittenden endeared himself to Republicans by urging Vermonters to volunteer for service in New York. After the battle was over, he issued a proclamation announcing that the character of the war had changed and urging everyone to unite in the country's defense.[80] The state, however, continued to insist on its prerogatives to officer the militia. Shortly after Chittenden's proclamation was issued, the Vermont council adopted a resolution proclaiming that the militia could serve only under their own officers.[81]

❖ ❖ ❖ ❖ ❖ ❖

While all five New England states feuded with the federal government over the militia, the problem was most serious in southern New England because of mounting defense costs there. In Massachusetts, the cost ran about $200,000 a month and eventually totaled $850,000; in Connecticut the monthly bill was $50,000 and the final cost close to $150,000; and in Rhode Island the monthly figure was $15,000 and the total more than $50,000.[82] In discharging these bills, state officials could expect little help from Washington. Government agents were so strapped for funds that they could not even supply those militia that were in federal service.[83] Moreover, the administration made it clear that it would neither advance money nor promise reimbursement for any militia serving under state officers in violation of federal rules. These expenses, the secretary of war said, "are chargeable to the State, and not to the United States."[84]

With little prospect of securing federal aid, state officials turned to local sources. But raising money in wartime New England was no easy task. The federal tax burden was already heavy and still growing at a time when the region was in the throes of a depression. With business so slow, only Rhode Island, whose economy was cushioned by a healthy textile industry, was bold enough to impose new taxes, and then only to the extent of $25,000.[85]

Unwilling to raise taxes, New England officials looked to their banks for relief, but these institutions could provide only limited aid. The suspension of specie payments in the middle and southern states had put such a premium on specie that speculators were buying up New England bank notes in order to redeem them for cash. This forced the banks to retrench, which meant they could not meet the states' needs. In Massachusetts only $631,000 of a $1,000,000 loan offering was taken; in Connecticut, only $50,000 of a $500,000 offering, and in Rhode Island, only $23,000 of a $100,000 offering.[86]

The financial situation in Connecticut was particularly chaotic. The state was inundated with depreciated New York bank paper, which drove specie and Connecticut banks notes out of circulation and created an acute shortage of legal money.[87] Some businessmen issued their own currency, but these notes were easily counterfeited and of doubtful value.[88] For most people, finding enough legal currency to pay their debts and taxes was difficult, if not impossible. "The People cry for relief," said one Federalist. "All say something must be done."[89] The state finally authorized the payment of taxes in New York notes and permitted Connecticut banks to issue special notes—known as "facilities"—that did not have to be redeemed until after the war. The banks were also allowed to issue notes whose face value was less than a dollar.[90]

New England's defense problem was not unique. Other states were also forced to pay for defense measures in the last year of the war.[91] "So far as regards the common defence," Rufus King concluded, "the Genl. Govt. has deserted its duties."[92] Virginia ran up the largest bill. Extensive British operations in the Chesapeake forced the Old Dominion to advance the federal government close to $1,000,000, and the state's Federalist congressmen insisted that Virginia was "in the most deplorable situation."[93] Unlike New England, however, Virginia officials had ready access to cheap bank paper and a firm promise of federal reimbursement. The financial crisis was therefore less acute. In New England, on the other hand, Federalists bitterly complained that the administration had squandered its resources in Canada while leaving the region defenseless.[94]

❖ ❖ ❖ ❖ ❖ ❖

The defense problem was one of New England's chief grievances in 1814, but it was not the only one. Ever since Jefferson's presidency, Federalists had been critical of Republican foreign policy. Virtually all Federalists agreed that the rejection of the Monroe-Pinkney Treaty, followed by the enactment of commercial sanctions and the declaration of war—in short the whole policy of confrontation with England—was disastrous. The costs of this policy, in blood and treasure, had mounted steadily since 1807, and yet (except for the belated repeal of the Orders in Council) the nation had little to show for its sacrifices. Indeed, by 1814 any hope of winning concessions from the enemy had all but vanished.

Equally disheartening, New England Federalists could see little prospect of winning control of the national government to effect longterm policy changes. In spite of the Federalists' wartime election gains, the Virginia Dynasty remained firmly in control. In addition, the Louisiana Purchase had brought vast new territories under American control, and the flood of immigration (which was only temporarily halted by the war) promised to populate these territories with Republican voters. For New England Federalists seeking a voice in national affairs, the prospects were bleak indeed.

Some Federalists in New England compared their plight to that of Americans in 1776 and saw a corresponding need for radical action. The press was filled with articles that echoed the spirit of Seventy-Six. Typical of these was an essay in the Salem *Gazette* that called for Massachusetts to sequester federal tax money, make a separate peace with England, and invite neighboring states to sign "a convention of alliance, amity and commerce."[95] Most New England Federalists, however, shrank from such extremism, hoping no doubt that the mere threat of action would force the national government to change its policies.

❖ ❖ ❖ ❖ ❖ ❖

Traditionally, Americans had dealt with crises by calling a convention.[96] The Albany Congress (1754), the Stamp Act Congress (1765), the First Continental Congress (1774), and the Philadelphia Constitutional Convention (1787) were all convened to deal with crises. In New England there was recurring talk of calling a convention: first in 1808–1809, when the long embargo brought trade to a halt; then in the summer of 1812, when the declaration of war threatened to drive America into an alliance with France; and finally in 1814, after a new embargo had been imposed.[97]

The demand for a convention in 1814 was particularly strong in the interior of Massachusetts. "[T]he people in this part of the Country," recalled one Federalist, "were much more excited than in most other parts of New England."[98] According to Noah Webster, the movement began in January when leaders in Northampton called a meeting of "the principal inhabitants" of Old Hampshire (which had recently been divided into three counties) to "consider whether any measures could be taken to arrest the continuance of the war, and provide for the public safety."[99] At a meeting held on January 19, Federalist leaders approved an address drawn up by Webster and circulated under Joseph Lyman's name. Arguing that New England's problems grew out of defects in the Constitution as well as the war, the address urged the towns in Old Hampshire to send memorials to the state legislature requesting "a convention of all the Northern and Commercial States . . . to consult upon measures in concert, for procuring . . . alterations in the Federal Constitution."[100]

As a result of this address, the Massachusetts legislature was flooded with memorials—more than forty in all—which voiced similar complaints about the war, the restrictive system, executive tyranny, and the lack of New England's influence in the Union.[101] Eleven suggested a northern convention. Although the tone of most was moderate, a few bristled with extremism. The memorial from Newbury, for example, declared that people there were "READY TO RESIST UNTO BLOOD" to secure their rights.[102]

The memorials were particularly critical of the recent embargo, and there was considerable support in the legislature for taking action against this measure. Francis Blake announced that if the American constitution permitted embargoes, he preferred the British constitution "monarchy and all," and Samuel Fessenden told cheering galleries that the state should legalize the coasting trade and raise an army to protect its rights.[103] According to Samuel Putnam, it was "the settled determination *not to petition Congress again,*" and proposals to legalize the coasting trade and outlaw seizures made without a search warrant were "received with great unanimity."[104]

Much to the dismay of the extremists, however, the moderates refused to condone any radical action. "You cannot sufficiently realize the embarrassments which the Politicks of the Boston Stamp have occasioned," complained Putnam.[105] The petitions were referred to a committee chaired by former United States senator James Lloyd, and a document was prepared—known as Lloyd's Report—which condemned the war and the embargo. Although the report recognized the right of nullification, it argued that no action was necessary because the embargo was unconstitutional and therefore void. The report conceded that a convention might be called to deal with New England's problems but recommended waiting until the will of the people had been registered in the spring elections. By skirting the issue of nullification and postponing a convention, Lloyd's Report was a clear victory for moderation.[106]

The Federalists won the ensuing elections, but when the Massachusetts legislature met again in May of 1814, the convention project was quietly shelved. The embargo had been repealed, which eliminated one source of complaint. In addition, Napoleon's defeat had ended the war in Europe, and Great Britain's offer to open direct negotiations with the United States had raised hopes for an end to the Anglo-American war as well.[107]

In the summer of 1814, however, circumstances again changed. The negotiations with Britain were delayed, and when they did begin, the envoys found themselves deadlocked. In addition, the war moved closer to New England's shores as the British occupied eastern Maine and stepped up their raids on the coast. Harassed by the enemy and abandoned by the federal government, New England officials watched hopelessly as their defense costs mounted. A crisis appeared to be at hand, and Massachusetts Federalists responded by reviving the project for a convention.[108]

On September 7, the day after breaking with Dearborn over the command issue, Governor Strong summoned the Massachusetts legislature to a special session.[109] According to Harrison Gray Otis, prior to the session, "a few influential members of the Legislature" met to discuss the possibility of a convention. Although Otis opposed the project, other Federalists argued that it was necessary to satisfy their "country friends." Accordingly, the decision was made to summon a convention to obtain "security against Conscription, taxes & the danger of invasion" and to restrain "the tendency to excess."[110]

The defense problem played a central role in the proceedings that followed. In his opening address to the legislature on October 5, Governor Strong focused almost exclusively on this issue. The special session was necessary, he said, because the war had "assumed an aspect so threatening and destructive" that the state had been forced to call out more militia than at any time in its history. "It is an obvious reflection," the governor said, "that the limited sources of revenue which the state has retained in its own power, bear no proportion to the expenses hereby incurred." If the state did not find relief, it would be "extremely difficult, if not impossible, to provide even in the first instance for the requisite expenditures."[111]

The Massachusetts legislature responded to the governor's address with a report drawn up by Otis. Echoing the governor's complaints, the report said that the war had "assumed an aspect of great and immediate danger" and that the people could not continue to pay federal taxes and at the same time finance local defense measures. The alternatives were "submission to the enemy, or the control of their own resources." The report also declared that the Constitution had failed to secure "equal rights and benefits" to New England. To remedy these problems, the report recommended calling a convention of New England states.[112] This proposal was approved 260–90 in the house and 22–12 in the senate, and twelve delegates were chosen to represent the state in the proposed convention.[113]

When the Connecticut legislature met in mid-October, Governor Smith devoted his address exclusively to the defense problem. Because the federal government had withdrawn its support, he said, "we are left to defend ourselves against a formidable and exasperated enemy."[114] The state legislature responded with a report that concentrated on the same issue. In this "odious and disastrous war," the report said, "the national government are dooming us to enormous taxation, without affording any just confidence that we shall share in the expenditure of the public revenue." The report concluded by recommending that Connecticut take part in the proposed convention.[115] The Connecticut house approved this recommendation by a vote of 153 to 36 and chose seven delegates to attend the meeting.[116]

In Rhode Island the concern over defense was no less pronounced. Both the governor's address in November and the legislative report that followed focused almost exclusively on this issue. Governor Jones declared that the state was "as defenceless as at the commencement of the war" and that the federal government "refused to make the necessary advances for expenses which their own officers have ordered and approved." Complaining of "great pecuniary embarrassments," Jones said that even one half of the federal tax money collected in the state "would increase, in a very respectable degree our means of defence."[117] The legislature agreed. By a margin of 39 to 28, the Rhode Island house voted to take part in the convention and chose four delegates to represent the state.[118]

Although New Hampshire and Vermont were also invited to the convention, Federalist leaders in both states opposed the project. However, two counties in each state chose a pair of delegates each to attend. Although one of the Vermont delegates was denied a seat because he represented a minority in a Democratic district, the other three were seated. This bought the total number of delegates to twenty-six.[119]

❖ ❖ ❖ ❖ ❖ ❖

Many moderates supported the convention at least partly to silence the extremists, and the prospect of a convention probably did control unrest. "[I]t is the opinion of my best informed friends from the Country," said Otis, "that a reliance on some *effectual suggestions* from that body, alone prevents a violent ferment and open opposition in many places."[120] Nevertheless, the demand for extreme action did not entirely subside. Francis Blake, who thought "the Legislature of Massachusetts should speak to the National Government in a voice as loud as thunder," recommended that the state sequester federal tax money.[121] Although no one in the legislature supported this proposal, innkeepers and retailers in Old Hampshire promised to withhold their federal taxes until after the convention had met.[122] The people of Reading, Massachusetts, made a similar pledge. "[U]ntil the public opinion shall be known," said a resolution they adopted, "*we will not enter our carriages [on the tax rolls]—pay our continental taxes—or aid, inform or assist any officer in their collection.*"[123]

Timothy Pickering, who described the convention as "the best hope of our best men," deprecated "every thing which shall *simply be put on paper*" and called for bold action.[124] Some newspapers echoed his cry. "Advance boldly," said the Boston *Centinel.* "Suffer yourselves not to be entangled by the *cobwebs* of a compact which has long since ceased to exist."[125] The *Centinel* even suggested that a new nation was in the making. An article describing the appointment of the Connecticut delegates was headlined "Second Pillar of a new Federal Edifice reared," and a story on Rhode Island's action was entitled "Third Pillar Raised."[126] Josiah Quincy, on the other hand, had a much better sense of what the convention was likely to do. When asked what the result would be, he replied: "A GREAT PAMPHLET!"[127]

Federalists in the middle and southern states did not favor rash action but were sympathetic to the plight of their friends in New England. The Pittsburgh *Gazette,* for example, said that Otis's report summoning the convention "breathes the spirit of Old Massachusetts, is dignified and patriotic."[128] There was hope, too, that the convention would force the administration to modify its policies. John Stanly of North Carolina was not sure what the convention would do, but "if it frighten Madison from his course, I shall be glad of it."[129]

Republicans, on the other hand, vigorously condemned the project. William Plumer's view was typical. "I expect no good, but evil from it," he said; "it will embarrass us, aid the enemy, & protract the war."[130] Most Republicans, however, were confident—or at least hopeful—that the convention would pursue a moderate course. "With respect to the object of the convention," said an army officer, "I cannot believe that it is open Rebellion, an actual division of the States, or undisguised union with the public enemy."[131] "The publick," added a Republican newspaper, "do not feel any distressing anxiety about the proceedings of the Convention of *'choice spirits'* at Hartford. . . . There will be much *smoke* and no *fire.*"[132]

Some Republicans called for the federal government to suppress New England disaffection. "The people," said one southerner, "wish now to see some strong steps taken with those traitors in Massachusetts[;] it will not do to temporize."[133] The administration, however, preferred a more cautious approach. The War Department dispatched Colonel Thomas Jesup to Hartford—ostensibly on a recruiting mission but actually to keep an eye on the convention. Jesup was instructed to pay special attention to the armory at Springfield (which had been threatened by Shays's rebels thirty years earlier), and to assure "the friends of the union" in New England that the government would aid and protect them.[134] The War Department also made plans to raise volunteers and to send additional regulars to New England if trouble arose.[135]

Republicans need not have worried because by the time the convention met in December, the crisis atmosphere in New England had largely abated. The campaigning season was over, and although the bills were still coming in, New England could expect a lull in British raids until the spring. Moreover, the new British terms, published on December 1, boded well for peace. With the publication of these terms, a wave of optimism swept through the country, and rumors of peace began to circulate freely.[136]

The character of the twenty-six delegates at the convention also boded well. George Cabot, Nathan Dane, and Otis headed the Massachusetts delegation; Chauncey Goodrich and James Hillhouse, the Connecticut delegation; and Daniel Lyman and Samuel Ward, the Rhode Island delegation. Except for Timothy Bigelow and perhaps one or two others, all the delegates were moderates, hardly the sort to promote violent measures. Radicals like Blake, Quincy, and Fessenden were purposely excluded from the meeting.[137] "I do not know that we have among [the] delegates a Single bold & ardent man," lamented John Lowell, Jr.[138]

Although Otis talked of taking bold measures—of treating "the administration as having *abdicated* the Government"—it was not in his character.[139] As Lowell said: "Mr Otis is naturally timid & frequently wavering. . . . He is sincere in wishing thorough measures but a thousand fears restrain him."[140] The other delegates did not even promise boldness. Dane reportedly said that he agreed to attend the meeting because "somebody must go to prevent mischief," and Cabot made the same point.[141] "We are going," he told a friend, "to keep you young hot-heads from getting into mischief."[142]

❖ ❖ ❖ ❖ ❖ ❖

Although no site for the convention was mentioned in the official documents, Federalist leaders chose Hartford, probably to avoid the appearance of Massachusetts domination. Goodrich, who was mayor of Hartford as well as Connecticut's lieutenant governor, procured the use of the state council chamber.[143] Democrats welcomed the delegates to the city by flying their flags at half-mast and ringing bells, and later the town crier marched a body of regulars around the meeting house "playing the *Death* march with muffled drums and colors furled."[144] Although some people turned out to see what the convention would do, most ignored the proceedings. "I am astonished," said Jesup, "at the little interest excited by the Meeting."[145]

The Hartford Convention met from December 15, 1814, to January 5, 1815. "We sit *twice* a day Connecticut fashion," Otis wrote, "and in the evenings talk politicks over the fire."[146] At the opening session Cabot was unanimously chosen president, and Theodore Dwight, editor of the Hartford *Connecticut Mirror,* was chosen secretary. To avoid the intrusion of popular feeling, the delegates conducted their proceedings in secret.[147] Although public bodies often met behind closed doors, in this case the secrecy gave "more plausibility to the cry of treason."[148] The delegates were remarkably faithful in keeping their pledge of secrecy. Such an injunction, said a Connecticut delegate,

Harrison Gray Otis, by Chester Harding. Courtesy of the National Portrait Gallery, Smithsonian Institution

"was never more faithfully observed."[149] Indeed, Federalists in Washington complained of the lack of information.[150]

No record of the debates was kept—only a bare-bones journal of the proceedings.[151] "The wise speeches," said Goodrich, "[were] all left behind within the walls of the venerable chambers."[152] Even though Otis had originally opposed the convention, he became the driving force in its deliberations. The only known radical, Bigelow, was given no committee assignments and apparently did not play a major role in the proceedings. Nor was there any sign of dissension. "We are progressing very pleasantly, & with great unanimity," said one delegate, "& shall, I am confident, arrive at a result which *ought* to satisfy every reasonable man & true friend of his country."[153]

At their first meeting the delegates established a committee headed by Goodrich to draw up an agenda. It was indicative of the moderate bent of the delegates—and the passing of the crisis atmosphere—that the first draft of the agenda was devoted exclusively to war-related issues: the need for local defense, the waste of money on Canada, the dispute over the militia, and the administration's plans for enlisting minors and conscripting militia. There was no mention of New England's long-term problems nor any reference to constitutional amendments. Since this was hardly likely to satisfy radical opinion— particularly among the party's "country friends"—the delegates subsequently added constitutional reform to their agenda.[154]

The final report of the convention was largely the work of Otis.[155] About half of the report was devoted to immediate concerns: the defense problem, the minor enlistment law, and the proposals for drafting men into the army and navy. To finance defense measures, the report recommended that the states seek authority from the national government to preempt federal tax money collected within their borders. To deal with unconstitutional measures for filling the ranks of the army and navy, the report recommended nullification, asserting that it was the right and the duty of a state "to interpose its authority" to protect its citizens.[156]

The other half of the report was devoted to long-term problems. After cataloguing the failures of Republican policies, the report recommended seven constitutional amendments "to strengthen, and if possible to perpetuate, the union of the states."[157] These amendments called for: (1) a two-thirds vote in Congress to declare war, interdict trade with a foreign nation, or admit new states to the Union; (2) a sixty-day limit on embargoes; (3) an end to counting three-fifths of slaves in apportioning representation in Congress; (4) a ban against naturalized citizens holding federal office; and (5) a provision that would limit presidents to one term and bar the election of a president from the same state twice in succession.[158]

These amendments represented a catalogue of New England's grievances over the past decade. They struck at the over-representation of white southerners in Congress, the growing political power of the West, the restrictive system and the war, the influence of foreign-born office holders (like Albert Gallatin), and the Virginia Dynasty and its domination of national politics. Federalists hoped that the adoption of these amendments would restore sectional balance and prevent a renewal of those policies that had been most damaging to New England's interests.

Although the report of the Hartford Convention called for nullifying federal laws, the tone of the document was generally moderate. The report expressly opposed any "irrevocable" step that might lead to disunion and recommended instead "a course of moderation and firmness."[159] Even if New England's grievances were not redressed, the report simply recommended that another convention be held in June of 1815, or sooner if necessary.[160]

❖ ❖ ❖ ❖ ❖ ❖

The report of the Hartford Convention was published as an extra in the Hartford *Connecticut Courant* on January 6 and subsequently reprinted in many newspapers around the country.[161] The publication of the report, Otis later recalled, "had the immediate effect of calming the public mind throughout New England."[162] Federalists everywhere praised the results. Theodore Dwight called the report "an able performance," and Christopher Gore claimed that the delegates had executed "a difficult task . . . with wisdom and discretion."[163] Daniel Webster described the proceedings as "moderate, temperate & judicious" and reported that Federalists from the middle and southern states were "very highly gratified" with the results.[164] A Virginia paper predicted that the report would "command respect" and "diffuse light," and the New York *Evening Post* said that alarmists would "read with vast satisfaction this masterly report, and rejoice to find [their] fears and alarms groundless."[165]

Even the extremists professed satisfaction. Pickering thought the report "bears the high character of wisdom, firmness and dignity," and William Sullivan said that even though he was "prepared to pursue much more efficient measures," he was satisfied with the results. "It must be born in mind," he said, "that this may be considered as the first of a series of well considered measures."[166] A Boston paper made the same point. "No sensible man," said the *Gazette*, "ought to expect, that the *first* New England Convention would do as much as the *last* out of several congresses of the patriots of the revolution."[167]

Republicans were relieved by the moderation of the report. The Washington *National Intelligencer* said that "the proceedings were tempered with more moderation than was to have been expected," and John Armstrong claimed that the report proved that New England was engaged in nothing more than "a game of bragge."[168] The Worcester *Aegis* considered the report laughable, and the Boston *Patriot* said that the entire convention project was "so pitiful and insignificant, and so truly contemptible" that no counter-convention was necessary.[169] Andrew Jackson, on the other hand, later said that if he had been stationed in New England, he would have court-martialed the "monarchists & Traitors" who were behind the Hartford Convention.[170] Given his record in the Southwest and later in Florida, this was probably no idle boast.

The Massachusetts and Connecticut legislatures formally approved the convention report.[171] Both states also sent emissaries to Washington to secure federal tax money. Otis was opposed to the mission because he thought the state's congressional delegation "could do all which can be done."[172] Other Federalists disagreed, and Otis was chosen to head a three-man commission that included William Sullivan and merchant Thomas H. Perkins. Connecticut sent Calvin Goddard, a delegate to the Hartford Convention, and General Nathaniel Terry, head of the state army.[173]

On their way to Washington, the delegates learned of Jackson's victory at New Orleans, and news of peace soon followed. "The joyful event of peace," said Perkins, "has suspended the mission on which I came."[174] The delegates were the butt of much humor as they completed the final leg of their journey to the nation's capital. "The *grievance deputies* from Massachusetts & Connecticutt," said Winfield Scott from Baltimore, have "afforded a fine Subject of jest & merriment to men of all parties."[175]

In Washington Madison was careful to keep his distance from the "ambassadors." That "mean and contemptible little blackguard," complained Otis, ignored the delegates and told everyone their mission would have failed anyway.[176] The administration had already rebuffed attempts by Ohio and Virginia to preempt federal tax money, so in all likelihood Massachusetts and Connecticut would have fared no better even if the war had continued.[177]

The delegates remained in Washington in the hope of persuading Congress to reimburse the states for their militia costs. Massachusetts Republican Joseph Varnum shepherded a bill for this purpose through the Senate, but it was postponed in the House after "a very animated and rather acrimonious debate."[178] Massachusetts and Connecticut were partially reimbursed in 1831, but not until thirty years later—when the nation faced a secessionist threat from another quarter—did Congress finally authorize full payment.[179]

Massachusetts and Connecticut approved the seven constitutional amendments recommended by the convention, but they were the only states to do so.[180] Although the amendments were introduced in Congress, no action was taken on them. Eight states, including Vermont, adopted resolutions against the amendments.[181] The New York legislature declared that their effect "would be to create dissentions among the different members of the union, to enfeeble the national government, and to tempt all nations to encroach upon our rights."[182]

The Hartford Convention was the climax of New England's opposition to the war. As one scholar has put it, it was "a normal product of abnormal conditions."[183] New England Federalists called the meeting to let off steam and to insure that the moderates in their party retained control. They were also looking for a solution to their defense problem and a vehicle for airing their long-term grievances. The Hartford Convention, in other words, was designed to meet several needs. It was not only a party caucus and constitutional convention but a defense conference as well. Although it represented a triumph for moderation, few people remembered it that way in the rush of events at the end of the war.

CHAPTER 11

The Treaty of Ghent

IN THE MILITARY and naval campaigns, the record of the United States during the War of 1812 was decidedly mixed. There were some successes—most notably on the northern lakes and at New Orleans—and some failures—particularly in the Chesapeake Bay and on the Canadian frontier. In the peace negotiations, however, the nation's record was much better, not because of what the envoys won but because of what they avoided losing. No single campaign in the field loomed as large as these negotiations. It was here—in Ghent, Belgium, rather than on the Canadian-American frontier—that the United States consistently outmaneuvered the enemy, and it was here that Americans could claim their most significant victory.[1]

American success at the negotiating table was fitting because it was here that Republicans expected to win the war. Some Republicans—the "scarecrow" party—had supported military preparations in the War Congress in the hope of persuading the British to make concessions. When this failed, some voted for the declaration of war for the same reason. Although most Republicans believed that the conquest of Canada would be a mere matter of marching, many hoped that no marching would be necessary—that the decision for war itself would be enough to win concessions from the enemy. In this sense, the declaration of war was a bluff designed to force the British to take American demands seriously.[2]

That the president himself harbored these views is suggested by the haste with which he sent out peace feelers in the early days of the war. "The sword was scarcely out of the scabbard," Madison said, "before the enemy was apprised of the reasonable terms on which it would be resheathed."[3] On June 18, 1812, the day that war was declared, Secretary of State James Monroe summoned the British minister, Augustus J. Foster, both to inform him of the decision for war and to urge him to work for peace.[4] Five days later Madison invited Foster to the White House to outline America's terms. Expressing a desire to avoid "any serious collision," the president told Foster that the British could restore peace by giving up the Orders in Council and impressment.[5] Although Foster had no authority to negotiate on these issues, he was expected to pass the terms on to London.

The United States also pursued peace through Jonathan Russell, the American chargé d'affaires in London. On June 26, barely a week after the declaration of war, the administration dispatched a note to Russell authorizing him to open negotiations for an armistice. The British would have to give up the Orders in Council and impressment, but in return the United States promised to bar all British seamen from American ships.[6] By the time Russell made this offer in late August, the Orders in Council had already been repealed. Hence impressment was the only issue that stood in the way of peace.

The British, however, showed no interest in Russell's offer. Having made one important concession—on the Orders in Council—they were in no mood to make another. "[N]o administration," said Britain's foreign secretary, Lord Castlereagh, "could expect to remain in power that should consent to renounce the right of impressment, or to suspend the practice, without the certainty of an arrangement . . . to secure its object." With the war only a few weeks old, Castlereagh expressed surprise at America's eagerness for peace. "[I]f the American Government was so anxious *to get rid of the war*," he told Russell, "it would have an opportunity of doing so on learning the revocation of the orders in council."[7]

That the repeal of the Orders in Council would end the war the British did not doubt. For years British restrictions on neutral trade had been the leading source of Anglo-American friction, while impressment had not been a major issue since the loss of the Monroe-Pinkney Treaty and the attack on the *Chesapeake* in 1807. Confident that the repeal of the Orders would avert war, the British government in July of 1812 instructed the Royal Navy to ignore any attacks from privateers sent to sea before news of the British concession reached America.[8] Even after learning of the declaration of war, Castlereagh told Russell that British officials still entertained "great hopes . . . of the favorable effect" which the repeal of the Orders would have on American policy.[9]

The British government waited until October 13—ten weeks after receiving the news of war—before authorizing general reprisals against the United States.[10] In the meantime, the ministry instructed Sir John Borlase Warren, the new British naval commander on the American station, to propose an armistice. Foster, who had heard of the repeal of the Orders after leaving the United States, was already trying to arrange a cease-fire in Halifax. At his suggestion, British officials in Canada signed an armistice with General Henry Dearborn. The United States, however, repudiated this agreement because it did not provide for an end to impressment.[11] Hence the negotiations in 1812 ended in failure even though both sides were interested in peace.

❖ ❖ ❖ ❖ ❖ ❖

In March of 1813, Andrei Dashkov, the Russian minister in Washington, invited the United States to take part in a new round of negotiations, this time under the auspices of his government.[12] Aside from any prestige they might garner, the Russians had several reasons for acting. Great Britain was their most important ally, and they wanted her to concentrate on the war in Europe. In addition, the United States was an important commercial partner whose ships normally carried tropical produce to Russian ports in the Baltic. This trade had come to an abrupt halt with the outbreak of war, and it was not likely to resume until peace was restored.[13]

The administration welcomed the Russian offer.[14] Russia had long championed neutral rights, and American officials expected to profit from her mediation. "There is not a single [maritime] interest," Monroe said, "in which Russia and the other Baltic powers may not be considered as having a common interest with the United States."[15] American officials were anxious for peace for several reasons. The campaign against Canada had not gone well, Federalist opposition remained as adamant as ever, and the nation's financial situation was already deteriorating. Furthermore, Napoleon's retreat from Russia had greatly strengthened Britain's hand on the Continent. If Britain prevailed in Europe, the United States might find itself alone in the field against her. To avoid this prospect, American officials hoped to liquidate the war in the New World while Britain was still tied up in the Old.[16]

Without even waiting to hear Britain's response, Madison chose three peace commissioners and dispatched them to Europe. Albert Gallatin, who had grown weary of his duties at the Treasury Department, was chosen to head the mission. He was joined by John Quincy Adams, the American minister in St. Petersburg, and James A. Bayard, a moderate Delaware Federalist. The Senate rejected Gallatin's nomination because he was still a member of the cabinet, but by this time he was already in Europe.[17]

The instructions the commissioners carried with them called for British concessions on a broad range of maritime issues.[18] Later Monroe suggested that England might consider tossing Canada into the bargain as well. "[I]t may be worth while," he told the envoys, "to bring to view, the advantages to both Countries which is promised, by a transfer of the upper parts and even the whole of Canada to the United States."[19] Only one of the American demands, however, was a *sine qua non*—a point deemed essential to any settlement—and that was an end to impressment. Bayard, who had earlier declared that if this point were insisted upon he was likely to "grow grey in the war," suggested an informal understanding on the subject, but the administration was unyielding.[20] Privately Monroe told Gallatin that an informal agreement "would not only ruin the present admn., but the republican party & even the [republican] cause."[21]

Gallatin and Bayard joined Adams in St. Petersburg in July of 1813. There they cooled their heels—attending an unending round of parties—waiting for Britain's official response to the mediation offer.[22] In fact, the British had already rejected the proposal. They had no desire (as Castlereagh put it) to allow the United States "to mix directly or indirectly Her Maritime Interests with those of another State"—certainly not with those of a great inland power that favored a broad definition of neutral rights.[23]

The British rejection was common knowledge, but because the Russians were reluctant to give up the project, the American envoys received no official notice.[24] By December the lack of any official word had become a source of "much impatience and embarrassment."[25] Finally in January of 1814, six months after arriving in Russia, Gallatin and Bayard took their leave, refusing to wait any longer. The two envoys headed for London, ostensibly en route home but actually to scout out the prospects for peace in the enemy's capital.[26]

Before leaving Russia, the American envoys had conducted informal negotiations with Alexander Baring, an ardent friend of the United States who had married a Philadelphia socialite and was the nation's banker in London. Although the Americans had hoped that the foreign seaman act, which authorized the president to bar British tars from American ships, would provide a basis for ending impressment, Baring disabused them of this notion.[27] No British government, he said, could agree to renounce impressment on this basis alone, and even the best friends of peace "would not be bold enough to recommend it."[28]

❖ ❖ ❖ ❖ ❖ ❖

Although British officials rejected the mediation offer, they felt obliged to make a counter offer to demonstrate their peaceful intentions. Having already raised the possibility of direct talks through various other channels, Castlereagh sent a message to Monroe in November of 1813 offering "to enter upon a direct negociation for the restoration of Peace." The talks, Castlereagh said, would have to be conducted "upon principles of perfect reciprocity not inconsistent with the established maxims of Public Law, and with the maritime Rights of the British Empire."[29] This was a thinly disguised promise to insist on the right of impressment.

President Madison accepted this offer and appointed four men to serve on the commission. Adams headed the mission; the other members were Bayard, Kentucky War Hawk Henry Clay, and Jonathan Russell, who had conducted the early armistice negotiations in London. Three weeks later, when Madison learned that Gallatin was still in Europe, his name was added to the list. Since everyone now agreed that Gallatin had given up his place in the cabinet, the Senate approved his nomination.[30]

The American commission was exceptionally strong. Four of the envoys already had distinguished themselves in public life, and Adams and Clay still had long and important careers ahead of them. Only Russell would never achieve any great distinction. With such a strong mission, differences of opinion were inevitable. Clay and Adams were frequently at odds, though usually on minor issues. "Upon almost all the important questions," Adams said, "we have been unanimous."[31] Gallatin played a particularly important role in forging this consensus. According to Adams, the former secretary of the treasury contributed "the largest and most important share to the conclusion of the peace."[32]

In contrast to the United States, Great Britain had to rely on second-rate men because her top officials were busy with European affairs. The British peace mission was headed by Dr. William Adams, an admiralty lawyer selected because American diplomats were known to favor legal arguments. Also on the commission was Lord Gambier, a veteran naval officer who was expected to look after Britain's maritime rights, and Henry Goulburn, an undersecretary in the Colonial Office who was supposed to protect Britain's interests in Canada. Goulburn was the most ambitious and energetic of the three, and he took charge of the negotiations.[33]

The British envoys were appointed in May but were slow to depart for Ghent. According to an American observer in London, they did "not appear in a hurry to leave this Country."[34] British officials dragged their feet, hoping that victories in America would enhance their bar-

John Quincy Adams, by Pieter van Huffel. Courtesy of the National Portrait Gallery, Smithsonian Institution

gaining position at Ghent. Now that the war in Europe was over, the mood in England was vindictive. "War with America, and most inveterate war," said a friendly Englishman, "is in the mouth of almost every one you meet in this wise and thinking nation."[35] The British press contributed to this mood with inflammatory pieces. The American people, said the London *Sun*, must not be "left in a condition to repeat their insults, injuries, and wrongs." "Our demands," added the *Times*, "may be couched in a single word, *Submission*."[36]

American officials had hoped that the great powers on the Continent would serve as a counterpoise to British strength, but it soon became apparent that British influence was everywhere paramount, even in the press. "It is something singular," reported Bayard, "that on the continent you get no news but what comes from England." "If the War is to be continued," Clay warned, "we must rely for its prosecution exclusively upon our own resources." "From Europe," added Gallatin, "no assistance can for some time be expected."[37]

Few Europeans gave much thought to the American war. According to Jonathan Russell, the "Great Congress at Vienna" (which was forging a general European settlement) overshadowed "the little congress at Ghent."[38] Nevertheless everyone—the British included—recognized that the American war hampered Britain's freedom of action on the Continent, and as time passed, sympathy for the United States mounted. By December of 1814 Gallatin reported that the continental powers "rejoiced at any thing which might occupy & eventually weaken our Enemy," and an American in Paris said that "enthusiasm here in our favor is in full flood."[39]

The United States profited from this undercurrent of sympathy. Napoleon had allowed American ships to arm in French ports and to bring their prizes in for adjudication, but after his fall the British put pressure on the new regime to halt this practice. Although French officials revoked the authority of American ships to arm in French ports, they refused to close their ports to American privateers. British merchants raised a clamor, and British officials protested, but in vain. American privateers were still cruising from French ports when the war ended.[40]

❖ ❖ ❖ ❖ ❖ ❖

The peace negotiations were originally planned for Gothenburg, Sweden, but the end of the war in Europe made Ghent more convenient because it afforded quicker access to both capitals.[41] The negotiations lasted from August 8, 1814, to December 24, 1814—far longer than anyone expected though not as long as the Congress of Vienna, which met from September 1814 to June 1815.

The negotiations were conducted behind closed doors, but President Madison kept the American people informed of the progress. British officials, on the other hand, kept their people in the dark. "The proceedings at Ghent," said the London *Morning Chronicle*, "continue to excite the chief interest in the public mind, but Ministers persist in their silence both with regard to their progress and result."[42] The *Times* was reduced to making deductions from the number of messages that were carried between the hotels of the two delegations, and the paper complained that the first real news of the negotiations came from America.[43] In mid-December gamblers were still offering three-to-one odds that peace would not be concluded before the end of the year, and as late as December 24, the very day the treaty was signed, the *Morning Chronicle* reported that the talks "afforded no prospect of an amiable issue," and the *Times* repeated rumors that the negotiations had broken off.[44]

Adams claimed that the tone of the British notes in the negotiations was "arrogant, overbearing, and offensive," while that of American notes was "neither so bold nor so spirited as I think it should be."[45] The Massachusetts envoy need not have worried because the British representatives were overmatched and thus easily outmaneuvered. A London newspaper later complained that the British envoys showed neither "adroitness or skill" and accused them of presenting their demands in a "crude and undigested state."[46] After overplaying their hand in the early rounds, the British envoys were put on a tight leash by officials in London. Thereafter, as Adams put it, they "were little more than a medium of communication between us and the British Privy Council."[47] The American envoys were quick to exploit this advantage. "[T]he Americans," complained Goulburn, "have rather hoaxed us for the number of our references home."[48]

When the negotiations began, the American envoys were still bound to insist on an end to impressment. Six months earlier Monroe had written that even if the war in Europe ended the British still had to give up impressment. "This degrading practice," he said, "must cease, our flag must protect the crew, or the United States, cannot consider themselves an independent Nation."[49]

Like other American diplomats in this era, the envoys at Ghent were prepared to violate their instructions if necessary. As early as November of 1813, Adams reported that Bayard "seemed anxious to discuss the expediency of giving up the point of impressment."[50] Six months later Clay said that the issue had become "a mere theoretic pretension" and that if "the interests of our Country demanded of me the personal risk of a violation of instructions I should not hesitate to incur it."[51] Adams and Gallatin also hinted at a willingness to give up the point.[52]

The envoys never had to take this risk because in June of 1814 the administration decided to drop impressment.[53] The news reached the envoys just as the negotiations were getting under way.[54] Although Republican leaders later justified their decision by claiming that the end of the European war had brought an end to impressment, privately they conceded that Napoleon's defeat had killed any chance of winning concessions on the issue.[55]

❖ ❖ ❖ ❖ ❖ ❖ ❖

With impressment out of the way, the envoys were able to focus on other issues, and in the first two weeks of the negotiations the British presented their terms. As a *sine qua non* for peace, they insisted that the western Indians be included in the settlement and that a permanent barrier or reservation be established for them in the Old Northwest. In addition, they demanded American territory in northern Maine (to facilitate overland traffic between Quebec and Halifax) and in present-day Minnesota (to assure access to the Mississippi River). They also called on the United States to demilitarize the Great Lakes—removing all warships from those waters and all fortifications from the shores. Finally, the British declared that the American right to fish in Canadian waters and to dry their catch on Canadian shores would not be renewed without an equivalent.[56]

The British terms were based on several considerations, but uppermost was their concern for Canadian security. It was "notorious to the whole world," the British said, "that the conquest of Canada and its permanent annexation to the United States was the declared object of the American Government."[57] When the American envoys denied this, the British produced the annexationist proclamations issued by William Hull and Alexander Smythe in 1812.[58] The American envoys, however, blandly replied that neither of these proclamations "was authorized or approved by the Government."[59] Unable to find any official statement on the subject, the British could only repeat that American designs on Canada were a "matter of notoriety."[60]

British officials had talked about the desirability of an Indian barrier ever since the early 1790s.[61] Such a barrier would enhance Canadian security by establishing a buffer zone between British and American territories and by insuring that the western tribes remained loyal to Britain. Control of the lakes and a direct overland route between

Quebec and Halifax were also expected to increase Canadian security by making it easier to ward off attacks from the south. The British were also anxious to protect their Indian allies. Having abandoned them in the Peace of 1783 and again in the Jay Treaty of 1794, British officials had repeatedly promised not to desert them again. In February of 1814 Sir George Prevost told an assemblage of western Indians: "Our Great Father considers you as his children and will not forget you or your interests at a peace."[62] Several months later, Lieutenant Colonel Robert McDouall told the Indians at Mackinac that the king would help them recover their "old boundaries." Great Britain, he added, would make peace only "on the express condition that your interests shall be first considered, your just claims admitted, and no infringement of your rights permitted in future."[63] Several British newspapers echoed this pledge. "[T]hese sable heroes," said the *Sun,* must "be for ever secured against Yankee encroachment and barbarity."[64]

As a boundary for the Indian reservation, the British suggested the line established by the Treaty of Greenville in 1795, though subject to "such modifications as might be agreed upon."[65] This treaty had been superseded by others, but if resurrected, it would have secured to the Indians about a third of Ohio, half of Minnesota, and almost all of Indiana, Illinois, Michigan, and Wisconsin. This territory was not, as the American envoys claimed, a third of the land mass of the United States, but 250,000 square miles, or about 15 percent.[66] The region was inhabited by some 20,000 Indians and about 100,000 whites.[67] When asked what would become of those Americans who found themselves on the wrong side of the new boundary, the British replied that "they must shift for themselves"—meaning that they would have to abandon their homes.[68]

In presenting their demand for an Indian barrier, the British envoys exceeded their instructions in two ways. First, they presented the Indian reservation as a *sine qua non,* though officials in London saw the barrier as simply one possible means of protecting the Indians.[69] Secondly, even though the British government was only interested in preventing Americans from purchasing land in the barrier, the British envoys demanded that the United States refrain from acquiring territory "by purchase or otherwise."[70] This would prevent Americans from acquiring lands inside the barrier by conquest in "defensive" wars.

The British terms need not have surprised anyone since they were anticipated by newspaper articles on both sides of the Atlantic.[71] Nevertheless, the American envoys were stunned. Although aware of the strident anti-American feeling in England, they had assumed that the British government would be more conciliatory.[72] They failed to realize that with the war in Europe over, British leaders were anxious to end the American war on terms that would insure that Canada and its Indian allies were amply protected in the future.

The American envoys flatly rejected the British proposals. "A Treaty concluded upon such terms," they said, "would be but an armistice. It cannot be supposed that America would long submit to conditions so injurious and degrading."[73] The Indian barrier was particularly objectionable. It undermined American sovereignty, ran counter to a tradition of national control over the Indians, and threatened the westward movement. Adams told Goulburn that to condemn such a vast expanse of territory "to perpetual barrenness and solitude [so] that a few hundred savages might find wild beasts to hunt upon it, was a species of game law that a nation descended from Britons would never endure."[74] This unyielding attitude surprised Goulburn. "Till I came here," he later said, "I had no idea of the fixed determination which there is in the heart of every American to exterpate the Indians & appropriate Their territory."[75]

Convinced that the prospects for peace were remote, the American envoys sent a truce ship home to notify the administration. In mid-October, President Madison sent copies of the envoys' dispatches to Congress. Several days later he also gave Congress the instructions that authorized the envoys to drop impressment. These documents were published to show the world—and particularly the Federalists—how reasonable the administration was and how unreasonable the British had become. Publication of these documents had the dual effect of generating support for the war at home and embarrassing British officials abroad.[76]

British leaders were annoyed by the publication of the documents. "Mr. Madison has acted most scandalously," declared the prime minister, Lord Liverpool. To publish terms with a negotiation still in progress was unprecedented "on the part of any civilized government."[77] British officials were also exasperated by the intransigence of the Americans—their unwillingness to make any concessions. "The doctrine of the American government is a very convenient one," Liverpool said; "they will always be ready to keep what they acquire, but never to give up what they lose."[78]

Members of the opposition, on the other hand, attacked the government for making excessive demands. Alexander Baring charged the ministry with setting up "extraordinary pretensions," and the Marquis of Lansdowne made it clear that he was "no supporter of these new principles upon which the contest was conducted."[79] The *Morning*

Chronicle declared that the British terms "were any thing but wise and moderate" and accused the cabinet of fighting "a war of aggression and conquest."[80]

❖ ❖ ❖ ❖ ❖ ❖ ❖

With the talks apparently stalled, the mood of the American envoys became gloomy. Only Clay retained even a shred of hope for peace.[81] An inveterate gambler who sometimes stayed up all night playing cards, Clay thought the British might be bluffing.[82] The Kentucky War Hawk found it difficult to believe that the British would allow the talks to break up over the issues in question. "Such a rupture," he said, "would entirely change the whole character of the War, would unite all parties at home, and would organize a powerful opposition in Great Britain." Perhaps, Clay suggested, the British were "attempting an experiment upon us"—dragging out the negotiations in the hope that "they will strike some signal blow, during the present campaign." If this were the case, then there was still hope that the British "would ultimately abandon [their] pretensions."[83]

Clay's suspicions were well founded. The British demands were what one scholar has called "a probing operation."[84] Their purpose was to provide a basis for negotiation and to determine what concessions the Americans were willing to make. Even the Indian barrier was not supposed to be a *sine qua non,* even though it was presented as one by the British envoys. "Our Commissioners," Liverpool lamented, "had certainly taken a very erroneous view of our policy." They failed to appreciate "the inconvenience of the continuance of the war."[85]

Clay's suspicion that British officials were trying to buy time was also correct. With the balance of power in the New World shifting in their favor, the British were confident that victories in the field would soon strengthen their hand at Ghent. In early September, Liverpool said: "If our commander [Sir George Prevost] does his duty, I am persuaded we shall have acquired by our arms every point on the Canadian frontier which we ought to insist on keeping." Later that month he suggested that the discussions be drawn out until news arrived on "the progress of our arms." And the following month he said that the best policy to pursue was "to gain a little more time before the negotiation is brought to a close."[86]

Unwilling to end the negotiations, the British gradually retreated from their demands. Instead of an Indian barrier, they agreed to settle for a pledge to restore the Indians to their status as of 1811.[87] "[T]heir sine qua non," said Clay, "has dwindled down to a demand that the Indians shall be included in the peace and put in the condition they

James A. Bayard, by [Edward?] Wellmore. Courtesy of the Historical Society of Delaware

stood in prior to the battle of Tippacanoe."[88] This stipulation was too vague to be meaningful. For all practical purposes, the British once again had abandoned the Indians.

Having retreated from their initial terms, the British offered a new basis for peace in October—*uti possidetis,* which meant that each side would retain whatever territory it held at the war's end.[89] If this offer were accepted, the British would gain eastern Maine, Mackinac, and Fort Niagara, while the United States would get Fort Malden and Fort Erie. The British suggested that the agreement be "subject to such modifications as mutual convenience may be found to require."[90] Their hope was to retain northern Maine (for the overland route between Quebec and Halifax) as well as Mackinac and Fort Niagara, but to trade the rest of eastern Maine for forts Malden and Erie.[91] The British gave little thought to the possibility of retaining New Orleans because by this time their projected campaign against the Crescent City had assumed only minor importance in their overall strategy for ending the war.[92]

Britain's new offer was far more moderate than her original terms, but the American envoys were too close to the situation to appreciate its significance. A week later Bayard said: "It is impossible to tell what is the real intentn. of the British Govt. on the question of Peace or War. They probably mean to be govd by events."[93] Even Clay thought that obstacles "of a serious and difficult character" still remained and that "the safest opinion to adopt is . . . that our Mission will terminate unsuccessfully."[94]

Rejecting the new British offer, the American envoys again sent a truce ship to Washington to bring the administration up to date. Madison transmitted the envoys' dispatches to Congress on December 1. The publication of these documents convinced many people that peace was near, and the result was a steady flow of peace rumors that continued until the conflict was over.[95]

❖ ❖ ❖ ❖ ❖ ❖

When it became evident that the Americans would not agree to *uti possidetis,* the British dropped this demand just as they had their others. By this time the shrill attacks against the United States in the British press had given way to protests over war taxes. "Economy & relief from taxation are not merely the War Cry of Opposition," said one official, "but they are the real objects to which public attention is turned."[96] The British were also disillusioned by the lack of military progress in America. Reports of the fall of Washington and the occupation of eastern Maine had raised their hopes, but news soon followed of the failures at Baltimore and Plattsburgh.[97] "If we had either burnt Baltimore or held Plattsburgh," Goulburn said, "I believe we should have had peace on [our] terms."[98]

The failures in America suggested that another campaign—whose projected cost was £10,000,000 ($44,000,000)—would be necessary if the British were to exact any concessions.[99] "[T]he contest with America," grumbled an opposition leader, "was likely to plunge the country in[to] frightful expense."[100] According to the *Morning Chronicle*, the prospect of renewing the property tax was greeted everywhere with "a sense of horror and indignation."[101]

Another year of fighting was also likely to undermine Britain's position in Europe. "We are certainly anxious to make Peace before the next Campaign," said a British official. "We do not think the Continental Powers will continue in good humour with our Blockade of The whole Coast of America beyond that Period."[102] The allies at Vienna were already feuding among themselves, and British officials were wondering how quickly they could recall troops from America.[103] "The negotiations at Vienna are not proceeding in the way we could wish," said Liverpool, "and this consideration itself was deserving of some weight in deciding the question of peace with America."[104]

To buttress their position at home and in the field, British officials asked the Duke of Wellington to take charge of the American war.[105] The Iron Duke agreed, but he refused to leave Europe until the spring or to guarantee success. "I feel no objection to going to America," he told Liverpool, "though I don't promise to myself much success there." What the British needed was "not a General, or General officers and troops, but a naval superiority on the Lakes." Without this, there was little hope of success. Given the existing circumstances, Wellington concluded, "you have no right . . . to demand any concession of territory from America."[106]

Wellington's opinion was all that British officials needed to jettison their last territorial demands. On November 18 Liverpool wrote to Castlereagh: "I think we have determined, if all other points can be satisfactorily settled, not to continue the war for the purpose of obtaining or securing any acquisition of territory."[107] The only important issues that remained unsettled were the status of the American fishing rights in Canadian waters and British navigation rights on the Mississippi River. Since both rights were guaranteed by the Treaty of 1783, both were likely to stand or fall together.

These rights caused a deeper division in the American delegation than any other issue. Clay, representing western interests, wanted to close the Mississippi to the British, while Adams, representing Massachusetts fishermen, insisted on retaining the fisheries. Ultimately, both issues were left out of the treaty. This was a tacit admission that both rights continued, which was a victory for Adams.[108]

The American and British envoys spent close to a month hammering the treaty into final form. Their handiwork—completed on December 24, 1814—is known as the Treaty of Ghent or the Peace of Christmas Eve.[109] The treaty mentioned none of the maritime issues that had caused the war. It simply restored the *status quo ante bellum*—the state that existed before the war. Each side agreed to evacuate all enemy territory, though the British were allowed to retain several islands in Passamaquoddy Bay (between Maine and Nova Scotia) until their ownership was determined. Each side agreed not to carry off any enemy property and to return all prisoners of war "as soon as practicable."[110] Any prizes taken beyond a certain time—ranging from twelve days off the American coast to 120 days in distant parts of the world—had to be restored to their owners.

Each nation also promised to make peace with the Indians and "to restore to such tribes . . . all the possessions, rights, and privileges which they may have enjoyed, or been entitled to, in one thousand eight hundred and eleven, previous to such hostilities."[111] In addition, the treaty established commissions—three in all—to fix the Canadian-American boundary and to establish the rightful owner of the Passamaquoddy Islands.[112] Both nations also promised to "use their best endeavors" to stamp out the slave trade.[113]

On three earlier occasions—in connection with the Jay Treaty in 1794, a boundary convention in 1803, and the Monroe-Pinkney Treaty in 1806—the United States had insisted on modifications after an agreement had been signed by its envoys. This time the British would settle for nothing less than unconditional ratification. They also wanted hostilities to end not when the treaty was signed (which was customary) but only after ratifications had been exchanged. Since this would entail a delay if the British instrument of ratification were lost at sea, the envoys agreed that hostilities would cease when both sides had ratified the agreement. The treaty, however, would not be binding until ratifications had been exchanged.[114]

❖ ❖ ❖ ❖ ❖ ❖

British officials welcomed the Treaty of Ghent because it undercut criticism at home and gave them a freer hand in Europe. Castlereagh called the restoration of peace "a most auspicious and seasonable event" and congratulated Liverpool on "being released from the mill-stone of an American war."[115] In Vienna a British official reported that peace had "produced an astonishing effect," helping to foil a Russian bid for aggrandizement.[116]

The British people also welcomed peace, though somewhat grudgingly. The *Courier, Naval Chronicle,* and *Annual Register* all praised the results of the negotiations, and an army officer said that most soldiers agreed because they "saw that neither fame nor any military distinction could be acquired in this species of milito-nautico-guerilla-plundering-warfare."[117] The *Morning Chronicle* also rejoiced at the restoration of peace but said that British leaders had "humbled themselves in the dust" and "thereby brought discredit on the country."[118] The *Times* and *Globe,* on the other hand, criticized the government for failing to win any concessions. Calling the treaty "deadly" and "disgraceful," the *Times* lamented that the United States had escaped "a sound flogging."[119]

In Parliament, members of the opposition tried to make political capital out of the negotiations. The Marquis of Wellesley said that "the American commissioners had shown the most astonishing superiority over the British" and that "peace had been concluded under circumstances in which neither honour nor security had been provided for."[120] Opposition motions that challenged the government's handling of the negotiations, however, were decisively defeated.[121] In the heady days of the postwar *Pax Britannica,* few people were interested in this kind of criticism. Indeed, according to the *Morning Chronicle,* such was the buoyant mood of the British people that, even before peace was restored, "purchases to an immense amount" were made in the stock market, generating "the greatest Bull Account which has been known for years."[122]

The American envoys feared that they too might be criticized by their constituents. Clay called the agreement "a damned bad treaty" and predicted that "we should all be subject to much reproach."[123] Except for Bayard, the other envoys shared his apprehension. The only thing the envoys would say in defense of the treaty was that it was the best that circumstances allowed and that it ended the war without sacrificing any honor, territory, or right.[124]

❖ ❖ ❖ ❖ ❖ ❖

On January 2, 1815, Henry Carroll, Clay's personal secretary, boarded the ship *Favourite* in London to take a copy of the treaty to the United States. He was joined by Anthony Baker, who carried a copy of the British instrument of ratification. The ship encountered bad weather in the Chesapeake Bay and hence headed for New York harbor, docking around 8:00 P.M. on February 11. Carroll made no secret of his mission. Word quickly spread that peace was at hand, and soon the entire city was celebrating.[125]

From New York reports of the treaty spread in all directions. An express rider carried the news in a record thirty-two hours to Boston, where handbills announcing the treaty were distributed. Schools in Boston were closed, people left their jobs, and the legislature adjourned. In the boisterous celebration that followed, bells were rung, the city was illuminated, troops turned out to fire a salute, and cartmen formed a procession of sleighs, parading around the city with the word "peace" on their hats.[126] Celebrations of this sort took place all over the country.[127] "Grand illuminations are making throughout the United States," said one American.[128] Everywhere, too, the news of peace drove up the price of war bonds and treasury notes. Goods that were normally shipped to foreign markets also rose in value, while war materiel and imported goods generally declined.[129]

The British were prepared to offer a separate peace to New England if the treaty were not ratified, but there was no danger of this happening.[130] News of the treaty reached the nation's capital on February 13, and an official copy arrived the following day. Madison submitted the treaty to the Senate on February 15, and the next day the Senate voted unanimously (35–0) to approve it. Madison gave his own approval later that day, thus completing the ratification process. Since the British had already ratified, this marked the end of hostilities. The war formally came to an end at 11:00 P.M. the following day—February 17—when Monroe exchanged ratifications with Baker, who had arrived in Washington earlier that evening.[131]

❖ ❖ ❖ ❖ ❖ ❖

Although Americans of both political parties rejoiced at the restoration of peace, Federalists had special cause to celebrate. The war, after all, had achieved none of the nation's maritime goals. Instead, the Treaty of Ghent seemed to confirm what Federalists had been saying all along about the futility of the conflict. Many Federalists expected to reap significant political dividends. As Christopher Gore put it: "The treaty must be deemed disgraceful to the government who made the war and the peace, and will be so adjudged by all, after the first effusions of joy at relief have subsided."[132]

There was one Federalist, however, who was not so optimistic. James Robertson of Philadelphia said that the strategy of Republicans was already apparent. They would ignore the causes of the conflict and portray it as "a war on our part of pure self defence against the designs of the British to reduce us again to subjection." By portraying the war in this light, they could claim that it was a great triumph. "The President," Robertson concluded, "will only have to call it a glorious peace, and the party here will echo it."[133]

Robertson's prophecy proved correct. In a message to Congress announcing the end of the war, President Madison congratulated Americans "upon an event which is highly honorable to the nation, and terminates, with peculiar felicity, a campaign signalized by the most brilliant successes." The war, Madison claimed, "has been waged with a success which is the natural result of the wisdom of the Legislative councils, of the patriotism of the people, of the public spirit of the militia, and of the valor of the military and naval forces of the country."[134]

All across the country Republican orators and editors echoed the president's cry. "Never did a country occupy more lofty ground," said Joseph Story; "we have stood the contest, single-handed, against the conqueror of Europe." "This second war of independence," crowed the New York *National Advocate*, "has been illustrated by more splendid achievements than the war of the revolution."[135] The nation had attained all of its objectives, added a writer for the *National Intelligencer:* "the administration has succeeded in asserting the principles of God and nature against the encroachments of human ambition and tyranny." "Yes," echoed the Worcester *National Aegis,* "*we have triumphed—* let snarling malcontents say what they will, *we have gloriously triumphed!"*[136] Republicans exaggerated, for the United States could not in justice claim to have won the war. But because of the clear-headed determination shown by the American envoys at Ghent, the nation could at least claim that it had won the peace.

Conclusion

THE WAR OF 1812 is often called America's "second war of independence." The issues and ideology of this conflict echoed those of the
Revolution. In addition, this was the nation's second and last struggle
against Great Britain, the second and last time that it was the underdog
in a war, and the second and last time that it tried to conquer Canada.
Nevertheless, the supposed threat to American independence in 1812
was more imagined than real. It existed mainly in the minds of thin-
skinned Republicans who were unable to shake the ideological legacy
of the Revolution and interpreted all British actions accordingly.

British encroachments on American rights were certainly both real
and serious. But throughout this period the focus of British policy was
always on Europe. The overriding objective of the British government
was to secure the defeat of France, and all else was subordinated to
this aim. Britain's policy, in other words, was preeminently European.
Her aim was not to subvert American independence but to win the
war in Europe. Once this objective was achieved, her infringements
on American rights would cease.

Not only did Republicans misread British intentions, but throughout
this turbulent era they consistently overrated America's ability to win
concessions. Daniel Sheffey, a Virginia Federalist, made this point in
a speech delivered on the eve of war in 1812. "We have considered
ourselves of too much importance in the scale of nations," he said. "It
has led us into great errors. Instead of yielding to circumstances, which
human power cannot control, we have imagined that our own destiny,
and that of other nations, was in our hands, to be regulated as we

thought proper."[1] Sheffey's analysis was borne out, not only by the restrictive system but also by the war.

The War of 1812 lasted only two years and eight months—from June 18, 1812, to February 17, 1815. Though the war was not long, the United States was beset by problems from the beginning. Many of the nation's military leaders were incompetent, and enlistments in the army and navy lagged behind need. The militia were costly and inefficient and repeatedly refused to cross into Canada or to hold their positions under enemy fire. It was difficult to fill the war loans, and the nation's finances became increasingly chaotic. There was also extensive trade with the enemy—trade that Federalists and Republicans alike freely took part in. A combination of Federalist opposition, Republican factionalism, and general public apathy undermined the entire war effort.

Congress was partly responsible for this state of affairs. Endless debate and deep divisions delayed or prevented the adoption of much-needed legislation. Congress was particularly negligent on financial matters. Hoping for a quick war and fearing the political consequences of unpopular measures, Republicans postponed internal taxes and delayed a national bank. As a result, public credit collapsed in 1814, and a general suspension of specie payments ensued. By the end of the war, the administration had to rely on depreciated bank paper and treasury notes. If the contest had continued much longer, the Revolutionary War phrase "not worth a continental" might have been replaced by "not worth a treasury note."

A strong president might have overcome some of these problems, but Madison was one of the weakest war leaders in the nation's history. Although his opponents called the contest "Mr. Madison's War," it never bore his stamp. Cautious, shy, and circumspect, Madison was unable to supply the bold and vigorous leadership that was needed. In some respects, to be sure, his caution served the nation well. Unlike other war presidents, he showed remarkable respect for the civil rights of his domestic foes. Despite pleas from other Republicans, he refused to resort to a sedition law. Thus, even though Federalists had to face mob violence (particularly at the beginning of the war), they never had to contend with government repression. Madison's treatment of enemy aliens and prisoners of war was also commendably humane, and his circumspect policy toward New England disaffection was undoubtedly well judged, too.

In other ways, however, Madison's cautious brand of leadership undermined the nation's war effort. He allowed incompetents like

Eustis and Hamilton to hold key positions, he tolerated Armstrong's intrigues and Monroe's backbiting in the cabinet, and he retained Gideon Granger as postmaster general long after his hostility to the administration had become notorious. Madison was also slow to get rid of incompetent generals in the field or to promote officers who had proven themselves in battle. Because he lacked a commanding influence in Congress, he was unable to secure vital legislation, and because he lacked a strong following in the country, he was unable to inspire people to open their hearts and purses.

Contemporaries were aware of Madison's shortcomings, and even Republicans criticized his leadership. "Our President," said John C. Calhoun in 1812, "has not . . . those commanding talents, which are necessary to controul those about him." "[H]is spirit and capacity for a crisis of war," declared a Pennsylvania congressman in 1814, "are very generally called in question." "Mr. Madison," added a western congressman in 1815, "is perhaps 'too good' a man for the responsible office he holds. He does not like to offend his fellow men for any cause."[2] Even Virginia Republicans considered Madison "*too tender* of the feelings of other people." "The amiable temper and delicate sensibility of Mr Madison," declared one Virginian, "are the real sources of our embarrassments."[3]

No doubt poor leadership in Washington and in the field drove up the cost of this war. At the beginning of the contest, a Federalist newspaper predicted that the war would cost 30,000 lives and $180,000,000 and lead to a French-style conscription.[4] This prediction was close to the mark. Official sources, which are not entirely reliable, indicate that the total number of American troops engaged in the contest was 528,000: 57,000 regulars, 10,000 volunteers, 3,000 rangers, and 458,000 militia.[5] Another 20,000 served in the navy and marines.[6] The battle casualties were comparatively light. The official figures are 2,260 killed and 4,505 wounded.[7]

There is no record of how many soldiers died from disease, but before the advent of modern medicine, deaths from disease invariably exceeded those from enemy fire. Epidemics were common, and field commanders sometimes reported 30, 40, or even 50 percent of their troops on the sick list.[8] There were numerous reports of multiple deaths from dysentery, typhoid fever, pneumonia, malaria, measles, typhus, and smallpox. In 1812, a soldier at Buffalo said: "Every day three or four are carried off to their Graves." In 1813, Governor Isaac Shelby said: "They are dying more or less every day on our March." And in 1814, General George Izard called the mortality rate from disease and exposure among his troops "prodigious."[9]

After sampling army records, one scholar has concluded that two and a half times as many soldiers died from disease or accident as were killed or wounded in battle.[10] If this sample is representative, the total number of non-battle military deaths must have been about 17,000. The army executed an additional 205 men, mainly for repeated desertion, and the navy executed a few men, too.[11] Some privateersmen also died in the war, primarily from disease in British prisons. There were a few civilian casualties as well—mostly victims of Indian raids in the West. Adding all the pertinent figures together suggests that the total number of deaths attributable to the war must have been about 20,000.[12]

The cost of the war (excluding property damage and lost economic opportunities) was $158,000,000. This includes $93,000,000 in army and navy expenditures, $16,000,000 for interest on the war loans, and $49,000,000 in veterans' benefits.[13] (The last veteran died in 1905, the last pensioner—the daughter of a veteran—in 1946.)[14] The government also awarded land bounties to some 224,000 people who had served in the war.[15] The national debt, which Republicans had reduced from $83,000,000 in 1801 to $45,000,000 in 1812, rose to $127,000,000 by the end of 1815. The government borrowed $80,000,000 during the war, but because of discounts offered and paper money received, it got only $34,000,000 specie value.[16]

What did the war accomplish? Although militarily the conflict ended in a draw, in a larger sense it represented a failure for Republican policy makers. The nation was unable to conquer Canada or to achieve any of the maritime goals for which it was contending. Indeed, these issues were not even mentioned in the peace treaty, which merely provided for restoring all conquered territory and returning to the *status quo ante bellum.*

In other ways, however, the war was fraught with consequences for the future. The United States annexed part of Spanish West Florida in 1813—the only permanent land acquisition made during the war, though it came at the expense of a neutral power rather than the enemy.[17] The war also broke the power of the Indians in the Northwest and the Southwest. Tecumseh's confederacy was the last great attempt to unite American Indians against further encroachments on their lands. Although this confederacy had the support of the British, it collapsed when Tecumseh was killed in the Battle of the Thames in 1813. In the peace negotiations at Ghent, Great Britain failed to secure a permanent reservation for the Indians, leaving them at the mercy of an expansive people determined to engross lands up to and even beyond the Mississippi River.

The Indians never recovered from this blow. The western tribes, said the secretary of war in 1818, "have, in a great measure, ceased to be an object of terror, and have become that of commiseration."[18] Never again would Indians seriously threaten the United States, and never again would a foreign nation tamper with American Indians. The subjugation of the Indians, in turn, promoted manifest destiny and the westward movement. The heady nationalism and expansionism that characterized American foreign policy throughout the nineteenth century was at least partly a result of the War of 1812.

The war also contributed to the growth of Canadian nationalism. The British never considered the war more than a sideshow—a footnote in their history. For Canadians, however, the war was more important. In 1812 the various provinces in Canada were little more than outposts in the British Empire populated by a jarring combination of French Canadians, native-born British subjects, Loyalists who had fled from the United States during the Revolution, and Americans who had migrated across the border in search of greater economic opportunities. The War of 1812 helped cement these disparate groups into a nation. The war also produced a host of patriotic legends—centering on the exploits of Isaac Brock, Laura Secord, and others—that contributed further to the development of Canadian nationalism.

Even though the war stimulated nationalism, it was an important benchmark in the history of American sectionalism. New England Federalists were determined to insulate themselves from the war. In order to retain control over their militia and obstruct war measures, they resurrected the states' rights doctrine that Virginia Republicans had used in the late 1790s to fight the alien and sedition laws. Later on, this same doctrine would be employed by southern Democrats to block the tariff and to protect slavery. New England's opposition to the war was thus part of a larger tradition of sectionalism, one that flourished until the northern victory in the Civil War delivered a body blow to the whole notion of states' rights.

The war also stimulated peacetime defense spending. In his message to Congress announcing the end of hostilities, President Madison echoed an old Federalist plea by calling for preparedness. "Experience has taught us," he said, "that a certain degree of preparation for war is not only indispensable to avert disasters in the onset, but affords also the best security for the continuance of peace."[19] Congress agreed. The peacetime army was fixed at 10,000 men in 1815 (three times what it had been in 1802), and the construction of nine ships-of-the-line and twelve heavy frigates was authorized in 1816.[20] Congress also launched a far-reaching program to fortify the coast, appropriating almost $8,500,000 for this purpose between 1816 and 1829.[21]

The war affected the American military establishment in another way. Those officers who had outlived their usefulness—Smyth, Wilkinson, Hampton, Dearborn, and the like—were cast aside to make room for younger men, such as Brown, Scott, Gaines, Macomb, and Jackson. As a result, the American army had a decidedly new look by 1815. A number of navy officers also burned their names into the history books during the conflict. Among these were Perry, Macdonough, Hull, Bainbridge, Decatur, and Stewart.

The war had a dramatic impact on the American economy, too. Unlike most American wars, this one did not generate a general economic boom. According to Thomas Jefferson, whose heavy debts became unmanageable during the war, the conflict "arrested the course of the most remarkable tide of prosperity any nation ever experienced."[22] Although people in the middle and western states prospered, those in New England and the South did not. Manufacturing thrived because of the absence of British competition, but whatever gains were made in this sector of the economy were dwarfed by heavy losses in fishing and commerce. For most Americans, the economic opportunities were greater before and after the war than during it.

The war also sparked an interest in suppressing illegal trade. Throughout the war, trade with the enemy had been widespread, particularly on the northern frontier. "[Y]ou may always buy a Yankee," a British naval officer observed, "in almost any rank and station!"[23] Congress had tried to halt this traffic with a series of trade restrictions, culminating in the enemy trade act of 1815. Although this measure had expired with the end of the war, there was every indication that smuggling, which had always existed on the Canadian frontier, would continue. Hence Congress adopted a new measure that granted customs officials the same extensive powers in peacetime that they had enjoyed under the enemy trade act.[24]

The war left an enduring legacy of anglophobia in the United States. Hatred of England, originally kindled by the American Revolution, was further inflamed by the War of 1812—particularly by the Indian atrocities in the West and British depredations in the Chesapeake. William Henry Harrison predicted that Americans would long remember the "horrible species of warfare" practiced by the Indians allied to Britain. "Ages yet to come," he told a British officer, "will feel the effect of the deep-rooted hatred and enmity which [this warfare] must produce between the two nations."[25] People in the Chesapeake felt the same way about the ravages of Cockburn's men.

Britain's treatment of American prisoners of war further intensified this anglophobia. At one time or another about 20,000 Americans, mostly privateersmen, were held in British prisons.[26] British officials often treated these prisoners roughly to induce them to enlist in the Royal Navy and to discourage privateering. Even before the war was over, stories of abuse began to filter back to the United States. In March of 1814 a captured sailor on board a British prison ship in the Bahamas reported that Americans "have been suffering every deprivation on board of this old prison ship. . . . We are used with as much barbarity as though we were Turks."[27]

After the war ended, the trickle of stories became a torrent. "The return of our people from British prisons," said *Niles' Register*, "have filled the newspapers with tales of horror."[28] Some of the stories came from Halifax, where most Americans captured on the northern frontier were held. "All the prisoners that we have yet seen," said the Boston *Patriot*, "agree that their treatment in the Halifax prisons was brutal and barbarous in the extreme."[29]

Other stories came from Dartmoor, a damp and dreary prison in southwestern England. By the end of the war, "this accursed place," as one prisoner called it, housed some 6,500 Americans.[30] A group of former prisoners from Massachusetts (most of whom were Federalists) said that their experience at Dartmoor had extinguished "every impression we formerly entertained in favor of the British nation, as magnanimous, pious, liberable, and honorable or brave." The "regular and systematic oppression" practiced by the British was "calculated to render our existence uncomfortable, and by breaking down our spirits and abusing our feelings, to hurry us out of this world into eternity."[31]

Trouble at Dartmoor reached a climax on April 6, 1815—almost two months after the war ended—when a dispute over responsibility for transporting the men home delayed repatriation. Anxious to regain their freedom, the prisoners became unruly, and British soldiers fired on them, killing six and wounding sixty others. Although an Anglo-American commission tried to whitewash the affair, a committee of prisoners issued several reports on the "Dartmoor massacre" that were widely circulated in the United States.[32] "The blood of every man, in whose bosom beats a sound *American* heart," said the Richmond *Enquirer*, "will run cold at the narrative of the base and premeditated murder which was perpetrated within the walls of Dartmoor Prison." The *Enquirer* even urged parents to share the prisoners' story with their children to show the depravity of British leaders.[33]

Americans did not soon forget the brutality of the war. As early as 1813, the House of Representatives published a study—with extensive documentation—that criticized Great Britain for the Indian atrocities, the Chesapeake depredations, and the mistreatment of prisoners.[34] Other stories kept the embers of hatred alive for decades. Long after the conflict was over, *Niles' Register* published war-related anecdotes and documents that showed the British in a bad light.[35] Nineteenth-century histories—culminating in Henry Adams's magisterial study of the Age of Jefferson—continued this tradition by focusing on Britain's misdeeds.[36]

Another legacy of the war was the enhanced reputation that the United States enjoyed in Europe. Although the nation's performance in this war was mixed, it nonetheless earned the respect of Europe. "[T]he Americans," said Augustus J. Foster, "have had the satisfaction of proving their courage—they have brought us to speak of them with respect." According to another Englishman, the war had "humbled the tone of our ministry and of the nation, and made the United States much more respected in Europe."[37]

The British were careful not to impress any Americans when the Royal Navy went back on a war footing during Napoleon's Hundred Days in 1815.[38] In fact, Americans were never again subjected to those dubious maritime practices that had caused the war. With Europe generally at peace in the century after Waterloo, the Great Powers had no interest in regulating American trade or in tampering with the nation's merchant marine. The United States had ample time to grow and to husband its strength so that it could meet the Great Powers on an equal footing in the next world war—the one touched off at Sarajevo in 1914.

The war also left an enduring political legacy. A number of statesmen—James Monroe, John Quincy Adams, Andrew Jackson, and William Henry Harrison—were able to parlay their public service during the war into the presidency. A host of lesser lights also made political capital out of the war. The Battle of the Thames, which became a kind of Bunker Hill in western legend, helped create one president, one vice president, three governors, three lieutenant governors, four senators, and twenty congressmen. In addition, countless other participants in the battle were elected to lesser offices.[39]

The war confirmed Republican hegemony and ushered in an era of one-party rule. "Never was there a more glorious opportunity," crowed Joseph Story, "for the Republican party to place themselves permanently in power."[40] The Republicans laid claim to all the victories in the war and blamed the defeats on the Federalists. The Republicans also charged the Federalists with prolonging the war, though the available evidence suggests that opposition in both countries shortened the conflict by making each of the governments more amenable to a compromise peace.[41]

What did the Federalists reap from their opposition to the war? According to a Republican paper, it was "Disappointment!—Disgrace!— Detection!—Despair!"[42] Opposition to the war was popular during the conflict but not afterwards, and Federalists found it particularly difficult to live down the notoriety of the Hartford Convention. Almost twenty years after the war, the convention's secretary complained that "from the time of its coming together to the present hour, [it] has been the general topic of reproach and calumny." Even after the convention journal was published in 1823, "the weak, the designing, and the wicked, still made use of the Hartford Convention as a countersign of party, and as a watchword to rally the ignorant and vicious around the standard of the ambitious."[43] Like "blue lights" and "Henryism," the phrase "Hartford Convention" entered the political vocabulary as a synonym for treason.

Federalists protested that they were made the scapegoats for the failure of Republican policies. "The charge that opposition encourages the enemy and injures the cause," said Rufus King, "has at all times been made as an excuse for the failure and defeat of a weak administration."[44] Federalists also pointed out that Republicans never achieved their war aims and never admitted the war's true costs. "What we have suffered and what we have lost are carefully concealed," said a Federalist address. "A Treaty, which gives us peace, is represented as glorious, when it has given us nothing else. And it is attempted to make us believe that all the objects of the war have been obtained, when every thing, for which it was declared has been abandoned."[45]

These protests fell on deaf ears. The decline of the Federalist party—begun in 1800 but arrested by the restrictive system and the war—continued apace after the war was over. It mattered not that the war had vindicated so many Federalist policies—particularly the importance of military and naval preparedness and the need for internal taxes and a national bank—and that Republicans themselves admitted as much by adopting these policies during or after the war. It mattered not that Federalists had predicted the futility of the conflict and that the Treaty of Ghent had proven them right. What mattered was that the nation had emerged from the war without surrendering any rights or territory and with just enough triumphs—both on land and on sea—to give the appearance of victory.

The Battle of New Orleans, though fought after Great Britain had signed and ratified the peace treaty, played a particularly important role in forging the myth of American victory. Even before the peace terms were known, Republicans were touting this battle as a decisive turning point in the war. "The terms of the treaty are yet unknown to us," said Congressman Charles J. Ingersoll in early 1815. "But the victory at Orleans has rendered them glorious and honorable, be they what they may. . . . Who is not proud to feel himself an American—our wrongs revenged—our rights recognized!"[46]

Republicans boasted of how they had defeated "the heroes of Wellington," "Wellington's *invincibles*," and "the conquerors of the conquerors of Europe."[47] "[W]e have unqueened the self-stiled Queen of the Ocean," crowed the Boston *Yankee,* and "we have beaten at every opportunity, *Wellington's Veterans!*"[48] The myth of American victory continued to grow so that by 1816 *Niles' Register* could unabashedly claim that "we did virtually dictate the treaty of Ghent."[49] Several months later a Republican congressman declaimed on the nation's triumph. "The glorious achievements of the late war," said Henry Southard of New Jersey, "have sealed the destinies of this country, perhaps for centuries to come, and the Treaty of Ghent has secured our liberties, and established our national independence, and placed this nation on high and honorable ground."[50]

As the years slipped by, most people forgot the causes of the war. They forgot the defeats on land and sea and lost sight of how close the nation had come to military and financial collapse. According to the emerging myth, the United States had won the war as well as the peace. Thus the War of 1812 passed into history not as a futile and costly struggle in which the United States had barely escaped dismemberment and disunion, but as a glorious triumph in which the nation had single-handedly defeated the conqueror of Napoleon and the Mistress of the Seas.

Map 1. The Northern Theater

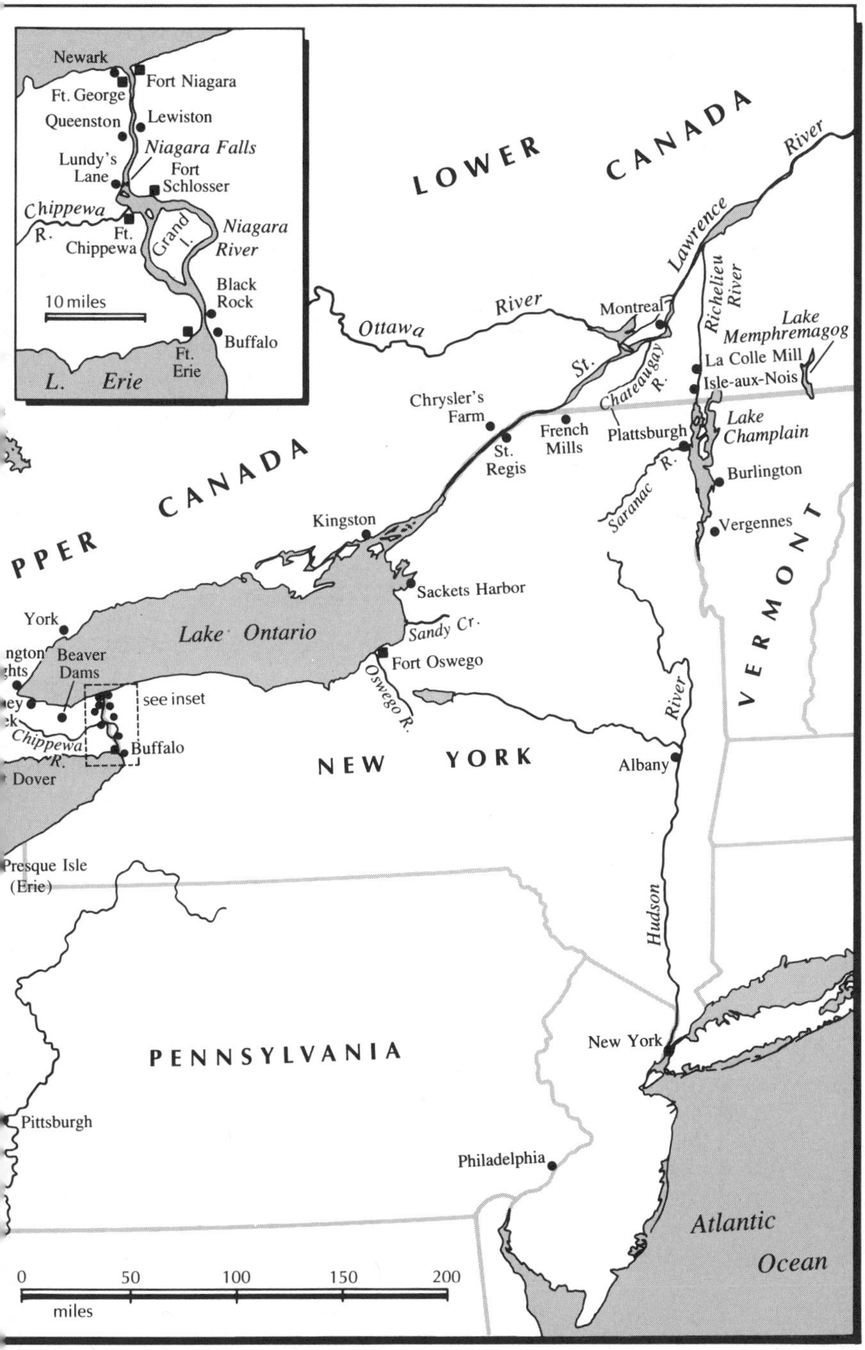
Newark
Fort Niagara
Ft. George
Queenston
Lewiston
Niagara Falls
Lundy's Lane
Fort Schlosser
Chippewa R.
Ft. Chippewa
Grand I.
Niagara River
Black Rock
Buffalo
Ft. Erie
L. Erie
10 miles
LOWER CANADA
St. Lawrence River
Ottawa River
Montreal
Richelieu River
Lake Memphremagog
La Colle Mill
Isle-aux-Nois
Chateaugay R.
Chrysler's Farm
St. Regis
French Mills
Plattsburgh
Lake Champlain
Burlington
Saranac R.
Vergennes
UPPER CANADA
Kingston
Sackets Harbor
York
Lake Ontario
Sandy Cr.
Fort Oswego
Oswego R.
Beaver Dams
see inset
Chippewa R.
Buffalo
Dover
VERMONT
NEW YORK
Albany
Hudson River
Presque Isle (Erie)
PENNSYLVANIA
New York
Pittsburgh
Philadelphia
Atlantic Ocean
0 50 100 150 200
miles

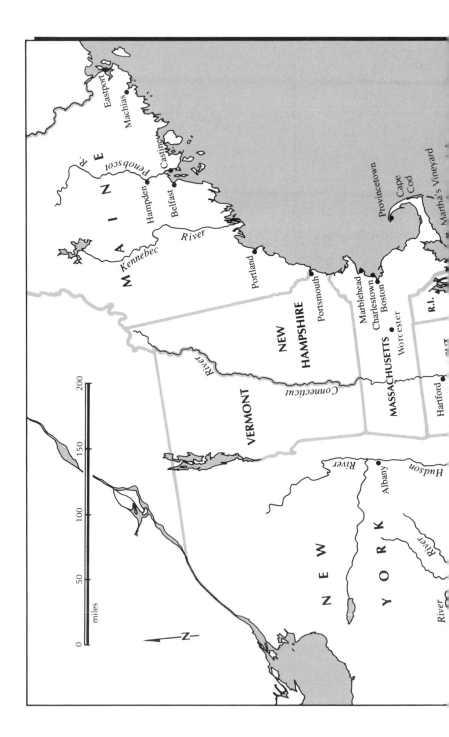

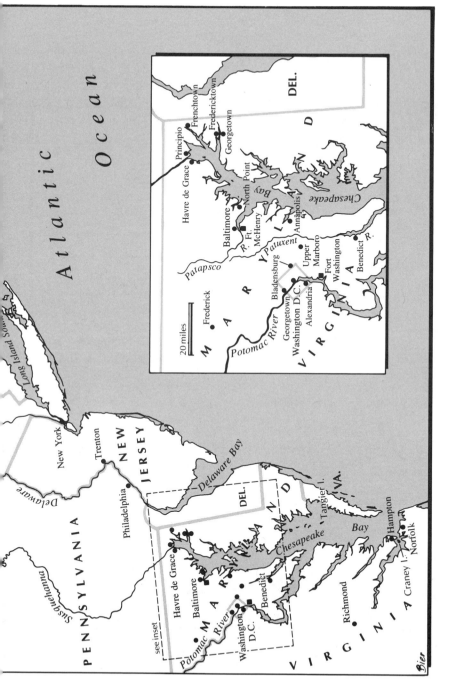

Map 2. The Atlantic Theater

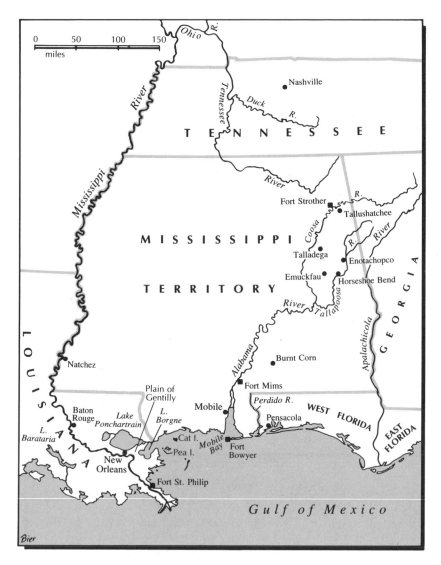

Map 3.   The Southern Theater

314

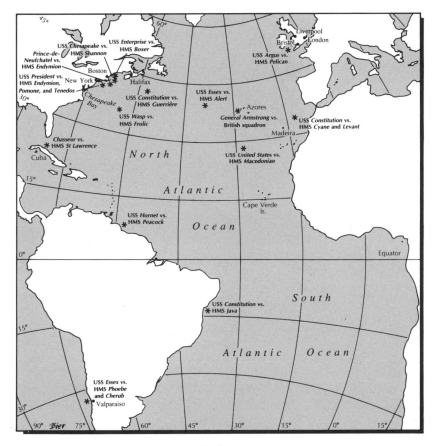

Map 4. The War at Sea

A Note on Sources

The best starting point for any research on the War of 1812 is the comprehensive bibliography compiled by John C. Fredriksen, *Free Trade and Sailors' Rights: A Bibliography of the War of 1812* (1985). Although replete with errors and marred by an index that is difficult to use, this work is indispensable for identifying the principal published sources on any aspect of the war. Also useful is Dwight L. Smith, *The War of 1812: An Annotated Bibliography* (1985), and the bibliography at the end of John K. Mahon's study, *The War of 1812* (1972).

Primary Sources

The primary sources available for the study of this war are voluminous. Fortunately, most have been published or are available in microform. Especially valuable is the congressional record: U.S. Congress, *Annals of Congress: Debates and Proceedings in the Congress of the United States, 1789–1824*, 42 vols. (1834–56). Compiled retrospectively from newspapers and official sources, this work is far from complete. Most speeches delivered in the Senate were never recorded, and many House speeches were lost, too. Nevertheless, the *Annals* is indispensable for tracing the history of bills, fathoming the intentions of the government, and understanding the opposition. In the course of the debates, congressmen also revealed a great deal about the times in which they lived and the problems they were trying to solve.

Members of the cabinet periodically submitted reports to Congress. Most of these were published in U.S. Congress, *American State Papers: Documents, Legislative and Executive, of the Congress of the United States*, 38 vols. (1832–61). Many of these reports, as well as a number of other government documents, have been published by Scholarly Resources in a new collection under the general editorship of Thomas C. Cochran: *The New American State Papers*, 205 vols. (1972–81).

Many of the official cabinet records are available on microfilm at regional depositories of the National Archives, and there is an excellent guide: National Archives and Records Service, *Catalog of National Archives Microfilm Publications* (1974). The National Archives also has more detailed guides for each of its series. I used the War and Navy department records to trace the military and naval history, to understand the system of supply, and to follow the flow of money. I used the Treasury Department records to explore the wartime restrictive system and the State Department records to trace the diplomacy of the war.

The most valuable War Department records I used were *Letters Sent by the Secretary of War Relating to Military Affairs, 1800–1889* (M6); *Confidential and Unofficial Letters Sent by the Secretary of War, 1814–1847* (M7); *Letters Received by the Secretary of War, Registered Series, 1801–1870* (M221); and *Letters Received by the Secretary of War, Unregistered Series, 1789–1861* (M222). The most valuable Navy Department Records have been *Letters Received by the Secretary of the Navy: Captains' Letters, 1805–1885* (M125); *Letters Received by the Secretary of the Navy from Commanders, 1804–1886* (M147); and *Letters Sent by the Secretary of the Navy to Officers, 1798–1868* (M149). The Treasury Department records I found most useful have been *Letters Sent by the Secretary of the Treasury to Collectors of Customs at All Ports (1789–1847) and at Small Ports (1789–1847)* (M175); and *Correspondence of the Secretary of the Treasury with Collectors of Customs, 1789–1833* (M178). The most useful State Department Records I examined were *Records of Negotiations Connected with the Treaty of Ghent, 1813–1815* (M36); *Diplomatic Instructions to All Countries, 1801–1906* (M77); and *War of 1812 Papers, 1789–1815* (M588).

I found the correspondence of contemporaries—Republicans and Federalists alike—essential for understanding many aspects of the war. The best guide to collections available on microfilm is Richard W. Hale, Jr., ed., *Guide to Photocopied Historical Materials in the United States and Canada* (1961). A more current guide that is periodically updated but is less informative is Lynn Sabol, ed., *Guide to Microforms in Print* (1985). Another useful guide is National Historical Publications and Records Commission, *Historical Documentary Editons* (1986). For other manuscript collections, the best guide is still Philip Hamer, ed., *A Guide to Archives and Manuscripts in the United States* (1961).

I have indicated in the notes which collections I examined on film by appending a reel number. The most valuable were the papers of James Madison (LC), James Monroe (LC), Thomas Jefferson (LC), Andrew Jackson (LC), William Plumer (LC), Timothy Pickering (MHS), Robert Goodloe Harper (MdHS), William Gaston (UNC), Albert Gallatin (SR), and Richard Rush (SR). I also examined a microfilm edition of the papers of James Monroe (NYPL), but there were no reel numbers.

I consulted many other collections in manuscript form, the most valuable of which were the papers of Harrison Gray Otis (MHS), Henry D. Sedgwick (MHS), Jonathan Russell (BU), Jonathan Roberts (HSP), William Jones (HSP),

Sources

Alexander Dallas (HSP), Charles J. Ingersoll (HSP), Joseph H. Nicholson (LC), Galloway-Maxcy-Markoe (LC), Thomas Jesup (LC), Jacob Brown (LC), Wilson Cary Nicholas (UVA), and Timothy Pitkin (HL).

Newspapers are another invaluable source—one that few scholars of this period have fully exploited. According to *Niles' Register,* 1 (October 19, 1811), 116, there were 345 newspapers in the United States on the eve of the war, and this does not count country editions of city papers. The vast majority were weeklies, though there were 25 dailies and another 49 that came out two or three times a week.

Though only four pages long, most papers devoted considerable space to printing government documents and excerpts from the debates and proceedings of Congress—which suggests that the reading public was remarkably well informed about public affairs. Most papers also published editorials, news from home and abroad, long-winded essays, bits of local gossip, literary pieces, poetry, humor, and advertisements. Some also carried reports from correspondents in Washington, providing information about national affairs not available elsewhere.

The papers in the big coastal cities usually had the largest budgets, the widest circulation, and the best access to information. As the Boston *Yankee* (January 3, 1812), put it: "Our cities have more of that floating intelligence called news than our country towns. They are the eyes through which we perceive what is going on abroad." Articles and editorials from the city papers were often reprinted in other papers. In fact, the number of times a paper's material was reprinted was a measure of its influence.

The standard guide to early American newspapers is still Clarence S. Brigham, *History and Bibliography of American Newspapers, 1690–1820,* 2 vols. (1947). The best guide to papers available in microform is U.S. Library of Congress, *Newspapers in Microform: United States, 1948–1983,* 2 vols. (1984). The Readex Corporation is committed to putting all newspapers published before 1820 on microform, and most of the important ones have already been filmed by Readex or others. Since newspapers often underwent minor title changes, I have cited all uniformly with the city in roman type followed by the title in italics.

I profited most from the following Republican papers (which are listed roughly in order of their importance and influence): Washington *National Intelligencer* (which was the semi-official organ of the government), Philadelphia *Aurora* (which was hostile to the administration), Boston *Independent Chronicle,* New York *National Advocate,* Lexington *Reporter,* Richmond *Enquirer,* Baltimore *Whig* (which was anti-administration), Worcester *National Aegis,* Boston *Yankee,* Trenton *True American,* Salem *Essex Register,* Concord *New-Hampshire Patriot,* and Hartford *American Mercury.* I also mined *Niles' Register,* a Republican magazine that specialized in publishing government documents, statistical data, and articles from other magazines and newspapers.

The following are the Federalist papers I profited most from (again listed roughly in order of their importance and influence): Boston *Columbian Centinel,* New York *Evening Post,* Philadelphia *United States' Gazette,* Baltimore/

Georgetown *Federal Republican,* Boston *New-England Palladium,* Hartford *Connecticut Courant* (the oldest newspaper still in publication), Alexandria *Gazette,* Charleston *Courier,* Raleigh *Minerva,* Boston *Gazette,* Trenton *Federalist,* Salem *Gazette,* Keene *Newhampshire Sentinel,* Pittsburgh *Gazette,* and Chillicothe *Supporter.*

There are a number of good documentary collections devoted to the military and naval history of the war. The standard collection of American documents is John Brannan, ed., *Official Letters of the Military and Naval Officers of the United States, during the War with Great Britain in the Years 1812, 13, 14, & 15* (1823). There is a good documentary history of the war at sea in progress: William S. Dudley and Michael J. Crawford, eds., *The Naval War of 1812: A Documentary History,* 1 vol. to date (1985).

For the British side of the story, I used William Wood, ed., *Select British Documents of the Canadian War of 1812,* 3 vols. (1920-28), which is the standard collection of military documents. In addition, I used the documentary collections (which contain American material, too) edited by one of the deans of Canadian scholarship, Ernest A. Cruikshank. The most important of these is *The Documentary History of the Campaign on the Niagara Frontier,* 9 vols. (n.d.–1908).

I consulted several British periodicals as well: the London *Times,* a ministerial paper that published many government documents; the London *Morning Chronicle,* an anti-ministerial print; the *Annual Register,* which summarized events and opinion for each year; and the *Naval Chronicle,* a treasure trove of British naval lore and documents. The *Naval Chronicle* (which was remarkably moderate on the American war) provided a public forum for debating the naval issues of the day and devoted considerable space to letters seeking to explain (or explain away) the American victories at sea.

To understand British foreign policy, I used the Foreign Office Papers (PRO). There are photocopies of 5/88, 5/101, and 5/102 in the Library of Congress. I also used the papers of Henry Goulburn (UM), a superb collection that contains most of the pertinent British documents on the peace negotiations. For public debate on the war, I consulted T. C. Hansard, ed., *The Parliamentary Debates from the year 1803 to the Present Time,* [First Series], 41 vols. (1803–20). I also used various documentary collections, memoirs, and autobiographies. The most valuable were: Duke of Wellington, ed., *Dispatches, Correspondence, and Memoranda of Field Marshall Arthur, Duke of Wellington,* 15 vols. (1858–72), and the memoirs attributed to George R. Gleig, particularly *A Subaltern in America, Comprising His Narrative of the Campaigns of the British Army . . . during the Late War* (1833).

Secondary Sources

There are several good military histories of the war. I relied heavily on three: John K. Mahon's *War of 1812* (1972), which is the most detailed; Reginald Horsman, *The War of 1812* (1969), which is the most accurate; and Harry L. Coles, *The War of 1812* (1965), which is the liveliest. James R. Jacobs and Glenn

Tucker, *The War of 1812: A Compact History* (1969), is a good popular account with a valuable appendix that explains ordnance, tactics, uniforms, and nautical terminology. Glenn Tucker wrote a longer popular study that is also valuable: *Poltroons and Patriots: A Popular Account of the War of 1812*, 2 vols. (1954). Also useful is Benson J. Lossing, *The Pictorial Field-Book of the War of 1812* (1868). Lossing traveled 10,000 miles in the 1850s and 1860s, visiting battle sites and interviewing survivors. His text is a compendium of fascinating detail that includes songs, poems, battle maps, and other illustrations.

The best account of the war at sea is still Theodore Roosevelt, *The Naval War of 1812*, 2 vols., 3rd ed. (1900). Roosevelt's second volume is not as good as his first, but his judicious work is nonetheless a good antidote to the ill-tempered standard British account, William James, *A Full and Correct Account of the Chief Naval Occurrences of the Late War between Great Britain and the United States of America* (1817). Another valuable work is Alfred T. Mahan, *Sea Power and Its Relations to the War of 1812*, 2 vols. (1905), though Mahan had a tendency to rework quotations from his source material so that they read better.

For the domestic history of the war, Henry Adams, *History of the United States during the Administrations of Jefferson and Madison,* 9 vols. (1889-91) has long been standard, though Adams sought to make almost everyone look bad except his ancestors, John and John Quincy Adams. Characteristically, he criticized the Republicans for declaring war and the Federalists for opposing the war. Scholars have long since discarded his assessment of the Republicans, though most still accept his view of the Federalists. Adams's history is still valuable, but his judgments (many of which are cleverly disguised as facts) must be treated with caution.

The best corrective of Henry Adams is Irving Brant, *James Madison,* 6 vols. (1941–61). Brant went over much of the same ground as Adams and frequently shows where Adams distorted or misread the evidence. But like so many biographers, Brant became enamored of his subject. He was reluctant to acknowledge Madison's mistakes, and he labored mightily (though in vain) to prove that Madison was a strong president.

Charles J. Ingersoll, a bright and knowledgeable Republican who sat in the Thirteenth Congress, wrote two valuable treatises that further illuminate the domestic history of the war. These are *Historical Sketch of the Second War between the United States of America, and Great Britain,* 2 vols. (1845–49), and *History of the Second War between the United States of America and Great Britain,* 2 vols. (1853). J. C. A. Stagg's modern work, *Mr. Madison's War: Politics, Diplomacy, and Warfare in the Early American Republic, 1783-1830* (1983), is a superb study that traces the inner history of the Republican party during the war and explores the impact of politics on the prosecution of the war.

Several regional studies deserve mention. Allan S. Everest, *The War of 1812 in the Champlain Valley* (1981), is a very good treatment of the subject. Sarah M. Lemmon, *Frustrated Patriots: North Carolina and the War of 1812* (1973), is a model state study; James W. Hammack, Jr., *Kentucky and the Second American Revolution: The War of 1812* (1976), is good on Kentucky's role in the war; and Victor Sapio, *Pennsylvania & and War of 1812* (1970), is good on Pennsylvania and the coming of the war. Jerome R. Garitee, *The Republic's Private Navy: The American Privateering Business as Practiced by Baltimore during the War of 1812* (1977), is a superb study of the in-port side of privateering.

Future Work

In spite of all that has been written about the war, there is still work to be done. The Jonathan Roberts Papers (HSP) are so informative, especially on the proceedings of the War Congress, that they should be published in their entirety. So too should the Joseph H. Nicholson Papers (LC), since they contain a large number of valuable letters from Nathaniel Macon. Also worthy of publication is Anthony G. Dietz's informative dissertation, "The Prisoner of War in the United States during the War of 1812" (American University, 1964).

In addition, we need modern studies of the naval, economic, and financial history of the war; the history of disease and medicine; the system of supply; the British treatment of American prisoners of war; the weapons of the war; privateering; the war in the Chesapeake, especially in 1814; trade with the enemy; the treatment of enemy aliens in the United States and Great Britain; the role of Indians; and the role of Republican dissidents, particularly De Witt Clinton and the Clintonians. In short, the War of 1812 is still a fertile field for study.

Notes

Location and Publisher Abbreviations

AAS:	American Antiquarian Society, Worcester, MA
BEHS:	Buffalo and Erie County Historical Society, Buffalo, NY
BU:	Brown University, Providence, RI
ChHS:	Chicago Historical Society, Chicago, IL
CHS:	Connecticut Historical Society, Hartford, CT
DU:	Duke University, Durham, NC
EI:	Essex Institute, Salem, MA
HL:	Huntington Library and Art Gallery, San Marino, CA
HSP:	Historical Society of Pennsylvania, Philadelphia, PA
HSW:	State Historical Society of Wisconsin, Madison, WI
HU:	Harvard University, Cambridge, MA
JHU:	Johns Hopkins University, Baltimore, MD
LC:	Library of Congress, Washington, DC
MdHS:	Maryland Historical Society, Baltimore, MD
MeHS:	Maine Historical Society, Portland, ME
MHS:	Massachusetts Historical Society, Boston, MA
MNY:	Museum of the City of New York, New York, NY
NHHS:	New Hampshire Historical Society, Concord, NH
NYPL:	New York Public Library, New York, NY
PRO:	Public Record Office, London, England
SR:	Scholarly Resources, Wilmington, DE
UM:	University of Michigan, Ann Arbor, MI
UNC:	University of North Carolina, Chapel Hill, NC
UVA:	University of Virginia, Charlottesville, VA

Source Abbreviations

AC: U.S. Congress, *Annals of Congress: Debates and Proceedings in the Congress of the United States, 1789–1824,* 42 vols., Washington, DC, 1834–56, (12–1 refers to the 12th Congress, 1st session, and similarly for other sessions)

Adams, *History:* Henry Adams, *History of the United States during the Administrations of Jefferson and Madison,* 9 vols., New York, 1889–91

ASP: C: U.S. Congress, *American State Papers: Claims,* Washington, DC, 1834

ASP: C & N: U.S. Congress, *American State Papers: Congress and Navigation,* 2 vols., Washington, DC, 1832–34

ASP: F: U.S. Congress, *American State Papers: Finance,* 5 vols., Washington, DC, 1832–59

ASP: FR: U.S. Congress, *American State Papers: Foreign Relations,* 6 vols., Washington, DC, 1833–59

ASP: IA: U.S. Congress, *American State Papers: Indian Affairs,* 2 vols., Washington, DC, 1832–34

ASP: MA: U.S. Congress, *American State Papers: Military Affairs,* 7 vols., Washington, DC, 1832–61

ASP: NA: U.S. Congress, *American State Papers: Naval Affairs,* 4 vols., Washington, DC, 1834–61

Brannan, *Official Letters:* John Brannan, ed., *Official Letters of the Military and Naval Officers of the United States, during the War with Great Britain in the Years 1812, 13, 14, & 15,* Washington, DC, 1823

Cruikshank, *Niagara Frontier:* Ernest A. Cruikshank, ed., *The Documentary History of the Campaign on the Niagara Frontier,* 9 vols., Welland, Ontario, n.d.–1908

DAB: Allen Johnson and Dumas Malone, eds., *Dictionary of American Biography,* 20 vols., New York, 1928–36

Dudley and Crawford, *Naval Wars:* William S. Dudley and Michael J. Crawford, eds., *The Naval War of 1812: A Documentary History,* 1 vol. to date, Washington, DC, 1985

Ingersoll, *Historical Sketch:* Charles J. Ingersoll, *Historical Sketch of the Second War between the United States of America, and Great Britain,* 2 vols., Philadelphia, 1845–49

Ingersoll, *History:* Charles J. Ingersoll, *History of the Second War between the United States of America and Great Britain,* 2 vols., Philadelphia, 1853

Mahan, *Sea Power:* Alfred T. Mahan, *Sea Power and Its Relations to the War of 1812,* 2 vols., Boston, 1905

Mahon, *War of 1812:* John K. Mahon, *The War of 1812,* Gainesville, 1972

NASP: C & N: Stephen E. Salsbury, ed., *The New American State Papers: Commerce and Navigation,* 47 vols., Wilmington, 1973

NASP: MA: Benjamin F. Cooling, ed., *The New American State Papers: Military Affairs,* 19 vols., Wilmington, 1979

NASP: NA: K. Jack Bauer, ed., *The New American State Papers: Naval Affairs,* 10 vols., Wilmington, 1981

ND (M125): U.S. Department of the Navy, *Letters Received by the Secretary of the Navy: Captains' Letters, 1805–1885,* Microfilm Series M125, National Archives, Washington, DC

ND (M147): U.S. Department of the Navy, *Letters Received by the Secretary of the Navy from Commanders, 1804–1886,* Microfilm Series M147, National Archives, Washington, DC

ND (M149): U.S. Department of the Navy, *Letters Sent by the Secretary of the Navy to Officers, 1798–1868,* Microfilm Series M149, National Archives, Washington, DC

Parliamentary Debates: T. C. Hansard, ed., *The Parliamentary Debates from the Year 1803 to the Present Time,* [First Series], 41 vols., London, 1803–20

RD: U.S. Congress, *Register of Debates in Congress [1824–1837],* 29 vols., Washington, DC, 1825–37 (19–1 refers to the 19th Congress, 1st session, and similarly for other sessions)

Senate Journal: U.S. Congress, *Journal of the Executive Proceedings of the Senate [1789–1828],* 3 vols., Washington, DC, 1828

SD (M30): U.S. Department of State, *Dispatches from United States Ministers to Great Britain, 1791–1906,* Microfilm Series M30, National Archives, Washington, DC

SD (M36): U.S. Department of State, *Records of Negotiations Connected with the Treaty of Ghent, 1813–1815,* Microfilm Series M36, National Archives, Washington, DC

SD (M77): U.S. Department of State, *Diplomatic Instructions to All Countries, 1801–1906,* Microfilm Series M77, National Archives, Washington, DC

SD (M588): U.S. Department of State, *War of 1812 Papers, 1789–1815,* Microfilm Series M588, National Archives, Washington, DC

TD (M175): U.S. Department of the Treasury, *Letters Sent by the Secretary of the Treasury to Collectors of Customs at All Ports (1789–1847) and at Small Ports (1847–1878),* Microfilm Series M175, National Archives, Washington, DC

TD (M178): U.S. Department of the Treasury, *Correspondence of the Secretary of the Treasury with Collectors of Customs, 1789–1833,* Microfilm Series M178, National Archives, Washington, DC

WD (M6): U.S. Department of War, *Letters Sent by the Secretary of War Relating to Military Affairs, 1800–1889,* Microfilm Series M6, National Archives, Washington, DC

WD (M7): U.S. Department of War, *Confidential and Unofficial Letters Sent by the Secretary of War, 1814–1847,* Microfilm Series M7, National Archives, Washington, DC

WD (M221): U.S. Department of War, *Letters Received by the Secretary of War, Registered Series, 1801–1870,* Microfilm Series M221, National Archives, Washington, DC

WD (M222): U.S. Department of War, *Letters Received by the Secretary of War, Unregistered Series, 1789–1861,* Microfilm Series M222, National Archives, Washington, DC

Wood, *British Documents:* William Wood, ed., *Select British Documents of the Canadian War of 1812,* 3 vols., Toronto, 1920–28

Zaslow, *Defended Border:* Morris Zaslow, ed., *The Defended Border: Upper Canada and the War of 1812*, Toronto, 1964

❖ ❖ ❖ ❖ ❖ ❖

The poetry at the beginning of this study was taken from the Trenton *True American*, June 29, 1812, and Fred L. Pattee, ed., *The Poems of Philip Freneau: Poet of the American Revolution*, 3 vols. (Princeton, 1902–7), 3: 345–46.

Introduction

1. A recent bibliography lists more than 6,000 items on the War of 1812. Although some of these items are unpublished—manuscripts, typescripts, and dissertations—the amount of published material is nonetheless staggering. See John C. Fredriksen, *Free Trade and Sailors' Rights: A Bibliography of the War of 1812* (Westport, 1985).

2. For more on the debate on the causes of the war, see Warren H. Goodman, "The War of 1812: A Survey of Changing Interpretations," *Mississippi Valley Historical Review* 28 (September, 1941), 171–86, and Clifford L. Egan, "The Origins of the War of 1812: Three Decades of Historical Writing," *Military Affairs* 38 (April, 1974), 72–75.

3. See Lord Hawkesbury to Anthony Merry, September 16, 1803, in Bernard Mayo, ed., *Instructions to the British Ministers to the United States, 1791–1812* (Washington, 1941), 200; Cartel for the Exchange of Prisoners of War, May 12, 1813, in Wood, *British Documents*, 3:797; Albert Gallatin, Memorandum of Voyage to St. Petersburg, June 21, 1813, in Gallatin Papers (SR), reel 26.

Chapter 1: The Road to War, 1811–1812

1. Jefferson's entire inaugural was spartan. See Merrill D. Peterson, *Thomas Jefferson and the New Nation: A Biography* (New York, 1970), 654–55.

2. The literature on the first political parties is extensive, though most studies focus on party organization and ideology rather than on policies. The best Federalist studies (which concentrate on the party after it fell from power) are Linda Kerber, *Federalists in Dissent: Imagery and Ideology in Jeffersonian America* (Ithaca, 1970); David H. Fischer, *The Revolution of American Conservatism: The Federalist Party in the Era of Jeffersonian Democracy* (New York, 1965); James M. Banner, Jr., *To the Hartford Convention: The Federalists and the Origins of Party Politics in Massachusetts, 1789–1815* (New York, 1970); Shaw Livermore, Jr., *The Twilight of Federalism: The Disintegration of the Federalist Party, 1815–1830* (Princeton, 1962); Lisle A. Rose, *Prologue to Democracy: The Federalists in the South, 1789–1800* (Lexington, 1968); and James H. Broussard, *The Southern Federalists, 1800–1816* (Baton Rouge, 1978). The best Republican studies are Drew R. McCoy, *The Elusive Republic: Political Economy in Jeffersonian America* (Chapel Hill, 1980); Lance Banning, *The Jeffersonian Persuasion: Evolution of a Party Ideology* (Ithaca, 1978); Stuart G. Brown, *The First Republicans:*

Political Philosophy and Public Policy in the Party of Jefferson and Madison (Syracuse, 1954); and Noble E. Cunningham, Jr., *The Jeffersonian Republicans: The Formation of Party Organization, 1789–1801* (Chapel Hill, 1957), and *The Jeffersonian Republicans in Power: Party Operations, 1801–1809* (Chapel Hill, 1963).

3. For Washington's views, see Washington to Congress, December 3, 1793, in *AC*, 3–1, 12.

4. Speech of Benjamin Tallmadge, April 6, 1808, in *AC*, 10–1, 1982; Boston *Weekly Messenger*, reprinted in Boston *Gazette*, December 26, 1811.

5. The best analysis of Hamilton's financial program, which stresses his aim to monetize American society, is Forrest McDonald, *Alexander Hamilton: A Biography* (New York, 1979), chs. 7–13.

6. For the development of Federalist defense policies, see Richard H. Kohn, *Eagle and Sword: The Federalists and the Creation of the Military Establishment in America, 1783–1802* (New York, 1975); James R. Jacobs, *The Beginnings of the U.S. Army, 1783–1812* (Princeton, 1947), chs. 1–9; Harold Sprout and Margaret Sprout, *The Rise of American Naval Power, 1776–1918*, rev. ed. (Princeton, 1966), 13–53; Marshall Smelser, *The Congress Founds a Navy, 1787–1798* (Notre Dame, 1959); and Donald R. Hickey, "Federalist Defense Policy in the Age of Jefferson, 1801–1812," *Military Affairs* 45 (April, 1981), 63–70.

7. See documents in *ASP: MA*, 1:6, 41, 112, 120, 153, 155, 192–97; Sprout and Sprout, *Rise of American Naval Power*, 13–15, 25–53.

8. The Jay Treaty can be found in *ASP: FR*, 1:520–25. The standard account of the treaty is Samuel F. Bemis, *Jay's Treaty: A Study in Commerce and Diplomacy*, rev. ed. (New Haven, 1962). For an excellent analysis of the ideological background, see Jerald A. Combs, *The Jay Treaty: Political Battleground of the Founding Fathers* (Berkeley, 1970).

9. Boston *Yankee*, reprinted in Philadelphia *Aurora*, February 24, 1812.

10. Curtis P. Nettels, *The Emergence of a National Economy, 1775–1815* (New York, 1962), 396. For a superb account of the development of Anglo-American friendship in this period, see Bradford Perkins, *The First Rapprochement: England and the United States, 1795–1805*, 2nd ed. (Berkeley, 1967).

11. The standard accounts of the Quasi-War are Gardner W. Allen, *Our Naval War with France* (Boston, 1909), and Alexander DeConde, *The Quasi-War: The Politics and Diplomacy of the Undeclared Naval War with France, 1797–1801* (New York, 1966). See also William Stinchcomb, *The XYZ Affair* (Westport, 1980), and Michael A. Palmer, *Stoddart's War: Naval Operations during the Quasi-War with France, 1798–1801* (Columbia, SC, 1987).

12. The estimate of losses can be found in Report of the Secretary of State, January 18, 1799, in *ASP: FR*, 2:232.

13. Report of the House Naval Committee, January 17, 1799, in *ASP:NA*, 1:69; Robert G. Albion and Jennie B. Pope, *Sea Lanes in Wartime: The American Experience*, 2nd ed. ([Hamden, Conn.], 1968), 81–83.

14. The convention is printed in *ASP: FR*, 2:295–301.

15. Jefferson to Nathaniel Macon, May 14, 1801, in Jefferson Papers (LC), reel 23.

16. Republican financial policies can be followed in Davis R. Dewey, *Finan-*

cial History of the United States, 12th ed. (New York, 1934); Bray Hammond, *Banks and Politics in America from the Revolution to the Civil War* (Princeton, 1962); Alexander Balinky, *Albert Gallatin: Fiscal Theories and Policies* (New Brunswick, 1958); and Adams, *History.*

17. For Republican defense policies, see Jacobs, *Beginnings of the U.S. Army,* chs. 10–14; and Sprout and Sprout, *Rise of American Naval Power,* 53–85.

18. *AC,* 7–1, 1306–12. For an excellent account of Jefferson's attempt to reform and republicanize the army, see Theodore J. Crackel, *Mr. Jefferson's Army: Political and Social Reform of the Military Establishment, 1801–1809* (New York, 1987).

19. Jacobs, *Beginnings of the U.S. Army,* 253; Crackel, *Mr. Jefferson's Army,* 45–53.

20. *AC,* 10–1, 2849–52; Crackel, *Mr. Jefferson's Army,* 169–76.

21. Winfield Scott, *Memoirs of Lieut.-General Scott,* 2 vols. (New York, 1864), 1:35–36. See also Jacobs, *Beginnings of the U.S. Army,* 270.

22. Speech of Nathaniel Macon, April 16, 1810, in *AC,* 11–2, 1863.

23. Speeches of James Fisk, January 25, 1812, and Samuel McKee, January 18, 1812, in *AC,* 12–1, 841 and 968–69.

24. Report of the Secretary of the Navy, December 3, 1811, in *ASP:NA,* 1:249–50; *AC,* 7–2, 1565; Sprout and Sprout, *Rise of American Naval Power,* 53–85.

25. Adam Seybert, *Statistical Annals . . . of the United States of America* (Philadelphia, 1818), 712. The figure excludes $100,000 appropriated in the 1790s but spent in 1801–1802.

26. For more on the militia and privateers, see John K. Mahon, *The American Militia: Decade of Decision, 1789–1800* (Gainesville, 1960); Lawrence D. Cress, *Citizens in Arms: The Army and the Militia in American Society to the War of 1812* (Chapel Hill, 1982); and Edgar Maclay, *A History of American Privateers* (New York, 1899).

27. See Jefferson to Congress, February 10, 1807, in *AC,* 9–2, 63–65. The quoted words are from speech of John Randolph, December 16, 1811, in *AC,* 12–1, 541.

28. See Report of the Secretary of the Navy, June 9, 1809, in *ASP:NA,* 1:200; Madison to Congress, May 23, 1809, in *AC,* 11–1, 12; Dudley and Crawford, *Naval War,* 1:12.

29. Nettels, *Emergence of a National Economy,* 396.

30. Monroe to [Secretary of State], July 1, 1804, in Monroe Papers (LC), reel 3. See also Monroe to Secretary of State, August 7, 1804, ibid., reel 11.

31. Monroe to Secretary of State, October 18, 1805, ibid., reel 11.

32. Perkins, *First Rapprochement,* 86–89; Nettels, *Emergence of a National Economy,* 396.

33. Lords Holland and Auckland to Lord Howick, October 20, 1806, in Foreign Office Papers 5/51 (PRO).

34. The *Essex* decision is printed in Dudley and Crawford, *Naval War,* 1:17–20. See also Perkins, *First Rapprochement,* 177–81; and Perkins, *Prologue to War: England and the United States, 1805–1812* (Berkeley, 1961), 77–84.

35. Anthony Merry to Lord Mulgrave, September 30, 1805, in Adams, *History*, 3:97.

36. Monroe to Secretary of State, September 25, 1805, in Monroe Papers (LC), reel 11.

37. Perkins, *Prologue to War*, 104–6.

38. Most of the petitions are printed in *ASP:FR*, 2:737–73.

39. The standard work on impressment is James F. Zimmerman, *Impressment of American Seamen* (New York, 1925).

40. For estimates on the size of the merchant marine, see Gallatin to Madison, April 13, 1807, in Madison Papers (LC), reel 25; speech of Langdon Cheves, January 17, 1812, in *AC*, 12–1, 818; Adams, *History*, 6:455; Zimmerman, *Impressment*, 272. See also Timothy Pickering to Francis J. Jackson, April 8, 1812, in Pickering Papers (MHS), reel 14.

41. Zimmerman, *Impressment*, 266–67.

42. Ibid., 55–61, 67–68; Georgetown *Federal Republican*, February 8, 1813. There are copies of "protections" in ND (M147), reel 4; Foreign Office Papers 5/55 (PRO); and Zimmerman, *Impressment*, 69n.

43. Admiralty to [Rueben G. Beasley], May 26, 1813, in *NASP: NA*, 8:23.

44. The analysis of the issues in the ensuing paragraphs is based mainly on the following sources: Perkins, *Prologue to War;* Reginald Horsman, *The Causes of the War of 1812* (Philadelphia, 1962); A. L. Burt, *The United States, Great Britain, and British North America from the Revolution to the Establishment of Peace after the War of 1812* (New Haven, 1940); Charles S. Hyneman, *The First American Neutrality: A Study of the American Understanding of Neutral Obligations during the Years 1792–1815* (Urbana, 1934); W. Allison Phillips and Arthur H. Reede, *Neutrality, Its History, Economics and Law: The Napoleonic Period* (New York, 1936); Carlton Savage, *Policy of the United States toward Maritime Commerce in War*, 2 vols. (Washington, 1934–36).

45. Speech of Barnabas Bidwell, March 8, 1806, in *AC*, 9–1, 653.

46. Speech of Samuel Smith, March 10, 1806, in *AC*, 9–1, 168.

47. Fisher Ames, "Political Review III," in W. B. Allen, ed., *Works of Fisher Ames*, 2 vols. (Indianapolis, 1984), 1:472–73. See also Boston *Repertory*, cited in Richmond *Enquirer*, October 11, 1805.

48. *AC*, 9–1, 90–91, 109, 112; Merry to Mulgrave, February 2, 1806, in Foreign Office Papers 5/48 (PRO); Jefferson to Monroe, March 10, 1808, in Jefferson Papers (LC), reel 41.

49. Jefferson to William Short, October 3, 1801, in Jefferson Papers (LC), reel 24.

50. Henry S. Randall, *The Life of Thomas Jefferson*, 3 vols. (New York, 1858), 3:315. For British attempts to renew the Jay Treaty, see Lord Harrowby to Merry, August 4, 1804, in Mayo, *Instructions to British Ministers*, 207–8.

51. Jefferson to Monroe, March 10, 1808, in Jefferson Papers (LC), reel 41.

52. Madison to Monroe and Pinkney, May 17, 1806, in SD (M77), reel 1.

53. Lords Holland and Auckland to Monroe and Pinkney, November 8, 1806, in SD (M30), reel 10. Monroe and Pinkney claimed that privately the

British promised that if their deserters were returned they would give up impressment except "in cases of an extraordinary nature." The British envoys, however, denied making this pledge. See Monroe and Pinkney to Madison, January 3 and April 22, 1807, and Monroe to Madison, February 28, 1808, in *ASP:FR*, 3:146, 160–61, 174; Lords Holland and Auckland to George Canning, July 28 and August 10, 1807, in Foreign Office Papers 5/54 (PRO). Quotation from p. 174.

54. The Monroe-Pinkney Treaty is printed in *ASP:FR*, 3:147–51. The analysis in the following paragraphs is based on Donald R. Hickey, "The Monroe-Pinkney Treaty of 1806: A Reappraisal," *William and Mary Quarterly*, 3rd ser., 44 (January, 1987), 65–88.

55. The established duty for re-exported goods was 3 percent of their value. Under the Monroe-Pinkney Treaty, this duty would be lowered to 2 percent for goods shipped to Europe and 1 percent for goods shipped to the Caribbean.

56. Note of Holland and Auckland, December 31, 1806, in SD (M30), reel 10.

57. Quoted in Jacob Wagner to Pickering, July 21, 1813, in Pickering Papers (MHS), reel 30. For more on Jefferson's views, see Hickey, "Monroe-Pinckney Treaty," 85–87.

58. See Jefferson's cabinet notes, February 3, 1807, (filed under March 5, 1806), in Jefferson Papers (LC), reel 35.

59. There is a good account of the *Chesapeake* affair in Perkins, *Prologue to War*, 140–49.

60. Nicholson to Gallatin, July 14, 1807, in Gallatin Papers (SR), reel 14.

61. For an analysis of the Orders in Council, see Perkins, *Prologue to War*, chs. 6–7, and Horsman, *Causes of the War of 1812*, chs. 6–8.

62. Napoleon, quoted in Perkins, *Prologue to War*, 69.

63. Spencer Perceval, quoted in Adams, *History*, 6:279.

64. William Lee to Gallatin, May 22, 1812, in Gallatin Papers (SR), reel 24; Perkins, *Prologue to War*, 206–7, 304–7.

65. Charles Francis Adams, ed., *Memoirs of John Quincy Adams*, 12 vols. (Philadelphia, 1874–77) (December 29, 1809), 2:92.

66. See American Ships Seized by Danish Privateers, October 16, 1809, George Erving to Secretary of State, June 23, 1811, and Report of the Secretary of State, July 6, 1812, all in *ASP:FR*, 3:332, 521, 584.

67. The best account of the restrictive system is Herbert Heaton, "Non-Importation, 1806–1812," *Journal of Economic History* 1 (November, 1941), 178–98. There are also good treatments in Adams, *History*, vols. 3–6; Perkins, *Prologue to War*, chs. 4–7; and Horsman, *Causes of the War of 1812*, chs. 3–12.

68. Boston *Independent Chronicle*, reprinted in Washington *National Intelligencer*, December 11, 1805.

69. The law is printed in *AC*, 9–1, 1259–62.

70. The law is printed in *AC*, 10–1, 2814–15. There are several good books on the embargo, each of which approaches the subject from a different angle.

See Louis M. Sears, *Jefferson and the Embargo* (Durham, 1927); Walter W. Jennings, *The American Embargo, 1807–1809* (Iowa City, 1921); and Burton Spivak, *Jefferson's English Crisis: Commerce, Embargo, and the Republican Revolution* (Charlottesville, 1979).

71. Speech of John Randolph, April 14, 1808, in *AC*, 10–1, 2136.

72. Perkins, *Prologue to War*, 160–63.

73. Gallatin to Jefferson, July 29, 1808, and Jefferson to Gallatin, August 11, 1808, in Jefferson Papers (LC), reels 41 and 42.

74. See *AC*, 10–2, 1798–1804. For an excellent analysis of this law, see Leonard W. Levy, *Jefferson & Civil Liberties: The Darker Side*, 2nd ed. (New York, 1973), ch. 6. Levy's study is a compelling analysis of Jefferson's disregard for civil liberties. The "Preface to the Paperback Edition," which examines the reception of the first edition, is a remarkable commentary on the history profession.

75. Nettels, *Emergence of a National Economy*, 396.

76. See Jennings, *American Embargo*, chs. 7–9.

77. John Armstrong, quoted in Perkins, *Prologue to War*, 166. For the impact of the embargo abroad, see Jennings, *American Embargo*, 70–93, and Sears, *Jefferson and the Embargo*, 276–301, 312–17.

78. Horsman, *Causes of the War of 1812*, 141–42; Clifford L. Egan, *Neither Peace nor War: Franco-American Relations, 1803–1812* (Baton Rouge, 1983), 97.

79. Robert Ferguson, quoted in Horsman, *Causes of the War of 1812*, 143.

80. The law is printed in *AC*, 10–2, 1824–30.

81. For more on the Erskine Agreement, see Perkins, *Prologue to War*, 210–20.

82. The act is printed in *AC*, 10–2, 2582–83.

83. Quoted in Perkins, *Prologue to War*, 246.

84. Egan, *Neither Peace nor War*, 120–22.

85. *AC*, 11–3, 1338–39. The legislative history of this bill is significant because it marked the first time that the previous question was successfully used to cut off debate. See *AC*, 11–3, 1091–95.

86. Adams, *History*, 6:37–45; Burt, *United States and Great Britain*, 292–95; Perkins, *Prologue to War*, 274–82.

87. See documents in Dudley and Crawford, *Naval War*, 1:41–49, and *ASP:FR*, 3:471–99. See also Adams, *History*, 6:25–37; and Perkins, *Prologue to War*, 271–73.

88. Quoted in Perkins, *Prologue to War*, 273.

89. *Niles' Register*, 2 (March 7, 1812), 5.

90. There are two excellent studies of the Shawnee leaders by R. David Edmunds: *The Shawnee Prophet* (Lincoln, 1983), and *Tecumseh and the Quest for Indian Leadership* (Boston, 1984). Edmunds argues that the Prophet was the more important of the two leaders. The conventional view—which stresses Tecumseh's role—can be found in Glenn Tucker, *Tecumseh: Vision of Glory* (Indianapolis, 1956).

91. William Henry Harrison to William Eustis, July 10, August 6, and

August 7, 1811, in Logan Esarey, ed., *Messages and Letters of William Henry Harrison*, 2 vols. (Indianapolis, 1922), 1:533, 544, 549; Robert B. McAfee, *History of the Late War in the Western Country* (Lexington, 1816), 17.

92. Harrison to Eustis, July 2, 1811, in Esarey, *Messages and Letters of William Henry Harrison*, 1:526.

93. Eustis to Harrison, July 17 and 20, 1811, and Harrison to Eustis, August 7 and 13, 1811, ibid., 1:535–37, 550, 554; McAfee, *History of the Late War*, 18–19.

94. Harrison to Eustis, November 18, 1811, in WD (M221), reel 44; McAfee, *History of the Late War*, 18–36; Alec R. Gilpin, *The War of 1812 in the Old Northwest* (East Lansing, 1958), 16–19.

95. R. I. Snelling to Harrison, November 20, 1811, in WD (M221), reel 44.

96. Harrison to Eustis, May 6, 1812, ibid., reel 45.

97. Trenton *True American*, December 2, 9, 16, 1811, and January 6, 1812; Salem *Essex Register*, December 21, 1811; Concord *New-Hampshire Patriot*, December 24, 1811.

98. Lexington *Reporter*, November 23, 1811, and March 14, 1812. See also ibid., May 23 and 30, 1812.

99. For an excellent analysis of Republican thinking on the eve of the war, see Roger H. Brown, *The Republic in Peril: 1812* (New York, 1964), and Steven Watts, *The Republic Reborn: War and the Making of Liberal America, 1790–1820* (Baltimore, 1987).

100. William Plumer to John Quincy Adams, August 18, 1812, in Plumer Papers (LC), reel 2.

101. Lexington *Reporter*, December 10, 1811.

102. Philip S. Klein, ed., "Memoirs of a Senator from Pennsylvania: Jonathan Roberts, 1771–1854," *Pennsylvania Magazine of History and Biography* 61 (April, 1938), 240; speech of John C. Calhoun, May 6, 1812, in *AC*, 12–1, 1399. See also speech of Nathaniel Macon, January 4, 1812, in *AC*, 12–1, 661.

103. Washington *National Intelligencer*, November 7, 1811; A. McLane to Peter B. Porter, February 28, 1812, in Porter Papers (BEHS), reel 2. See also Philadelphia *Aurora*, October 26, 1812; Jonathan Roberts to Matthew Roberts, April 12, 1812, in Roberts Papers (HSP).

104. John Binns to Jonathan Roberts, May 5, 1812, in Roberts Papers (HSP); Felix Grundy to Andrew Jackson, December 24, 1811, in Jackson Papers (LC), reel 5; Jonathan Roberts to Richard F. Leech, June 14–16, 1812, in Roberts Papers (HSP). See also Gideon Granger to John Tod, December 26, 1811, in Granger Papers (LC).

105. John W. Eppes to Jefferson, March 20, 1811, in Edgehill-Randolph Papers (UVA). For an excellent article on the political origins of the war, see J.C.A. Stagg, "James Madison and the 'Malcontents': The Political Origins of the War of 1812," *William and Mary Quarterly*, 3rd ser., 33 (October, 1976), 557–85.

106. The *Annals of Congress* and contemporary newspapers are replete with Federalist attacks on the restrictive system. For a sampling, see *AC*, 9–2, 157–58; *AC*, 10–1, 1704–6, 1850–54, 2118–25; *AC*, 10–2, 20–27, 29–35, 51–60,

767–79, 865–86; *AC*, 11–2, 1637–38, 1651–53, 1708–9; *AC*, 11–3, 910–32, 1011–27; New York *Evening Post*, December 26, 1811; Hartford *Connecticut Mirror*, February 10, 1812; Chillicothe *Supporter*, February 29, 1812; Philadelphia *United States' Gazette*, June 26, 1812; and Boston *Columbian Centinel*, July 25, 1812.

107. Plumer to John A. Harper, April 27, 1812, in Plumer Papers (LC), reel 3; Gerry to Madison, May 19, 1812, in Madison Papers (LC), reel 14. See also John G. Jackson to Madison, March 30, 1812, ibid., reel 13; John Binns to Jonathan Roberts, May 3, 1812, in Roberts Papers (HSP).

108. Madison to South Carolina House of Representatives, January 8, 1812, in Madison Papers (LC), reel 13.

Chapter 2: The Declaration of War

1. Boston *Independent Chronicle*, September 30, 1812; Washington *National Intelligencer*, November 7, 1811; Salem *Essex Register*, October 30, 1811. For similar sentiments, see Philadelphia *Aurora*, October 26, 1811; Concord *New-Hampshire Patriot*, October 29, 1811; and Worcester *National Aegis*, November 6, 1811.

2. The most reliable contemporary guide to party affiliation in the War Congress is in *Niles' Register*, 1 (November 30, 1811), 233–34. For tests that can be used to establish the affiliation of doubtful members, see Donald R. Hickey, "The Federalists and the War of 1812" (Ph.D. dissertation, University of Illinois, 1972), Appendix A; and Hickey, Letter to the Editor, *William and Mary Quarterly*, 3rd ser., 30 (April, 1973), 371–73.

3. Jonathan Roberts to William Jones, May 24, 1812, in Jones Papers (HSP).

4. The standard work on the Old Republicans is Norman K. Risjord, *The Old Republicans: Southern Conservatism in the Age of Jefferson* (New York, 1965). See also William C. Bruce, *John Randolph of Roanoke, 1773–1833*, 2 vols. (New York, 1922); and Russell Kirk, *John Randolph of Roanoke* (Chicago, 1951). The Old Republicans are sometimes called the "Tertium Quids" or simply the "Quids," meaning a third thing or party. Contemporaries applied the term *Quid* to several different Republican factions, but (except for occasionally allying with Federalists in state politics) these factions had little in common. For an illuminating discussion of this subject, see Noble E. Cunningham, Jr., "Who Were the Quids?" *Mississippi Valley Historical Review* 50 (September, 1963), 252–63.

5. There is no monograph on the Clintonians, but for a good introduction, see Steven E. Siry, "The Sectional Politics of 'Practical Republicanism': De Witt Clinton's Presidential Bid, 1810–1812," *Journal of the Early Republic* 5 (Winter, 1985), 441–62.

6. For a good analysis of the Invisibles, see John S. Pancake, "The 'Invisibles': A Chapter in the Opposition to President Madison," *Journal of Southern History* 21 (February, 1955), 17–37. See also John S. Pancake, *Samuel Smith and the Politics of Business: 1752–1839* (University, AL, 1972); Frank A. Cassell, *Merchant Congressman in the Young Republic: Samuel Smith of Maryland, 1752–*

1839 (Madison, 1971); and Dice R. Anderson, *William Branch Giles: A Study in the Politics of Virginia and the Nation from 1790 to 1830* (Menasha, WI, 1914). For a good illustration of the Invisibles' hostility to Gallatin, see speech of William Branch Giles, December 17, 1811, in *AC*, 12–1, 47–51.

7. [Jonathan Roberts] to ———, February 3, 1812, in Roberts Papers (HSP).

8. Scholars differ over who (if anyone) ought to be classified as a War Hawk. My list is traditional. It includes those House members who were outspoken proponents of war and supplied leadership to the war movement. Harry W. Fritz makes a good case for the traditional War Hawks in "The War Hawks of 1812," *Capitol Studies* 5 (Spring, 1977), 25–42. For alternative views, see Reginald Horsman, "Who Were the War Hawks?" *Indiana Magazine of History* 60 (June, 1964), 121–36; Roger H. Brown, "The War Hawks of 1812: An Historical Myth," ibid., 137–51; and Ronald L. Hatzenbuehler, "The War Hawks and the Question of Congressional Behavior in 1812," *Pacific Historical Review* 65 (February, 1976), 1–22. My critique of Hatzenbuehler's work, as well as his reply, can be found in *Pacific Historical Review* 45 (November, 1976), 642–45.

9. William Reed to Timothy Pickering, February 18, 1812, in Pickering Papers (MHS), reel 30.

10. *AC*, 12–1, 330.

11. John A. Harper to William Plumer, December 2, 1811, in Plumer Papers (LC), reel 3.

12. A correspondent from Washington, quoted in Boston *Columbian Centinel*, November 16, 1811.

13. Klein, "Memoirs of Jonathan Roberts," 230. See also Jonathan Roberts to Alexander Dallas, December 19, 1813, in Dallas Papers (HSP).

14. Albert Gallatin, notes on president's message [Fall, 1811], in Madison Papers (LC), reel 26.

15. Madison to Congress, November 5, 1811, in *AC*, 12–1, 11–15. Quotation from p. 13.

16. Philadelphia *Aurora*, November 7, 1811; Worcester *National Aegis*, November 27, 1811. For similar sentiments, see Petersburg (VA) *Republican*, reprinted in Lexington *Reporter*, December 17, 1811; Benjamin Rush to James Monroe, November 8, 1811, and John Adams to Monroe, December 19, 1811, in Monroe Papers (LC), reel 4; Henry Dearborn to Monroe, November 14, 1811, in Monroe Papers (NYPL).

17. Josiah Quincy to Harrison Gray Otis, November 8, 1811, in Otis Papers (MHS).

18. Four of the nine committee members were War Hawks: Porter, Calhoun, Grundy, and Harper. Two other members—Joseph Desha and John Sevier—are sometimes classified as War Hawks and could be counted on to support war measures.

19. Lowndes to Elizabeth Lowndes, December 7, 1811, in Lowndes Papers (UNC), reel 1. See also William A. Burwell to Wilson Cary Nicholas, December 29, 1811, in Nicholas Papers (LC); Grundy to Andrew Jackson, November 28,

1811, in Jackson Papers (LC), reel 5; Alexandria *Herald*, reprinted in Richmond *Enquirer*, December 10, 1811.

20. Report of the House Foreign Relations Committee, November 29, 1811, in *AC*, 12–1, 373–77. Quotation from p. 376.

21. Speech of Peter B. Porter, December 6, 1811, in *AC*, 12–1, 417.

22. *AC*, 12–1, 419–20, 545–48, 565–66.

23. *AC*, 12–1, 556–57, 560–66; Washington *National Intelligencer*, December 17, 1811; Baltimore *Whig*, reprinted in Philadelphia *Aurora*, December 18, 1811.

24. Letter from a Federalist, January 6, 1812, reprinted from Alexandria *Herald* in Richmond *Enquirer*, January 23, 1812.

25. Speech of Daniel Sheffey, January 3, 1812, in *AC*, 12–1, 635. See also speech of William Branch Giles, December 17, 1811, in *AC*, 12–1, 44; Timothy Pickering to Samuel W. Dana, January 16, 1812, in Pickering Papers (MHS), reel 14; Samuel Taggart to Rev. John Taylor, January 20, 1812, in Mary R. Reynolds, ed., "Letters of Samuel Taggart, Representative in Congress, 1803–1814," *Proceedings of the American Antiquarian Society* 33 (October, 1923), 376–77.

26. Thomas R. Gold to Nathan Appleton, [December, 1811?], in Appleton Papers (MHS); Bleecker to Henry D. Sedgwick, December 27, 1811, in Sedgwick Papers (MHS). See also Quincy to Otis, November 8 and 26, 1811, in Otis Papers (MHS); James Milnor to Samuel Bradford, December 10, 1811, in Bradford Papers (HSP); William Reed to Timothy Pickering, January 20, 1812, and Samuel W. Dana to Pickering, January 30, 1812, in Pickering Papers (MHS), reel 30; James A. Bayard to William H. Wells, January 12, 1812, in Elizabeth Donnan, ed., *Papers of James A. Bayard, 1796–1815* (Washington, 1915), 188; Taggart to Taylor, December 14, 1811, in Reynolds, "Letters of Samuel Taggart," 370. For a fuller analysis of Federalist strategy in the War Congress, see Donald R. Hickey, "The Federalists and the Coming of the War, 1811–1812," *Indiana Magazine of History* 75 (March, 1979), 70–88.

27. For Federalist votes on these measures, see Hickey, "Federalists and the Coming of the War," 84–86. See also Nathaniel Macon to Joseph H. Nicholson, January 10, 1812, in Nicholson Papers (LC).

28. *AC*, 12–1, 33, 566–67, 2227–28. The new cash bounty was actually $16 plus three months' pay. Privates were paid $5 a month. For the old bounty (which was set in 1802), see *AC*, 7–1, 1309.

29. *AC*, 12–1, 85, 99, 112, 192–93, 691, 697, 800–801, 1035–36, 2229–37, 2267–69.

30. See Madison to Jefferson, February 7, 1812, in Madison Papers (LC), reel 13; Monroe to John Taylor, June 13, 1812, in Monroe Papers (LC), reel 5; Jonathan Roberts to Matthew Roberts, December 20, 1811, in Roberts Papers (HSP); speeches of Joseph Anderson, December 17, 1811, and George W. Campbell, December 18, 1811, in *AC*, 12–1, 54–84.

31. Speech of William Branch Giles, December 17, 1811, in *AC*, 12–1, 35–54.

32. See debate in *AC*, 12–1, 728–801.

33. See Report of House Committee, January 2, 1806, Ebenezer Huntington to Benjamin Tallmadge, January 5, 1810, and Resolutions of Kentucky Legislature, February 8, 1812, in *ASP: MA*, 1:189, 263–66, 318; Hartford *Connecticut Mirror*, February 17, 1812.

34. *AC*, 12–1, 195, 1004, 1021, 1040, 1084–85, 1298.

35. Speech of Langdon Cheves, January 17, 1812, in *AC*, 12–1, 803–22; Paul Hamilton to Cheves, December 3, 1811, in *ASP: NA*, 1:248–52.

36. John Adams, quoted in Edmund Quincy, *Life of Josiah Quincy of Massachusetts*, 4th ed. (Boston, 1868), 248; Philadelphia *Aurora*, February 27, 1812.

37. Speech of Josiah Quincy, January 25, 1812, in *AC*, 12–1, 949–68. Quotation from p. 957. Almost every Federalist newspaper in the country (and many Republican ones, too) carried Quincy's speech.

38. Speech of Adam Seybert, January 18, 1812, in *AC*, 12–1, 830, 833. For the rest of the debate on naval expansion, see *AC*, 12–1, 859–1005.

39. *AC*, 12–1, 164, 999. Lloyd's speech in support of his proposal is in *AC*, 12–1, 131–47. This speech was widely reprinted in the press, and in pamphlet form an edition of 12,000 copies sold out in Boston. See Philadelphia *United States' Gazette*, June 1, 1812.

40. *AC*, 12–1, 1002–4.

41. *AC*, 12–1, 166, 1005, 2261–62. Most Federalists were so disgusted with the failure of naval expansion that they abstained on the final vote of this bill.

42. *AC*, 12–1, 163, 1030, 1160–61, 2251–52.

43. See Alexander S. Balinky, "Gallatin's Theory of War Finance," *William and Mary Quarterly*, 3rd ser., 16 (January, 1959), 73–82.

44. Gallatin to Ezekiel Bacon, January 10, 1812, in *ASP: F*, 2:523–27. See also Report of the Secretary of the Treasury, November 22, 1811, in *ASP: F*, 2:495–97.

45. Plumer to John A. Harper, February 4, 1812, in Plumer Papers (LC), reel 2.

46. *AC*, 12–1, 846–47.

47. Speech of Robert Wright, March 2, 1812, in *AC*, 12–1, 1123; John A. Harper to William Plumer, February 17, 1812, in Plumer Papers (LC), reel 3.

48. New York *Columbian*, reprinted in Philadelphia *Aurora*, January 27, 1812; Baltimore *Sun*, reprinted in Philadelphia *Aurora*, January 31, 1812; Albany *Register*, reprinted in Hartford *Connecticut Mirror*, March 16, 1812; Washington *National Intelligencer*, January 28, 1812.

49. Baltimore *Whig*, January 31, 1812; Concord *New-Hampshire Patriot*, February 11, 1812; Lexington *Reporter*, February 15, 1812; Bennington (VT) *Green-Mountain Farmer*, February 25, 1812. See also Worcester *National Aegis*, February 5, 1812; Edward Fox to Jonathan Roberts, February 23, 1812, in Roberts Papers (HSP); Henry Dearborn to Gallatin, March 29, 1812, in Gallatin Papers (SR), reel 24; and George Hay to Monroe, January 23, 1812, in Monroe Papers (NYPL).

50. *AC*, 12–1, 167, 1092, 2253–55.

51. James A. Bayard to Caesar A. Rodney, March 9, 1812, in "James Asheton Bayard Letters, 1802–1814," *Bulletin of the New York Public Library* 4 (July, 1900), 236.

52. *AC*, 12–1, 1094–1155.

53. Madison to Jefferson, March 6, 1812, in Madison Papers (LC), reel 13.

54. Madison to Congress, March 9, 1812, in *AC*, 12–1, 1162. The analysis that follows is based on Samuel Elliot Morison, "The Henry-Crillon Affair of 1812," *Proceedings of the Massachusetts Historical Society* 69 (October, 1947–May, 1950), 207–31; and E. A. Cruikshank, *The Political Adventures of John Henry: The Record of an International Imbroglio* (Toronto, 1936). The pertinent documents are printed in *AC*, 12–1, 1163–81, and in Henry Adams, ed., "Count Edward de Crillon," *American Historical Review* 1 (October, 1895), 51–69.

55. Gerry to Madison, January 29, 1812, in Madison Papers (LC), reel 26.

56. Madison to Jefferson, March 9, 1812, ibid.

57. Madison to Congress, March 9, 1812, in *AC*, 12–1, 1162.

58. Sir James Craig to Henry, February 6, 1809, in *AC*, 12–1, 1164.

59. Washington *National Intelligencer*, March 10, 1812.

60. John A. Harper to William Plumer, March 11, 1812, in Plumer Papers (LC), reel 3.

61. Nathaniel Macon to Joseph H. Nicholson, March 23, 1812, in Nicholson Papers (LC).

62. Leonard White to Daniel Appleton White, March 11, 1812, in White Papers (EI).

63. Report of the Secretary of State, March 12, 1812, in *AC*, 12–1, 169.

64. Baltimore *Federal Republican*, March 12, 1812; statement of Samuel Sterett, in Philadelphia *Aurora*, March 19, 1812; Benjamin Tallmadge to James McHenry, March 16, 1812, in McHenry Papers (LC); Samuel Elliot Morison, *The Life and Letters of Harrison Gray Otis, Federalist, 1765–1848*, 2 vols. (Boston, 1913), 2:46.

65. Abijah Bigelow to Hannah Bigelow, March 22, 1812, in Clarence S. Brigham, ed., "Letters of Abijah Bigelow, Member of Congress, to His Wife, 1810–1815," *Proceedings of the American Antiquarian Society* 40 (October, 1930), 332–33. See also Quincy to Otis, March 19, 1812, in Otis Papers (MHS); Taggart to Taylor, March 13, 1812, in Reynolds, "Letters of Samuel Taggart," 389.

66. John A. Harper to William Plumer, March 11, 1812, in Plumer Papers (LC), reel 3. See also Plumer to William Claggett, March 24, 1812, in Plumer Papers (NHHS), reel 2; Boston *Independent Chronicle*, March 26, 1812.

67. Cruikshank, *John Henry*, 7; David W. Parker, ed., "Secret Reports of John Howe, 1808," *American Historical Review* 17 (October, 1911–January, 1912), 70–102, 332–54; Dumas Malone, *Jefferson and His Time*, 6 vols. (Boston, 1948–1981), 5:519–20.

68. Louis Serurier to Duc de Bassano, March 23, 1812, in Adams, *History*, 6:194.

69. Clay to Monroe, March 15, 1812, in Monroe Papers (LC), reel 5; Irving

Brant, *James Madison*, 6 vols. (Indianapolis and New York, 1941–1961), 5:428. See also Bayard to Andrew Bayard, May 2, 1812, in Donnan, *Papers of James A. Bayard*, 196.

70. Madison to Congress, April 1, 1812, in *AC*, 12–1, 186–87.

71. *AC*, 12–1, 189, 1598, 1612–14, 2262–64.

72. *AC*, 12–1, 203, 1622–23, 2269–70.

73. Speech of Henry Clay, April 1, 1812, in *AC*, 12–1, 1588. See also speeches of Felix Grundy, Adam Seybert, and John Smilie, April 1, 1812, in *AC*, 12–1, 1587–88, 1592; Richard M. Johnson to Frankfort (KY) *Palladium*, April 4, 1812, reprinted in Lexington *Reporter*, April 18, 1812; John C. Calhoun to James Macbride, April 18, 1812, in Robert L. Meriwether et al., eds., *The Papers of John C. Calhoun*, 16 vols. to date (Columbia, SC, 1959—), 1:100.

74. William Reed to Timothy Pickering, April 25, 1812, in Pickering Papers (MHS), reel 30.

75. Madison to Jefferson, April 24, 1812, in Madison Papers (LC), reel 14.

76. Speeches of John C. Calhoun and Josiah Quincy, April 7, 1812, in *AC*, 12–1, 1265–66; Nathaniel Macon to Joseph H. Nicholson, April 7–8, 1812, in Nicholson Papers (LC); broadside, April 3, 1812, in Shaw Broadside Collection (AAS); Washington *National Intelligencer*, April 2, 1812; Philadelphia *United States' Gazette*, April 14, 1812; Hartford *Connecticut Mirror*, May 18, 1812.

77. Nathan Appleton to Samuel Appleton, April 5, 1812, in Appleton Papers (MHS). See also Macon to Nicholson, April 6, 1812, in Nicholson Papers (LC); diary of Henry Thompson, April 3, 1812 (MdHS); Washington *National Intelligencer*, April 9, 1812; Richmond *Enquirer*, April 10, 1812; Eliza C. Harrison, ed., *Philadelphia Merchant: The Diary of Thomas P. Cope, 1800–1851* (South Bend, 1978) (April 2, 1812), 269; W. Freeman Galpin, "The Grain Trade of Alexandria, Virginia, 1801–1815," *North Carolina Historical Review* 4 (October, 1927), 421; Brant, *James Madison*, 5:426.

78. *Niles' Register* 2 (April 11, 1812), 101. See also John Taylor to Monroe, May 10, 1812, in Monroe Papers (LC), reel 5.

79. *Niles' Register* 2 (April 11, 1812), 101.

80. *Boston Gazette*, March 26, 1812; Brant, *James Madison*, 5:401.

81. Lowndes to Elizabeth Lowndes, [March 23, 1812], in Lowndes Papers (UNC), reel 1; Plumer to Harper, May 11, 1812, in Plumer Papers (LC), reel 3. For similar sentiments, see John Taylor to Monroe, January 2, 1812, in Monroe Papers (LC), reel 4; Edward Fox to Jonathan Roberts, May 4, 1812, in Roberts Papers (HSP); Alexander Campbell to [Jeremiah Morrow?], May 6, 1812, in Campbell Papers (ChHS); Lexington *Reporter*, January 11 and 25 and February 1, 1812; Philadelphia *Aurora*, March 24, 1812.

82. Speech of Josiah Quincy, January 19, 1809, in *AC*, 10–2, 1112.

83. Quincy to Otis, November 8 and 26, 1812, in Otis Papers (MHS).

84. *Boston Gazette*, December 19, 1811. For other examples of Federalist skepticism, see Tallmadge to McHenry, January 16, 1812, in McHenry Papers (LC); Nathaniel Saltonstall, Jr., to Nathaniel Saltonstall, May 1, 1812, in Saltonstall Papers (MHS); Nathan Appleton to Samuel Appleton, May 12 and June 1, 1812, in Appleton Papers (MHS); Theodore Sedgwick to Daniel Dewey,

June 11, 1812, in Sedgwick Papers (MHS); Samuel Yorke and James Schott to Patrick Tracy Jackson, April 2, 1812, in Kenneth W. Porter, ed., *The Jacksons and the Lees: Two Generations of Massachusetts Merchants, 1765–1844*, 2 vols. (Cambridge, 1937), 1:728.

85. James Monroe, quoted in memorandum of [John Randolph?], March 31, 1812, in Samuel Smith Papers (LC), reel 4.

86. Washington *National Intelligencer*, March 19 and April 7, 9, and 14, 1812; Leonard White to Daniel Appleton White, April 11, 1812, in White Papers (EI); Brant, *James Madison*, 5:448.

87. Madison to Jefferson, April 24, 1812, in Madison Papers (LC), reel 14.

88. Richard Beale Davis, ed., *Jeffersonian America: Notes on the United States of America Collected in the Years 1805–6–7 and 11–12 by Sir Augustus John Foster, Bart.* (San Marino, 1954), 92.

89. Foster to Barclay, May 10, 1812, in George L. Rives, ed., *Selections from the Correspondence of Thomas Barclay, Formerly British Consul-General at New York* (New York, 1894), 309.

90. Taggart to Taylor, January 20, 1812, in Reynolds, "Letters of Samuel Taggart," 377.

91. Macon to Nicholson, March 31, 1812, in Nicholson Papers (LC).

92. George W. Campbell to Andrew Jackson, April 10, 1812, Jackson Papers (LC), reel 5.

93. *AC*, 12–1, 219, 1342, 1353. The Senate voted for a recess, but the House refused to concur.

94. Macon to Nicholson, April 30, 1812, in Nicholson Papers (LC); Bayard to Rodney, May 6, 1812, in "James Asheton Bayard Letters," 237. See also Jonathan Roberts to Matthew Roberts, May 7, 1812, in Roberts Papers (HSP). The Senate adjourned on May 4 because it had a bare quorum and on May 13 because it had no quorum. See *AC*, 12–1, 225, 239.

95. Baltimore *American*, reprinted in Boston *Gazette*, February 17, 1812. See also Raleigh *Minerva*, February 21, 1812; Philadelphia *Aurora*, February 13 and 14, 1812; London *Times*, March 10, 1812; Edward Fox to Jonathan Roberts, April 7, 1812, in Roberts Papers (HSP); William Reed to Pickering, February 6, 1812, and Abraham Shepherd to Pickering, Feburary 20, 1812, in Pickering Papers (MHS), reel 30. The editor of a widely read Republican magazine later published the treaty because it was "frequently referred to;— and its insertion in the *Register* has been earnestly solicited." See *Niles' Register* 3 (November 28, 1812), 196–201.

96. Augustus J. Foster to Monroe, November 1, 1811, and Monroe to Foster, November 12, 1811, in *ASP:FR*, 3:499–500. The return of the impressed Americans took place after the two nations were at war. See William Bainbridge to Paul Hamilton, July 11, 1812, in ND (M125), reel 24; Boston *Independent Chronicle*, July 13, 1812.

97. Baltimore *Whig* and Lexington *Reporter*, reprinted in New York *Evening Post*, November 19 and December 12, 1811. For similar sentiments, see Trenton *True American*, November 25, 1811; and Thomas J. Rogers to Jonathan Roberts, December 1, 1811, in Roberts Papers (HSP).

98. Bradford Perkins, *Castlereagh and Adams: England and the United States, 1812–1823* (Berkeley, 1964), 11.

99. Ibid.; Mahan, *Sea Power*, 1:386.

100. The number of licenses issued annually is often reported incorrectly. The correct figures can be found in "An Account of the Number of Commercial Licenses, Granted during the Last Ten Years," February 13, 1812, in *British Sessional Papers: House of Commons, 1812,* 343, and in Seybert, *Statistical Annals,* 70.

101. Perkins, *Prologue to War,* 401.

102. London *Times,* June 17 and 24, 1812; *The Annual Register . . . for the Year 1812,* new ed. (London, 1821), *[State Papers],* 379–81.

103. Madison to Henry Wheaton, February 26–27, [1827], in Madison Papers (LC), reel 21; Brown, *Republic in Peril,* 37–38. For similar sentiments, see Madison to Wheaton, July 11, 1824, in Madison Papers (LC), reel 20; Jefferson to Robert Wright, August 8, 1812, in Jefferson Papers (LC), reel 46; speech of William King, February 5, 1813, in *AC,* 12–2, 1001.

104. Perkins, *Prologue to War,* 310–12.

105. Washington *National Intelligencer,* May 23, 1812; Adams, *History,* 6:215–18.

106. Adams, *History,* 6:216–18; Perkins, *Prologue to War,* 399–400.

107. Richard C. Knopf, ed., *The Diary of Thomas Worthington: 1812* (n.p., n.d.) (May 27, 1812), 15. For similar sentiments, see Lexington *Reporter,* June 6, 1812.

108. Clay to William W. Worsley, February 9, 1812, in James F. Hopkins and Mary W. M. Hargreaves, eds., *The Papers of Henry Clay,* 8 vols. to date (Lexington, 1959—), 1:630. See also Bayard to Andrew Bayard, February 1, 1812, in Donnan, *Papers of James A. Bayard,* 191.

109. Madison to Congress, June 1, 1812, in *AC,* 12–1, 1624–29.

110. Ibid., 1626.

111. Ibid., 1629.

112. Report of House Foreign Relations Committee, June 3, 1812, in *AC,* 12–1, 1546–54. Quotations from pp. 1547 and 1554. There has been some debate over whether Calhoun or Monroe wrote this report. The weight of evidence favors the former. See Charles M. Wiltse, "The Authorship of the War Report of 1812," *American Historical Review* 49 (January, 1944), 253–59; Meriweather et al., *Papers of John C. Calhoun,* 1:123n–124n; and Brant, *James Madison,* 5:473.

113. Ingersoll, *History,* 1:94.

114. *AC,* 12–1, 1630–37; Bayard to Andrew Bayard, June 4, 1812, in Donnan, *Papers of James A. Bayard,* 198.

115. There is a good treatment of Senate action on the war bill in Leland R. Johnson, "The Suspense Was Hell: The Senate Vote for War in 1812," *Indiana Magazine of History* 65 (December, 1969), 247–67.

116. Monroe to Gallatin, June 1, 1812, in Gallatin Papers (SR), reel 24.

117. Brown, *Republic in Peril,* 116–17.

118. There is a good discussion of the attractions of maritime war in Brown,

Republic in Peril, 108–10. See also James A. Bayard to Andrew Bayard, May 2, 1812, in Donnan, *Papers of James A. Bayard,* 196–97.

119. *AC,* 10–1, 1852; *AC,* 10–2, 171, 779, 812, 1191, 1362; Rufus King to Pickering, January 19, 1808, January 15, 1809, and January 26, 1810, in Charles R. King, *The Life and Correspondence of Rufus King,* 6 vols. (New York, 1894–1900), 5:65, 128, 189; Henry Cabot Lodge, *Life and Letters of George Cabot,* 2nd ed. (Boston, 1878), 491; Quincy, *Josiah Quincy,* 146.

120. See *AC,* 9–1, 1064; *AC,* 10–1, 1064–65; *AC,* 11–1, 155–56; *AC,* 11–2, 1324; *AC,* 12–1, 199–201, 208–9, 220–22, 1353–54.

121. Speech of Josiah Quincy, January 25, 1812, in *AC,* 12–1, 949.

122. Baltimore *Federal Republican* [December 4, 1811], reprinted in *Niles' Register* 1 (December 7, 1811), 251–52. See also Boston *Gazette,* December 5, 1811; Philadelphia *United States' Gazette,* December 9, 1811, and May 30, 1812; Newport *Mercury,* December 14, 1811, and June 20, 1812; Charleston *Courier,* December 17, 1811; address of New Jersey Federalist Convention, July 4, 1812, in Newport *Mercury,* August 8, 1812.

123. *AC,* 12–1, 265–71.

124. *AC,* 12–1, 271–97.

125. On the liabilities of triangular war, see Madison to Jefferson, May 25, 1812, in Madison Papers (LC), reel 14; Jefferson to Madison, May 30, 1812, in Jefferson Papers (LC), reel 46; William A. Burwell to Wilson Cary Nicholas, May 23, 1812, in Nicholas Papers (UVA).

126. Jonathan Roberts to Matthew Roberts, June 17, 1812, in Roberts Papers (HSP).

127. *AC,* 12–1, 297.

128. The act declaring war is printed in *AC,* 12–1, 2322–23.

129. The causes of the war are developed more fully in chapter 1: The Road to War, 1801–1812.

130. Porter to Eustis, April 19, 1812, in WD (M221), reel 47. See also memorandum of [John Randolph?], March 31, 1812, in Samuel Smith Papers (LC), reel 4.

131. Quoted in William A. Burwell to Wilson Cary Nicholas, May 23, 1812, in Nicholas Papers (UVA).

132. Monroe to John Taylor, June 13, 1812, in Monroe Papers (LC), reel 5; Cutts to Plumer, December 11, 1811, in Plumer Papers (LC), reel 3.

133. For Madison's diplomatic initiative, see chapter 11: The Treaty of Ghent.

134. For Madison's role in the development of the restrictive system, see Donald R. Hickey, "American Trade Restrictions during the War of 1812," *Journal of American History* 68 (December, 1981), 518–19.

135. Speech of Henry Clay, December 7, 1812, in *AC,* 12–2, 299–300.

136. See, for example, Gallatin to Thomas Coles, April 28, 1812, in TD (M175), reel 2; Coles to Gallatin, April 29, May 2 and 6, 1812, in TD (M178), reel 29.

137. Alexander Dallas to Gallatin, April 5, 1812, in Gallatin Papers (SR), reel 24; Boston *Gazette,* May 23, 1812.

138. Speech of John C. Calhoun, June 24, 1812, in *AC*, 12–1, 1541; speech of Langdon Cheves, April 10, 1812, in *AC*, 12–1, 1310. See also speech of William Lowndes, April 9, 1812, in *AC*, 12–1, 1289.

139. See *AC*, 12–1, 692, 1280–1314. For other attempts to modify the non-importation law, all of which failed, see *AC*, 12–1, 188–89, 228–35, 239, 1633–34.

140. *AC*, 12–1, 1511.

141. Gallatin to Cheves, June 10, 1812, in *AC*, 12–1, 1512–13.

142. *AC*, 12–1, 1543–44.

143. *AC*, 12–1, 1545–46.

144. Jefferson to Madison, August 5, 1812, in Madison Papers (LC), reel 26. See also Jefferson to Madison, April 17 and June 29, 1812, ibid.; Jefferson to Richard M. Johnson, January 29, 1813, and to William Short, June 18, 1813, in Jefferson Papers (LC), reel 46.

145. Madison to Jefferson, April 24, 1812, in Madison Papers (LC), reel 14. See also Madison to Congress, November 5, 1812, in *AC*, 12–2, 14.

146. *AC*, 12–1, 319, 1532, 1570, 1572, 1574. This act is printed in *AC*, 12–1, 2354–56, but a crucial word—"such"—is omitted from section 7 so that the law appears to prohibit the use of British licenses to trade with *any* port in the world. For a more accurate version, see U.S. Congress, *The Public Statutes at Large of the United States of America from the Organization of the Government in 1789, to March 3, 1815*, 8 vols. (Boston, 1845–1848), 2:778–81.

147. Gallatin to Bacon, June 24, 1812, in *ASP: F*, 2:539. Eventually $8,000,000 was raised under the $11,000,000 loan act. See Revised Statement of the Public Debt, April 14, 1814, in *ASP:F*, 2:839.

148. *AC*, 12–1, 305, 1509–10, 2335–37.

149. *AC*, 12–1, 311, 1531, 2338. See also speech of John C. Calhoun, April 7, 1814, in *AC*, 13–2, 1989.

150. *AC*, 12–1, 1555–59.

151. James Breckinridge to Dr. Campbell, June 29, 1812, in Breckinridge Papers (UVA).

152. Speech of Harmanus Bleecker, June 22, 1812, in *AC*, 12–1, 1523. See also speech of Elijah Brigham, June 22, 1812, in *AC*, 12–1, 1526.

153. Speech of Abijah Bigelow, June 22, 1812, in *AC*, 12–1, 1517.

154. *AC*, 12–1, 303, 316, 318, 1516, 1573–74, 1580–81, 2327–32, 2353, 2362.

155. Boston *Yankee*, July 17, 1812.

156. The War Congress met from November 4, 1811, to July 6, 1812, or for 246 days. The first session of the Fifth Congress, which was in session from November 13, 1797, to July 16, 1798, also met for 246 days. These were the longest sessions until the second session of the Twenty-Seventh Congress, which met for 269 days from December 6, 1841, to August 31, 1842. See U.S. Congress, *Biographical Directory of the American Congress, 1774–1949* (Washington, 1950), 65, 99, 197. Of the 143 laws adopted in this session, 115 were public. See *AC*, 12–1, 2225–62; and Philadelphia *Aurora*, July 13, 1812.

157. Washington *National Intelligencer*, July 8, 1812. For similar sentiments, see New York *National Advocate*, May 22, 1813.

158. See, for example, the long editorial in the premier issue of the New York *National Advocate*, December 15, 1812.

Chapter 3: The Baltimore Riots

1. Samuel G. Goodrich, *Recollections of a Lifetime*, 2 vols. (New York, 1856), 1:439. See also Richard Sedgwick to Henry D. Sedgwick, June 20, 1812, in Sedgwick Papers (MHS); Henry Lee to Andrew Cabot, January 20, 1813, and to Patrick Tracy Jackson, January 30, 1813, in Porter, *Jacksons and Lees*, 2:1071, 1076.

2. Charles J. Ingersoll to Alexander Dallas, June 23, 1812, in Ingersoll Papers (HSP).

3. James W. Hammack, Jr., *Kentucky and the Second American Revolution: The War of 1812* (Lexington, 1976), 14–15.

4. Thomas Rogers to Jonathan Roberts, June 21, 1812, in Roberts Papers (HSP); *Niles' Register* 2 (July 11, 1812), 305.

5. Gerry to Madison, July 5, 1812, in Madison Papers (LC), reel 14. See also Richard Rush to Benjamin Rush, June 29, 1812, in Richard Rush Papers (SR), reel 1.

6. Christian Ellery to Madison, June 24, 1812, in Madison Papers (LC), reel 14; John Bach McMaster, *A History of the People of the United States, From the Revolution to the Civil War*, 8 vols. (New York, 1883–1913), 3:550.

7. Theodore Sedgwick, Jr., to Henry D. Sedgwick, June 30, 1812, in Sedgwick Papers (MHS); G. Terry Madonna, "The Lancaster Federalists and the War of 1812," *Journal of the Lancaster County Historical Society* 71 (Trinity, 1967), 146–47.

8. Gilbert to Sarah Hillhouse, June 20, 1812, in Alexander-Hillhouse Papers (UNC).

9. Philadelphia *Freeman's Journal*, reprinted in Chillicothe *Supporter*, July 4, 1812. For similar sentiments, see Oration of William Winder, July 4, 1812, in Wilmington *American Watchman*, July 15, 1812; B. D. Rounsaville to citizens of Rowan County, July 1, 1812, in Raleigh *Minerva*, July 10, 1812; Resolutions of Fayetteville County (NC) June 27, 1812, in Charleston *Courier*, July 10, 1812; Address of Isaac Auld, quoted ibid., July 21, 1812; Baltimore *Federal Gazette*, reprinted in Chillicothe *Supporter.*, July 11, 1812.

10. James Lloyd, quoted in Richard Rush to Benjamin Rush, June 29, 1812, in Rush Papers (SR), reel 1.

11. Lloyd, quoted in Charles J. Ingersoll to Alexander Dallas, June 23, 1812, in Ingersoll Papers (HSP).

12. Trenton *True American*, July 13, 1812.

13. Address of Massachusetts House, June 26, 1812, in *Niles' Register* 2 (August 29, 1812), 417–18; Declaration of Connecticut Assembly, August 25, 1812, ibid. 3 (September 12, 1812), 24. See also *Boston Gazette*, June 29, 1812;

Boston *New-England Palladium*, June 9–26, 1812; Hartford *Connecticut Courant*, July 7, 1812; Hartford *Connecticut Mirror*, August 17, 1812; and sermons printed in Providence *Gazette*, July 25 and August 8, 1812.

14. Otis to John Rutledge, Jr., July 31, 1812, in Rutledge Papers (UNC). For similar sentiments, see Boston *Columbian Centinel*, July 11, 1812; Address of Middlesex County (MA) Convention, August 10, 1812, in Providence *Gazette*, August 22, 1812; William Ellery Channing, "Extracts from Sermons," in *The Works of William E. Channing*, 6 vols. (Boston, 1841–43), 1:682.

15. Address of Massachusetts House, June 26, 1812, in *Niles' Register* 2 (August 29, 1812), 418.

16. Baltimore *Federal Republican*, June 20, 1812; Alexandria *Gazette*, June 20, 1812; Philadelphia *United States' Gazette*, June 23, 24, 25, 26, 29, 1812; New York *Evening Post*, June 29, 1812. The Charleston *Courier* reversed itself, initially calling for everyone "to rally around the Rulers of the Nation," but later upholding the right to criticize policy and calling for the election of men who would restore peace. See issues of June 25, and August 5 and 10, 1812. For other anti-war sentiments, see Address of New Jersey Federalist Convention, July 4, 1812, in Newport *Mercury*, August 8, 1812.

17. The address was usually referred to as the "Address of the Minority to Their Constituents." The citations that follow are to the version in *AC*, 12–1, 2196–2223. For the pamphlet editions, see Ralph R. Shaw and Richard H. Shoemaker, *American Bibliography: A Preliminary Checklist for 1812* (New York, 1962), 6–7.

18. "Address of the Minority," 2196. The previous question was used several times to end debate in the War Congress; secret sessions were employed in both houses when the prewar embargo and the war bill were under consideration; and Federalists thought that House Republicans had treated an anti-war resolution offered by John Randolph arbitrarily in May, 1812. For an excellent contemporary sketch of the history of the previous question, see speech of William Gaston, January 19, 1816, in *AC*, 14–1, 699–718. For Randolph's motion, see *AC*, 12–1, 1451–78.

19. "Address of the Minority," 2196, 2218–19.

20. Ibid., 2220–21.

21. "Review of an Address of . . . Members of the House . . . on the subject of war with Great Britain," in Washington *National Intelligencer*, July 18 and 23, and August 1, 1812.

22. Speech of Felix Grundy, May 6, 1812, in *AC*, 12–1, 1410; Washington *National Intelligencer*, May 14, 1812.

23. *Niles' Register* 1 (December 7, 1811), 251; Thomas J. Rogers to Jonathan Roberts, May 16, 1812, in Roberts Papers (HSP). For similar sentiments, see Philadelphia *Aurora*, April 7, 1812; Richard Rush to Benjamin Rush, May 16, 1812, in Rush Papers (SR), reel 1; Republican sources quoted in Alexandria *Gazette*, November 4, 1811, and May 7 and 15, 1812, and in Baltimore *Federal Republican*, June 4, 1812; Simon Snyder, quoted in Madonna, "Lancaster Federalists," 143; speech of John Randolph, May 6, 1812, in *AC*, 12–1, 1400.

24. Washington *National Intelligencer*, June 27, 1812; Address of Massachu-

setts Senate, June 26, 1812, in *Niles' Register* 2 (July 11, 1812), 309; Augusta *Chronicle*, quoted in John E. Talmadge, "Georgia's Federalist Press and the War of 1812," *Journal of Southern History* 19 (November, 1953), 493. See also Thomas Rogers to Jonathan Roberts, June 21, 1812, in Roberts Papers (HSP).

25. Baltimore *American*, July 16, 1812; Wilmington *American Watchman*, June 26, 1812; John G. Jackson to Madison, June 26, 1812, in Madison Papers (LC), reel 14.

26. Speech of Robert Wright, May 6, 1812, in *AC*, 12–1, 1413.

27. Jefferson to Madison, June 29, 1812, in Madison Papers (LC), reel 26 (also in Jefferson Papers [LC], reel 46). This letter has been discreetly omitted from the various published works of Jefferson and Madison. See also Jefferson to William Duane, August 4, 1812, in Jefferson Papers (LC), reel 46.

28. Boston *Yankee*, May 15, 1812. See also Baltimore *Sun*, reprinted in Wilmington *American Watchman*, July 4, 1812; *Niles' Register* 2 (June 27, 1812), 284; Governor William Plumer to New Hampshire legislature, November 18, 1812, ibid. 3 (December 5, 1812), 210; New York *Military Moniter*, reprinted in Washington *National Intelligencer*, March 24, 1813.

29. My understanding of Baltimore is based on the following sources: J. Thomas Scharf, *History of Baltimore City and County* (Philadelphia, 1881); Clayton C. Hall, ed., *Baltimore: Its History and Its People*, 3 vols. (New York, 1912); Hamilton Owens, *Baltimore on the Chesapeake* (Garden City, 1941); Gary L. Browne, *Baltimore in the Nation, 1789–1861* (Chapel Hill, 1980); James W. Livingood, *The Philadelphia-Baltimore Trade Rivalry, 1780–1860* (Harrisburg, 1947); Frank R. Rutter, *South American Trade of Baltimore* (Baltimore, 1897); William T. Howard, Jr., *Public Health Administration and the Natural History of Disease in Baltimore, Maryland, 1797–1820* (Washington, 1924); [Jared Sparks], "Baltimore," *North American Review* 20 (January, 1825), 99–138; Clarence P. Gould, "The Economic Causes of the Rise of Baltimore," in Leonard W. Labaree, ed., *Essays in Colonial History Presented to Charles McLean Andrews by His Students* (New Haven, 1931), 225–51.

30. Howard, *Public Health Administration*, 178; J. Thomas Scharf, *History of Maryland, From the Earliest Period to the Present Day*, 3 vols. (Baltimore, 1879), 3:782.

31. By contrast, there were 99 females for every 100 males in New York, 104 for every 100 in Philadelphia, and 107 for every 100 in Boston. See Seybert, *Statistical Annals*, 49. All figures are from the 1810 census.

32. Irish editors aside, Wright was probably the leading Anglophobe in the country. For his pardon (issued on January 28, 1809), see *Interesting Papers Illustrative of the Recent Riots at Baltimore* [Baltimore, 1812?], 80–81. For the history of rioting in Baltimore, see Scharf, *History of Baltimore*, 778–94; Scharf, *History of Maryland*, 2:503–4, 590–91; L. Marx Renzulli, Jr., *Maryland: The Federalist Years* (Rutherford, 1972), 107–11, 167, 253n; Cassell, *Samuel Smith*, 88, 257–59; Francis F. Beirne, *The Amiable Baltimoreans* (New York, 1951), 222; W. Bird Terwilliger, "William Goddard's Victory for the Freedom of the Press," *Maryland Historical Magazine* 36 (June, 1941), 139–49.

33. *Niles' Register* 3 (September 19, 1812), 47.

34. Katherine J. Gallagher, "Alexander Contee Hanson," in *DAB*, 8:231; Clarence S. Brigham, *History and Bibliography of American Newspapers, 1690–1820*, 2 vols. (Worcester, 1947), 1:235; Scharf, *History of Baltimore*, 88. Hanson's father was chancellor of Maryland, and his grandfather was president of the Continental Congress.

35. Benjamin Merrill to Timothy Pickering, January 14, 1815, in Pickering Papers (MHS), reel 30.

36. Baltimore *Whig*, June 6, 1812.

37. Richmond *Enquirer*, June 26, 1812; Baltimore *Whig*, reprinted ibid., June 30, 1812. See also Salem *Essex Register*, October 2, 1813.

38. Gallagher, "Alexander Contee Hanson," 231.

39. Renzulli, *Maryland*, 248.

40. The most valuable source for the Baltimore riots is *Report of the Committee of Grievances and Courts of Justice of the House of Delegates of Maryland, on the Subject of the Recent Mobs and Riots in the City of Baltimore* (Annapolis, 1813) (hereafter cited as *Maryland Legislative Report*). The report itself is only twelve pages long and was widely reprinted in the press, but the official edition has over 300 pages of depositions appended. Other sources are "Report of the Baltimore City Council," August 6, 1812; A. C. Hanson et al., "An Exact and Authentic Narrative of the Events Which Took Place in Baltimore on the 27th and 28th of July Last"; "Narrative of John E. Hall"; "Narrative of John Thomson"; and "Narrative of Otho Sprigg." These accounts were widely reprinted in the press and were collected (along with other papers bearing on the riots) in two contemporary pamphlets: *Interesting Papers Illustrative of the Recent Riots at Baltimore* [Baltimore, 1812?], and *A Portrait of the Evils of Democracy* (Baltimore, 1816). (The citations that follow are to the first of these pamphlets.) Another source is Henry Lee, *A Correct Account of the Baltimore Mob* (Winchester, VA, 1814). I presented a shorter account of the riots in "The Darker Side of Democracy: The Baltimore Riots of 1812," *Maryland Historian* 7 (Fall, 1976), 1–19. For other treatments, see Thomas Boyd, *Light-horse Harry Lee* (New York, 1931), ch. 18; Frank Cassell, "The Great Baltimore Riot of 1812," *Maryland Historical Magazine* 70 (Fall, 1975), 241–59; and Paul A. Gilje, "The Baltimore Riots of 1812 and the Breakdown of the Anglo-American Mob Tradition," *Journal of Social History* 13 (Summer, 1980), 547–64.

41. Deposition of Isaac Caustin, in *Maryland Legislative Report*, 318. See also deposition of James P. Heath, ibid., 284; Alexandria *Gazette*, November 4, 1811, and May 15, 1812.

42. Baltimore *Federal Republican*, June 1, 1812.

43. Baltimore *Federal Republican*, June 20, 1812, partially reprinted in *Niles' Register* 2 (August 8, 1812), 379.

44. Depositions of William Gwynn, William Merryman, Edward Johnson, and Isaac Caustin, in *Maryland Legislative Report*, 22, 107, 174, 318.

45. Deposition of William Gwynn, ibid., 21; Hanson et al., "Exact and Authentic Narrative," 26–27; Georgetown *Federal Republican*, July 27, August 3, and October 19, 1812.

46. Deposition of Peter L. White, in *Maryland Legislative Report*, 66.

47. Deposition of John Worthington, ibid., 241.

48. Deposition of Samuel Hollingsworth, ibid., 336.

49. Although two prominent Federalists were assaulted during the night of violence, the only serious casualty was one of the rioters, who perished when he fell from the upper story of the *Federal Republican* building.

50. Depositions of William Stewart and William Gwynn, in *Maryland Legislative Report*, 22–23, 63.

51. Depositions of James Sterett, Samuel Sterett, and William Barney, ibid., 200, 203, 278.

52. Deposition of David R. Geddes, ibid., 50; Boston *New-England Palladium*, July 3, 1812; New York *Commercial Advertiser*, reprinted in Hartford *Connecticut Mirror*, July 20, 1812.

53. Depositions of Nixon Wilson, Edward Johnson, and John S. Abel, in *Maryland Legislative Report*, 149, 163, 307; David Hoffman to Virgil Maxcy, July 11, 1812, in Galloway-Maxcy-Markoe Papers (LC).

54. *Maryland Legislative Report*, 3.

55. Deposition of John Worthington, ibid., 242.

56. [Henry Lee] to Hanson, July 20, 1812, in *Niles' Register* 2 (August 8, 1812), 378. Jefferson's actual words were: "The mobs of great cities add just so much to the support of pure government, as sores do to the strength of the human body." See Thomas Jefferson, *Notes on the State of Virginia*, ed. William Peden (Chapel Hill, 1955), 165.

57. John Hanson Thomas to Hanson, [June 28, 1812], in *Niles' Register* 2 (August 8, 1812), 375.

58. Hanson to Robert Goodloe Harper, July 24, 1812, in Harper Papers (MdHS), reel 2.

59. Depositions of John Howard Payne and Peter L. White, in *Maryland Legislative Report*, 14–15, 68; sublease of Jacob Wagner, July 23, 1812, in *Interesting Papers*, 10.

60. Deposition of John Howard Payne, in *Maryland Legislative Report*, 15–16; Lee, *Correct Account*, 5–6. See also John Lynn to Hanson, July 19, 1812, and [Lee] to Hanson, July 20, 1812, in *Niles' Register* 2 (August 8, 1812), 376, 378.

61. Georgetown *Federal Republican*, July 27, 1812, reprinted in *Niles' Register* 2 (August 8, 1812), 379–80.

62. Hanson et al., "Exact and Authentic Narrative," 28; "Report of Baltimore City Council," 2.

63. Deposition of Peter L. White, in *Maryland Legislative Report*, 70. See also "Narrative of John Hall," 53.

64. Hanson et al., "Exact and Authentic Narrative," 28; *Maryland Legislative Report*, 4–5.

65. Deposition of John Howard Payne, in *Maryland Legislative Report*, 16.

66. Deposition of James P. Heath, ibid., 282–83; Hanson et al., "Exact and Authentic Narrative," 29. There were additional injuries on both sides during

the night. A spectator in the street was shot to death, and a number of Federalists who left the house were beaten and one was nearly hanged. See depositions of William Stewart, Dennis Nowland, James Gittings, William Barney, and Middleton B. Magruder, in *Maryland Legislative Report*, 64, 189, 235, 259, 305; Hanson et al., "Exact and Authentic Narrative," 29; James W. Williams to John W. Stump, July 28, 1812, in War of 1812 File (MdHS).

67. Deposition of Peter L. White, in *Maryland Legislative Report*, 71.

68. Stricker had the authority to call out the militia without such an order. See letter of Governor Robert Bowie, August 21, 1812, in Annapolis *Maryland Gazette*, September 3, 1812.

69. Depositions of John Howard Payne, William Gwynn, George H. Steuart, and William Barney, in *Maryland Legislative Report*, 16–17, 24–26, 216, 256–62. Barney was the son of Joshua Barney, the naval hero of the Revolution and War of 1812.

70. Hanson et al., "Exact and Authentic Narrative," 29.

71. Testimony of Richard H. Owen, in Georgetown *Federal Republican*, October 23, 1812 (emphasis omitted).

72. Hanson et al., "Exact and Authentic Narrative," 30.

73. Testimony of Richard H. Owen, in Georgetown *Federal Republican*, October 19, 1812.

74. Deposition of John Stone, in *Maryland Legislative Report*, 98; Georgetown *Federal Republican*, August 31, 1812. See also deposition of William Gwynn, in *Maryland Legislative Report*, 27.

75. Hanson et al., "Exact and Authentic Narrative," 30–31; deposition of Middleton B. Magruder, in *Maryland Legislative Report*, 304–5.

76. Quoted in Boyd, *Harry Lee*, 319.

77. Lee, *Correct Account*, 10–12; "Narrative of John Hall," 55–56; "Narrative of John Thomson," 43–44; deposition of William Barney, in *Maryland Legislative Report*, 271–73.

78. Depositions of Joel Vickers, Thomas Buchanan, and James P. Heath, in *Maryland Legislative Report*, 41, 104, 283; "Narrative of John Hall," 56; "Narrative of Otho Sprigg," 49.

79. Baltimore *Whig*, reprinted in Georgetown *Federal Republican*, August 5, 1812 (emphasis omitted).

80. Deposition of Edward Johnson, in *Maryland Legislative Report*, 169, 174. See also ibid., 7; and deposition of Thomas Buchanan, ibid., 105.

81. John Stricker to governor, August 6, 1812, in *Niles' Register* 2 (August 22, 1812), 405–6; depositions of William Gwynn and William Barney, in *Maryland Legislative Report*, 50, 273–74.

82. Deposition of Edward Johnson, in *Maryland Legislative Report*, 169–70. Wooleslager may have been involved in the tarring and feathering of the British shoemaker in 1808. One of the people pardoned for the crime was "George Wallaslagar." See pardon of Governor Robert Wright, January 28, 1809, in *Interesting Papers*, 81.

83. Deposition of William Merryman and Thomas Robinson, in *Maryland*

Legislative Report, 111, 347; Hanson et al., "Exact and Authentic Narrative," 37–38; "Narrative of John Hall," 57–58.

84. *Maryland Legislative Report,* 8.

85. Hanson et al., "Exact and Authentic Narrative," 38; "Narrative of John Hall," 58–59.

86. J.P. Boyd to James McHenry, August 2, 1812, in McHenry Papers (LC).

87. Hanson et al., "Exact and Authentic Narrative," 38–39.

88. "Narrative of John Hall," 59 (emphasis omitted).

89. Hanson et al., "Exact and Authentic Narrative," 39; "Narrative of John Hall," 59.

90. Deposition of Dr. John Owen, in *Maryland Legislative Report,* 297.

91. Hanson et al., "Exact and Authentic Narrative," 40–41. See also Felix Gilbert to David Hillhouse, August 12, 1812, in Alexander-Hillhouse Papers (UNC).

92. "Narrative of John Thomson," 45–46.

93. Letter from Baltimore, July 29, 1812, printed in *Hartford Connecticut Courant,* August 4, 1812.

94. Deposition of William Merryman, in *Maryland Legislative Report,* 109.

95. Deposition of William R. Smith, in *Maryland Legislative Report,* 100. Stansbury repeated these sentiments after the riot. See deposition of William Gwynn, ibid., 32. See also Georgetown *Federal Republican,* August 17, 1812.

96. Hanson et al., "Exact and Authentic Narrative," 37. See also depositions of Richard B. Magruder and John E. Dorsey, in *Maryland Legislative Report,* 83–84.

97. Hanson et al., "Exact and Authentic Narrative," 40–41; "Narrative of John Hall," 59–60.

98. Letter of A.C. Hanson, August 3, 1812, in Boston *New-England Palladium,* August 14, 1812; John Pierce, "Memoirs," 18 vols. in MS form, 2:79 (MHS); Hanson to John E. Hall, August 22, 1812, and October 15, 1813, in Hanson Papers (MdHS); Timothy Pickering to Elizabeth Pickering, November 13, 1814, in "Unpublished Letters," *Maryland Historical Magazine* 20 (June, 1925), 127.

99. J.P. Boyd to James McHenry, August 2, 1812, in McHenry Papers (LC).

100. Pierce, "Memoirs," 2:62; Boston *New-England Palladium,* January 5, 1813; Lee to Monroe, January 7, 1813, in Monroe Papers (NYPL); Lee to Rufus King, November 19, 1813, in King, *Rufus King,* 5:352; Boyd, *Harry Lee,* 327–29.

101. Madison to J. Montgomery, August 13, 1812, in John W. Garrett Papers (JHU).

102. Georgetown *Federal Republican,* August 3 and 7, 1812; testimony of Richard Owen, ibid., October 19, 1812; depositions of Charles Burrall and Edward Johnson, in *Maryland Legislative Report,* 155–58, 170–72.

103. Depositions of Edward Johnson and Dr. John Owen, in *Maryland Legislative Report,* 172, 296–97.

104. Deposition of John Scott, ibid., 122. See also deposition of Charles

Burrall, ibid., 157; proclamation of Edward Johnson, August 5, 1812, in *Niles'
Register* 2 (August 8, 1812), 378–79. Burrall's firmness made him so unpopular
in Baltimore that the administration later removed him from office. See
Burrall to Madison, March 6 and 7, 1814, in Madison Papers (LC), reel 16;
Scharf, *History of Baltimore*, 493.

105. Georgetown *Federal Republican*, August 31, October 28, and November
27, 1812; *Maryland Legislative Report*, 9; deposition of Thomas Kell, ibid., 139.
Mayor Johnson said that he was "astonished" at the acquittal of Lewis and
Wooleslager. See his deposition, ibid., 176.

106. Deposition of William R. Smith, ibid., 101.

107. A. C. Hanson et al. *ats.* State of Maryland, July, 1812, in Harper Papers
(MdHS), reel 2; Georgetown *Federal Republican*, August 28, September 7, and
October 19, 1812; Renzulli, *Maryland*, 285.

108. Deposition of Nicholas Brice, in *Maryland Legislative Report*, 251. James
Williams to John W. Stump, July 29, 1812, and A. Robinson to James Mc-
Henry, August 12, 1812, in War of 1812 File (MdHS); William Lansdale
to Virgil Maxcy, August 3, 1812, in Galloway-Maxcy-Markoe Papers (LC);
Trenton *Federalist*, August 17, 1812; Baltimore *American*, August 11, 1812;
Alexandria *Gazette*, August 8, 1812; Baltimore *Whig*, reprinted in Philadelphia
Aurora, August 1, 1812.

109. Mary Grundy, quoted in Jerome R. Garitee, *The Republic's Private Navy:
The American Privateering Business as Practiced by Baltimore during the War of 1812*
(Middleton, 1977), 80. See also J.P. Boyd to James McHenry, August 2, 1812,
in McHenry Papers (LC).

110. Georgetown *Federal Republican*, August 17 and 19, 1812.

111. See documents in *Interesting Papers*, 62–78; Renzulli, *Maryland*, 281–
82, 287–88.

112. Renzulli, *Maryland*, 290–92; *Maryland Legislative Report*, 1–12.

113. *Maryland Legislative Report*, 12–13.

114. *Niles' Register* 3 (February 20, 1813), 388–89.

115. Newport *Mercury*, August 8, 1812; Pittsburgh *Gazette*, August 14, 1812.

116. Report of Boston Town Meeting, August 6, 1812, in Boston *New-
England Palladium*, August 7, 1812.

117. Hartford *Connecticut Courant*, August 25, 1812. For similar sentiments,
see Raleigh *Minerva*, August 14, 1812; Georgetown *Spirit of Seventy-Six*, reprinted in Charleston *Courier*, August 8, 1812; Charleston *Courier*, August 28,
1812; Trenton *Federalist*, July 27 and August 3, 1812.

118. Letter of John Mitchell, in Georgetown *Federal Republican*, August 3,
1812; Alexandria *Gazette*, June 22, August 17, 18, and 25, 1812; Talmadge,
"Georgia's Federalist Press," 493–99; Myron F. Wehtje, "Opposition in Virginia to the War of 1812," *Virginia Magazine of History and Biography* 78 (January, 1970), 84.

119. Baltimore *Federal Republican*, May 2, 1812; Georgetown *Federal Republican*, March 22, June 21, September 24, 1813, and July 2, 1814; Morristown
(NJ) *Herald*, reprinted in Trenton *Federalist*, January 25, 1813.

120. Abel M. Grosvenor to brother, November 25, 1812, in Annapolis

Maryland Gazette, December 13, 1812; Georgetown *Federal Republican,* November 4 and December 21, 1812.

121. Concord *Gazette,* reprinted in Keene *Newhampshire Sentinel,* October 31, 1812; Constant Freeman to Secretary of War, August 23, 1812, in WD (M221), reel 44.

122. *Niles' Register* 3 (September 19, 1812), 47; Joseph Story to Nathaniel Williams, August 24, 1812, in William W. Story, *Life and Letters of Joseph Story,* 2 vols. (Boston, 1851), 1:228–29. See also Washington *National Intelligencer,* August 13 and 27, 1812.

123. Resolutions of Montgomery County (MD) Republican Meeting, August 29, 1812, in *Interesting Papers,* 71; Samuel Carswell to Madison, August 29, 1812, in Madison Papers (LC), reel 14. See also Samuel Smith to William Jones, August 1, 1812, in Jones Papers (HSP); Trenton *True American,* August 10, 1812; Concord *New-Hampshire Patriot,* August 18, 1812.

124. "Report of Baltimore City Council," August 6, 1812, in *Interesting Papers,* 1–4, 71; Madison to J. Montgomery, August 13, 1812, in John W. Garrett Papers (JHU).

125. Annapolis *Maryland Republican,* quoted in Georgetown *Federal Republican,* August 3, 1812 (emphasis omitted); New York *Columbian,* August 4, 1812; James W. Williams to John W. Stump, July 29, 1812, in War of 1812 File (MdHS). See also Felix Gilbert to David Hillhouse, August 12, 1812, in Alexander-Hillhouse Papers (UNC); Baltimore *American,* reprinted in Washington *National Intelligencer,* September 5, 1812; and Republican sources cited in Hartford *Connecticut Courant,* August 11, 1812.

126. Hartford *American Mercury,* August 5 and 12, 1812; Concord *New-Hampshire Patriot,* August 11, 1812; Washington *National Intelligencer,* July 28, August 6 and 13, 1812, and August 14, 1813; Baltimore *American,* August 1, 12, and 13, 1812; Boston *Chronicle,* August 17, 1812.

127. Salem *Essex Register,* August 12, 1812; Hartford *American Mercury,* August 5, 1812. For similar sentiments, see Worcester *National Aegis,* July 20, 1814.

128. Joseph Story to William Pinkney, June 26, 1812, Pinkney to Madison, July 5, 1812, and Mathew Carey to Madison, October 30, 1814, in Madison Papers (LC), reels 16 and 26; Lexington *Reporter,* January 23, 1813; Philadelphia *Democratic Press,* reprinted in Bennington *Green-Mountain Farmer,* February 17, 1813.

129. Story to Nathaniel Williams, October 8, 1812, and May 27, 1813, in Story, *Joseph Story,* 1:243–44.

130. The Alexandria *Gazette,* August 11, 1812, explicitly compared the legal method of repressing dissent in 1798 with the violent methods employed by Republicans in 1812.

131. George H. Stewart to Lemuel Shaw, August 13, [1812], in Record Book, Washington Benevolent Society Papers, 77 (MHS); Charleston *Courier,* August 26 and 28, 1812; Newport *Mercury,* August 22, 1812; Resolution of Franklin County Federalists, August 10, 1812, in *Interesting Papers,* 66–67. Aging Federalist Paul Revere took out a two-year subscription (for $10). See receipt, October 21, 1813, in Revere Papers (MHS).

132. Hanson to Robert Goodloe Harper, November 30, 1812, in Harper Papers (LC).

133. *Maryland Legislative Report*, 2; Hanson to Harper, July 6, 1812, in Harper Papers (LC).

134. For more on the elections of 1812, see chapter 5: Raising Men and Money.

Chapter 4: The Campaign of 1812

1. Speech of John Randolph, December 16, 1811, in *AC*, 12–1, 533.

2. The works that propounded this thesis were long on speculation and short on evidence. See Howard T. Lewis, "A Re-Analysis of the Causes of the War of 1812," *Americana* 6 (1911), 506–16, 577–85; Louis M. Hacker, "Western Land Hunger and the War of 1812: A Conjecture," *Mississippi Valley Historical Review* 10 (March, 1924), 365–95; and Julius W. Pratt, *Expansionists of 1812* (New York, 1925).

3. For the general thrust of American expansion in this era, see Arthur P. Whitaker, *The Spanish-American Frontier, 1783–1795: The Westward Movement and the Spanish Retreat in the Mississippi Valley* (Boston, 1927), and *The Mississippi Question, 1795–1803: A Study in Trade, Politics, and Diplomacy* (New York, 1934); Alexander DeConde, *This Affair of Louisiana* (New York, 1976); Isaac J. Cox, *The West Florida Controversy, 1798–1813: A Study in American Diplomacy* (Baltimore, 1918); Rembert W. Patrick, *Florida Fiasco: Rampant Rebels on the Georgia-Florida Border, 1810–1815* (Athens, 1954); and Reginald Horsman, *Expansion and American Indian Policy, 1783–1812* (East Lansing, 1967).

4. Clay to Thomas Bodley, December 18, 1812, in Hopkins and Hargreaves, *Papers of Henry Clay*, 1:842. See also Monroe to John Taylor, June 13, 1812, in Monroe Papers (LC), reel 5. For works that stress the maritime causes, see Adams, *History*, vols. 3–6; Burt, *United States and Great Britain;* Perkins, *Prologue to War;* and Horsman, *Causes of the War.*

5. *Niles' Register* 1 (November 30, 1811), 236; C. P. Lucas, *The Canadian War of 1812* (London, 1906), 5. Great Britain, by contrast, had a population of 12,600,000. See *Niles' Register* 2 (June 27, 1812), 284.

6. The strength of the American army has been estimated from figures in J. C. A. Stagg's illuminating article, "Enlisted Men in the United States Army, 1812–1815: A Preliminary Survey," *William and Mary Quarterly,* 3rd ser. 43 (October, 1986), 621. For British troop strength in Canada, see General Return of Troops in Upper Canada, July 4, 1812, and General Return of Troops in Lower Canada, July 4, 1812, in Cruikshank, *Niagara Frontier,* 3:98–99.

7. Harry L. Coles, *The War of 1812* (Chicago, 1965), 38–39.

8. Quoted in Ernest A. Cruikshank, "A Study of Disaffection in Upper Canada, 1812–15," in Zaslow, *Defended Border,* 206.

9. Reginald Horsman, *The War of 1812* (New York, 1969), 27.

10. Brock to George Prevost, July 12, 1812, and to Edward Baynes, July 29, 1812, in Wood, *British Documents,* 1:352, 396.

11. Tompkins to Robert Macomb, July 12, 1812, in Hugh Hastings, ed.,

Public Papers of Daniel D. Tompkins, Governor of New York, 1807–1817, 3 vols. (New York and Albany, 1898–1902), 3:26–27.

12. Jefferson to William Duane, August 4, 1812, in Jefferson Papers (LC), reel 46; speech of Henry Clay, February 22, 1810, in *AC,* 11–2, 580. For similar sentiments, see Jefferson to Pierre Dupont de Nemours, November 29, 1813, and to Thaddeus Kosciusko, November 30, 1813, in Jefferson Papers (LC), reel 47; Thomas Rogers to Jonathan Roberts, November 17, 1811, in Roberts Papers (HSP); Washington *National Intelligencer,* April 14, 1812; Boston *Yankee,* November 6, 1812; speech of John C. Calhoun, May 6, 1812, in *AC,* 12–1, 1397.

13. Speech of John Randolph, December 10, 1811, in *AC,* 12–1, 447.

14. Speech of Samuel Taggart, reprinted from *Alexandria Gazette,* June 24, 1812, in *AC,* 12–1, 1640. See also speeches of Elijah Brigham, January 4, 1813, and Josiah Quincy, January 5, 1813, in *AC,* 12–2, 512–14, 545–48; speech of Artemas Ward, March 5, 1814, in *AC,* 13–2, 1818; and William Gribbin, *The Churches Militant: The War of 1812 and American Religion* (New Haven, 1973), 28.

15. Memorial of Maryland House of Delegates [early 1814], in *AC,* 13–2, 1207; A New-England Farmer [John Lowell, Jr.], *Mr. Madison's War* (Boston, 1812), 41; speech of Henry Ridgely, January 4, 1813, in *AC,* 12–2, 518. See also speeches of Elijah Brigham, January 4, 1813, Lyman Law, January 5, 1813, Benjamin Tallmadge, January 7, 1813, and Laban Wheaton, January 8, 1813, in *AC,* 12–2, 513, 537–38, 646, 653–55; speech of Timothy Pitkin, February 10, 1814, in *AC,* 13–2, 1286–87.

16. Speech of Joseph Pearson, February 16, 1814, in *AC,* 13–2, 1454.

17. Boston *Independent Chronicle,* November 22, 1813; William H. Crawford to Madison, February 18, 1814, in Madison Papers (LC), reel 16. See also speech of Richard M. Johnson, December 11, 1811, in *AC,* 12–1, 457; speech of Thomas Robertson, January 11, 1813, in *AC,* 12–2, 709; Philadelphia *Aurora,* September 9, 1812; Washington *National Intelligencer,* November 9, 1813; Lexington *Reporter,* December 4, 1813; Reginald Horsman, "On to Canada: Manifest Destiny and United States Strategy in the War of 1812, *Michigan Historical Review* 13 (Fall, 1987), 12–18, 21–22.

18. Lexington *Reporter,* November 13, 1813, and January 8, 1814; Lexington *Kentucky Gazette,* reprinted ibid., January 22, 1814. See also Hammack, *Kentucky and the Second American Revolution,* 86–87.

19. Speech of Joseph Pearson, February 16, 1814, in *AC,* 13–2, 1453.

20. Monroe to Jonathan Russell, June 26, 1812, in SD (M77), reel 2.

21. *AC,* 12–1, 322–26.

22. See, for example, William Eustis to William Hull, June 24, 1812, in WD (M6), reel 5.

23. Proclamation of William Hull, [July 12, 1812], printed in Boston *Columbian Centinel,* August 5, 1812.

24. Proclamation of Alexander Smyth, November 17, 1812, in Cruikshank, *Niagara Frontier,* 4:215. Smyth's proclamation also offered $40 for "the arms and spoils of each savage warrior who shall be killed." ibid., 216.

25. Secretary of War to Hull, August 1 and 8, 1812, and to Smyth, November 25, 1812, in WD (M6), reel 6.

26. Davis, *Notes by Augustus John Foster*, 100.

27. Richard Rush to Benjamin Rush, June 20, 1812, in Rush Papers (SR), reel 1.

28. Speech of George M. Troup, April 30, 1812, in *AC*, 12–1, 1359–62.

29. Statement on clerks in War Department, January 29, 1813, in WD (M222), reel 6; speech of Felix Grundy, April 30, 1812, in *AC*, 12–1, 1355.

30. Madison to Congress, April 20, 1812, in *AC*, 12–1, 209. See also *AC*, 12–1, 219, 226, 258, 1354–76.

31. William H. Crawford to Monroe, September 9, 1812 in Monroe Papers (LC), reel 5; Jonathan Roberts to Matthew Roberts, March 27, 1812, in Roberts Papers (HSP). See also Richard Rush to Charles J. Ingersoll, February 26, 1812, in Rush Papers (SR), reel 1; Philadelphia *Aurora*, April 27, 1812; Jacobs, *Beginnings of the U.S. Army*, 363, 383; Claude M. Fuess, "William Eustis," in *DAB*, 6:193–95; Mahon, *War of 1812*, 63.

32. Scott, *Memoirs*, 1:31. See also Jacobs, *Beginnings of the U.S. Army*, 383–86.

33. Richard Rush to [Charles J. Ingersoll], February 11, 1812, in Rush Papers (SR), reel 1.

34. Scott to Monroe, November 6, 1814, in Monroe Papers (NYPL). See also petition of Ferah Jones et al., May 10, 1813, in Madison Papers (LC), reel 26.

35. Porter to John Armstrong, July 27, 1813, in WD (M222), reel 9.

36. Proclamation of James Madison, October 8, 1812, in WD (M222), reel 6.

37. *AC*, 12–1, 2300; John S. Hare, "Military Punishments in the War of 1812," *Journal of the American Military Institute* 4 (Winter, 1940), 230, 235–36.

38. See *AC*, 12–1, 2229; *AC*, 12–2, 1314–15.

39. *AC*, 12–1, 2227–28; *AC*, 12–2, 1318; *AC*, 13–2, 2789–90; *AC*, 13–3, 1838.

40. See chapter 2: The Declaration of War.

41. Richard Rush to Charles J. Ingersoll, August 16, 1812, in Rush Papers (SR), reel 1.

42. Joseph Wheaton to Madison, December 10, 23, and 29, 1812, and January 8, 1813, in Madison Papers (LC), reel 14. Quotation from December 10 letter. See also *AC*, 12–1, 2237; speech of David R. Williams, December 29, 1812, in *AC*, 12–2, 462–63; speech of George M. Troup, February 3, 1814, in *AC*, 13–2, 1230; Monroe to House and Senate military committees, December 23, 1812, in *ASP: MA*, 1:610.

43. Henry Dearborn to Madison, September 30, 1812, in Madison Papers (LC), reel 14. See also Madison to Monroe, August 19, 1813, in Monroe Papers (LC), reel 5; Jacobs, *Beginnings of the U.S. Army*, 381–82.

44. *AC*, 7–1, 1307; *AC*, 10–1, 2850–51; *AC*, 12–1, 2230.

45. *AC*, 12–2, 1314–15.

46. For civilian wage rates, see Dearborn to Madison, September 30, 1812,

in Madison Papers (LC), reel 14; Timothy Dwight, *Travels; in New-England and New-York*, 4 vols. (New Haven, 1821–22), 4:352; Donald R. Adams, "Wage Rates in the Early National Period: Phildelphia, 1785–1830," *Journal of Economic History* 28 (September, 1968), 406–9; Carroll D. Wright, *History of Wages and Prices in Massachusetts: 1752–1883* (Boston, 1885), 77–82.

47. *AC*, 12–1, 2232.

48. Ezekiel Bacon to Gallatin, October 13, 1812, in Madison Papers (LC), reel 14. See also statement of Alexander Smyth, [late 1812], in *ASP: MA*, 1:497.

49. See, for example, Thomas Pinckney to Secretary of War, September 24, 1814, and George W. Hight to Madison, Janaury 23, 1815, in WD (M221), reels 62 and 65; Timothy Upham to Monroe, December 7, 1814, in WD (M222), reel 14; George Izard to Secretary of War, November 26, 1814, and January 15, 1815, in George Izard, ed., *Official Correspondence with the Department of War . . . in the Years 1814 and 1815* (Philadelphia, 1816), 122, 133; [Secretary of War] to John W. Eppes, December 6, 1814, in *NASP: MA*, 5:154–55.

50. For a general analysis of the supply system, see Marguerite M. McKee, "Service of Supply in the War of 1812," *Quartermaster Review* 6 (March–April, 1927), 45–55; Erna Risch, *Quartermaster Support of the Army: A History of the Corps, 1775–1939* (Washington, 1962), 81–180; Leonard D. White, *The Jeffersonians: A Study in Administrative History, 1801–1829* (New York, 1951), 224–32.

51. *AC*, 7–1, 1307.

52. A. Parker to [William Eustis], November 29, 1809, in *ASP: MA*, 1:257.

53. *AC*, 12–1, 127, 1215, 2257–61. The quartermaster was authorized "to purchase military stores, camp equipage, and other articles requisite for the troops," while the commissary was "to conduct the procuring and providing of all arms, military stores, clothing, and generally all articles of supply requisite for the military service." *AC*, 12–1, 2258–59.

54. Madison to William Wirt, September 30, 1813, in Gaillard Hunt, ed., *The Writings of James Madison*, 9 vols. (New York, 1900–1910), 8:264. See also Secretary of War to Thomas Pinckney, June 13, 1812, in WD (M6), reel 5.

55. See, for example, James Winchester to Eustis, November 20, 1812, J. Bryant to Willis Alston, January 27, 1813, William Blackledge to Secretary of War, January 19, 1813, Thomas Pinckney to Secretary of War, December 31, 1812, and February 23, 1813, in WD (M221), reels 49, 50, and 55; Stephen Van Rensselaer to Henry Dearborn, September 1, 1812, in Solomon Van Rensselaer, *A Narrative of the Affair of Queenstown: In the War of 1812* (New York, 1836), 37–38.

56. Armstrong to Jacob Brown, June 19, 1814, in Ernest A. Cruikshank, ed., *Documents Relating to the Invasion of the Niagara Peninsula by the United States Army, Commanded by General Jacob Brown, in July and August, 1814* (Niagara-on-the-Lake, Ontario, [1920?]), 36.

57. Thomas Jesup to ———, September 8, 1814, in Jesup Papers (LC).

58. The ration was mandated by Congress. See *AC*, 12–1, 2230.

59. Statement of Winfield Scott, [July, 1814], in WD (M221), reel 66.

60. Ibid.

61. Alexander Smyth to Henry Dearborn, November 9, 1812, and William Winder to Smyth, November 7, 1812, in *ASP: MA*, 1:497, 509.

62. Testimony of Dr. W. M. Ross, [fall, 1813], in James Wilkinson, *Memoirs of My Own Times*, 3 vols. (Philadelphia, 1816), 3:111, 308.

63. Edmund P. Gaines to Monroe, [late 1814], in WD (M222), reel 11.

64. Morgan Lewis to Monroe, November 22, 1814, in Monroe Papers (NYPL); Jacob Brown to Monroe, November 28, 1814, in Brown Papers (LC). For other evidence of the failure of the supply system, see Harrison to Eustis, December 12, 1812, Charles Boerstler to [Secretary of War], January 20, 1813, and John Graham to Monroe, October 20, 1814, in WD (M221), reels 45, 50 and 61; George W. Hight to Monroe, December 31, 1814, in WD (M222), reel 11; B. Tappan to Monroe, January 13, 1813, in Monroe Papers (NYPL); H. Goddard to John Cotton Smith, May 29, 1814, in Smith Papers (CHS); inspection reports of William King, October 5, 1812, Smyth to Secretary of War, October 20, 1812, statement of John R. Fenwick, December 23, 1814, and John S. Gano to William Henry Harrison, January 27, 1814, in *ASP: MA*, 1:491–93, 601, 657.

65. For recognition of the importance of cleanliness, see Division Orders at Fort Niagara, May 12, 1813, in WD (M222), reel 8; and James Mann, *Medical Sketches of the Campaigns of 1812, 13, 14* (Dedham, MA, 1816), 38.

66. Mann, *Medical Sketches*, passim.

67. Ibid. See also John Duffy, *The Healers: A History of American Medicine* (New York, 1976), chs. 4–8; Mary C. Gillett, *The Army Medical Department, 1775–1818* (Washington, 1981), ch. 1.

68. Mann, *Medical Sketches*, passim. The quotation is from p. 81. See also Isaac Van Voorhis to Eustis (with enclosure), December 1, 1811, Francis Le Baron to Eustis, November 13, 1812, and to Armstrong, March 30, 1813, in WD (M221), reels 46, 49, and 54; list of Medicine and Hospital Stores, June 30, 1813, in Esarey, *Messages and Letters of William Henry Harrison*, 2:486.

69. *AC*, 12–1, 238, 1376, 2297–98.

70. Eustis to Adam Seybert, December 9, 1811, and Decius Wadsworth to George M. Troup, June 19, 1813, in *ASP: MA*, 1:303, 337. The returns of weapons manufactured and repaired at Harpers Ferry and Springfield are scattered through WD (M221) and (M222).

71. Eli Whitney to Eustis, August 17, 1812, in WD (M221), reel 49; White, *Jeffersonians*, 226n; Jeannette Mirsky and Allan Nevins, *The World of Eli Whitney* (New York, 1952), ch. 17.

72. Jeffrey Kimball, "The Battle of Chippewa: Infantry Tactics in the War of 1812," *Military Affairs* 31 (Winter, 1967–1968), 169; James R. Jacobs and Glenn Tucker, *The War of 1812: A Compact History* (New York, 1969), 194–95. For a discussion of other ordnance used in the war, see Alan R. Douglas, "Weapons of the War of 1812," *Michigan History* 47 (December, 1963), 321–26.

73. Report of House Committee, December 16, 1811, in *ASP: MA*, 1:303; Callender Irvine to John Armstrong, March 1, 1813, in WD (M221), reel 54.

74. Chauncey to William Jones, November 5, 1814, in ND (M125), reel 40.

75. Madison to [Jefferson], August 17, 1812, in Madison Papers (LC), reel 14; Brant, *James Madison*, 6:45.

76. William Hull, *Memoirs of the Campaign of the Northwestern Army of the United States, A.D. 1812* (Boston, 1824), 17. See also Hull to Eustis, December 17, 1811, in WD (M221), reel 44.

77. Hull, *Memoirs of the Campaign*, 17. See also Julius W. Pratt, "William Hull," in *DAB*, 9:363–64.

78. Philadelphia *Aurora*, June 13, 1812.

79. Hull to Eustis, June 15, 1811, and March 6, 1812, in Ernest A. Cruikshank, ed., *Documents Relating to the Invasion of Canada and the Surrender of Detroit, 1812* (Ottawa, 1912), 3, 22; Hull, *Memoirs of the Campaign*, 18–23.

80. Quoted in Mahan, *Sea Power*, 1:341. See also Hull to Secretary of War, June 24, July 3 and 7, 1812, in WD (M221), reel 45; letter from Detroit, August 17, 1812, in Philadelphia *Aurora*, September 16, 1812; Thomas B. St. George to Brock, July 8, 1813, in Cruikshank, *Surrender of Detroit*, 44; McAfee, *History of the Late War*, 52–58.

81. Brock to Lord Liverpool, August 29, 1812, in Adams, *History*, 6:318–19. See also Matthew Elliott to William Claus, July 15, 1812, and Daniel Springer to Brock, July 23, 1812, in Wood, *British Documents*, 1:358, 376; Mahon, *War of 1812*, 45–46.

82. Hull to Secretary of War, August 13, 1812, in Cruikshank, *Surrender of Detroit*, 139–41; Hull, *Memoirs of the Campaign*, 72–73; McAfee, *History of the Late War*, 77–82; Gilpin, *War of 1812 in the Northwest* 95–104.

83. Porter Hanks to Hull, August 4, 1812, in WD (M222), reel 8. See also Louise P. Kellogg, "The Capture of Mackinac in 1812," *Proceedings of the State Historical Society of Wisconsin* 60 (October 24, 1912), 124–45.

84. Hull to Eustis, August 26, 1812, in WD (M221), reel 45.

85. Lewis Cass to Eustis, September 10, 1812, ibid., reel 43.

86. Adams, *History*, 6:315–16.

87. Thomas Jesup to ———, August 2, 1812, in Jesup Papers (LC).

88. Mahon, *War of 1812*, 48–49.

89. Hull, *Memoirs of the Campaign*, 73; McAfee, *History of the Late War*, 91.

90. Brock to brothers, September 3, 1812, in Ferdinand B. Tupper, *The Life and Correspondence of Major-General Sir Isaac Brock*, rev. ed. (London, 1847), 284. See also M. C. Dixon to R. H. Bruyeres, July 8, 1812, in Wood, *British Documents*, 1:351.

91. Mahon, *War of 1812*, 49–50; Coles, *War of 1812*, 53.

92. Brock to Hull, August 15, 1812, in Brannan, *Official Letters*, 41.

93. Quoted in Gilpin, *War of 1812 in the Northwest*, 117. See also Hull to Eustis, August 26, 1812, in WD (M221), reel 45.

94. Adams, *History*, 6:333; Mahon, *War of 1812*, 50.

95. Cass to Eustis, September 10, 1812, in WD (M221), reel 43. See also

Hull to Eustis, August 26, 1812, ibid., reel 45; Brock to Prevost, August 17, 1812, in Wood, *British Documents*, 1:465–70.

96. Edward Baynes to Brock, September 10, 1812, in Cruikshank, *Niagara Frontier*, 3:250; Return of Ordnance and Ordnance Stores Taken at Detroit, in Cruikshank, *Surrender of Detroit*, 154.

97. William Hull to Citizens of the United States, June 1, 1814, in *Niles' Register* 6 (July 23, 1814), 346.

98. General Order of April 25, 1814, in Washington *National Intelligencer*, May 3, 1814.

99. See especially Hull, *Memoirs of the Campaign*, and Maria Campbell and James Freeman Clarke, *Revolutionary Services and Civil Life of General William Hull . . . together with the History of the Campaign of 1812, and Surrender of the Post of Detroit* (New York, 1848). Campbell was Hull's daughter and Clarke his grandson.

100. Nathan Heald to Thomas H. Cushing, October 23, 1812, in Brannan, *Official Letters*, 84–85; Walter K. Jordan to Betsy Jordan, October 12, 1812, in Esarey, *Messages and Letters of William Henry Harrison*, 2:165; McAfee, *History of the Late War*, 98–101; Gilpin, *War of 1812 in the Northwest*, 127–28.

101. Pittsburgh *Mercury*, reprinted in Philadelphia *Aurora*, September 12, 1812.

102. Zachary Taylor to Harrison, September 10, 1812, in WD (M221), reel 44; McAfee, *History of the Late War*, 153–54; Gilpin, *War of 1812 in the Northwest*, 137–39.

103. J.G. Jackson to Madison, August 31, 1812, and Isaac Shelby to [Secretary of War], September 5, 1812, in WD (M221), reels 46 and 48; petition from Harrison County (IN), December 24, 1812, in WD (M222), reel 6; E. Munger to John S. Gano, August 23, 1812, in Philadelphia *Aurora*, September 9, 1812.

104. Secretary of War to William Henry Harrison, September 1, 1812, in WD (M6), reel 6.

105. Secretary of War to Harrison, September 17, 1812, in WD (M6), reel 6; John Gibson to William Hargrove, August 20, 1812, in Esarey, *Messages and Letters of William Henry Harrison*, 2:91; Richard M. Johnson to Madison, September 18, 1812, in Madison Papers (LC), reel 14; Mahon, *War of 1812*, 64–66.

106. Secretary of War to Ebenezer Denny, September 1, 1812, in WD (M6), reel 6; James Morrison to Henry Clay, December 24, 1812, in WD (M222), reel 6.

107. Washington *National Intelligencer*, November 8, 1813. Harrison's papers teem with references to purchases of large quantities of supplies. See Esarey, *Messages and Letters of William Henry Harrison*, 2:156–359.

108. Harrison to Eustis, December 12, 1812, in WD (M221), reel 45. See also James Morrison to Henry Clay, December 24, 1812, in WD (M222), reel 6; Morrison to Monroe, January 19, 1813, in Monroe Papers (NYPL).

109. Harrison to Eustis, September 27 and December 12, 1812, in WD (M221), reel 45.

110. Harrison to Monroe, January 24 and 26, 1813, McClanahan to Harrison, January 26, 1813, and Winchester to Secretary of War, February 11, 1813, ibid., reels 53 and 58; Henry Proctor to Roger Sheaffe, January 25, 1813, in Wood, *British Documents*, 1:7–9; McAfee, *History of the Late War*, 211–22. See also documents in *ASP: MA*, 1:367–75.

111. Statement of American officers, February 20, 1813, in Brannan, *Official Letters*, 135.

112. Harrison to [Secretary of War] (with enclosures), December 24, 1812, and (with enclosures) January 3, 1813, in William Henry Harrison Papers (LC), reel 1; McAfee, *History of the Late War*, 162–63, 177–82; Mahon, *War of 1812*, 68–70.

113. Julius W. Pratt, "Solomon Van Rensselaer" and "Stephen Van Rensselaer," in *DAB*, 19:210–11; James E. Walmsley, "Alexander Smyth," in *DAB*, 17:373–74; Horsman, *War of 1812*, 43–44; Coles, *War of 1812*, 59–60.

114. Stephen Van Rensselaer to Daniel Tompkins, September 17, 1812, in Van Rensselaer, *Narrative of Queenstown*, 17; Mahon, *War of 1812*, 76–77; Coles, *War of 1812*, 60–62.

115. John Lovett to Joseph Alexander, October 14, 1812, and John Chrystie to Thomas Cushing, February 22, 1813, in Cruikshank, *Niagara Frontier*, 4:86, 95–102; letter of John Robinson, October 14, 1812, in Wood, *British Documents*, 1:610–14; Mahon, *War of 1812*, 77–80.

116. Brant, *James Madison*, 6:91; Philadelphia *Aurora*, reprinted in Cruikshank, *Niagara Frontier*, 4:125.

117. Van Rensselaer to [Dearborn], October 14, 1812, in WD (M221), reel 43.

118. Ibid.; Winfield Scott to Secretary of War, December 29, 1812, in WD (M221), reel 57; John Chrystie to Gallatin, March 11, 1813, in Gallatin Papers (SR), reel 26; John Chrystie to Thomas Cushing, February 22, 1813, in Cruikshank, *Niagara Frontier*, 4:102–3; letter of John Robinson, October 14, 1812, and General Orders of October 20, 1812, in Wood, *British Documents*, 1:614–17, 628; Ernest A. Cruikshank, "The Battle of Queenston Heights," in Zaslow, *Defended Border*, 21–44; Van Rensselaer, *Narrative of Queenstown*, passim.

119. Statement of John Burkholder, October 31, 1812, in Wood, *British Documents*, 1:641–42; Solomon Van Rensselaer to Morgan Lewis, September 11, 1812, in Cruikshank, *Niagara Frontier*, 3:254.

120. Allan S. Everest, *The War of 1812 in the Champlain Valley* (Syracuse, 1981), 88; Thomas G. Ridout to cousin, January 5, 1813, in Matilda Edgar, *Ten Years of Upper Canada in Peace and War, 1805–1815* (Toronto, 1890), 168.

121. General Orders of November 29, 1812, in Cruikshank, *Niagara Frontier*, 4:313.

122. William Winder to Alexander Smyth, December 7, 1812, in WD (M222), reel 6; Smyth to Dearborn, December 4, 1812, in WD (M221), reel 43; statement of Peter B. Porter, December 14, 1812, in Philadelphia *Aurora*, December 30, 1812; Cecil Bisshop to Roger Sheaffe, December 1, 1812, and statement of Alexander Smyth, January 28, 1813 in Cruikshank, *Niagara Frontier*, 4:253–56, 308–10.

123. Quoted in Tupper, *Isaac Brock*, 335.

124. Letter from Mifflin County volunteer (militiaman), December 3, 1812, in Philadelphia *Aurora*, December 25, 1812. See also New York *Mercantile Advertiser*, reprinted in Philadelphia *Aurora*, December 17, 1812; New York *Evening Post*, December 15, 1812; Peter B. Porter to Buffalo *Gazette*, December 8, 1812, reprinted in Philadelphia *Aurora*, December 22, 1812; Cyrenus Chapin to Solomon Van Rensselaer, December 13, 1812, in Cruikshank, *Niagara Frontier*, 4:301.

125. Walmsley, "Alexander Smyth," 374.

126. George Howard to Sarah Howard, July 7, 1813, in George Howard Journal (CHS); Georgetown *Federal Republican*, November 26, 1813.

127. Julius W. Pratt, "Henry Dearborn," in *DAB*, 5:175; Adams, *History*, 6:305–9; Horsman, *War of 1812*, 49.

128. Eustis to Dearborn, July 9, 1812, in Adams, *History*, 6:308. See also Secretary of War to Dearborn, July 9 and August 15, 1812, in WD (M6), reel 6.

129. Zebulon M. Pike to Dearborn, November 20, 1812, and Dearborn to Eustis, November 24, 1812, in WD (M221), reel 43; H. A. S. Dearborn, "The Life of Major General Henry Dearborn," 7 vols. in MS form, 5:passim (MeHS); Mahon, *War of 1812*, 94–95; Everest, *War of 1812 in Champlain Valley*, 90–92.

130. Ingersoll, *Historical Sketch*, 1:102.

131. Bennington *Green-Mountain Farmer*, January 13, 1813. See also Bolling Hall to Madison, July 8, 1813, in Madison Papers (LC), reel 15.

132. Gallatin to Jefferson, December 18, 1812, in Gallatin Papers (SR), reel 25.

133. Washington *National Intelligencer*, December 22, 1812.

134. Philadelphia *Aurora*, October 29, 1812.

135. Macon to Joseph H. Nicholson, March 25, 1812, in Nicholson Papers (LC). See also Rush to Ingersoll, February 26, 1812, in Rush Papers (SR), reel 1; Mahon, *War of 1812*, 5.

136. Hamilton to Langdon Cheves, December 3, 1811, in Dudley and Crawford, *Naval War*, 1:53–56; John G. Van Deusen, "Paul Hamilton," in *DAB*, 8:189–90.

137. Hamilton to Cheves, December 3, 1811, in Dudley and Crawford, *Naval War*, 1:56–57. Two frigates, the *Boston* and *New York*, had rotted beyond repair.

138. John H. Frederick, "Joshua Humphreys," in *DAB*, 9:376–77.

139. Theodore Roosevelt, *The Naval War of 1812*, 2 vols., 3rd ed. (New York, 1900), 1:60–69.

140. Samuel Evans to Secretary of the Navy, June 24, 1812, Charles Gordon to Hamilton, June 28, July 17 and 28, 1812, Robert T. Spence to William Jones, September 4, October 8, and November 16, 1813, Thomas Macdonough to Jones, March 7, 1814, and Daniel Patterson to Jones, November 18, 1814, in ND (M147), reels 4 and 5; John H. Dent to Hamilton, July 14, 1812, Isaac

Hull to Hamilton, October 29, 1812, and William Bainbridge to Jones, April 30, 1814, in ND (M125), reels 24, 25, and 35.

141. Alexander Murray to Jones, March 21, 1813, Hugh G. Campbell to Jones, July 30, 1814, and John H. Dent to Benjamin Crowninshield, January 28, 1815, in ND (M125), reels 27, 38, and 42; John Downes to Jones, November 17, 1814, in ND (M147), reel 5; Jones to Hull, May 31, 1814, in ND (M149), reel 11.

142. John Shaw to Hamilton, February 17, 1812, in ND (M125), reel 23.

143. Hamilton to Stephen Cassin, November 30, 1812, Hamilton to Jacob Jones, [December, 1812], and William Jones to Jacob Lewis, February 26, 1813, in ND (M149), reel 10.

144. John Shaw to Hamilton, February 17, 1812, and Samuel Evans to Jones, February 8, 1814, in ND (M125), reels 23 and 34; Jacob Jones to William Jones, February 16, 1813, Lewis Warrington to Jones, October 18, 1813, Macdonough to Jones, March 18, 1814, and Thomas Brown to Crowninshield, January 31, 1815, in ND (M147), reel 5; Crowninshield to Dent, February 4, 1815, to Bernard Henry, February 6, 1815, to Joshua Barney, February 6, 1815, and to commanding naval officer at Erie, February 9, 1815, in ND (M149), reel 12.

145. *Niles' Register* 1 (November 2, 1811), 144–45, and 2 (March 14, 1812), 18; London *Morning Chronicle*, December 31, 1812; Disposition of British Ships, July 1, 1812, in Dudley and Crawford, *Naval War*, 1:180–82.

146. Mahan, *Sea Power*, 1:388–89, 400–401; Horsman, *War of 1812*, 57–58; Richard Glover, "The French Fleet, 1807–1814: Britain's Problem and Madison's Opportunity," *Journal of Modern History* 39 (September, 1967), 233–52.

147. Monroe to Jefferson, June 16, 1813, in Jefferson Papers (LC), reel 46; Gallatin to Madison, [June 20, 1812], in Gallatin Papers (SR), reel 25; Rodgers to Hamilton, June 3, 1812 (filed at the end of February, 1812), and Decatur to Hamilton, June 8, 1812, in ND (M125), reels 23 and 24; Mahan, *Sea Power*, 1:318.

148. Hamilton to Rodgers, June 22, 1812, in ND (M149), reel 10. See also Hamilton to Decatur, June 22 and September 9, 1812, and to Rodgers, September 9, 1812, ibid.

149. Rodgers to Hamilton, September 1, 1812, in ND (M125), reel 25.

150. Letter from British naval officer at Halifax, October 15, 1812, in *Naval Chronicle* 28 (July–December, 1812), 426. See also Thomas Saumarez to Brock, July 22, 1812, in Tupper, *Isaac Brock*, 215; London *Times*, September 4, 1812; Hartford *Connecticut Mirror*, August 3, 1812; Mahan, *Sea Power*, 1:401–4.

151. Tompkins to New York legislature, November 3, 1812, in Hastings, *Papers of Daniel D. Tompkins*, 3:180. See also Madison to Congress, November 4, 1812, in *AC*, 12–2, 13.

152. George Coggeshall, *History of American Privateers, and Letters-of-Marque, during Our War with England in the Years 1812, '13 and '14* (New York, 1856), 6.

153. Hull to Hamilton, July 21, 1812, in ND (M125), reel 24; Roosevelt,

Naval War, 1:122–27; Edgar S. Maclay, *A History of the United States Navy from 1775 to 1884*, 2 vols., rev. ed. (New York, 1897), 1:334–43.

154. Quoted in Oliver H. Perry to Hamilton, July 26, 1812, in Dudley and Crawford, *Naval War*, 1:200.

155. Hull to Hamilton, July 28 and August 2, 1812, in ND (M125), reel 24.

156. *Naval Chronicle* 28 (July–December, 1812), 343.

157. Quoted in Coggeshall, *American Privateers*, 26–27.

158. Hull to Hamilton, August 28, 1812, in Dudley and Crawford, *Naval War*, 1:241. See also Hull to Hamilton, August 30, 1812, in ND (M125), reel 24; James R. Dacres to Herbert Sawyer, September 7, 1812, in *Naval Chronicle* 28 (July–December, 1812), 347–48; extract from *Guerrière* Log Book, in Philadelphia *Aurora*, October 12, 1812; Roosevelt, *Naval War*, 1:127–36; Maclay, *United States Navy*, 1:345–60; Linda M. Maloney, *The Captain from Connecticut: The Life and Naval Times of Isaac Hull* (Boston, 1986), 186–91.

159. Lexington *Reporter*, January 6, 1815; Louis H. Bolander, "Constitution," in James T. Adams, ed., *Dictionary of American History*, 5 vols. (New York, 1940), 2:29.

160. Philadelphia *Aurora*, April 9, 1812; New York *Public Advertiser*, reprinted ibid., September 5, 1812; London *Times*, January 2, 1812; Hamilton to Decatur, April 9, 1812, in ND (M149), reel 10.

161. Quoted in Maclay, *United States Navy*, 1:379.

162. Quoted, ibid., 1:384. See also Decatur to Hamilton, October 30, 1812, in ND (M125), reel 25; B. F. Bournne to Thomas Welsh, Jr., October 29, 1812, in Philadelphia *Aurora*, December 13, 1812; John S. Carden to J. W. Croker, October 28, 1812, in *Naval Chronicle* 29 (January–June, 1813), 77–78; Roosevelt, *Naval War*, 1:147–57; Maclay, *United States Navy*, 1:368–92.

163. Decatur to Hamilton, December 4, 1812, in ND (M125), reel 25; Maloney, *Isaac Hull*, 204, 283.

164. Bainbridge to Hamilton, January 3, 1813, in ND (M125), reel 26.

165. Journal of William Bainbridge, December 29–30, 1812, ibid. Henry D. Chads to J.W. Croker, December 31, 1812, and testimony of Chads, in *Naval Chronicle* 29 (January–June, 1813), 346–48, 403–6; Roosevelt, *Naval War*, 1:160–71; Maclay, *United States Navy*, 1:401–10.

166. David Porter to Paul Hamilton, July 12, August 15, and September 3, 1812, statement of David Porter and C. S. Hopkins, July 11, 1812, and James Lawrence to William Jones, March 19, 1813, in ND (M125), reels 24, 25, and 27; Jacob Jones to Hamilton, November 24, 1812, in ND (M147), reel 4; William Crane to Paul Hamilton, July 29, 1812, Thomas Whinyates to John Borlase Warren, October 23, 1812, and James L. Yeo to Charles Sterling, November 22, 1812, in Dudley and Crawford, *Naval War*, 1:209–11, 539–41, 594; Roosevelt, *Naval War*, 1:118–20, 139–45, 176, 210–17.

167. John Binns to Jonathan Roberts, November 13, 1812, in Roberts Papers (HSP).

168. London *Times*, March 20, 1813; Roosevelt, *Naval War*, 1:180.

169. Joseph Marx to [Wilson Cary Nicholas], September 9, 1812, in Nicholas Papers (UVA).

170. A. Wanderer [Noah Johnson], *Journals of Two Cruises aboard the American Privateer* Yankee (New York, 1967), 61–156; Philadelphia *Aurora*, September 14, 1812; Log-Book of the *Rossie*, July 12–October 22, 1812, in *Niles' Register* 3 (November 7, 1812), 158; Maclay, *American Privateers*, 269.

171. Washington *National Intelligencer*, August 11, 1812; Salem *Essex Register*, December 16, 1812. See also London *Morning Chronicle*, August 22, 1812.

172. London *Morning Chronicle*, September 17 and 18, 1812; London *Times*, December 30, 1812.

173. London *Times*, January 1, 1813. See also London *Morning Chronicle*, December 31, 1812, and January 1, 1813.

174. John Borlase Warren to J. W. Croker, February 26, 1813, in *Naval Chronicle* 29 (January–June, 1813), 250–55.

175. Warren, quoted in Mahan, *Sea Power*, 1:402.

176. Letter of "Faber," March 5, 1813, in *Naval Chronicle* 29 (January–June, 1813), 198.

177. Thomas Jesup to James Taylor, December 28, 1812, in Jesup Papers (LC); Wilson Cary Nicholas to ———, December 24, 1812, in Nicholas Papers (LC).

178. Speech of Lemuel Sawyer, December 16, 1812, in *AC*, 12–2, 405.

179. Maclay, *United States Navy*, 1:vi, 442.

180. *London Times*, October 21, 1812; London *Evening Star*, reprinted in New York *National Advocate*, December 16, 1812.

181. The Earl of Harrowby, quoted in Perkins, *Castlereagh and Adams*, 18.

182. London *Times*, March 18, 1813. See also *Naval Chronicle* 29 (January–June, 1813), 113–19, 465–70, 472–74.

183. *Naval Chronicle* 29 (January–June, 1813), 37, 288, 472; John Quincy Adams to Thomas Boylston Adams, January 31, 1813, in Worthington C. Ford, ed., *Writings of John Quincy Adams*, 7 vols. (New York, 1913–17), 4:428; William James, *The Naval History of Great Britain*, 6 vols., rev. ed. (London, 1837), 6:6.

184. London *Times*, October 29 and 30, 1812, and January 6, 1813.

185. Ibid., December 29, 1812.

186. London *Morning Chronicle*, March 20, 1813. See also ibid., October 23 and December 28, 1812.

187. *Naval Chronicle* 29 (January–June, 1813), 198. See also ibid., 12.

188. Statement of British Naval Force on North American Stations, 1810–1813, in Charles Vane, ed., *Memoirs and Correspondence of Viscount Castlereagh*, 12 vols. (London, 1848–53), 8:292.

189. Report of the Admiralty, February 1, 1815, in *Niles' Register* 8 (May 20, 1815), 198; David Milne to George Hume, April 26, 1814, in Edgar E. Hume, ed., "Letters Written during the War of 1812 by the British Naval Commander in American Waters (Admiral Sir David Milne)," *William and Mary Quarterly*, 2nd ser., 10 (October, 1930), 292; James, *Naval History*, 6:143–48; Albion and Pope, *Sea Lanes in Wartime*, 389–91.

190. Admiralty circular, in Louis J. Jennings, ed., *The Croker Papers: The*

Correspondence and Diaries of the Late Right Honourable John Wilson Croker, 3 vols. (London, 1884), 3:44–45.

191. Order of Admiralty, July 31, 1812, in *Naval Chronicle* 28 (July–December, 1812), 139.

192. *Naval Chronicle* 28 (July–December, 1812), 343.

193. *Niles' Register* 3 (December 5, 1812), 221.

Chapter 5: Raising Men and Money

1. William A. Burwell to [Wilson Cary Nicholas], February 1, 1813, in Nicholas Papers (UVA); Joshua Clibbons to Jonathan Russell, February 15, 1813, in Russell Papers (BU).

2. Knopf, *Diary of Thomas Worthington* (December 1, 1812), 39.

3. The best study of the election is Norman K. Risjord, "Election of 1812," in Arthur M. Schlesinger, Jr., et al., eds., *History of American Presidential Elections, 1789–1968*, 4 vols. (New York, 1971), 1:249–96.

4. Philadelphia *Aurora*, March 11, 1812.

5. Address of Pennsylvania Committee of Correspondence, September 16, 1812, in Washington *National Intelligencer*, October 10, 1812.

6. Jonathan Roberts to Matthew Roberts, May 20, 1812, in Roberts Papers (HSP); Report of J. B. Varnum, May 18, 1812, and Richard M. Johnson to Joseph Gales, May 29, 1812, in *Niles' Register* 2 (May 23, 1812), 192–93; John Langdon to John Smilie, William H. Crawford, and Charles Cutts, May 28, 1812, and Report of J. B. Varnum, June 8, 1812, in *Niles' Register* 2 (June 27, 1812), 276; Richard P. McCormick, *The Presidential Game: The Origins of American Presidential Politics* (New York, 1982), 96–97.

7. DeAlva S. Alexander, *A Political History of the State of New York*, 3 vols. (New York, 1906–9), 1, 184, 201–2; Craig R. Hanyan, "De Witt Clinton and Partisanship: The Development of Clintonianism from 1811 to 1820," *New York Historical Society Quarterly* 57 (April, 1972), 111; McCormick, *Presidential Game*, 97.

8. Address of New York Committee of Correspondence, August 17, 1812, in *Niles' Register* 3 (September 12, 1812), 17–19.

9. New York Committee of Correspondence to Harrison Gray Otis, August 25, 1812, in Otis Papers (MHS); Abraham Shepherd to Timothy Pickering, October 4, 1812, in Pickering Papers (MHS), reel 30; William Gaston and John Stanly to Philadelphia Committee of Correspondence, [Summer, 1812], in Gaston Papers (UNC), reel 1; Boston *Columbian Centinel*, October 7, 1812; Benjamin Stoddert to John Steele, September 3, 1812, in H. M. Wagstaff, ed., *The Papers of John Steele*, 2 vols. (Raleigh, 1924), 2:682–85; Broussard, *Southern Federalists*, 144–47; Marvin R. Zahniser, *Charles Cotesworth Pinckney, Founding Father* (Chapel Hill, 1967), 258–59.

10. William Coleman, quoted in statement of Rufus King, July 27, 1812, in King, *Rufus King*, 5:266.

11. Philadelphia Committee of Correspondence to Joseph Porter, August

10, 1812, in Gaston Papers (UNC), reel 1. See also Philadelphia Committee of Correspondence to Harrison Gray Otis, July 27, 1812, and Charles W. Hare to Otis, June 24, 1812, in Otis Papers (MHS); Robert Goodloe Harper to Benjamin Stoddert, September 10, 1812, in Harper Papers (MdHS), reel 2.

12. Philadelphia Committee of Correspondence to John Stanly and William Gaston, August 13, 1812, in Gaston Papers (UNC), reel 1; Robert Goodloe Harper to John Lynn, September 25, 1812, in Bernard C. Steiner, *The Life and Correspondence of James McHenry* (Cleveland, 1907), 583–86; [William Sullivan], *Familiar Letters on Public Characters, and Public Events*, 2nd ed. (Boston, 1834), 327; John S. Murdock, "The First National Nominating Convention," *American Historical Review* 1 (July, 1896), 680–83.

13. Statement of Rufus King, August 5, 1812, in King, *Rufus King*, 5:270. See also David B. Ogden to William Gaston, September 21, 1812, in Gaston Papers (UNC), reel 1.

14. Pickering to Edward Pennington, July 12, 1812, in Pickering Papers (MHS), reel 14. For similar sentiments, see Joseph Pearson to Otis, November 9, 1812, in Otis Papers (MHS).

15. William Sullivan, *The Public Men of the Revolution*, ed. John T. S. Sullivan (Philadelphia, 1847), 351n.

16. Memorandum of [Harrison Gray Otis], [1812], in Alexander Washburn Collection (MHS).

17. Madonna, "Lancaster Federalists," 149; Risjord, "Election of 1812," 258.

18. Benjamin Romaine to Albert Gallatin, December 13, 1812, in Gallatin Papers (SR), reel 25. See also David Jones to Madison, September 17, 1812, in Madison Papers (LC), reel 26.

19. Address of South Carolina Assembly, September 1, 1812, in Risjord, "Election of 1812," 285.

20. Address of Pennsylvania Committee of Correspondence, October 12, 1812, in Washington *National Intelligencer*, October 24, 1812.

21. Boston *Yankee*, October 2, 1812.

22. Pennsylvania newspaper, quoted in Victor Sapio, *Pennsylvania & the War of 1812*, (Lexington, 1970), 178–79.

23. The play, "Election Scene," is reprinted from the Worcester *National Aegis* in Philadelphia *Aurora*, October 13, 1812. See also William Plumer to John Adams, January 2, 1813, in Plumer Papers (LC), reel 2; Risjord, "Election of 1812," 259–60.

24. John A. Harper to Plumer, February 6, 1813, in Plumer Papers (LC), reel 3.

25. John Stokely to Monroe, January 30, 1813, in Monroe Papers (LC), reel 5. See also William A. Burwell to [Wilson Cary Nicholas], February 1, 1813, in Nicholas Papers (UVA); William Wirt to Madison, August 29, 1813, in Madison Papers (LC), reel 26.

26. Clay to Caesar A. Rodney, December 29, 1812, in Hopkins and Hargreaves, *Papers of Henry Clay*, 1:750. For similar sentiments, see John C. Calhoun to James Macbride, April 18, 1812, in Meriwether et al., *Papers of John*

C. Calhoun, 1:99–100; Thomas Flournoy to Jefferson, August 29, 1812, in Jefferson Papers (LC), reel 46; Baptist Irvine to Peter Porter, January 6, 1813, in Cruikshank, *Niagara Frontier*, 4:343.

27. Thomas Rogers to Jonathan Roberts, November 1, 1812, in Roberts Papers (HSP); Lexington *Reporter*, June 17, 1812; Worcester *National Aegis*, November 18, 1812.

28. Address of Association of Democratic Young Men, in Philadelphia *Aurora*, October 29, 1812; Thomas Rogers to Jonathan Roberts, November 1, 1812, in Roberts Papers (HSP). See also Anthony Baker to Lord Castlereagh, October 31, 1812, in Foreign Office Papers 5/88 (PRO).

29. Samuel Latham Mitchill to Elizabeth Mitchill, November 24, 1812, in Mitchill Papers (MNY).

30. Morgan Lewis to Gallatin, November 10, 1812, in Gallatin Papers (SR), reel 25; John C. Fitzpatrick, ed., *The Autobiography of Martin Van Buren* (Washington, 1920), 40–41; Alexander, *Political History of New York*, 1:209–10.

31. Sanford W. Higginbotham, *The Keystone in the Democratic Arch: Pennsylvania Politics, 1800–1816* (Harrisburg, 1952), 268–69.

32. Rush to Charles J. Ingersoll, November 14, 1812, in Ingersoll Papers (HSP).

33. Address of Pennsylvania Committee of Correspondence, October 12, 1812, in Washington *National Intelligencer*, October 24, 1812.

34. *AC*, 12–2, 79; Irving Brant, "Election of 1808," in Schlesinger et al., *History of American Presidential Elections*, 1:2460. In the contest for the vice presidency, Gerry won 131 votes to Ingersoll's 86.

35. See *Niles' Register* 4 (June 26, 1813), 268–69; and Hickey, "Federalists and the War of 1812," Appendix A. At the opening session of the 13th Congress, the Republicans controlled 114 of 182 seats in the House and 28 of 36 seats in the Senate. These proportions changed slightly later on because of deaths, contested elections, and resignations.

36. The Federalists had pockets of support in Ohio, Kentucky, and New Orleans, but elsewhere in the West their strength was negligible. Except for Savannah, their strength in Georgia was also negligible. For the election results elsewhere east of the Appalachian Mountains in 1812, see Washington *National Intelligencer*, October 22, 1812 (for VT); Keene *Newhampshire Sentinel*, January 9, March 6, and May 22, 1813, (for NH); Banner, *Hartford Convention*, 361, 367 (for MA); Richard J. Purcell, *Connecticut in Transition, 1775–1818* (Washington, 1918), 290 (for CT); Samuel H. Allen, "The Federal Ascendency of 1812," *Narragansett Historical Register* 7 (October, 1889), 390–94 (for RI); Alexander, *Political History of New York*, 1:213, 215 (for NY); Higginbotham, *Keystone in the Democratic Arch*, 267 (for PA); Walter R. Fee, *The Transition from Aristocracy to Democracy in New Jersey, 1789–1829* (Sommerville, NJ, 1933), 179–82 (for NJ); John A. Munroe, *Federalist Delaware, 1775–1815* (New Brunswick, NJ, 1954), 233–35 (for DE); Renzulli, *Maryland*, 288 (for MD); Broussard, *Southern Federalists*, 294–95 (for VA, NC, and SC).

37. Calhoun to James Macbride, December 25, 1812, in Meriwether et al., *Papers of John C. Calhoun*, 1:146; Adam Seybert to Gallatin, October 3, 1812,

in Gallatin Papers (SR), reel 25; William H. Crawford to Monroe, September 9, 1812, in Monroe Papers (LC), reel 5. See also speech of Felix Grundy, April 30, 1812, in *AC*, 12–1, 1354; Nathaniel Macon to Joseph H. Nicholson, April 22, 1812, in Nicholson Papers (LC); George Hay to Monroe, November 1, 1812, in Monroe Papers (NYPL); Clay to Caesar A. Rodney, December 29, 1812, in Hopkins and Hargreaves, *Papers of Henry Clay*, 1:750; Jonathan Roberts to William Jones, December 28, 1812, in Dudley and Crawford, *Naval War*, 1:635; Gallatin to Jefferson, December 18, 1812, in Gallatin Papers (SR), reel 25; Augustus J. Foster to Lord Wellesley, March 12, 1812, in Cruikshank, *John Henry*, 129.

38. [Eustis] to Madison, December 3, 1812, in Madison Papers (LC), reel 26; John A. Harper to William Plumer, January 5, 1813, in Plumer Papers (LC), reel 3.

39. John H. Frederick, "William Jones," in *DAB*, 10:205; *Senate Journal*, 2:315.

40. Madison to Henry Lee, February, 1827, in Madison Papers (LC), reel 21.

41. Macon to Nicholson, March 22, 1814, in Nicholson Papers (LC).

42. Gallatin to Madison, [January 4, 1813?] and [January 7, 1813], in Madison Papers (LC), reel 26; Gallatin to Jefferson, December 18, 1812, in Gallatin Papers (SR), reel 25.

43. Gallatin to Madison, [January 4, 1813?], and Crawford to Madison, January 6, 1813, in Madison Papers (LC), reel 26; George Hay to Monroe, October 9 and December 13, 1812, in Monroe Papers (NYPL).

44. For an excellent study of this enigmatic figure, see C. Edward Skeen, *John Armstrong, Jr., 1758–1843: A Biography* (Syracuse, 1981).

45. Jonathan Roberts to Matthew Roberts, January 12, 1813, in Roberts Papers (HSP).

46. For an example of Armstrong's penchant for intrigue, see answers to War Department circular, March 24, 1813, in WD (M222), reel 10, and Armstrong to William Duane, April 3, 1814, in WD (M6), reel 7. Armstrong had asked senior army officers to evaluate Duane's military handbook and then had passed their comments on to Duane. The officers were almost uniformly critical of the handbook, and Armstrong was careful to tell Duane precisely what each officer had said. Apparently his aim was to isolate Duane (who was an army staff officer) and thus render him more dependent on the secretary of war.

47. Plumer to Harper, January 13, 1813, in Plumer Papers (LC), reel 3. See also Rush to Ingersoll, January 13, 1813, in Rush Papers (SR), reel 2.

48. *Senate Journal*, 2:316. See also Benjamin Tallmadge to John Cotton Smith, January 18, 1813, in Smith Papers (CHS).

49. Monroe to Madison, December 27, 1813, in Madison Papers (LC), reel 26.

50. Gallatin to William Few, May 9, 1813, in Gallatin Papers (SR), reel 26. See also Gallatin to James W. Nicholson, May 5, 1813, ibid.

51. Jones to Alexander Dallas, July 19, 1813, in Dallas Papers (HSP).

52. *AC*, 12–2, 139–42.

53. Benjamin Tallmadge to James McHenry, December 2, 1812, in McHenry Papers (LC).

54. Madison to Congress, November 4, 1812, in *AC*, 12–2, 11–16.

55. Ibid., 11.

56. Ibid., 11–12, 16.

57. John A. Harper to William Plumer, January 8, 1813, in Plumer Papers (LC), reel 3.

58. Speech of John Randolph, January 9, 1813, in *AC*, 12–2, 678.

59. Speech of Josiah Quincy, January 5, 1813, in *AC*, 12–2, 562, 600n.

60. Harper to Plumer, November 21, 1812, in Plumer Papers (LC), reel 3.

61. Speech of Stevenson Archer, January 6, 1813, in *AC*, 12–2, 594, 596.

62. Speech of Jonathan O. Moseley, January 2, 1813, in *AC*, 12–2, 485.

63. For more on this proposal, see chapter 11: The Treaty of Ghent.

64. Speech of Israel Pickens, February 5, 1813, in *AC*, 12–2, 1007. For similar sentiments, see Charles Kenny to Jonathan Roberts, February 12, 1813, in Roberts Papers (HSP).

65. *AC*, 12–2, 1339–42.

66. See letter from Washington, January 28, 1813, in Lexington *Reporter*, February 20, 1813.

67. Speech of John Clopton, February 12, 1813, in *AC*, 12–2, 1031; speech of Joseph Desha, February 5, 1813, in *AC*, 12–2, 995.

68. Speech of Charles Goldsborough, February 12, 1813, in *AC*, 12–2, 1053. See also Abijah Bigelow to Hannah Bigelow, February 7, 1813, in Brigham, "Letters of Abijah Bigelow," 357; Samuel Taggart to John Taylor, February 4, 1813, in Reynolds, "Letters of Samuel Taggart," 424; Washington *National Intelligencer*, February 13, 1813.

69. *AC*, 12–2, 108, 111, 1055.

70. Speech of David R. Williams, December 29, 1812, in *AC*, 12–2, 461–62; speech of George M. Troup, December 30, 1812, in *AC*, 12–2, 476.

71. John Devereux to William Gaston, July 6, 1813, in Gaston Papers (UNC), reel 2.

72. See [Secretary of War] to David R. Williams, November 11, 18, 20, and 25, 1812, in *NASP: MA*, 5:21–26; Monroe to Congress, December 23, 1812, in Monroe Papers (LC), reel 5.

73. *AC*, 12–2, 63, 459–844, 1322–25.

74. Lowndes to Elizabeth Lowndes, January 16, 1813, in Mrs. St. Julien Ravenel, *Life and Times of William Lowndes of South Carolina, 1782–1822* (Boston, 1901), 119.

75. For more on contemporary wage rates, see chapter 4: The Campaign of 1812.

76. *AC*, 12–2, 26, 44–45, 193, 481, 1314–15, 1318–19.

77. *AC*, 12–2, 1314.

78. Speech of Ezekiel Bacon, November 9 and 20, 1812, in *AC*, 12–2, 145, 157–58. For the Federalist view, see speech of Laban Wheaton, November 20, 1812, in *AC*, 12–2, 157.

79. Story to Nathaniel Williams, May 27, 1813, in Story, *Joseph Story*, 1:245.

80. Thomas Jesup to Monroe, January 20, 1815, in Jesup Papers (LC).

81. *AC*, 12–2, 108–9, 114, 1146, 1157, 1346–51.

82. *AC*, 12–2, 1350; "Rules and Regulations of the Army of the United States," May 1, 1813, in *ASP: MA*, 1:425–37; Skeen, *John Armstrong*, 128–29.

83. Speeches of James Milnor and Thomas R. Gold, November 20, 1812, and Josiah Quincy and Timothy Pitkin, November 21, 1812, in *AC*, 12–2, 161–64, 168–69, 179.

84. Speech of Laban Wheaton, November 21, 1812, in *AC*, 12–2, 178.

85. *AC*, 12–2, 24.

86. *AC*, 12–2, 110, 922–23, 946; Washington *National Intelligencer*, February 1, 1813.

87. Thomas Jesup to James Taylor, December 28, 1812, in Jesup Papers (LC). See also Boston *Yankee*, January 1, 1813.

88. Madison to Congress, November 4, 1812, in *AC*, 12–2, 15.

89. Washington *National Intelligencer*, November 28, 1812; letter from Washington, December 9, 1812, reprinted from New York *Mercantile Advertiser* in New York *National Advocate*, December 15, 1812.

90. *AC*, 12–2, 32, 119, 449–50, 1061, 1315–16, 1352.

91. *AC*, 12–2, 866–69.

92. Speech of Langdon Cheves, January 23, 1813, in *AC*, 12–2, 868–69.

93. Memorial of Baltimore Privateering Interests, November 10, 1812, in *NASP: NA*, 1:273–74; John Ferguson and John Lawrence to Cheves, November 23, 1812, in *AC*, 12–2, 433–34. See also John Binns to Jonathan Roberts, November 13, 1812, in Roberts Papers (HSP); Garitee, *Republic's Private Navy*, 183.

94. Gallatin to Cheves, December 8, 1812, in *AC*, 12–2, 434–36.

95. Report of House Ways and Means Committee, December 21, 1812, in *ASP: F*, 2:591; *AC*, 12–2, 36, 76, 106, 167, 908, 1168, 1346, 1319–21, 1328–29.

96. Statement of Jonathan Russell, [November, 1812], in *AC*, 12–2, 1267. See also Gallatin to Cheves, November 18, 1812, in *AC*, 12–2, 1251–52.

97. Statement of Jonathan Russell, [November, 1812], in *AC*, 12–2, 1267.

98. London *Morning Chronicle*, August 1, 3, 4, 6, 13, 1812; letter from Liverpool, July 20, 1812, in Philadelphia *Aurora*, September 7, 1812; Worcester *National Aegis*, October 7, 1812; Jonathan Russell to Reuben Beasley, August 1, 1812, in Russell Papers (BU); Anthony Baker to Castlereagh, December 18, 1812, in Foreign Office Papers 5/88 (PRO).

99. Lemuel Trescott to Gallatin, July 4, 1812, Peter Sailly to Gallatin, July 7, 1812, Samuel Buell to Gallatin, July 12 and August 8, 1812, and Gallatin to Cheves, December 10, 1812, all in Gallatin Papers (SR), reel 25.

100. William Montgomery to Madison, August 25, 1812, in Madison Papers (LC), reel 14; Harrison, *Diary of Thomas P. Cope* (August 24, 1812), 277.

101. Circular of Paul Hamilton, August 28, 1812, in ND (M149), reel 10; Richard Rush to U.S. district attorneys, October 5, 1812, in *AC*, 12–2, 1257–

58; Rush to U.S. district attorneys, October 15, 1812, in Philadelphia *Aurora,* October 26, 1812.

102. Gallatin to Cheves, November 18, 1812, in *AC,* 12–2, 1252–54; Samuel Taggart to John Taylor, December 8, 1812, in Reynolds, "Letters of Samuel Taggart," 412.

103. Gallatin to Peter Sailly, August 6, 1812, Gallatin to customs collectors, October 5, 1812, and Gallatin to Larkin Smith, October 6, 1812, all in Gallatin Papers (SR), reel 25.

104. Gallatin to Cheves, November 18, 1812, in *AC,* 12–2, 1255. For Gallatin's authority to remit fines and forfeitures, see *AC,* 4–2, 2953–54, and *AC,* 6–1, 1437.

105. Examination of merchants, [November, 1812], in *AC,* 12–2, 1259–61; Nathan Appleton et al. to New York committee of merchants, November 2, 1812, John Gore to Appleton, November 23, 1812, and Joseph Sewall and Giles Lodge to Appleton, November 27, 1812, all in Appleton Papers (MHS).

106. Speech of William M. Richardson, December 7, 1812, in *AC,* 12–2, 297. For similar sentiments, see speech of Langdon Cheves, December 4, 1812, in *AC,* 12–2, 255; Plumer to Harper, November 28, 1812, in Plumer Papers (LC), reel 2.

107. Giles to Wilson Cary Nicholas, December 10, 1812, in Nicholas Papers (UVA); speech of Langdon Cheves, December 4, 1812, in *AC,* 12–2, 254.

108. Klein, "Memoirs of Jonathan Roberts," 244. See also Elisha Tracy to Gallatin, December 14, 1812, and Joseph Whipple to Gallatin, December 19, 1812, in Gallatin Papers (SR), reels 25 and 26; Nathaniel Saltonstall to Leverett Saltonstall, November 25, 1812, in Saltonstall Papers (MHS).

109. Speech of Richard M. Johnson, December 3, 1812, in *AC,* 12–2, 234. See also Lexington *Reporter,* December 19, 1812.

110. *AC,* 12–2, 33–34, 100, 450–51, 855, 1126, 1316, 1321–22, 1334–35. See also circular of Albert Gallatin, February 16, 1813, and James Lloyd to Gallatin, February 19, 1813, in Gallatin Papers (SR), reels 25 and 26.

111. Report of House Ways and Means Committee, February 15, 1813, Gallatin to Cheves, February 9, 1813, and Bill Partially to Suspend Non-Importation, in *AC,* 12–2, 1062–65.

112. Speech of Langdon Cheves, December 4, 1812, in *AC,* 12–2, 249.

113. Memorial of the Citizens of Baltimore, February 18, 1813, in Madison Papers (LC), reel 15.

114. Speech of Thomas P. Grosvenor, February 26, 1813, in *AC,* 12–2, 1138.

115. *AC,* 12–2, 110, 1099–1100, 1112–13.

116. Benjamin Romaine to Gallatin, December 13, 1812, in Gallatin Papers (SR), reel 25; London *Morning Chronicle,* August 12 and September 18, 1812; Anthony Baker to Lord Castlereagh, March 22, 1813, in Foreign Office Papers 5/88 (PRO); Edward Fox to Jonathan Roberts, November 10, 1812, in Roberts Papers (HSP); Philadelphia *Democratic Press,* reprinted in Richmond *Enquirer,* January 21, 1813; British Order in Council, November 13, 1812, in *Niles' Register* 3 (February 20, 1813), 400; W. Freeman Galpin, "The American Grain

Trade to the Spanish Peninsula, 1810–1814," *American Historical Review* 28 (October, 1922), 29–33; Walter R. Copp, "Nova Scotian Trade during the War of 1812," *Canadian Historical Review* 18 (June, 1937), 150; Mahan, *Sea Power*, 1:265, 410–11; Carl Seaburg and Stanley Paterson, *Merchant Prince of Boston: Colonel T. H. Perkins, 1764–1854* (Cambridge, 1971), 237.

117. Galpin, "American Grain Trade," 25.

118. Statement of John Purviance and William Pinkney, October 12, 1812, in Boston *Columbian Centinel*, October 5, 1814; Gallatin to Larkin Smith, July 24, 1812, in Gallatin Papers (SR), reel 25. The government did threaten to prosecute the British agent for prisoners of war in Philadelphia and the former British consul at Boston for issuing licenses, but both men were allowed to leave the country instead. See *Niles' Register* 5 (September 4, 1813), 4; Brant, *James Madison*, 6:171.

119. British circular, November 9, 1812, in *Niles' Register* 3 (February 27, 1813), 415.

120. Madison to Congress, February 24, 1813, in *AC*, 12–2, 1116–17.

121. *AC*, 12–2, 121, 1150–51.

122. Speech of Langdon Cheves, December 4, 1812, in *AC*, 12–2, 250.

123. *AC*, 12–2, 142–44, 212–14, 216–17.

124. *AC*, 12–2, 121, 1146, 1153, 1163–64.

125. Report of the Secretary of the Treasury, December 1, 1812, in *ASP: F*, 2:580.

126. Gallatin's revised estimates are summarized in speech of Langdon Cheves, January 23, 1813, in *AC*, 12–2, 870. See also Report of the Secretary of the Treasury, December 1, 1812, in *ASP: F*, 2:580–81.

127. Gallatin to Madison, [November, 1812], in Gallatin Papers (SR), reel 25.

128. *AC*, 12–2, 75, 97, 907–8, 919–20, 1326–28, 1330–33.

129. *AC*, 12–2, 1065.

130. See *AC*, 12–2, 1076–79. See also Artemas Ward to Josiah Quincy, June 9, 1813, in Quincy, *Josiah Quincy*, 320.

131. *AC*, 12–2, 110, 1082–90, 1101, 1110, 1114, 1120–23, 1334.

132. New York *National Advocate*, March 9, 1813.

133. For more on the Russian proposal, see chapter 11: The Treaty of Ghent.

134. Adams, *History*, 7:41–43; Brant, *James Madison*, 6:153–59; Raymond Walters, Jr., *Albert Gallatin: Jeffersonian Financier and Diplomat* (New York, 1957), 259.

135. John Lovett to Joseph Alexander, June 17, 1813, and to Solomon Van Rensselaer, July 16, 1813, in Catharina V. R. Bonney, *A Legacy of Historical Gleanings*, 2 vols., 2nd ed. (Albany, 1875), 1:300, 302.

136. Lovett to Alexander, July 17, 1813, ibid., 303.

137. *AC*, 13–1, 106, 108, 110.

138. Charles Cutts to Plumer, June 8, 1813, in Plumer Papers (LC), reel 3.

139. Jonathan Roberts to Matthew Roberts, May 25, 1813, in Roberts Papers (HSP).

140. Madison to Gallatin, August 2, 1813, and to Dearborn, August 8, 1813, in Madison Papers (LC), reel 15; Charles J. Ingersoll to [Alexander Dallas], July 6, 1813, in Ingersoll Papers (HSP); Washington *National Intelligencer*, July 1, 1813; Lexington *Reporter*, August 21, 1813; Daniel Webster to Charles March, June 26, 1813, in Claude H. Van Tyne, ed., *The Letters of Daniel Webster* (New York, 1902), 45; Brant, *James Madison*, 6:187–88, 192–93.

141. Jonathan Roberts to Matthew Roberts, June 21, 1813, in Roberts Papers (HSP).

142. Jeremiah Mason to Jesse Appleton, July 20, 1813, in George S. Hillard, *Memoir, Autobiography and Correspondence of Jeremiah Mason*, ed. G. J. Clark (Boston, 1917), 61; Calhoun to James Macbride, June 23, 1813, in Meriwether et al., *Papers of John C. Calhoun*, 1:177. See also Andrei Dashkov to Nikolai P. Rumiantsev, August 7, 1813, in Nina K. Bashkina et al., eds., *The United States and Russia: The Beginning of Relations, 1765–1815* [Washington, 1980], 995.

143. Madison to Congress, May 25, 1813, in *AC*, 13–1, 14–17. Quotation from p. 17.

144. Madison to Senate, July 6, 1813, in Madison Papers (LC), reel 15; *Senate Journal*, 2:347–51, 381–84.

145. Jeremiah Mason to Mary Means Mason, July 11, 1813, in Hillard, *Jeremiah Mason*, 60–61.

146. Jesse Bledsoe to Isaac Shelby, July 21, 1813, in Gallatin Papers (SR), reel 26; Christopher Gore to [Timothy Pickering], June 15, 1813, in Pickering Papers (MHS), reel 30.

147. *Senate Journal*, 2:346, 389–90.

148. Philadelphia *Aurora*, January 30, 1812. See also ibid., February 11, 1812.

149. Charles Cutts to Plumer, June 8, 1813, in Plumer Papers (LC), reel 3. See also Joseph Alston to William Lowndes, June 23, 1813, in Lowndes Papers (UNC), reel 1.

150. Thomas Hart Benton to Andrew Jackson, June 15, 1813, in Jackson Papers (LC), reel 6.

151. *Senate Journal*, 2:355.

152. *Senate Journal*, 2:389.

153. Jeremiah Mason to Jesse Appleton, July 20, 1813, in Hillard, *Jeremiah Mason*, 62.

154. *AC*, 13–1, 149–52.

155. Speech of Harmanus Bleecker, January 7, 1813, in *AC*, 12–2, 621.

156. Speech of Felix Grundy, June 18, 1813, in *AC*, 13–1, 225–26.

157. Speeches of Zebulon R. Shipherd, Alexander C. Hanson, and Joseph Pearson, June 18, 1812, in *AC*, 13–1, 235–36, 254–56, 285–286.

158. *AC*, 13–1, 302–3, 308–11.

159. Report of the Secretary of State, July 12, 1813, in *ASP: FR*, 3:609–12.

160. Gallatin to Madison, March 5, 1813, in Madison Papers (LC), reel 15.

161. Report of the Secretary of the Treasury, July 28, 1813, in *ASP: F*, 2:646–47.

162. James Breckinridge to Andrew Hamilton, July 4, 1813, in Breckin-

ridge Papers (UVA); J. L. Shevinester (?) to Andrew Jackson, June 18, 1813, in Jackson Papers (LC), reel 6.

163. Quoted in Daniel Webster to Charles March, May 31, [1813], in Charles M. Wiltse et al., eds., *The Papers of Daniel Webster: Correspondence*, 7 vols. (Hanover, NH, 1974–1986), 1:142. See also Charles Cutts to William Plumer, June 8, 1813, in Plumer Papers (LC), reel 3; Artemas Ward to Thomas Ward, June 19, 1813, in Thomas Walter Ward Papers (AAS).

164. Benjamin Tallmadge to James McHenry, June 10, 1813, in McHenry Papers (LC).

165. Report of House Ways and Means Committee, June 10, 1813, in *AC*, 13–1, 149–50. The taxes were supposed to yield $6,365,000, but a proposed tax on foreign tonnage (expected to yield $900,000) was never adopted. This reduced the anticipated yield to $5,465,000. Expenses and losses were expected to reduce the total by an additional $750,000.

166. The tax laws are printed in *AC*, 13–1, 2717–73.

167. Gallatin to President of Senate, December 27, 1809, in *ASP: F*, 2:388; U.S. Department of the Treasury, *Report of the Secretary of the Treasury on the State of the Finances for the Year 1866* (Washington, 1866), 306.

168. *AC*, 13–1, 2759. A state was entitled to a 15 percent discount if it paid its quota by February 10, 1814, and to a 10 percent discount if it paid by May 1, 1814.

169. Ingersoll, *Historical Sketch*, 1:240.

170. Report of Rhode Island Assembly, in Hartford *Connecticut Courant*, March 15, 1814.

171. William Jones to William Bibb, July 19, 1813, in *ASP: F*, 2:644.

172. *AC*, 13–1, 78, 477, 2766–68; Report of the Secretary of the Treasury, January 8, 1814, in *ASP: F*, 2:661–62.

173. Story's decision is printed in the New York *National Advocate*, June 26, 1813. See also Washington *National Intelligencer*, March 8, 1814; Story, *Joseph Story*, 1:248; Ingersoll, *Historical Sketch*, 2:40.

174. *AC*, 13–1, 55, 485, 2777–79. Ships sailing to the United States from Europe, Africa, and the Orient were given a grace period of three to five months before being subject to the law.

175. Madison to Congress, July 20, 1813, in *AC*, 13–1, 499–500.

176. *AC*, 13–1, 98–101, 500–504.

177. Quoted in Brant, *James Madison*, 6:197.

178. *AC*, 13–1, 38–39, 382, 486–87.

179. General Order of the Secretary of the Navy, July 29, 1813, in ND (M149), reel 11; Order of the Secretary of War, August 5, 1813, in *Niles' Register* 4 (August 14, 1813), 386.

180. Jones to Hugh Nelson, July 21, 1813, in *ASP: F*, 2:645–46. See also Washington *National Intelligencer*, August 4, 1813.

181. *AC*, 13–1, 81, 479, 2766.

182. John Lovett to Joseph Alexander, July 17, 1813, in Bonney, *Legacy of Historical Gleanings*, 1:304.

183. *AC*, 13–1, 82, 483, 2773–74.

184. Dallas to Hannah Gallatin, July 22, 1813, in Gallatin Papers (SR), reel 26; and Dallas, quoted in Brant, *James Madison*, 6:191. For similar sentiments, see William Jones to Dallas, July 19, 1813, in Dallas Papers (HSP); Worcester *National Aegis*, November 17, 1813.

185. Washington *National Intelligencer*, July 26, 1813; John Lovett to Joseph Alexander, July 27, 1813, in Bonney, *Legacy of Historical Gleanings*, 1:306.

186. *AC*, 13–1, 83; speech of Elbridge Gerry, April 18, 1814, in *AC*, 13–2, 776–78; Henry B. Larned, "Gerry and the Presidential Succession in 1813," *American Historical Review* 22 (October, 1916), 95–97.

Chapter 6: The Campaign of 1813

1. William Bradford et al., to U.S. Senate, May 2, 1813, in *ASP: MA*, 1:336; C. Edward Skeen, "Mr. Madison's Secretary of War," *Pennsylvania Magazine of History and Biography* 100 (July, 1976), 345.

2. Estimate based on figures in Stagg, "Enlisted Men in the United States Army," 621.

3. Skeen, *John Armstrong*, 129.

4. Pierce Butler to Monroe, May 2, 1813, in Monroe Papers (LC), reel 5.

5. Armstrong to cabinet, February 8, 1813, in *ASP: MA*, 1:439; Armstrong to Henry Dearborn, February 10 and 24, March 29, and April 19, 1813, and to Peter B. Porter, February 23, 1813, in WD (M6), reel 6; J.C.A. Stagg, *Mr. Madison's War: Politics, Diplomacy, and Warfare in the Early American Republic, 1783–1830* (Princeton, 1983), 284–86.

6. Mahan, *Sea Power*, 1:301–3.

7. Paul Hamilton to Langdon Cheves, December 3, 1811, and to Isaac Chauncey, September 4, 1812, in Dudley and Crawford, *Naval War*, 1:56, 302; Roosevelt, *Naval War*, 1:182–84.

8. Madison to Dearborn, October 7, 1812, in Madison Papers (LC), reel 14; William Jones to Isaac Chauncey, January 27, 1813, in ND (M149), reel 10. See also Secretary of War to William Henry Harrison, April 3, 1813, in WD (M6), reel 6.

9. Quoted in Mahan, *Sea Power*, 1:361. See also Hamilton to Chauncey, August 31, 1812, in Dudley and Crawford, *Naval War*, 1:297–300.

10. Chauncey to Hamilton, September 3 and 26, October 8, 21, 22 and 27, and November 4 and 5, 1812, in ND (M125), reel 25; Mahan, *Sea Power*, 1:374–77.

11. Brock to George Prevost, October 11, 1812, in Dudley and Crawford, *Naval War*, 1:332.

12. Report on the Provincial Marine of the Canadas, n.d., A. Gray to George Prevost, January 29, 1812, Appointment of Sir J. L. Yeo, March 19, 1813, and General Order of April 22, 1813, in Wood, *British Documents*, 1:240, 250–51, 2:77–78, 81–84; speech of Francis Horner, December 1, 1814, in *Parliamentary Debates*, 29:644; Chauncey to Jones, November 5, 1814, in ND (M125), reel 40; C. P. Stacey, "Another Look at the Battle of Lake Erie," *Canadian Historical Review* 39 (March, 1958), 41–51. Most of the equipment for the American

fleet on Lake Erie was manufactured in Pittsburgh. See William W. Dobbins, "The Dobbins Papers," *Publications of the Buffalo Historical Society* 8 (1905), 313–14.

13. Chauncey to Secretary of the Navy, August 13, and October 1 and 6, 1813, in ND (M125), reels 30 and 31; Morgan Lewis to Daniel Tompkins, August 15, 1813, and Buffalo *Gazette*, August 17, 1813, in Cruikshank, *Niagara Frontier*, 7:24, 34; Daniel A. Nelson, "*Hamilton & Scourge*: Ghost Ships of the War of 1812," *National Geographic* 163 (March, 1983), 289–313.

14. Chauncey to Jones, March 18, 1813, in ND (M125), reel 27; Secretary of War to Dearborn, March 29, 1813, and Dearborn to Secretary of War, [early 1813], in *ASP: MA*, 1:442; Jones to Chauncey, April 8, 1813, in *NASP: NA*, 4:278–81; Mahan, *Sea Power*, 2:31–34.

15. Dearborn to Armstrong, April 28, 1813, in WD (M221), reel 52; Chauncey to Jones, April 28, 1813, in ND (M125), reel 28; Roger Sheaffe to Prevost, May 5, 1813, in Wood, *British Documents*, 2:89–94; William Chewett et al. to John Strachan et al., May 8, 1813, in Cruikshank, *Niagara Frontier*, 5:192–202; Charles Humphries, "The Capture of York," in Zaslow, *Defended Border*, 251–70; C. P. Stacey, *The Battle of Little York* (Toronto, 1977), passim.

16. Samuel S. Conner to Armstrong, May 4, 1813, in WD (M221), reel 51.

17. Journal of Dr. William Beaumont, April 27, 1813, in Genevieve Miller, ed., *Wm. Beaumont's Formative Years: Two Early Notebooks, 1811–1821* (New York, 1946), 46.

18. George Howard to Sarah Howard, May 7, 1813, in George Howard Journal (CHS).

19. Penelope Beikie, quoted in Stacey, *Battle of Little York*, 17. See also William Chewett et al. to John Strachan et al., May 8, 1813, in Cruikshank, *Niagara Frontier*, 5:200.

20. Chauncey to Jones, June 4, 1813, in ND (M125), reel 29; letter to Baltimore *Whig*, May 7, 1813, E. W. Ripley to William D. Powell, n.d., and Kingston *Gazette*, August 17, 1813, in Cruikshank, *Niagara Frontier*, 5:171–73, 8:25; Francis de Rottenburg to Bathurst, October 25, 1813, in Wood, *British Documents*, 2:220; Stacey, *Battle of Little York*, 22.

21. Prevost to Bathurst, July 20, 1813, in Cruikshank, *Niagara Frontier*, 6:256.

22. William Allan to Edward Baynes, August 3, 1813, in Wood, *British Documents*, 2:195.

23. Chauncey to Jones, August 4, 1813, in ND (M125), reel 30; Winfield Scott to John Boyd, August 3, 1813, in *ASP: MA*, 1:450; Grant Powell to Prevost, August 1, 1813, John Strachan and Grant Powell to Baynes, August 2, 1813, and William Allan to Baynes, August 3, 1813, in Wood, *British Documents*, 2:189–96.

24. E.B. Brenton to Noah Freer, May 30, 1813, in Cruikshank, *Niagara Frontier*, 5:281–82.

25. Brown to Henry Dearborn, July 25, 1813, in Adams, *History*, 7:165. See also Brown to Armstrong, June 1, 1813, in Franklin B. Hough, *A History of Jefferson County in the State of New York, from the Earliest Period to the Present Time*

(Albany, 1854), 490–91; Chauncey to Jones, June 2, 1813, in ND (M125), reel 29; Baynes to Prevost, May 30, 1813, E. B. Brenton to Noah Freer, May 30, 1813, and Brown to Tompkins, June 1, 1813, in Cruikshank, *Niagara Frontier,* 5:276–87.

26. Chauncey to Hamilton (with enclosure), September 26, 1812 in ND (M125), reel 25.

27. Elliott to Hamilton, October 9, 1812, in Dudley and Crawford, *Naval War,* 1:328.

28. Ibid., 328–31; Nathan Towson to J. D. Elliott, July 6, 1843, and Report of British Court of Inquiry, in Cruikshank, *Niagara Frontier,* 4:50–52, 54–57.

29. Brock to Prevost, October 11, 1812, in Dudley and Crawford, *Naval War,* 1:332.

30. Chauncey to Perry, February 1, 1813, in Alexander Slidell Mackenzie, *The Life of Commodore Oliver Hazard Perry,* 2 vols. (New York, 1840–41), 1:125. See also Perry to Hamilton, November 28, 1812, in ND (M147), reel 4; Chauncey to Secretary of the Navy, January 21, 1813, in ND (M125), reel 26.

31. Chauncey to Secretary of the Navy, May 29, 1813, in ND (M125), reel 28.

32. Perry to Jones, August 4, 1813, in ND (M147), reel 5; Dearborn to Secretary of War, June 8, 1813, and Perry to Chauncey, June 13, 1813, in Cruikshank, *Niagara Frontier,* 6:55, 7:272; Mahan, *Sea Power,* 2:62–64, 69–73.

33. Perry to Secretary of the Navy, July 23 and 30, 1813, in ND (M147), reel 5.

34. Perry to Secretary of the Navy, August 10, 1813, ibid.

35. Perry to Chauncey, July 27, 1813, ibid.

36. Harrison to Armstrong, August 22, 1813, in Esarey, *Messages and Letters of William Henry Harrison,* 2:525.

37. Perry to Secretary of the Navy, August 21 and September 2, 1813, in ND (M147), reel 5.

38. Speech of Tecumseh, September 18, 1813, in *Niles' Register* 5 (November 6, 1813), 174. See also John Sugden, *Tecumseh's Last Stand* (Norman, 1985), 19.

39. Barclay to Yeo, September 1, 1813, in Wood, *British Documents,* 2:268; testimony of Thomas Stokoe, in Charles O. Paullin, ed., *The Battle of Lake Erie: A Collection of Documents* (Cleveland, 1918), 151.

40. Narrative of Robert H. Barclay, in Wood, *British Documents,* 2:303.

41. Barclay to Yeo, September 1 and 12, 1813, and narrative of Barclay, ibid., 268, 274, 304. See also Robert Gillmor to Edward Couche, September 5, 1813, ibid., 291.

42. Barclay to Yeo, September 12, 1813, ibid., 277.

43. Perry to Jones, September 13, 1813, in *ASP: NA,* 1:295.

44. Quoted in Edgar, *Ten Years of Upper Canada,* 324.

45. Perry to Jones, September 13, 1813, in *ASP: NA,* 1:295; Barclay to Yeo, September 12, 1813, and Yeo to Warren, October 10, 1813, in Wood, *British Documents,* 2:274–77, 287–88; *Niles' Register* 7 (Supplement), 41; Paullin, *Battle of Lake Erie,* 140n; Maclay, *United States Navy,* 1:517; Ernest A. Cruikshank,

"The Contest for the Command of Lake Erie in 1812–13," in Zaslow, *Defended Border*, 96–104; Mackenzie, *Oliver Hazard Perry*, 1:215–61.

46. Perry to Harrison, September 10, 1813, in Benson J. Lossing, *The Pictorial Field-Book of the War of 1812* (New York, 1868), 530. Perry actually took two ships, *two* schooners, *one* brig, and a sloop. Although the original note to Harrison has been lost, the copy reproduced in Lossing is a facsimile.

47. Jones to Perry, September 21, 1813, in ND (M149), reel 11. See also Richmond *Enquirer*, September 28 and October 15, 1813.

48. *AC*, 13–2, 2838–39, 2855–56; Samuel Hambleton to Jones, May 23, 1814 (filed under June 10, 1814), in ND (M149), reel 11.

49. *Naval Chronicle* 30 (July–December, 1813), 431.

50. Gallatin to Madison, March 5, 1813, in Madison Papers (LC), reel 15.

51. Armstrong to Harrison, March 17, 1813, in Esarey, *Messages and Letters of William Henry Harrison*, 2:386; Armstrong to Harrison, April 4, 1813, in Harrison Papers (LC), reel 1; Secretary of War to Harrison, April 27, 1813, in WD (M6), reel 6.

52. Pittsburgh *Gazette*, reprinted in Richmond *Enquirer*, April 13, 1813; Mahon, *War of 1812*, 159–61.

53. Procter to Prevost, May 14, 1813, in Wood, *British Documents*, 2:34.

54. General Orders of May 9, 1813, in Brannan, *Official Letters*, 156.

55. William G. Erving to John H. James, May 2, 1818, in Benjamin Drake, *Life of Tecumseh, and His Brother the Prophet* (Cincinnati, 1858), 182.

56. Harrison to Secretary of War, May 9 and 13, 1813, in WD (M221), reel 53; Procter to Prevost, May 14, 1813, in Wood, *British Documents*, 2:33–37; Diary of the Siege of Fort Meigs, April 25–May 9, 1813, reprinted from Chillicothe *Fredonian*, in *Niles' Register* 4 (June 12, 1813), 242–44; McAfee, *History of the Late War*, 256–77; Gilpin, *War of 1812 in the Northwest*, 182–89.

57. Croghan to Harrison, [July 30, 1813], in McAfee, *History of the Late War*, 323. See also Croghan to Cincinnati *Liberty Hall*, September 14, 1813, in Esarey, *Messages and Letters of William Henry Harrison*, 2:527–29.

58. Prevost to Procter, August 9, 1813, in Wood, *British Documents*, 2:44–47. Quotation from p. 46. See also Croghan to Harrison, August 5, 1813, in Brannan, *Official Letters*, 184–86; McAfee, *History of the Late War*, 321–28; Gilpin, *War of 1812 in the Northwest*, 206–7.

59. Procter to de Rottenburg, September 12, 1813, in Wood, *British Documents*, 2:273.

60. Speech of Tecumseh, September 18, 1813, in *Niles' Register* 5 (November 6, 1813), 175.

61. McAfee, *History of the Late War*, 338; Shelby to Kentucky militia, July 30, 1813, in Washington *National Intelligencer*, August 18, 1813.

62. Shelby to ———, September 10, 1813, in Isaac Shelby Papers (LC).

63. McAfee, *History of the Late War*, 331–32; Mahon, *War of 1812*, 178.

64. Harrison to Armstrong, October 9, 1813, in WD (M222), reel 8.

65. Quoted in Thomas D. Clark, "Kentucky in the Northwest Campaign," in Philip P. Mason, ed., *After Tippecanoe: Some Aspects of the War of 1812* (East Lansing, 1963), 94.

66. Harrison to Armstrong, October 9, 1813, in WD (M222), reel 8; Richard M. Johnson to Armstrong, November 21, 1813, in WD (M221), reel 54; Harrison to Armstrong, September 27, 1813, in Esarey, *Messages and Letters of William Henry Harrison*, 2:551; Procter to de Rottenburg, October 23 and November 16, 1813, in Wood, *British Documents*, 2:323–27, 338–41; General Order of September 9, 1815, in Cruikshank, *Niagara Frontier*, 8:160–64; Edgar, *Ten Years of Upper Canada*, 144; Bennett H. Young, *The Battle of the Thames* (Louisville, 1903), 29–109; Sugden, *Tecumseh's Last Stand*, passim.

67. Harrison to Secretary of War, October 16, 1813, in Esarey, *Messages and Letters of William Henry Harrison*, 2:579–81.

68. Harrison to Armstrong, May 11, 1814, in Harrison Papers (LC), reel 2.

69. Harrison and Cass to Armstrong, July 17, 1814, in WD (M221), reel 62; Treaty of Peace and Friendship, July 22, 1814, in *ASP: IA*, 1:326; Gilpin, *War of 1812 in the Northwest*, 240–41; Sugden, *Tecumseh's Last Stand*, 182–207.

70. Memorandum of J. B. Glegg, May 3 and 5, 1813, in Cruikshank, *Niagara Frontier*, 5:221.

71. Dearborn to Secretary of War, May 27, 1813, and Darby Noon to Tompkins, May 27, 1813, ibid., 246–47, 249; Chauncey to Jones, May 28, 1813, in ND (M125), reel 28; John Vincent to Prevost, May 28, 1813, in Wood, *British Documents*, 2:103–7.

72. Dearborn to Secretary of War, May 29, 1813, in Cruikshank, *Niagara Frontier*, 5:266–67.

73. Military Journal of William H. Merritt, in Wood, *British Documents*, 3:579.

74. Chandler to Dearborn, June 18, 1813, in WD (M222), reel 7; James Burns to Dearborn, n.d., in *ASP: MA*, 1:447–48; James Fitzgibbon to James Somerville, June 7, 1813, and letter to Buffalo *Gazette* [June, 1813], in Cruikshank, *Niagara Frontier*, 6:12–15, 105–6; Harvey to [Baynes], June 6, 1813, and Vincent to Prevost, June 6, 1813, in Wood, *British Documents*, 2:139–45; Herbert F. Wood, "The Many Battles of Stoney Creek," in Zaslow, *Defended Border*, 56–60.

75. Narrative of Charles Boerstler, in Cruikshank, *Niagara Frontier*, 6:130–37; Fitzgibbon to de Haren, June 24, 1813, Boerstler to Dearborn, June 25, 1813, Memoir of Laura Secord, February 18, 1861, in Wood, *British Documents*, 2:159–62, 164–65; S. A. Curzon, "The Story of Laura Secord, 1813," in Zaslow, *Defended Border*, 306–10.

76. Ingersoll to [Alexander Dallas], July 6, 1813, in Ingersoll Papers (HSP). See also Secretary of War to Dearborn, July 6, 1813, in WD (M6), reel 7; Dearborn to Madison, August 17, 1813, in Madison Papers (LC), reel 15.

77. Dearborn to Armstrong, July 6, 1813, in WD (M221), reel 52; Peter B. Porter to Dearborn, July 13, 1813, in *Niles' Register* 8 (Supplement), 146–47; Buffalo *Gazette*, July 13, 1813, statement of James Fitzgibbon, and Recollections of James Sloan, in Cruikshank, *Niagara Frontier*, 6:226–31; Thomas Clark to Harvey, July 5 and 12, 1813, in Wood, *British Documents*, 2:174–77.

78. McClure to Tompkins, December 10, 1813, in WD (M221), reel 55.

79. McClure to Armstrong, December 6, 10, and 13, 1813, in WD (M221),

reel 55; McClure to Tompkins, December 6 and 10, 1813, John A. Rogers et al. to Buffalo *Gazette*, [December, 1813], in Cruikshank, *Niagara Frontier*, 8:254, 264, 9:10; Military Journal of William H. Merritt, in Wood, *British Documents*, 3:607–8.

80. McClure to Armstrong, December 13, 1813, in WD (M221), reel 55.

81. McClure to Armstrong, December 22, 1813, ibid.

82. Tompkins to Armstrong, December 24, 1813, in Hastings, *Papers of Daniel D. Tompkins*, 3:407. See also McClure to Armstrong, December 22 and 25, 1813, in WD (M221), reel 55; Lewis Cass to Armstrong, January 12, 1814, in *ASP: MA*, 1:488; Lt. Driscoll, "The Capture of Fort Niagara," in Cruikshank, *Niagara Frontier*, 9:18–20; Gordon Drummond to Prevost, December 20 and 22, 1813, and General Order of December 19, 1813, in Wood, *British Documents*, 2:490–92, 494–97.

83. McClure to Secretary of War, December 22, 1813, in WD (M221), reel 55; Riall to Drummond, December 19, 1813, and Timothy Hopkins to Tompkins, December 20, 1813, in Cruikshank, *Niagara Frontier*, 9:14, 24.

84. Letter to Albany *Argus*, December 26, 1813, ibid., 55. See also Tompkins to Armstrong, January 2, 1814, in Hastings, *Papers of Daniel D. Tompkins*, 3:408.

85. McClure to [Secretary of War], December 20, 1813, in WD (M222), reel 8.

86. McClure to Erastus Granger, December 28, 1813, in Cruikshank, *Niagara Frontier*, 9:61. See also Timothy Hopkins to Tompkins, December 20, 1813, McClure to Tompkins, December 20, 1813, and John C. Spencer to Tompkins, December 26, 1813, ibid., 24–25, 53.

87. Riall to Drummond, January 1, 1814, and Amos Hall to Tompkins, January 6, 1814, ibid., 70–72, 92–97.

88. Cass to Secretary of War, January 12, 1814, in *ASP: MA*, 1:487.

89. Tompkins to Armstrong, January 2, 1814, in Hastings, *Papers of Daniel D. Tompkins*, 3:408. See also Amos Hall to [Tompkins], December 30, 1813, in *Niles' Register* 5 (February 12, 1814), 394.

90. Secretary of War to David R. Williams, August 5, 1813, and to James Wilkinson, August 8, 1813, in WD (M6), reel 7; Secretary of War to Dearborn, April 19, 1813, Secretary of War to Wilkinson, September 6 and 22, 1813, Memoranda of Wilkinson and Armstrong, October 5, 1813, and Secretary of War to Wilkinson, October 19 and 20, 1813, in Cruikshank, *Niagara Frontier*, 5:148–49, 7:106, 163–64, 197–98, 8:81–82, 85–86; Secretary of War to Hampton, October 16, 1812, in *ASP: MA*, 1:461; Stagg, *Mr. Madison's War*, 331–43; Skeen, *John Armstrong*, 145–63.

91. Isaac Clark to Armstrong, June 4, 1813, in WD (M222), reel 7; George Taylor to Richard Stovin, June 3, 1813, in Wood, *British Documents*, 2:221–23; Rodney Macdonough, *Life of Commodore Thomas Macdonough, U.S. Navy* (Boston, 1909), 115–20.

92. Madison to Armstrong, September 8, 1813, in Madison Papers (LC), reel 15.

93. Scott, *Memoirs*, 1:94n; Randolph to Joseph H. Nicholson, June 25, 1807,

in Nicholson Papers (LC). See also Charles W. Elliott, *Winfield Scott: The Soldier and the Man* (New York, 1937), 32–33.

94. Allan B. Magruder to [Secretary of War], January 16, 1813, in WD (M221), reel 55. See also William H. Crawford to Madison, January 15, 1812, and March 3, 1813, in Madison Papers (LC), reels 13 and 15; Jacobs, *Beginnings of the U.S. Army*, 344–52.

95. Mahon, *War of 1812*, 202–5.

96. Secretary of War to Hampton, October 16, 1813, in *ASP: MA*, 1:461; Secretary of War to Wilkinson, October 19, 1813, in Cruikshank, *Niagara Frontier*, 8:81–82.

97. Hampton to Armstrong, September 25, 1813, in WD (M222), reel 8.

98. Michael O'Sullivan, "Account of the Battle of Chateauguay," November 3, 1813, reprinted from Quebec *Mercury*, in Wood, *British Documents*, 2:406.

99. Hampton to Armstrong, November 1, 1813, and Report of L. Thayer [early 1814], in WD (M221), reels 53 and 57; Robert Purdy to Wilkinson, n.d., in *ASP: MA*, 1:479–80; de Salaberry to father, October 29, 1813, Prevost to Bathurst, October 30, 1813, and O'Sullivan, "Account of the Battle of Chateauguay," November 3, 1813, in Wood, *British Documents*, 2:391–95, 401–12.

100. Hampton to Armstrong, November 1, 1813, in WD (M221), reel 53.

101. Wilkinson to Armstrong, October 19, 1813, in WD (M222), reel 9.

102. Wilkinson to Secretary of War, September 16, 1813, in Cruikshank, *Niagara Frontier*, 7:133; Ellery Harrison, ed., *The Memoirs of Gen. Joseph Gardner Swift* (Worcester, MA, 1890), 116. See also Wilkinson to Dearborn, December 4, 1813, in Dearborn Papers (MeHS).

103. John P. Boyd to Wilkinson, November 12, 1813, in *Niles' Register* 5 (December 18, 1813), 266–67; Wilkinson to Armstrong, November 16, 1813, and Journal of Wilkinson, October 21—November 12, 1813, in *ASP: MA*, 1:475–78; J. W. Morrison to de Rottenburg, November 12, 1813, in Wood, *British Documents*, 2:441–44; Ronald L. Way, "The Day of Crysler's Farm," in Zaslow, *Defended Border*, 56–83.

104. George Howard to Sarah Howard, December 19, 1813, in George Howard Journal (CHS).

105. Dr. Lovell, quoted in Mann, *Medical Sketches*, 119. See also Journal of Wilkinson, November 12, 1813, in *ASP: MA*, 1:478; Secret Information from French Mills, February 7, 1812, in Cruikshank, *Niagara Frontier*, 9:168; Mahon, *War of 1812*, 215–18.

106. Wilkinson to Armstrong, March 25, 1814, in WD (M221), reel 58.

107. Wilkinson to Dr. Bule, March 31, 1814, in Wilkinson Papers (LC); Wilkinson to [Armstrong?], March 31, 1814, in Brannan, *Official Letters*, 325–26; William Williams to Vincent, March 31, 1814, in Wood, *British Documents*, 3:14–16; Albany *Register* and Middlebury *Columbian Patriot*, reprinted in Richmond *Enquirer*, April 16, 1814.

108. *Niles' Register* 5 (October 2, 1813), 77; John R. Swanton, *Social Organization and Social Usages of the Indians of the Creek Confederacy* (Washington, 1928), *passim*; Angie Debo, *The Road to Disappearance*, 2nd ed. (Norman, 1967), 3–

71; Michael D. Green, *The Politics of Indian Removal: Creek Government and Society in Crisis* (Lincoln, 1982), chs. 1–2; J. Leitch Wright, Jr., *Creeks & Seminoles: The Destruction and Regeneration of the Muscogulge People* (Lincoln, 1986), chs. 1–3.

109. *Niles' Register* 5 (September 13, 1813), 43.

110. Quoted in Robert V. Remini, *Andrew Jackson*, 3 vols. (New York, 1977–84), 1:188.

111. Mahon, *War of 1812*, 232.

112. Benjamin Hawkins to Eustis, July 20, 1812, in WD (M221), reel 45; Hawkins to Secretary of War, September 7, 1812, and William Henry to John J. Henry, June 26, 1812, in *ASP: IA*, 1:812–13; Shelbyville *Tennessee Herald*, reprinted in *Niles' Register* 2 (June 13, 1812), 256; letter from Creek Agency, July 27, 1813, in *Niles' Register* 5 (September 25, 1813), 56.

113. Harry Toulmin to Willie Blount, July 28–30, 1813, in WD (M221), reel 50; H. S. Halbert and T. H. Ball, *The Creek War of 1813 and 1814* (Chicago, 1895), 125–42; Frank L. Owsley, Jr., *Struggle for the Gulf Borderlands: The Creek War and the Battle of New Orleans, 1812–1815* (Gainsville, 1981), 30–33.

114. Quoted in John F. H. Claiborne, *Life and Times of Gen. Sam. Dale, The Mississippi Partisan* (New York, 1860), 128–29.

115. William Claiborne to Thomas Flournoy, September 2, 1813, in WD (M221), reel 52; Henry Toulmin to Raleigh *Register*, September 7, 1813, in *Niles' Register* 5 (October 16, 1813), 105–7; Halbert and Ball, *Creek War*, 147–64; Owsley, *Struggle for the Borderlands*, 35–39.

116. William Claiborne, quoted in Halbert and Ball, *Creek War*, 299.

117. Toulmin to Raleigh *Register*, September 7, 1813, in *Niles' Register* 5 (October 16, 1813), 105.

118. James White to John Cocke, November 24, 1813, in Richmond *Enquirer*, December 25, 1813; J. Hoyt to Thomas Pinckney, December 4, 1813, and John Floyd to Thomas Pinckney, January 27, 1814, in WD (M221), reel 56; Owsley, *Struggle for the Borderlands*, 42–60.

119. Quoted in Coles, *War of 1812*, 197.

120. General Orders of November 7, 1813, in Jackson Papers (LC), reel 61. See also Remini, *Andrew Jackson*, 1:191–93.

121. Coffee to Jackson, November 4, 1813, in Brannan, *Official Letters*, 255–56. See also Owsley, *Struggle for the Borderlands*, 64–65.

122. Coffee to Jackson, November 4, 1813, in Brannan, *Official Letters*, 256.

123. Jackson to Willie Blount, November 11 and 15, 1813, in Jackson Papers (LC), reel 61; Owsley, *Struggle for the Borderlands*, 65–66.

124. Jackson to Secretary of War, December 16, 1813, in Jackson Papers (LC), reel 7.

125. Jackson to Coffee, December 11, 1813, and to John Floyd, December 26, 1813, and Blount to Jackson, December 22, 1813 (two letters), in Jackson Papers (LC), reel 7; Jackson to Rachel Jackson, December 29, 1813, in Jackson Papers, Supplement (SR), reel 3; Jackson to Floyd, December 27, 1813, in Sam B. Smith et al., eds., *The Papers of Andrew Jackson*, 2 vols. to date (Knoxville, 1980–), 2:510; statement of J.W. Sittler, in John S. Bassett, ed., *Correspondence of Andrew Jackson*, 6 vols. (Washington, 1926–33), 1:434.

126. Jackson to Armstrong, December 16, 1813, and to Rachel Jackson, January 28, 1814, in Jackson Papers (LC), reels 7 and 8; Jackson to Thomas Pinckney, January 29, 1814, in Bassett, *Correspondence of Andrew Jackson*, 1:447–54; Owsley, *Struggle for the Borderlands*, 73–76.

127. Jackson to William Lewis, February 21, 1814, in Jackson Papers, Supplement (SR), reel 3.

128. General Orders of [March 14, 1814], in Jackson Papers (LC), reel 62.

129. John Reid and John Eaton, *The Life of Andrew Jackson* (Philadelphia, 1817), 143. See also James Parton, *Life of Andrew Jackson*, 3 vols. (New York, 1860), 1:504–12.

130. Jackson to Rachel Jackson, April 1, 1814, in Jackson Papers (LC), reel 9.

131. Jackson to Willie Blount, March 31, 1814, in Jackson Papers, Supplement (SR), reel 3; Jackson to Armstrong, April 2, 1814, in WD (M221), reel 54; Jackson to Pinckney, March 28, 1814, and to Blount, April 2, 1814, in Jackson Papers (LC), reels 9 and 10; Jackson to Blount, March 28, 1814, in Brannan, *Official Letters*, 321–23; Owsley, *Struggle for the Borderlands*, 79–81.

132. Address of Andrew Jackson, April 2, 1814, in Jackson Papers (LC), reel 10.

133. Quoted in letter of Anne Royall, December 15, 1817, in Lucille Griffith, ed., *Letters from Alabama, 1817–1822, by Anne Royall* (University, AL, 1969), 91–92. See also Jackson to Blount, April 18, 1814, in Jackson Papers (LC), reel 10.

134. Jackson to [Thomas Pinckney], May 18, 1814, in Jackson Papers (LC), reel 10.

135. Articles of Agreement and Capitulation, August 9, 1814, in *ASP: IA*, 1:326–27; Parton, *Andrew Jackson*, 1:535; Owsley, *Struggle for the Borderlands*, 86–94; Remini, *Andrew Jackson*, 1:225–32.

136. For more on British naval policy in 1812, see chapter 4: The Campaign of 1812.

137. Statement of British Naval Force on North American Stations, 1810–1813, in Vane, *Memoirs and Correspondence of Viscount Castlereagh*, 8:292.

138. Quoted in Mahan, *Sea Power*, 2:151.

139. Thomas Pinckney to Secretary of War, October 17, 1812, in WD (M221), reel 48; Dudley and Crawford, *Naval War*, 1:561.

140. [Lord Castlereagh?] to Anthony Baker, February 3, 1813, in Foreign Office Papers 5/88 (PRO); Notice of Foreign Office, December 26, 1812, in *Naval Chronicle* 28 (July–December 1812), 507; Proclamation of John Borlase Warren, November 16, 1813, in *Niles' Register* 5 (December 18, 1813), 264–65; Mahan, *Sea Power*, 2:9–10.

141. John Hollins to Wilson Cary Nicholas, April 8, 1813, in Nicholas Papers (UVA).

142. Mahan, *Sea Power*, 2:182.

143. Nathaniel Macon to Joseph H. Nicholson, March 1, 1813, in Nicholson Papers (LC); John Lovett to Joseph Alexander, May 18, 1813, in Bonney, *Legacy of Historical Gleanings*, 1:297.

144. *Niles' Register* 5 (September 13, 1813), 41.

145. John Lovett to Joseph Alexander, May 18, 1813, in Bonney, *Legacy of Historical Gleanings*, 1:297.

146. Harrison, *Diary of Thomas P. Cope* (December 18, 1813), 287.

147. New York *Columbian*, reprinted in Richmond *Enquirer*, December 28, 1813.

148. Philadelphia *Democratic Press*, reprinted in Richmond *Enquirer*, December 28, 1813; Hartford *American Mercury*, December 21, 1813.

149. Washington *National Intelligencer*, December 30, 1813, and January 10, 1814; Hartford *American Mercury*, December 21, 1813; Philadelphia *Democratic Press*, reprinted in Richmond *Enquirer*, December 30, 1813; Manuel Eyre to William Jones, January 5, 1814, in Jones Papers (HSP); Harrison, *Diary of Thomas P. Cope* (January 5, 1814), 289.

150. See James Pack, *The Man Who Burned the White House: Admiral Sir George Cockburn, 1772–1853* (Annapolis, 1987).

151. Mahan, *Sea Power*, 2:155–56.

152. Quoted in deposition of William T. Killpatrick, June 25, 1813, in *ASP: MA*, 1:365.

153. See documents in *ASP: MA*, 1:358–67; Cockburn to Warren, May 3 and 6, 1813, in *Naval Chronicle* 30 (July–December, 1813), 164–68; Mahon, *War of 1812*, 115–16; Pack, *George Cockburn*, 151–55.

154. Ingersoll, *Historical Sketch*, 1:198.

155. Littleton W. Tazewell to Armstrong, June 22, 1813, H. Beatty to Robert Taylor, June 22, 1813, and Taylor to [Secretary of War], June 23, 1813, in WD (M221), reel 57; Norfolk *Herald* and Beatty to Robert Taylor, June 25, 1813, in Washington *National Intelligencer*, June 28 and July 10, 1813.

156. See documents in *ASP: MA*, 1:375–81. See also S. Crutchfield to James Barbour, June 28, 1813, in Washington *National Intelligencer*, July 5, 1813.

157. Journal of Charles Napier, August 12, 1813, in William F. P. Napier, *The Life and Opinions of General Sir Charles James Napier*, 4 vols. (London, 1857), 1:221.

158. John Sherbrooke to Prevost, July 20, 1813, in Wood, *British Documents*, 3:713. See also James Scott, *Recollections of a Naval Life*, 3 vols. (London, 1934), 3:153; James, *Naval History of Great Britain*, 6:234–35.

159. *Niles' Register* 4 (May 15, 1813), 182; ibid. 5 (January 8, 1814), 312; ibid. 6 (June 25, 1814), 279.

160. Ibid. 5 (October 16, 1813), 119; ibid. 5 (January 8, 1814), 312; ibid. 6 (April 30, 1814), 150; Scott, *Recollections of a Naval Life*, 3:118–20; Mahon, *War of 1812*, 122; Mahan, *Sea Power*, 2:157.

161. John Lovett to Joseph Alexander, July 17, 1813, in Bonney, *Legacy of Historical Gleanings*, 1:304.

162. William Jones to American navy captains, February 22, 1813, in ND (M149), reel 10. See also Edward K. Eckert, *The Navy Department in the War of 1812* (Gainesville, 1973), 21.

163. Samuel Evans to William Jones, April 20, 1813, and James Lawrence to William Jones, May 18, 1813, in ND (M125), reel 28.

164. Roosevelt, *Naval War*, 1:223–24.

165. Quoted in Mahan, *Sea Power*, 2:134. See also Roosevelt, *Naval War*, 1:225–26.

166. Broke to captain of the *Chesapeake*, June [1], 1813, in ND (M125), reel 29.

167. George Budd to William Jones, June 15, 1813, in *Niles' Register* 4 (July 3, 1813), 290–91; Broke to T. Bladen Capel, June 6, 1813, in *Naval Chronicle* 30 (July–December, 1813), 83–84; Halifax newspapers, reprinted in London *Times*, August 16 and 24, 1813; Roosevelt, *Naval War*, 1:226–43; Maclay, *United States Navy*, 1:450–68.

168. London *Morning Chronicle*, July 9, 1813.

169. *Naval Chronicle* 30 (July–December, 1813), 41; Maclay, *United States Navy*, 1:461.

170. Halifax underwriters to Broke, August 25, 1813, John W. Croker to Warren, July 9, 1813, and "Biographical Memoir of Sir Philip Bowes Vere Broke," in *Naval Chronicle* 30 (July–December, 1813), 398–99, 486; ibid. 33 (January–June, 1815), 17–19.

171. Salem *Gazette*, September 25, 1813.

172. Philip Freneau, "In Memory of James Lawrence, Esquire," in Pattee, *Poems of Philip Freneau*, 3:313–14.

173. Annapolis *Maryland Republican*, reprinted in Washington *National Intelligencer*, July 2, 1813.

174. Porter to Hamilton, October 14, 1812, in Dudley and Crawford, *Naval War*. 1:528.

175. Porter to Secretary of the Navy, July 3, 1814, in ND (M125), reel 37.

176. Ibid. See also David Porter, *Journal of a Cruise Made to the Pacific Ocean . . . in the Years 1812, 1813, and 1814,* 2 vols., 2nd ed. (New York, 1822), 2: 144–58.

177. Porter to Secretary of the Navy, July 3, 1814, in ND (M125), reel 37; Porter, *Journal of a Cruise*, 2:175; Hillyar to John W. Croker, March 30, 1814, in *Naval Chronicle* 32 (July–December, 1814), 168–70; Roosevelt, *Naval War*, 2:15–37.

178. Edward R. McCall to [Isaac Hull], September 7, 1813, in ND (M125), reel 31; Roosevelt, *Naval War*, 1:252–65; Mahan, *Sea Power*, 2:187–92, 216–19.

179. Quoted in Mahan, *Sea Power*, 2:20.

180. *Niles' Register* 6 (March 26, 1814), 69. See also London *Morning Chronicle*, December 1, 1814.

181. Quoted in Maclay, *American Privateers*, 275.

182. *Niles' Register* 5 (November 20, 1813), 200; ibid. 6 (June 18, 1814), 269; Coggeshall, *American Privateers*, 219–25.

Chapter 7: The Last Embargo

1. Speech of William H. Murfree, January 10, 1814, in *AC*, 13–2, 856; William Hunter to James A. Bayard, January 29, 1814, in Donnan, *Papers of*

James A. Bayard, 266. See also speech of Charles J. Ingersoll, February 14, 1814, in *AC*, 13–2, 1431.

2. Richard Rush to Charles J. Ingersoll, October 28, 1813, in Rush Papers (SR), reel 3.

3. Madison to Congress, December 7, 1813, in *AC*, 13–2, 538–44.

4. *Senate Journal,* 2:451–52, 470; Adams, *History,* 7:370.

5. Charles Goldsborough to Harmanus Bleecker, February 4, 1814, in Harrier Rice, *Harmanus Bleecker: An Albany Dutchman, 1779–1849* (Albany, 1924), 37; William R. Davie to John Steele, February 4, 1814, in Kemp P. Battle, ed., "Letters of William R. Davie," *James Sprunt Historical Monograph* 7 (1907), 74. See also John Hoffman to Virgil Maxcy, January 16, 1814, in Galloway-Maxcy-Marcoe Papers (LC); William Hunter to James A. Bayard, January 29, 1814, in Donnan, *Papers of James A. Bayard,* 266.

6. *Senate Journal,* 1:453–54, 471.

7. *AC,* 13–2, 1057.

8. *AC,* 13–2, 600, 631; Jeremiah Mason to Marsha Mason, February 10, 1814, in Hillard, *Jeremiah Mason,* 83.

9. Jones to Alexander Dallas, December 21, 1813 in Dallas Papers (HSP).

10. Dallas to Jones, February 3, 1814, in Jones Papers (HSP); *Senate Journal,* 1:471; Adams, *History,* 7:396–97.

11. Klein, "Memoirs of Jonathan Roberts," 366; Jones to Dallas, September 15, 1814, in Dallas Papers (HSP). For similar sentiments, see Nathaniel Macon to Joseph H. Nicholson, February 17, 1814, in Nicholson Papers (LC).

12. Macon to Nicholson, February 8, 1814, in Nicholson Papers (LC).

13. *AC,* 13–2, 766, 852–53, 1114–15, 2023–24; Pinkney to Madison, January 25, 1814, in Madison Papers (LC), reel 15.

14. Macon to Nicholson, February 17, 1814, in Nicholson Papers (LC).

15. *Senate Journal,* 2:472; Adams, *History,* 7:398–99.

16. Brant, *James Madison,* 6:243.

17. John A. Harper to William Plumer, November 1, 1812, in Plumer Papers (LC), reel 3.

18. Charles J. Ingersoll to Madison, January 5, 1814, in Madison Papers (LC), reel 15.

19. Dolley Madison to Hannah Gallatin, January 21, [1814], in Gallatin Papers (SR), reel 26; *Niles' Register* 7 (January 14, 1815), 320; Brant, *James Madison,* 6:243–44.

20. Memorial of Harrisburg merchants, [1814], and John Binns to Madison, July 11, 1814, in Madison Papers (LC), reel 16. See also Chandler C. Price to William Jones, February 14, 1814, in Jones Papers (HSP); Higginbotham, *Keystone in the Democratic Arch,* 285–86.

21. *AC,* 13–2, 1245–47, 1837–38; *Senate Journal,* 2:511; Brant, *James Madison,* 6:244–45.

22. John Smith to Gallatin, March 27, 1814, in Gallatin Papers (SR), reel 26. For similar sentiments, see Lexington *Reporter,* April 2, 1814.

23. Roberts to Alexander Dallas, December 12, 1813, in Dallas Papers (HSP).

24. Speech of William Baylies, February 24, 1814, in *AC*, 13–2, 1656. See also speeches of Elijah Brigham, January 20, 1814, and Artemas Ward, Jr., March 5, 1814, in *AC*, 13–2, 1061, 1818.

25. *AC*, 13–2, 939, 1054.

26. Speech of Thomas B. Robertson, January 15, 1814, in *AC*, 13–2, 982.

27. *AC*, 13–2, 939, 1056.

28. Speech of John C. Calhoun, January 15, 1814, in *AC*, 13–2, 995. See also speeches of Charles J. Ingersoll, January 15, 1814, and John Bowen, January 20, 1814, in *AC*, 13–2, 1005, 1071.

29. Speech of Zebulon R. Shipherd, January 17, 1814, in *AC*, 13–2, 1030.

30. Speech of James Fisk, January 13, 1814, in *AC*, 13–2, 934.

31. Speech of Felix Grundy, January 15, 1814, in *AC*, 13–2, 993. See also Baltimore *Whig*, reprinted in Richmond *Enquirer*, May 4, 1814.

32. *AC*, 13–2, 664, 1807–31.

33. Macon to Nicholson, January 24, 1814, in Nicholson Papers (LC); Washington *National Intelligencer*, January 28, 1814. Timothy Pickering delivered one speech (over two days) that lasted six hours. See speech of Timothy Pickering, February 26 and 28, 1814, in *AC*, 13–2, 1695, 1697–1767.

34. Macon to Nicholson, February 14, 1814, in Nicholson Papers (LC).

35. Washington *National Intelligencer*, December 28, 1813; Henry G. Conner, "William Lewis, 1778–1844," in William D. Lewis, ed., *Great American Lawyers*, 8 vols. (Philadelphia, 1907–9), 3:46.

36. Macon to Nicholson, January 8, 1814, in Nicholson Papers (LC).

37. Stagg, *Mr. Madison's War*, 366–67.

38. Monroe to Madison, December 27, 1813, in Madison Papers (LC), reel 26.

39. *AC*, 13–2, 597, 979, 2789–90.

40. Speech of Robert Wright, January 13, 1814, in *AC*, 13–2, 931. See also speech of Cyrus King, January 13, 1814, in *AC*, 13–2, 931.

41. *AC*, 13–2, 573, 623, 643, 1113–14, 1191, 1866, 2791–92, 2814–16; [Secretary of War] to George W. Campbell, January 14, 1814, in *NASP: MA*, 5:107; James Monroe to William Branch Giles, October 17, 1814, in *ASP: MA*, 1:514.

42. *AC*, 13–2, 764, 1931, 2847–50.

43. *AC*, 13–2, 881. See also speeches of George M. Troup, James Fisk, and Daniel Webster, January 10, 1814, in *AC*, 13–2, 881–83, 885–86.

44. Speech of Richard Stockton, January 10, 1814, in *AC*, 13–2, 881. For similar sentiments, see speeches of Thomas P. Grosvenor, Daniel Webster, and Alexander Hanson, January 10, 1814, in *AC*, 13–2, 883–87.

45. *AC*, 13–2, 887–88.

46. *AC*, 13–2, 633, 1803–4, 2799–2800.

47. Speeches of Jotham Post, Jr., Charles Goldsborough, Cyrus King, Alexander McKim, and William S. Smith, March 4, 1814, in *AC*, 13–2, 1802–3.

48. *AC*, 13–2, 614, 1807, 2804.

49. Speeches of Jotham Post, Jr., Artemas Ward, Jr., Charles Goldsborough, and Alexander McKim, March 5, 1814, in *AC*, 13–2, 1804–6.

50. John Mason to William Plumer, January 20, 1814, in Plumer Papers (LC), reel 2. See also Madison to Armstrong, November 15, 1813, in Madison Papers (LC), reel 27.

51. Speech of Alexander McKim, March 5, 1814, in *AC*, 13–2, 1805.

52. Report of the Secretary of the Treasury, January 8, 1814, in *ASP: F*, 2:651–53.

53. *AC*, 13–2, 645, 675, 1588–89, 1798, 2811–12, 2795–98.

54. Speech of Alexander Hanson, February 14, 1814, in *AC*, 13–2, 1374. See also speeches of Joseph Pearson, February 16, 1814, and Zebulon R. Shipherd, February 18, 1814, in *AC*, 13–2, 1447–53, 1504–7.

55. Speech of John C. Calhoun, February 25, 1813, in *AC*, 13–2, 1689; Washington *National Intelligencer*, March 12, 1814.

56. *AC*, 11–3, 346–47, 826; Hammond, *Banks and Politics*, 209–22.

57. Petition of inhabitants of New York City, December 18, 1813, in *AC*, 13–2, 873–74. See also Alexander Hanson to Robert Goodloe Harper, April 3, 1814, in Harper Papers (MdHS), reel 2.

58. *AC*, 13–2, 1578–85, 1949–54, 2023; Raymond Walters, Jr., "The Origins of the Second Bank of the United States," *Journal of Political Economy* 53 (June, 1945), 120.

59. Speeches of Zebulon R. Shipherd, June 18, 1813, and Solomon Sharp, June 19, 1813, in *AC*, 13–1, 236, 295; Philadelphia *United States' Gazette*, May 5, 1812; Charles S. Hall, *Benjamin Tallmadge, Revolutionary Soldier and American Businessman* (New York, 1943), 332.

60. Morison, *Harrison Gray Otis*, 2:66–67; John D. Forbes, *Israel Thorndike, Federalist Financier* (New York, 1953), 112–16.

61. Memorandum of James Lloyd, [April, 1814], and Charles W. Hare to Otis, April 13 and 26, 1814, in Morison, *Harrison Gray Otis*, 2:72–75; Otis to George Cabot, July 2, 1819, and Cabot to Otis, July 3, 1819, in [Harrison Gray Otis], *Letters in Defence of the Hartford Convention, and the People of Massachusetts* (Boston, 1824), 96–97.

62. Pickering to Rebecca Pickering, January 9, 1814, in Pickering Papers (MHS), reel 3. For similar sentiments, see Nathaniel Saltonstall, Jr., to Nathaniel Saltonstall, May 6, 1814, in Saltonstall Papers (EI).

63. See Boston *Independent Chronicle*, April 14, 1814; and Boston *Gazette*, April 14, 1814.

64. James Lloyd to Harrison Gray Otis, May 16, 1814, in Otis Papers (MHS); George Campbell to Madison, May 4, 1814, in Madison Papers (LC), reel 16; Madison to Campbell, May 7, 1814, in Hunt, *Writings of James Madison*, 8:277.

65. Georgetown *Federal Republican*, July 13, 1814; Report of the Secretary of the Treasury, September 23, 1814, in *ASP: F*, 2:845–46; petition of Jacob Barker, December 22, 1821, in *ASP: C*, 828.

66. Report of the Secretary of the Treasury, September 23, 1814, in *ASP: F*, 2:846–47.

67. Worcester *National Aegis*, January 5, 1814.

68. For prewar evasions of the non-importation act, see Thomas Coles to Gallatin, October 26 and December 4, 1811, John Barnes to Gallatin, Decem-

ber 27, 1811, and [Joseph Whipple] to Gallatin, February 18, 1812, in TD (M178), reels 26, 29, and 34; Albert Gallatin to Thomas Newton, November 26, 1811, in *ASP: C & N*, 1:873–74; L. Trescott to Henry Dearborn, August 21, 1811, Peter Sailly to Gallatin, September 10, 1811, Samuel Buck to Gallatin, October 18, 1811, Isaac Smith to Gallatin, November 15, 1811, and David Gelston to Gallatin, November 20, 1811, in *NASP: C & N*, 47: 510–11, 522, 529–30, 533; Gallatin to customs collectors, October 7, 1811, in Madison Papers (LC), reel 13.

69. Proclamation of John C. Sherbrooke, July 3, 1812, in Wood, *British Documents*, 1:204–5. See also Order of George Prevost, July 11, 1812, in *Niles' Register* 4 (March 20, 1813), 46.

70. Walter R. Copp, "Nova Scotian Trade during the War of 1812," *Canadian Historical Review* 18 (June, 1937), 141–55; John D. Forbes, "Boston Smuggling, 1807–1815," *American Neptune* 10 (April, 1950), 152.

71. Letter from Halifax, November 9, 1812, in Salem *Essex Register*, December 16, 1812. See also Henry A. S. Dearborn to Gallatin, September 8, 1812, in TD (M178), reel, 11; speech of Robert Wright, January 20, 1814, in *AC*, 13–2, 1089.

72. Joseph Whipple to Gallatin, June 20, 1812, in Gallatin Papers (SR), reel 25; J. Clason to Madison, December 17, 1813, in Madison Papers (LC), reel 15; Henry A. S. Dearborn to William Jones, October 22, 1813, in TD (M178), reel 12; George Ulmer to William King, January 10, 1813, in WD (M221), reel 52; Manuel Eyre to Jonathan Roberts, January 24, 1813, in Roberts Papers (HSP).

73. Quoted in Samuel Eliot Morison, *Harrison Gray Otis, 1765–1848: The Urbane Federalist* (Boston, 1969), 338. See also R. Kent Newmyer, "Joseph Story and the War of 1812: A Judicial Nationalist," *Historian* 26 (August, 1964), 489–98.

74. Boston *Columbian Centinel*, September 1, 1813. See also speech of Thomas P. Grosvenor, January 25, 1814, in *AC*, 13–2, 1138; Thomas Coles to Gallatin, July 27 and 31, 1813, in TD (M178), reel 29; Raymond Walters, Jr., *Alexander James Dallas: Lawyer—Politician—Financier, 1759–1817* (Philadelphia, 1943), 171–72.

75. Henry A.S. Dearborn to William Jones, September 21 and October 22, 1813, in TD (M178), reel 12; John Lawrence to Jonathan Russell, June 14, 1814, in Russell Papers (BU).

76. Henry A.S. Dearborn to William Jones, October 30, 1813, in TD (M178), reel 12.

77. George Ulmer to Henry Dearborn, March 3, 1813, in WD (M222), reel 9; Martin Jennison to John Armstrong, March 23, 1814, in WD (M221), reel 54; H.N. Muller III, "A 'Traitorous and Diabolic Traffic': The Commerce of the Champlain-Richelieu Corridor during the War of 1812," *Vermont History* 44 (Spring, 1976), 95–96; Barry J. Lohnes, "A New Look at the Invasion of Eastern Maine, 1814," *Maine Historical Society Quarterly* 15 (Summer, 1975), 8–9.

78. Gallatin to Abraham Bessent, March 17, 1812, in TD (M175), reel 2.

See also Hugh Campbell to Paul Hamilton, January 4, 1812, in ND (M125), reel 23; Edward Channing, *A History of the United States*, 6 vols. (New York, 1905–25), 4:540–41.

79. William J. McIntosh to William H. Crawford, April 18, 1813, TD (M178), reel 38.

80. See Jane Lucas de Grummond, *The Baratarians and the Battle of New Orleans* (Baton Rouge, 1961), passim.

81. John Shaw to Paul Hamilton, October 27, 1812, in ND (M125), reel 25.

82. [John Windship] to William Plumer, Jr., April 2, 1814, in Plumer Papers (NHHS), reel 2.

83. Daniel Patterson to William Jones, November 22, 1813, in ND (M147), reel 5.

84. Undated newspaper clipping, in WD (M221), reel 54; Wilburt S. Brown, *The Amphibious Campaign for West Florida and Louisiana, 1814–1815: A Critical Review of Strategy and Tactics at New Orleans* (University, AL, 1969), 40.

85. T.H. Williams to Wilkinson, March 14, 1813, in WD (M222), reel 9.

86. Shaw to Hamilton, January 18, 1813, in ND (M125), reel 26.

87. Jones to P.T. Du Bourg, September 27, 1813, in TD (M178), reel 16. See also Jones to Du Bourg, August 24, 1813, ibid.

88. Hart Massey to Gallatin, March, 1812, in TD (M178), reel 31.

89. Cornelius Van Ness, quoted in Muller, "Commerce of the Champlain-Richelieu Corridor," 86. See also John Chandler to Armstrong, March 3, 1813, in WD (M222), reel 7; Keene *Newhampshire Sentinel,* November 6, 1813; Chilton Williamson, *Vermont in Quandary: 1763–1825* (Montpelier, 1949), 275.

90. Pike to Armstrong, February 15, 1813, in WD (M221), reel 55.

91. George Ulmer to Armstrong, March 29, 1813, ibid., reel 58.

92. "Marcellus" to Armstrong, [early 1814], in WD (M222), reel 10.

93. Henry A. S. Dearborn to William Jones, December 16, 1813, in TD (M178), reel 12.

94. Lexington *Reporter,* August 7, 1813.

95. Thomas Coles to William Jones, January 27, 1814, in TD (M178), reel 29; John Smith to Madison, January 24, 1814, and Cushing Eells to Madison, May 17, 1813, in Madison Papers (LC), reel 15; Caesar Rodney to Gallatin (with enclosure), March 20, 1813, in Gallatin Papers (SR), reel 26; William Hawkins to James Iredell, October 8, 1813, in Iredell Papers (DU); Boston *Independent Chronicle,* July 5, 1813; Pack, *George Cockburn,* 151, 159.

96. Henry A.S. Dearborn to William Jones, December 16, 1813, in TD (M178), reel 12.

97. H. Crittenden to Lewis Cass, November 5, 1814, in WD (M222), reel 10; Muller, "Commerce of the Champlain-Richelieu Corridor," 83, 87.

98. Quoted in John P. Cranwell and William B. Crane, *Men of Marque: A History of Private Armed Vessels out of Baltimore during the War of 1812* (New York, 1940), 72. See also Alan S. Taylor, "The Smuggling Career of William King," *Maine Historical Society Quarterly* 17 (Summer, 1977), 19–38.

99. Georgetown *Federal Republican,* May 3 and 31, 1813. Quotation from May 3 issue.

100. Charles Goldsborough to Harmanus Bleecker, April 27, 1813, in Rice, *Harmanus Bleecker*, 31–34.

101. Madison to Congress, December 9, 1813, in *AC*, 13–2, 2031–32.

102. Washington *National Intelligencer*, December 28, 1813. See also Georgetown *Federal Republican*, December 1, 1813; Jeremiah Mason to Jesse Appleton, December 21, 1813, in Hillard, *Jeremiah Mason*, 69–70; Resolutions of Tennessee Legislature [late 1813], in Lexington *Reporter*, January 1, 1814. The three men were William Branch Giles of Virginia, David Stone of North Carolina, and Joseph Anderson of Tennessee.

103. *AC*, 13–2, 551–61, 2032–53.

104. Speech of Zebulon R. Shipherd, February 9, 1814, in *AC*, 13–2, 1266; Memorial of Maryland House of Delegates, [January, 1814], in *AC*, 13–2, 1208.

105. Washington *National Intelligencer*, December 28, 1813.

106. *AC*, 13–2, 554, 2053, 2781–88.

107. Speech of Jeremiah Mason, December 16, 1813, in *AC*, 13–2, 555.

108. *AC*, 13–2, 2781–88.

109. Jones to Customs Collectors, December 24, 1813, in *Niles' Register* 5 (January 29, 1814), 353–54.

110. *AC*, 13–2, 594, 639, 1121–22, 1269, 2788–89, 2793–95. See also speeches of Cyrus King, January 18, 1814, and John Reed, January 22, 1814, in *AC*, 13–2, 1048, 1117–21; Gideon Granger to Madison, January 4, 1814, in Madison Papers (LC), reel 15.

111. Henry A.S. Dearborn to William Jones, January 4, 1814, in TD (M178), reel 12.

112. Petition of Boston Fishermen, [January, 1814], printed in Boston *Columbian Centinel*, February 2, 1814.

113. Speech of Richard Stockton, December 11, 1813, in *AC*, 13–2, 2037.

114. Adams, *History* 7:370.

115. See *AC*, 13–2, 613, 678–79, 773–74, 1134–35, 1144, 1229.

116. *AC*, 13–2, 682, 1867–68. See also speech of John C. Calhoun, April 4, 1814, in *AC*, 13–2, 1946–47; circular letters of Thomas K. Harris, April 15, 1814, Israel Pickens, April 16, 1814, and John Sevier, April 20, 1814, in Noble E. Cunningham, Jr., ed., *Circular Letters of Congressmen to Their Constituents, 1789–1829*, 3 vols. (Chapel Hill, 1978), 2:878–81, 889, 901.

117. Speech of Robert Wright, March 2, 1814, in *AC*, 13–2, 1772.

118. Madison to Congress, March 31, 1814, in *AC*, 13–2, 694.

119. Salem *Essex Register*, April 16, 1814. For similar sentiments, see Washington *National Intelligencer*, April 7, 1814; Lexington *Reporter*, April 15, 1814; Edward Gray to William Jones, April 4, 1814, in Jones Papers (HSP).

120. Circular letter of William Gaston, April 19, 1814, in Cunningham, *Circular Letters*, 2:896; Nathaniel Macon to Joseph H. Nicholson, March 3, 1814, in Nicholson Papers (LC).

121. Nicholas Gilman to Pierre Van Cortlandt, Jr., April 3, 1814, in Jacob Judd, ed., *Van Cortlandt Family Papers*, 4 vols. (Tarrytown, 1976–81), 3:696.

122. *Niles' Register* 6 (April 9, 1814), 100.

123. Macon to Joseph H. Nicholson, April 6, 1814, in Nicholson Papers (LC).

124. *AC*, 13–2, 741, 2001–2, 2830.

125. *AC*, 13–2, 773, 2017–18.

126. Speeches of John C. Calhoun and Elisha R. Potter, April 12, 1814, in *AC*, 13–2, 2012–13.

127. There is a good discussion of America's treatment of enemy aliens in Dwight F. Henderson, *Congress, Courts, and Criminals: The Development of Federal Criminal Law, 1801–1829* (Westport, 1985), ch. 5.

128. See returns of marshals, in SD (M588), reels 2–3. The returns indicate that around 4,000 enemy aliens lived in New York and about 2,000 in Pennsylvania. Another 4,000 were probably scattered through the rest of the country. Though these returns are far from complete, they contain considerable data on each alien and thus offer excellent material for a quantitative study.

129. See *AC*, 5–1, 3753–54. This law should not be confused with the more infamous alien act, which authorized the deportation of aliens in time of peace and expired in 1802.

130. The grace period was established by a provision in the enemy trade act. See *AC*, 12–1, 2356.

131. State Department Notice, July 7, 1812, in Richard Bache, ed., *The Case of Alien Enemies, Considered and Decided upon a Writ of Habeas Corpus, Allowed on the Petition of Charles Lockington, an Enemy Alien, by the Hon. William Tilghman . . . The 22nd Day of November, 1813* (Philadelphia, 1813), iii-iv. Most of the government's regulations on enemy aliens are printed in this pamphlet, which can be found in SD (M588), reel 3.

132. Monroe to Anthony Baker, December 30, 1812, in Foreign Office Papers 5/88 (PRO); Monroe to American commissioners, January 30, 1814, in Gallatin Papers (SR), reel 26; John Graham to John Mason, October 12, 1814, in SD (M588), reel 4.

133. State Department Notice, February 23, 1813, and Monroe to U.S. marshals, March 12, 1813, in Bache, *Case of Alien Enemies*, v, vii.

134. Monroe to Thomas Barclay, May 13, 1813, in SD (M588), reel 1.

135. State Department Notice, February 6, 1813, and Monroe to U.S. marshals, February 6, 1813, in Bache, *Case of Alien Enemies*, v, vii.

136. Monroe to William Johnson, February 16, 1814, in SD (M588), reel 5.

137. Mason to U.S. marshals, November 12, 1813, in Bache, *Case of Alien Enemies*, viii.

138. The best study on prisoners in this war is Anthony G. Dietz, "The Prisoner of War in the United States during the War of 1812" (Ph.D. dissertation, American University, 1964), which is practically definitive for the American side of the story. For the British side, see Ira Dye, "American Maritime Prisoners of War, 1812–1815," *Proceedings of the North American Society of Oceanic History, March 19–20, 1977, at Peabody Museum of Salem, Massachusetts,* ed. Clark G. Reynolds (n.p., n.d.); and Reginald Horsman, "The Paradox of Dartmoor Prison," *American Heritage* 26 (February, 1975), 13–17, 85.

139. See, for example, Isaac Baker to James Winchester, February 26, 1813,

in WD (M221), reel 50; statement of Abraham Walter, November 22, 1813, in Worcester *National Aegis,* December 22, 1813; "Thomas King's Narrative," in Salem *Essex Register,* November 6, 1813; statement of W. L. Churchill et al., [Fall, 1814], in *Niles' Register* 8 (April 22, 1815), 129; statement of John Stewart and Charles Lyford, October 3, 1813, William M. Scott to C. K. Gardner, October 8, 1813, and Thomas Barclay to John Mason, December 21, 1813, in Wood, *British Documents,* 3:814–17, 834–35.

140. Dietz, "Prisoner of War," passim; Dye, "Maritime Prisoners," passim.

141. Reuben Beasley to Jonathan Russell, October 23, 1812, in Russell Papers (BU); British Transport Office to [Beasley], May 26, 1813, and Beasley to Monroe, June 10, 1813, in *NASP: NA,* 8:24–25, 40; Dye, "Maritime Prisoners," 8; Roosevelt, *Naval War,* 1:77n.

142. Isaac Hull to Paul Hamilton, June 20, 1812, in ND (M125), reel 24; Hamilton to Hull, July 1, 1812, in ND (M149), reel 10; Christopher Gadsden to [Secretary of the Navy], July 4, 1812, in ND (M147), reel 4.

143. Porter to Hamilton, June 28, 1812, in ND (M147), reel 3; Hamilton to Porter, June 30, 1812, in ND (M149), reel 10.

144. Dietz, "Prisoner of War," 17, 41–42, 348–52, 378; Dye, "Maritime Prisoners," 2, 8–9.

145. Provisional Agreement for Exchange of Prisoners, November 28, 1812, in *NASP: NA,* 8:14–16; Dietz, "Prisoner of War," 28–34.

146. Cartel for Exchange of Prisoners, May 12, 1813, in *NASP: NA,* 8:19–22; Dietz, "Prisoner of War," 35–47. Quotation from p. 19.

147. Dietz, "Prisoner of War," 47–50; Dye, "Maritime Prisoners," 10, 15.

148. Thomas Barclay to Prevost, December 20, 1813, in Wood, *British Documents,* 3:830–31; Dietz, "Prisoner of War," 22.

149. Robert Goodloe Harper, *Speech . . . Delivered at Annapolis, January 20, 1814* (Boston, 1814), 77; Ralph Robinson, "Retaliation for the Treatment of Prisoners in the War of 1812," *American Historical Review* 49 (October, 1943), 65; Dietz, "Prisoner of War," 258–59.

150. Scott to Secretary of War, January 30, 1813, in *ASP: FR,* 3:634.

151. *AC,* 12–2, 90, 1145–46, 1362–63; Armstrong to Henry Dearborn, May 15, 1813, *ASP: FR,* 3:635; Robinson, "Retaliation," 65–67.

152. Prevost to James Wilkinson, October 17, 1813, in *ASP: FR,* 3:635.

153. Wilkinson to Prevost, December 3, 1813, and Prevost to Wilkinson, December 11, 1813, in *ASP: FR,* 3:637–38; Dietz, "Prisoner of War," 277.

154. London *Courier,* quoted in Adams, *History,* 7:362; London *Times,* January 27, 1814. See also London *Times,* December 25, 1813.

155. Memorial of Maryland House of Delegates [January, 1814], in *AC,* 13–2, 1205; Gouverneur Morris to Rufus King [Spring, 1814], in Anne C. Morris, ed., *The Diary and Letters of Gouverneur Morris,* 2 vols. (New York, 1888), 2:565. For similar sentiments, see Timothy Pickering to James Pindall, January 27, 1814, in Pickering Papers (MHS), reel 15; Sermon of Rev. Latrop, printed in Boston *New-England Palladium,* February 25, 1814; speech of William Gaston, February 18, 1814, in *AC,* 13–2, 1560.

156. Worcester *National Aegis,* December 8, 1813.

157. Ibid., January 19, 1814; statements of Francis Blake and James Prince, in Boston *Columbian Centinel,* January 19, 26, 29, and February 5, 1814; Boston *New-England Palladium,* February 11, 1814; *Niles' Register* 5 (January 29, 1814), 359–61; ibid. 6 (March 12, 1814), 38–39; Thomas Walter Ward to James Prince, January 17, 1814, in Ward Papers (AAS); broadside, [January, 1814], in Miscellaneous Broadside Collection (AAS); J. Snelling to Armstrong, January 13, 1814, in WD (M221), reel 57; Dietz, "Prisoner of War," 170.

158. Speech of Langdon Cheves, February 24, 1814, in *AC,* 13–2, 1649.

159. Winder to Madison, February 1 and 8, 1814, and Monroe to Winder, May 7, 1814, in Madison Papers (LC), reels 15 and 26; Prevost to Monroe, May 31, 1814, in Wood, *British Documents,* 3:842–44; Robinson, "Retaliation," 68–69; Dietz, "Prisoner of War," 292–96.

160. John Mason to Armstrong, July 25, 1814, in WD (M222), reel 12; Reuben Beasley to Mason, March 18, 1814, in *ASP: FR,* 3:727; Convention with Supplementary Article, July 16, 1814, and Prevost to Barclay, July 31, 1814, in Wood, *British Documents,* 3:844–48; Robinson, "Retaliation," 69–70; Dietz, "Prisoner of War," 296–99, 336–37.

161. See documents in *ASP: FR,* 3:632–34; Dietz, "Prisoner of War," 224–68.

162. *AC,* 13–2, 979, 1113, 1797–98.

163. Madison to Congress, December 7, 1813, in *AC,* 13–2, 542.

164. *AC,* 13–2, 545, 785; Adams, *History,* 7:395.

165. Madison to Congress, March 31, 1814, in *AC,* 13–2, 694.

166. Speech of Daniel Webster, April 6, 1814, in *AC,* 13–2, 1972.

167. Ibid., 1969.

Chapter 8: The British Counteroffensive

1. Leo Gershoy, *The French Revolution and Napoleon,* 2nd ed. (New York, 1964), 513–21.

2. See Guillaume de Bertier de Sauvigny, "The American Press and the Fall of Napoleon in 1814," *Proceedings of the American Philosophical Society* 98 (October, 1954), 337–76. See also Hartford *Connecticut Courant,* June 14, 1814; and William H. Channing, *Memoir of William Ellery Channing,* 3 vols. (London, 1848), 2:98–99.

3. Jefferson to Samuel Brown, April 28, 1814 in Jefferson Papers (LC), reel 47. See also Gallatin to Marquis de Lafayette, April 21, 1814, in Gallatin Papers, Supplement (SR), reel 3; speech of William Gaston, February 18, 1814, in *AC,* 13–2, 1557.

4. William Wirt to Dabney Carr, February 15, 1814, in Wirt Papers (MdHS), reel 2; Philip Nicholas to Wilson Cary Nicholas, July 13, 1814, in Nicholas Papers (LC); Rutland (VT) *Herald,* June 1, 1814.

5. Joseph H. Nicholson to William Jones, May 20, 1814, in Jones Papers (HSP). See also Hartford *American Mercury,* June 7, 1814; Philadelphia *Aurora,* June 8, 1814; speech of George M. Troup, February 8, 1814, in *AC,* 13–2, 1256; [John Armstrong] to state governors, July 4, 1814, in *ASP: MA,* 1:549.

6. *Niles' Register* 7 (September 10, 1814), 2, 11; Boston *Yankee*, October 28, 1814; Trenton *True American*, November 28, 1814; Philadelphia *United States' Gazette*, reprinted in Georgetown *Federal Republican*, November 19, 1814.

7. Mahon, *War of 1812*, 317; C. P. Stacey, ed., "An American Plan for a Canadian Campaign: Secretary James Monroe to Major General Jacob Brown, February, 1815," *American Historical Review* 46 (January, 1941), 352; Brown, *Amphibious Campaign*, 93.

8. Cochrane, quoted in Mahan, *Sea Power*, 2:330–31; London *Times*, May 24, 1814.

9. Letter from a congressman, January 8, 1815, in Lexington *Reporter*, February 8, 1815. See also Jacob Brown to Secretary of War, May 8, 1814, in Brown Papers (LC).

10. See Monroe to Giles, November 10, 1814, in *ASP: MA*, 1:519; Hartford *American Mercury*, March 22, 1814.

11. Estimate based on figures in Stagg, "Enlisted Men in the United States Army," 621.

12. Cabinet notes, June 7, 1814, in Madison Papers (LC), reel 16; Secretary of War to Jacob Brown, March 20 and June 10, 1814, and to George Izard, June 10, 1814, in WD (M6), reel 7; Secretary of War to George Izard, May 14, 1814, in Izard, *Official Correspondence*, 15–16; Armstrong to Jacob Brown, June 19, 1814, in Cruikshank, *Documents Relating to the Invasion of Jacob Brown*, 35–37.

13. Commodore Chauncey's estimate of naval forces on Lake Ontario, [1814], in Jacob Brown Papers (LC); C. Winton-Clare, "A Shipbuilder's War," in Zaslow, *Defended Border*, 167; C.P. Stacey, "Naval Power on the Lakes, 1812–1814," in Mason, *After Tippecanoe*, 56; Roosevelt, *Naval War*, 2:86–87.

14. Arthur Sinclair to William Jones, June 22, and July 3 and 22, 1814, in ND (M125), reels 37 and 38; A. H. Holmes to George Croghan, July 27, 1814, and Croghan to Armstrong, August 9, 1814, in WD (M221), reel 60.

15. Sinclair to Jones, August 9, 1814, in ND (M125), reel 38.

16. Ibid.; Croghan to Armstrong, August 9, 1814, in WD (M221), reel 60; Robert McDouall to George Prevost, August 14, 1814, in Wood, *British Documents*, 3:273–77; Gilpin, *War of 1812 in the Northwest*, 242–45.

17. McDouall to Gordon Drummond, September 9, 1814, and A. H. Bugler to McDouall, September 7, 1814, in Wood, *British Documents*, 3:277–81.

18. John B. Campbell to John B. Walbach, May 18, 1814, in WD (M221), reel 51.

19. Narrative of Alexander McMullen, in Cruikshank, *Niagara Frontier*, 2:370.

20. Campbell to Walbach, May 18, 1814, in WD (M221), reel 51; deposition of Mathias Steele, May 31, 1814, opinion of court of enquiry, June 20, 1814, and Narrative of Alexander McMullen, in Cruikshank, *Niagara Frontier*, 1:16–18, and 2:369–71; Thomas Talbot to Phineas Riall, May 16, 1814, and Drummond to Prevost, May 27, 1814, in Wood, *British Documents*, 3:88–92.

21. George Mitchell to Jacob Brown, May 8, 1814, and Brown to Armstrong, May 9, 1814, in WD (M221), reel 51; Drummond to Prevost, May 7,

1814, and George Yeo to John W. Croker, May 9, 1814, in Wood, *British Documents*, 3:52–57, 61–63.

22. Melancthon Woolsey to Isaac Chauncey, June 1, 1814, and Chauncey to William Jones, June 2, 1814, in ND (M125), reel 37; William Carpenter to Peter B. Porter, June 1, 1814, in Porter Papers (BEHS), reel 3; Drummond to Prevost, June 2, 1814, in Wood, *British Documents*, 3:73–75.

23. George Howard to Sarah Howard, May 22, 1814, in George Howard Journal (CHS); Lossing, *Field-Book of the War of 1812*, 806.

24. Brown to Armstrong, July 6, 1814, and Brown, "Memoranda of . . . the Campaign on the Niagara in 1814," 1–7, in Brown Papers (LC); Peter B. Porter to Daniel D. Tompkins, July 3, 1814, in Cruikshank, *Niagara Frontier*, 1:26.

25. Quoted in Mahon, *War of 1812*, 269.

26. Brown to Secretary of War, July 7, 1814, in WD (M221), reel 59; Brown, "Memoranda of . . . the Campaign on the Niagara in 1814," 8–24; Thomas Jesup, "Memoir of the Campaigns on the Niagara," in Jesup Papers (LC); Riall to Drummond, July 6, 1814, and Porter to W. L. Stone, May 26, 1840, in Cruikshank, *Niagara Frontier*, 1:31–32, and 2:362–65; Kimball, "Battle of Chippewa," 169–86.

27. Brown to Chauncey, July 13, 1814, in Brown Papers (LC).

28. Chauncey to Brown, August 10, 1814, in ND (M125), reel 38. See also Chauncey to Jones, August 10, 1814 (2 letters), ibid.; Brown to Armstrong, July 25, 1814, in Brown Papers (LC).

29. Letter from Halifax newspaper, reprinted in *Niles' Register* 7 (February 25, 1815), 410.

30. Letter of James Miller, July 28, 1814, in Cruikshank, *Niagara Frontier*, 1:105.

31. Brown to Armstrong, [August 7, 1814], in WD (M221), reel 59; Brown to Judge Barker, August 7, 1814, in Brown Papers (LC); Brown, "Memoranda of . . . the Campaign on the Niagara in 1814," 24–50; Jesup, "Memoir of the Campaigns on the Niagara"; letter of James Miller, July 28, 1814, and Drummond to Prevost, July 27, 1814, in Cruikshank, *Niagara Frontier*, 1:87–92, 105–6.

32. John Tucker to Henry Conran, August 4, 1814, in Cruikshank, *Niagara Frontier*, 1:120.

33. Drummond to Prevost, August 4, 1814, and Tucker to Conran, August 4, 1814, ibid., 116, 120; Lodowick Morgan to Brown, August 5, 1814, in Brannan, *Official Letters*, 383–84.

34. Secret Orders of August 14, 1815, in Cruikshank, *Niagara Frontier*, 1:139–41.

35. Edmund P. Gaines to Armstrong, August 23, 1814, in WD (M221), reel 61.

36. Ibid.

37. Drummond to Prevost, August 15, 1814, in Cruikshank, *Niagara Frontier*, 1:142.

38. Jesup, "Memoir of the Campaigns on the Niagara"; Drummond to

Prevost, August 15, 1814, and Ripley to Gaines, August 17, 1814, in Cruikshank, *Niagara Frontier*, 1:141–44, 156–58; Gaines to Armstrong, August 23, 1814, in Brannan, *Official Letters*, 394–99; Ernest A. Cruikshank, "Drummond's Night Assault upon Fort Erie, August 15–16, 1814," in Zaslow, *Defended Border*, 154–64.

39. Brown to Secretary of War, September 29, 1814, in WD (M221), reel 59.

40. Brown to Secretary of War, September 29, 1814, and Peter B. Porter to Brown, September 22, 1814, ibid.; Drummond to Prevost, August 21, and September 2 and 17, 1814, and Louis de Watteville to Drummond, September 19, 1814, in Cruikshank, *Niagara Frontier*, 1:183, 190–91, 201–4.

41. Jesup, "Memoir of the Campaigns on the Niagara."

42. Brown to Tompkins, September 20, 1814, in Brown Papers (LC).

43. George Izard to Secretary of War, November 8, 1814, in WD (M221), reel 62.

44. Quoted in Lucas, *Canadian War of 1812*, 196–97.

45. [Frederick Robinson] to Merry, September 22, 1814, in Francis Bickley, ed., *Report on the Manuscripts of Earl Bathurst, Preserved at Cirencester Park* (London, 1923), 291.

46. Everest, *War of 1812 in the Champlain Valley*, 161–62.

47. Secretary of War to Izard, July 27 and August 12, 1814, in Izard, *Official Correspondence*, 64–65, 69–71. See also Armstrong to Brown, August 16, 1814, in Brown Papers (LC).

48. General Orders of September 5, 1814, in Plattsburgh *Republican*, September 24, 1814.

49. Alexander Macomb to Secretary of War, September 15, 1814, in WD (M221), reel 64. See also Macomb to Secretary of War, September 8, 1814, ibid.

50. Macomb to Secretary of War, September 15, 1814, ibid.

51. For the capture of the *Eagle* and *Growler*, see chapter 6: The Campaign of 1813.

52. Testimony of Henry Cox, in Wood, *British Documents*, 3:421; Roosevelt, *Naval War*, 2:109–15.

53. *Niles' Register* 7 (October 1, 1814), 48.

54. Mahon, *War of 1812*, 324–25; Roosevelt, *Naval War*, 2:128.

55. James Robertson to Daniel Pring, September 12, 1814, in Wood, *British Documents*, 3:374.

56. Thomas Macdonough to William Jones, September 11, 1814, in ND (M125), reel 39. See also Charles Budd to Macdonough, September 13, 1814, and Macdonough to Jones, September 13, 1814, ibid.; Pring to Yeo, September 12, 1814, Robertson to Pring, September 12, 1814, and statement of Robertson, in Wood, *British Documents*, 3:368–77, 468–75; Macdonough, *Thomas Macdonough*, 157–93; Everest, *War of 1812 in the Champlain Valley*, 179–85.

57. [Frederick Robinson] to Merry, September 22, 1814, in Bickley, *Manuscripts of Earl Bathurst*, 292.

58. Quoted in Everest, *War of 1812 in the Champlain Valley*, 187.

59. Macomb to Secretary of War, September 12 and 15, 1814, in WD (M221), reel 64; Prevost to Bathurst, September 22, 1814, in Wood, *British Documents*, 3:364–66; Everest, *War of 1812 in the Champlain Valley*, 185–90.

60. Bathurst to Henry Goulburn, September 1, 1814, in Goulburn Papers (UM), reel 1; Dudley Mills, "The Duke of Wellington and the Peace Negotiations at Ghent in 1814," *Canadian Historical Review* 2 (March, 1921), 22.

61. Alicia Cockburn to Charles Sandys, October 20, 1814, in Wood, *British Documents*, 3:387–88; London *Morning Chronicle*, November 18, 1814. See also speech of Samuel Whitbread, November 18, 1814, in *Parliamentary Debates*, 29:364–65; *The Annual Register . . . for the Year 1814* (London, 1815), *[General History]*, 191; Lord Liverpool to Lord Castlereagh, October 21, 1814, in Duke of Wellington, ed., *Dispatches, Correspondence, and Memoranda of Field Marshall Arthur, Duke of Wellington*, 15 vols. (London, 1858–72), 9:367.

62. AC, 13–3, 23, 387, 1962–63; Macdonough, *Thomas Macdonough*, 193.

63. Quoted in Glenn Tucker, *Poltroons and Patriots: A Popular Account of the War of 1812*, 2 vols. (Indianpolis, 1954), 2:636.

64. Quoted in Lohnes, "Invasion of Eastern Maine," 9.

65. Perley Putnam to Henry Dearborn, July 12, 1814, and John Brewer to Armstrong, July 16, 1814, in WD (M221), reels 59 and 61; Charles Morris to William Jones, September 8 and 20, 1814, in ND (M125), reel 39; Andrew Pilkington to John Sherbrooke, July 12, 1814, Sherbrooke to Bathurst, September 10, 1814, Henry John to Sherbrooke, September 3, 1814, Robert Barrie to Edward Griffith, September 3, 1814, and Pilkington to Sherbrooke, September 14, 1814, in Wood, *British Documents*, 3:301–3, 308–18, 323–27, 329–31; William D. Williamson, *The History of the State of Maine*, 2 vols. (Hallowell, 1832), 2:640–51.

66. Proclamation of John Sherbrooke and Edward Griffith, September 21, 1814, in *Niles' Register* 7 (October 29, 1814), 117–18; Williamson, *History of Maine*, 2:650–53; John Abbott, *The History of Maine* (Boston, 1875), 420–23.

67. Salem *Essex Register*, August 3, 1814.

68. Strong to Secretary of War, December 9, 1814, in WD (M221), reel 66.

69. Secretary of War to Dearborn, November 14 (filed under November 22) and December 19, 1814, Monroe to Strong, December 1, 1814, and Monroe to William King, January 2, 1815, in WD (M6), reels 7 and 8; Monroe to King, December 26, 1814, in WD (M7), reel 1; Caleb Strong to Harrison G. Otis, Thomas H. Perkins, and William Sullivan, January 31, 1815, in Otis Papers (MHS); Lohnes, "Invasion of Eastern Maine," 17; Williamson, *History of Maine*, 2:653–54.

70. Robert Ross, quoted in Adams, *History*, 8:124.

71. Prevost, quoted ibid., 125.

72. Ibid., 127.

73. Jones to Barney, August 20 and 27, 1813, in ND (M149), reel 11.

74. Richmond *Enquirer*, April 30, 1814; Decius Wadsworth to Armstrong, June 26, 1814, in WD (M221), reel 67; William Barney to William Jones, June

11, 13, and 25, 1814, in Brannan, *Official Letters*, 340–43; William M. Marine, *The British Invasion of Maryland, 1812–1815*, ed. Louis H. Dielman (Baltimore, 1913), 58–69.

75. Georgetown *Federal Republican*, August 11, 1814.

76. Armstrong, quoted in John P. Van Ness to Richard M. Johnson, November 23, 1814, in *ASP: MA*, 1:581.

77. Armstrong to Johnson, October 17, 1814, in *ASP: MA*, 1:539.

78. Skeen, *John Armstrong*, 187–90. See also John S. Williams, *History of the Invasion and Capture of Washington* (New York, 1857), 15–123.

79. John Harvey to Edward Baynes, June 11, 1813, in Cruikshank, *Niagara Frontier*, 6:68; General Order of July 2, 1814, in *ASP: MA*, 1:549; Adams, *History*, 8:122.

80. Skeen, *John Armstrong*, 191–97; Walter Lord, *The Dawn's Early Light* (New York, 1972), 22–27.

81. Quoted in Mahon, *War of 1812*, 291.

82. Robert Ross to Bathurst, August 30, 1814, in London *Times*, September 28, 1814.

83. Statement of James Monroe, November 13, 1814, in *ASP: MA*, 1:536.

84. Memorandum of James Madison, August 24, 1814, in Madison Papers (LC), reel 16; statement of James Monroe, November 13, 1814, and Report of Tobias Stansbury, November 15, 1814, in *ASP: MA*, 1:536–37, 561.

85. [George R. Gleig], *A Subaltern in America, Comprising His Narrative of the Campaigns of the British Army . . . during the Late War* (Philadelphia, 1833), 66–67.

86. See, for example, notice of a new poem, "Bladensburg Races, or, The Devil Take the Foremost," in Georgetown *Federal Republican*, January 7, 1815.

87. Ross to Bathurst, August 30, 1814, in London *Times*, September 28, 1814.

88. William Winder to Armstrong, August 27, 1814, in Brannan, *Official Letters*, 400–402; Narrative of William Winder, September 26, 1814, and Barney to Jones, August 29, 1814, in *ASP: MA*, 1:557–58, 579–80; Ross to Bathurst, August 30, 1814, in *Niles' Register* 7 (December 31, 1814), 277–78; Bulletin of Admiralty, September 27, 1814, in *Naval Chronicle* 32 (July–December, 1814), 247–49; Ingersoll, *Historical Sketch*, 2:156–80; Tucker, *Poltroons and Patriots*, 2:501–51; Lord, *Dawn's Early Light*, 59–143.

89. Dolley Madison to Anna Cutts, August 23, 1814, in Lucia B. Cutts, ed., *Memoirs and Letters of Dolley Madison* (Boston, 1887), 110–11; Tucker, *Poltroons and Patriots*, 2:570–74.

90. S. Burch and J. T. Frost to Patrick Magruder, September 15, 1814, in *AC*, 13–3, 307. See also Magruder to Speaker of the House, December 17, 1814, in *AC*, 13–3, 953–57.

91. Memorandum of [James Monroe], [August, 1814], in Madison Papers (LC), reel 16; Brant, *James Madison*, 6:306–8; Tucker, *Poltroons and Patriots*, 2:574–75; Lord, *Dawn's Early Light*, 151–53.

92. G. C. Moore Smith, ed., *The Autobiography of Lieutenant-General Sir Harry Smith*, 2 vols. (London, 1902), 1:200. See also [George R. Gleig], *A Narrative of the Campaigns of the British Army at Washington, Baltimore, and New Orleans*

(Philadelphia, 1821), 134–35; letter from midshipman on H.M.S. *Espoir*, in *Niles' Register* 7 (Supplement), 150.

93. William Wirt to Elizabeth Wirt, October 24, 1814, in Wirt Papers (MdHS), reel 2.

94. Mrs. A. Peter to Timothy Pickering, August 28, 1814, in Pickering Papers (MHS), reel 30; Cockburn to Cochrane, August 27, 1814, in London *Times*, September 28, 1814; Scott, *Recollections of a Naval Life*, 3:298–312; Ingersoll, *Historical Sketch*, 2:180–210.

95. Letter of William Thornton, August 30, 1814, in Washington *National Intelligencer*, September 7, 1814; Ingersoll, *Historical Sketch*, 2:184.

96. Thomas Tingey to William Jones, August 27 and October 18, 1814, in ND (M125), reels 38 and 40; Dudley and Crawford, *Naval War*, 1:91, 128.

97. Washington *National Intelligencer*, August 30 and 31, 1814. See also letter from Washington, August 27, [1814], in Philadelphia *Aurora*, August 30, 1814; Margaret Bayard Smith to Jane Kirkpatrick, August, [1814], in Gaillard Hunt, ed., *The First Forty Years of Washington Society, Portrayed by the Family Letters of Mrs. Samuel Harrison Smith (Margaret Bayard)* (New York, 1906), 113.

98. [Gleig], *Narrative of the Campaigns*, 132.

99. Washington *National Intelligencer*, September 1, 1814; [Gleig], *Narrative of the Campaigns*, 132–33, 140–41; Scott, *Recollections of a Naval Life*, 3:313; Moore Smith, *Autobiography of Harry Smith*, 1:203.

100. Washington *National Intelligencer*, August 31, 1814. See also Scott, *Recollections of a Naval Life*, 3:312–13.

101. Moore Smith, *Autobiography of Harry Smith*, 1:204.

102. John Rogers to Jones, September 9, 1814, in ND (M125), reel 39; General Orders of November 17, 1814, in WD (M221), reel 66; Report of Alexandria Common Council, September 7, 1814, and Samuel T. Dyson to Armstrong, August 29, 1814, in *ASP: MA*, 1:589–91; Elers Napier, *The Life and Correspondence of Admiral Sir Charles Napier*, 2 vols. (London, 1862), 1:80.

103. Report of Alexandria Common Council, September 7, 1814, in *ASP: MA*, 1:591; James Gordon to Cochrane, September 9, 1814, in *Naval Chronicle* 33 (January–June, 1815), 167–70; Edward Codrington to wife, September 10, 1814, in Jane Bourchier, *Memoir of the Life of Admiral Sir Edward Codrington*, 2 vols. (London, 1873), 1:319; Napier, *Admiral Charles Napier*, 1:80–86.

104. Scott, *Recollections of a Naval Life*, 3:314–15. For similar sentiments, see Codrington to wife, September 10, 1814, in Bourchier, *Edward Codrington*, 2:319; and James, *Naval History of Great Britain*, 6:311–12.

105. Memorandum of James Madison, [August 29, 1814], in Madison Papers (LC), reel 16; Brant, *James Madison*, 6:312; Hammack, *Kentucky and the Second American Revolution*, 93–94.

106. Quoted in Lord, *Dawn's Early Light*, 216.

107. Margaret Bayard Smith to Jane Kirkpatrick, August, [1814], in Hunt, *First Forty Years of Washington Society*, 115; Mrs. A. Peter to Pickering, August 28, 1814, in Pickering Papers (MHS), reel 30. See also George Hay to Monroe, September 10, 1814, in Monroe Papers (NYPL).

108. Memorandum of James Madison, [August 29, 1814], in Madison Papers (LC), reel 16; Armstrong to Baltimore *Patriot,* September 3, 1814, reprinted in Washington *National Intelligencer,* September 8, 1814; Williams, *Invasion of Washington,* 105–6.

109. Armstrong to Joseph Desha, October 2, 1814, in Desha Papers (LC).

110. *Annual Register for 1814 [General History],* 185. See also Trenton *True American,* December 5, 1814.

111. Quoted in *Niles' Register* 7 (December 31, 1814), 275 (most capital letters omitted). See also ibid., (February 18, 1815), 392; *Annual Register for 1814 [General History],* 206; speeches of Samuel Whitbread, November 8, 1814, and James Mackintosh, April 11, 1815, in *Parliamentary Debates,* 29:47 and 30:526; London *Morning Chronicle,* November 2, 1814; Trenton *True American,* December 5, 1814.

112. Prince Regent to Parliament, November 8, 1814, in *Parliamentary Debates,* 29:2. See also *Naval Chronicle* 32 (July–December, 1814), 247, 249; London *Morning Chronicle,* September 28, 1814.

113. *Cobbett's Weekly Register,* reprinted in *Niles' Register* 8 (Supplement), 34. See also ibid. 7 (December 31, 1814), 276.

114. Codrington to wife, September 10, 1814, in Bourchier, *Edward Codrington,* 1:320. See also John K. Mahon, "British Command Decisions Relative to the Battle of New Orleans," *Louisiana History* 6 (Winter, 1965), 63.

115. The details of Baltimore's preparations can be followed in Samuel Smith Papers (LC), reels 3–4. See also Frank A. Cassell, "Baltimore in 1813: A Study of Urban Defense in the War of 1812," *Military Affairs* 33 (December, 1969), 349–61; and Cassell, *Samuel Smith,* 182–204.

116. John Stricker to Samuel Smith, September 15, 1814, in Brannan, *Official Letters,* 420–24; Cockburn to Cochrane, September 15, 1814, in *Naval Chronicle* 33 (January–June, 1815), 162–64; Arthur Brook to Bathurst, September 17, 1814, in London *Times,* October 18, 1814; [Gleig], *Subaltern in America,* 128; *Niles' Register* 7 (December 3, 1814), 200–201.

117. [Gleig], *Narrative of the Campaigns,* 178.

118. Smith to Monroe, September 19, 1814, in WD (M221), reel 66; Cockburn to Cochrane, September 15, 1814, in *Naval Chronicle* 33 (January–June, 1815), 162–64; Arthur Brook to Bathurst, September 17, 1814, in London *Times,* October 18, 1814; [Gleig], *Narrative of the Campaigns,* 197.

119. Quoted in Pancake, *Samuel Smith,* 130.

120. George Armistead to Monroe, September 24, 1814, in WD (M221), reel 59; Cochrane to Croker, September 17, 1814, in *Niles' Register* 7 (December 3, 1814), 199–200; ibid. (September 24, 1814), 24.

121. Washington *National Intelligencer,* September 26, 1814; Tucker, *Poltroons and Patriots,* 2:585–90; Lord, *Dawn's Early Light,* 240–46, 291–97; Oscar Sonneck *"The Star Spangled Banner,"* rev. ed. (Washington, 1914), 9–63.

122. Letter of Robert Wright, October 19, 1814, in Brannan, *Official Letters,* 449–50. See also William Wirt to ———, August 21, 1814, in Wirt Papers

(LC), reel 1; Nathaniel Fenwick to Monroe, September 26, 1814, in WD (M221), reel 61.

123. *Niles' Register* 7 (October 27, 1814), 110, and (Supplement), 158.

124. Proclamation of Alexander Cochrane, April 2, 1814, in Jackson Papers (LC), reel 10.

125. Quoted in Frank A. Cassell, "Slaves of the Chesapeake Bay Area and the War of 1812," *Journal of Negro History* 57 (April, 1972), 151.

126. Ibid., 153–54. See also Pack, *George Cockburn*, 167–69. Americans claimed that the British sold the runaways they carried off in the West Indies. Though in general this was untrue, at least one American saw some Virginia slaves sold in the Bahamas in 1813. See statement of Patrick Williams, November 17, 1813, in Jonathan Russell Papers (BU).

127. There are several excellent accounts of the Gulf Coast campaign, most notably A. Lacarriere Latour, *Historical Memoir of the War in West Florida and Louisiana in 1814–15*, trans. H. P. Nugent (Philadelphia, 1816); Charles B. Brooks, *The Siege of New Orleans* (Seattle, 1961); Wilburt S. Brown, *The Amphibious Campaign for West Flordia and Louisiana, 1814–1815: A Critical Review of Strategy and Tactics at New Orleans* (University, AL, 1969); and Frank L. Owsley, Jr., *Struggle for the Gulf Borderlands: The Creek War and the Battle of New Orleans, 1812–1815* (Gainesville, 1981).

128. London *Courier*, reprinted in *Niles' Register* 5 (December 11, 1813), 250; John K. Mahon, "British Strategy and Southern Indians: War of 1812," *Florida Historical Quarterly* 44 (April, 1966), 285–302; Frank L. Owsley, Jr., "The Role of the South in the British Grand Strategy in the War of 1812," *Tennessee Historical Quarterly* 31 (Spring, 1972), 22–38.

129. Brown, *Amphibious Campaign*, 36, 172.

130. Latour, *Historical Memoir*, 255–56. See also George Poindexter to Nachez *Mississippi Republican*, reprinted in Washington *National Intelligencer*, February 13, 1815; *Niles' Register* 7 (February 25, 1815), 410, and 8 (Supplement), 190; letter from army officer, January 20, 1815, in Lexington *Reporter*, February 13, 1815.

131. Admiralty, quoted in Mahan, *Sea Power*, 2:385, and Bathurst, quoted in Adams, *History*, 8:314.

132. Andrew Jackson to Armstrong, June 27, 1814, in WD (M221), reel 63; Owsley, *Struggle for the Borderlands*, 98–100; Mahon, *War of 1812*, 341–43.

133. Owsley, *Struggle for the Borderlands*, 105–7; Mahon, *War of 1812*, 345–47.

134. Proclamation of Edward Nicolls, August 29, 1814, in *Niles' Register* 7 (November 5, 1814), 134–35.

135. William Lawrence to Andrew Jackson, September 15–16, 1814, in WD (M221), reel 63; Latour, *Historical Memoir*, 34–40.

136. Jackson to Armstrong, July 30, 1814, in WD (M221), reel 63.

137. Monroe to Jackson, October 21, 1814, in Jackson Papers (LC), reel 13.

138. Jackson to Monroe, November 14, 1814, in WD (M221), reel 63; Jackson to Blount, November 14, 1814, in Jackson Papers (LC), reel 14; Latour, *Historical Memoir*, 44–51.

139. Brooks, *Siege of New Orleans*, 71.

140. Brown, *Amphibious Campaign*, 47.

141. [John Windship] to William Plumer, Jr., March 20, 1814, in Plumer Papers (NHHS), reel 2.

142. Thomas Flournoy to Armstrong, March 14 and 25, 1814, in WD (M221), reel 52. Quotation from March 14 letter.

143. Latour, *Historical Memoir*, 72; Francois-Xavier Martin, *The History of Louisiana, From the Earliest Period*, 2 vols. (New Orleans, 1827–29), 2:340. See also letter from New Orleans, December 16, 1814, in Richmond *Enquirer*, January 14, 1815; George Poindexter to Monroe, February 5, 1815, in Monroe Papers (NYPL).

144. Jackson to Monroe, December 27, 1814, in WD (M221), reel 63; Brooks, *Siege of New Orleans*, 74–75, 84–87; Brown, *Amphibious Campaign*, 63–69.

145. General Orders of December 16, 1814, in *Niles' Register* 7 (January 14, 1815), 316–17.

146. Latour, *Historical Memoir*, 73.

147. Proclamation of Andrew Jackson, September 21, 1814, and Claiborne to Jackson, October 17 and 24, 1814, in Jackson Papers (LC), reels 13 and 62; General Order of December 14, 1814, in *Niles' Register* 7 (January 28, 1814), 345; Jackson to Monroe, December 27, 1814, in WD (M221), reel 63; Jackson to Claiborne, October 31, 1814, in Bassett, *Correspondence of Andrew Jackson*, 2:88; Latour, *Historical Memoir*, 67; Brooks, *Siege of New Orleans*, 118.

148. Daniel Patterson to William Jones, October 10, 1814 (2 letters), in ND (M147), reel 5.

149. George Poindexter to Monroe, February 5, 1815, in Monroe Papers (NYPL).

150. Proclamation of Andrew Jackson, September 21, 1814, in Jackson Papers (LC), reel 62.

151. See documents in Latour, *Historical Memoir*, ix-xv; Jackson to Daniel B. Morgan, January 8, 1815, in Jackson Papers (LC), reel 62; Proclamation of James Madison, February 6, 1815, in *AC*, 13–3, 1829–30; Brown, *Amphibious Campaign*, 86; William Bridgwater, "Jean Laffite," in *DAB*, 10:540–41; de Grummond, *Baratarians*, passim.

152. Brown, *Amphibious Campaign*, 93.

153. Moore Smith, *Autobiography of Harry Smith*, 1:247.

154. Brooks, *Siege of New Orleans*, 68.

155. Quoted in Mahon, *War of 1812*, 352.

156. Ibid., 352–53; Mahon, "British Strategy and Southern Indians," 298.

157. Brown, *Amphibious Campaign*, 76–77; Owsley, *Struggle for the Borderlands*, 126–27.

158. Thomas Ap Catesby Jones to Daniel Patterson, March 12, 1814, in Brannan, *Official Letters*, 487–89; Latour, *Historical Memoir*, 57–62; Brooks, *Siege of New Orleans*, 90–97.

159. Codrington to wife, December 23 and 27, 1814, in Bourchier, *Edward Codrington*, 1:332–33.

160. Letter of Eligius Fromentin, December 30, 1814, in *Niles' Register* 7 (February 4, 1815), 360; Latour, *Historical Memoir*, 82–83, 87; Brooks, *Siege of New Orleans*, 129–35.

161. Patterson to Secretary of the Navy, December 28, 1814, in ND (M147), reel 5; Codrington to wife, December 27, 1814, in Bourchier, *Edward Codrington*, 1:333; Brooks, *Siege of New Orleans*, 140–44.

162. [Gleig], *Subaltern in America*, 221.

163. Jackson to Monroe, December 27, 1814, in WD (M221), reel 63; John Keane to Edward Pakenham, [December, 1814], in *The Annual Register . . . for the Year 1815* (London, 1816) *[Appendix to Chronicle]*, 144–47; [Gleig], *Subaltern in America*, 219; Latour, *Historical Memoir*, 105–12; Brooks, *Siege of New Orleans*, 144–50.

164. Brooks, *Siege of New Orleans*, 164–73.

165. [Gleig], *Narrative of the Campaigns*, 310. See also Brown, *Amphibious Campaign*, 179.

166. Jackson to Secretary of War, December 29, 1814, in WD (M221), reel 63; John D. Henley to Patterson, December 28, 1814, and Patterson to Secretary of the Navy, December 29, 1814, in ND (M147), reel 5; Brooks, *Siege of New Orleans*, 178–79.

167. Jackson to Secretary of War, December 29, 1814, in WD (M221), reel 63; Brooks, *Siege of New Orleans*, 183–93.

168. Brooks, *Siege of New Orleans*, 197–98; Brown, *Amphibious Campaign*, 119–20.

169. [Gleig], *Subaltern in America*, 250.

170. Codrington to wife, January 4, 1815, in Bourchier, *Edward Codrington*, 1:334; Latour, *Historical Memoir*, 132–36; Brooks, *Siege of New Orleans*, 198–206; Brown, *Amphibious Campaign*, 121–28.

171. Brooks, *Siege of New Orleans*, 213.

172. Ibid., 210–12; Brown, *Amphibious Campaign*, 128–31.

173. Brooks, *Siege of New Orleans*, 220–25.

174. Patterson to Secretary of the Navy, January 13, 1815, ND (M147), reel 5; William Thornton to Edward Pakenham, [January, 1815], in *Annual Register for 1815 [Appendix to Chronicle]*, 147–49; Brooks, *Siege of New Orleans*, ch. 19; Brown, *Amphibious Campaign*, ch. 9.

175. Letter from New Orleans, January 13, 1815, in Richmond *Enquirer*, February 11, 1815.

176. Moore Smith, *Autobiography of Harry Smith*, 1:247. For similar sentiments, see [Gleig], *Subaltern in America*, 260–62.

177. Letter from New Orleans, January 13, 1815, in *Niles' Register* 7 (February 11, 1815), 379.

178. Letter from New Orleans, in *Niles' Register* 7 (February 11, 1815), 378.

179. Quoted in *Niles' Register* 8 (Supplement), 184.

180. Moore Smith, *Autobiography of Harry Smith*, 1:241.

181. Ibid., 244.

182. Jackson to [Secretary of War], January 9, 1815, in WD (M221), reel 63; Jackson to Secretary of War, January 13, 1815, in Jackson Papers, Supplement

(SR), reel 4; John Lambert to Bathurst, [January, 1815], in *Annual Register for 1815 [Appendix to Chronicle]*, 141–44; Moore Smith, *Autobiography of Harry Smith*, 1:238; Brooks, *Siege of New Orleans*, ch. 19; Brown, *Amphibious Campaign*, ch. 9.

183. Report of American Loss, in Brannan, *Official Letters*, 461; Return of [British] Casualties, in Latour, *Historical Memoir*, cliv; Brooks, *Siege of New Orleans*, 250–52.

184. Washington *National Intelligencer*, February 7, 1815.

185. Report of American Loss, in Brannan, *Official Letters*, 461; Return of [British] Casualties, in Latour, *Historical Memoir*, cliv; Brooks, *Siege of New Orleans*, 151, 192, 206, 250–52.

186. W.H. Overton to Jackson, January 19, 1815, in Jackson Papers (LC), reel 15; Latour, *Historical Memoir*, 187–97.

187. Jackson to Secretary of War, January 19, 1815, in Jackson Papers (LC), reel 15; Brooks, *Siege of New Orleans*, 260–63.

188. Jackson to Secretary of War, January 19, 1815, in Jackson Papers (LC), reel 15.

189. Quoted in de Grummond, *Baratarians*, 106.

190. Resolutions of Louisiana Legislature, in Latour, *Historical Memoir*, cxxiv-cxxix.

191. General Orders of December 16, 1814, in *Niles' Register* 7 (January 14, 1815), 317.

192. Jackson to Lambert, March 13, 1815, in Jackson Papers (LC), reel 17; Address of Andrew Jackson, February 19, 1815, and General Orders of March 13, 1815, in Latour, *Historical Memoir*, xc, cii.

193. *Niles' Register* 8 (June 3, 1815), 245–48, (June 10, 1815), 249–253, and (June 17, 1815), 272–74; Alexander Dallas to Jackson, April 12, 1815, in Jackson Papers (LC), reel 18; Parton, *Andrew Jackson*, 2:300–321.

194. Report of Court, [March 21, 1815], in Jackson Papers (LC), reel 17.

195. Bassett, *Correspondence of Andrew Jackson*, 2:ix.

196. Proceedings of General Court Martial Held at Mobile, December 5, 1814, in Jackson Papers (LC), reel 64; Parton, *Andrew Jackson*, 2:277–300.

197. William Lawrence to Jackson, February 12, 1815, and James Winchester to Monroe, February 17, 1815, in WD (M221), reel 63; Lambert to Bathurst, February 14, 1815, in Latour, *Historical Memoir*, clxxii-clxxv.

198. Proclamation of Alexander Cochrane, April 25, 1814, in *Niles' Register* 6 (May 14, 1814), 182–83.

199. Proclamation of James Madison, June 29, 1814, in Savage, *Policy toward Maritime Commerce*, 1:287–88. See also Monroe to American commissioners and ministers, May 24, 1814, in SD (M77), reel 2.

200. Nettels, *Emergence of a National Economy*, 385, 396.

201. Ibid., 399.

202. For more on the war economy, see chapter 9: The Crisis of 1814.

203. *Niles' Register* 6 (July 9, 1814), 317.

204. Ibid.

205. William Williams to John Cotton Smith, April 9, 1814, and Selectmen of Saybrook to Smith, April 12, 1814, in Thompson R. Harlow et al., eds., *John Cotton Smith Papers*, 7 vols. (Hartford, 1948–67), 2:226–28, 235; *Naval Chronicle* 32 (July–December, 1814), 171.

206. A total of 410,603 militia were called out during the war, the vast majority for coastal defense. See Militia in Service during War, April 15, 1820, in *ASP: MA*, 2:280–81.

207. Hartford *Connecticut Courant*, August 16 and September 6, 1814; Reginald Horsman, "Nantucket's Peace Treaty with England in 1814," *New England Quarterly* 54 (June, 1981), 180–98; Edward Byers, *The Nation of Nantucket: Society and Politics in an Early American Commercial Center, 1660–1820* (Boston, 1987), 277–89.

208. Walter M. Whitehill, ed., *New England Blockaded in 1814: The Journal of Henry Edward Napier* (Salem, 1938) (July 9, 1814), 33; McMaster, *History of the United States*, 4:134.

209. Proclamation of John O. Creighton, October 8, 1814, in *NASP: NA*, 4:246. See also *Niles' Register* 7 (November 19, 1814), 167–68.

210. Whitehill, *Journal of Henry Edward Napier* (May 29, 1814), 18.

211. For more on this problem, see chapter 4: The Campaign of 1812.

212. William Bainbridge to William Jones, October 5, 1812, in Dudley and Crawford, *Naval Documents*, 1:510.

213. Stephen Decatur to Benjamin W. Crowninshield, January 18, 1815, in ND (M125), reel 42.

214. Ibid.; New York *National Advocate*, reprinted in Washington *National Intelligencer*, April 11, 1815; *Naval Chronicle* 33 (January–June, 1815), 283; Roosevelt, *Naval War*, 2:137–46; Maclay, *United States Navy*, 2:65–73.

215. *Niles' Register* 8 (April 8, 1815), 103–4.

216. Charles Stewart, Minutes of Chase and Action of *Constitution*, [May, 1815], in ND (M125), reel 44; *Naval Chronicle* 33 (January–June, 1815), 466–67; Roosevelt, *Naval War*, 2:155–67; Maclay, *United States Navy*, 2:48–54.

217. Lewis Warrington to Jones, April 29 and May 12, 1814, and Joseph Bainbridge to Jones, June 3, 1814, in ND (M147), reel 5; Johnston Blakeley to Jones (with enclosure), July 8, 1814, in *ASP: NA*, 1:315–16; W. H. Watson to Benjamin Crowninshield, March 2, 1815, in *NASP: NA*, 4:264–65; Roosevelt, *Naval War*, 2:38–43, 48–55, 57–63, 167–73.

218. William Bainbridge to Jones, June 23, 1814, and Isaac Hull to Jones, October 2, 1814, in ND (M125), reels 37 and 40; Fulton to Madison, November 5, 1814, in Madison Papers (LC), reel 16; New York *National Advocate*, November 22, 1814; *Naval Chronicle* 30 (July–December, 1813), 403; Howard I. Chapelle, "The Ships of the American Navy in the War of 1812," *Mariner's Mirror* 18 (July, 1932), 299; Wallace Hutcheon, Jr., *Robert Fulton: Pioneer of Undersea Warfare* (Annapolis, 1981), 120–24, 129–38.

219. *Naval Chronicle* 32 (July–December, 1814), 244; London *Morning Chronicle*, November 2, 1814. See also John M. Forbes to Jonathan Russell, September 27, 1814, in Russell Papers (BU).

220. Concord *New-Hampshire Patriot*, December 13, 1814.

221. Letter to London *Statesman*, September 29, 1814, reprinted in Lexington *Reporter*, December 31, 1814.

222. Speech of Joseph Marryat, December 1, 1814, in *Parliamentary Debates*, 29: 650. See also John W. Croker to James Fowler, September 16, 1814, in *Niles' Register* 8 (Supplement), 187.

223. Ingersoll, *History*, 1:38–39.

224. *Naval Chronicle* 32 (July–December, 1814), 244.

225. Letter to the Editor, August 18, 1814, Ibid., 211.

226. Memorial of Bristol merchants, reprinted from London *Statesman* in *Niles' Register* 8 (Supplement), 186.

227. Resolutions of Glasgow meeting, September 7, 1814, in *Niles' Register* 7 (November 26, 1814), 190–91.

228. London *Times*, September 6, 1814; John W. Croker to London Assurance Corporation, August 19, 1814, in *Niles' Register* 7 (November 19, 1814), 174–75.

229. Speech of Alexander Baring, December 1, 1814, in *Parliamentary Debates*, 29:651.

230. Notice of Admiralty, April 30, 1814, in *Naval Chronicle* 31 (January–June, 1814), 497–98; letter to the editor, September 10, 1814, ibid. 32 (July–December, 1814), 219.

231. Croker to London Assurance Corporation, August 19, 1814, in *Niles' Register* 7 (November 19, 1814), 174–75.

232. London *Times*, February 11, 1815. See also [Gleig], *Narrative of the Campaigns*, 213–14.

233. *Parliamentary Debates*, 29:640–70.

234. *Niles' Register* 7 (October 29, 1814), 120 and (January 7, 1815), 291; Adams, *History*, 7:196; Cranwell and Crane, *Men of Marque*, 321–28.

235. Proclamation of Thomas Boyle, [August, 1814], in *Niles' Register* 7 (January 7, 1815), 290–91.

236. Quoted in Maclay, *American Privateers*, 498.

237. Samuel C. Reid to New York *Mercantile Advertiser*, October 4, 1814, in Brannan, *Official Letters*, 445–49; John B. Dabney to Secretary of State, October 5, 1814, in *Niles' Register* 7 (December 17, 1814), 253–55; Maclay, *American Privateers*, 493–502.

238. *Niles' Register* 7 (October 29, 1814), 120–21; Maclay, *American Privateers*, 377–90.

239. Thomas Boyle to George P. Stephenson, March 2, 1815, in *Niles' Register* 8 (March 25, 1815), 62.

240. Ibid., 61–62

Chapter 9: The Crisis of 1814

1. Hartford *American Mercury*, October 25, 1814.

2. William Jones to Alexander Dallas, September 15, 1814, in Dallas Papers (HSP); New York *National Advocate*, September 10, 1814.

3. See Stagg, *Mr. Madison's War*, 456n.

4. James Monroe to George M. Troup, October 17, 1814, and to William Branch Giles, October 26, 1814, in *ASP: MA*, 1:515, 519. See also Memorial of Baltimore Committee of Vigilance and Safety, January 26, 1815, ibid., 602–3.

5. Jefferson to Monroe, October 16, 1814, in Monroe Papers (LC), reel 5.

6. [Secretary of War] to Izard, May 25, 1814, in Izard, *Official Correspondence*, 25; Madison to [Armstrong], August 13, 1814, in Madison Papers (LC), reel 27; Washington *City Gazette*, reprinted in Bennington *Green-Mountain Farmer*, August 23, 1814.

7. Izard to Secretary of War, July 3, 1814, in WD (M221), reel 62.

8. Stagg, "Enlisted Men," 624. Both sides relied heavily on deserters for information, though frequently they had little to offer but camp gossip.

9. See, for example, Hartford *American Mercury*, February 1, April 19, May 31, June 28, August 9, October 4, and November 22, 1814, and January 17, 1815.

10. J. Laval to [Secretary of War], December 21, 1812, in WD (M221), reel 46.

11. See, for example, Thomas Pinckney to Secretary of War, December 25, 1812, Robert Taylor to Secretary of War, November 15, 1813, Alexander Macomb to Daniel Parker, January 20, 1815, in WD (M221), reels 55, 57, and 64; Proclamation of James Madison, July 22, 1812, and December 20, 1814, and Secretary of War to Pinckney, January 7, 1813, in WD (M6), reels 6 and 7.

12. William Jones to Arthur Sinclair, May 19, 1814, in *NASP: NA*, 4:348; Lexington *Reporter*, December 31, 1814.

13. Proclamation of James Madison, June 17, 1814, in *Niles' Register* 6 (June 25, 1814), 279; Order of Secretary of War, in Lexington *Reporter*, July 9, 1814.

14. There were 24 additonal executions in 1815. See Hare, "Military Punishments," 238.

15. See chapter 7: The Last Embargo.

16. Jones to Dallas, September 15, 1814, in Dallas Papers (HSP).

17. Jones to Madison, [October 15, 1814], in Madison Papers (LC), reel 16.

18. Decatur to Jones, September 8, 1814, and Chauncey to Jones, August 30, 1814, in ND (M125), reels 38 and 39.

19. John H. Dent to Secretary of the Navy, January 28, 1815, Hugh G. Campbell to Benjamin Crowninshield, February 13, 1815, and William Bainbridge to Crowninshield, January 26, 1815, in ND (M125), reel 42.

20. Secretary of War to Daniel Tompkins, November 21, 1814, in WD (M6), reel 7; Pinckney to Secretary of War, May 20, 1814, in WD (M221), reel 56.

21. Georgetown *Federal Republican*, November 24, 1814; William Plumer to Charles Cutts, November 21, 1814, in Plumer Papers (LC), reel 2. See also John Kerr to [Monroe?], January 31, 1815, in WD (M221), reel 63; John T. Gilman to Monroe, November 17, 1814, in WD (M222), reel 11.

22. Moses Porter to Armstrong, July 25 and August 3, 1814, in WD (M221), reel 65.

23. See chapter 4: The Campaign of 1812.

24. Speech of Alexander Hanson, November 28, 1814, in *AC*, 13–3, 656.

25. J. Willcocks to Armstrong, July 1, 1814, in WD (M221), reel 67.

26. Timothy Upham to Monroe, December 7, 1814, in WD (M222), reel 14.

27. John Graham to John Mason, November 7 and December 13, 1814, in SD (M588), reel 2.

28. Francis Le Baron to Monroe, January 20, 1815, in WD (M221), reel 63.

29. Dearborn to Monroe, December 22, 1814, and Joseph Wingate to Monroe, January 4, 1815, in WD (M222), reels 11 and 18; Wright Hall to Armstrong, August 15, 1814, William D. Cheever to Monroe, October 7, 1814, Samuel Russell to Monroe, October 18, 1814, and Robert McCoy to Thomas Cadwallader, December, 1814, and January 16, 1815, in WD (M221), reels 60, 62, 64, and 65; Tompkins to Monroe, December 24, 1814, in Hastings, *Papers of Daniel D. Tompkins*, 3:629; Dietz, "Prisoner of War," 73; Adams, *History*, 8:283.

30. Gallatin to Secretary of the Treasury, December 24, 1814, in Gallatin Papers (SR), reel 27; Ralph W. Hidy, *The House of Baring in American Trade and Finance: English Merchant Bankers at Work, 1763–1861* (Cambridge, MA, 1949), 52.

31. Dallas to Eppes, December 2, 1814, in *ASP: F*, 2:878; Dallas to Commissioner of Loans at Boston, November 9, 1814, in *Niles' Register* 7 (December 24, 1814), 270.

32. Thomas H. Cushing to Monroe, December 4, 1814, in WD (M222), reel 10; Dearborn to Monroe, November 5, 1814, and James Byers to Monroe, January 4, 1815, in WD (M221), reels 59 and 61; Oliver H. Perry to Benjamin Crowninshield, February 12, 1815, in ND (M125), reel 42; *Niles' Register* 7 (Supplement), 176; Keene *Newhampshire Sentinel*, December 3, 1814; speeches of Charles J. Ingersoll, November 17, 1814, Elijah Brigham, November 21, 1814, and Thomas P. Grosvenor, November 28, 1814, in *AC*, 13–3, 609, 626, 669; Perkins & Co., Boston, to Perkins & Co., Canton, November 17, 1814, in Thomas G. Cary, *Memoir of Thomas Handasyd Perkins* (Boston, 1856), 300; Ingersoll, *Historical Sketch*, 1:249; Seybert, *Statistical Annals*, 749.

33. Dallas to Eppes, December 2, 1814, in *ASP: F*, 2:878; James Robertson to Pickering (with enclosure), November 22, 1814, in Pickering Papers (MHS), reel 30.

34. See, for example, Samuel Smith to Monroe, October 5, 1814, William D. Cheever to Monroe, October 22, 1814, Dearborn to Monroe, November 10 and 21, 1814, and Thomas Cadwallader to Monroe, December 22, 1814, in WD (M221), reels 60, 61, and 66; John T. Gilman to Monroe, November 17, 1814, in WD (M222), reel 11.

35. John Langdon, Jr., to Monroe, November 1, 1814, in WD (M222), reel 12.

36. James Morrison to Monroe, November 16, 1814, in WD (M221), reel 64. See also John Anderson to Andrew Jackson, November 25, 1814, in Jackson Papers (LC), reel 14.

37. J. Van Fenstermaker, *The Development of American Commercial Banking, 1782–1837* (Kent, OH, 1965), 111.
38. Washington *National Intelligencer*, March 28, 1814.
39. Fenstermaker, *Commercial Banking*, 111.
40. Christopher Gore to Rufus King, July 28, 1814, in King, *Rufus King*, 5:403; Ingersoll, *Historical Sketch*, 2:48; Dewey, *Financial History*, 145. See also John Haff to Madison, January 28, 1814, in Madison Papers (LC), reel 15; James Robertson to Pickering, March 17, 1814, in Pickering Papers (MHS), reel 30; Washington *National Intelligencer*, July 22, 1814; *Niles' Register* 6 (July 23, 1814), 353; Hammond, *Banks and Politics*, 182–83.
41. Gore to King, July 28, 1814, in King, *Rufus King*, 5:403.
42. Joseph and George Marx to Wilson Cary Nicholas, July 27, 1814, in Nicholas Papers (UVA). See also Harrison, *Diary of Thomas P. Cope* (June 28, 1814), 293.
43. *Niles' Register* 7 (Supplement), 175–77; Erick Bollman to James A. Bayard, August 24, 1814, in Donnan, *Papers of James A. Bayard*, 319; Albert S. Bolles, *The Financial History of the United States, From 1789 to 1860*, 3rd ed. (New York, 1891), 273; Paul Studenski and Herman E. Krooss, *Financial History of the United States*, 2nd ed. (New York, 1963), 74.
44. Dallas to Eppes, December 2, 1814, in *ASP: F*, 2:877–81; Bolles, *Financial History*, 268.
45. William D. Cheever to Monroe, October 7, 1814, in WD (M221), reel 60.
46. Joseph Whipple to Dallas, December 21, 1814, in TD (M178), reel 26; Rutland (VT) *Herald*, August 17, 1814; Portland *Gazette*, reprinted in Salem *Gazette*, November 29, 1814.
47. J. A. Douglas to Henry A. S. Dearborn, November 23, 1814, in TD (M175), reel 2. The administration later reversed this policy, ordering the seizure of all goods imported from Castine. See *Niles' Register* 7 (December 24, 1814), 270.
48. Eustis to Rush, December 10, 1814, in Rush Papers (SR), reel 3. See also John Chandler to Monroe, November 21, 1814, in WD (M221), reel 60; Jacob Ulmer to John Brooks, September 29, 1814, in *ASP: MA*, 3:859.
49. Izard to Secretary of War, July 31, 1814, in WD (M221), reel 62.
50. George Prevost to Earl Bathurst, August 27, 1814, in Cruikshank, *Niagara Frontier*, 1:180. See also Joseph Whipple to George W. Campbell, August 23, 1814, in TD (M178), reel 26; Thomas Macdonough to William Jones, July 23, 1814, in ND (M147), reel 5; letter from Burlington, VT, August 15, 1814, in Boston *Gazette*, August 29, 1814; Bennington *Green-Mountain Farmer*, August 23 1814; Thomas G. Ridout to George Ridout, February 19 and May 15, 1814, in Edgar, *Ten Years of Upper Canada*, 275, 282; Muller, "Commerce of the Champlain-Richelieu Corridor," passim.
51. Macdonough to Jones, June 29, and July 9 and 23, 1814, in ND (M147), reel 5. See also Plattsburgh *Republican*, reprinted in Bennington *Green-Mountain Farmer*, August 9, 1814; Concord *New-Hampshire Patriot*, January 3, 1815.
52. Macdonough to Jones, June 8, 1814, in ND (M147), reel 5.

53. Dallas to Eppes, November 19, 1814, in *ASP: F*, 2:881–82.

54. Richard Rush to U.S. district attorney for Massachusetts, July 28, 1814, in *AC*, 13–3, 1823–27. Quotation from p. 1823.

55. *Niles' Register* 8 (Supplement), 149. See also Henderson, *Congress, Courts, and Criminals*, ch. 6.

56. Salem *Gazette*, September 2, 1814. See also Windsor *Vermont Republican*, reprinted in Bennington *Green-Mountain Farmer*, March 15, 1814.

57. H. Storrs to Monroe, October 21, 1814, in WD (M221), reel 66; Henry A. S. Dearborn to Dallas, November 14, 1814, in TD (M178), reel 12; Washington *National Intelligencer*, April 4, 1814.

58. Izard to Secretary of War, July 31, 1814, in WD (M221), reel 62.

59. Statement of Callender Irvine, December 26, 1812, in WD (M222), reel 8; Eustis to John Shelby, September 17, 1812, in McAfee, *History of the Late War*, 118; Sapio, *Pennsylvania & the War of 1812*, 192–93; Higginbotham, *Keystone in the Democratic Arch*, 288–89; Jacobs, *Beginnings of the U.S. Army*, 375. See also correspondence scattered through WD (M6), reels 5–6.

60. Harrison, *Diary of Thomas P. Cope* (October 25, 1813), 287; Philadelphia *United States' Gazette*, October 11, 1813.

61. Harrison, *Diary of Thomas P. Cope* (July 18 and September 28, 1814), 294, 300.

62. Jacobs, *Beginnings of the U.S. Army*, 375.

63. Dearborn to Elbert Anderson, Jr., September 28, 1812, in WD (M222), reel 5. The figure for wages is based on the scale approved by Congress in late 1812. See *AC*, 12–2, 1314–15.

64. Elbert Anderson, Jr., to Armstrong, February 6, 1813, and August 13, 1814, in WD (M221), reels 50 and 59; Anderson to Armstrong, September 3, 1813, and statement of William D. Cheever, December 1, 1814, in WD (M222), reels 7 and 10.

65. Washington Lee to Armstrong, September 2, 1813, in WD (M222), reel 8.

66. Tompkins to New York Legislature, November 3, 1812, in Hastings, *Papers of Daniel D. Tompkins*, 3:180.

67. Victor S. Clark, *History of Manufactures in the United States*, 2 vols. (Washington, 1916–28), 1:chs. 9, 18–20.

68. Simon Snyder to Pennsylvania Legislature, December 5, 1811, in *Niles' Register* 1 (December 21, 1811), 282. For similar sentiments, see Madison to Congress, December 7, 1813, and speech of Charles J. Ingersoll, February 14, 1814, in *AC*, 13–2, 543, 1431; Washington *National Intelligencer*, November 25, 1813; Boston *Independent Chronicle*, August 16, 1813.

69. James Morrison to Henry Clay, December 24, 1812, in WD (M222), reel 6. See also Secretary of War to Morrison, October 29, 1812, in WD (M6), reel 6; and Morrison to Monroe, January 28, 1813, in WD (M221), reel 55.

70. Martin Baum to Armstrong, March 25, 1813, in WD (M221), reel 50.

71. Armstrong to William Duane, April 29, 1813, in William Duane, ed.,

"Selections from the Duane Papers," *Historical Magazine*, 2nd ser., 4 (August, 1868), 62.

72. Clay to Armstrong, June 25, 1813, in Hopkins and Hargreaves, *Papers of Henry Clay*, 1:806–7.

73. Speech of Joseph Hawkins, January 18, 1815, in *AC*, 13–3, 1081. See also Albert Gallatin to Secretary of War, April 17, 1813, in Madison Papers (LC), reel 15; Lewis Sanders to [Wilson Cary Nicholas], June 2, 1814, in Nicholas Papers (UVA); Thomas P. Abernethy, "Andrew Jackson and the Rise of Southwestern Democracy," *American Historical Review* 33 (October, 1927), 65.

74. Richard C. Wade, *The Urban Frontier: The Rise of Western Cities, 1790–1830* (Cambridge, MA, 1959), 39–71.

75. Letter from Boston merchant, October 17, 1813, in Boston *Patriot*, November 10, 1813.

76. See Ebenezer Denny to Armstrong, April 10 and 23, 1814, in WD (M221), reel 52; Thomas P. Abernethy, *The South in the New Nation, 1789–1819* ([Baton Rouge], 1961), 456–57.

77. Shelby to Kentucky Legislature, December 6, 1814, in Lexington *Reporter*, December 17, 1814.

78. State of Georgia, *Acts of the General Assembly of the State of Georgia [1812]* (Milledgeville, 1812), 3–8; State of Maryland, *Laws Made and Passed by the General Assembly of the State of Maryland [1813]* (Annapolis, 1813), 15–20; State of North Carolina, *Laws of North Carolina [1812]* ([Raleigh, 1813]), 8–9; State of North Carolina, *Laws of North Carolina [1813]* ([Raleigh, 1814]), 6–7; Peter Early to Georgia Senate, November 11, 1814, in Lexington *Reporter*, February 8, 1815.

79. Jefferson to Monroe, October 16, 1814, and to William Duane, November 24, 1814, in Jefferson Papers (LC), reel 47.

80. Nathaniel Macon to Joseph H. Nicholson, December 23, 1812, in Nicholson Papers (LC); Jefferson to William Short, November 28, 1814, in Jefferson Papers (LC), reel 47.

81. Randolph to Josiah Quincy, August 30, 1813, in Quincy, *Josiah Quincy*, 336. See also John Hollins to [Wilson Cary Nicholas], June 1, 1814, and Joseph and George Marx to [Wilson Cary Nicholas], August 9 and 23, 1814 in Nicholas Papers (UVA); W. Freeman Galpin, "The Grain Trade of Alexandria, Virginia, 1801–1815," *North Carolina Historical Review* 4 (October, 1927), 424–27; Garitee, *Republic's Private Navy*, 52–54.

82. William Lowndes to Elizabeth Lowndes, November 6, 1814, in Lowndes Papers (UNC), reel 1. See also Sarah Lemmon, *Frustrated Patriots: North Carolina and the War of 1812* (Chapel Hill, 1973), 192–96.

83. *Niles' Register* 7 (December 3, 1814), 193–97. For similar sentiments, see New York *National Advocate*, reprinted in Philadelphia *Aurora*, March 1, 1814; Memorandum of [Virgil Maxcy], March 15, 1814, in Galloway-Maxcy-Markoe Papers (LC); William C. Bradley to Armstrong, May 5, 1814, in WD (M221), reel 51; Adams, *History*, 8:14–15; Channing, *History of the United States*, 4:542–

43; Morison, *Harrison Gray Otis*, 2:52–53; Marshall Smelser, *The Democratic Republic, 1801–1815* (New York, 1968), 292.

84. W. B. Smith, "Wholesale Commodity Prices in the United States, 1795–1824," *Review of Economic Statistics* 9 (October, 1927), 177.

85. John Quincy Adams, *An Eulogy on the Life and Character of James Monroe* (Boston, 1831), 74. See also Rufus King to Christopher Gore, July 11, 1814, in King, *Rufus King*, 5:398.

86. For more the state loans, see chapter 10: The Hartford Convention.

87. Paul Revere & Son to Eustis, May 4, 1812, and Eli Whitney to Armstrong, March 8, 1813, in WD (M221), reels 56 and 58.

88. The command problem is dealt with in chapter 10: The Hartford Convention.

89. Statement of Third Auditor's Office, December 12, 1820, in *ASP: MA*, 2:280–81.

90. Tonnage for the Year 1813, in *ASP: C & N*, 1:1018.

91. Samuel Eliot Morison, *The Maritime History of Massachusetts, 1783–1860*, rev. ed. (Cambridge, MA, 1961), 205–6; Charles Warren, *Jacobin and Junto; or, Early American Politics as Viewed in the Diary of Dr. Nathaniel Ames, 1758–1822* (Cambridge, MA, 1931), 264.

92. Perkins & Co., Boston, to Perkins & Co., Canton, November 17, 1814, in Cary, *Thomas Handasyd Perkins*, 300.

93. Gore to King, July 28, 1814, in King, *Rufus King*, 5:403; Benjamin W. Labaree, *Patriots and Partisans: The Merchants of Newburyport, 1764–1815* (Cambridge, MA, 1962), 200.

94. Gore to King, July 28, 1814, in King, *Rufus King*, 5:403.

95. Speech of Daniel Sargent, [October 11, 1814], in *Synopsis of Debates in the Massachusetts Legislature* [Boston, 1814], 13. See also Timothy Pitkin, *A Statistical View of the Commerce of the United States* (Hartford, 1816), 41–42, 45–46; Robert A. East, "Economic Development and New England Federalism, 1803–1814," *New England Quarterly* 10 (September, 1937), 442–44; Mahan, *Sea Power*, 2:179–83.

96. Speech of Richard Stockton, December 10, 1814, in *AC*, 13–3, 849.

97. William Duane to Jefferson, September 26, 1814, in Jefferson Papers (LC), reel 46.

98. James Ronaldson to Jonathan Russell, February 17, 1814, in Russell Papers (BU); Andrei Dashkov to Nikolai Rumiantsev, January 1, 1815, in Bashkina et al., *United States and Russia*, 1100.

99. William Wirt to Elizabeth Wirt, October 25, 1814, in Wirt Papers (MdHS), reel 2.

100. Madison to Wilson Cary Nicholas, November 25, 1814, in Madison Papers (LC), reel 16.

101. See chapter 5: Raising Men and Money.

102. Federalists had little strength in Georgia or the West. For the election results elsewhere in 1813–1814, see Keene *Newhampshire Sentinel*, October 23 and 30, 1813, and Zadock Thompson, *History of Vermont*, 3 vols., rev. ed. (Burlington, 1853), 2:94–95, 118 (for VT); Keene *Newhampshire Sentinel*, June

12 and 19, 1813, and April 2 and June 11, 1814 (for NH); Banner, *Hartford Convention*, 361, 367 (for MA); Hartford *Connecticut Courant*, October 25, 1814, and Purcell, *Connecticut in Transition*, 291–92 (for CT); Allen, "Federal Ascendancy," 390–94 (for RI); Alexander, *Political History of New York*, 217, 226 (for NY); Higginbotham, *Keystone in the Democratic Arch*, 284, 299 (for PA); Fee, *From Aristocracy to Democracy*, 195, 203 (for NJ); Munroe, *Federalist Delaware*, 233–35 (for DE); Renzulli, *Maryland*, 307–10 (for MD); Broussard, *Southern Federalists*, 294–95 (for VA, NC, and SC).

103. See *Niles' Register* 9 (December 16, 1815), 280–81.

104. Hay to Monroe, March 14, 1814, in Monroe Papers (NYPL); Macon to Joseph H. Nicholson, February 4, 1814, in Nicholson Papers (LC). For similar sentiments, see Thomas Jesup to————, July 15, 1813, in Jesup Papers (LC); Robert Whitehill to James Hamilton, July 25, 1813, in Hamilton Papers (HSP); William Jones to Alexander Dallas, January 4, 1814, in Jones Papers (HSP).

105. Harrison, *Diary of Thomas P. Cope* (September 2, 1814), 298; George Hay to Monroe, September 10, 1814, in Monroe Papers (NYPL); King to Jeremiah Mason, September 2, 1814, in King, *Rufus King*, 5:414.

106. See chapter 8: The British Counteroffensive.

107. George W. Campbell to Madison, September 26, 1814, in Madison Papers (LC), reel 16; Campbell to John Norvell, January 19, 1815, in Campbell Papers (LC); Stagg, *Mr. Madison's War*, 432.

108. Jones to Madison, September 11, 1814, in Madison Papers (LC), reel 16.

109. Madison to Monroe, October 1, 1814, in Monroe Papers (NYPL); *Senate Journal*, 2:530.

110. Madison to Tompkins, September 28, 1814, and Tompkins to Madison, October 6 and 8, 1814, in Madison Papers (LC), reels 16 and 26.

111. Madison to Rodgers, November 24, 1814, Memorandum of Attorney General, December 4, 1814, Madison to Crowninshield, December 15, 1814, and Crowninshield to Madison, December 26 and 28, 1814, in Madison Papers (LC), reel 16; *Senate Journal*, 2:597; Dashkov to Rumiantsev, January 1, 1815, in Bashkina et al., *United States and Russia*, 1100.

112. Dallas to William Jones, October 2, 1814, in Jones Papers (HSP).

113. J. Harold Ennis, "Alexander James Dallas," in *DAB*, 5:36–38; Walters, *Alexander James Dallas*, passim.

114. George Hay to Monroe, October 16, 1814, in Monroe Papers (LC), reel 10.

115. Abner Lacock, quoted in Ingersoll, *Historical Sketch*, 2:253; *Senate Journal*, 2:533.

116. *AC*, 13–2, 766, 2003, 2835.

117. Proclamation of James Madison, August 8, 1814, in *AC*, 13–3, 9.

118. Jonathan Roberts to Matthew Roberts, September 27, 1814, in Roberts Papers (HSP). See also Nathaniel Macon to Joseph H. Nicholson, September 22, 1814, in Nicholson Papers (LC).

119. Washington *National Intelligencer*, September 9, 1814; Brant, *James Madison*, 6:323.

120. Dashkov to Rumiantsev, November 14, 1814, in Bashkina et al., *United States and Russia*, 1097.

121. William Wirt to Elizabeth Wirt, October 24, 1814, in Wirt Papers (MdHS), reel 2.

122. Jones to Dallas, September 25, 1814, in Dallas Papers (HSP).

123. Daniel Webster, quoted in speech of Joseph Lewis, February 8, 1815, in *AC*, 13–3, 1137; Jesse Bledsoe to William Worsely, September 26, 1814, in Worsely Papers, Lyman C. Draper Collection (HSW), reel 6cc. See also Ingersoll, *History*, 2:264.

124. Madison to Congress, September 20, 1814, in *AC*, 13–3, 12–15.

125. These documents are printed in *ASP: FR*, 3:695–710.

126. Speeches of Joseph Varnum, November 16, 1814, and John C. Calhoun, October 25, 1814, in *AC*, 13–3, 58, 465.

127. Speech of Jeremiah Mason, November 16, 1814, in *AC*, 13–3, 78.

128. Memorandum of Rufus King, October, 1814, in King, *Rufus King*, 5:422–24; Alexander Hanson to Robert Goodloe Harper, October 9, 1814, in Harper Papers (MdHS), reel 2; Timothy Pickering to Gouverneur Morris, October 29, 1814, in Pickering Papers (MHS), reel 15.

129. Speech of Alexander Hanson, October 10, 1814, in *AC*, 13–3, 382. Hanson reported that his speech was received "almost with acclamation" by the Republicans. "Even old [Robert] Wright was ready to embrace me . . . but while I am willing to go all honourable lengths to defend the country I can have no connection or understanding with scoundrels." Hanson to Harper, October 11, 1814, in Harper Papers (MdHS), reel 2.

130. Alexandria *Gazette*, October 15, 1814. See also Speech of Thomas J. Oakley, October 10, 1814, in *AC*, 13–3, 382–83; Stephen Van Rensselaer to Rufus King, October 25, 1814, in King, *Rufus King*, 5:431; Charles Cotesworth Pinckney to F. D. Petit de Villers, October 31, 1814, in Pinckney Papers (DU); Robert Goodloe Harper to William Sullivan, November 2, 1814, in Harper Papers (MdHS), reel 2; Robert Patterson to Jonathan Russell, November 6, 1814, in Russell Papers (BU); Samuel Dana to [Eustis], November 2, 1814, in Eustis Papers (LC), reel 2; William Polk to William Hawkins, October 17, 1814, in Raleigh *Minerva*, October 21, 1814; Georgetown *Federal Republican*, October 11, 1814; Resolutions of New York Legislature, ibid., October 31, 1814; New York *Evening Post*, October 12 and 13, 1814; Philadelphia *United States' Gazette*, October 14, 1814; Norfolk *Ledger*, reprinted in Salem *Essex Register*, November 19, 1814.

131. Boston *Gazette*, November 7, 1814.

132. Pickering to Caleb Strong, October 12, 1814, in Pickering Papers (MHS), reel 15.

133. Otis to Robert Goodloe Harper, October 27, 1814, in Morison, *Harrison Gray Otis*, 2:181. See also Caleb Strong to Pickering, October 12, 17, and 18, 1814, John Lowell, Jr., to Pickering, October 19, 1814, Pickering to Gouverneur Morris, October 29, 1814, and Manasseh Cutler to Pickering, November 28, 1814, in Pickering Papers (MHS), reels 15 and 30; Samuel Taggart to John Taylor, November 2, 1814, in Reynolds, "Letters of Samuel

Taggart," 430–31; Henry Lee to————, February 18, 1815, in Porter, *Jacksons and the Lees*, 2:1122; Boston *New-England Palladium*, October 18 and 28, 1814; Boston *Columbian Centinel*, October 19 and 26, 1814; Keene *Newhampshire Sentinel*, October 22, 1814; Boston *Daily Advertiser*, reprinted in Salem *Gazette*, November 1–15, 1814.

134. Letter from Washington, December 24, 1814, in New York *National Advocate*, December 28, 1815. See also Nathaniel Macon to Joseph H. Nicholson, October 24, 1814, in Nicholson Papers (LC).

135. Monroe to George M. Troup, October 17, 1814, in *ASP: MA*, 1:515.

136. Monroe to Brown, February 10, 1815, in WD (M7), reel 1. See also Monroe to Daniel D. Tompkins, February 4, 1815, ibid.; Monroe to Chairman of Senate Military Committee, December 23, 1814, in *ASP: MA*, 1:610; speech of John C. Calhoun, October 25, 1814, in *AC*, 13–3, 467; New York *National Advocate*, September 10 and November 6, 1814; William Wirt to Elizabeth Wirt, October 25, 1814, in Wirt Papers (MdHS), reel 2; Lexington *Reporter*, January 6, 1815.

137. Speech of Lyman Law, December 17, 1814, in *AC*, 13–3, 944; Gouverneur Morris to Harrison Gray Otis, November 8, 1814, in Morison, *Harrison Gray Otis*, 2:183. See also speeches of Jeremiah Mason, November 16, 1814, Morris Miller, November 28 and December 8, 1814, Thomas P. Grosvenor, December 3, 1814, and Zebulon R. Shipherd, December 9, 1814, in *AC*, 13–3, 90–91, 687–88, 739, 742, 791–92, 821; Alexandria *Gazette*, December 17, 1814; New York *Evening Post*, November 4 and 5, 1814; Ontario (NY) *Repository*, reprinted in Pittsburgh *Gazette*, January 10, 1815.

138. Memorandum of Rufus King, October, 1814, in King, *Rufus King*, 5:424. See also Frederick Wolcott to Oliver Wolcott, October 16, 1814, in Wolcott Papers (CHS); John Jacob Astor to Monroe, September 2, 1814, in Monroe Papers (LC), reel 5; speeches of Thomas Bayly and Cyrus King, October 22, 1814, Zebulon R. Shipherd, October 25, 1814, and Lyman Law, December 17, 1814, in *AC*, 13–3, 440, 452, 472, 948; Boston *Columbian Centinel*, August 31, 1814; Boston *New-England Palladium*, September 2, 6, and 9, 1814; Boston *Gazette*, September 5, 1814; Portsmouth *Oracle*, reprinted in Chillicothe *Supporter*, November 19, 1814; Baltimore *Federal Gazette*, reprinted in Pittsburgh *Gazette*, January 21, 1815.

139. George Hay to Monroe, November 27, 1814, in Monroe Papers (LC), reel 5; Monroe to [Hay?], December 2, 1814, in Monroe Papers (NYPL); Alexander Hanson to Robert Goodloe Harper, October 9, 1814, in Harper Papers (MdHS), reel 2; Dallas to William Jones, September 18, 1814, in Jones Papers (HSP); Elkanah Watson to Madison, September 8, 1814, in Madison Papers (LC), reel 16.

140. Hanson to Harper, October 9, 1814, in Harper Papers (MdHS), reel 2.

141. John Lovett to Solomon Van Rensselaer, June 22, 1813, in Bonney, *Legacy of Historical Gleanings*, 1:301. See also Jonathan Roberts to [Matthew Roberts], March 16, 1814, in Roberts Papers (HSP).

142. Georgetown *Federal Republican*, November 25, 1814; *AC*, 13–3, 110–11.

143. Letter from Washington, November 25, 1814, in Salem *Gazette*, December 9, 1814.

144. Georgetown *Federal Republican*, November 26, 1814. See also Ingersoll, *History*, 2:292–93.

145. These documents are printed in *ASP: FR*, 3:710–26.

146. Washington *National Intelligencer*, December 2, 1814. See also Boston *New-England Palladium*, December 9, 1814; *AC*, 13–3, 701.

147. Plumer to Jeremiah Mason, December 29, 1814, in Plumer Papers (LC), reel 2. For similar sentiments, see William Lowndes to Elizabeth Lowndes, November 30, 1814, in Lowndes Papers (UNC), reel 1; Ebenezer Stott to Duncan Cameron, December 12, 1814, in Cameron Papers (UNC); Worcester *National Aegis*, December 14, 1814; New York *Evening Post*, December 5, 7, and 8, 1814; Trenton *Federalist*, December 5, 1814; Philadelphia *United States' Gazette*, December 13, 1814; Georgetown *Federal Republican*, December 2, 1814; Alexandria *Gazette*, December 3, 1814; Baltimore *Federal Gazette*, reprinted in Charleston *Courier*, December 20, 1814.

148. For the peace rumors, see Joseph Lyman to John Treadwell, December 14, 1814, in Morison, *Harrison Gray Otis*, 2:188; Edward Lloyd to Elijah Davis, December 21, 1814, in "Unpublished Letters," *Maryland Historical Magazine* 21 (September, 1926), 283; Salem *Gazette*, January 13, 1815; Boston *Columbian Centinel*, January 14, 18, and 28, 1815; Providence *Gazette*, January 14, 1815; Newport *Mercury*, January 14, 1815; New London *Connecticut Gazette*, January 18, 1815; Chillicothe *Supporter*, December 24, 1814; *Niles' Register* 4 (January 15, 1815), 331.

149. Ingersoll, *History*, 2:282.

150. Adams to Louisa Catherine Adams, September 27, 1814, in Ford, *Writings of John Quincy Adams*, 5:149.

151. Resolution of Philadelphia City Council, August 27, 1814, in Madison Papers (LC), reel 16. See also *AC*, 13–3, 19, 335.

152. Nathaniel Macon to Joseph H. Nicholson, October 7, 1814, in Nicholson Papers (LC).

153. Speech of Jonathan Fisk, September 26, 1814, in *AC*, 13–3, 312, 314. For similar sentiments, see Charles J. Ingersoll to [Dallas], September 30, 1814, in Ingersoll Papers (HSP).

154. Speech of Nathaniel Macon, September 26, 1814, in *AC*, 13–3, 313. See also Washington *National Intelligencer*, September 2, 1814.

155. *AC*, 13–3, 311–12, 323, 341–42.

156. Speech of Langdon Cheves, October 3, 1814, in *AC*, 13–3, 342.

157. *AC*, 13–3, 387–88, 395–96.

158. *AC*, 13–3, 396; Ingersoll, *History*, 2:264.

159. *AC*, 13–3, 223, 1143, 1911–12.

160. *AC*, 13–3, 120, 1105–6; Jefferson to Samuel H. Smith, September 21 and October 29, 1814, in Jefferson Papers (LC), reel 47; *Niles' Register* 7 (December 31, 1814), 285.

161. Monroe to George M. Troup, October 17, 1814, in *ASP: MA*, 1: 514–17.

162. Ibid., 515.

163. For the New York law, see State of New York, *Laws of the State of New-York [1814]* (Albany, 1815), 15–20. Pennsylvania rejected a similar plan. See Mathew Carey, *The Olive Branch; or Faults on Both Sides, Federal and Democratic,* 10th ed. (Philadelphia, 1818), 355n.

164. For Knox's plan, see Report of the Secretary of War, January 18, 1790, in *ASP: MA,* 1:6–13.

165. The bill is printed in *Niles' Register* 7 (November 26, 1814), 181–83. See also Bibb to Monroe, November 1, 1814, in WD (M221), reel 59; Stagg, *Mr. Madison's War,* 459–61.

166. *AC,* 13–3, 38.

167. Varnum to Eustis, November 12, 1814, in Eustis Papers (LC), reel 2.

168. Speech of Joseph Varnum, November 16, 1814, in *AC,* 13–3, 58–70. Quotations from pp. 69–70.

169. Speeches of Robert H. Goldsborough, November 22, 1814, and David Daggett, November 16, 1814, in *AC,* 13–3, 73, 104.

170. *AC,* 13–3, 109.

171. Speech of Charles J. Ingersoll, December 9, 1814, in *AC,* 13–3, 808–19. Quotation from p. 815.

172. *AC,* 13–3, 713–14, 869–70, 928–29.

173. *AC,* 13–3, 132, 136, 141, 976, 993–94.

174. Ingersoll, *History,* 2:297. See also Harrison, *Diary of Thomas P. Cope* (January 5, 1815), 302.

175. James Hillhouse to Timothy Pitkin, November 7, 1814, in Pitkin Papers (HL).

176. Resolutions of Northampton Convention, November 16, 1814, in Boston *New-England Palladium,* November 29, 1814.

177. Speech of Daniel Webster, December 9, 1814, in Claude H. Van Tyne, ed., *The Letters of Daniel Webster* (New York, 1902), 67; Resolution of Connecticut Legislature, [Fall, 1814], in *Niles' Register* 7 (Supplement), 107–8. The Maryland House of Delegates also threatened to nullify the law. See Resolution of Maryland House, December 17, 1814, in Boston *Columbian Centinel,* December 28, 1814.

178. Bibb to Monroe, November 1, 1814, in WD (M221), reel 59; *AC,* 13–3, 38; Stagg, *Mr. Madison's War,* 461–62.

179. Speeches of Cyrus King and Thomas P. Grosvenor, December 3, 1814, in *AC,* 13–3, 725–26, 733–34.

180. Webster's speech is not printed in the *Annals,* but his argument is summarized in the speech of Thomas P. Grosvenor, December 3, 1814, in *AC,* 13–3, 734.

181. *AC,* 13–3, 45, 753–54, 756, 1837–38.

182. Theodore Dwight to Timothy Pitkin, January 9, 1815, in Pitkin Papers (HL).

183. Joseph L. Smith to John R. Bell, October 29, 1814, in Rush Papers (SR), reel 3; Thomas Jesup to Monroe, January 20, 1815, in Jesup Papers (LC).

184. George W. Hight to Monroe, January 12, 1815, in WD (M221), reel 62.

185. State of Connecticut, *The Public Laws of the State of Connecticut [1814]* (Hartford, [1815]), 186, 189–90; State of Massachusetts, *Laws of the Commonwealth of Massachusetts [1814–1815]*, (Boston, [1815]), 640–41; Jesup to Monroe, January 31 and February 3, 1815, in Jesup Papers (LC).

186. *AC*, 13–3, 162, 755, 1896–99.

187. Richard Hildreth, *The History of the United States*, 6 vols., rev. ed. (New York, 1854–55), 6:402, 404.

188. Armstrong to Nathaniel Searle, Jr., July 9, 1814, in *ASP: MA*, 1:608; Robert Taylor to Monroe, September 29, 1814, and Daniel D. Tompkins to Monroe, December 12, 1814, in WD (M221), reel 66; Hartford *Connecticut Courant*, September 8 and November 10, 1812; Boston *New-England Palladium*, October 28, 1814; Hildreth, *History of the United States*, 6:554–55; Adams, *History*, 8:282–83. Connecticut actually had state troops in federal service as early as 1813. See chapter 10: The Hartford Convention.

189. Report of the Secretary of the Navy, November 15, 1814, in *ASP: NA*, 1:323–24.

190. *AC*, 13–3, 223, 1085, 1908.

191. Report of the Secretary of the Navy, November 15, 1814, in *ASP: NA*, 1:322–23.

192. Speech of James Pleasants, November 8, 1814, in *AC*, 13–3, 542.

193. *AC*, 13–3, 35, 548, 1834.

194. George W. Campbell to Senate, September 23, 1814, in *ASP: F*, 2:840–43. Quotation from p. 843.

195. Jefferson to Thomas Cooper, September 10, 1814, in Jefferson Papers (LC), reel 47; Jefferson to Madison, October 15, 1814, in Madison Papers (LC), reel 16.

196. Nathaniel Macon, quoted in Ingersoll, *Historical Sketch*, 2:254. See also speech of Nathaniel Macon, January 4, 1812, in *AC*, 12–1, 663; Monroe to Jefferson, September 10, 1814, in Jefferson Papers (LC), reel 47; Monroe to Jefferson, December 21, 1814, in Monroe Papers (LC), reel 5.

197. Madison to Monroe, October 23, 1814, in Madison Papers (LC), reel 16.

198. Report of House Way and Means Committee, October 10, 1814, in *AC*, 13–3, 378–81. Quotation from p. 378.

199. Ingersoll, *Historical Sketch*, 2:254.

200. Dallas to Eppes, October 17, 1814, in *ASP: F*, 2:866–69. Quotation from p. 866.

201. Dallas to Eppes, December 2, 1814, in *ASP: F*, 2:877–81.

202. Report of the Secretary of the Treasury, January 17, 1815, in *ASP: F*, 2:885–89.

203. George Ticknor to Edward T. Channing, January 22, 1815, in George S. Hillard et al., *Life, Letters, and Journals of George Ticknor*, 2 vols. (Boston 1876), 1:30–31.

204. *AC*, 13–3, 134, 771, 1855–57.

205. Dutch bankers later told American agents that this loan could probably

be filled at 75—a 25 percent discount—but the peace treaty was signed before any action was taken. See American commissioners to Dallas, December 25, 1814, in Gallatin Papers (SR), reel 27.

206. *AC,* 13–3, 38, 511–513, 1834–36.

207. Dallas to Speaker of the House, April 12, 1816, in *ASP: F,* 3:121; Bolles, *Financial History,* 233–34.

208. Report of the Secretary of the Treasury, January 17, 1815, in *ASP: F,* 2:887.

209. *AC,* 13–3, 258, 291, 1148, 1264, 1921–24, 1939–41.

210. Hanson to Harper, October 9, 1814, in Harper Papers (MdHS), reel 2.

211. These laws can be found in *AC,* 13–3, 1839–925.

212. Ingersoll, *Historical Sketch,* 1:240.

213. As revised in 1792, the tax on whiskey was 7 to 18 cents per gallon, depending on the proof of the product. See *AC,* 2–1, 1375.

214. Jefferson to William Short, November 28, 1814, in Jefferson Papers (LC), reel 47. For similar sentiments, see Daniel Webster to Moody Kent, December 22, [1814], in Van Tyne, *Letters of Daniel Webster,* 69.

215. Speech of Thomas P. Grosvenor, November 29, 1814, in *AC,* 13–3, 698.

216. William H. Crawford to Henry Clay, December 31, 1816, in *ASP: F,* 3:190, 209.

217. Timothy Pickering to John Pickering, February 11, 1815, in Pickering Papers (MHS), reel 3, part 1.

218. Dallas to Eppes, October 17, 1814, in *ASP: F,* 2:867.

219. Ingersoll, *Historical Sketch,* 2:252–53.

220. *AC,* 13–3, 534–35.

221. Speech of William Gaston, November 14 and 15, 1814, in *AC,* 13–3, 564–65, 568–81, esp. 574.

222. *AC,* 13–3, 587–88, 631–34, 655–56.

223. Joseph Anderson to George W. Campbell, November 23, 1814, in Campbell Papers (LC).

224. Dallas to Lowndes, November 27, 1814, in *ASP: F,* 2:872.

225. Jonathan Roberts to Matthew Roberts, November 20, 1814, in Roberts Papers (HSP).

226. *AC,* 13–3, 686.

227. *AC,* 13–3, 119, 126–27, 1025–26.

228. Speech of Langdon Cheves, January 2, 1815, in *AC,* 13–3, 1025.

229. *AC,* 13–3, 1030–32.

230. *AC,* 13–3, 177, 1039, 1044–45.

231. Daniel Webster to Ezekiel Webster, January 22, 1815, in Fletcher Webster, ed., *The Private Correspondence of Daniel Webster,* 2 vols. (Boston, 1875), 1:250.

232. Dallas to William Jones, January 29, 1815, in Jones Papers (HSP). See also John Norvell to George W. Campbell, February 10, 1815, in Campbell Papers (LC).

233. Madison to Senate, January 30, 1815, in *AC*, 13–3, 189–91. Quotation from p. 189.

234. Jonathan Roberts to Matthew Roberts, February 2, 1815, in Roberts Papers (HSP); Washington *National Intelligencer*, February 4, 1815.

235. *AC*, 13–3, 226, 229, 231–32, 1151–53, 1168.

236. *AC*, 13–3, 305.

237. Dallas to Eppes, November 19, 1814, in *ASP: F*, 2:881–82.

238. *AC*, 13–3, 757.

239. Georgetown *Federal Republican*, January 6, 1815.

240. *AC*, 13–3, 1889–1906.

241. *AC*, 13–3, 181–88, 1033–38; Washington *National Intelligencer*, January 6, 1815.

242. *AC*, 13–3, 188, 1061–62.

243. Robert Patterson to Jonathan Russell, February 20, 1815, in "Letters of Jonathan Russell," *Proceedings of the Massachusetts Historical Society* 54 (November, 1920), 80.

244. Peter Du Ponceau to Dallas, January 5, 1815, in Dallas Papers (HSP); John Norvell to George W. Campbell, February 10, 1815, in Campbell Papers (LC); Jonathan Roberts to Matthew Roberts, November 4, 1814, in Roberts Papers (HSP).

245. Varnum to Eustis, February 17, 1815, in Eustis Papers (LC), reel 1.

246. Worcester *National Aegis*, December 21, 1814; Boston *Yankee*, December 23, 1814.

247. New York *National Advocate*, December 28, 1814; Philadelphia *Aurora*, January 14, 1815. See also Georgetown *Federal Republican*, November 30, 1814.

248. Worcester *National Aegis*, February 1, 1815.

249. Speech of Charles J. Ingersoll, November 17, 1814, in *AC*, 13–3, 612.

250. Hartford *American Mercury*, November 8, 1814.

Chapter 10: The Hartford Convention

1. Salem *Gazette*, July 4, 1814.

2. A party's cohesion is measured by dividing the party majority on roll-call votes by the party's total vote and then converting the result to a percentage. For example, if there were 10 Federalists and they divided 10–0, 9–1, and 8–2 on three roll call votes, the party's cohesion would be 27/30, or .9, which is 90 percent. See Lee F. Anderson et al., *Legislative Roll-Call Analysis* (Evanston, 1966), 36. For a fuller analysis of party voting during the war, see Harry Fritz, "The Collapse of Party: President, Congress, and the Decline of Party Action, 1807–1817" (Ph.D. dissertation, Washington University, 1970), 250–308; and Donald R. Hickey, "Federalist Party Unity and the War of 1812," *Journal of American Studies* 12 (April, 1978), 26–31.

3. King to Christopher Gore, July 17, 1812, in King, *Rufus King*, 5:272; Philadelphia *United States' Gazette*, June 23, 1812. For similar sentiments, see

[William Sullivan], *Familiar Letters*, 311–12, 354; Felix Gilbert to David Hillhouse, July 24, 1812, in Alexander–Hillhouse Papers (UNC); Hartford *Connecticut Courant*, April 26, 1814.

4. Speech of Harmanus Bleecker, January 7, 1813, in *AC*, 12–2, 619; Wilkes-Barre *Gleaner and Luzerne Advertiser*, reprinted in Pittsburgh *Gazette*, May 1, 1812; Richard Peters to Timothy Pickering, April 4, 1814, in Pickering Papers (MHS), reel 30. For similar sentiments, see speech of Daniel Sheffey, January 11, 1813, in *AC*, 12–2, 698; speech of Alexander Hanson, June 16, 1813, in *AC*, 13–1, 180–82; speech of Richard Stockton, December 11, 1813, in *AC*, 13–2, 2040; Rufus King to Sir William Scott, December 11, 1814, in King, *Rufus King*, 5:443; and Report of Connecticut Legislature, October, 1814, in *Niles' Register* 7 (November 19, 1814), 164.

5. Timothy Dwight, *A Discourse, in Two Parts, Delivered July 23, 1812* (Utica, 1812), 43; Channing, *William Ellery Channing*, 1:337. For a sampling of similar sentiments, see [John Lowell, Jr.], *Mr. Madison's War*, 5; Boston *New-England Palladium*, August 7, 1812; Resolutions of Providence (RI) Meeting, April 7, 1812, in Newport *Mercury*, April 11, 1812; and Georgetown *Federal Republican*, September 30, October 2 and 7, 1812.

6. Speech of Morris Miller, January 14, 1814, in *AC.*, 13–2, 958. For similar sentiments, see speech of Josiah Quincy, November 21, 1812, in *AC*, 12–2, 170; and speech of John Culpepper, February 12, 1814, in *AC*, 13–2, 1364.

7. Alexandria *Gazette*, June 5, 1812.

8. Speech of James A. Bayard, June 16, 1812, in *AC*, 12–1, 293.

9. Federalist predictions that the war would prove both costly and futile are legion. See, for example, speech of Daniel Sheffey, January 3, 1812, in *AC*, 12–1, 625; Hartford *Connecticut Mirror*, January 20 and February 10, 1812; Hartford *Connecticut Courant*, June 30, 1812; Newport *Mercury*, March 7, 1812; Boston *Columbian Centinel*, May 20, 1812; Philadelphia *United States' Gazette*, June 24, 1812; Trenton *Federalist*, June 22, 1812; New York *Herald*, reprinted in Chillicothe *Supporter*, May 23, 1812; and Charleston *Courier*, August 19, 1812.

10. David Osgood, *A Solemn Protest against the Late Declaration of War*, 2nd ed. (Cambridge, MA, 1812), 9. See also Gribbin, *Churches Militant*, chs. 1–2; and Lawrence D. Cress, "'Cool and Serious Reflection': Federalist Attitudes toward War in 1812," *Journal of the Early Republic* 7 (Summer, 1987), 123–45.

11. Joseph Smith to Monroe, December 26, 1814, and Thomas Jesup to Monroe, January 23, 1815, in WD (M221), reels 63 and 66; Goodrich, *Recollections of a Lifetime*, 2:51–52.

12. Resolutions of New Bedford Town Meeting, July 21, 1814, in *Niles' Register* 6 (August 6, 1814), 386. See also Samuel M. Worcester, *The Life and Labors of Samuel Worcester*, 2 vols. (Boston, 1852), 2:226.

13. Report of Massachusetts Legislature, June 10, 1813, in *Niles' Register* 4 (June 19, 1813), 252–53. Massachusetts finally got the arms she demanded. See Caleb Strong to Massachusetts Legislature, January 13, 1814, in Boston *New-England Palladium*, January 14, 1814.

14. Resolution of Massachusetts Senate, June 15, 1813, in *Niles' Register* 4 (July 3, 1813), 287. For the Republican criticism that prompted this resolution, see Boston *Independent Chronicle*, March 6 and 15, 1813.

15. Ingersoll, *Historical Sketch*, 2:23.

16. Decatur to William Jones, December 20, 1813, in Washington *National Intelligencer*, December 28, 1813. See also Ingersoll, *Historical Sketch*, 2:53–54; Adams, *History*, 7:279–80.

17. *Niles' Register* 5 (January 1, 1814), 299.

18. See *AC*, 13–2, 1123–28.

19. Speech of Jonathan O. Moseley, January 24, 1814, in *AC*, 13–2, 1126.

20. Some of the material that follows in this chapter has been taken from Donald R. Hickey, "New England's Defense Problem and the Genesis of the Hartford Convention," *New England Quarterly* 50 (December, 1977), 587–604.

21. See *AC*, 2–1, 1392–95; Adams, *History*, 8:220; Mahon, *American Militia*, 65.

22. Dearborn to Caleb Strong, June 22, 1812, in *ASP: MA*, 1:322; Eustis to Strong, July 21, 1812, in WD (M6), reel 6; Dearborn to Roger Griswold, June 22, 1812, in Hartford *Connecticut Courant*, September 1, 1812; William Jones to Rhode Island Legislature, November 6, 1812, in *Niles' Register* 3 (November 21, 1812), 179–80.

23. John Cotton Smith to William Eustis, July 2, 1812, Griswold to Eustis, August 13, 1812, Strong to Eustis (with enclosure, giving state supreme court advisory opinion), August 5, 1812, and Jones to Eustis, August 22, 1812, in *ASP: MA*, 1:326, 610–12, 615, 621; Hartford *Connecticut Mirror*, reprinted in Hartford *Connecticut Courant*, August 11, 1812.

24. Speech of John Holmes, [October 10, 1814], in *Synopsis of Debates in Massachusetts Legislature*, 8; Hartford *Connecticut Courant*, November 17, 1812; Theodore Dwight, *History of the Hartford Convention* (New York, 1833), 255.

25. For the use of militia on the Canadian frontier, see Eustis to Daniel D. Tompkins, March 24, 1812, and to Return J. Meigs, March 26, 1812, in WD (M6), reel 5; Eustis to Joseph Anderson, June 6, 1812, in WD (M222), reel 5.

26. Madison to Congress, November 4, 1812, in *AC*, 12–2, 13. See also Memorandum of [Albert Gallatin?], June, 1812, in Madison Papers (LC), reel 25.

27. Eustis to [Dearborn], July 1, 1812, in Eustis Papers (LC), reel 1; Dearborn to Monroe, July 8, 1812, in Monroe Papers (LC), reel 5; Dearborn to Monroe, July 30, 1812, in Monroe Papers (NYPL); Lynn W. Turner, *William Plumer of New Hampshire, 1759–1850* (Chapel Hill, 1962), 220. In *Martin v. Mott* in 1827, the Supreme Court ruled that the president had the authority to determine when to call out the militia. See Lodge, *George Cabot*, 513.

28. Madison to Dearborn, August 9, 1812, in Madison Papers (LC), reel 14.

29. Smith to Eustis, June 7, 1813, in *ASP: MA*, 1:615.

30. For documents bearing on this matter—too voluminous to cite in detail—see John Cotton Smith Papers (CHS). Most of the pertinent documents have been published in Harlow et al., *John Cotton Smith Papers*, vols. 1 and

2. See also Decatur to Jones, July 7, 1813, in ND (M125), reel 29; and Hartford *Connecticut Courant*, November 10, 1813.

31. Benjamin Waterhouse to Monroe, July 21, 1813, in Monroe Papers (LC), reel 5; Nicoll Fosdick et al. to Madison, January 6, 1814, in WD (M222), reel 11.

32. Madison to Armstrong, May 24, 1814, in Madison Papers (LC), reel 27.

33. Jirah Isham to J. C. Smith, May 16, 1814, and Smith to Isham, September 21, 1814, in Harlow et al., *John Cotton Smith Papers*, 3:62 and 4:89.

34. Quoted in Isham to Smith, May 16, 1814, ibid., 3:62.

35. Smith to Cushing, August 4, 1814, ibid., 182.

36. Isham to Smith, August 22, 1814, ibid., 221; Cushing to Secretary of War, September 8, 1814, in *ASP: MA*, 4:888.

37. Isham to Smith, August 18, 1814, in Smith Papers (CHS).

38. Smith to Taylor, August 27, 1814, in Harlow et al., *John Cotton Smith Papers*, 4:12.

39. Taylor to Lusk, September 11, 1814, ibid., 44.

40. Quoted in Lusk to Smith, September 14, 1814, in Smith Papers (CHS). See also Taylor to Smith, September 11, 1814, and [September 12, 1814], ibid.

41. Taylor to Smith, [September 12, 1814], ibid.

42. Order of P. P. Schuyler, September 12, 1814, in *ASP: MA*, 1:621.

43. Jacob Ulmer to Eustis, September 26, 1812, in WD (M221), reel 49; Strong to Eustis, August 5 and 21, and September 10, 1812, and Statement of Massachusetts Militia in U. S. Service, January 30, 1828, in *ASP: MA*, 1:324–25, 610–11, and 3:922–23.

44. Bainbridge to Arnold Welles, April 6 and 20, 1814, and Report of Third Auditor's Office, August 1, 1825, in *ASP: MA*, 3:77–78, 87, 179; Bainbridge to Henry A. S. Dearborn, September 27, 1814, in ND (M125), reel 39; Ingersoll, *Historical Sketch*, 2:121; Alden Bradford, *History of Massachusetts*, 3 vols. (Boston, 1822–29), 3:184; Henry A. S. Dearborn, *The Life of William Bainbridge*, ed. James Barnes (Princeton, 1931), 192–93.

45. Sarah Dearborn to Henry Dearborn, September 1, 1814, in Dearborn Papers (MeHS).

46. Secretary of War to Cushing, June 2, 1814, in WD (M6), reel 7; Strong to John Brooks, June 12 and October 1, 1814, and Alden Bradford to Brooks, November 22, 1814, in *ASP: MA*, 3:13–14, 78–79.

47. Dearborn to Armstrong, July 14, 1814, in WD (M221), reel 61.

48. Rules and Regulations of the Army of the United States, May 1, 1813, Dearborn to Strong, July 8, 1812, Strong to Dearborn, July 12, 1812, Report of House Committee, March 10, 1818, and Alden Bradford to Brooks, November 22, 1822, in *ASP: MA*, 1:433, 612, and 3:13–14, 84; William H. Sumner, *A History East Boston* (Boston, 1858), 739; speech of John Davis, March 25, 1826, in *RD*, 19–1, 1778–79.

49. Dearborn to Secretary of War, September 5, 1814, in WD (M221), reel 61; Strong to Monroe, September 7, 1814, in *ASP: MA*, 1:613.

50. Dearborn to Monroe, September 26, 1814, in WD (M221), reel 61; Dearborn to Strong, September 4, 1814, James Lloyd and William H. Sumner

to George Graham, February 3, 1817, Report of House Committee on Massachusetts Claims, March 10, 1818, Report of Third Auditor's Office, July 28, 1825, in *ASP: MA*, 3:63–64, 84, 179, 881; speech of Peleg Sprague, April 7, 1826, in *RD*, 19–1, 2115–16; Bradford, *History of Massachusetts*, 3:185.

51. Commissioners for Seacoast Defense to Sumner, September 10, 1814, and Strong to Sumner, September 10, 1814, in *ASP: MA*, 3:890–91.

52. Selectmen of Portland to Armstrong, [Spring, 1813], in WD (M222), reel 9.

53. Sumner to Brooks, September 15, 1814, Report of Third Auditor's Office, May 11, 1825, in *ASP: MA*, 3:171, 896–97; Sumner, *East Boston*, 734–42.

54. Sumner to Brooks, September 19, 1814, and Brooks to Sumner, September 24, 1814, in *ASP: MA*, 3:897–98.

55. Richardson to Sumner, September 24, 1814, Sumner to Brooks, September 22 and 28, 1814, Bradford to Brooks, November 22, 1822, in *ASP: MA*, 3:13–16, 897, 899–900; Alden Bradford, *Biography of the Hon. Caleb Strong* (Boston, 1820), 24n.

56. Pelatiah Smith et al. to Richardson, September 24, 1814, and Richardson to Sumner, September 24, 1814, in *ASP: MA*, 3:898–99.

57. For the political character of Oxford County, see election results in Banner, *Hartford Convention*, 359.

58. Sumner to Brooks, September 25 and 28, 1814, in *ASP: MA*, 3:899–900.

59. Sumner to Richardson, September 30 and October 1, 1814, in *ASP: MA*, 3:900.

60. Brooks to Sumner, September 27, 1814, in *ASP: MA*, 3:899.

61. Secretary of the Navy to President, April 25, 1800, in *ASP: NA*, 1:87; Dearborn to Samuel L. Mitchill, November 20, 1807, and Eustis to William Branch Giles, January 20, 1810, in *ASP: MA*, 1:220, 258; John O. Creighton to William Jones, October 6, 1814, in ND (M147), reel 5.

62. Petition of the inhabitants of Newport, [Summer, 1814], in WD (M221), reel 66. See also Jeremiah Howell and [Arthur?] Fenner to Armstrong, June 27, 1814, ibid., reel 62.

63. William Jones to Secretary of War, September 8, 1814, in *ASP: MA*, 1:622; Report of Rhode Island Assembly, November 5, 1814, in *Niles' Register* 7 (November 26, 1814), 180–81; Clarence S. Brigham, "History of the State of Rhode Island and Providence Plantations," in Edward Field, ed., *State of Rhode Island and Providence Plantations at the End of the Century: A History*, 3 vols. (Boston, 1902), 1:299.

64. Secretary of War to William Jones, October 4, 1814, in WD (M6), reel 7.

65. William Plumer to Dearborn, June 24, and July 6 and 20, 1812, in Plumer Papers (LC), reel 2; Turner, *William Plumer*, 209–13, 219.

66. Gilman to Armstrong, May 20 and June 30, 1814, in WD (M221), reels 53 and 61. Quotation from May 20 letter.

67. Thomas H. Cushing to Armstrong, May 21, 1814, ibid., reel 60; Ingersoll, *Historical Sketch*, 2:120; John N. McClintock, *History of New Hampshire* (Boston, 1889), 502.

68. Dearborn to Monroe, September 26, 1814, in WD (M221), reel 61.

69. Order of Martin Chittenden, November 10, 1813, in *Niles' Register* 5 (November 27, 1813), 212.

70. Ibid. (December 4, 1813), 229.

71. Vermont militia officers to Chittenden, November 15, 1813, ibid., 230.

72. John L. Heaton, *The Story of Vermont* (Boston, 1889), 123–24; Hildreth, *History of the United States*, 6:452–53.

73. Hartford *American Mercury*, November 30, 1813.

74. Speech of Solomon Sharp, January 6, 1814, in *AC*, 13–2, 859.

75. Quoted in Morison, *Harrison Gray Otis*, 2:64–65.

76. Resolutions of New Jersey Legislature, February 12, 1814, in *Niles' Register* 6 (March 5, 1814), 11. See also Resolutions of Pennsylvania Legislature, ibid. 5 (February 26, 1814), 423.

77. Wilkinson to Chittenden, April 5, 1814, and Alexander Macomb to Armstrong, April 19, 1814, in WD (M221), reels 55 and 58.

78. Samuel Mackay to Macomb, April 24, 1814, ibid., reel 55.

79. Macomb to Armstrong, May 24, 1814, ibid. Pennsylvania also had trouble over reorganization. According to the governor, William Duane's "rudeness & tyrannical conduct" in reorganizing a regiment "so disgusted the officers and influenced the men that he was obliged precipitately to retreat from the camp, where he never after showed himself." Simon Snyder to Monroe, January 16, 1815, in WD (M221), reel 66.

80. Chittenden to John Newell, September 4 and 5, 1814, in *Niles' Register* 7 (Supplement), 103; Proclamation of Martin Chittenden, September 19, 1814, ibid. (October 15, 1814), 65.

81. Resolution of Vermont Council, October 28, 1814, ibid. (Supplement), 105–6.

82. Report of Connecticut Comptroller, October 31, 1816, Statement of Militia Claims, January 13, 1817, and Report of Third Auditor's Office, January 30, 1828, in *ASP: MA*, 1:667, 3:926–27, and 4:878–82.

83. See A. Stetson to Secretary of War, September 12, 1814, in WD (M221), reel 66; John O. Creighton to Secretary of Navy, December 12, 1814, in ND (M147), reel 5; and documents in *ASP: MA*, 3:901–8, 4:883.

84. Monroe to governors of Massachusetts and Connecticut, September 17, 1814, *ASP: MA*, 1:614.

85. Newport *Mercury*. September 17, 1814; Clark, *History of Manufactures*, 1:538; Brant, *James Madison*, 6:236.

86. Newport *Mercury*, November 12, 1814; Ebenezer Huntington to J. C. Smith, September 14, 1814, Andrew Kingsbury to Smith, September 20 and November 30, 1814, Smith to Elizur Goodrich, November 9, 1814, and Goodrich to Smith, November 25, 1814, in Harlow et al., *John Cotton Smith Papers*, 6:61, 85, 167–68, 196, 204; Adams, *History*, 8:302–3.

87. Chauncey Goodrich to [Timothy Pitkin], January 10, 1815, in Pitkin Papers (HL); William W. Woolsey to Smith, January 11, 1815, in Harlow et al., *John Cotton Smith Papers*, 4:241; Dwight, *Hartford Convention*, 339.

88. Goodrich, *Recollections of a Lifetime*, 1:493.

89. Goodrich to [Pitkin], January 30, 1815, in Pitkin Papers (HL).

90. State of Connecticut, *Public Statute Laws of Connecticut [1815]*, 174, 187–91; Goodrich to Pitkin, February 6, 1815, in Pitkin Papers (HL).

91. Statement of Militia Claims, January 13, 1817, in *ASP: MA*, 1:667.

92. King to Jeremiah Mason, September 2, 1814, in King, *Rufus King*, 5:414.

93. Quoted in Pickering to Samuel P. Gardner, November 23, 1814, in Pickering Papers (MHS), reel 38. See also N. Everett to Monroe, September 29, 1814, in WD (M221), reel 61.

94. Boston *Gazette*, September 1 and 15, 1814; Boston *Weekly Messenger*, reprinted ibid., October 17, 1814; Boston *New-England Palladium*, September 30, 1814; Hartford *Connecticut Mirror*, August 29, September 12, and October 3, 17, and 24, 1814.

95. Salem *Gazette*, September 23, 1814. For similar sentiments, see Hartford *Connecticut Courant*, September 13, and December 6 and 13, 1814; Frank M. Anderson, "A Forgotten Phase of the New England Opposition to the War of 1812," *Proceedings of the Mississippi Valley Historical Association* 6 (May, 1913), 178–79.

96. Morison's *Harrison Gray Otis* still has the best account of the Hartford Convention although it understates the importance of the defense problem. This study should be supplemented with Morison's shorter revised study of Otis, *Urbane Federalist*, with Banner's *Hartford Convention*, and with my article, "New England's Defense Problem and the Genesis of the Hartford Convention."

97. For details on these convention movements, see L. Nash to Daniel Appleton White, July 24, 1812, in White Papers (EI); Worcester *National Aegis*, September 23, 1812; James T. Adams, *New England in the Republic, 1776–1850* (Boston, 1926), 270; Morison, *Harrison Gray Otis*, 2:4–13, 59–61, 85–95; Morison, *Urbane Federalist*, 305–11, 342–43, 355–56; Banner, *Hartford Convention*, 303–6, 308–10, 313–21.

98. Joseph Lyman to Noah Webster, January 2, 1835, in Emily E. F. Ford, *Notes on the Life of Noah Webster*, ed. Emily E. F. Skeel, 2 vols. (New York, 1912), 2:498.

99. Noah Webster, "Origin of the Hartford Convention in 1814," in *A Collection of Papers on Political, Literary and Moral Subjects* (New York, 1843), 311.

100. Address of Joseph Lyman, January 5, 1814, in Ford, *Noah Webster*, 2:125–28. Quotation from p. 128.

101. Banner, *Hartford Convention*, 314–17.

102. Petition of Newbury, January 31, 1814, in *Niles' Register* 6 (March 5, 1814), 8.

103. Francis Baylies to William Baylies, January 24, 1814, in Miscellaneous Bound Collection (MHS); Morison, *Harrison Gray Otis*, 2:89.

104. Putnam to Pickering, February 11, 1814, in Pickering Papers (MHS), reel 30.

105. Putnam to Pickering, February 12, 1814, ibid.

106. Boston *Columbian Centinel*, February 23, 1814; Report of the Massachusetts Legislature, February 18, 1814, in *Niles' Register* 6 (March 5, 1814), 4–8.

107. Worthington C. Ford, ed., "A Letter of Noah Webster to Daniel Webster, 1834," *American Historical Review* 9 (October, 1903), 103; Morison, *Harrison Gray Otis*, 2:95; Banner, *Hartford Convention*, 320–21.

108. Webster, "Origin of the Hartford Convention," 314; Ford, "Letter of Noah Webster," 103; Morison, *Harrison Gray Otis*, 2:96.

109. Morison, *Harrison Gray Otis*, 2:99.

110. Otis, quoted ibid., 101–2.

111. Strong to Massachusetts Legislature, October 5, 1814, in *Niles' Register* 7 (October 29, 1814), 113–14.

112. Report of Massachusetts House, October 8, 1814, ibid. (November 12, 1814), 149–51. See also John Phillips and Timothy Bigelow to New England governors, October 17, 1814, ibid. (November 26, 1814), 179.

113. Morison, *Harrison Gray Otis*, 2:103–5.

114. Smith to Connecticut Legislature, October, 1814, in *Niles' Register* 7 (November 19, 1814), 162–63.

115. Report of Connecticut Legislature, October, 1814, ibid., 164–65.

116. Morison, *Harrison Gray Otis*, 2:106.

117. Jones to Rhode Island Legislature, November 1, 1814, in *Niles' Register* 7 (November 26, 1814), 177–78.

118. Report of Rhode Island House, November 5, 1814, ibid., 180–81; Morison, *Harrison Gray Otis*, 2:107.

119. Keene *Newhampshire Sentinel*, December 10, 1814; Morison, *Harrison Gray Otis*, 2:107–8.

120. Otis to Christopher Gore, December 3, 1814, in Samuel Eliot Morison, ed., "Two Letters of Harrison Gray Otis on the Hartford Convention, 1814–1815," *Proceedings of the Massachusetts Historical Society* 60 (November, 1926), 27.

121. Speech of Francis Blake, October 7, 1814, in *Synopsis of Debates in Massachusetts Legislature*, 5.

122. Ibid., 6; Resolutions of Innkeepers and Retailers of Hampshire, Franklin, and Hampden Counties, December 28, 1814, in Hartford *Connecticut Courant*, January 3, 1815.

123. Resolutions of Reading Meeting, January 5, 1815, in Salem *Gazette*, January 10, 1815.

124. Pickering to John Lowell, Jr., November 28, 1814, and to James Hillhouse, December 16, 1814, in Pickering Papers (MHS), reel 15.

125. Boston *Columbian Centinel*, December 21, 1814.

126. Ibid., November 9, 1814.

127. Quincy, *Josiah Quincy*, 358. For similar sentiments, see Lowell to Pickering, December 3, 1814, in Pickering Papers (MHS), reel 30.

128. Pittsburgh *Gazette*, October 26, 1814.

129. John Stanly to William Gaston, November 11, 1814, in Gaston Papers (UNC), reel 2. See also Robert Goodloe Harper to William Sullivan, November 2, 1814, in Harper Papers (MdHS), reel 2; Georgetown *Federal Republican*, November 9, 1814, and January 11, 1815.

130. Plumer to Jeremiah Mason, December 29, 1814, in Plumer Papers (LC), reel 2.

131. Joseph L. Smith to [Thomas Jesup], December 26, 1814, in Jesup Papers (LC).

132. Worcester *National Aegis*, December 28, 1814. For similar sentiments, see Bennington *Green-Mountain Farmer*, November 28, 1814; Hartford *American Mercury*, December 13, 1814; and Lexington *Reporter*, December 31, 1814.

133. William Pope to Monroe, October 28, 1814, in Monroe Papers (NYPL).

134. Monroe to Thomas Jesup, November 26, 1814, in WD (M7), reel 1.

135. Monroe to Daniel D. Tompkins, November 26, 1814, and to Jacob Brown, November 26, 1814, ibid.; Brown to Monroe, December 29, 1814, in Brown Papers (LC); Memorandum of Tench Ringgold, January 10, 1815, in Monroe Papers (NYPL).

136. For the peace rumors, see chapter 9: The Crisis of 1814.

137. Morison, *Harrison Gray Otis*, 2:130–37; Morison, *Urbane Federalist*, 358–62.

138. Lowell to Pickering, December 3, 1814, in Pickering Papers (MHS), reel 30.

139. Otis to Gore, December 3, 1814, in Morison, "Two Letters," 27.

140. Lowell to Pickering, December 3, 1814, in Pickering Papers (MHS), reel 30. For similar sentiments, see Pickering to Putnam, February 3, 1814, ibid., reel 15.

141. Nathan Dane, quoted in Robert C. Winthrop to Henry Cabot Lodge, August 23, 1878, in Lodge, *George Cabot*, 602.

142. Cabot, quoted ibid., 519.

143. Ingersoll, *Historical Sketch*, 2:233.

144. Letter from Hartford, December 16, 1814, in Boston *Gazette*, December 19, 1814. See also letter from Hartford, December 16, 1814, in Concord *New-Hampshire Patriot*, December 22, 1814; Goodrich, *Recollections of a Lifetime*, 2:53.

145. Jesup to Monroe, December 15, 1814, in Jesup Papers (LC). See also Hartford *American Mercury*, December 20, 1814.

146. Otis to Sally Foster Otis, [December 22, 1814], in Morison, *Harrison Gray Otis*, 2:190.

147. Secret Journal of the Hartford Convention, December 15, 1814, in Dwight, *Hartford Convention*, 383.

148. Zilpah Longfellow, quoted in Morison, *Harrison Gray Otis*, 2:140.

149. Calvin Goddard to David Daggett, January 3, 1815, in William E. Buckley, ed., "Letters of Connecticut Federalists, 1814–1815," *New England*

Quarterly 3 (April, 1930), 327. See also Concord *New-Hampshire Patriot*, January 3, 1815.

150. George Ticknor Curtis, *Life of Daniel Webster*, 2 vols., 4th ed. (New York, 1872), 1:136.

151. The Secret Journal of the Hartford Convention is printed in Dwight, *Hartford Convention*, 383–98.

152. Goodrich to [Pitkin], January 10, 1815, in Pitkin Papers (HL).

153. Stephen Longfellow, Jr., to Zilpah Longfellow, December 22, 1814, in Morison, *Harrison Gray Otis*, 2:189.

154. Secret Journal of the Hartford Convention, December 16 and 24, 1814, in Dwight, *Hartford Convention*, 386–87, 392.

155. Morison, *Harrison Gray Otis*, 2:148. The Report of the Hartford Convention is printed in Dwight, *Hartford Convention*, 352–79.

156. Report of the Hartford Convention, in Dwight, *Hartford Convention*, 361.

157. Ibid., 370.

158. Ibid., 377–78.

159. Ibid., 353.

160. Ibid., 378–79.

161. Morison, *Harrison Gray Otis*, 2:147.

162. Otis, quoted in Morison, *Urbane Federalist*, 396.

163. Dwight to Timothy Pitkin, January 9, 1815, in Pitkin Papers (HL); Gore to Strong, January 14, 1815, in Lodge, *George Cabot*, 560.

164. Webster to————, January 11, 1815, in Daniel Webster Papers (HU).

165. Winchester (VA) *Gazette*, reprinted in Salem *Gazette*, February 7, 1815; New York *Evening Post*, January 7, 1815. See also [Robert Goodloe Harper] to [Alexander Hanson], January 19, 1815, in Galloway-Maxcy-Markoe Papers (LC); William R. Davie to William Gaston, February 4, [1815], in Gaston Papers (UNC), reel 2; letter from a congressman, January 10, 1815, in Boston *Columbian Centinel*, January 21, 1815; Gore to Strong, January 14, 1815, in Lodge, *George Cabot*, 560.

166. Pickering to Lowell, January 23, 1815, in Pickering Papers (MHS), reel 15; Sullivan to Henry D. Sedgwick, January 6, 1815, in Sedgwick Papers (MHS).

167. Boston *Gazette*, January 9, 1815.

168. Washington *National Intelligencer*, January 13, 1815; Armstrong to Joseph Desha, January 16, 1815, in Desha Papers (LC).

169. Worcester *National Aegis*, January 11, 1815; Boston *Patriot*, January 7, 1815. For similar sentiments, see Salem *Essex Register*, January 18, 1815; and Warren, *Jacobin and Junto*, 280.

170. Jackson to Monroe, January 6, 1817, in Jackson Papers (LC), reel 71.

171. Hartford *Connecticut Courant*, January 31, 1815; Adams, *History*, 8:301–2.

172. Otis to Gore, January 21, 1815, in Morison, "Two Letters," 28.

173. See documents in Samuel Eliot Morison, ed., "The Massachusetts Embassy to Washington, 1815," *Proceedings of the Massachusetts Historical Society*

48 (March, 1915), 343–51; Smith to Calvin Goddard and Nathaniel Terry, February 4, 1815, in Smith Papers (CHS).

174. Perkins to John P. Cushing, February 16, 1815, in Cary, *Thomas Handasyd Perkins*, 219.

175. Scott to Monroe, February 15, 1815, in Monroe Papers (NYPL).

176. Otis to Sally Foster Otis, February 23, 1815, in Morison, *Harrison Gray Otis*, 2:168.

177. Alexander Dallas to Monroe, January 14, 1815, and to Thomas B. Worthington, January 17, 1815, in WD (M221), reels 61 and 67.

178. *AC*, 13–3, 225, 230, 250, 1264–65, 1279. The quotation (from the stenographer) is on p. 1264. See also Georgetown *Federal Republican*, March 3, 1815.

179. J. R. Poinsett to James K. Polk, December 23, 1837, in *ASP: MA*, 7:775; James Schouler, *History of the United States under the Constitution*, 7 vols., rev. ed. (New York, 1894–1913), 2:508n.

180. Boston *New-England Palladium*, February 7 and 10, 1815.

181. *AC*, 13–3, 280–81, 284, 1269–70; Herman V. Ames, *The Proposed Amendments to the Constitution of the United States during the First Century of Its History* (Washington, 1897), 46.

182. Report of New York Legislative Committee, in *Niles' Register* 8 (April 8, 1815), 100. See also Report of New Jersey House, ibid. (March 4, 1815), [16].

183. Morison, *Harrison Gray Otis*, 2:80.

Chapter 11: The Treaty of Ghent

1. There are three excellent studies of the diplomatic history of the war. The standard account is Frank A. Updyke, *The Diplomacy of the War of 1812* (Baltimore, 1915); Fred L. Engelman, *The Peace of Christmas Eve* (New York, 1962), is a first-rate popular study; and Bradford Perkins presents a brilliant and incisive modern analysis in *Castlereagh and Adams: England and the United States, 1812–1823* (Berkeley, 1964).

2. See chapter 2: The Declaration of War.

3. Madison to Congress, March 4, 1813, in *AC*, 12–2, 123. For similar sentiments, see speech of Stevenson Archer, January 6, 1813, in *AC*, 12- 2, 597.

4. Perkins, *Castlereagh and Adams*, 3–4.

5. Davis, *Notes by Augustus John Foster*, 100.

6. Monroe to Russell, June 26, 1812, in SD (M77), reel 2.

7. Russell to Monroe, September 17, 1812, in *ASP: FR*, 3:594–95.

8. Perkins, *Castlereagh and Adams*, 11.

9. Russell to Monroe, September 17, 1812, in *ASP: FR*, 3:593.

10. British Order in Council, October 13, 1812, in *Naval Chronicle* 28 (July–December, 1812), 303–5.

11. John Graham to Russell (with enclosure), August 10, 1812, and Monroe to Russell, August 21, 1812, in SD (M77), reel 2; Dearborn to Secretary of

War, August 9, 1812, in Cruikshank, *Surrender of Detroit*, 127–28; Articles of Agreement for an Armistice, August 21, 1812, in Cruikshank, *Niagara Frontier*, 3:197–98; Warren to Secretary of State, September 30, 1812, and Secretary of State to Warren, October 27, 1812, in *ASP: FR*, 3:595–97; Anthony Baker to Lord Castlereagh, October 31, 1812, in Foreign Office Papers 5/88 (PRO).

12. Dashkov to Monroe, March 8, 1813, in Bashkina et al., *United States and Russia*, 933–34.

13. Gallatin to Alexander Baring, August 27, 1813, in SD (M36), reel 1; letter of Pavel P. Svin'in, [April, 1812], and Levett Harris to Monroe, October 27, 1812, in Bashkina et al., *United States and Russia*, 836, 894; Alfred W. Crosby, Jr., *America, Russia, Hemp, and Napoleon: American Trade with Russia and the Baltic, 1783–1812* ([Columbus, OH], 1965), ch. 14.

14. Monroe to Dashkov, March 11, 1813, in Bashkina et al., *United States and Russia*, 937.

15. Monroe to American commissioners, April 15, 1813, in SD (M77), reel 2. See also Monroe to American commissioners, April 27, 1813, ibid.

16. Perkins, *Castlereagh and Adams*, 20–21.

17. See chapter 5: Raising Men and Money.

18. Monroe to American commissioners, April 15, 1813, in *ASP: FR*, 3:695–700, and (for confidential paragraphs) in Donnan, *Papers of James A. Bayard*, 204–6.

19. Monroe to American commissioners, June 23, 1813, in SD (M77), reel 2. See also Robert Walsh to Robert Goodloe Harper, December 2, 1813, in Harper Papers (MdHS), reel 2.

20. Bayard to Andrew Bayard, February 14, 1813, in Donnan, *Papers of James A. Bayard*, 203.

21. Monroe to Gallatin, May 6, 1813, in Gallatin Papers (SR), reel 26.

22. Engelman, *Peace of Christmas Eve*, ch. 2.

23. Castlereagh to Goulburn, October 8, 1813, in Henry Goulburn Papers (UM), reel 1.

24. Baring to Gallatin, July 22, 1813, in SD (M36), reel 1; John Quincy Adams to William H. Crawford, November 15, 1813, and to Abigail Adams, December 30, 1813, in Ford, *Writings of John Quincy Adams*, 4:531, 534.

25. Bayard, European Diary, December 14, 1813, in Donnan, *Papers of James A. Bayard*, 493.

26. Gallatin to Monroe, November 21, 1813, in SD (M36), reel 1; Gallatin to Monroe, January 7, 1814, and to Baring, January 7, 1814, in Gallatin Papers (SR), reel 26.

27. See American commissioners to Emperor Alexander, August 14, 1813, in Henry Adams, ed., *The Writings of Albert Gallatin*, 3 vols. (Philadelphia, 1879), 1:559–61.

28. Baring to Gallatin, July 22, 1813, in SD (M36), reel 1. See also Charles King to Rufus King, January 20, 1814, in King, *Rufus King*, 5:366.

29. Castlereagh to Secretary of State, November 4, 1813, in SD (M36), reel 1.

30. See chapter 7: The Last Embargo.

31. John Quincy Adams to John Adams, December 26, 1814, in Ford, *Writings of John Quincy Adams,* 5:253.

32. John Quincy Adams to Louisa Catherine Adams, January 13, 1815, ibid., 267.

33. Perkins, *Castlereagh and Adams,* 59–61.

34. Reuben Beasley, quoted in Engelman, *Peace of Christmas Eve,* 120.

35. Letter from England, March 29, 1814, reprinted from *Baltimore American* in Lexington *Reporter,* June 18, 1814. See also Georgetown *Federal Republican,* June 9, 1814.

36. London *Times,* June 2, 1814; London *Sun,* quoted in Perkins, *Castlereagh and Adams,* 63. For similar sentiments, see Captain Fairman, quoted in *Naval Chronicle* 30 (July–December, 1813), 225; London *Evening Star,* reprinted in Washington *National Intelligencer,* April 2, 1813; Reuben Beasley to Russell, February 16, 1813, and Thomas O'Reilly to Russell, August 5, 1814, in Russell Papers (BU); Bayard to Clay and Russell, April 20, 1814, in SD (M36), reel 2; Gallatin to Clay, April 22, 1814, in Gallatin Papers (SR), reel 26; Crawford to Clay, June 10, 1814, in Hopkins and Hargreaves, *Papers of Henry Clay,* 1:932; Adams, *Memoirs of John Quincy Adams* (October 26, 1814), 3:58.

37. Bayard to Andrew Bayard, March 19, 1814, in Donnan, *Papers of James A. Bayard,* 281; Clay to Monroe, August 18, 1814, in Monroe Papers (LC), reel 5; Gallatin to Monroe, June 13, 1814, in SD (M36), reel 1. See also King to Gouverneur Morris, October 11 and 13, 1814, in King, *Rufus King,* 5:417, 419.

38. Russell to John L. Lawrence, October 7, 1814, in Russell Papers (BU).

39. Gallatin to Monroe, December 25, 1814, in Gallatin Papers (SR), reel 27; William Shaler to Russell, December 8, 1814, in Russell Papers (BU). See also Duke of Wellington to Castlereagh, October 4, 1814, in Wellington, *Dispatches of the Duke of Wellington,* 9:314.

40. Letter from Washington, January 28, 1813, and French Imperial Decree, April 14, 1813, in Lexington *Reporter,* February 20 and October 9, 1813; Castlereagh to Bathurst, March 3, 1814, in Vane, *Correspondence of Viscount Castlereagh,* 10:4; Crawford to American commissioners, May 28, 1814, in Hopkins and Hargreaves, *Papers of Henry Clay,* 1:926; R. Gordon to Comte de la Forest, May 10, 1814, and to Bathurst, May 19, 1814, in Wellington, *Dispatches of the Duke of Wellington,* 9:92–3; James Fowler to Admiralty, September 15, 1814, and J. W. Croker to Fowler, September 16, 1814, in *Niles' Register* 8 (Supplement), 186–87; Crawford to [Monroe], November 1, 1814, in Madison Papers (LC), reel 26; Crawford to Monroe, December 16 and 21, 1814, in Monroe Papers (LC), reel 5; Lawrence Kaplan, *Entangling Alliances with None: American Foreign Policy in the Age of Jefferson* (Kent, OH, 1987), 147–49.

41. Clay to Russell, May 1, 1814, in Hopkins and Hargreaves, *Papers of Henry Clay,* 1:887–88.

42. London *Morning Chronicle,* September 7, 1814. See also *Naval Chronicle* 32 (July–December, 1814), 247.

43. London *Times,* September 26 and November 21, 1814.

44. For the gambling odds, see London *Morning Chronicle,* December 16,

1814. For the erroneous reports, see ibid., December 24, 1814, and London *Times,* December 24, 1814.

45. Adams, *Memoirs of John Quincy Adams* (October 12, 1814), 3:51.

46. London *Morning Chronicle,* November 21, 1814. For similar sentiments, see Worcester *National Aegis,* January 4, 1815.

47. Quoted in Engelman, *Peace of Christmas Eve,* 297.

48. Goulburn to Bathurst, December 13, 1814, in Bickley, *Manuscripts of Earl Bathurst,* 316.

49. Monroe to American commissioners, January 28, 1814, in SD (M77), reel 2. See also Monroe to American commissioners, February 14, 1814, ibid.

50. Adams, *Memoirs of John Quincy Adams* (November 19, 1813), 2:550.

51. Clay to [Crawford], July 2, 1814, in Hopkins and Hargreaves, *Papers of Henry Clay,* 1:938.

52. Gallatin to Monroe, June 13, 1814, in SD (M36), reel 1; Gallatin to Emperor Alexander, June 19, 1814, in Gallatin Papers (SR), reel 27; Adams to John Adams, February 17, 1814, in Ford, *Writings of John Quincy Adams,* 5:22.

53. Notes of cabinet meeting, June 23, 24, and 27, 1814, in Madison Papers (LC), reel 27.

54. Monroe to American commissioners, June 25 and 27, 1814, in SD (M77), reel 2; Perkins, *Castlereagh and Adams,* 72.

55. Washington *National Intelligencer,* November 5, 1814; Monroe to American commissioners, June 25, 1814, in SD (M77), reel 2.

56. See Castlereagh to British commissioners, July 28 and August 14, 1814, in Goulburn Papers (UM), reel 1; and documents in *ASP: FR,* 3:705–10.

57. British commissioners to American commissioners, September 4, 1814, in SD (M36), reel 1.

58. American commissioners to British commissioners, September 9, 1814, in Goulburn Papers (UM), reel 1; British commissioners to American commissioners, September 19, 1814, in *ASP: FR,* 3:718.

59. American commissioners to British commissioners, September 26, 1814, in Goulburn Papers (UM), reel 1. In fact, the administration had approved of Hull's proclamation. See chapter 4: The Campaign of 1812.

60. British commissioners to American commissioners, October 8, 1814, in SD (M36), reel 1. See also Adams to Secretary of State, September 5, 1814, ibid.; Castlereagh to British commissioners, July 28, 1814, in Goulburn Papers (UM), reel 1; Bayard, Memorandum of Conferences, August 27, 1814, in Donnan, *Papers of James A. Bayard,* 338.

61. Bemis, *Jay's Treaty,* esp. ch. 6.

62. George Prevost, quoted in Sugden, *Tecumseh's Last Stand,* 196.

63. Robert McDonall, quoted ibid., 205.

64. London *Sun,* quoted in Perkins, *Castlereagh and Adams,* 82.

65. Adams, *Memoirs of John Quincy Adams* (August 19, 1814), 3:18.

66. American commissioners to British commissioners, August 24, 1814, in Goulburn Papers (UM), reel 1; U.S. Bureau of the Census, *Historical Statistics of the United States, Colonial Times to 1970,* 2 vols. (Washington, 1975), 1:39.

67. American commissioners to Monroe, August 19, 1814, in *ASP: FR,* 3:709; American commissioners to British commissioners, August 24, 1814, in Goulburn Papers (UM), reel 1; U.S. Bureau of the Census, *Historical Statistics of the United States,* 1:27–37.

68. Adams, *Memoirs of John Quincy Adams* (August 19, 1814), 3:19.

69. Castlereagh to British commissioners, July 28, 1814, in Goulburn Papers (UM), reel 1; Castlereagh to Liverpool, August 28, 1814, in Vane, *Correspondence of Viscount Castlereagh,* 10:100–101.

70. British commissioners to American commissioners, August 19, 1814, in SD (M36), reel 1. See also Goulburn to Bathurst, August 21, 1814, in Wellington, *Dispatches of the Duke of Wellington,* 9:188–89; Liverpool to Bathurst, September 14, 1814, in Bickley, *Manuscripts of Earl Bathurst,* 287.

71. See, for example, London *Times,* May 24, 1814; Portland *Eastern Argus,* August 18, 1814; New London *Connecticut Gazette,* August 17 and September 7, 1814; Quebec *Gazette,* reprinted in Boston *Gazette,* September 1, 1814; New York *Evening Post,* September 23, 1814.

72. Gallatin to William H. Crawford, April 21, 1814, in Gallatin Papers (SR), reel 26.

73. American commissioners to British commissioners, August 24, 1814, in Goulburn Papers (UM), reel 1.

74. Adams, *Memoirs of John Quincy Adams* (September 1, 1814), 3:28.

75. Goulburn to Bathurst, November 26, 1814, in Goulburn Papers (UM), reel 2.

76. See chapter 9: The Crisis of 1814.

77. Liverpool to Wellington, November 26, 1814, in Wellington, *Dispatches of the Duke of Wellington,* 9:456; speech of Liverpool, November 21, 1814, in *Parliamentary Debates,* 29:368.

78. Liverpool to Wellington, October 28, 1814, in Wellington, *Dispatches of the Duke of Wellington,* 9:384.

79. Speeches of Alexander Baring and Marquis of Lansdowne, November 21, 1814, in *Parliamentary Debates,* 29:383, 414. See also speeches of Earl Donoughmore and George Ponsonby, November 21, 1814, ibid., 385, 415–16.

80. London *Morning Chronicle,* November 22, 1814. For similar sentiments, see *Naval Chronicle* 32 (July–December, 1814), 425.

81. Adams to Crawford, October 5, 1814, in Ford, *Writings of John Quincy Adams,* 5:152.

82. See Adams, *Memoirs of John Quincy Adams* (September 8 and 21, 1814), 3:32, 39. Clay had once reportedly bet $50,000 on a hand of cards, but the hand was never played out because "a bystander swept the cards from the table & thus broke up the game." The story may be apocryphal, but it illustrates Clay's reputation for high stakes gambling. See Harrison, *Diary of Thomas P. Cope* (May 15, 1812), 272.

83. Clay to Monroe, August 18, 1814, in Monroe Papers (LC), reel 5; Clay to Crawford, August 22, 1814, in Hopkins and Hargreaves, *Papers of Henry Clay,* 1:972.

84. Perkins, *Castlereagh and Adams,* 69.

85. Liverpool to Castlereagh, September 2, 1814, in Wellington, *Dispatches of the Duke of Wellington,* 9:214; Liverpool to Bathurst, September 15, 1814, in Bickley, *Manuscripts of Earl Bathurst,* 289. See also Liverpool to Castlereagh, September 23, 1814, and Liverpool to Wellington, September 27 and November 4, 1814, in Wellington, *Dispatches of the Duke of Wellington,* 9:278, 290, 406.

86. Liverpool to Castlereagh, September 2, 1814, to Bathurst, September 11, 1814, and to Wellington, October 28, 1814, in Wellington, *Dispatches of the Duke of Wellington,* 9:214, 240, 384.

87. British commissioners to American commissioners, September 19, 1814, in *ASP: FR,* 3:718. See also Bathurst to Goulburn, September 20, 1814, and to British commissioners, September 27, 1814, in Goulburn Papers (UM), reel 1.

88. Clay to Crawford, September 20, 1814, in Hopkins and Hargreaves, *Papers of Henry Clay,* 1:979.

89. British commissioners to American commissioners, October 21, 1814, in SD (M36), reel 1.

90. Ibid.

91. Bathurst to British commissioners, October 17, 18 and 20, 1814, in Goulburn Papers (UM), reel 1.

92. See James A. Carr, "The Battle of New Orleans and the Treaty of Ghent," *Diplomatic History* 3 (Summer, 1979), 273–82. The British also gave little thought to Prairie du Chien, a frontier outpost they had captured in July of 1814.

93. Bayard to Erick Bollman, October 29, 1814, in Donnan, *Papers of James A. Bayard,* 351.

94. Clay to Monroe, October 26, 1814, in Monroe Papers (LC), reel 5.

95. See chapter 9: The Crisis of 1814.

96. Nicholas Vansittart, quoted in Perkins, *Castlereagh and Adams,* 99.

97. See London *Times,* September 27, and October 18 and 19, 1814; Liverpool to Bathurst, September 30, 1814, in Bickley, *Manuscripts of Earl Bathurst,* 294–95; Liverpool to Castlereagh, October 21, 1814, in Wellington, *Dispatches of the Duke of Wellington,* 9:367.

98. Goulburn to Bathurst, October 21, 1814, in Wellington, *Dispatches of the Duke of Wellington,* 9:366.

99. Liverpool to Castlereagh, October 28 and November 2, 1814, ibid., 383, 402.

100. Speech of Samuel Whitbread, November 18, 1814, in *Parliamentary Debates,* 29:364.

101. London *Morning Chronicle,* November 17, 1814. See also ibid., November 3, 1814.

102. Bathurst to Goulburn, September 12, 1814, in Goulburn Papers (UM), reel 1.

103. Liverpool to Canning, December 28, 1814, in Charles D. Yonge, *The Life and Administration of Robert Banks, Second Earl of Liverpool,* 3 vols. (London, 1868), 2:74–77; Perkins, *Castlereagh and Adams,* 100–101.

104. Liverpool to Canning, December 28, 1814, in Yonge, *Earl of Liverpool*, 2:76.

105. Liverpool to Castlereagh, November 4, 1814, and to Wellington, November 4, 1814, in Wellington, *Dispatches of the Duke of Wellington*, 9:405–6.

106. Wellington to Liverpool, November 9, 1814, ibid., 425–26.

107. Liverpool to Castlereagh, November 18, 1814, ibid., 438.

108. Adams, *Memoirs of John Quincy Adams* (November 28, 1814), 3:71–76; Bathurst to Goulburn, November 21, 1814, and Goulburn to Bathurst, November 26, 1814, in Goulburn Papers (UM), reel 2.

109. The treaty is printed in *ASP: FR*, 3:745–48.

110. Ibid., 746. Great Britain later paid $1,204,960 for slaves carried off at the end of the war. Updyke, *Diplomacy of the War*, 404.

111. Treaty of Ghent, in *ASP: FR*, 3:747. This clause was a dead letter from the beginning. See Colin G. Calloway, *Crown and Calumet: British-Indian Relations, 1783–1815* (Norman, OK, 1986), 240–48.

112. The commissions rendered their decisions between 1817 and 1842. See Updyke, *Diplomacy of the War*, 421–36.

113. Treaty of Ghent, in *ASP: FR*, 3:748.

114. Ibid., 746, 748; Castlereagh to British commissioners, July 28, 1814, and Goulburn to Bathurst, December 30, 1814, in Goulburn Papers (UM), reels 1 and 2; Worthington C. Ford, ed., "Intended Instructions [to the British commissioners at Ghent]," *Proceedings of the Massachusetts Historical Society* 48 (December, 1914), 161; Perkins, *Castlereagh and Adams*, 121.

115. Castlereagh to Liverpool, January 2, 1815, in Wellington, *Dispatches of the Duke of Wellington*, 9:523.

116. Edward Cooke (an undersecretary in the Foreign Office), quoted in Liverpool to Bathurst, January 16, 1815, in Bickley, *Manuscripts of Earl Bathurst*, 324.

117. London *Courier*, reprinted in Washington *National Intelligencer*, February 16, 1815; *Naval Chronicle* 33 (January–June, 1815), 70–71; *Annual Register for 1814 [Preface]*, v; Moore Smith, *Autobiography of Harry Smith*, 1:251.

118. London *Morning Chronicle*, December 27, 1814.

119. London *Times*, December 27 and 30, 1814. See also London *Globe*, reprinted in *Niles' Register* 7 (February 25, 1815), 407.

120. Speech of Marquis Wellesley, April 13, 1815, in *Parliamentary Debates*, 30:589 and 598. See also ibid., 205–6, 209, 500–533, 587–607, 649–52.

121. Ibid., 513–14, 533, 600, 607.

122. London *Morning Chronicle*, December 31, 1814.

123. Adams, *Memoirs of John Quincy Adams* (December 11 and 14, 1814), 3:104, 118.

124. Gallatin to Monroe, December 25, 1814, in Gallatin Papers (SR), reel 27; Clay to Monroe, December 25, 1814, in Monroe Papers (LC), reel 5; Bayard to Andrew Bayard, December 24, 1814, in Donnan, *Papers of James A. Bayard*, 364; John Quincy Adams to Louisa Catherine Adams, December 23, 1814, and January 3, 1815, and to Abigail Adams, December 24, 1814, in Ford, *Writings of John Quincy Adams*, 5:245–46, 248, 260–61.

125. Bathurst to British commissioners, December 26, 1814, in Goulburn Papers (UM), reel 2; Perkins, *Castlereagh and Adams*, 142.

126. Benjamin Russell to Jonathan Goodhue, February 11, 1815, in Boston *Columbian Centinel*, February 15, 1815; McMaster, *History of the United States*, 4:275.

127. Boston *Yankee*, February 17, 1815; Hartford *American Mercury*, February 21 and 28, 1815; Washington *National Intelligencer*, February 18 and 20, 1815; Updyke, *Diplomacy of the War*, 365–66; Lemmon, *North Carolina*, 200–201.

128. Otis Ammidon to Jonathan Russell, February 20, 1815, in "Letters of Jonathan Russell," 78.

129. Washington *National Intelligencer*, February 16 and 17, 1815; Hartford *Connecticut Courant*, February 21, 1815; Boston *Gazette*, February 13 and March 6, 1815; Georgetown *Federal Republican*, February 20, 1815; Updyke, *Diplomacy of the War*, 368–69; Adams, *History*, 9:61–62.

130. Liverpool to Castlereagh, December 23, 1814, in Wellington, *Dispatches of the Duke of Wellington*, 9:495.

131. Washington *National Intelligencer*, February 14, 15, and 18, 1815; *Senate Journal*, 2:618–20; *Parliamentary Debates*, 30:218.

132. Gore to Strong, February 18, 1815, in Lodge, *George Cabot*, 563.

133. Robertson to Pickering, February 14, 1815, in Pickering Papers (MHS), reel 30.

134. Madison to Congress, February 18, 1815, in *AC*, 13–3, 255.

135. Story to Nathaniel Williams, February 22, 1815, in Story, *Joseph Story*, 1:254: New York *National Advocate*, February 20, 1815.

136. Washington *National Intelligencer*, February 23, 1815; Worcester *National Aegis*, February 22, 1815. For similar sentiments, see Boston *Yankee*, February 17, 1815; Richmond *Enquirer*, February 18, 1815; Philadelphia *Aurora*, February 20, 1815; Trenton *True American*, March 6, 1815; Concord *New-Hampshire Patriot*, March 7 and April 11, 1815; Address of Massachusetts Republicans, February 23, 1815, and Address of John Dickinson, March 18, 1815, in Washington *National Intelligencer*, March 27, 1815; speech of John C. Calhoun, February 27, 1815, in *AC*, 13–3, 1236; *Niles' Register* 8 (March 4, 1815), 417–19.

Conclusion

1. Speech of Daniel Sheffey, January 3, 1812, in *AC*, 12–1, 627.

2. Calhoun to James Macbride, April 18, 1812, in Meriwether et al, *Papers of John C. Calhoun*, 1:99–100; Charles J. Ingersoll to Monroe, June 8, 1814, in Monroe Papers (LC), reel 5; letter from a congressman, January 8, 1815, in Lexington *Reporter*, February 8, 1815.

3. Richmond *Enquirer*, December 24, 1812; William A. Burwell to [Wilson Cary Nicholas], February 1, 1813, in Nicholas Papers (UVA).

4. Annapolis *Maryland Gazette*, October 15, 1812.

5. Robert B. Atkinson to John B. Floyd, February 22, 1858, in *NASP: MA*,

5:339; U.S. Congress, *Report of the Third Auditor relative to the Officers, Non-Commissioned Officers, and Soldiers of the Militia, Volunteers, and Rangers of the Late War,* [U.S. Serial Set, #302] (Washington, 1836), 78–79.

6. U.S. Department of Defense, *Selected Manpower Statistics* ([Washington], 1974), 19.

7. Ibid., 63.

8. See Edmund P. Gaines to Armstrong, August 11, 1814, and Moses Porter to Secretary of War, July 25, August 10, and September 10 and 21, 1814, in WD (M221), reels 61 and 65; James Wilkinson to Armstrong, August 16, 1813, in WD (M222), reel 9; Dr. G. Proctor to F. K. Huger, July 31, 1813, in Lowndes Papers (UNC), reel 1; Alexander Smyth to Dearborn, November 9, 1812, Report of Hospital Surgeon, 1814, and Izard to Secretary of War, November 8, 1814, in Cruikshank, *Niagara Frontier,* 2:298, 452–53, and 4:187; Harrison to Armstrong, September 8, 1813, in Esarey, *Messages and Letters of William Henry Harrison,* 2:538; Mann, *Medical Sketches,* 66, 89, 125; McAfee, *History of the Late War,* 183–86; Gilpin, *War of 1812 in the Northwest,* 230; Lemmon, *North Carolina,* 44, 51, 89, 91, 199.

9. I. A. Coles to Richard Rush, November 16, [1812], in Monroe Papers (NYPL); Shelby to Susannah Shelby, October 28, 1813, in Shelby Papers (LC); Izard to [Secretary of War], June 25, 1814, in Izard, *Official Correspondence,* 38. See also Samuel Huntington to Eustis, October 1, 1812, in WD (M221), reel 45.

10. Stagg, "Enlisted Men in the United States Army," 624.

11. Hare, "Military Punishments," 238; Benjamin Homans to Chauncey, December 19, 1814 in ND (M149), reel 11. Andrew Jackson's military courts handled a particularly large number of desertion cases. See Proceedings of General Court Martial Held at Nashville, October 19, 1814, in Jackson Papers (LC), reel 64.

12. The British have not tabulated their losses. Their casualties were probably higher because of the Battle of New Orleans, but their deaths from disease were probably lower because their armies were smaller and their troops more seasoned.

13. U.S. Bureau of the Census, *Historical Statistics of the United States,* 2:1140.

14. New York *Times,* January 16, 1946, p. 17, and January 17, 1947, p. 10; President's Commission on Veterans' Pensions, *The Historical Development of Veterans' Benefits in the United States* (Washington, 1956), 100.

15. George C. Whiting to J. Thompson, March 2, 1858, in *NASP: MA,* 5:341.

16. U.S. Department of the Treasury, *Report of the Secretary of the Treasury for 1866,* 304; Report of Ways and Means Committee, April 13, 1830, in *RD,* 21–1, Appendix, 115.

17. See Cox, *West Florida Controversy,* ch. 16.

18. Report of the Secretary of War, December 5, 1818, in *ASP: IA,* 2:183.

19. Madison to Congress, February 18, 1815, in *AC,* 13–3, 255–56.

20. See *AC,* 13–3, 297–98, 1272–73, 1934–35; *AC,* 14–1, 363, 1374, 1886–87; K. Jack Bauer, "Naval Shipbuilding Programs, 1794–1860," *Military Affairs*

29 (Spring, 1965), 34. The Senate preferred an army of 15,000 men, and the administration favored 20,000. See *AC*, 13–3, 286; and Monroe to Giles, February 22, 1815, in Monroe Papers (LC), reel 5.

21. C. Gratiot to John Eaton, March 8, 1830, in *ASP: MA*, 4:305. See also Board of Engineers to Calhoun, February 7, 1821, ibid., 2:305–12; speech of Samuel Smith, March 9, 1820, in *AC*, 16–1, 1620.

22. Jefferson to William Short, November 28, 1814, in Jefferson Papers (LC), reel 47.

23. Whitehill, *Journal of Henry Edward Napier* (May 29, 1814), 20.

24. *AC*, 13–3, 285, 1271, 1945–49. For the renewal of this act, see *AC*, 14–2, 1343–45.

25. Harrison to John Vincent, November 3, 1813, in Esarey, *Messages and Letters of William Henry Harrison*, 2:592–94. See also Georgetown *Federal Republican*, March 31, 1813.

26. *Annual Register for 1814 [General History]*, 205; Horsman, "Paradox of Dartmoor," 14. The United States held about the same number of British prisoners. See Dietz, "Prisoner of War," 106–7.

27. Samuel Davis to mother, March 10, 1814, in *Niles' Register* 8 (Supplement), 120.

28. *Niles' Register* 8 (April 22, 1815), 127.

29. Boston *Patriot*, March 25, 1815. See also Salem *Essex Register*, April 5, 1815; statements of W. L. Churchill et al., and of Ebenezer A. Lewis et al., in Washington *National Intelligencer*, April 6, 1815. See also ibid., April 7, 1815.

30. Letter of J. Odiorne, November 1, 1814, in *Niles' Register* 8 (March 25, 1815), 56. See also Horsman, "Paradox of Dartmoor," 13.

31. Resolutions of William Harmon et al., August 31, 1815, in *Niles' Register* 9 (October 28, 1815), 154.

32. For the official view, see Report of Charles King and Francis S. Larpent, April 26, 1815, in *Niles' Register* 8 (July 22, 1815), 354–57. For the prisoners' side of the story, see their reports ibid. (June 17, 1815), 269–71, (July 8, 1815), 321–28, and (August 5, 1815), 389–92.

33. Richmond *Enquirer*, June 17, 1815. See also Washington *National Intelligencer*, May 31 and June 1, 1815. A student of this subject has concluded that the Americans adhered more closely to international law than the British. Robin F. A. Farbel, "The Laws of War in the 1812 Conflict," *Journal of American Studies* 14 (August, 1980), 199–218.

34. Report on Spirit and Manner in Which the War is Waged by the Enemy, July 31, 1813, in *ASP: MA*, 1:339–82.

35. *Niles' Register* ran a column entitled "War Events" for eight months after the war and continued to publish this kind of material long after the column had been discontinued.

36. Henry Adams, *History*, displays the same Anglophobia that is evident in the writings of John Adams and John Quincy Adams.

37. Davis, *Notes by Augustus John Foster*, 5; letter from an Englishman, July 21, 1815, in *Niles' Register* 9 (October 28, 1815), 156.

38. Perkins, *Castlereagh and Adams*, 160–62.

39. Young, *Battle of the Thames*, ch. 8; Stagg, *Mr. Madison's War*, 330n.
40. Story to Nathaniel Williams, February 22, 1815, in Story, *Joseph Story*, 1:254.
41. See Richard Archer, "Dissent and the Peace Negotiations at Ghent," *American Studies* 18 (Fall, 1977), 5–16.
42. Boston *Yankee*, March 3, 1815.
43. Dwight, *Hartford Convention*, 4, 382.
44. Statement of Rufus King, [1814?], in King, *Rufus King*, 5:405. For similar sentiments, see speech of Daniel Webster, January 14, 1814, in *AC*, 13–2, 942.
45. Address of Boston Federalists, February 27, 1815, in Boston *Gazette* (Supplement), March 2, 1815.
46. Speech of Charles J. Ingersoll, February 16, 1815, in *AC*, 13–3, 1159, 1161. See also Dwight, *Hartford Convention*, 381.
47. Latour, *Historical Memoir*, 100; *Niles' Register* 8 (March 4, 1815), [1]; speech of George M. Troup, February 16, 1815, in *AC*, 13–3, 1156. See also letter from New Orleans, January 19, 1815, in Richmond *Enquirer*, February 15, 1815; Address of Andrew Jackson, March, 1815, in Brannan, *Official Letters*, 469.
48. Boston *Yankee*, March 3, 1815.
49. *Niles' Register* 11 (September 14, 1816), 40.
50. Speech of Henry Southard, January 17, 1817, in *AC*, 14–2, 584.

Index

Adams, John, 34, 35

Adams, John Quincy, 2, 19, 230, 240, 284, 307; appointed to peace commission, 120, 160, 283, 285; and peace negotiations, 287–96; in Russia, 284; portrait, 286

Adams, William, 285

Adams, U.S.S., 90–91; burned by U.S., 194, 216

Address of Minority (Federalist anti-war address), 54–55

Albany Congress (1754), 270

Alert, H.M.S.: defeated by U.S.S. *Essex,* 96

Alexander, Czar, 16

Alexandria (VA): surrender and plunder of, 201, 263

Amelia Island (FL): illegal trade with, 169

American Revolution, 3, 19, 26, 51, 149, 236, 264, 265, 269, 290, 300. *See also* War of 1812: as second war of independence

Ames, Fisher, 13

Anderson, Joseph, 172

Anglo-French wars (1793–1815), 5, 300

Anglophobia, 7, 305–7

Apalachicola River, 205, 206

Apothecary general, 223

Archer, Stevenson, 109

Argus, U.S.S. (10 guns): defeated by H.M.S. *Pelican,* 157

Argus, U.S.S. (22 guns): burned by U.S., 199, 216

Armistead, George: and defense of Fort McHenry, 203–4

Armistice: agreement of 1812, 283; rumors of, 166

Armories, U.S., 79, 223, 274

Armstrong, John, 119, 126, 229, 302; appointed secretary of war, 106; blamed for capture of Washington, 202; and campaign of 1813, 129, 135, 143, 144; character of, 107, 367n.46; draws up army code of regulations, 112, 263; and defense of Washington, 196; favors conscription, 164; as judge of talent, 183; resignation of, 202, 233; portrait, 108

Army, U.S.: actual size, 73, 126, 183, 221; authorized size, 6, 8, 33, 111, 165; bounty, 33, 76–77, 111, 164, 243; code of regulations, 112, 263; condition of, 8, 76, 126, 183; conscription into, 164, 241–43; desertion, 76, 222, 407n.8; discipline, 76, 222; disease in, 78–79, 302–3; dueling in, 222; enlistment period, 76, 111; officers, 8, 76, 112, 214; pay, 77, 111, 223; rations, 78–79; recruiting problems, 111, 164, 221–22; supply, 78–79, 149; weapons, 79–80

Astor, John Jacob, 122; and illegal trade, 171

441

Index

U.S. naval strategy in 1812, 92; portrait, 36

Galusha, Jonas, 266

Gambier, Lord: appointed to British peace commission, 285

Gaston, William, 247; proposal to restrict war, 163

General Armstrong, American privateer: attacked by G.B., 219

Georgetown (MD): British raid on, 153

Gerry, Elbridge, 28, 37, 52; death of, 238; elected vice president, 101, 366n.34; as president pro tem of Senate, 125

Ghent (Belgium), 281, 285, 287

Ghent, Treaty of, 2, 308, 309; negotiated, 287–96; ratified, 297, 298; reception of, 296–99; terms of, 296

Gibson, Jacob, 171

Gilbert, Felix H., 52

Giles, William Branch, 30, 116, 125, 172, 232, 242, 243; and act to increase army, 33; and war bill, 46

Gilman, John T.: and New Hampshire militia problem, 266

Girard, Stephen, 122

Glasgow (Scotland), 218

Goddard, Calvin: and Connecticut embassy to Washington, 279

Goldsborough, Charles, 110

Goldsborough, Robert H., 242

Goodrich, Chauncey: and Hartford Convention, 275, 277

Goodrich, Samuel G., 52

Gordon, James: and plunder of Alexandria (VA), 201

Gore, Christopher, 278

Gothenburg (Sweden), 287

Goulburn, Henry: appointed to British peace commission, 285; and peace negotiations, 287–96

Governor Tompkins, American privateer, 218

Grand Terre Island (LA), 169, 204, 207

Granger, Gideon, 302; and election of 1812, 101; removed as postmaster general, 162

Grant, Ulysses, 1

Great Britain: army, 73, 182–83; authorizes reprisals against U.S., 282–83; blockades U.S. coast, 152–53, 214–16;

and European war, 99, 158, 181, 182, 287, 296–97, 300; navy of, 92, 99, 151; offers direct negotiations, 160, 284–85; peace terms, 236, 238, 240, 274, 289–91, 294; policy of conciliation in 1812, 42–43; rejects Russian mediation, 284; response to naval defeats, 97–99; strategy, 92–93, 135, 151–53, 190, 194, 195, 204–5; vindictiveness, 287

Great Lakes: command of, 127–28, 183; G.B. calls for U.S. demilitarization of, 236, 289

Greenock (Scotland), 218

Greenville (OH), Treaty of, 290

Gregg, Andrew: and war bill, 46

Grenville, Lord, 10

Griffith, Edward: and British occupation of Maine, 194

Griswold, Roger, 261; and Connecticut militia problem, 259–60

Grosvenor, Thomas P., 244, 248

Growler, U.S.S.: captured by G.B., 143–44, 190

Grundy, Felix, 30, 55, 334n.18; accuses Federalists of moral treason, 121, 163; defeated for speaker, 160

Guadaloupe (West Indies), 97

Guerrière, H.M.S.: defeated by U.S.S. *Constitution*, 93–94; depicted, frontispiece

Gulf Coast: British invasion of, 204–14

Gunboats, 9, 34, 131, 190, 191, 193, 195–96, 208

Halifax (Canada), 97, 168, 194, 217, 283, 289, 294

Hall, Amos: and defense of Niagara frontier, 142–43

Hamilton, Alexander, 6, 7, 249

Hamilton, Paul: resigns from cabinet, 106; as secretary of the navy, 90, 302

Hamilton, U.S.S.: lost in storm, 129

Hampden (ME), 194, 225

Hampton, Wade, 183, 305; and Battle of Chateaugay, 144–45, 266

Hampton (VA): British raid on, 154

Hannibal: tactics of, 148

Hanson, Alexander C., 166, 238; and Baltimore riots, 57–68; court-martialed, 57; founds *Federal Republican*, 57; pledges support for war, 237; portrait, 58

447

Index

UNIVERSITY OF ILLINOIS PRESS
1325 SOUTH OAK STREET
CHAMPAIGN, ILLINOIS 61820-6903
WWW.PRESS.UILLINOIS.EDU